TOM STOPPARD

Also by Ira Nadel

Biography: Fiction, Fact & Form

Joyce and the Jews: Culture and Texts

Various Positions: A Life of Leonard Cohen

TOM STOPPARD:
A
Life

Ira Nadel

palgrave
macmillan

TOM STOPPARD

Grateful acknowledgement is made to the following for permission to print previously published and unpublished material. All previously unpublished Stoppard material copyrighted by Tom Stoppard; the right to reproduce requires his permission. Quotations from the published plays of Tom Stoppard reprinted with the permission of Faber and Faber, Grove Press and Samuel French. Others to be thanks for allowing the inclusion of material include Miriam Stoppard, Peter Stoppard, Harold Pinter, the estate of Richard Imison, Derek Balmer, Anthony Smith, David Foot, Peter Brook, Emanuel Azenberg, David Mamet, Richard Dreyfuss, and the Harry Ransom Humanities Research Center of the University of Texas at Austin. The photographs which appear in this book are reproduced by the kind permission of Peter Stoppard, Yosi Studio, Pocklington School, Derek Balmer, Lord Snowdon, Camera Press, Anthony Crickmay, V&A Picture Library, New York Times, Donald Cooper, Photostage, Herald Photographic Services, Miriam Stoppard, Karan Kapoor, Chris Pizzello, AP Photo. Every attempt has been made to race copyright holders. We apologise for any omissions.

First published 2002 by
PALGRAVE MACMILLAN™
175 Fifth Avenue, New York, N.Y. 10010 and
Houndmills, Basingstoke, Hampshire, England RG21 6XS.
Companies and representatives throughout the world.

PALGRAVE MACMILLAN IS THE GLOBAL ACADEMIC IMPRINT OF THE PALGRAVE MACMILLAN
division of St. Martin's Press, LLC and of Palgrave Macmillan Ltd. Macmillan® is a registered trademark in the United States, United Kingdom and other countries. Palgrave is a registered trademark in the European Union and other countries.

ISBN 0-312-23778-2 hardback

Library of Congress Cataloging-in-Publication Data available from the Library of Congress.

First published in the United Kingdom in 2002 by Methuen

First palgrave macmillan edition: July 2002
10 9 8 7 6 5 4 3 2 1

Printed in the United States of America

CONTENTS

For Dara & Ryan

I have been leading a double life – at least!
Stoppard, *The Real Inspector Hound*

I should obviously be part of a double act.
Stoppard, 1991

INTRODUCTION

QUESTIONER: *Do you often find your past revisits you?*
STOPPARD: *Sometimes it seeks me out.*
Stoppard, 1995

He glanced from the train as it cut across the countryside. He had just left the Pinkas Synagogue in the Jewish ghetto of Prague, its walls filigreed with nearly 80,000 names of Czech Jews killed in the Holocaust – including those of his paternal and maternal grand-parents. He had visited the site with two Czech relatives and now, as the train took him to the south-east, he unfolded a gazetteer of 'Jewish monuments in Moravia and Silesia'. Zlín, his destination, merited three lines, two of interest: one of the cemeteries had a small Jewish section, and it was the birthplace of the English playwright Tom Stoppard 'in proper name Tomáš Straüssler (born 1937)'.

Stoppard's surprise at seeing his name – both of his names – was as immediate as his decision to return. He had been in Prague to meet with a cousin he hadn't seen since he was an infant and to learn more of his obscured family past. Spontaneously, he decided to revisit the family home to duplicate a photograph he had just been shown of his parents sitting on a bench against the wall of their house. Having his picture taken in the same spot would connect him to his past. He took the train, checked into a hotel and the next morning went to the house on Zálesná III, the carefully laid-out street in a complex near the Bat'a Hospital where his father had practised medicine. But, try as he might, he could not find the right angle or perspective. He walked round the red-brick cube of the house. He stopped. He tried different views. In the end, he left in frustration and bewilderment. His parents and his home remained elusive; he understood that the past could not be reproduced, only invented.

Stoppard's desire to replicate the scene underlined his need to relive it, but his failure allowed him to imagine it, emotionally as well as physically. The memory of the original photo would have to suffice, while he reconstructed in his mind the moment and the place where his parents had sat. Stoppard's scepticism of biography's ability to re-create the past – expressed often in his work – now matched his own inability to re-create his parents' picture. Such an attitude has made the job of writing his biography doubly challenging: not only must it be as accurate as possible, but it must also construct a narrative that convincingly relates the nature of the events outlined by such 'facts'. Eleanor Swan's caveat in *Indian Ink* – '*biography* is the worst possible excuse for getting people wrong' – has remained a constant warning, while Oscar Wilde's claim in *The Invention of Love* has been a persistent challenge: 'biography,' he explains to A. E. Housman, 'is the mesh through which our real life escapes'.[1] Happily, biographers do not agree; they believe in the capacity of biography to uncover the patterns that shape their subjects' lives and aid in understanding their origins and actions. Facts become a key to interpretation, although *what* is a fact is always at issue.

Stoppard complicates the matter by taking pleasure in dramatizing both sides of any situation, enjoying the double perspective of renouncing and yet succumbing to biography. Over the years, he has often complicated biographers' efforts, while simultaneously offering limited glimpses of his early life in India, his arrival in England and, most recently, the discovery of his Jewish past. Yet he resists any biographical reading of his works, and closely guards any private details about his life. Affable and open in interviews, he also establishes inviolable borders.

Comic confusion, as well as comic action, often results. Rumours abound: was the dialogue in the original version of *Rosencrantz and Guildenstern are Dead* actually a massive typing error? Did he actually submit an A Level essay on one of his plays for one of his sons? Did he have a romance with Mia Farrow in the summer of 1998? These and other stories are untrue, yet the contradictions, which provide little problem for the playwright, whose own life has been a collection of opposing issues and experiences, become the very centre of the biographical undertaking. He, of course, celebrates the very confusion, telling a reporter that he wants his biography 'to be as inaccurate as possible', although he made a point of personally explaining to me the woven story of his Jewish past.[2] The dialectic of Stoppard's life – immigrant and Englishman, dramatist and screenwriter, public figure and private man – has, indeed, lacked a synthesis, which is just the way he likes it. Such oppositions and resulting inventions, however, are the foundation of this account, which attempts to clarify the elements of his character, the details of his life and the evolution of his work, while avoiding the charge made to the biographer Eldon Pike in *Indian Ink*: 'You are constructing an edifice of speculation on a smudge of paint on paper, which no longer exists'.[3]

Stoppard himself encourages such behaviour. In a 1963 review of James Saunders's play, *Next Time I'll Sing to You*, Stoppard cleverly remarked that in writing about a hermit who spent nearly forty-two years in a barricaded hovel, Saunders 'quickly discards the documentary evidence as the clue to the essential *why* of the man'.[4] This would be Stoppard's ideal biography: one that does not try to document but instead understands the life of its subject, as Virginia Woolf anticipated. In one of her notebooks, she wrote 'let the biographer present fully, completely, accurately, the known facts without comment; then let him write the life as fiction'.[5] Yet facts cannot be discounted and the facts of Stoppard's life immediately disclose a series of disruptions and antitheses which he has rewritten into a part that he beautifully plays, appropriate for a playwright who once identified himself as 'the kind of person who embarks on an endless leapfrog down the great moral issues. I put a position, rebut it, refute it, refute the rebuttal, and rebut the refutation. Forever. Endlessly'.[6]

Stoppard in many ways resists biography. When I first approached him with the idea of writing his life, he asked me who would read such an account? 'I told you. I'm not self-analytical,' he declared to a *Boston Globe* reporter.[7] Nevertheless, the absence of self-analysis or intro- spection, a quality he shares with many of his characters, does not limit audiences from identifying autobiographical elements in his work. From his understanding of journalism in *Night and Day* to the situa- tion of the dramatist Henry in *The Real Thing* and his involvement with an actress, there are similarities. And, like his characters, Stoppard is driven, intelligent and ferociously articulate.

Stoppard's characteristic pose of not knowing or arguing against himself is not so much equivocation as keeping his alternatives available. 'No symbolism admitted and none denied' was the inscription he wanted on the doorpost to his study, he declared in 1987. The openness of interpretation is the openness that comes from inclusiveness. Or, as he explained in his 1999 essay, 'Pragmatic Theatre',

> Art which stays news, in Ezra Pound's phrase, is art in which the question 'what does it mean?' has no correct answer. Every narrative has, at least, a capacity to suggest a metanarrative . . .[8]

Stoppard opposes fixity, remaining elusive and elliptical. Beneath his geniality and image of a dandy resides a figure engaged in trying to understand himself as well as others. Yet he has long been accustomed to disguising his identity and concealing his emotions. Several around him have sensed this emotional reserve and his unwillingness to reveal personal feelings or doubts. One friend told a story of how, after he felt a certain frostiness from Stoppard, the playwright unexpectedly phoned him to apologize for his rudeness, recalling a book he had seen at the friend's home entitled *Absent Friends*. 'That's what I've been,' he confided. But while he has numerous professional friends and acquaintances, they remain just that.

Until recently, he was at ease in his self-protective garb, buttressed by the kind of domestic stability that defined his private life for some eighteen years. Between 1972 and 1990, his years with his second wife, Miriam Stoppard, he repeatedly showed the world an accomplished, ingenious writer who regularly had projects on the go, from original works to adaptations and screenplays. His public life mirrored his private happiness as he moved from one grand home to another with a wife who had an equally successful career as a physician, TV host and writer. But the period preceding his arrival in England (1937–46) and the period after his second marriage (1992 to the present) have provided less internal assurance and outward balance, although he has achieved unmatched triumphs which include the international success of *Arcadia*, a knighthood and an Oscar for the screenplay of *Shakespeare in Love*.

A biographer of Stoppard, however, knows that he hasn't quite pinned him down. Stoppard's own admission that he often misleads, misdates and misconstrues the past generates this doubt. His wilful, but not malicious, encouragement that he hopes his biographer will misinterpret many details of his life is both a lively challenge and a warning. But would one expect otherwise? No, because, as his plays repeatedly display, it is not so much the possession of fixed knowledge that matters but the truth such knowledge reveals. 'Mere untruth is a very poor reason for restraint,' he once quipped, adding that 'accuracy is a high price to pay for truth'.[9] Wilde echoes this in *The Invention of Love* when he declares that he was said to have walked down Piccadilly with a lily in his hand. But 'there was no need. To do it is nothing, to be said to have done it is everything. It's the truth about me,' he tells Housman.[10] Stoppard shares this view: when he reads something inaccurate about himself, 'I never demand corrections. I quite like it really. If enough things that are untrue are said about you, no one will know what really is true.'[11]

Yet even this is contradictory. In *Arcadia*, the false assumptions of the academic Bernard must be exposed. And the audience knows (and takes pleasure in) the errors of the biographer Eldon Pike in *Indian Ink*. But as Hannah, the novelist in *Arcadia*, explains, 'it's wanting to know that makes us matter'.[12] So even if Stoppard unintentionally misleads, setting false traps for his biographer and offering explanations that don't quite match either with the record or with other statements of his, it is nonetheless the *effort* of getting it right that matters. When he jested that he hoped the would-be biography would be as inaccurate as possible, he also added that he knew he was behaving badly.[13]

> *There are many things I know which are not verifiable but*
> *nobody can tell me I don't know them . . .*
> Stoppard, *Jumpers*

The personal and theatrical contradictions that dominate Stoppard's life are the subjects of this biography, with one fuelling the other as he incorporates strategies that address the displacements he has encountered. His display of intellect masks the intensity of his feelings, while he discards autobiography yet constantly explores identity. 'Who am I?' is a question repeatedly posed not only by Rosencrantz and Guildenstern but by the playwright himself.

How Stoppard's emotions have shaped his work is another concern, from the impact of his geo-political dislocations to the discovery of his Jewish identity. The paradoxes that have resulted have influenced not only his writing but his reception: while there is a widespread admiration of his wit and intellect, there is discomfort over his supposed lack of feelings. A restlessness with his thoughtful, quasi-realistic works (*Night and Day* and *The Real Thing*) counters audiences' pleasure in his early, overcharged comedies. His vision of a romantic English past seen in *Arcadia* or the clubby world of Victorian Oxford in *The Invention of Love* has been explained by some as England only as an outsider might imagine it. His origins in Central Europe, which value curtailed if not suppressed emotions and an embedded irony, seem at odds with his sense of what he wants English life to be: open, uplifting and, above all, instilled with a comic logic. His Central European outlook constantly sees the absurd, instead of the rational, dominating experience, or rather, sees both at the same time.

Other contradictions include his productivity and his constant procrastination; his fertile mind and his repeated declarations that he lacks ideas; his youthful disavowal of education and his lifelong enthusiasm for books; his flamboyance and his severe reticence; his appreciation of popular culture and study of the most difficult philosophical or scientific concepts; his satire of academics and appeal to erudite audiences; his non-intellectual air and instinctive attraction to complex ideas; his conservative values and his political activism.

These antitheses take other forms as well, namely his preference for polished dramatic forms yet reliance on radical structures; his outward reserve but genuine concern for others; his declared indifference to character and his ability to create memorable and affecting figures on the stage; his success in marrying the play of ideas with the unlikely form of farce; his commitment to the text but his equally strong commitment to its alteration in rehearsals and even performances; the reconstruction of language through the destruction of cliché; the revitalization of the work of others (Nestroy, Molnár, Chekhov) without limiting the originality of his own drama; his resistance to egotism but oblique self-representation in his texts; his skill in perfecting the surface while exposing the subversive; his alternate celebration and criticism of the usefulness of art; his pronounced commitment to marriage yet his difficulty in meeting its requirements.

Stoppard has said that his favourite line in English drama is from Christopher Hampton's *The Philanthropist:* 'I'm a man of no convictions. At least, I think I am.'[14] But this glib summary fails to convey the depth of Stoppard's resistance to taking sides which this biography seeks to unravel at the same time as it identifies the confusions that have formed it. Stoppard's life has been, in his words, an advance through a 'series of small, large and microscopic ambushes', which characterize his plays as well.[15] Facts and events support this view, but one must not feel complacent with the documentary or historical element which a line from his radio play *The Dog it Was that Died* neatly summarizes. A policeman, assisting a spy, perceptively remarks that 'I'm just showing that the facts would fit more than one set of possibilities'.[16] But neither should the facts be dismissed.

Complicating the process of Stoppard's own efforts to understand his past was his mother's reticence in discussing it, especially after they arrived in England. It was preferable to keep the past distant, partly because she believed it might put Stoppard and his brother at risk as they began their English life. As a result, a protective screen descended which until recently Stoppard was happy to keep in place. Adopting a new name and country forced a certain self-protection. Instead of the displaced refugee beginning again in a new country, he became a fully realized English schoolboy who made the First XI in cricket and went off to investigate English life as a provincial journalist rather than to a classroom as a university student. Absorbed by English moral life as well as social manners, Stoppard substituted England for his original home, which was at best unclear, although his accent, which he did not lose (nor did his mother, who spoke English with a Czech accent throughout her life), identified him as 'other'. Even the unexpected discovery in Prague in 1994 that his mother had several older siblings, a number of whom had died in concentration camps, did not fundamentally alter his identity. However, the information, coinciding with new details about the Straüsslers in Zlín, resulted in a return to the city in the spring of 1998 with his brother after a fifty-nine-year absence. But the return and confirmation of his Jewish identity did not change his outlook: 'I was vaguely pleased when I found out. But it's too late to pretend that somehow you're different because you've learned something.' The experience left him, he said, 'with a combination of feeling detached or engaged'.[17] The statement typically contradicts and reveals Stoppard's awkward relationship to his past. His reserve and privacy on such matters battles with his desire to know: 'the fact that my past is largely missing from my consciousness is something that doesn't bother me . . . Maybe I'm undisturbed by the past because I jumped the rails. The rails I'm on only began in 1946,' he once explained.[18]

Stoppard knows that you can revisit but not recapture the past, that history and biography are unable to reconstitute exactly what happened; consequently, he understands that the truth remains uncertain – except perhaps in science. Or so he hopes. Hence his interest and articulation of science and its development in his plays. Mathematics, an early and sustaining interest of his, remained, along with physics, a means to situate a degree of fixedness. *Galileo*, his unproduced screenplay, *Hapgood* and *Arcadia* are his three most ambitious encounters with science and the examination of its ability to fix nature. But he also knows that uncertainty is its basis: 'the act of observing determines the reality . . . You get what you interrogate for,' a physicist summarizes in *Hapgood*.[19] Yet even in *The Invention of Love*, the search continues: Housman eloquently celebrates textual editing as a science. The future may be disorder but it doesn't prevent us from seeking ways to predict it.

The paradox of Stoppard, however, has another dimension, since it is this very freedom from, or absence of, home which has allowed him to create. Released from a fixed past and allowed to invent a fluid history, he has constructed a special marginality which has permitted him to accept antithesis, critically and culturally. This he repeatedly celebrates as his freedom to see *both* sides of every issue or situation. His origins in the 'Deserts of Bohemia' (Shakespeare's phrase in *The Winter's Tale* for what became Czechoslovakia) encouraged a vision which was satiric, comic and intellectual as a form of survival, accompanied by a resistance to exposing the private or the personal. Camouflage, masking itself as display, would be its best expression. Self-invention emerged because Stoppard appeared to possess no visible past – or too much of one which, ironically, needed to be hidden to survive in England.

But like the characters in *The Winter's Tale*, Stoppard has encountered a strange sense of fortune. Antithetical elements constantly rub up against each other, from the family's exchange of Nairobi for Singapore as their haven from the Nazis – only to be caught in the Japanese invasion of the island in 1942 – or their sudden, unplanned change of direction from Australia to India when they transferred ships after escaping from Singapore. Antithesis seems to define Stoppard's life, but rather than attempt to resolve it, he capitalizes on it, exploring the freedoms it offers, rather than its contradictions, recalling Richard Ellmann's remark about Oscar Wilde: given a choice of alternatives, he managed to choose both.[20]

Although Stoppard left central Europe at the age of two, it has never left him, frequently returning to the foreground of his work. *Professional Foul* and *Squaring the Circle* are obvious examples but so, too, are his actions in 1977 related to the Charter 77 movement, his continued friendship with Václav Havel, his support of Russian dissidents and his continuous championing of human rights, all made possible, in a sense, because of his life in post-war England, which Arthur Koestler once labelled the 'Davos for internally bruised veterans of the totalitarian age'.[21]

But the question remains: why, from his mid-fifties to the present, has Stoppard been so keen to recover his past? What has occurred to overcome his resistance to the past and his determination to certify its reality? Psychologically, the answer may lie in the freedom to do so, now that his mother and stepfather have died. Historically, it might be that the past is catching up with him. Following his cursory attempt in the mid 1980s to have his mother retell their past, he discovered in the early nineties that relatives in the Czech Republic were seeking him out and, to his chagrin, he learned that for several years before her death his mother had been in contact with a retired Bat'a chemist who was researching the fate of the Jewish employees of the company. Stoppard decided to let down his guard and no longer felt that he must hide his feelings or his life. 'The older I get, the less I care about self-concealment,' he admitted in 1997.[22] Returning to his parents' home in Zlín to duplicate their photo was not an act of nostalgia but of reclaiming and acknowledging his origins.

Biography , as Virginia Woolf once noted, should be 'the record of things that change rather than of the things that happen'. Housman incisively summarizes this view at the end of Act One of *The Invention of Love* when, to a student who tells him she doesn't mind being chastised, he exclaims – 'but life is *in* the minding'.[23] Biography is the narrative of such 'minding' and for one involved with constructing, rather than inventing, Stoppard's life, the challenge is to display that activity, while remaining aware of what biography can – and cannot – do.

Diffident on the surface but apprehensive underneath, cautious about being thought too serious, yet writing works of high ideas, Stoppard resorted to masking complicated concepts in the frivolous or the farcical. The reasons for this posture emerge from the details of his life which will also elucidate his resistance to commitment as a response to the knowledge that order does not ensure meaning nor guarantee security. 'The way I see it, life is lived off the record. It's altogether too human for the written word, it happens in pictures . . . metaphors,' says the Inspector in Stoppard's *Cahoot's Macbeth*: a view Stoppard repeatedly endorses.[24] This biography, however, challenges such an attitude by sharpening our sense of Stoppard the man while examining the origins of Stoppard the dramatist.

CHAPTER 1

DESERTS OF BOHEMIA

If you think I have an accent now,
you should have heard me then.
Stoppard, 1996

In the twilight of the first Czechoslovakian Republic, Tomáš
Straüssler, later known as Tom Stoppard, was born. The year was 1937,
a time of contrast and confusion as Nazis threatened the country and
international powers remained indifferent. It was another period of
transition and terror for a country that did not officially exist until 1918
and would cease to do so in 1938 – only to be reborn in 1989.

Marginalized in the imagination of Europe although geographically
at its centre, Czechoslovakia asserted an independent identity, despite
being, historically, an appendage of Vienna, Berlin or Moscow.
Divided between 'empire and nation, Fascism and democracy,
capitalism and Communism', the country was a frontier open to
others but cut off from itself.[1] The shifting chiaroscuro of its society
and politics generated radical yet ironic incongruities of language and
culture: until recently, German, the official language since the late
eighteenth century, dominated all public exchanges; although it was
bounded by Austria, Germany, Poland and Hungary, Paris rather than
central Europe eclipsed its culture. Jews were Germans in one census,
Czechs in the next. Alternately a frontier and a nation, urban and
rural, modern and traditional, the Czech Republic had as many
identities as it had rulers.

Art as well as politics contributed to the disorder. Shakespeare
provided Czechoslovakia with a coastline in *The Winter's Tale*,
Apollinaire an existence outside modern Europe in his poem 'Zone'.
Kafka presented Prague as the anonymous city of *The Trial*, while

Chamberlain summarized its status in the west as 'a far-away country' in his notorious 1938 appeasement speech. Yet, ironically, this 'far-away' country was bordered by four central powers. The hands on the medieval clock tower in the Jewish Quarter run backwards, suggesting to Sir Walter Scott (and others) the paralysis of the country in time as well as place.[2]

Originally divided into the regions of Bohemia in the north and Moravia in the south, the Czech Republic nevertheless attempted to assert an identity rooted in an indigenous culture and adventurous imagination. Sometimes it succeeded, although it more often failed. Linked to 'Eastern Europe' since 1945, despite its geographic placement in the centre of Europe, the Czech Republic's artistic and cultural drives constantly pointed towards the west. Vienna and Paris, rather than Budapest or Moscow, were its natural direction.

In the fractious culture of modern Czechoslovakia, torn between dislocation and centrism, German and Slav, freedom and oppression, artists found original ways to reshape expression. The ambiguity of their identities became the source of their confident originality. Surrealism, Constructivism, Poetism made their way into Czech art, illustrating the creativity of the Czech imagination, caught at times between cultural nationalism and artistic cosmopolitanism. A Czech 'futurist' manifesto published in 1913 declared 'long live the liberated word, the new word . . . the poetry of noise, the civilization of inventions and of journeys of discovery'. It claims 'Death To! . . . folklore, Moravian–Slovak embroidery, Alfons Mucha [and] old Prague sentimentality'.[3] The Prague Linguistic Circle or the experimental Liberated Theatre of Jiřís Voskovec and Jan Werich continued to push the edges of artistic expression originating in the Devěstil group, which celebrated film as the epitome of art for the modern world.

The year of Stoppard's birth, 1937, also marked the beginning of the end of contemporary Czech culture and nationhood, symbolically underscored by the death of the revered President Masaryk. This was followed in 1938 by the death of Karel Čapek, revolutionary dramatist and author not only of *R. U. R.* but *The Insect Play*, an allegorical satire of bureaucracy, and the Czech children's classic, *Dáenka: The Life of a Puppy*. Yet the politics of the period and Čapek's perceived radicalism meant that neither the National Museum nor the National Theatre would organize his funeral, the latter even refusing to fly the traditional black flag to honour his memory.

In 1939, Alfons Mucha died. The artist who returned from Paris to Prague, not only to design the first postage stamps and banknotes for the new country in 1918, but to complete his monumental cycle of paintings on Czechoslovak history, *The Slav Epic*, was also one of the first to be arrested by the Gestapo when the Germans invaded Prague in March 1939. He was released shortly afterwards, but in poor health, and he died that July. The Germans, now occupying the country under the terms of a protectorate, knew the potential danger of a public funeral and banned Mucha's. Such individual losses were symbolic of an even greater one: that of the first Czech Republic which would not be reconstituted until 1989, following years of Communist rule.

Throughout these changes, the resilient Czech identity survived, its continuity dependent on its constant reconstruction. In the face of continual renewal, disruptions and inversions, Czech identity remakes itself and endures, much as Tom Stoppard, through various dislocations and shifting worlds, builds an identity that is equally attractive and elusive. Born into a country defined by antithesis, Stoppard learned to capitalize on a series of extravagant oppositions, translating them into marvellous plays and an appealing public persona. Like the Czech Republic itself, Stoppard paradoxically seems on the fringe of the European consciousness and at its very centre.

> *The whole disorderliness of history, concealed under*
> *artificial order for years, suddenly spurts out.*
> Václav Havel, Letter to Dr Gustáv Husák,
> General Secretary of the Czechoslovak Communist Party, 1975

Tom Stoppard's often-cited quip that once he left his native homeland he became a 'bounced Czech' disguises the importance of his origin in Zlín, a small city in south-east Moravia, today some four and half hours from Prague and only forty miles from present-day Slovakia.[4] Lying among low, forested foothills, Zlín originated as a settlement in the thirteenth century on the left bank of the River Drevnice. It survived various wars and renewal, although by the end of the nineteenth century it was still a provincial town, but with a rail link to Otrokovice and onwards to the capital of Moravia, Brno.

In September 1894, Tomáš Bat'a (1876–1932) established a shoe factory near the railway station where by 1900 one hundred and twenty people worked. By 1904, Bat'a's vision of overseas markets had led him to travel to the States and he had returned with new ideas of production and efficiency partly based on the idea of Henry Ford's assembly line. Within decades, Bat'a's own factories would be known as the 'Detroit of Czechoslovakia'. Over the next thirteen years, the company quickly expanded through the rapid production and sale of boots to the Austrian army during the first World War. Most notable in this growth was Bat'a's vision of a uniform architectural and social environment for his workers. He commissioned a series of homes, schools, sports facilities and hospitals that were harmonious and unified not only in architecture but in social outlook. Such advanced planning received notice throughout Europe.

Bat'a dominated the city, both in manufacturing and institutions, employing 4,000 people and operating eighteen shoe stores through-out Moravia and Bohemia by the end of the First World War. Peace, however, brought unemployment and the company had to be scaled down. But in 1922 Bat'a took a bold step: to stimulate business and renew his industry, while combating the economic downturn, he cut his prices in half and glutted the market with his cheap shoes. His *Batovky*, light linen shoes that everyone could afford, became an international success. The result was phenomenal as his empire grew throughout the country and Europe, leading him, in the 1930s, to undertake an important new building programme which created some of the finest examples of modern city planning in the country.

Bat'a sought uniformity which he thought would bring stability to the social and personal lives of his employees: by 1930, there were more than 17,000 people involved with his company, which that year pro-duced 22 million pairs of shoes. The work-force grew to 36,000 during the thirties. New factory buildings were constructed, as well as housing and hospitals. Le Corbusier was invited to design several civic buildings, though he produced no more than a preliminary sketch. Two architects drew up the principal plans in the late 1920s: František Gahura and Vladimir Karfík favoured a functionalist modernism of brick and plate glass, stressing square lines and flat roofs derived from the Bauhaus school. The centrepiece of the Bat'a complex was a sixteen-storey administration building built by Karfík which still looms over the eastern end of the factory buildings that housed the production lines. The paternalistic though autocratic Bat'a had an office built in an elevator so that he could keep an eye on his workers on every floor while continuing with his own work. His death in a plane crash in 1932 was a blow to the city, although his son immediately took over.

Zálcsná was one of several workers' housing areas planned by the two architects. Situated across the River Drevnice, in carefully laid-out streets given only numerical names, neat two-storey, square brick homes built between 1925 and 1927 sat on plots of greenery, separated from, but visible to, their neighbours. Zálesná III was sometimes called the street of doctors because so many lived there, ten short blocks from the new hospital. At number 2619 lived Doctor Eugen Straüssler and his wife Martha who, in July 1937, would become the parents of a second son, Tomáš Straüssler.

A scar, a trace

Eugen Straüssler was born on 7 January 1908 in Podmokly, situated in North Bohemia, now part of the Czech Republic. A year later, his sister Edita was born. His father, Julius Straüssler (born 1878), was an employee of the state railways who, in about 1915, was transferred to Vienna, where Eugen attended primary school. After the formation of the Czechoslovak railways, Julius Straüssler moved to Brno, where he became a senior inspector. His wife, Hildegard (born 1883), was a housewife. In Brno, Eugen attended grammar school and then the medical faculty of the T. G. Masaryk University in the city. The university was one of the finest in the country, with Brno, the capital of Moravia, one of the leading cities. A dedicated student, Eugen did well in his studies and impressed his professors.

At the age of twenty-four, in 1932, he applied to work at the newly founded Bat'a Hospital in Zlín; he was hired without references, which was unusual, but a testimony to his accomplishments and his family's reputation for reliability and hard work. He began work on 4 February 1932; his official letter of appointment, dated 1 February 1932, stated that his employment included lodging 'consisting of 1 room with help, heating and light board of hospital standard for [a] physician. To cover your sundry expenses you will be paid 200 Kc, in words two hundred crowns after deduction of health and old age pension insurance rates.' He was entitled to three weeks' vacation for which he would receive 10 Kc as 'reimbursement for unconsumed meals'. Work at the hospital was under the guidance of a senior consultant and any private practice or 'gainful activity' was not permitted, but 'if you prove successful, you may be promoted to the rank of assistant physician'.[5] Bat'a clearly provided for its employees, whether on the factory floor or hospital corridor.

Dr Straüssler was a favourite of the head physician, Dr Albert, who valued the up-and-coming young physician. When there was a problem, he would be called by the chief to sort it out. He was also known for his kind and caring manner. In the late 1990s, when Stoppard met the daughter of Dr Albert in Prague, she told him how his father had stitched up a severe cut caused when she put her hand through a pane of glass. The scar, a trace of Eugen Straüssler, stared at him as he touched it fifty-six years after his father's death, the only tangible sign of his existence.[6]

Eugen Straüssler met Martha Becková (later shortened to Beck), born to Rudolf and Regina Becková near Brno in Rousinov on 11 July 1911, on a ski trip. She was the youngest of six children, following four older sisters and one older brother. When she left school, Martha took a secretarial course and then joined Bat'a at the age of about eighteen. She also began skiing and attending dances, with her mother present. On one ski outing, a young doctor with a group of university students invited her to a dance at the hospital; his name was Eugen Straüssler. In an unpublished and unfinished memoir started in the 1980s, Martha described him as having unconventional good looks, intelligence, modesty and much charm (qualities that would be evident in his younger son). He was also good-humoured, optimistic and empathetic; his outlook on life was positive and pictures always show him smiling. In a recently discovered piece of film from the 1930s, Dr Straüssler smiles and comforts a male patient as he is being transferred outdoors from one pavilion to another at the Bat'a Hospital; the same film later shows him in a crowd, greeting visitors to what may be the newly opened Bat'a museum. The two images reveal a well-dressed man, socially at ease and graceful. His goal was to be a heart and lung specialist. When he met Martha, he was still studying medicine and working at the Bat'a hospital during his vacations.

Martha, who had short, dark hair, large eyes and an attractive face, began work at the hospital on 19 July 1927, performing secretarial and then some nursing duties, although she was not officially certified as a nurse. Her parents were Catholic, although they were originally Jewish; in order to secure their safety, her grandparents converted from Judaism to Catholicism and she listed Catholic as her religion on her employment form. Eugen Straüssler was Jewish – or at least acknowledged that one of his grandparents was Jewish. He did not celebrate the Jewish holidays and was not observant, but neither did he hide his Jewishness. It was simply not an issue; nor was intermarriage. In Martha's family, there were so many mixed marriages that the matter lost importance; the ratio was about fifty–fifty.[7]

On 23 June 1934, the couple married in Zlín. A wedding photo shows a beaming Eugen Straüssler in profile, looking at his new wife who proudly stares at the camera with an equally happy smile. She wears a brocaded dress and an elegant but simple bracelet and holds a pair of gloves. Her husband is neatly turned out in a dark suit with a distinctive white handkerchief in the breast pocket. An earlier photo of Martha taken in 1927, when she was sixteen, shows her looking beautiful as a flapper in beads, slave bracelet, Charleston shoes and party dress. A 1930 picture reveals a glamorous woman with plucked eyebrows in a fur-collared coat.

On 26 July 1934, a month after their wedding, the couple moved to Zálesná III. Martha Straüssler soon stopped working for the company, expecting her first child, a son, Petr (later anglicized to Peter), born on 21 August 1935. To advance her skills, Martha had taken and passed a training course on voluntary nursing sponsored by the Czecho-slovakian Red Cross in May 1935.

A company report described the orderliness of the Straüssler home: 'very nice dining room, dormitory grey, gentleman's room upstairs, furniture from Iris [a local store], carpets downstairs from Bat'a dept. store for 1000 Kc, wicker furniture not yet delivered for the hall. Two small rooms upstairs joined into one, so that mother's room is bigger.'

As an intern, Straüssler worked hard and after four years, at the age of twenty-eight, he was promoted to assistant chief consultant. Personnel files praise his ability and attitude. A 1937 assessment commended his work as 'very good', his nature as 'upright', his leadership capacity as that of an 'organizer', his attitude towards the factory as 'very good' and his general references as 'ascendant'. As deputy senior consultant in 1937, he received a 2000 Kc raise to 7000 Kc. In addition to Czech, Dr Straüssler knew German and a smattering of French. Marking the birth of his second son, Tomáš, on 3 July 1937, Dr Straüssler received a gift of 200 Kc from the company. The family nicknamed the baby Tomik.

At 2 a.m. on 21 September 1938, a year to the day after the death of the former President and national hero, Masaryk, the British and French ambassadors in Prague pressured President Edvard Beneš to accept a partitioned country, the result of intense negotiations with Hitler and a prelude to a meeting with the English and French at Godesberg; Russia, who assured the inviolability of Czech borders, was not even consulted by the two western countries. A demonstration of some 100,000 that evening in St Wenceslas Square, the traditional gathering place for free demonstrations, did not provide the Czech government with the necessary strength to stand against the Germans and their demands, nor did it provide the courage for the British and the French to oppose Hitler's orders.[8] The march to Hradčany Castle, the residence of the president and seat of government, only led to a brief appearance by Beneš on a balcony to announce that the government had resigned. The leader of *The Times* for 22 September 1938 declared, 'There is nothing sacrosanct about the present frontiers of Czechoslovakia'.

The Munich agreement of 29 September 1938, in which Britain and France appeased Hitler by satisfying his claims to the Sudetenland (a section of Eastern Czechoslovakia populated with nearly three million German-speaking Czechs) and agreed to the partition of the country, destroyed Czechoslovakia. Announcement of the agreement over loudspeakers in Prague the next day led to public weeping.[9] Sacrificed to preserve peace in Europe, so Chamberlain and the British argued, Czechoslovakia lost three-tenths of its territory, one-third of its population and four-tenths of its national income.[10]

Poland and Hungary also took advantage of the country's humiliation and presented long-standing claims. As a result, nearly five million people were transferred to German, Polish or Hungarian jurisdiction. More importantly, public confidence in the international system and its leaders was eroded. A five-stage German occupation of the Sudetenland occured between 1 and 10 October; in the midst of this, Beneš resigned on 5 October 1938, leaving the country in turmoil.

He who wants to be a Czech must cease to be a Jew.
Karel Havlíček, 1844

Jewish life in Czechoslovakia had always been tenuous but tolerated. Joseph II in 1780 proclaimed religious tolerance of the Jews and others, and sought to integrate them into civil society and make them loyal Austrian subjects since the Czech lands were under Austro-Hungarian control. But in the nineteenth century, during the period of national rebirth, Bohemia's German speakers and Jewish communities were transformed into 'national minorities'. Over time, the Jews of Bohemia were forced to define their identities in ethnic terms, becoming more excluded from the nation.

Anti-Semitism in Czechoslovakia has a complex past, emerging in the nineteenth century as a forceful reaction to the revival of Czech nationalism. As early as 1811, there were anti-Jewish riots in Prague; in 1869, a widely-read article by Jan Neruda entitled 'The Jewish Fear' fuelled the idea of Jews as foreigners, exacerbated by the decision of many to speak German rather than Czech as a sign of their identity with Austro-Hungary and the tolerant ideas initiated by Joseph II. But the nationalist drive alienated the Jews from their Czech identity, as Karel Havlíček made clear, a view that persisted for more than a century. The November 1920 Prague riots caused Kafka to write, 'I have been spending every afternoon outside on the streets, bathing in anti-Semitic hate,' to his translator and lover, Milena Jesenska.[11] Language, more than religion, doubly disenfranchised the Jews from Czech life: they were ostracized for speaking German, which was thought to be anti-Czech, but criticized for speaking Czech because they were thought to be foreign and impure. Should they abandon the imperial cosmopolitanism which speaking German had previously represented and switch to a Czech national affiliation? Ironically, at the beginning of the twentieth century, German itself was being purified, which meant they were excluded from both languages. Kafka underscores the difficulty: 'I have never lived among Germans.

German is my mother tongue and as such more natural to me, but I consider Czech much more affectionate.'[12]

The Czech revival put Jews at risk; the German occupation and establishment of the protectorate put them in danger. The year the Sträusslers escaped Czechoslovakia, more than 118,000 people in the Protectorate of Bohemia–Moravia were deemed to be 'of the Jewish race' as defined by the Nuremberg Laws. Some 26,000 emigrated, 14,000 survived and almost 80,000 died, the great majority of Czech and Moravian Jews interned first at Terezin, a Bohemian fortress town some sixty kilometres from Prague. Ironically, the camp was simultaneously a stop on the way to Auschwitz and a model ghetto inspected by the International Red Cross in 1944. A powerful and silent testimony to those who died are the 77,297 names of Jewish men, women and children that today line the walls of the restored Pinkas Synagogue in the Old Town of Prague. Yet those names, first inscribed in the fifties, were removed by the Communists in 1968, the synagogue having become the State Jewish Museum after the war. The pretext for removal was renovation; only after public pleas for support and a change in government were the names restored, beginning in 1992. Stereotypes typified the anti-Semitic attitude toward Jews before and during war which forced those assimilated Jews to be publically designated as Jews. Jiří Weil's 1960 comic novel set in wartime Prague, *Mendelssohn on the Roof*, satirized the view. Seeking a statue of Mendelssohn among numerous figures on the roof of the Rudolfinum concert hall for the Reichstag Protector Reinhard Heydrich, the searchers despair because the statues are not labelled. The answer is to find the statue with the biggest nose: 'that'll be the Jew!' cries a character. They quickly spot one with an appropriate profile and mistakenly haul down Richard Wagner.

The impact of these devastating changes on Czech Jewish life were becoming more and more obvious. On 30 October 1938, Hitler expelled 13,000 Polish Jews from Germany, compelling them to leave their money and property behind. Taken by train to the Polish border, they fled across as machine-guns fired behind them. On 7 November 1938, Herschel Grynszpan, appalled at the treatment of his sister, one of those from Germany forced to return to Poland, entered the German Embassy in Paris and shot the diplomat von Rath, who died two days later. Hitler responded with a pogrom against the Jews of

Berlin on 9 November 1938, the infamous Kristallnacht.

To be a Jew in Czechoslovakia was to experience a triple dis-enfranchisement: one was condemned for being Jewish, for speaking German and then for speaking Czech, since that was a sign of a false assimilation, one which would dilute the nationalist revival. To be a Jew in Czechoslovakia between the wars was to be an alien, dislocated and uncertain about one's place, linguistically, culturally and socially. Intellectually and artistically, the pull was towards Vienna, but politically and socially the anchor was Prague; the dilemma was that one could feel at home in neither. The Prague Jewish bourgeoisie considered itself secure on the basis of its Bohemian–Austrian descent, its patriotism and preference for German. But this made it hated by the Czech nationalists and, ironically, by a large part of the German population of the Czechoslovak Republic. 'National Jews' or 'German Bohemians' were among the catchphrases invented to identify the Jews who were considered to be Germans and/or Austrians and were made to prove their loyalty as Czechs. The Czechs in fact considered the Jews to be German, and anti-Semitism rubbed off on the Czechs, as expressed by even the tolerant Tomáš Masaryk: 'I do not believe that they [the Jews] can become Czech through a declaration.' Such confusion not surprisingly led to Jewish dislocation from their religion, as Kafka noted in a diary entry from 1911: 'today . . . I saw before me the fate of European Jewry, which is in the process of an unpredictable transition. Those directly concerned do not worry, but bear what is upon them as truly transitional people.'[13] The result was at best an indifference to Jewish custom and an inbred cultural and social restlessness, the product of an ironic sense of security.

Chameleon-like behaviour became necessary among Jews in an attempt to find a cultural or social footing, but at the same time a readiness to depart was prompted by a persistent feeling of uncertainty. One moment you were, or believed you were, Czech, but the next you were labelled German or, worse in that situation, a Jew and ordered to register or to give up your possessions. Such unease and anxiety might be overcome by assimilating, but that flight from the cultural ghetto only led to new entrapments. On 21 June 1939, for example, several months after the Sträusslers left, the Reich Protector von Neurath issued a decree implementing the Nuremberg racial laws of 1935 for Bohemia–Moravia, including the law that Jews were excluded from economic activity, prevented from selling or transferring real estate, businesses or securities without permission; furthermore, all possession of precious metals, pearls and art had to be reported by 31 July 1939 – all this in the face of what the first Czechoslovak Republic (1918–38) had enacted: equal rights for Jews as citizens of the state who no longer had to choose between Czech or German nationality because Jewish nationality was also recognized, a step thought to be a positive social development. But by the summer of 1939, old fears were realized and new ones were on their way.

Such events as the expulsion of Polish Jews from Germany or new changes to the status of Jews in Czechoslovakia did not go unnoticed in Zlín, which seemed insulated from the major disturbances but was actually central to the events since the Bat'a company had the capacity to provide war materials, from shoes to motors. Dr Straüssler could not overlook the sudden threats to Jews that spread throughout the country and neither could the Bat'a Shoe Company, which became concerned over its fate and that of its Jewish employees even before Hitler's rise to power and the Munich accord. Top officials in the company were anxious about their own well-being, given their fear of Nazi control over their business and capital, plus the anticipated restriction on their freedom as Czechs. As early as 1932, Tomáš Bat'a had called a meeting of top executives to share concerns over Hitler's likely coming to power and what preparations were necessary. With the loss of the Sudetenland in 1938, Bat'a began to formulate a policy of transfer rather than dismissal for a number of its employees, including Jews, at every level of the organization. Jan Bat'a, Tomáš's stepbrother, who took over the company after the founder died in a plane crash in 1932, initiated this policy, which began with the relocation of some forty Jewish employees (mostly executives) and their families to branches in other parts of the world.[14] For more than two decades, Bat'a had relied on Jews in senior posts: their senior corporate counsel in Germany was Jewish, as well as their US representative, the former owner of a Berlin shoe agency. Bat'a had earlier established trading companies around the world under the name 'Kotva' (Czech for anchor) and numerous Jews and others were transferred through the offices of this company.[15] Thomas J. Bat'a himself, son of the founder, fled the country as Slovakia declared its separation from Bohemia and Moravia.

Well informed through various governmental contacts, Bat'a executives learned of the imminent separation of Slovakia before it became public, a clear sign to them of immediate hostilities. On the morning the Germans crossed the frontier, 14 March 1939, Dr Albert called a meeting of all the Jewish doctors at his home. He told them that, for their safety and that of their families, they would have to leave the country and that Bat'a would immediately begin to seek transfers, passports and papers for them. Bat'a quickly initiated a plan to disperse these physicians – fifteen in all – to other Bat'a operations in Africa, Singapore and the Philippines. However, in order not to draw attention to the programme, these transfers were presented as a rotation or addition to overseas staff necessary to meet the growing activities of the firm outside Czechoslovakia. Jewish employees were actually dismissed at their own request on 22–3 of March 1939, four months before the Nuremberg laws came into force in the protectorate.[16]

The Straüsslers, anxious over their future in Czechoslovakia, had prepared for their journey early by securing passports on 19 September 1938, several days in advance of the 21 September Prague demonstration and some two weeks before the Munich agreement. Worry over an impending sense of anti-Semitism and protection against any future repression prompted their action. Indeed, following the Munich agreement, organized acts of anti-Semitism began, and suddenly large groups of refugees began to make their way across the country to centres like Brno and Prague. And once the Germans established the Protectorate of Bohemia–Moravia after March 1939, no one could legally leave the country without approval of the Gestapo. The danger of such departures was evident, but the Straüsslers' determination to leave was unwavering.

In preparation for his departure and in response to the increasing anti-Semitism following Munich, Dr Straüssler took a series of courses in February and March 1939, according to a document dated 11 March 1939: he attended shoemaking school for two weeks, worked in a shoe shop for half a week, a chiropody clinic for half a week and ended his training with a week as an Assistant Staff Clerk in the staff department of the factory and shops. He would need these qualifications to justify his transfer, medicine being too valuable a profession to permit a Jewish doctor to travel with his family from Czechoslovakia to

Singapore. In late March 1939, a letter from the Social and Health Institute of Bat'a confirmed the fitness of the family 'for journey and stay in the tropics'.

Dismissed at his own request from the Bat'a company of Zlín on 23 March 1939 – the Nazis occupied the country on the 15th – Dr Straüssler miraculously departed with his family and other Bat'a employees on their journey. The date stamped by British Passport Control in Prague for their departure to the Straits Settlements (Singapore) is 19 April 1939. Travelling in a group, with officially sanctioned papers but false jobs, they managed to make their way, avoiding arrest, detention or return, across Austria to Genoa. This may have been partly because the group was not one of refugees, like so many others, but a properly designated, company-protected entourage with papers and a clear purpose. It is unlikely, however, that the Nazi authorities could have overlooked the group's Jewishness, but perhaps they allowed them transit because they, too, were pleased to see them leave. Their departure reduced the number of Jews that had to be dealt with by the Germans in what had become an overwhelming refugee problem.

The Straüsslers, one of eighty-six Jewish families employed by Bat'a, joined approximately thirty-six families who left; two remarkable photographs appear of the family on the eve of their departure. The first is of the Straüssler family and the Becks (relatives on his mother's side) standing together in front of the Straüssler home the day before leaving Czechoslovakia; melancholy and anxiety shows in the family's eyes, with the young Stoppard, his brother and a cousin in the foreground unaware of the imminent change. The second photo is of the two-year-old Stoppard and his three-year-old brother Petr encircled by a life preserver on the deck of the SS *Victoria* from Genoa, bound for Singapore, in March 1939.[17] With the sea surrounding them, they look with innocence and curiosity directly into the camera. For the anticipated journey, Martha Straüssler had obtained thirty English pounds on 28 February 1939, a bank document explaining that she 'is going with her husband who will stay in Singapore three years at least'.[18]

Their departure was timely: shortly after the arrival of German troops in the country, some 5,000 Jewish refugees, anti-Nazi journalists and Communists were detained in a special camp at

Milovice, near Prague. The arrests were made by Czech police under orders from the Gestapo. It soon became impossible to leave the Protectorate, but in the spring of 1939, the Sträusslers, as well as Tomáš Bat'a, left Zlín.[19]

For the Sträusslers, departure meant upheaval, dislocation and loss, but it also ensured safety. The fear within the family was that the Germans who had overrun Czechoslovakia might begin to investigate the history of the Sträusslers and discover that Stoppard's grandparents on his father's side had some Jewish relations in Austria. The result could be catastrophic – but up to that moment, no one in Zlín gave it a thought, since the family did not practise Judaism and had assimilated. The Sträusslers were 'not Jews to themselves'. This typified a situation and pattern for many Jews in the Czech–Slovak region who had to choose between Orthodox Judaism or estrangement since the Reform Movement in the Czech lands was very limited. Signalling the family's confusion over their Judaism, one of their sons was circumcised and the other was not. Stoppard himself has explained the dilemma, especially that of his mother, who in later life would not talk about this period, when, as he put it, 'Hitler made her Jewish'.[20]

Why Singapore, which in 1939 was still a safe haven? Stoppard explained this in a 1998 interview, commenting that Sträussler family legend was probably fact. Their immediate neighbours and family friends, Dr Gellert and his family, actually had the papers to go to Singapore; the Sträusslers had orders for Nairobi. Dr Gellert had no interest in Singapore but was intrigued by Nairobi. Eugen Sträussler simply wanted to get his family out and had no preference. To satisfy his friend, he switched papers, ending up with the passage to Singapore. His neighbour headed for Nairobi and remained there for the rest of his life.[21] Other Jewish families from Bat'a went to the Phillippines, Hong Kong and Borneo.

Some members of the Sträusslers' extended family were not so lucky, although at the time no one knew of their fate. Julius and Hildegard Sträussler, Stoppard's paternal grandparents, were sent to the Terezin deportation camp in northern Bohemia in the first transport on 2 December 1941; by 9 January 1942, they had been sent onwards to the east, towards Riga, where a Jewish ghetto held some 40,000 Latvian Jews. Most were liquidated in mass killings or sent on to Salaspils concentration camp. They were never heard from again. Rudolph and Regina Beck, Martha's parents, died at Terezin in April and July 1944. A similar fate awaited his aunt Edita, who had married a Mr Eckerman and was living in Brno. She and her two-year-old daughter Hana were deported to a ghetto in Minsk, departing on 16 November 1941. They, too, were never heard from again. Wilma and Berta, sisters of Martha, died at Auschwitz; Anny, another sister, died in another camp. Their names are among those that line the walls of Pinkas Synagogue. Only Martha's brother, Ota, who remained in Czechoslovakia, and Irma, an older sister, who had married and gone to live in Argentina, survived. By October 1941, all 'Protectorate Jews' had to have registration numbers and display the yellow Star of David in public.

CHAPTER 2

LAVENDER STREET

―――――

The very name 'Singapura' was a paradox, for no lion had
ever set foot in this Lion City.
C. M. Turnbull, *A History of Singapore 1819–1988*

Colonial grandeur and oriental exoticism greeted the Straüssler family as they stood at the rail of their ship when it docked at Singapore Harbour on 15 May 1939. They had travelled for more than two weeks, from Genoa through the Tyrrhenian Sea into the Mediterranean and, via the Suez Canal, to the Red Sea and Indian Ocean, until they stopped at Colombo on 10 May 1939. From there, they entered the Strait of Malacca and finally reached Singapore. They were greeted by unfamiliar cries at the dock as runners from the largest Singapore hotels tried to identify passengers and trunks for the short journey to Raffles, the Grove or the Adelphi. The Straüsslers were not going to any hotel, but to the Bat'a compound, where they would take up residence in this exotic, tropical land that strangely contrasted English habits with Asiatic life.

The perilous situation in the Straüsslers' Czech homeland gave way to a temporary idyll in Singapore. Set between the South China Sea and the Indian Ocean, the 622-square-kilometre, diamond-shaped island of Singapore was a thriving colonial centre primed for business and trade. And in springtime it looked glorious. The Straüsslers' small house, offering temporary accommodation, belonged to a Dutch shipping company. There was even a small Jewish neighbourhood along Meyer Road, with a synagogue on Waterloo Road. An earlier settler, a Venetian Jew from Calcutta, a Mr Belilios, had done well importing cattle and sheep to the island. The Straüsslers, happy in their situation, intended to move to a house nearer the sea, until war broke out and shattered their plans.

For over a century, Singapore had been south-east Asia's most modern and outward-looking city. Yet colonial Singapore was still visible to refugees arriving in 1939 at Clifford Pier at Collyear Quay, which crossed in front of the Victorian General Post Office, near Change Alley, where moneylenders had their booths. The imposing, high-domed Supreme Court stood where the Hotel de l'Europe once dominated the Padang and Esplanade. To its left was the Victoria Theatre and to its right, the Municipal Hall, all examples of English neo-classical architecture, with tall columns supporting rigid porticos. A statue of Sir Thomas Stamford Raffles, who had founded modern Singapore as a trading post in 1819, approved the city's expansion from a stone alcove in Empress Place.

Lavender Street

Singapore was striking in its contrasts: between its Eastern mystery and reconstructed Englishness, it blended two worlds. A 1936 traveller remarked on the mix of Chinese, Japanese, Siamese, Filipinos, Malays, Sinhalese, Indians, Australians and English vying with each other in 'many shades of orange, and pink and red and blue and green, magenta and cherry colours predominating. Many of them are half naked; and their brown skins throw the colours of their robes into strange relief.' Indian saris mixed with Malay batik sarongs and Chinese silk cheongsams. The Chinese amahs wore short black baggy trousers and starched white jackets with their hair tied in long queues hanging down their backs.[1]

Central Singapore had numerous arcaded streets filled with rickshaws, carts, cars and trams. Vendors would offer bolts of silks and cottons, sacks of dried food; goldsmiths, furniture-makers, money-changers and food shops were everywhere. Streets like Lavender Street, Jalan Besar Road or Malay Street teemed with businesses, brothels, cafés and restaurants. The New World Amusement Park could accommodate up to 700 dancers, who gathered among its eating stalls, shops, sideshows, opera halls and musical performers. Exoticism extended to the wealthy Chinese of Singapore. One of the wealthiest, Aw Boon Haw, the founder of Tiger Balm ointment, had his car painted a vivid yellow with black stripes while the hood and radiator were made to represent an enormous tiger's head with the mouth wide open to show rows of large, white teeth.

Humidity was a constant problem. Situated only eighty miles north of the Equator, Singapore suffered from a tropical climate which Kipling referred to as 'the heat of the orchid-house, – a remorseless, steam-sweat that knows no variation between night and day'.[2] One perspiring diner at Raffles had to eat in his beret because his bald head collected condensed water under the dining-room's electric fans. Some resorted to changing their clothes three times a day. Nevertheless, for many, Singapore provided remarkable opportunities, as the journalist Mona Gardner wrote in 1939: 'to the young clerk out from home, it means joining the master caste and letting his complexion take him to places his salary never could. A tour of duty here spells malaria to army officers, to the bride it means orchids after marriage and to Japanese imperialists it is the place where 18 inch guns are waiting to say "Keep off the Grass".' The key to Singapore's success was rubber, since it was the departure point for much of the rubber grown and processed in Malaysia. Dominating the marine highway, Singapore was the hinge for trade between Asia and Europe.[3]

Curious evocations of England and Scotland in Singapore were the place names, ranging from the Cameron Highlands Hotel, to the Gleneagles Hospital. Estates often had names like Swiss Cottage or Holland Park, with individual homes called 'Brean Down'. Recreation was similarly a blend of English and Indian pastimes, with cricket, horse racing and tennis the most popular pursuits. 'In both India and Singapore,' writes one commentator, 'English attitudes were adopted and adapted to colonial circumstances and often extended to influence the recreation habits of the indigenous population.'[4] Not surprisingly, the British Regimental Band performed every Tuesday and Friday afternoon on the Esplanade.

For Martha Straüssler, Singapore represented security and stability. In the beginning, it was 'marvellous. I liked the heat, the exotic fruit, the food and the local people,' she wrote in her memoir. A Malayan ayah pushed the boys about in a double cane pushchair and tried hard to speak Czech to them. As Peter Stoppard confirmed to me, 'we arrived in Singapore as Czech-speaking children', but the boys left, three years later, with a marginal knowledge of English.[5]

Linguistically, Singapore was a polyglot mixture of English, Chinese and Tamil and it was rare to find a monolingual family or home; multilingualism was the norm. English dominated, though it took a unique form, officially Singapore Colloquial English, informally shaped into 'Singlish', a colloquial blend of words drawing on disparate linguistic sources. At home, Stoppard spoke a child's Czech, while around him was a remarkable chorus of unusual languages. He was introduced to 'Singlish' at the English convent nursery school he attended from the age of three with his brother, travelling there by rickshaw. His parents needed to speak English outside the home, his mother possibly familiar with the language through the study of primary-grade English in Czechoslovakia, his father slightly advanced through his medical studies. In India, Stoppard's English would become more formalized, but there, too, it would reflect a remarkable diversity: his school was an American Methodist one and the English spoken there was more American than British. One visitor to Singapore in the thirties, in fact, ironically criticized the type of English spoken by the British, especially at Raffles: 'after hearing their English in the lounge, it is a relief to talk one's mother tongue with the Indian servants, who have a pleasing voice and a pure pronunciation . . .'[6]

Like Zlín, Singapore was neatly divided: downtown were offices and docks; to the east was an airport; to the west, the industrial city of Jurong, while offshore was the island of Sentosa and some fifty-nine smaller islands serving either as oil refineries or beach escapes from the city. The Bat'a rubber plantations in Malaysia, connected to Singapore by a railway that crossed the kilometre-long causeway across the narrow Straits of Johor, provided constant activity for the Bat'a factory and administrative offices on the island.

J. G. Farrell's novel *The Singapore Grip*, set between 1937 and 1942, vividly investigates the unexpected impact of war on Singapore life, suddenly caught between tennis matches and air raids. The novel captures, if only briefly, the extravagant contrasts of the city: a hectic Chinatown, the more sedate Indian sector and a rural Malay section counterbalanced the stateliness of the Colonial enclave. This was a world where the traffic police still wore basketwork wings strapped across their backs so that they did not have to wave their arms in the heat but could casually turn their feet to direct the cars. Robinson's restaurant, newly air-conditioned, dominated Raffles Place, and became the focal point of much social life. Orchids could still be picked on the roadside. Japanese belligerency did not worry the Straüsslers or anyone else in 1939. They were greeted by wide avenues, beautiful lawns, monolithic government buildings and ageless banks.

A greater attention to class was apparent in Singapore, where, according to Stoppard's mother, people were obsessed with one's religion and background. In Czechoslovakia, ancestry, before the German take-over, did not matter; Stoppard's parents were not religious in any way, although they celebrated Christmas and Easter. From central Europe to colonial Britain via Singapore was a strange and dislocating experience for Stoppard, but the intersection of these disparate cultures taught him that life was contrast and antithesis. To be in south-east Asia as framed by colonial Britain was disorienting for a young Czech boy learning a new language in a foreign land. He responded in a way which he would later repeat: by appropriating the new as a defence against further change.

In advance of the Straüsslers' arrival in 1939, the storm clouds of Europe were already darkening the skies of south-east Asia, although war had not yet been declared. Pressure on the government for more bomb-proof shelters and gas masks mounted in the papers. Frequent drills for poison-gas attacks were held, as well as public lectures on protecting oneself from air attack. Preparations for a conflict were under way but there was no great worry because it was thought that Japan would exhaust herself financially in trying to subdue the Chinese. By 1941, however, there were frequent rehearsals for battle and a constant call for volunteer nurses, air-raid wardens and defence aides; sufficient food had been stored for six months and medical supplies for two years. But while a war raged in Europe, there was little disturbance in Singapore. There was no food rationing, social restrictions or limitations on drink. The beaches remained undefended. A similarly false sense of security existed in Malaya, where some 18,000 Europeans worked with the Malays, Chinese, Indians and Tamils on the rubber estates and railways.

On 8 December 1941, this serenity and stability shattered. Early that morning, the Japanese began landing at Kota Bahru, a coastal town on the east coast of Malaysia, 400 miles to the north. The Governor of Singapore, Sir Shenton Thomas, awakened by a call telling him of the invasion, took only minor precautions until 4.15 a.m., when, with only fifteen minutes' warning, Japanese bombs began to fall on his unprepared city. Most thought it was a practice raid; one startled woman who had been hurled from her bed complaining to the police that 'they're overdoing it – Robinson's [a department store/restaurant] has just been hit!'[7] But the seventeen Japanese planes killed sixty-one people and injured 133. There were no more air raids that month, creating a false sense of business as usual, while the crisis surrounded them. Passenger ships left harbour half-empty. At the end of December, Japanese leaflets fell on the city, calling for its surrender.

The Straüsslers did not panic when war broke out; at least they were together, although the situation was traumatic. From late December until mid-February, Singapore was under frequent attack by waves of bombers and fighter planes in V formations, dropping bombs or strafing the city and ships. Initially, the naval station, commercial docks, oilfields and air bases were the targets, but increasingly, by accident and intention, homes, hospitals and hotels were hit. Constant dark clouds billowed up around the city centre from the burning oil depots and flaming warehouses stuffed with rubber, tin, whisky and gin. The city was in a permanent dark haze, silhouetted at night by the fires burning out of control, intensified by exploding ammunition stores.

In eight weeks, the Japanese advanced from close to the Thai border to the southern tip of the Malay Peninsula. By 31 January 1942, the Japanese breached the Johor causeway; on 8–9 February, troops began to land on Singapore Island. Yet a strange denial of the imminent danger persisted and calm balanced the terror. Two popular cinemas remained open as late as 11 February 1942, while the *Straits Times* on that day advertised a dinner dance at Raffles Hotel. Shortly before the fall of the city, the Singapore Club in the Fullerton Building began to destroy its liquor stock, inviting its members to assist by offering free drinks; the place was packed. Singapore's population had increased to nearly one million by January 1942, with the largest influx of civilian refugees coming from Malaya. Military personnel, arriving to reinforce the island, as well as fleeing from the north, added another 500,000. People were housed in the basements of hotels, schools, churches and any other available space. Stoppard himself recalled that his 'earliest memories were of bomb shelters and air raids', although he also remembered going to school with his brother in a rickshaw, hiding under the dining-room table, covered with blankets, during an air raid and being driven to the docks at night.[8] The arrival of reinforcements in merchant ships, commercial ships and naval transports meant that the women and children on the island would be evacuated – on the very same ships that had brought the troops and supplies, although this was not part of their original mission. Embarkations had to take place at night because of the constant daylight raids.

Women and children would hurriedly board ships while cargo was being offloaded. Conditions were often unsanitary and primitive, since the troops had to be unloaded immediately and the refugees boarded as quickly as possible because of Japanese attacks. Gaining passage was immensely difficult, since up until two weeks before Singapore fell the civil administration had made little attempt to organize a proper evacuation.[9] Officials caused numerous delays because of their insistence on passport checks. Individuals also had to pay for their own passage, with the P & O company charged with organizing passages. The booking office, surprisingly, still operated, although for safety it moved out of the harbour to the manager's home in a residential neighbourhood; people had to make their way past the Botanical Gardens and up sedate Cluny Road to queue for long hours in the tropical heat to get a ticket or pass to leave. Two desks stood in the booking room, one with a sign which read 'Colombo', the other 'UK'.[10] If one received a ticket, it meant a single suitcase and space for a mattress which the passenger had to provide. No one at the time could assess the risks of sailing or the length of separation between husbands and wives. There was also little time to prepare, sometimes only hours; at the docks, where launches would ferry passengers out to waiting ships in the harbour, there was congestion and confusion as cars, trucks, rickshaws and taxis converged, with many vehicles forced to divert because of bomb craters, blocked streets, air raids, burning buildings, abandoned vehicles and unexploded bombs. Artillery fire, fighter attacks and bombing runs made a trip to the waterfront extremely dangerous. In the middle of the afternoon of 30 January 1942, the day British forces retreated across the causeway to Singapore Island, an air-raid siren was sounded near the docks, but the bombs dropped on another part of the island. Peter Stoppard believes that was the day he, his brother and mother departed. A stamp permitting their passage from Singapore to India in their passport reads 29 January 1942.

A good number of women and children had already left by the middle of January, but by the end of the month all were ordered to evacuate. Martha Sträussler stayed as long as she could because she did not want to leave her husband and travel on her own with her two sons, Petr and Tomáš, to Australia, the destination for most Bat'a employees. It was impossible to leave with her husband, however, and she and the children most likely left Singapore between 30 January and 2 February 1942, although possibly as late as 6 February: all was chaos, with boats, departure times and dates constantly changing. The *Felix Roussel* departed on the 6th, one day before the Japanese intensified their shelling of the city. In her memoir, Martha indicated that she waited longer than the other women to depart in the hope that her husband might join her or that the Japanese would be repelled. Censored information on just how badly the battle on the Malay Peninsula was going generated false hopes, since the authorities were reluctant to tell the public the truth.[11]

Overcrowding on board was common and ships that might carry a few hundred were forced to take over a thousand. There was no privacy. It is estimated that the four ships that left on 30–31 January 1942 carried between 5,000 and 6,000 evacuees. Another two ships left a week later, carrying nearly 2,400 women and children.[12] By February 1942, when bombing raids at the docks were as constant as the plumes of dark smoke from the burning oil storage tanks or the devastated naval base to the north, numerous burned-out ships littered the waterway, one of them the 17,000-ton *Empress of Asia*. Ships that escaped relatively unscathed headed for safety in Colombo, Sri Lanka or Fremantle, Australia before heading on to Durban and/or Bombay or Liverpool.

With British and Australian naval escorts protecting the convoy from constant bombing, the ship carrying Stoppard, his brother and mother made it to sea under cover of darkness, though its intended destination was unclear. It stood for three days just off Singapore, then headed to Australia before inexplicably turning back to Singapore only to stop at Colombo where a number of the passengers, including Petr, Tomáš and their mother, transferred to a vessel bound for India. Stoppard remembered that their destination changed at sea from Australia to India, another moment in his life where accident intervened. In the hurry and confusion of changing ships at Colombo, a small brown suitcase containing family photographs, personal items, mementoes and papers was lost. Stoppard's documented past was gone; so, too, was anything belonging to his father. (Peter Stoppard thinks that the lighter or small boat ferrying their luggage sank.) Years later, Martha recalled her unhappiness when one night she lost two silver medallions engraved with the names of her sons that her best friend had given her. Without their father, or knowledge of his fate, the family was displaced for a second time.

Circumstances on the *Felix Roussel* were typical of the escaping vessels. The captain was Irish, the officers French and the crew Lascars, sailors from India. On board were thirty seamen from the bombed *Empress of Asia* and eight American bankers, survivors from another sinking.[13] Water was rationed, food limited and sanitary facilities intolerable. Mattresses on the deck were preferable to sleeping in the overcrowded cabins. But worry over those left behind in Singapore outweighed the discomfort or any danger from Japanese planes, and tears often covered Martha Straüssler's face. The family finally disembarked in Bombay on 14 February 1942.

Dr Straüssler had joined the Local Defence Corps of the Straits Settlements Volunteer Force, as did all the Czechoslovakian Bat'a men remaining in Singapore, a result of the complete mobilization of the island. As the situation worsened in early February, Mr Jugas, in charge of Bat'a operations, told the men that they had to decide whether to stay or depart. Each had to make up his own mind. As a physician, Dr Straüssler felt obliged to stay and help, postponing his departure to join his family. Hospitals were drastically overcrowded, with admissions reaching over 2,000 patients a day and the unclaimed dead being buried in pits dug on the front lawns of the buildings. Dr Straüssler worked part-time at a first-aid station. One day, a bomb fell nearby, collapsing the sandbags at the post and injuring several, including Dr Straüssler: he apparently had a crushed rib. As a consequence, it was impossible for him to leave the next day, when most Bat'a people departed.

By 10 February, a general call to evacuate went through Singapore; on the 12th, the British retreated to their final perimeter around Singapore City. By then, about one million people were crowded into a three-mile radius from the waterfront, bombed by day, shelled by night. Until recently, what happened to Dr Straüssler remained something of a mystery: he was thought to be part of a handful of other Bat'a men trying to board some of the last boats able to leave on 12 or 13 February. In fact, Dr Straüssler died at sea on 13 or 14 February 1942, when his ship and others were spotted by Japanese fighter planes in the straits between Sumatra and Bangka Island and attacked from the air as well as torpedoed. Historians refer to 13 February as 'Black Friday'.[14]

The details of Dr Straüssler's death remained unknown to his wife, despite many enquiries, until the mid 1990s, when, through the efforts of, first, Dr Emil Máčel of Zlín, who has studied the fate of the Bat'a doctors, and then of Stoppard himself, the story became clear. According to Dr Máčel, a friend of Dr Straüssler's, Josef Varmuža, drove Dr Straüssler and others to the harbour on 12 February, but one of them, a Mr Koš, forgot some documents and had to go back. The remaining Bat'a employees, including Dr Straüssler, boarded a ship which had departed by the time Mr Varmuža returned. The ship was soon attacked in the strait.

Stoppard's own research presents a different picture. Contacted by Mr Leslie Smith, a former neighbour in their Singapore compound who was now living in England, Stoppard pieced together a new narrative. Smith was a family friend, managing the Singapore branch of a British corporation that made optical and navigational equipment. One night, he was visited at his office by Dr Straüssler and a Mr Heim, asking for help to leave. Although there was chaos at the docks as thousands of civilians streamed down to Clifford Pier and Telok Ayer Basin, seeking any means of escape, Smith had a pass to the docks and that night they entered the secure area and gained passage on a ship because Smith knew the captain. Dr Straüssler tried to convince Smith to stay on board, but he refused, citing loyalty to his staff. The ship left that Friday night, only to be bombed by the Japanese in the strait known as 'Bomb Alley'. It was part of a forty-four-ship evacuation armada that ranged from naval sloops to outboard motor launches sailing south for Java and then Australia. The next day, confirmation reached Singapore that the ship carrying Dr Straüssler had been sunk.[15] Two days after Dr Straüssler's death, on 15 February 1942, Singapore fell: facing potentially immense loss of life, combined with dwindling supplies, staggering damage and intense over-crowding, the British had little choice but to surrender.

Dr Straüssler died the same year his parents and sister were killed by the Nazis and his name appears on memorials in Singapore and Zlín of those Bat'a employees and Czechs who sacrificed their lives. But the meaning of his loss was not immediately understood by the young Stoppard boys. 'I'm afraid I don't recall worrying about my father,' Stoppard told an interviewer in 1987. 'But my memory really begins after I'd lost him. Fatherlessness didn't strike me as being an event. It was a state of life.'[16] As his mother remarked, for the first two years in India they spoke of little else. In Stoppard's drama, fathers are rarely present.

Martha Straüssler was understandably reluctant to speak to her sons about their Czech roots or Singapore past: the former, perhaps the happiest period of her life, was taken away from her; the latter, the most dangerous, entailed the loss of her husband and a run for their lives. Ironically, while she strove to have both her sons assimilate fully into English life (encouraged and promoted by her new husband) after their move there in 1946, she herself 'remained engagingly foreign'.[17]

So far, India likes me.
Stoppard, *Indian Ink*

India was the first country that gave Stoppard clear memories of his youth. He was nearly five when he arrived and eight and a half when he left, old enough for the country to make a lasting impression on him. He and his family crisscrossed the country following their landing in Bombay, eventually settling in Darjeeling.[18] It would be remembered as a haven from the turmoil and tragedy of Singapore. India was the first country where Stoppard became conscious of his status as a refugee. 'We had no choice about leaving Singapore or indeed about where we were going. We got on a boat going to Australia,' he remembers. 'For some reason while we were at sea the boat decided to go to India.' (Stoppard is forgetting the transfer at Colombo.) But unlike his experiences in Czechoslovakia or even Singapore, which largely evaporated, those in India remained with him: 'I retain quite a nostalgia for the heat and smells and sounds of India,' he remarked in February 1995.[19] Martha, his mother, was less sanguine. Her persistent worry about her husband – had he survived? Did he know where they were? – constantly plagued her. Her efforts to find out something via the Red Cross and the Czech Consulate in Calcutta were largely unsuccessful.

Martha Straüssler's four years in India seemed to her 'like a lifetime and a nightmare'. They arrived in Bombay without their personal belongings. They had no more than their papers and the clothes they wore. She was also anxious about her husband's fate and depressed. Settling finally in the hill town of Darjeeling on the edge of the Himalayas, however, lifted her spirits and revived her health: she worked, looked after the boys and awaited word of her husband.

Eventually, she was invited to visit the consulate in Calcutta, where she was told that Dr Straüssler was still among those missing and presumed lost. She returned the next day to Darjeeling but initially did not tell her sons the news, believing they had enough to cope with. But, one day, Martha asked a friend to tell the boys: the woman took them for a walk and told them that their father was dead. They returned to their worried mother, concerned for their reaction. Stoppard remembers that 'for my part, I took it well, or not well, depending on how you look at it. I felt almost nothing. I felt the significance of the occasion but not the loss.'[20] His language is not ironic but verbally antithetical, very much in line with the way his plays, arabesques of antithesis, operate.

I could find Minto Villa in my sleep and often have in the
forty-five years since we left India.
Stoppard, 1991

When they first arrived in India, Bat'a moved the Straüsslers from Singapore around the country, first to Naini Tal, a nineteenth-century hill town; Lahore, in the east, where Bat'a had a factory in nearby Batapur, followed, then Kanpur (formerly Cawnpore), the largest city in the state of Uttar Pradesh; teeming Calcutta, once the capital of British India, and ancient Delhi, the industrial centre of the north, were next. Such movement, however, did not ease Martha Straüssler's worries as they followed the pattern of Europeans, alternating between the cooler hill stations during the summer and the temperate plains during the winter. Several times they moved to Batanagar, the Bat'a town built downriver from Calcutta. At one point during this shuffling, several of the mothers, including Martha Sträussler, asked for something to do and this was how the family found themselves settled in Darjeeling, where Martha Sträussler began to manage the Bat'a shoe shop.

On a map of India, Darjeeling is a finger pointing to Tibet, surrounded by Nepal to the west and Bhutan to the west. Next to the hill town of Simla, made famous by Kipling, Darjeeling is the most celebrated of all the hill stations, those mountain locales established in the nineteenth century as sanatoria for government officials, army officers and ordinary civilians, villages that in their social structure and architecture duplicated British life. Perched on a ridge 7,000 feet up in the Himalayan foothills of north-east India, overlooking the Bengali plain and originally discovered by intrepid horticulturalists, Darjeeling is said to have derived its name from Dorje Ling, 'the land of the thunderbolt'. Terraced tea gardens and thickly forested hills surround the city. Its cool temperatures, due to its altitude, made it one of the most sought-after destinations.

Darjeeling sits in privacy, observing from its diminutive perspective the majesty of the Himalayas. The twin peaks of Kanchenjunga at 8,585 metres and the surrounding mountains startle the visitor but not the inhabitants, as the travel writer Jan Morris so accurately describes: 'The town lives in the knowledge of them, and so acknowledges another scale of things. Its littleness is not inferiority complex, but self-awareness, and it gives the community a particular intensity and vivacity.'[21] Stoppard himself underscored the power of the view when he revisited Darjeeling in 1990: 'the genius of the place is the view of the Kanchenjunga range of the Himalayas.' And when the mist seems to lift the mountains off the earth, 'they float in the sky, infinitely far off and yet sharply detailed . . . lit like theatre, so ageless and permanent as to make history trivial. It is perhaps the most mesmerizing view of the earth from anywhere on the earth.'[22]

Another traveller – the actor Geoffrey Kendal, father of Felicity Kendal (later to have an important role in Stoppard's life) – wrote to his daughter Jennifer during the time of the Sträusslers' stay that the climate was 'like the best of English summer'. 'There are no cars in the town, only rickshaws and riding ponies. Everyone rides, it is 2 rs an hour. And you can get a pony anywhere – children ride to school on them . . . the hills are covered in tea plants.'[23]

Darjeeling is built in layers, with the posh hotels and villas at the top, a jumbled bazaar at the bottom. The dense, tiered buildings reveal a vibrant life, partly the product of the brilliant mountain air, which is seldom hot. Strolling at the Chaurasta, the triangular piazza half-way along the ridge, became a ritual; the large, green-shuttered Oxford Bookshop with its open wooden floors looming over the square a relic of the Raj. Nearby is the essential symbol of traditional English values, the yellow-painted, Gothic-style St Andrew's Church, dominating the steep landscape of tin-roofed, multi-gabled wood and fretwork chalet-style buildings, in the idiom of all the Raj hill stations.

Like Singapore, Darjeeling presented Stoppard with two cultures in contrast. Evoking British village life in their physical configuration, the hill stations replicated particular features of the natural and social environment of Britain. The social practices of the British inhabitants created a kind of nostalgic world, outfitting the locales with trees and flowers indigenous to England, cultivating English fruit orchards and vegetable gardens and constructing homes and hotels as gabled Gothic villas, half-timbered Tudor cottages or ornamented Swiss chalets, against a dramatic landscape peopled with exotic individuals.[24]

Darjeeling is a frontier settlement, bordering Bhutan, Sikkim, Nepal and Tibet, and is more an *entrepôt* of central-Asian trade than a city. Founded by Captain G. S. Lloyd, it long stood as a restorative locale for those suffering from the heat of Calcutta and the Bengal plains; for the English, it represented relaxation and recreation. Visitors came to recover from illness, escape the heat and revive the social habits left back in England. Emily Eden, whose journal *Up the Country* would be helpful to Stoppard when he wrote *In the Native State* (1991), recounts how her three children made a restorative journey in 1838 to Mussoorie, the nearest hill station to Delhi. The first British residence in Darjeeling was built in 1826 and the city soon became a centre for tea plantations, with the Planter's Club its centre. The city was also a crossroads for many: Lepchas, the original inhabitants, Nepalese, Tibetans, Chinese, Indians and Americans, as well as various refugees, made up the diverse populace. On the eastern end of the ridge, at Jalapahar Hill, a small military fort perched, reminding all of the extended danger of war. Counterbalancing this was Observatory Hill, rising directly above the Chaurasta, holy to the Buddhists who have a shrine at its summit with trees along the way often covered with white prayer flags.

Certain traditions prevailed, from the authority of the Planter's Club and the Gymkhana Club, sponsor of the annual horse races, to the Victorian-style Windamere [sic] Hotel and the Mount Everest Hotel, set back from the road with a Frenchified elegance from its dunce's-cap towers in the château style. The appropriately named main thoroughfare to the plains remains Hill Cart Road. In the centre of the city was The Dell, where four roads met, but also near a popular level walk around Observatory Hill. It is not, however, shielded from weather, and the monsoon season, from June to September, often causes landslides.

Linking Tibet and India made Darjeeling an exotic world, similar to and yet different from Singapore. The marketplace was an international crossroads with Marwaris moneylending, Kashmiris and Punjabis dealing in silks, skins and furs, Nepalese selling turquoise, coral, amber, jade and knives, Parsees offering silverware and Bhutanese functioning as pawnbrokers. Trade with Tibet meant importing horses, blankets, tea, wool, musk, musical instruments and shoes; in turn, various items would be exported to Tibet, such as brass, copper and salt. There was also an important trade in tea – and all this trans-frontier trade generated an international character for the town which, for Stoppard, equalled his experience in Singapore. During the war, the population expanded with the numerous English and American soldiers who found the city ideal for rest and recreation.

It is unlikely that the young Stoppard and his brother were aware of more than the physical attributes of Darjeeling and its astonishing similarity, despite the geographical contrast, to Singapore when they arrived in 1942. They did recall the first rail trip, however, because the train was derailed twice and had to be levered back on to the tracks. The second time it happened, the floorboards in their carriage were ripped up and their mother insisted they be transferred to another car. He also remembers receiving his first snowball from an American officer travelling in the same railcar.

From the 1860s on, the hill stations had boarding-schools for British, Anglo-Indian and Indian children: the climate and isolation from the distractions and illness of the cities was thought to be beneficial. The Stoppard boys would board at the Mount Hermon School at North Point, a co-educational institution and slightly down-scale, given the reputation and history of the more formal, all-boys school nearby, St Paul's, founded by Bishop Cotton, who had been a master at Marlborough and taught for fifteen years at Rugby. He was said to be the model young master in *Tom Brown's Schooldays*. St Joseph's, an imposing Jesuit school in a detailed Gothic structure, was the other school in Darjeeling. The slightly *déclassé* Mount Hermon was founded in 1895 by Emma Knowles, an American Methodist. The original location, situated in the centre of the town, was a rented house called 'Arcadia', foreshadowing the title of Stoppard's 1993 play.

As the school grew, it needed larger premises and soon acquired the Mount Hermon Estate which had formerly belonged to the Lebong Tea Company. In 1926, the school formally reopened as the Queens Hill School, its original name, which changed in 1930 to the Mount Hermon School. Founded by Nonconformist missionaries, the school was run by the Methodist Episcopal Church of America and it was, in a word, inclusive. In the 1940s, for example, the co-ed student body consisted of English, American, Anglo-Indian, Scandinavian, Tibetan, Australian, Anglo-Burman, Armenian and Austrian children, refugee and non-refugee.[25] Social class was not an issue since a large proportion of the children were those of American missionaries. Stoppard and his brother started in 1942 and left in January 1946.

Out of the classroom, students were free to roam the Mount Hermon estate. Excursions to Black Rock, a huge promontory down the hillside, or the yearly troop to Tiger Hill, 11 kilometres away, at 2 a.m. to watch the sunrise on Kanchenjunga, were much-anticipated school events. But nothing compared with a visit to Hafiz's shop, which sold sweets, tinned fruit and gram, a spicy mixture of cereal, pasta and nuts. A trip to Keventer's, a dairy shop, was also a treat, as much as tea at Pliva's restaurant on special occasions when parents came to visit. Next to Keventer's was the Bat'a shoe store managed by Stoppard's mother, who introduced the chiropody corner in the niche created by the rear window with its view of Kanchenjunga.

Stoppard clearly remembers these experiences and the anxiously awaited visits of his mother: he would often stare at the long, straight driveway to the school and 'watch an amorphous dot at the far end of this road slowly turn into his mother', a friend remarked. She would visit on Sundays, walking down the long zigzag from the Lebong Road. Stoppard and his brother would wait for her beneath a large *Cryptomeria*, a fir tree which grew all over the hills. They would spot her in the distance but have to wait some minutes to be sure it was their mother, 'but it was always her in the end, turning off the hill on to the flat driveway, laden with good things to eat'.[26] They would run and bring her back to a bench beneath the tree where they would unpack her gifts, mostly food. Returning to Darjeeling, in Stoppard's memory, often meant returning to that tree.

Stoppard's report card from November 1944, when he was seven, is a useful record of his interests and progress. Among his subjects were History ('good'), Geography ('very good'), Grammar and Reading ('good' ['fair' is crossed out]), Writing ('good') and Arithmetic ('very good'). His only 'excellent' was, appropriately, in Literature. Out of thirty students, he ranked tenth.

Other memories of Mount Hermon School recalled by Stoppard included his youthful crush on the matron's daughter who would sometimes dry his hair. The event still resonates: 'the smell of damp hair cooking in the blast of an electric dryer is still a Proustian trigger for pleasurable and disturbing emotions,' he wrote in 1991.[27] The Matron was Mrs Callow and her daughter was Joy, according to a letter reminding Stoppard in 1983. The two dormitories where the small boys slept at the end of the corridor had iron beds with interlocking springs that served as trampolines. But if boys were out of bed after lights out, Mrs Callow would reprimand them by making them sit on the carpet in her room and feeding them cookies while she got ready to listen to the news. Stoppard also remembers his first musical performance: playing the triangle with a school percussion band in 1944 in the Darjeeling town square – anticipating, perhaps, the triangle-playing prisoner in his play *Every Good Boy Deserves Favour*.

What Mount Hermon really meant for Stoppard was security and a feeling that, despite the disruptive past, there might be order in the present and possibly the future: one day, he recalled, walking down the corridor to the playground 'trailing a finger along a raised edge on the wall, and it suddenly came upon me that *everything was all right*, and would always be'.[28] The image remained and he used it in his 1973 radio play, *Where Are They Now?*, presenting two parallel school dinners, one in 1945, the other in 1969. Gale, reminiscing, recalls that at age seven, during his first term at school, he trailed his finger along the raised edge of the wall:

and I was suddenly totally happy . . . I experienced happiness as a state of being: everywhere I looked, in my mind, *nothing was wrong*. You never get that back when you grow up; it's a condition of maturity that almost *everything* is wrong, *all the time*.[29]

Marking the relaxed and accepting atmosphere at the school, Stoppard was known as 'Tommy Straüssler'.

The dignified, large, grey bulk of the two-storey Mount Hermon school building meant protection for Stoppard – and secrecy, as he remembered that the ayah or manservant 'would appear like a ghost in the night to smuggle me and my brother a parcel of tuck from Minto Villa', the family home.[30] And the plateau of the playing field below the building meant a chance to learn baseball, cricket and other sports favoured by the American headmaster.

In Darjeeling, Stoppard also frequented the Oxford Book and Stationery Company on the Chaurasta (a Cambridge shop was further down the hill) and remembered buying the *Dandy* and *Beano* in a shop near the Capital Cinema in Darjeeling. His mother also remembered the two of them planning to open a bookshop in India when he was older.

The Straüsslers lived in several places, starting with a brief stay at the Swiss Hotel. They then moved to Minto Villa, on the right-hand side of Auckland Road (now Gandhi Road), past the Capitol Cinema, remembered by Stoppard for its grey stone pillars and its name chiselled on one of the two square stone pillars at the front. Struan Lodge was their second home, an apricot-coloured stone house on the slope overlooking the bazaar. Curiously, he later noted, most of the homes in Darjeeling reflected a Scottish style and had Scottish names, like Killarney Lodge and Gleneagles, or Auckland Road.

Other memories of Darjeeling focus on the American officers who were to him:

figures of radiant, almost mythological glamour . . . far more exotic then to me than the Nepalese population or even the Tibetan traders who were common enough in the narrow street that climbed up past the Bat'a shoe shop and the Planter's Club to the town square where ponies waited for hire.[31]

Their smart, thin soled shoes, unlike the heavy-duty British version, and non-khaki uniforms suggested 'an unmilitary debonair spirit borne out by [their] easy manners'.[32] When Stoppard encountered a generous American officer, he asked if he had any gum, and this led to an invitation to visit him the next morning at the Mount Everest Hotel. Stoppard arrived to find the officer had gone; however, his visit to the imposing Mount Everest had a magical effect, as he entered past a liveried major-domo, which he remembered some fifty years later. On another occasion, a brigadier humorously showed him how to aim his toy revolver in the lounge of the Swiss Hotel where the Straüsslers stayed briefly. Across the street and steeply set below the imposing Mount Everest, the Swiss Hotel's corrugated roof was level with the road. Reminiscing about times past and the impact of the war, Stoppard realized that 'one of the problems about war is that it is not until afterwards that you find out whether it is a four-year war or a six-week war'.[33]

Emotionally, I like to conserve. I don't like impulsive change.
Stoppard, 1994

The past coloured Stoppard's view of India: 'When Bengal was replaced by Derbyshire, India misted over, a lost domain of uninterrupted happiness'.[34] Despite his positive recollections of this time, Stoppard concedes that he and his family led a precarious if not marginalized existence. To an interviewer in 1991, he admitted: 'we weren't actually English, as you know, so one was, I think, really neither in the British Raj world nor in the Indian world for most of the time I was there'.[35]

On 25 November 1945, however, things changed dramatically. Almost, it seemed, without warning, his mother married Kenneth Stoppard in Calcutta. Stoppard was a British major originally stationed in New Delhi and attached to the Indian army. Martha had met Kenneth during one of the major's frequent R & R visits to Darjeeling and he fell in love with the Czech widow with two small boys. Kenneth Stoppard came from northern England, not far from Sheffield, and had lost his own father at a young age. He understood something of the absence of a father and sensed the role he would have to play in the lives of Tommy and Peter Straüssler.

Major Stoppard embodied the dignified British officer who valued the colonial life in demeanour as well as attitude. After the war, he tried to uphold the colonial style and outlook back in England: the dignity of Britain must be maintained against all foreigners and foreignness, while respect for the monarchy and support of the Conservatives against Labour remained paramount. Major Stoppard's colonial paternalism contradicted the family's multicultural experiences in Singapore and Darjeeling. To Kenneth Stoppard, only selected races, adopting an English manner, such as Gurkhas, were admirable. But when ethnic groups like Jews or Indians, who might have honorary membership of the 'club' but remained outsiders, persisted in their 'tribal' ways, he saw this as sheer ingratitude and an insult to England. 'Don't you realize *that I made you British?*' was his persistent and not so rhetorical question to his Jewish stepsons.[36]

Tommy Sträussler had no idea of these attitudes as he prepared to leave India with his family and stepfather for an unexplored country, England, and an unknown life, that of an English schoolboy rather than a Czech refugee who had escaped from war-torn Singapore. And he was to have a new name: he was no longer to be Tomáš Sträussler, nor even Tommy Sträussler, but Tom Stoppard.

Uncertainty is the normal state.

Stoppard, *Rosencrantz and Guildenstern are Dead*

The first eight and a half years of Stoppard's life are a story of twentieth-century displacement and loss. Before he moved to England with a British stepfather, he had inhabited three countries; he had been a refugee thrown into at least three different cultures and four different languages: Czech, Chinese, Hindi and, finally, English. Not surprisingly, each element of this past found its way into his work, much as Stoppard might deny it. The repressive situation in Czechoslovakia, for example, under President Husák, led to Stoppard's support of Charter 77 and the writing of *Professional Foul*. His experience of Singapore found expression through his work on the screenplay of J. G. Ballard's novel *Empire of the Sun*, which Steven Spielberg released in 1987. Although set in Shanghai, it contained numerous parallels with Stoppard's life in the devastated city of Singapore which forced his family's evacuation and the death of his father. India, of course, appeared in *In the Native State*, his radio play, rewritten and mounted in the West End as *Indian Ink*.

Stoppard shared these experiences with his brother Peter and during this period of change and disruption they remained close. Two years older, Peter provided security and comfort for his younger brother. They attended the same schools in India and England, and lived together in Bristol for a period of time. While providing a link with their past, Peter also shared in their recent rediscoveries of family history. And as Stoppard's career developed, Peter would stay close to him, acting as his brother's financial manager during his career as an accountant in Bristol.

Another constant in the midst of Stoppard's shifting, fragmentary youth was his engagement with English, which he first began to understand in Singapore and gradually started to use in India. English quickly substituted for Czech, a peculiar American rather than British English, since the Mount Hermon School was run by American Methodists and many visitors were American. Colloquial speech, often filled with American expressions, blended with the more formal language used by the British in Darjeeling. Baseball, as he has noted, was his first sport, cricket his second. English, he has frequently remarked, was not a second language for him but his first. Yet his accent, in which he occasionally lisps and rolls his *r*-sounds, is a frequent reminder of the Czech origin of his English pronunciation. One ungenerous rumour was that Stoppard copied the expatriate drawl of his literary hero, Graham Greene, who used the same sound. Stoppard rejects this as caprice, as well as the idea that his talent with English and fascination with words originates, as did that of Conrad and Nabokov, with English being his second language. Nabokov, he fondly pointed out, spoke English from childhood and he, Stoppard, had never been literate in any other language *but* English: 'I spoke only toddler's Czech. I went to English-speaking school in India, and I was educated in English. English has been my first language ever since I could talk.'[37]

The most significant aspect of his early life, however, is the modern one of dislocation. As a refugee or outsider, even after he settled in England in 1946, Stoppard learned how to adjust, reject or adapt to his new environments through appropriation or invention. Such adaptability would be refined in England throughout his career, as he moved from provincial journalism to playwriting, short stories, novels and screenplays – and a possible explanation of why, unlike some of his contemporaries, he is happy to accommodate his work to the demands of a director, actor or audience. Plays are events, not texts, Stoppard is fond of repeating, emphasizing that they are to be acted rather than merely read. His view results from his acceptance of the fluidity and change necessary for survival as well as performance.

CHAPTER 3

ET IN ARCADIA EGO

He is English . . . but only sort of.
New York Post, December 1967

Stoppard's arrival in England in February 1946 was unplanned and his reaction unexpected. His mother, having met and married Major Kenneth Stoppard in India, accepted with some surprise and concern that she and her two sons would make this new country, their fourth, yet another invented home. But Stoppard's first response to Britain would last a lifetime: he welcomed his adopted country from the moment he arrived. 'As soon as we all landed up in England, I knew I had found a home. I embraced the language and the landscape, and the two came together for me in journalism'.[1] However, a 1967 article in the *New York Post* recalled a different perspective: that of the émigré or refugee who, despite his efforts to make his mark in his new country by adopting their ways as thoroughly as possible, was still thought of as an outsider. This contradiction is at the core of Stoppard's life.

The combination of countryside and tradition were irresistible for a young boy of eight and a half who, desperately needing stability, suddenly found the security of family and school. His change of name, he declared some years later, did not at first actually bother him, although he realized that 'in practically everything I had written there was something about people getting each other's names wrong – usually in a completely gratuitous way having nothing to do with character or plot.'[2]

Bitter cold and rain greeted the Stoppard family at the end of their journey from Bombay across the Indian Ocean, up the Red Sea, through the Suez Canal and across the Mediterranean until they passed Gibraltar and headed north to Southampton. The contrast with

India was immediate, although it was not so much the weather, since Darjeeling was often damp because of its mountain location. They arrived in February 1946, four years to the day after they had landed in Bombay. The move, according to Stoppard's mother, was sudden, drastic and unplanned, prompting her to decide that their only security from further upheavals would be to minimize, if not cover up, their Jewish past. She and the boys quickly proved their adaptability to the ways of their new country. With their stepfather, they boarded a train at the port, the first, Peter Stoppard remembered, they didn't have to sleep on. By Indian standards, their journey was relatively short: north from Southampton to East Retford, Nottinghamshire, the home of Major Stoppard's mother, north of Newark. A modestly-sized town, East Retford offered a pastoral beginning to their life in England. Martha Stoppard, at first anxious, irritable and unsure about their future, found their welcome warm and comforting.

Kenneth Stoppard returned to a job with the hundred-year-old steel manufacturer Firth-Brown of Sheffield as a technical sales representative of the steel fabricator's subsidiary, F. B. Tools, founded in 1946, specializing in magnesium drill bits. This venerable company had a reputation as a stable and solid employer, although the nationalization of the steel industry in 1951 brought uncertainty to the business until the Conservative government reversed the decision. F. B. Tools Ltd remained independent and for Kenneth Stoppard that meant job security and a steady income for the family, although they would have to move around the country in pursuit of advancement within the company. Never well off, the family was nonetheless comfortable. They soon moved from East Retford to Calver Sough, four miles north of Bakewell in Derbyshire. A short while later, they moved to 3 Meadway Drive, Dore, on the outskirts of Sheffield, to be closer to the head office of F. B. Tools in the city. The pattern of shifting about, this time within England, would continue: after some time in Dore, they moved again, to The Vicarage, Ockbrook, west of Nottingham, before settling in Bristol in the mid-1950s.

Seeking to normalize his relationship with his stepfather, Tom Stoppard often called him 'Daddy' or 'Father' or 'Dad'. However, Kenneth Stoppard objected to the last epithet as lower-class. Tall, with a moustache and military bearing, and a strong sense of being British, Kenneth Stoppard was also a bitter man: his father had died when he was very young, causing him to miss out on several educational opportunities. And because the war took five years out of his life, he also felt that England owed him something. Beneath his public charm was a private anger and his temper was often exposed. This caused tension in the home, more noticeable as the boys grew older. The combination of these attitudes made him something of a 'stuck-up Englishman who thought it was wrong to express one's feelings', except in anger. This was in direct contrast to Martha, who was an emotional and warm woman given to worrying about the well-being of her children. The marriage worked because she became subservient to her husband, putting up with anything for a quiet life, a tactic she followed to protect the children, including the two she had with her new husband. In the end, there was no point in fighting: 'that's what he's like', she seemed to be saying, a move which only amplified his selfishness and confirmed that he could get his way by being difficult or angry.[3]

He also admitted that he was not entirely pleased to be the stepfather of two half-Jewish children. Indeed, he was at times determined to minimize or eliminate their Czech identity. At age nine, when Stoppard innocently referred to his 'real father', Kenneth Stoppard reproached him. 'Don't you realise *that I made you British*?'

Rather than being allowed to maintain their émigré status, Stoppard and his brother were schooled by their stepfather in becoming proper Englishmen and Stoppard does credit his stepfather with teaching him to fish, love the countryside, speak properly and respect the monarchy. Nevertheless, stepfather and stepson were like 'chalk and cheese', according to Peter. Kenneth Stoppard became increasingly autocratic and outspoken in his conservative values. His passions were clear: fishing, deerstalking and business.[4]

Antithesis was again shaping Stoppard's life, this time defining his relationship with his stepfather who cultivated a rigid and emotionally restricted Englishness. Stoppard, by contrast, possessed a strong, central European emotionalism and energy, which he shared with his mother but which was also put in check.

Interestingly, in his plays, Stoppard rarely represents family life through brothers, sisters or parents of adult children. And although close to his own family, Stoppard would, in later years, consistently refrain from talking about them or publicly connecting them with his professional life. Other British dramatists of Stoppard's generation, notably Arnold Wesker and Harold Pinter, both Jewish, took a less adaptable view of British life: they maintained the rigid stance of an outsider in their work. Of course, the young Stoppard did not understand much of his stepfather's behaviour or attitudes until he was older. All he understood was that within three weeks of arriving in England, his last name was legally changed from Sträussler to Stoppard.

England in 1946 was attempting to recover from the harsh and limiting reality of the war and move towards the idealism and hope of reconstruction. Food, raw materials and consumer goods were still in short supply, partly due to Britain's huge post-war debt. Rationing for food, clothing, petrol and other domestic commodities continued until 1954. Austerity and a sense of disappointment characterized the country which, after the six-year siege of war, found itself demoralized. The sky itself, wrote Cyril Connolly in 1947, seemed 'permanently dull and lowering like a metal dish-cover'.[5] The vicious winter of 1947, the coldest in one hundred years, coupled with fuel shortages, contributed to the national depression. But amidst this background, the new Stoppard family found a moderate degree of stability.

Stoppard's English education began with books while he was at sea, on the troop-ship bringing him from India to England. A library aboard ship was his first European classroom and it was there he began to read, or attempt to read, seriously, trying to divine the contents of the books from their physical appearance alone. The first children's book he read was Arthur Ransome's *Peter Duck* – 'I mean a book which *looked* like a proper grown up book', because it had some 300 or so pages – during his early weeks in England.[6] He was surprised that such an intimidating object could be so gripping. He then started to search for other books by Ransome and by the time he arrived at public school, he began to read books in sets: the collected Arthur Ransome, Richmal Crompton's *Just William* series, Captain W. E. Johns' popular Biggles books, plus the usual classics, including one of his favourites, *Three Men in a Boat* by Jerome K. Jerome. His reading was 'utterly conventional except in its voracity'; at one point in his late teens, he chose to spend his bus fare on a second-hand book and risk the perils of hitchhiking rather than face a trip without something to read.

Stoppard's first real home in England was at Calver Sough, north of

Bakewell and close to Chatsworth, the Duke of Devonshire's grand estate. Contrast again: in the city, there were still the remnants of war, but Chatsworth was an idyllic world of landscape and architecture. Stoppard would visit the magnificent house of 175 rooms next to the meandering River Derwent in the Peak District of Derbyshire and be astonished by the garden and its landscaping, recalling the impact of the place some forty-five years later while working on *Arcadia*. The scenery was a mixture of the wild and the domestic: moors, rocks and bracken descended through woods to grazing land and the quiet riverside. Two waterfalls represented the contrasting styles: one came straight off the aqueduct, the other fell crookedly over rocks. The famous Empire Fountain at the end of the long Canal Pond at the south front of the house shot its water high in the sky 'like a plume of agitated white smoke', according to the current Duchess of Devonshire.

The fourth Duke of Devonshire had employed Lancelot 'Capability' Brown to wreck the first duke's 105-acre garden, replacing its sharply formal, ordered plot with a natural landscape. Terraces became slopes, parterres regressed into lawns, while the west garden became plain grass. In the mid-nineteenth century, Joseph Paxton was hired to redo the garden, building a magnificent conservatory which housed tropical flowers and fruits. Orchids, bananas, frangipani, oranges, lemons and limes grew rapidly, recalling the profusion of vegetation of both Singapore and Darjeeling for the young Stoppard. Plants were brought from India as well as the Himalayas for the garden, including dahlias, which figure in the final scenes of *Arcadia*. Although the conservatory had been destroyed by the time Stoppard began to visit Chatsworth – it was too costly to maintain and too strongly built to be dismantled (it had to be blown up!) – the exotic flora remained. Stoppard may also have learned something of Chatsworth's literary history: Defoe and Dr Johnson were among its visitors.

All was not entirely pastoral, as the various dukes relied on ingenious mechanical devices to pump the water, irrigate the plants and sustain the nature that surrounded the house. Four large man-made lakes were needed to maintain the waterworks and hydraulic machines in the building yard. The Swiss Lake, at nine acres the largest and the oldest, was designed to maintain the cascade. Chatsworth embodies the antitheses that characterize Stoppard's life: 'nothing fits exactly,' writes the present Duchess of Devonshire: 'none of the rooms except the Chapel is a set piece . . . There is no theme, no connecting style. Each room is a jumble of old and new, English and foreign.'[7] Like the first duke's formal garden, an artificial wonder which stood in contrast to the wild Peak country which contained it, Chatsworth, metaphorically and physically, demonstrated to Stoppard how to adapt the antithetical, something he himself was learning to do.

Pastoral England did survive at his prep school, the Dolphin School, founded by Charles Roach in Nottingham but since the war located at Okeover Hall in Derbyshire, near Ashbourne. Stoppard attended from 1946 to 1951 and, according to his brother who was also there, it was one of the happiest times in his life. One reason for this was Peter Roach, the son of the founder and a teacher at the school. He was an inspiring figure and Stoppard kept in contact with him throughout his career, even inviting him to his sixtieth birthday party. At Okeover, and later at Longford Hall near Newark, where the school moved during Stoppard's final two years, students 'were allowed to roam free in an arcadian landscape that had gone through several fashions'.[8] Peter Stoppard recalled that from the open windows at Okeover one often heard the farmhands yodelling for the cows, and the fire engines that were summoned when the ivy on the church caught fire.

As he adjusted to life in England during his early years, Stoppard welcomed a world of tradition while being sceptical about its permanence. At the Dolphin School, he and his brother experienced a British preparatory school that projected stability. Boarding at the school was not a trauma, given their experience living at the Mount Hermon School in Darjeeling. Order seemed to have arrived in his life and, with it, a kind of freedom which meant rambles in nature and a delight in a world that appeared to be under no outward threat. 'I was foreign, but I did not know it,' he later remarked. ' I pronounced "th" like "d" and a soft "s" into a hard "s". All that remains is that I have a very slightly idiosyncratic "r". I was teased a certain amount,' he admitted, adding that at that age, 'one simply accepts everything that happens as being one's due and adapts to it. I was very happy at my prep school.' But his impressions altered and his sense of difference emerged: 'when I finally came to England in 1946, I was under the impression I spoke the same English as anybody else spoke, but as soon as I got to my prep school it was quite clear that I didn't speak the same kind of English but it was my first language.'[9]

44

Stoppard remained at the Dolphin School until the age of thirteen, while his mother and stepfather organized their own lives and started their own family (a half-brother, Richard, would be born in 1949; a half-sister, Fiona, in 1955). He then followed his brother Peter to Pocklington Grammar School in Yorkshire, founded in 1514 by John Dowman, an eminent ecclesiastical lawyer whose family were once lords of the ancient manor of Pocklington. The school became affiliated with St John's College, Cambridge, which also benefited from John Dowman's generosity. After Stoppard arrived in 1951, he was known as 'Stoppard Two', and his brother Peter, who entered in 1949, 'Stoppard One'.

A useful bat.
R. G., 'Characters of the XI', *The Pocklingtonian*, 1953

Pastoral England was not a fantasy for the young Stoppard but a world he actually experienced at Pocklington, with its wide, expansive playing fields and magnificent, historic oak tree on its front lawn. The landscape was, and remains, welcoming to him: 'when I see English landscape . . . for some reason I just have always felt at home there. When I went to Czechoslovakia to visit – forests, castles, and so forth – that was foreign and touristy.' One of his favourite pieces of music would be Vaughan Williams's *Fantasia on a Theme of Tallis*, 'the most intense English sound one could possibly have', he has said, adding that 'I have an intense empathy for England'.[10]

For many years a guild school, Pocklington was more precisely a 'Free Grammar School' within a guild. Tuition was free and in Latin, properly called the science of grammar.[11] For many years, the school prepared clerics for St John's College, Cambridge, its most famous Old Boy being William Wilberforce, who attended between 1771 and 1776. Located at the edge of the Yorkshire Wolds in the market town of Pocklington, some thirteen miles east of York, off the road to Hull and connected then by a railway line which was the only divide between the town and the school (the station being a few hundred yards from the school), Pocklington enjoyed a solid reputation. There, Peter Stoppard and his brother began their more formal education, in a school that blended class and location, where boys from Yorkshire,

London and overseas easily mixed. The cross-section of society at Pocklington, from wealthy families to farmers' sons, meant a mix of attitudes and social levels which allowed for the easy acceptance of two young boys with a remarkable history.

The East Riding's reputation for being dour and failing to celebrate oneself may have crossed over to Stoppard who sought not so much to remove his past as to disguise it. His accent made this difficult, but he turned it into something positive: 'in England my Czecho-Chinese-American accent made me a subject of interest. It also gave one a certain cachet.'[12] Again the paradox: on the one hand, proud of the exoticism his accent bestowed, but on the other seeking to be as English as possible, encouraged by his mother and, in a different way, by his stepfather.

Subsequent oblique references to Stoppard's past and his modesty, at times bordering on embarrassment at his success, may be partly explained by the Pocklington ethos whereby one was not encouraged to excel in self-interest or ego. A central European dislike of showing off and a distrust of fame may also have indirectly contributed to this behaviour – or an insecurity as to its permanence. The school encouraged 'doing': acting rather than thinking about a problem. This directness, linked to Yorkshire attitudes and habits, might have prompted Stoppard to pursue the practical life of journalism, where 'doing' with words met the challenge of 'doing' with one's hands – and where one could turn experience into language and fact into narrative. Journalism, furthermore, encouraged the rewriting of the past, something that Stoppard may have been unconsciously enacting, although the boys did not speak freely about their history.

The school philosophy was and remains 'the enthusiastic use of talents for the benefit of society'.[13] The goal was to create 'all-rounders', to quote the former headmaster, David Gray: students who could resolve issues in practical terms. The Education Act of 1944 threatened to alter Pocklington's precarious independence as a direct-grant school, standing between a public school, entirely independent of state control, and controlled schools, directed by Local Education Authorities. Advocates of universal state control wanted to do away with these independent direct-grant schools, but the history of Pocklington and its educational contributions justified its continued if anomalous status.[14]

Latin and science remained a requirement of all the boys, although in its post-war period the school was somewhat mediocre.[15] However, athletically it remained rigorous: 'games are compulsory and all boys take open air exercise every day,' states an early school circular. The Parish Church of All Saints in Pocklington served as the school chapel and morning service was attended on Sundays by the boys, who marched into the town.

Stoppard was a scholarship student, winning a Governors' Scholarship worth £45 per year in July 1951 (his brother had an Exhibition, a bursary directly from school funds). As a student, he lived in School House, a dormitory on the second floor of the main building where he learned the history of a framed but cracked mirror. Intermittently attacked by German aircraft because of British Halifax bombers stationed at an air base on the far side of the playing fields during the Second World War, the school suffered peripheral damage. One day, a prefect narrowly missed being killed when a piece of shrapnel whizzed over his head and smashed into a mirror as he bent over. Framed, with a plaque, the mirror hangs on a dormitory wall of the School House.

A slightly above-average student, Stoppard elected the Classical Side (as opposed to the Modern) for the sixth form, his final year at Pocklington. In the Middle VIth, Stoppard took courses under the colourful Oxford classicist and Second Master of the school, J. H. Eggleshaw, who had a First in Greats and a detailed knowledge of fields other than his own which often embarrassed colleagues. He was a cultured figure who introduced boys to music, art, literature and the classics and may have been Stoppard's first exemplar of how the arts can enlighten. His home, to which he invited many students, was stuffed with books. He also coached rugby, track and, most importantly for Stoppard, cricket, showing that scholarship and athletics did not have to be divided. His high standards of self-discipline and attention to detail – he happily identified himself as a perfectionist – remained with Stoppard throughout his writing career.

Stoppard also took classes in divinity, English language, Latin, Greek, French and maths. His later interest in maths and the classics originated not only in these studies but with the Headmaster, Robert St John Pitts-Tucker, who held a first in Classics from Cambridge and, with Eggleshaw, made classical studies a persistent focus at the school.

Stoppard also had a bullying teacher who frightened him as a young boy; he reappears in the radio play, *Where Are they Now?* Rugby and tennis supplemented his main sport at Pocklington, cricket, which won Stoppard designation as 'a useful bat' in the school annual.

Other interests competed for his attention, principally debating, and he joined the Sixth Form Society early, becoming one of its two Treasurers in 1954. The previous year, he seconded the motion 'that this House considers that the Englishman's love of sport has degenerated into a financial racket'. Anticipating, as well as displaying, his comic outlook, Stoppard proposed at the final meeting of the society in March 'that this House considers a banana skin a more efficacious weapon than a Tommy-gun'. At a meeting with Bootham School a week later, Stoppard participated in a debate over whether or not 'life in the first Elizabethan era would have been preferable to existence in this Atomic Age'.[16]

Not only did the society hold debates on such topics as 'consistency a vice, not a virtue' (a very Stoppardian subject – could he have even proposed it?), but they invited various speakers to the school. The Open Meeting in 1953 was devoted to 'The Art of Charlie Chaplin', given by Bryant Peers, a friend of Chaplin's. After outlining the methods involved in making a film, Peers screened three old films, including Chaplin's *The Count*. This may have been Stoppard's first serious engagement with film, which he would later make a journalistic speciality and then, as a screenwriter, a profitable adjunct to his playwriting. These early experiences with verbal logic and well-argued positions probably contributed to his valuing what he calls his 'argument plays': 'I tend to write about oppositions and double acts ... I tend to write for two people rather than One Voice. Rosencrantz and Guildenstern were two sides of one temperament.'[17] Alluding to the world of debating, he explained this more fully in 1972: 'I'm the kind of person who embarks on an endless leapfrog down the great moral issues. I put a position, rebut it, refute it, refute the rebuttal, and rebut the refutation. Forever. Endlessly.'[18] Recalling his debating days to Kenneth Tynan, Stoppard added that 'I remember being completely indifferent as to which side of any proposition I should debate on.'[19] This, of course, was excellent training for a dramatist eager to remain open to all arguments.

Stoppard had little involvement with drama at the school, although he recalls writing a play about Charles I when he was twelve: 'it was surprisingly conventional: he died in the end'.[20] He had a limited association with the drama programme run by Charles Winour at Pocklington according to all accounts, although he did attend the largely obligatory school plays and played a backstage role with sound effects and props. The play for 1953 was Goldoni's *Servant of Two Masters*; in 1954, Sheridan's *The Critic* and *School for Scandal* were performed, plus comic scenes from Shakespeare. (In 1969, the school play would be *Rosencrantz and Guildenstern are Dead*.) These three works and Shakespearean scenes introduced Stoppard to the wit and humour possible on the stage. Another major production at the school was Dion Boucicault's *London Assurance*. The theatre visit that year was to see *The Mikado* at the York Theatre Royal; the year before it had been an authentic staging of the York Mystery Cycle.

Of equal importance culturally were the films regularly shown at the school. In 1954, the feature was Laurence Olivier's *Hamlet*. A review in *The Pocklingtonian* opened: 'despite an overdose of stone corridor, "Hamlet" was not only an entertaining film but a very helpful one to those who are studying for the General Certificate Examination.'[21] Alec Guinness in *The Card* and John Howard Davies's *Tom Brown's Schooldays* were the other screenings. Shakespeare at fourteen, however, was quite unappealing: 'we just sat around the class doing *The Merchant of Venice* and all having to read a part. All you did was to look ahead to see when it was Nerissa's turn and then you said your line. I didn't care at all about Shakespeare from that age until I was a journalist in Bristol and went to see Peter O'Toole's *Hamlet* in 1957.'[22]

Stoppard played cricket on the original 'Big Field' in front of a late-Victorian wedding-cake pavilion some distance from the school buildings. A poor drainage system often made the field more of a pudding, however, despite the efforts of G. N. Thornton, the coach, to improve the grounds. Although the season was short, cricket monopolized the months of May to July at Pocklington, producing a series of players who distinguished themselves in county, university and Test Match sides.[23] School records detail the achievement of the first century made on the school grounds – in 1896, by F. D. Cautley – and the highest score for the school, that of 126 by N. L. Lupton against Ripon in 1934. P. M. C. Bradshaw alone is credited with three centuries in one season (1946).[24]

In his final two years at Pocklington, Stoppard was selected for the First XI and became the team's Secretary in 1954. His position was wicket-keeper. The 1953 XI benefited from both brothers being on the team, Peter having a considerably better showing with 35 runs, Tom only 4.[25] According to 'Characters of the XI' for 1953, Peter 'has an excellent defence, which was very valuable to the team . . . but he should develop more attacking shots'. His brother 'is a keen and lively wicket-keeper who has improved steadily, but he must learn to take the ball more cleanly. A useful bat.'[26] Both brothers received praise for individual games, notably against the Old Pocklingtonians on 27 June 1953: 'The first eight wickets fell for only 26 runs, but P. Stoppard (20 n.o.), Wilcher and T. Stoppard, treating the bowling according to its merit, carried the total to 63'.[27] *The Pocklingtonian* for the summer of 1954 describes the season of 'T. Stoppard' in a comically understated manner: 'He has but rarely batted this season, and this may explain his lack of shots. His defence, however, is sound. A good close fielder.'[28] His total runs improved to 39 from the preceding season's 4. The accompanying team photo shows a youthful and confident Stoppard to the right of the team captain.

Cricket, of course, continued to fascinate and involve Stoppard, who kept wicket in Bristol when he began to write for the provincial papers, and again in London where his prowess, assisted by his increasing prominence as a playwright, found him playing for Harold Pinter's XI. In 1969, he was invited to keep wicket for Dame Peggy Ashcroft's XI at Stratford, organized to celebrate the two hundredth anniversary of Garrick's Shakespeare Jubilee at Stratford. Also on that team were Harold Pinter, Ian Carmichael, Tom Courtenay and David Warner. But as his commitments increased, Stoppard's cricket playing diminished. In 1981, for example, he managed only two games. In the first he had an opening knock of 25 followed by some impeccable wicket-keeping; going on to play for Pinter's XI, however, he 'managed to score six with great difficulty but no little elegance, though I did successfully stump someone out on the leg side. The truth is, I'm not as good at cricket as some people seem to think,' he disclosed.[29]

David Foot, a journalist and sportswriter from Bristol, recalled Stoppard as a solid wicket-keeper with sharp reflexes, although because of his height he often gave a slightly amusing and uncoordinated impression behind the stumps. At one London match, however, Stoppard was so absorbed in the game that he failed to notice when his lighted cigarette dropped behind one of his pads. Realization of his imminent immolation caused a minor delay and a major irritation. Cricket even had a role in bringing Stoppard and Miriam Moore-Robinson, later Stoppard's second wife, together. Although they originally met in September 1965, when Miriam and her then husband visited Anthony Smith, Stoppard and their families on holiday in the south of France, later encounters at various cricket matches organized by Smith intensified their contact. One of his constant companions at this time was *Wisden*.

Stoppard's love of cricket, however, was not entirely athletic. A game of strict form, history and discipline, it represented a kind of arcane regularity and order of an odd sort not often encountered in life. It also relies on individual excellence. It provides structure that exceeds time, since games can go on for days. It is also theatrical, with roles, costumes (the obligatory whites), directors (the umpires) and scripted behaviour. Its language, like that of the theatre, is specialized and abstruse, understood only by those schooled in the pastime. You also have an assigned position and an assigned time to enter or bat. An audience is present and there are formal intervals when refreshments are served. Applause rather than cheers celebrates fine play. The game's influence on Stoppard ranges from its use as a subject to its source for terms and even dress in his plays.

Cricket is the sport that reappears consistently throughout his work. In *The Boundary*, a 1975 television play written by Stoppard with Clive Exton, cricket affects the lives of the three characters, signalled by a cricketer in white flannels visible through the French windows of the opening scene. The title itself refers to the limits of the cricket field and becomes comically confused in the dialogue when Johnson says of the broken window, 'it's those damned bounders'. His associate Bunyans replies '(*correcting*) Boundaries.' Johnson's riposte is 'Hooked over square leg', which leaves Bunyans with 'Bouncers'. Johnson, attempting to clarify this statement, offers in frustration the final, ironic remark: 'Damn cricket.'[30] The first and second cricketers act as sentinels to the action. Cricket terms punningly appear in the play as *doubles entendres* while the two protagonists take note of a match being played outside their study. Brenda, the wife of one and mistress of the other, recovers from being hit by a ball to accuse both men of misbehaviour – only to be hit on the head a second time by a wayward ball, but this time killed. The order of cricket has unwittingly created chaos for a second time, not only of the papers in the room of these lexicographers (and in their language) but in their lives. Comically, Stoppard shows that overstepping a boundary will create havoc, a view that would appeal to his conservative temperament.

Metaphorically, the most important appearance of cricket in Stoppard's work is Henry's speech on writing in *The Real Thing*, when he develops the idea that a well-made bat represents a well-made piece of writing. Art and good writing launch ideas which just might shift the world – slightly. Years later, Stoppard kept a cricket bat in his study on the top floor of the massive, converted Victorian stable at his Iver Grove home in Buckinghamshire.

Minor references to cricket occur in his 1973 radio play, *Where Are They Now?*, and in other works, but other sports also surface in his plays, notably rugby, a strong Pocklington tradition – see the end of *Hapgood* and various passages in *The Invention of Love* – football, in *Professional Foul*, and tennis, which appears in *Rosencrantz and Guildenstern* and in his adaptation of Schnitzler's *Undiscovered Country*. Iver Grove had an outdoor floodlit tennis court on which Stoppard met, with unequal success, various challenges from his sons. Stoppard himself explains his absorption with sport as a fascination with matches and the clarity of the rules of play. His earliest thoughts which developed into *Professional Foul* originated with 'a vague idea that there was some sort of play to be written about the suspension of moral conduct on the sports field'.[31] Cricket combined individual heroics and team performance and is, in the words of the poet Henry Newbolt, 'the calling forth of order out of chaos'.

Stoppard left Pocklington on 27 July 1954 after completing his O Levels, choosing not to go on to A Levels as this would have meant another two years of study, followed by university. He matriculated in Middle VIth, his final term. He found school childish and the restrictions tiresome. It wasn't so much that he was rebellious as impatient. But, as the history of the school notes, 'leaving school at sixteen from a secondary school was in those days the rule rather than the exception'.[32] Nearly thirty per cent of the students left at that time. At graduation, he won the Use of English Prize for 1953 and was noted for his receipt of his General Certificate of Examination in Classics with a speciality in Ancient History.

At sixteen, Stoppard had no direction concerning a career: 'Until shortly before I left school, I had no idea what I wanted to do, but as soon as the idea of journalism occurred, I became really passionate about it and I was very lucky. I managed to get on to the local paper where my parents were living.'[33] This prosaic description contradicts his romantic image of journalists in the mid-fifties which became too strong for him to resist. At the age of seventeen, he headed for the family home in a Bristol suburb – Long Ashton – and went to work as a junior reporter.

School left a negative impression on Stoppard, although he did well, academically and athletically. His brother thinks this is because he quickly outgrew it. His frustration at the school derived largely from his maturity, finding life at a boarding-school in a small market town very confining: 'at seventeen, Tom was more like twenty'.[34] The origin of this frustration may also be linked to his disappointment over any intellectual or creative stimulation, since he found Pocklington stultifying and narrow, forming a counter-reaction: 'I left school thoroughly bored by the idea of anything intellectual, and gladly sold all my Greek and Latin classics to George's Bookshop in Park Street [Bristol]. I'd been totally bored and alienated by everyone from Shakespeare to Dickens besides.'[35] The Pocklington school history defends his decision not to go on to university in this comic manner: 'Tom Stoppard did not go through the full academic routine; it is the mark of genius not to do the obvious'.[36] In 1987, at the age of fifty, he admitted that 'university just seemed to me parole rather than freedom'.[37]

Wit in a Mackintosh

The seventeen-year-old Stoppard left the green fields of Pocklington for a congested semi-detached family home on sloping Providence Lane, Long Ashton, across the River Avon and fifteen minutes west of Bristol by car. The house, which had the Cornish name Tregenna, had been occupied by the Stoppards since 1950 and he joined his brother Peter, his half-brother Richard and his half-sister, Fiona, there with his mother and stepfather. With a Stoppardian sense of logical confusion, the address was 13, Providence Lane but the front door to the house was around the corner on Rayens Cross Road. From the rear, there was a view of Dundrey Hill and the Mendip Hills; to the west, rolling countryside. Approximately a year and a half later, when he became a sub-editor and kept late hours, preparing the paper, he moved out.

Domestic life was not enjoyable. Kenneth Stoppard found the career of his youngest stepson alien, partly because it was 'arty' and partly because it meant spreading the Stoppard name about in the papers, an undignified act. His interests remained fly fishing and deerstalking and he confined his reading only to these areas; no books on culture were to be found in the house. He was almost embarrassed by Stoppard's increasing success in an area of no particular interest to him. He had left school early and this probably distanced him from the benefits of culture. He was uncomfortable with literary or theatrical people, possibly feeling threatened by what he did not understand. If the topic of conversation was fishing, however, he was utterly charming. In later years, he rarely, if ever, attended any of his stepson's first nights. He found himself more of 'a frustrated squire, really'; there was a fair amount of snobbery in his family and he became embittered that the country did not recognize what he had done for it during the war and what he was trying to uphold. There was generally an unwelcoming air in the Stoppard home; the stepsons never felt comfortable about bringing friends over since the tense atmosphere in the home was not inviting. Not going to university meant the absence of freedom and friendships, which developed for Stoppard only after he moved out to work the night shift as a sub-editor.[38]

While family life was anti-cultural, Bristol itself was undergoing a cultural, if not literary and theatrical revival.[39] The theatre tradition was especially strong. Founded in 1766, the Theatre Royal on King Street was the oldest theatre in continuous use in Britain, and in 1946 was converted into a branch of the London Old Vic. Charles Kean, William Macready, Henry Irving, Ellen Terry and Herbert Beerbohm Tree all performed there; Garrick was in the audience for the inaugural performance of 1766. Bristol University had the country's first drama department and the first Chair of Drama in the country, held by Glynne Wickham. Sir Michael Redgrave and Cary Grant were born in Bristol, which soon became Stoppard's 'university', since his experiences there as reporter, theatre fan and young author began to shape his style, outlook and themes. He not only found encouragement for his work but discovered a tone and voice for his writing, and began to establish his identity as a writer. His fluency derived from deadlines as much as from language, as the eager reporter began to cover stories as diverse as cave-ins, criminal courts and visiting theatre personalities. Bristol might be said to have offered him courses in writing, theatre and cultural studies as it progressed in the late fifties and early sixties from a somewhat provincial community into a more artistically experimental centre. Its imprint on Stoppard would be lasting.

Stoppard's reading, which 'remained unintellectual' until he left school, also expanded at this period. His early passion was Damon Runyon, the American journalist, short-story writer and humorist best known for his accounts of New York hustlers, gangsters, gamblers, show people and crooks. Baseball, six-day bike races and murders were all part of Runyon's repertoire, as well as a natural, colloquial style that captured the street voice of the city. One of his stories was the source of the 1950 Broadway hit *Guys and Dolls*. A master of American slang and mobster speech – 'I long ago came to the conclusion that all life is 6 to 5 against' – Runyon was an early influence on Stoppard, especially in the tone and language of his short stories.[40] But other writers and books also came into view, especially the Americans: Salinger, Fitzgerald, Steinbeck, Dos Passos, Thurber, Mailer and, most importantly, Hemingway, whose breezy, open, unfussy, immediate style influenced Stoppard's prose. At one point, he owned Edmund Wilson's copy of Hemingway's *In Our Time,* his 1925 collection of short stories, but he sold it to buy a statue, 'a decision so weird that I cannot now bear to think of it, not least because Wilson is another of my heroes'. He took several of Wilson's books with him on holiday to Spain in the late fifties, including *To the Finland Station*, which was 'a seminal book for me, the first book which made me interested in history and politics'.[41]

The source of Stoppard's insouciant and occasionally irreverent prose style in his newspaper columns was A. G. Macdonell's comic novel, *England, Their England*, leavened with a dash of Evelyn Waugh. Stoppard had first encountered Macdonell's book at Pocklington and it remained the only work that ever directly influenced his writing style, he explained in a 1983 television interview with Richard Hoggart.

Witnessing a boy in the lower sixth actually laughing out loud while reading, Stoppard was intrigued to learn the title of the book, and 'for years after that my sentence structure was consciously and unconsciously based on this book': he wrote two or three hundred journalistic pieces 'of varying degrees of facetiousness which were directly influenced by this wonderful book'. Not only does the work include a satirical guide to drama criticism; it also contains a hilarious cricket match narrated in twenty-six pages.[42]

The allure of journalism for the seventeen-year-old had much to do with the romance of being a foreign correspondent: 'I wanted to be Noel Barber on the *Daily Mail* or Sefton Delmer on the *Daily Express* – that kind of big-name roving reporter. Noel Barber actually got shot in the head in Budapest [in 1956], which put him slightly ahead of Delmer as far as I was concerned.'[43] 'My first ambition', he explained to an interviewer in 1977, 'was to be lying on the floor of an African airport while machine-gun bullets zoomed over my typewriter.'[44] He shared the romantic view Evelyn Waugh satirized in *Scoop*, a novel Stoppard cherished for its tone as well as the portrait of a journalistic life and its possibilities. 'I am in consultation with my editors on the subject,' Lord Copper, newspaper owner, remarks on the choice of a foreign reporter to cover an overseas incident. 'We think it a very promising little war. A microcosm, as you might say, of world drama.' This was precisely the way Stoppard imagined incidents covered by journalists would be. The hero, William Boot, a name Stoppard would soon exploit in his early plays, is the parodic epitome of the reporter: 'Love, patriotism, zeal for justice, and personal spite flamed within him as he sat at his typewriter and began his message. One finger was not enough; he used both hands.'[45]

Waugh's style captivated Stoppard, who soon saw that writing about a contemporary subject in a light but satirical way could gain the public's attention. Drawing on the tradition of farce as much as the style of Ronald Firbank, Waugh had created a novel that condensed reference and comic image in sentences that embodied the comic tone of the time. The account of the creation of non-news and the importance of fiction rather than fact in *Scoop* would later be elaborated in Stoppard's *Night and Day*, with fictitious battles and false reports making instant headlines back in London. While the romanticized life of the journalist setting out for adventure in unknown lands appealed to the young writer, it was the satire and tone of Waugh's writing that caught Stoppard's imagination. Waugh, he admitted in 1990, 'became a literary god', along with Hemingway.[46]

Stoppard, however, did not get to cover wars, but flower shows, police courts and funerals. Feature writing and the odd colour piece – all of them unsigned – were among his earliest efforts; later, he became a second-string arts critic.

'Do you know, my first impression of you was not of a young man destined for great success in journalism?'
Evelyn Waugh, *Scoop*

Stoppard began as a junior or cub reporter on the morning paper the *Western Daily Press*, for £2 10*s*. 8*d*.; at seventeen, he was their youngest reporter at the time. The paper was suffering from falling circulation (10,000 or less) and was thought to be both staid and dull. Stoppard was an enthusiastic if undisciplined reporter, covering mundane events: car accidents, municipal meetings and bus strikes were among his early assignments. From the first, however, he was a colourful figure, with his cigarettes, flamboyant if slightly askew dress, and desperately thin appearance. He was also different, with a funny accent, and sometimes could be very brash, causing Geoffrey Reeves, who was then a postgraduate student at Bristol University, to quip that Stoppard was a 'cynical wit in a mackintosh'.[47] But he was also difficult to converse with and often terribly intense. Another young reporter, David Foot, later a distinguished cricket writer, remembers Stoppard at the antiquated Long Ashton Police Court, reading paperbacks most of the time – he was intent on his self-education – glancing up to get a quick sense of events, and then managing to write a rapid account of the crime despite his distraction. At the same time, he was taking in details which play a part in a short story he would publish in 1964, entitled 'The Story', concerning the tragic results of the publicity from a minor court case involving a schoolteacher and an indecency charge.

But the young reporter also exhibited a certain *naïveté*:

My first job was the West of England tennis tournament. I only had to get the results, but I got there half an hour before play – and found I had no paper to write on. I walked two miles to borrow some from a friend. The real reporter from my paper arrived 15 minutes from the end, having been to the cinema all afternoon.[48]

The changeable and long hours required of a cub reporter meant that it was easier for Stoppard to live in Bristol proper, rather than Long Ashton. He took a room on the top floor of a house owned by Dr John Wilders, at the time an English lecturer at the University of Bristol, who later became an Oxford don. Wilders remembered Stoppard as 'very sweet but disorganized'. He was called 'Big Tom', and was remembered with gratitude for helping to paint the stairs. 'There was no sign,' however, of 'the brilliant epigrammatic wit then. It's not spontaneous, of course. Stoppard is like Oscar Wilde. He works on it,' Wilders recalled.[49]

As a young reporter, Stoppard required some restraint. Dennis Frost, Stoppard's senior, remembered: 'He wasn't the most brilliant journalist . . . but he was just brilliant. The problem was to discipline his writing to the form of a provincial daily newspaper. I didn't know he was going to be a famous playwright. But he was going to be a famous *something*.'[50] His style was exuberant and literary rather than documentary and direct. He learned Pitman shorthand, an essential journalist's tool (and supposedly still retained it as late as 1991). But while he enthusiastically carried out his journalistic assignments, he was often distracted or detached in his relations with fellow reporters. He sometimes had a dreamy look in his eyes, with his mind miles away, some of his colleagues recalled. Later, at the *Bristol Evening World*, he avoided the crowded reporters' room, preferring to type up his stories in the small copy room among the female typists who took down reporters' phoned-in copy. David Foot felt him bohemian in outlook and approach, and felt that, while he took pride in the craft of journalism, he had probably turned to it because it 'was the nearest thing creatively to making a living'.[51] Others thought him indolent and absent-minded, a writer who preferred to wander off to King Street and the Old Vic rather than pursue the latest lead or scandal.

Often, there would be no story. Stoppard and another reporter were sent to cover a funeral of a local dignitary. The editor wanted a list of all who attended. It turned out to be a family funeral with only six people present. The two reporters left and went to the cinema, something most of the enthusiastic journalists did then. Four hours later, they returned. The editor queried them: 'What, four hours but only six names?' 'Ah, but one had three initials,' Stoppard replied.[52] Nevertheless, he covered a variety of subjects: agricultural shows, human interest stories and even, briefly, sports. When his first byline appeared on the front page in a story about a caving accident in the Mendip Hills, he later told his friend Anthony Smith that he wouldn't have minded dying that night. At the *Western Daily Press*, he also wrote a weekly motoring column (May–June 1958), even though he did not drive (he told friends he reviewed the upholstery); it would be ten years before he overcame his fear of driving and got a licence.

One of his early assignments was as a department-store Santa Claus, the subtitle of the column reading 'Unsuitable for children'; one of his last was a report on a child's first classical concert, which he presented as a comic dialogue between a child and mother.[53] Stoppard tended to work all night and sleep all day. In fact, he neglected to show up at a farewell lunch to which he invited Reg Eason, his editor, accidentally sleeping through the day. Good on puns, he wrote poetry in Bristol and once took an art course to improve his sketches. He would practise by writing dialogue and then the ideas would come. Often, he did what he called 'substitutions', taking, say, a speech by Noël Coward and revising it in his own words, seeking to combine absurdity and truth. This presumably laid the groundwork for his later reworking of *Hamlet* in *Rosencrantz and Guildenstern*, Agatha Christie in *The Real Inspector Hound* and *The Importance of Being Earnest* in *Travesties*.

Throughout this time, he always lacked money. At Marco's, the Italian restaurant favoured by Stoppard and his journalist friends (and shown in John Boorman's documentary *The Newcomers*), credit was often extended, although discrimination was evident: journalists had one week to pay, actors a month. In Bristol, Stoppard quickly became known as a wit rather than a clown, although he travelled from one assignment to another in a trilby hat and raincoat that always looked too big. Inventiveness was his trademark, especially when he was supposed to go out and interview the public. Instead of seeking 'man in the street' commentary on everything from Rhodesia to roads, he would sit in the canteen and 'make up quotes from people who always lived in one of Bristol's longest streets'. But when they brought cameras along to photograph the 'victims', his game was up.[54]

At the *Western Daily Press,* each reporter had three assignments, as Isabel Dunjohn, a co-reporter, features writer and early girlfriend of Stoppard's, explained: a morning, afternoon and evening story to pursue, but 'you did them in your own time'. Reporters often spent the day wandering the city, rarely phoning in stories: 'we were supposed to come back to the office and type up our stories on the manuals which were as antiquated and vast and noisy as parrots'. Stoppard and Isabel often escaped their 'duty runs' by sitting on a set of steps that ran into the river near the Old Duke pub, talking 'for hours about life and plans when no doubt we were supposed to be working'.[55] In print, Stoppard had definite, positive, mature views, but in conversation he was often inhibited and refrained from offering any definitive opinions – unless the topic was cricket, in which case he lost his detached if not bemused attitude. As wicket-keeper for a Sunday-afternoon team made up of actors and journalists (Anthony Smith was one of the main players), Stoppard often engaged batsmen in conversations of a surreal character, Foot recalled. He later kept wicket for the *Evening World* team: 'He was thin, gangling, all over the place: but very serious, very determined,' said a former colleague and player.[56]

Bill Bomford, deputy chief sub-editor at the paper, had a different view, that of the sub's room. The young Stoppard's 'slightly sibilant accent occasioned some mimicry among some of the subs,' Bomford recalls; more importantly, he remembers that Stoppard soon began to bypass the usual practice of handing copy to the chief sub and submitted it directly to Bomford, because he likely had 'been badly subbed once or twice and found my treatment of his work more sympathetic'.

Often, much of Stoppard's work had to be rewritten. Bomford remembers in particular a piece on a 'miraculous' escape from a telephone booth that was knocked down by a car; the entire piece needed revisions. Stoppard's attitude towards subbing was significant: he 'never minded being rewritten, provided the rewrite was justified and decently done; on the contrary, he was interested in different slants and nuances, and very keen to learn'. This attitude continued in the theatre: in rehearsal and even afterwards, Stoppard constantly rewrites, altering texts, shifting words and modifying scenes to fit a production. He also welcomes the input of directors if it enhances a scene. He did not enjoy working as a sub-editor himself, however, which he had to do from time to time, to fill in for those off on holiday or absent. The reason may have had to do with its lack of creativity and loss of freedom, Bomford suggests. Nevertheless, it profited his writing ability, what Bomford calls 'a stimulant in disguise. It demanded speed, accuracy and concision; to these qualities Tom added imagination and wit. Previously, Tom's work had been patchy – the patchiness that often signals a divergent thinker, someone who is potentially creative.'[57]

The working space of the subs at the *Western Daily Press* between 1954 and 1958 was hardly congenial. An ancient phone was attached to the wall, next to suction tubes which carried copy to the printing department and publishing room below. The latter tube, however, was used 'mainly for shouting messages down to the editor when he was writing the leader in the only room in which smoking was permissible'. Practical jokes and 'much general vulgarity helped to relieve the tedium of the job.' After midnight, the desks, placed end-to-end down the centre of the room and cleared of paper, phones, letters and paraphernalia, became a cricket pitch with subs taking turns to wield a child's sturdy wooden bat. The ball was made of paper, glue and string, although on one occasion it was a chunk of printing metal which gouged a hole in the panelling when it was struck the length of the room. 'In the wall bearing the antique telephone (and on the leg side of the batsman) were two or three large sash windows' out of which various items were frequently hurled, to the surprise of the pedestrians below.[58]

Amenities were few, since there was no canteen in the building located at the corner of Baldwin and Denmark Streets in the city centre. Subs brought sandwiches and were released in pairs for a mid-evening drink in the Windsor Castle pub across the street. A crate of beer provided by management on general election nights was the only perk. There was no extra pay. Only a few had cars; the others walked home at around 3 a.m. Bomford adds:

> The fact that a commodity as up-to-the-minute as a newspaper was produced amid such dilapidated surroundings, and always late at night, of course, gave the whole enterprise a surrealistic tinge – something that would appeal to Tom.

The oldest sub-editor at the time, still working in an office off the subs' room, had actually known W. G. Grace, the great cricketer.

The editor of the *Western Daily Press* was the unflappable and good-humoured Sam Shapcott, who provided 'a necessary buffer between an unruly editorial staff and a strait-laced management' who took umbrage at certain misbehaviour. Hiring the fire department to remove 'festoons of obsolete teleprinter tape which had been reeled out by some ring through the reporters' room windows' resulted in a full inquiry, although the perpetrator[s] were never identified. Shapcott, however, had a liberal attitude and was tolerant towards experimentation, although the paper itself was opposed to anything sensational. He was also acute in 'spotting and fostering talent [and] helped a number of novelists, broadcasters and journalistic high-fliers'.

Shortly after Bomford was appointed in 1954, Shapcott told him that 'that new chap Stoppard is going to be good'. Nevertheless, despite the originality of style, content and format, the paper was lifeless, something the management apparently equated with quality. Most of the writing was wordy and the headlines were merely labels; only the injection of some humour or a sensational headline varied the pattern. To be clever or daring were the only steps towards originality. Stoppard 'vented his frustration' at the mediocrity of the paper by writing 'witty and unorthodox headlines', one of which, intended for *Western Daily Press* readers undecided about whether or not to enrol for judo classes, read 'Get a Belt Round your Waist before You Get A Belt Round the Ear'.[59] The headline, said Bomford, signalled a watershed in Stoppard's writing and furnished proof of what he was capable of, at least comically, as a writer.

In late 1958, Stoppard was lured to the *Bristol Evening World* by Reg Eason, its news editor, who admired Stoppard's work.[60] He took up his new position in January 1959, receiving a small increase in salary but a much larger assignment sheet. He contributed to the daily gossip column, while covering a diverse set of subjects: home improvement, men's fashion, city librarians, drains ('perhaps the dullest word in the English language'), basketball, wrestling, Bristol buses, music and male hair-colouring (he declined to go blond, but did allow high-lights). He interviewed Albert Finney, reviewed Inland Revenue issues with the singer Connie Francis, wrote a profile of John Neville and participated for three minutes in the Marble Arch Marathon of 1959. Marking his increasing profile was the caption accompanying his picture for his column of 23 April 1959. It read 'World Reporter'.

Stoppard also continued to review amateur theatre groups – he had started to do so at the morning paper – with names like the Playgoers Club, the Kelvin Players and the Wayfarers Drama. He also went to Stratford-upon-Avon in the spring of 1960 to write about Peter Hall's productions of *Twelfth Night* with Dorothy Tutin and *Two Gentlemen of Verona* with Denholm Elliott as Valentine and Eric Porter as the Duke. Two years earlier, he had written on two productions of *Hamlet*, the first at Stratford, the second at Bristol. For Michael Redgrave's *Hamlet* at Stratford, he praised the way the speech to the players was handled, with Redgrave moving from confidential schemer when speaking to the First Player to confident critic when the rest of the players surrounded him as he concealed his plotting. The Bristol production was Peter O'Toole's, which Stoppard disliked because O'Toole allowed himself 'to be caught up in the excitement and strode around practically breathing fire through his nostrils. Mr Redgrave preferred to pick his way with a sort of wan grace.' This made Hamlet 'a very human figure, but never a heroic one', and this was his failing since his death did not seem heroic: 'perhaps had the balance of his emotions been tilted less towards remorse and more towards anger he would have been complete'.[61] In 1958, Stoppard tried to write his first play, beginning one for a competition sponsored by the *Observer*, 'but that one petered out after a dozen pages that were not unlike *Look Back in Anger*'.[62]

In 1960, when Stoppard decided it was time to be serious about playwriting and support himself by freelancing, the Bristol papers consolidated. He was soon offered various feature work by his old employer, the *Western Daily Press*, and new work began to appear, including occasional sports reports (tennis, basketball) and even 'Old Tom Stoppard's Almanack', a set of predictions for 1962. Representative prophecies began with 'Bristol Old Vic premières musical version of *War and Peace* . . . R.A.F. search for Bristol bus missing in snowdrift' (February), and continued: 'American spaceman lands in Leningrad: "Ill-timed" says rocket man . . . Cliff Richard and Lesley Caron in "The Peter Hall Story"' (August); 'Theatre Royal opens for bingo . . . . China liberates Wales; "Doctor in the Cathedral" chosen as Royal film' (November). 'The search for the bus, called off in April, was renewed in the spring and it was located in June.'[63]

In addition to wrestling and theatre, Stoppard had a strong interest in art and was reasonably knowledgeable about painters and painting. He would occasionally report on art shows and, when writing for the newly instituted arts page, would often comment on the state of galleries or the lack of support for painters. Once, in the late 1950s, when he stayed with Bomford and his wife, he asked him to draw his portrait. Bomford, a skilled artist, did a small pen-and-ink sketch, using stipple to suggest tone. Stoppard asked to keep it; Bomford agreed, but only after he titled it: 'Tom with measles'. When Bomford left the *Bristol Evening Post* and journalism to pursue a career as an artist, Stoppard turned up at his farewell party in a Bristol pub despite being desperately busy finishing his first novel, *Lord Malquist and Mr. Moon*. Bomford remembers him as being good-natured and calm, even when under such pressure. Dropping in unexpectedly at Stoppard's London flat in the spring of 1967, Bomford found Stoppard completing *Rosencrantz and Guildenstern* just before its opening at the National: 'It was quite late in the evening and he was still rewriting bits, but he had us in fits with his account of a disagreement over the script. Passages of dialogue were being cut by the director; Tom, when his turn came to direct, was reinstating them.'[64]

For the amalgamated papers, Stoppard not only did general news reporting, but was occasionally the second or third-string drama critic, again reporting on amateur theatrical productions and subbing for Peter Rodford, the first string. This would generate the situation he later developed in *The Real Inspector Hound*, originally called 'The Critics' and at one point 'The Stand-Ins'. He also did some film reviews, but generally had no bylines. His initials might occasionally appear at the bottom of a review or sports piece, although his editors quickly established an identity for him that was both familiar and slightly off-beat. Two headlines from October and November 1960 read: 'Look – There's A Completely Strange World – Tom Stoppard's, of course', and 'Gunpowder, Treason and Rot . . . By Stoppard, of course'. The first dealt with unusual traffic signals offered by lorry drivers to automobiles; the second with Stoppard's brief employment at a fireworks factory – or so we are led to believe in this piece of comic prose.

When Hilton Tims, the regular film critic, was on holiday, Stoppard stood in. On his return, Tims would often look at Stoppard's reviews and admire a turn of phrase or witticism 'which made me gnash my teeth in secret admiration . . . though I convinced myself he wrote more for effect than to give a realistic appraisal of the films he had seen'.[65] One of Stoppard's more colourful reviews, of *The Vikings*, starring Kirk Douglas, began 'THE VIKINGS: A Norse-opera', a clever but not entirely original phrase, as Tims soon discovered on a visit to Stoppard's Sion Hill flat near the Clifton Suspension Bridge, when he spotted an American magazine that had first used the phrase. When Tims left the *Evening World*, Stoppard took over as the film critic and columnist for 'Talk of the Town'. He was conscientious, seeing a slew of movies during the day and then working in the reporters' room until one or two in the morning, worrying over his column, asking colleagues: 'Have I done the right thing?' Occasionally, one of his pieces would appear under the pseudonym 'Tomik Straussler'.[66]

Stoppard remembers his early work as 'indefatigably facetious. There is a sort of second-rate journalism that presents the journalist more than the subject. I did that.'[67] There was also politics. In 1959, his failure to back a strike led to his censure: a meeting of the complaints committee of the National Union of Journalists sat in Bristol on 11 December 1959 and, after review from the National Executive, they found that Stoppard should be suspended from membership for two months from 18 December 1959.

I don't know why . . . but I just seized England and it seized me.
Stoppard, 1991

Journalism had another attraction for Stoppard: it was a way of writing the self, creating a persona that actually stood in for the real person. As a reporter, you were permitted certain freedoms, allowed to ask certain questions and encouraged to investigate areas that one would other-wise not be able to see. An entirely different self could be constructed that soon materialized through language, bylines and even, occa-sionally, a picture. But this could also be protective and shield one from one's origins and identity. Being a journalist allowed Stoppard to become intimate with England. It also became a passport to the discovery of his dramatic imagination.

Stoppard more than once noted that his mother feared that British chauvinism would put him and his brother at a disadvantage among his new peers if much was made of their foreignness. Consequently, just as she hid or denied their Jewish past, they, in turn, took to England and English boarding-school life with enthusiasm and energy manifesting itself in their drive to be as English as possible. Life in England as an Englishman was remedial and it worked: his receptiveness to England resulted in the very Englishness of his plays, exhibited early in his satire of British punctuality (*The Dissolution of Dominic Boot*), classic British writers such as Shakespeare and also Wilde and Agatha Christie (see *Rosencrantz and Guildenstern, Travesties* and *The Real Inspector Hound*), public-school education (*Where Are they Now?*), British empiricism (*Jumpers*), British espionage (*The Dog it Was that Died, Hapgood*), British absorption with landscape gardening and its history (*Arcadia*), and British academia (*Arcadia, The Invention of Love*).

Such an obsession with things British – indeed, for a while he collected English watercolours, as well as first editions of major English writers – might be understood as psychological compensation to overcome any trace of foreignness in his life. Mike Nichols, who would direct the successful New York production of *The Real Thing* in 1984 and later consider filming *Arcadia*, posed the issue succinctly when he asked, in speaking of his own immigrant situation in America, 'what must I do to be unnoticeable, to be like them?'[68]

In assimilating his new culture and language, Stoppard made it more expressive, balancing intellectualism with an appeal to popular culture. Being an outsider permitted him to get to the heart of English life with an enthusiasm and optimism not shared by other playwrights. David Hare commented that what separates Stoppard from other dramatists is that 'as an immigrant to England, he is unreservedly in love with England . . . We have a more jaundiced view.' A Romanian who grew up in Brazil but now lives in Monte Carlo, New York and London explained to me that a nomad or foreigner 'remains foreign to everything and everyone, but is foreign to nothing'.[69] By incorporating the very symbols and writers of Britain in his work – borrowing, imitating, or even stealing – Stoppard constructed an incontrovertible English identity which he constantly reaffirmed through film work, beginning with the screenplay for *The Romantic Englishman* and continuing with *Shakespeare in Love* and most recently *Enigma*. Ignoring, or at least isolating, his private past because he knew that if it emerged it would distress his mother and possibly himself became characteristic of his work, distinguished by its avoidance of autobiographical content.

Preventing disequilibrium by overlooking the past was a strategy surpassed only by Stoppard's eager pursuit of British customs and history in his writing. As he explained in 1968, 'I simply don't like very much revealing myself. I am a very private sort of person. But there again one has to distinguish between self-revelation and auto-biography.'[70] Honest though his work is, it nevertheless masks another self hidden behind the persona of journalist, playwright, novelist or screenwriter. Yet acculturation, based on a personal decision to avoid the past because of its pain, may be the overarching Stoppardian double act which has its source in the demands of a new life beginning in 1946. His mother never overcame her anxiety about her children, constantly worrying about their health, food and well-being. Her last words to Stoppard while he was driving her to the hospital before she died in October 1996 were an expression of worry that he didn't have enough sweets in the car for his long ride back to London. Earlier, in the mid-seventies, Martha Stoppard felt half-guilty for shutting her sons off from their past, explaining that she never really did so. She became unhappy about keeping the past under a protective covering and began to draft a personal history in 1981 at her son's request.[71]

Interestingly, when Stoppard began to be written about in his late twenties and early thirties, such attention made his mother anxious and upset because his Czech past would invariably come up. He could become a possible target for abuse of some sort or possibly jeopardize the safety of his children because of his public profile. The past remained an 'uncomfortable, impossible thing' for her, and so, in numerous interviews until the mid-1990s, he generally avoided it for her sake. A 1967 New York interview is representative: asked if he was Jewish, Stoppard replied, 'I don't know. There must be some Jewish somewhere. Jose [his first wife] insists I must be because she wants me to be.'[72] At the time, he also didn't much care, yet in his early twenties he came to regret that he had been given his stepfather's name when he was eight years old. He actually thought that he would rather be called by his father's name, Sträussler, but he knew it would upset his stepfather and, in turn, his mother. His mother's death in 1996, followed by his stepfather's in 1997, freed him to remark that 'left to myself, I'm not that inhibited' about the past. 'I don't mind talking about them; it doesn't bother me at all,' he added.[73] Such a transformation coincides with his recent investigation and rediscovery of his past through his visits to Prague and Zlín.

I wasn't much use as a reporter. I felt I didn't have the right to ask people questions. So I went on to theatre criticism.
Stoppard, 1967

Stoppard's drama criticism had begun with coverage of amateur as well as professional theatre productions in Bath and Bristol, many of which were not at all successful. A Bath production of *A Scent of Flowers* by James Saunders had an audience of seven, a lesson, as Anthony Smith repeated to Stoppard, for any promising playwright. That year he also saw a production of Pinter's *The Birthday Party* but didn't understand any of the new and redefining elements of Pinter's work; rather, 'I thought of Hemingway of Fifty Grand and The Killers.' 'Be cautious', he later warned, 'of people telling you what Pinteresque means in 200 words.'[74] He soon found that reporting did not allow for elaborate or even serious discussions about the theatre and subsequently confessed to a perpetual dis-ease with one of journalism's fixtures: deadlines. 'I've never handed anything in to a newspaper or magazine without being rushed and furious. I'm usually angry with myself for agreeing to do it. I end up doing it and in it goes.'[75]

In the process of reviewing the arts, Stoppard befriended members of the Bristol Old Vic, costuming himself as a quasi-bohemian: 'he used to turn up in sandals with no socks, like a beatnik. In the local café he would hang out with lots of poor unknown actors from the Old Vic who darned his socks and bummed cups of tea off him.'[76] The theatre, however, became an increasingly important home for him. Among his new friends was Peter O'Toole, who had joined the company in 1955 from RADA. O'Toole, who also started in journalism but after naval service pursued his acting career, left London for Bristol at twenty-three, his first performance at the Theatre Royal being seven lines as a cab-driver in Thornton Wilder's *The Matchmaker*. He next appeared in Jean Giraudoux's *Ondine*, which Ken Tynan reviewed in the *Observer*, neglecting O'Toole in favour of Eric Porter, Alan Dobie and

'Miss Yvonne Furneaux, a buxom temptress . . . more impressive in silhouette than in action'.[77] By the 1957–8 season, however, O'Toole could not be overlooked. He had the crowning role: Hamlet, with Margaretta Scott as Gertrude, Wendy Williams as Ophelia and Barry Wilsher as Horatio.

The headline of the *Times* review of *Hamlet* reflected the curious cross-over between the world of John Osborne and that of Shakespeare and the new change in British theatre. It read, 'Now an Angry Young Hamlet in Bristol Production'. Criticizing the sizzling pace of the play, the reviewer observed that 'the play is taken at such a pace that the play's deeper issues are glimpsed like some architectural masterpiece passed on a main road at 60 miles an hour . . . . Mr. John Moody's direction, set on a simple platform and curving ramp, presents an angry young bearded rebel.' The hero, said the paper, both dazzles and confuses, offering a 'restless interpretation, crudely staccato in diction and gesture yet blessed with uncommon energy and staying power'.[78]

Stoppard saw the production several times, but in parts, since his writing assignments often made it difficult for him to spend the entire evening in the theatre. Gradually he built up a sense of the whole. Equally important, he built up a friendship with O'Toole, who would often appear at Val Lorraine's Grosvenor Lodge home, a gathering place for actors where, after 1960, Stoppard lived. Later, O'Toole would indirectly help in getting Stoppard a London writing job and would even loan Stoppard some much-needed money. Indeed, it was the combination of O'Toole's acting and John Osborne's writing that worked as 'a delayed fuse' on Stoppard's desire to become a playwright. 'Not until I was about 20 did I begin to think that I would like to write something that lasted more than 24 hours.'[79]

O'Toole was clearly a Bristol personality; at parties at Val's, he would display extravagance, seductiveness and, more often than not, drunkenness. Women were not safe from his charm, but those who were insufferable were excluded from his circle. Often he would sit and feign sleep in a chair to avoid the idiocy of small talk. He was also a notorious driver, frequently crashing or getting into automotive mishaps; early on, he couldn't understand why he failed a driving test just because icy conditions made it impossible for him to control his car. One friend later quipped that O'Toole was better at driving a camel than a car. It was common to hear of him falling asleep at the wheel of his Riley on the M1, crashing the car and yet surviving, even though the car was demolished. On another occasion, he ignored a keep-left sign on the grounds that it made no sense, objected to people telling him to turn his lights on, and managed, on yet another occasion, to avoid driving down a flight of steps only at the last moment. His driving and drinking created such problems that a Bristol court banned him from driving for a year.

But O'Toole and Stoppard became fast friends, partly because the theatre was an education for both. O'Toole found his roles provided him with literary instruction. Despite his education at RADA, he was not well read, although his lack of a formal education actually allowed him to bring a freshness to the lines when, in actual performance rather than class, he learned how to act. In the seventy-three roles he played in his three years at the Bristol Old Vic, he discovered a presence that took him forward. Whether it was as Corvino in *Volpone*, Peter Shirley in *Major Barbara*, Jimmy Porter in *Look Back in Anger*, Vladimir in *Waiting for Godot*, or, of course, Hamlet, O'Toole found acting a challenge and a thrill.[80] Stoppard, who was undergoing a simultaneous education in the theatre, discovered in O'Toole a ready study of what an actor can become and what can happen to a text when it becomes a theatrical event.

Stoppard also found himself exposed to a range of British and European plays at the Bristol Old Vic that were new to him. These included not only Shakespeare, but works by Max Frisch, Shaw and a striking production of *War and Peace* staged by Erwin Piscator, a distinguished experimental European director. This innovative production used film and a strong rhythmic flow of action with staccato dialogue and was reviewed in the *Western Daily Press* on 29 January 1962. Nor did Stoppard neglect amateur theatre in the region, much of which he tolerated rather than enjoyed.

Theatre life, and in particular that at the Bristol Old Vic, became so enticing for Stoppard that he actually went on stage. Uniting his journalism with his budding interest in the theatre, he took his first and last theatrical role, a walk-on part as an Arab, for one performance only, in the Bristol Old Vic's production of Shaw's *Captain Brassbound's Conversion*. The September 1958 production called for Stoppard, who had once swished water in a tub to simulate surf lapping up against the backcloth of a school production, to move toward Emrys James when David King yelled 'Seize them!' He then had to twist one arm behind James's back and stick a knife at his throat. As the seventh Arab appearing briefly at the end of the second act, Stoppard was disappointed not to find his name on the marquee on the night of the performance.

In beard, skirt, blouse and kimono, Stoppard only required make-up: 'With my face, hands and feet a healthy Moorish brown, I looked like an attempt to keep death off the roads – which was about right.' But as the moment approached, he developed stage-fright 'and turned East for a minute in case it helped':

> Then we padded on barefoot behind David King (played by Abdul Krim) and leered picturesquely, looking like the dust-jacket of a cheap edition of 'Beau Geste'.
>
> I had a crafty look round for Mr. James and was unnerved to see that there were about six people between us. I had doubts about getting through to seize him before the curtain came down.
>
> For a moment I wondered whether the plot would suffer very much if I seized Miss Heal [the female lead] instead.

Engrossed in visualizing himself rushing about the stage trying to seize people who had just been seized by someone else, he missed his cue:

> But we theatre people stick together. Mr. James with great presence of mind ran towards me and held out a trailing limb for me to put the arm on.
>
> After that it was just a case of remembering which side my knife was, and I emoted until the curtain dropped.

He ends this comic account of his stage début with reference to a forthcoming production of *As You Like It*: 'I sort of see myself as Orlando done in the Method manner.'[81] In the introduction to a collection of memoirs on the Theatre Royal Bristol, Stoppard summarized the impact of the Bristol Old Vic on his theatrical development: 'I was a junior reporter when I entered the Theatre Royal for the first time, and it still feels more as if it entered me.'[82]

The world of the theatre, with its blend of language and performance, plus the general fascination at the time with dramatists

– 'after 1956 everybody of my age who wanted to write, wanted to write plays – after Osborne and the rest at the [Royal] Court, and with Tynan on the *Observer*, and Peter Hall about to take over the RSC' – led Stoppard to attempt his first full-length play in the late summer of 1960. Simultaneously, he became haunted by what he thought was lost time: when he read a rave for a new play, all he wanted to know was how old the writer was, and if he was a year younger than himself, he was desperate.[83] The romance of the dramatist exceeded that of the novelist; no one, in fact, wanted to write fiction any more.

CHAPTER 4

AT THE PARAGON

Theatre satisfies my capacity for safety and risk.
Stoppard, 1980

To celebrate his twenty-third birthday, Stoppard slipped off to Italy with Isabel Dunjohn. The trip wasn't entirely carefree. Since 1958, he had been nurturing the possibility of a new career in the theatre. By the summer of 1960, he also felt he had reached the end of his life as a journalist: 'there's a limit to the combination of stories you could write. Once past that you look for something new.'[1] On the island of Capri, he decided to abandon the press for playwriting. But why playwriting? Why not fiction or poetry? Stoppard himself has explained the choice often. After Osborne's *Look Back in Anger* (1956), the formation of the Royal Court's English Stage Company and Peter Hall's exciting work at Stratford, a new energy vibrated through English theatre. Playwrights had all the attention. Young writers found it to be the most dynamic medium with the most original possibilities for expression. And then there was Beckett, whose *Godot* 'was a shocking event because it completely redefined the minima of a valid theatrical transaction. Up till then, to have a play at all you had to have 'x', you couldn't have a tenth of 'x' and have a play.'[2]

Theatre was romantic, alluring and captivating for authors as well as audiences – who for two hours or more couldn't escape to the refrigerator, switch channels or answer the phone. Stoppard's fascination, however, had little to do with the theatre as a venue for social change or political ideas, as was emerging in the work of John Osborne, John Arden, Arnold Wesker or Harold Pinter. Stoppard approached the theatre as a magical place where unusual trans-formations could occur: for years, he recounted a unique performance of Shakespeare's *The Tempest* which took place at an Oxford college. At the end of the play, produced on a college lawn at the edge of a lake, the newly freed Ariel rushed off towards the lake in the dusk and *ran across the water*. As the transfixed audience witnessed this magical act (the director arranged for planks to be put just below the surface), Ariel reached the other side as darkness fell and fireworks were set off. The effect was sensational; Shakespeare's only direction in the text reads 'Exit Ariel'.[3] This, for Stoppard, was the essence of theatre – imagination and the freedom to create a scene that makes the text an event.

The plays that mattered to Stoppard created similar effects: N. F. Simpson's absurdist *One Way Pendulum* and James Saunders's *Next Time I'll Sing to You*. What fascinated him was making the irrational seem rational. Turning to the theatre, he explained in 1976, had little 'to do with the fact that Pinter, Wesker, Osborne and Arden suddenly showed up in the late fifties like the four horsemen – hoarse men – of the new apocalypse'.[4] It was, rather, the possibilities of theatre as a vehicle for ideas, concepts, abstractions and the totality of the effort involving actors, directors, producers, lighting designers, set designers and the audience that appealed to him. He was attracted by the risky, unstable business of putting on a play which 'owing to the chemistry of the performers and the entire situation is much more exciting than [publishing prose]'.[5]

Mythologizing drama in terms of its imaginative possibilities equalled Stoppard's earlier romanticizing of journalism, reflecting the extent to which his imagination, rather than reason, guided his life. 'Plays were sexy . . . a young writer having his or her play performed without decor on a Sunday night at the Royal Court would have more critical attention poured into this tyro piece than someone publishing an eighth novel. It was extraordinary and deeply attractive,' he recalled years later.[6] In the summer of 1960, Stoppard returned from Italy with a new goal: to write a play.

I told him that I'd had him down as a greasy-haired lout,
and he replied that he'd figured me as a poncey graduate.
Anthony Smith on first meeting Stoppard in 1960

Stoppard's closest Bristol friend and earliest supporter was Anthony Smith, who took an instant dislike to him when they first met as rival film critics in 1960. Smith describes their meeting in vivid, comical detail:

> In 1960 I was working for the *Evening Post*. I was sent to review a film, *Battle Inferno*. The only other reviewer at the press view was a greasy-haired, loose-lipped lout in a brown suit from the *Evening World* [the rival evening paper] called Tom Stoppard. We'd never met, and over a glass of sweetish sherry in the Embassy Cinema's office I formed no desire to meet him again. I went back and wrote that the film wasn't much cop, then waited to see what the *World* review would say. Just as I thought: he rated it. Provincial jerk.
>
> Some months later, the Editorial Director of the Bristol United Press, Richard Hawkins, decided to introduce a weekly Arts Page in the *Western Daily Press*, and invited me to edit it. The bad news was that he asked me to give plenty of work to a local freelance called Stoppard. I sniffed, and rang Stoppard. He said he'd like to kick off with a piece on the New Wave of French film directors. Mon Dieu, I thought to myself, I'll have my work cut out knocking that into shape. When it arrived it was knowledgeable, perceptive and beautifully written. I didn't change a word. Who *was* this provincial jerk?[7]

A friendship flourished, although not without its criticisms: 'he seemed to me the all-time greedy go-getting journalist in a smart suit and spotty with it. Well, not so smart perhaps. He looked like a bookies' runner aspiring to a sort of post teddy-boy provincial trendiness.'[8] His dress later improved – slightly: 'he now chose clothes with flair and wore them all at once,' Smith quipped.[9] Throughout Bristol, Stoppard was known for his trilby hat and mackintosh, the very image, he thought, of a dashing journalist. He also had a huge fur coat 'and he sat huddled in it while I was driving my open car to London. He had this slight Czech thing about his "r" sounds and he was rolling them, and I suddenly saw this growling bear next to me. He got it and we laughed so much we had to stop,' Smith recalled.[10]

Smith, who arrived in Bristol from Cambridge in 1960, lived for three years in a flat on top of The Paragon, a tall apartment building with a triangular balcony and commanding view from Redcliffe to the Mendip Hills, the River Avon and the Clifton Suspension Bridge, designed by Brunel. The panorama was astonishing: 'the terrace seems to be attached to the top corner of the world. It's fabulous, Bristol just spread out below, with the ships and all, the best view I've seen in this town,' Stoppard told Isabel Dunjohn.[11] There, Smith and Stoppard ran the weekly Arts Page for the revamped *Western Daily Press*, planning stories, designing layout and editing copy. Sometimes the work spilled over to Val Lorraine's long kitchen table. Before Smith moved to The Paragon, Stoppard had often crashed at Smith's first apartment, a garret flat in Hotwells, located at the bottom of the Avon Gorge.

Stoppard and Smith spent a great deal of time together, from vacations in the Vaucluse and trips to New York and Zagreb, to evenings arguing about writing and their literary futures. Smith wanted to be a novelist; Stoppard wanted to be known. Chess became a passion and over the coming years, when they were apart, they exchanged frequent postcards in an ongoing chess match. They also kept up with the London papers and journals; when the *Observer* revolutionized its use of space and typeface, they tried to imitate it on the Arts Page, experimenting with its format, photos and design.

They soon befriended a number of artists and writers, like Charles Wood, who did small drawings at the paper for display ads but also had a strong interest in radio drama (and whose play *Tie up the Ballcock* would première with Stoppard's *The Gamblers* in 1965). His actor pal was now Peter Nichols, another would-be playwright who was writing scripts for television. There was a creative surge in Bristol at the time, aided by people like John Arden, who was then playwright in residence at the university drama department (where he was succeeded by Martin Shuttleworth), in which Geoffrey Reeves, later to be an assistant to Peter Brook and to direct a Stoppard play, was a postgraduate student. John Hale ran the Bristol Old Vic, with Nat Brenner as the General Manager. Angela Carter was involved in a brief effort to establish a writers' group. Bristol had its own dance company and orchestra, as well as an Arts Centre in Kings Square and a new venue for experimental art, the Arnolfini Gallery, which opened in 1961. Zulfikar Ghose and B. S. Johnson, becoming established as a poet and novelist respectively, contributed to the Arts Page and became part of the Smith–Stoppard circle.

I'm a lover of and an apologist for journalism.
Stoppard, 1979

When the Bristol papers consolidated in the summer of 1960, Stoppard went freelance, a decision he did not take lightly. The Bristol United Press took control of the *Western Daily Press*. Eric Price became editor, reporting to Richard Hawkins, Editorial Director of the Bristol United Press. Redesigned as a populist paper by Price, a former sergeant-major, its circulation soared. It was Hawkins who decided to introduce the weekly Arts Page, though Price opposed it. Richard Hawkins was in conversation with Patrick Dromgoole (a radio producer, then at BBC Bristol) about Stoppard and how he 'was too good to stay on the *World*' and that he 'ought to do some serious writing instead of going to Fleet Street'. Hawkins agreed and was willing to give him enough work to keep him alive; 'if I wanted to risk getting off the *World*, stay in Bristol, and get on with writing as distinct from journalism,' Stoppard told Isabel, 'this truly . . . wd. be very good for me. I wd. stay at Val's . . . and just write and write, provided that Hawkins meant what he said.'[12] This was the opening Stoppard needed to leave full-time journalism and begin a writing career. He took it, although he kept on two columns.

Stoppard was in constant need of money and was always borrowing, repaying and borrowing again from friends. In 1960, when he set out as a freelance, he was elated to have Richard Hawkins offer him some work, telling Isabel 'I figure I can get by on £5 a week at a pinch, but £7 for safety (the main snag is that I CANNOT write without cigarettes!). It wd give me what I most lack now – time.' In that same letter, he reports on a meeting with John Hale, then director of the Bristol Old Vic, during which he informed him that he was writing a play. Excited, Hale told him to send it on as soon as it was finished. 'The value of this', Stoppard explained,

is not so much that he wd or cd put it on, but he is a man who really knows which theatres want which kind of plays. He cd not only criticise and suggest changes, but, if it was any good, send it to a management with his recommendation. This of course is worth rubies. I am determined to do this.[13]

Life was changing and he was eager, with this encouragement, to pursue his new direction.

During his journalism career, Stoppard had made an early attempt to move to Fleet Street. He was interviewed by the *Evening Standard* for a position on their 'Londoner's Diary' and got on well with Nick Tomalin, who was running it, but he also had to have an interview with Charles Wintour, editor of the paper. 'At one point,' Stoppard reported,

> Mr Wintour asked me if I were interested in politics. Thinking all journalists should be interested in politics, I told him I was. He then asked me who the current home secretary was. Of course, I had no idea who the current home secretary was, and, in any event, it was an unfair question. I'd only admitted to an interest in politics. I hadn't claimed I was *obsessed* with the subject.[14]

Stoppard contracted to provide two columns during 1960–2 for the *Western Daily Press*, one of them published under the pseudonym 'Brennus'. These were satirical treatments of issues of the day. Other contributions consisted of articles for the Arts Page, which Anthony Smith began to edit in 1960. There, Stoppard's writing was varied, but tended to film, theatre or literary criticism with the occasional cultural piece on art or dance. His pay was three guineas per article. Occasionally, when he had two items appearing on the same page, one would appear with the byline 'Tomik Straussler'.

One such article was 'A Slave to a Mural', his review of *Spartacus*, the Stanley Kubrick film starring Laurence Olivier, Peter Ustinov and Charles Laughton. Praising the spectacle, he then points out that epic is not Kubrick's style, which depends on 'a focal, microcosmic action and his direct and independent control over that action'. Control, says Stoppard acutely, is Kubrick's *métier*. 'Kubrick needs to have everything where he can touch it.' When the action moves out of his reach, nearly everything falls apart. Nevertheless, Stoppard admires the photography and script by Dalton Trumbo.[15] On the same page is his review of the work of Arnold Wesker, written to coincide with the

Bristol Old Vic's production of Wesker's *Roots*. This appears under Stoppard's own name.

> *The first time I reviewed a play the cast and director wrote*
> *[to] the editor with perfectly justifiable venom.*
> Stoppard, 1967

Theatre criticism by Stoppard began to appear on the Arts Page with regularity, one of his most important articles focusing on Brecht's *Mother Courage*. It opens with a comment on literary larceny, the 'borrowings' that great writers commit, anticipating, of course, his own later work: 'Lines, characters and whole plots reappear all the time to remind us that evolution is a matter of reproduction.' He then cites examples from drama, notably Thornton Wilder borrowing from Joyce and 'a long forgotten French farce' (Stoppard has the nationality wrong: it was the Austrian Nestroy who wrote *Einen Jux will er sich machen,* which Stoppard would later adapt as *On the Razzle;* Wilder used it for *The Merchant of Yonkers,* later reworked as *The Matchmaker*). He also cites Molière, Shakespeare and T. S. Eliot as examples of additional 'borrowers'.

The occasion for these remarks was the first production of Brecht in Bristol. Stoppard displays his own research, showing how Brecht modified a work by the Frenchmen Emile Erchmann and Alexandre Chatrian, *La Guerre,* with a strong female character, Hattouine, an old woman who follows the Russian army with her wagon. She is the chief fictitious character in the play, which is the point of departure for Brecht. 'As far as I know,' Stoppard adds, 'this curious sidelight on Brecht's most famous play has not been hitherto published.'[16] A box near two photographs from the Bristol Old Vic production notes that the play had been performed by Brecht's Berliner Ensemble in London in 1956 and that his wife, Helene Weigel, took the title role.

Another fascinating Stoppard article was on Harold Pinter. Stoppard never actually interviewed Pinter, but attended a talk he gave as part of the *Sunday Times* Festival, taking down quotes in shorthand. He found the remarks oblique and contradictory, but he structured them to invent an interview which gave the impression of a personal exchange between the increasingly important dramatist and the provincial journalist. The tone is almost satirical and always critical, complaining of a staccato delivery and grudging self-exposure, with contradiction rampant. 'I'm going to make categorical statements which should not be taken as categorical,' Pinter offered at one point as he satirized the ability of critics to criticize: 'You can't fool the critics for long. They can tell a dot from a dash a mile off.' The headline of the interview article read 'The Tense Present – Harold Pinter'.[17]

Stoppard's evaluation of popular culture also appears in these columns. An awareness that culture is not something segregated to the library, study, or common room but something that pervades society emerges. The importance of writing popular but educated drama finds early expression in a column on Arnold Wesker and his Centre 42 programme of bringing art to the masses. Critical of Centre 42's over-simplification that the division of culture lies somewhere between the Right and the Left, however, Stoppard editorializes: 'Art is necessary for itself', hinting at a position he will develop in the first ten years of his playwriting. The Wildean emphasis on style is enough justification for writing. 'Our culture', Stoppard explains,

> includes fishing, pigeon-racing, woodwork, rock'n'roll, Agatha Christie, gardening and Sunday Night at the Palladium . . . Too many people do nothing worthwhile, but many also can get as much spiritual benefit from their gardens or from Bartók. At the same time, the masses have no monopoly on unenlightenment . . . If the cultural revolution does come, it may have to start in the fourth form rather than the theatre stalls.[18]

This democratic view of culture identifies a position he would later transmit through his work as he manages to make the audience feel as knowledgeable about Shakespeare, Dada, Chaos Theory and the classics as he is.

Stoppard was similarly critical of the Bristol Old Vic and its programming. A 1962 article begins with the Old Vic's failure to put on Wesker's *Chips with Everything* when it was offered to them within a few days of its opening at the Royal Court in London. What did the director Val May mean by 'casting difficulties', Stoppard asks at the beginning of his piece. The issue is money, he says, but the more important question is the performance in Bristol of exciting new plays. Arguing for the existence of a sophisticated Bristol audience, he complains that 'few theatres will put on a new risky play unless there is a London tie-in'. He celebrates the Royal Court and its courage in experimenting with unorthodox work, somewhat ironic in light of the fact that Stoppard's own playwriting would not be produced at the Royal Court, although he did offer them *Rosencrantz and Guildenstern*. The National Theatre would become his more suitable 'home'.

The Bristol Old Vic, he argues, should be innovative and experimental *in advance* of London:

> The biggest ice-breaker of them all, *Look Back in Anger*, was offered to Bristol before the Royal Court and Bristol turned it down. When the Court had made Osborne's name, Bristol put the play on, and put on *The Entertainer*, too. But not the less successful *[Epitaph for] George Dillon* which has the best second act written for the English stage in the last 10 years.[19]

Bristol audiences were ready for Osborne and others, Stoppard argues in his assessment of contemporary British theatre which repeatedly holds up the Royal Court as the new standard alongside George Devine's plan to use the Cambridge Arts Theatre as a testing ground for new works to appear at the Royal Court, like Max Frisch's *The Fire Raisers*. He ends the piece by noting that he saw Ann Jellicoe's *The Knack*, originally produced at the Royal Court, in Bath, but with only thirty people in the audience. He could not understand the furore surrounding the work: was it obscene, shocking? No. Rather, it was funny, alive 'and built on verbal rhythms'. Two other works he saw in Bath, *Fred* and *A Slight Accident* by James Saunders – 'pitched somewhere in the Pinter–Beckett–Ionesco–N. F. Simpson syndrome' – were failures. But, he concludes, the plays of the 'new young' find it impossible to locate provincial audiences 'before they are held up, inspected and passed for consumption by London. This is irrational, and if we keep trying, at a loss, people may begin to pick plays on their merits instead of their reputations.'

Humour was another subject Stoppard covered for the Arts Page. His piece on James Thurber, 'Double-focus – the plight of the sane lunatic', is a virtual outline of his early comic sense, as he developed it in *After Magritte*, for example. Admiring Thurber's wit, he stresses how he united comedy and good writing. As if describing his own subsequent style, Stoppard writes that 'even when the fun is at its maddest, the style is rigidly lucid, beautifully worked'. Only Wodehouse competes; and both will be read 'not because they are funnier than S. J. Perelman but because they write better. Or rather, they *are* funnier *because* they write better.' A further comment acts as a manifesto for the first part of Stoppard's yet-to-be launched drama career: Thurber's mind, he says, 'was tuned to pick up the idiocies and surrealism masquerading as normality. This, if anything, was Thurber's speciality – the fantasy with the logical explanation.' Such is the 'plight of the sane lunatic ever so slightly at odds with the lunatic sane'. He further notes that 'the pattern is familiar: man finds himself in a ridiculous but logical position, tries to explain the inexplicable and then the wordless retreat that shrieks insanity'.[20] This itself becomes the pattern for some of Stoppard's early radio plays and shorter theatre pieces of the 1970s. His contributions to the Arts Page displayed his commitment to well-researched articles and gave him the confidence to compete successfully with university-trained critics like Johnson, Ghose and Philip Hobsbaum.

His enthusiasm for American writers displayed itself in various reviews and essays on the Arts Page, ranging from Hemingway to Raymond Chandler, John Dos Passos, Norman Mailer and Arthur Miller. This admiration for America partly originated in Darjeeling, not so much in his education at the American missionary school as in his encounters with the romantic and easy-going manners of American soldiers on leave. His respect for the clarity of American prose began with the stories of Damon Runyon he read in his teens and continued with Truman Capote. He imitated them all: 'as a (potential) writer I had no personality of my own, and as a reader I seemed to be a displaced American'. 'I found English writing slightly quaint and uninteresting', while 'I thought American writing was exciting and glamorous'. In his twenties, he went 'on an American binge: Fitzgerald, Steinbeck, Saroyan, Miller, Crane, cummings, Dos Passos, Thurber, O'Hara, Lardner, Mailer and Salinger and notably the first two anthologies of *New Yorker Short Stories*.' He also recalled the impression made on him by an excerpt from Joseph Heller's *Catch-22*.[21]

Hemingway, in particular, became a passion; from about the age of twenty, Stoppard soon read everything he had written: 'I was knocked sideways,' he said. And he 'remained at this angle for years, as is perfectly clear from Faber's *Introduction 2: Stories by New Writers* [where three of Stoppard's own works appear] and I'm not quite perpendicular yet'. Hemingway, he declared in 1984, had an 'atomic prose', explaining that Hemingway achieved his effects 'by making the reader do the work' through the pared-down sentences where 'the associative power of words rather than their "meaning" . . . makes prose work on its ultimate level'. 'Big Two-Hearted River' is his example, with its description of fishing, since he had fished for trout since childhood in England. Repetition also has persuasive meaning for him, as three passages from Hemingway show. But, as he notes, 'in trying to explain the attraction of art, the more indisputable a fact the less useful it becomes', for, in Hemingway, 'it is not simply physical action but the action of the physical world upon the individual that is important'.[22]

In his mid-twenties, Stoppard went to Paris and walked about, looking for Hemingway's address, and years later – when he could afford it – he began to collect Hemingway first editions. Another American writer, Jack Gelber, made Stoppard aware of a new and direct way of writing plays when he read *The Connection*. His later friendship with the American Ed Berman led to Stoppard's writing a celebration of America in the 1976 play *New-Found-Land*. At that time, he also considered writing a play about Hemingway, but nothing materialized. What did emerge from Stoppard's long-standing fascination with the writer was a talk at the Kennedy Library at Harvard on Hemingway for a conference in May 1982, reprinted as 'Reflections on Ernest Hemingway'.[23]

During the early 1960s, Stoppard also tried to publish freelance pieces. *Men Only* magazine, for example, bought his article on John Steinbeck in 1960 for £30, paid in instalments, although they wanted him to cut it from 5,500 to 2,000 words.

> I guess a true artist would say 'Never! You insult my artistic integrity! Take your filthy money and give me back my story!' Unfortunately, although it wd be unthinkable with a short story, I feel I have no alternative than to accept, and as it is merely a factual article it will not suffer so much by pruning.

The money, however, would be quickly spent, paying off debts, from loans to groceries and gas. 'Val [Lorraine] said, when I told her, "Aren't you thrilled to get £30 for your first proper freelance article?"

And you know, I just wasn't. I've lived with, breathed with that Steinbeck thing so long that all the excitement has gone out of it.'[24]

The article was a profile of Steinbeck, who had moved to a small Somerset village for eight months. Stoppard stresses how Steinbeck is a man of the people who identifies more with the villagers than with other writers. His hands, he notices, are 'large, capable hands that belong to the roving ranch-hand, labourer and newspaper man [with] none of the aesthetic delicacy of the artist'. And his mannerisms are not unlike Stoppard's: 'He smokes cigarette after cigarette as he talks, taking his time to find the phrase, searching the opposite wall for the right image . . .' Steinbeck complains of the competition others promote between himself and Hemingway and adds that he admires Kerouac. He also provides Stoppard with the rugged stereotypical image of the American writer who is 'untouched raw material, something primeval almost as if his body was shaped out of wood or clay. Conversely, he is capable of an emotion that is at first jarring in the pattern of civilized conventional thinking and then strangely logical in spite of it.'[25] Stoppard would himself soon exhibit this pattern in his own drama.

Stoppard would soon apply the habits he learned from journalism to playwriting. These habits were not only an efficacious, facile style that was comic in tone and experimental in form, but also a natural aptitude for research. His journalistic instincts meant he had to know his subject before he could write about it and he quickly learned what was essential and what was not for background and a good story. Anthony Smith recalled how Stoppard always read as much as was necessary (and often more), but where academics may get lost in the research, journalists do not; they know how to *use* what they are looking for. Stoppard became adept as a journalist, although sometimes he erred on the side of excessive research in his perfectionism. When asked by Smith to write a feature article on Norman Mailer, Stoppard read all of Mailer's work in two weeks, only to discover 'I over-researched on Mailer. Instead of knowing enough to write 1000 words, and writing 1200, I know enough to write 10,000 words and laboured mainly at compression, precis, discrimination, etc. to write 2000.' 'Cut at will,' he advised Smith. This, of course, carried over to his playwriting. Derek Marlowe described Stoppard's writing process, especially as it applied to *Jumpers*, in this manner: 'For Tom, writing a play is like sitting for an examination. He spends ages on research, does all the necessary cramming, reads all the relevant books, and then gestates the results.' As Stoppard earlier noted, 'a lot of my reading has resulted from the sheer necessity of having something to deliver.'[26]

But his disillusionment with journalism was growing, caused more by embarrassment than lack of talent, suggesting something of Stoppard's private side in conflict with the public:

> I felt I didn't have the right to ask people questions. I always thought they'd throw the teapot at me or call the police. For me, it was like knocking at the door, wearing your reporter's peaked cap, and saying: 'Hello, I'm from journalism. I've come to inspect you. Take off your clothes and lie down.'[27]

This didn't deter him from carrying out his assignments with panache and verbal disguises. In fact, it encouraged it and prompted further skill in masking himself between intellectual fireworks and verbal sophistication. In order to prepare himself for the tasks of journalism and perhaps his own imagined success, he would habitually conduct self-interviews while in the bath to polish his own epigrammatic and smart interview style.

Nevertheless, Stoppard disavowed his early journalism, preferring it not to be reprinted, whether it was his comic 'Brennus' columns, his clever movie reviews or his astute theatre criticism. The evidence of his Bristol apprenticeship seems to have been forgotten; or as Anthony Smith phrased it, Stoppard 'prefers to have been born aged 28 and the author of *Rosencrantz and Guildenstern are Dead*. Actually, he would most of all prefer to have been born aged 17 and the author of it.'[28]

In the late fifties, the playwright was the hottest thing in town.
Stoppard, 1977

Large printer's stones led from the street to the archway and garden at the front door of Val and Bob Lorraine's home, Grosvenor Lodge, on Gordon Road in Clifton, behind the Students Union of Bristol University, where Stoppard was now living. He had previously rented a room at 24 Sion Hill, where he had painted the fireplace a gorgeous red, to the chagrin of his landlord, Dr John Wilders. His new digs were appropriately linked to the theatre. An actress at the Bristol Old Vic, Val was a tremendous support and friend for Stoppard, who had a small room with tapering walls and a high window at the back of the house, on the second floor. Most importantly, she took his efforts at writing seriously: 'People like Val are so rare, I mean people who have faith in a promising writer or artist or actor or anyone like that and enough faith to think it so worthwhile to look after him.' 'She has more faith in me than I have in myself,' he added.[29] Val and her husband, Bob, a civil engineer, provided Stoppard with encouragement buttressed by frequent parties for visiting theatre companies, actors, agents and producers. Stoppard always enjoyed these parties, making new friends and helpful connections. He also grasped the existence of the theatrical world as a community.

One 'hilarious, hysterical, mad, incredible' event on his return to work in the summer of 1960 as film critic for the newly merged Bristol papers was a contest to win a trip to Pinewood Studios, dinner in London at the Pigalle with its floorshow, attendance at the première of the film *Doctor in Love* and an overnight stay at the Strand Palace. Contestants had to send in their funniest doctor stories. Stoppard, as the film critic, was to accompany the lucky winner and guest. Unexpectedly, Val Lorraine won. Stoppard and she went off on the jaunt, his editor telling him it was a good thing he had been in Italy during the contest, otherwise no one would have believed that it wasn't rigged. 'What made it a bigger farce was that the winner was supposed to be an innocent wide-eyed housewife being introduced to the glamour and mysteries of film making, and of course Val worked at Pinewood for years.'[30]

Efforts at writing his first serious play began at Grosvenor Lodge, when, in August 1960, Stoppard started *A Walk on the Water*, the title taken from the black American blues singer Leadbelly and his song, 'Ol' Riley'. The album, a favourite of Val's which she still owns, played repeatedly in the living-room of her home, the practice of listening to music while writing being a habit Stoppard would follow throughout his career. George Riley, the inventor-hero, represented the determination of Stoppard, who was inventing himself as a playwright. He told Val that his first play had to be accepted within two years or he would have to go back to journalism. After they had talked for most of the evening, Stoppard often wrote in longhand all night at her kitchen table, which could seat fourteen. One morning, Val came down to find a series of table knives, forks and teaspoons on the table spelling out the words, 'I've Finished!'

A letter dated 15 October 1960 from Stoppard to John Hale, Director of Productions at the Bristol Old Vic, describes his delivery of the typescript which Stoppard noted was 'a most unprofessional copy – unbound and probably spattered with typographical errors'. It is 'somewhere on your desk. Nat [Brenner] was there when I brought it in, and on the spur of the moment, I offered him a second copy.' Stoppard then added that since he left the paper, 'life has been one of ecstatic poverty; if anything, I am working harder, but of course it is very much more enjoyable. My weekly bits and pieces keep me in food and cigarettes, while I get on with other things', which included a good deal of writing: 'I myself have been inviting disaster by my unhealthy and nocturnal existence over this machine [his typewriter], but all I have developed so far is a pale, wan and interesting face.' The following day, Hale wrote to Stoppard at Grosvenor Lodge: 'Many thanks for your letter and the script. It will be read as soon as possible – not once but *twice*.'[31]

While he awaited comment on his submission – it took nine months before he had a definite reply – Stoppard wrote a one-act work, *The Gamblers,* and seventy-two additional newspaper columns. Around the same time, he also did a rough draft of what would be the ur-*Real Inspector Hound*, variously titled 'The Stand-Ins' or, in a later draft, 'The Critics'. In a letter to Isabel Dunjohn, he outlined his problems in structuring the play, calling it a 'surrealistic farce' because he was having trouble balancing between an Agatha Christie parody and his own play.

Stoppard by this time had an agent, Kenneth Ewing, who had recently joined the firm of Fraser and Dunlop in London, a talent and theatrical agency which was beginning to cultivate new writers and scripts. How he got in touch with Ewing is somewhat ambiguous. One account has Stoppard asking some friends at the Bristol Old Vic for a recommendation. They knew the Fraser and Dunlop agency and suggested he try their new literary agent, Ewing. Stoppard wrote to him. Another view is that John Hale of the Bristol Old Vic sent the script of *A Walk on the Water* to Peter Dunlop with the advice 'give it to your literary man'. That was Ewing, who read the work and liked it but wanted to see more. Stoppard sent him *The Gamblers*.[32] Meanwhile, Charles Landstone, dramaturg for the Bristol Old Vic, read *A Walk on the Water* and wrote an unfavourable report, none the less praising the well-drawn central character, 'though it is possible that, without good acting, he might become extremely boring . . . the difficulty lies in the limited projection of the writing' but 'the construction of the play is professional'.[33]

Unexpectedly, Stoppard received 'one of those Hollywood-style telegrams' that changed his life overnight: acceptance of *A Walk on the Water* from Ewing with a £10 advance, the largest lump sum Stoppard had ever earned; two weeks later, he received £100 when one of Britain's most important producing agencies, H. M. Tennent, bought an option on the work. With the money, he bought twenty books and a Picasso print.[34] This was in late January 1962, when Stoppard and Ewing formalized their arrangement through a letter of agreement.

Stoppard remained with Ewing, avoiding the ambitious and forceful agent Peggy Ramsay, who represented, or would soon be representing, James Saunders, John Osborne, Charles Wood, Peter Nichols, Joe Orton, Alan Ayckbourn and David Hare among others. She dismissed Stoppard's work, telling him – before she knew about *The Gamblers* – that 'all young writers seemed to be writing first plays about people in condemned cells'.[35] She found Stoppard's work flashy and glittery, but took credit for recommending *Rosencrantz and Guildenstern* to Kenneth Tynan at the National after seeing it at Edinburgh in 1966. Stoppard, however, said he knew nothing of her intervention.[36] Others simply assumed that Ramsay represented Stoppard, since she represented so many of the new dramatists of the sixties. Jeremy Brooks, at the Royal Shakespeare Company, for example, wrote to her in 1964 to ask if he might look at '"The Tragedy of Rosencrantz and Guildenstern" by Tom Stoppard'. Stoppard, however, found a more sympathetic and encouraging agent in Ewing, who would represent him for the next thirty-nine years. John Tydeman, Stoppard's principal BBC radio producer (who had sent Joe Orton to Ramsay), summed up their relationship: 'Tom was lucky in having him [Ewing]. Both looked after each other.'[37]

Meanwhile, *The Gamblers* made the rounds at the BBC, Michael Bakewell conveying news to Ewing that the Home Programmes 'thought it too heavy for a Saturday night play'.[38] Within weeks, however, rumours started to fly about *A Walk on the Water*: would Alec Guinness do it? He was reading the script in Rome. Ralph Richardson expressed interest. Was Peter Brook free to direct? What would happen? In fact, nothing happened; the option expired, although Ewing did succeed in eventually getting the play performed: first on British Independent Television in November 1963 and then in Hamburg in 1964, while Stoppard was on a fellowship in Berlin. (In 1968, retitled *Enter a Free Man*, it would be produced by Doris Cole Abrahams in the West End, against Stoppard's wishes.)

Stoppard would later comically refer to the work as his 'Flowering Death of a Salesman', the result of the heavy influence of Arthur Miller's *Death of a Salesman* and Robert Bolt's *Flowering Cherry*. At the memorial service for Kenneth Tynan in 1980, Stoppard admitted that he wrote the play fired by Tynan's enthusiasm for *Look Back in Anger* and the idea of receiving similar praise from the critic: 'He was still on the *Observer* when I started writing and I can say almost without licence that I wrote my first play in order that he might review it: at least opening the *Observer* was an important part of the fantasy which fuelled the operation.'[39] More exactly, his first effort was to have been for the *Observer*'s competition of 1958, 'but that one petered out after a dozen pages that were not unlike *Look Back in Anger*'.[40]

According to Stoppard, *The Gamblers* is the first play that was entirely his own.[41] Written in 1960, it opens with a prisoner in his cell singing when his jailer arrives. A sample of the dialogue, balancing cliché with rapid cross-talk, occurs on pages 25–6 of an early manuscript version:

J. For the people
P. By the people
J. Only it's two different lots of people
P. A mere quibble.
J. An evasion
P. Revolutionary double-talk.
J. Political jargon
P. There's no quarrelling with system.
J. It has resisted every –
P. resistance
J. It has to be challenged.

P.   Tested.

J.   Examined.

P.   Analysed.

J.   Scrutinised.

It doesn't ring true, does it?[42]

The exchange of identities, similar ideas, parallel confusions and mixed ideas suggests the themes Stoppard would explore in his later work, demonstrating the adage he outlined in 1974: 'I don't write about heroes. I tend to write about oppositions and double acts.'[43]

In *The Gamblers*, the Prisoner, who has that day been sentenced to death as the leader of an unsuccessful revolution against the state, pits his intellectual and articulate character against the duller character of the Jailer. Yet it is the latter who is romantic about death, martyrdom, socialism and religion; and ironically, just the other day, the Prisoner had himself been the town jailer, before his decision to join the aborted revolution led to his downfall. The two soon reverse positions so thoroughly that they begin to speak each other's lines in different contexts and partly change clothes. Ultimately, the Prisoner hangs the willing Jailer, who remains obsessed with the glory of martyrdom, convinced that he is more suitable for death than the Prisoner.

Unsophisticated in many ways – the lack of dramatic development, the absence of scene changes – the play none the less contains the seeds of situation and language that *Rosencrantz and Guildenstern* will display, epitomized in this short exchange. Commenting on a song the Prisoner has written, the Jailer remarks, 'Ah, they don't write songs like they used to.'

P.   Yes, I expect it will improve with age.

J.   It's not very old then?

P.   Very modern. I should say, recent. It's a recent traditional animal song with religious abstractions, one of the hardest kinds to write.

J.   It would take an educated man.

P.   A Scholar.

J.   A teacher.

P.   A genius.

J.   A *foreigner*.

P.   With a lightning brain.

In their discussions of religion, death and logic, passages also suggest some of the exchanges in *Jumpers*, summarized by the Jailer's remark that:

J.   Logicians have never found God.

P.   It's time. And yet they do make the effort in their way. It's the people who don't bother to search who always profess to have found Him[44]

Despite moments of clarity, wit and tested logic, the play lacked originality of situation. Stoppard himself has referred to the work as 'Waiting for Godot in the Condemned Cell' and as a play which is all mouth, lacking comedy and dramatic structure.[45] However, embedded in the unpublished text are moments of Stoppardian exchange and themes that would reappear in his work, constantly addressing the question his many doubles, from Rosencrantz and Guildenstern to the older and younger Housman in *The Invention of Love*, would ask: 'Which of us is which?'[46]

A letter received by Stoppard at about this time from Harry Corbett, head of the Theatre Workshop in London, offered some useful advice on *The Gamblers*, as well as an assessment of Stoppard's yet-to-be established reputation and the commercial theatre. In explaining why he wouldn't put on Stoppard's one-acter (an early version of *The Gamblers*), he begs him not to allow it to be produced in the West End

> before your first 3 act play is done on the avenue . . . Remember, your first one to the commercial mind is the one that will establish your leit motif; it will be your statement of account of the world. This is so even critically for example . . . Viewed in this light, your one acter is frivolous and facetious. Viewed in the light of acceptance of a first play it will be brilliant and revealing.[47]

Corbett was prescient: the success of *Rosencrantz and Guildenstern* in 1967 (a work in three acts) resulted in a 1968 West End production of *Enter a Free Man*, the retitled *A Walk on the Water*, a production Stoppard disliked and would rather have prevented. Reviewers tried to like the play but found it unamusing, especially after the brilliance of *Rosencrantz and Guildenstern*.

A kind of false exit.
Stoppard, 1961

Success as a dramatist in 1961 was elusive and Ewing soon encouraged Stoppard to write for television and radio, which were both eager for material. *The Gamblers* was still doing the rounds at the BBC drama department; an internal report, written on 8 January 1962, harshly dismissing the work in two sentences: 'A duologue between a man about to be hanged and his hangman, who hasn't the courage of his convictions. A diffuse, wordy nonsense by a writer who doesn't know what he's trying to say, and can't say it instinctively. No.' However, word did not reach Stoppard; a January update from Ewing stated that 'the Gamblers is still going through the mill, as apparently it was first read by Home Programme readers who thought it too heavy for a Saturday night play', adding 'don't feel you must rush the re-write on *Walk on the Water*'. A final report didn't get back to Ewing, however, until 22 June 1962, with language more circumspect than the in-house comments: 'there is a great deal in this that is very good, but it is much too diffuse and rambling to work in terms of sound alone. I think Stoppard is a writer well worth encouraging, and I would be very interested to hear of any ideas he may have for original radio plays . . .'[48]

The Gamblers would remain unproduced until June 1965, when it became the first of Stoppard's plays to be staged in England as an extramural exercise by students of the Bristol Old Vic Theatre School, performed in a former squash court in the Bristol University tower used by the drama department as a theatre. It had also been the venue for Pinter's début several years earlier, in May 1957, with his play *The Room*.

While trying to establish his career as a playwright, Stoppard was also combating his habit of disorganization. At 2 a.m. one morning in 1961, he explained in a letter that he was to be in London later that day for lunch with Binkie Beaumont of Tennent's theatrical agency and then set off to Spain. But all was chaos since he had neither traveller's cheques, clothes nor himself together. So, he'd come back to Bristol and start the trip over – 'a kind of false exit. If life is a stage I'm the guy who goes off to loud applause after a cameo of sustained brilliance only to return immediately for his umbrella.' He then summarized his efforts with his new play, 'The Critics', which would become *The Real*

Inspector Hound, at one point working sixteen continuous hours in order to finish it. Yet it was a mess and when he returned from Spain he would have to start over. 'Perhaps I'm being unduly a pessimist,' he adds, 'but I'm the kind of writer who constantly needs reassuring. If people don't immediately throw their hands in the air and say this is brilliant, I feel depressed.' The result of his round-the-clock effort was 'that I went to bed one day at 2pm and got up at 9 pm, and I'm out of step with myself. Today, I woke up too late for the bank (this is mainly why I must return to Bristol before Spain).' In an earlier letter, in June 1961, he noted that what really prompted him to write was fright. Of 'The Critics', he says, I 'finally got frightened enough to discipline myself to the typewriter for successive bouts, relying on some mystical process to write the play for me and as always it did'.[49] Such an explanation, however, masks his hard work.

Other trips, notably his first to New York, went more smoothly. With Anthony Smith as his accomplice, Stoppard took advantage of a charter flight for architects direct from Bristol to New York in April 1962, with his paper paying most of the fare on the promise of various reports and features. Arriving in New York without a place to stay, Stoppard began to phone a few contacts he had gathered from a copy of the *Village Voice* sent to him by an American girl he had met in 1960 in Italy. He located a radio engineer who was a friend of someone Stoppard had once met. The fellow invited them to come right over, but when they got there, their host had left the key and a note that he had gone out. In the morning, he rang to say he was at his girlfriend's. Stoppard had assumed he was walking all night in Central Park, too polite to return. Oddly, but much in the manner of a Stoppard play, he saw his benefactor only once during their week's stay, when he came back one morning to shave – 'and I was vaguely irritated when he woke me up!'

Stoppard, however, soon felt guilty, especially when he started to eat the food in the apartment, 'so on the Thursday I bought a loaf of bread, which I finished on Friday'. Occasionally, Stoppard and Smith, who was also enjoying the accommodation, would find a note from their host saying they should use the towels put out on the bath but Stoppard's remorse drove him to masochism: 'I'd leave notes back like "More peanut butter, please" and tear them up in nervous hysteria.' Smith started to wear the man's ties and began to leave notes like 'the rest of the team says they don't mind sleeping on the floor if you can get them some blankets. Where do you keep the butter?' Stoppard, who never knew his host's name, was by this time having giggling fits, and added to his account published in the *Village Voice*, 'if you read this, I feel terrible. Also, I used your razor.'[50]

Stoppard contacted Jerry Tallmer, the drama critic of the *Voice* who would later write a flattering piece on Stoppard when he arrived in New York to oversee David Merrick's production of *Rosencrantz and Guildenstern* in October 1967, recalling with some hyperbole that during Stoppard's first visit, 'he spent his two weeks here sleeping on the floor of the *Village Voice*. "I didn't know anybody in New York" says Stoppard, "but I knew whoever I wanted to know would be at the *Voice*, so I headed there."'[51] Five years earlier, when he had called Tallmer's number, he was startled by the casual response: 'No, I'm sorry Jerry isn't here any more; we're separated.' This was a shocking introduction to sixties New York, where personal details were so informally revealed to strangers on the phone. 'At that time, the word "separated" still sounded thrillingly American,' Anthony Smith recalled.[52]

Stoppard and Smith began to explore the city with Michael Smith, an Englishman who wrote for the *Voice*, and John Wanlock, also a contributor, offering suggestions. Three events stood out: an aborted interview with Lenny Bruce at the Village Vanguard after seeing his show, a baseball game and a tour of the Off-Off-Broadway theatres, clubs and revues led by Mel Brooks. The Bruce show, with its esoteric references and quick delivery, left the two Bristolians in the dark, but not so their visit to the Polo Grounds for a baseball game played by the Mets.

An article by Stoppard for the *Village Voice* detailed his slightly jaded impressions of New York, which began with the anxiety that came from watching New York cops whose swing of a night stick 'is the pause between two questions'. The baseball game 'was slightly less interesting than cricket but better therapy'. The therapy came from the encouragement to shout abuse, something never permitted at cricket. The height of the skyscrapers was not as unimaginable as he thought, and the Empire State Building only moderately intimidating. Two comedians at the Phase 2 put on the funniest show they saw, but the actors could not even find an agent. Exceeding his praise for Walter

Winchell is Stoppard's chagrin at the unintended humour of American tabloid headlines. 'I once parodied them in a press rag – "DOPE MODEL NUDE SLAIN FIEND LOVES PROBE MYSTERY QUIZ" – so there was something felicitous about the fact that the very first headline I saw in New York was "SLAIN EXEC LOVES PROBE". I felt good all day.'[53]

The most important aspect of the trip for Stoppard was his introduction to the Off-Off-Broadway theatre scene, with its unconventional if not avant-garde and experimental drama. Their guide was, appropriately, the gag-writer and comic, Mel Brooks, whom they met by chance at the offices of the *Voice*. An article by Anthony Smith entitled 'They Queue, They're Here to be Abused' in Bristol's *Western Daily Press* narrates their journey. It began with a visit to a Village coffee-house where they saw the comedy team of Grecco and Willard present traditional satire, not the sick-joke variety which was getting much attention then.

More importantly, Smith notes that the most heavily booked show on Off-Off-Broadway was *Brecht on Brecht*, a spoken anthology. Three new plays by Thornton Wilder were also produced in this 'other' venue where the myriad of coffee-houses offered revue cabaret, jazz, folk-songs and beat poetry. Not all of it good, of course, but what excited him (and, by implication, Stoppard) was 'Improv': with Brooks, they went to see Elaine May and Mike Nichols' Second City and their production of *The Premise*. The idea of instant theatre, which breaks down the barrier between stage and audience as the audience spontaneously 'scripts' the programme, was original and new for the two writers. It was not baseball, nor the ethnic diversity, nor the non-stop nightlife of New York that left the most important impression on the Bristol visitors. Rather, it was the idea that theatre could flourish in out-of-the-way places and, through innovation, break down the so-called 'fourth wall'.

Two weeks after his return, Stoppard reviewed Lenny Bruce's performance at The Establishment, which he dutifully reported in the *Voice*. The Establishment was Peter Cook's trendy night-club on Greek Street in Soho, London, which he opened with Nick Luard in October 1961 with jazz in the basement (often led by Dudley Moore) and comic entertainment on the main floor. Noting the contrasting reactions to Bruce's show – the man was both funny and disgusting – Stoppard documents the heckling, Bruce's nervousness and the programme which included a skit about a Catholic priest, a Christ-killing confession and drum-solo orgasm. 'Much callous laughter,' Stoppard wrote. But what really appealed to Stoppard was Bruce's stage manner, his 'eager confiding and his likeable personality. His main vice was unintelligibility, partly labial, partly in vocabulary.'

Making no concession to his British audience, Bruce was nevertheless popular, as Stoppard confirmed by citing other critics, especially Ken Tynan. In the *Observer,* Tynan recorded that it was his twenty-fourth visit to see Bruce perform and called him 'the most original free-speaking wild-thinking gymnast of language this inhibited island has ever engaged to amuse itself'. Most of the national papers, however, failed to cover Bruce. Stoppard adds that he sent a piece on the comic to his Bristol paper which included the word 'crap'. The features editor offered the choice of cutting it or killing the article. Stoppard countered this by smuggling the essay over to the Arts Page 'where the intellectual atmosphere makes blasphemy look sophisticated'. It appeared 30 April 1962 and celebrated the way Bruce made 'the unspeakable . . . eminently, hilariously speakable', with a detailed summary of the show, which was fixated on religion and sex.[54]

For a while, Stoppard continued to publish in the *Voice:* in May 1962, his article on Hemingway appeared; occasional London theatre pieces followed, often commentary focusing on the off-beat, such as Charles Marowitz's In-Stage, which he called London's best experimental theatre company. That spring, Stoppard also travelled to Scotland for some trout fishing, writing to Anthony Smith that he had to beat a trout over the head to kill it after he caught it, but 'that's how it is. Life. Insects eat microbe, fish eat insects, I eat fish. Somebody, sooner or later, will bring the process to its logical conclusion by eating me.' Working events out to their logical conclusion would soon characterize his seemingly irrational plays. 'Didacticism is the most gratuitous form of immaturity as I once remarked to George Eliot,' he comically adds in the same letter.[55] And for an aspiring playwright, the next logical step up the theatrical food chain was London.

Stoppard knew that after the Village, Lenny Bruce, Mel Brooks and New York, he could no longer stay in Bristol. During the spring and summer of 1962, he made up his mind to head for London. He preferred Bristol, but the law of diminishing returns is beginning to operate now. I want to get out for many reasons: can't get enough London work without living there, HATE writing for the press, can't write my plays in Grosvenor Lodge because I'm restricted all the time by the feeling that Val is kind of expecting me to write.[56]

The climate for writing had changed; he needed the freedom, stimulation and venues that London offered.

In the same letter, he mentions London contacts such as Peter Maddocks and Michael Wale and his efforts to drum up work, adding that 'I heard about a new showbiz magazine called Scene starting up, so wrote to them setting forth my ludicrous credentials and requesting an interview and freelance work. This is vaguely promising because Roger Beardwood is wrapped up in it . . . and I subsequently discovered that I had contacts there without knowing it . . . I'll have to hitch to London in a few days to try to see as many people as possible.' He also refers to Faber and Faber's plans for a second volume of new writing with six contributors and says he will submit several stories: 'what with that and the play I've got to rewrite [*A Walk on the Water*], I really have enough to keep me occupied if only I cd get with it.' He then outlines an idea for a radio play, originally thought of as a short story, which 'kicks off from Marilyn Monroe's suicide'. This would become *M is for Moon Among Other Things*, aired on the BBC in April 1964.

But before he reached London, there was a Hemingwayesque adventure. For his twenty-fifth birthday, Stoppard took off across Europe to Spain. The plan was to arrive in Pamplona by 3 July, then go up into the hills for a few days to do some fishing and reading. But his plans went awry, money again interfering:

I nearly had to put the whole thing off. You wouldn't believe it but I bloody well overslept; the bank again today, Saturday, with me due at Victoria at the time it would re-open. Didn't panic, just froze and felt sick. However, I phoned up told some lies about being delayed in London and they opened the bank for me during the afternoon, so now I have £25 in travellers cheques and £5 in pesetas, and a French quid [for] four hours in Paris. All this week I have missed things, connections, banks, interviews, shops, library, everything. I had an interview yesterday, no Thursday, with a BBC man re me doing a sound play, and I arrived half an hour late after killing half an hour in a coffee shop because I'd got the time wrong . . . the BBC man . . . was very kind about The Gamblers but sd it was too diffuse to do on radio – I pointed out that I hadn't submitted it for radio but for telly.

. . . I go to Spain with about 14 books, a play to write, and I'll come back with 14 unread books and an unwritten play and a very splendid feeling of self-indulgence . . . well, I have a choice of five trains and a boat to miss, but all being well I shall be among the bullfights and full brights in a few short days.[57]

During his trip to the continent, lack of funds forced him to hitch-hike frequently. At one point, he walked through the tunnel connecting Switzerland to France. After hitching rides to Paris, he arrived at midnight to find that he was locked out of the Gare du Nord. He walked around for hours, visited some all-night cafés and

then found 113 rue de Notre Dame de champs where the Hemingways lived in 1924 and where he learned and taught himself to kick the shit out of his writing . . . then the train and Calais, Dover, queuing, swearing, bloody English, England and London, had tea with Kenneth [Ewing] borrowed a couple of quid and came home. And here I am after two weeks of not trying to work and then trying and not being able to and generally getting jittery and depressed about writing and all the time getting broke, until now this moment I have 12sd left . . . [but] 12s is over 50 fags, so the immediate future is secure.[58]

Caught between the need for money and the desire to write, Stoppard was at an impasse. There was no place for journalism: it distracted and deflated his imagination. He also returned to a complicated family situation, finding himself quite out-of-favour with his stepfather. His mother had feared something serious must have happened to him because he hadn't written from abroad, even to inform her of his spontaneous decision to travel on to Italy. But she forgave him when she saw the Italian handbag he brought back for her. His stepfather did not react well to his decision to become a full-time author: 'apparently my papa was being very rude about me behind my back, and scornful of my life as "a writer".'[59]

Stoppard's departure for London was typically comical, and he wrote his farewell 'Brennus' column on the spur of the moment: I 'didn't have anything else to write about, and didn't tell anyone I was doing it. It appeared on Monday, and at 11.30 I was woken up by *Scene* to say I was it.' Later that day, his editor Richard Hawkins called, asking to see him: 'it occurred to me then for the first time that there might be something odd about an editor finding that a column was stopping only when he read it in the paper'. Hawkins told Stoppard it would have been nice to know in advance. 'I said that I hadn't known in advance myself.'[60] But he knew he needed the larger arena of London, and Hawkins offered to let him continue contributing his column from London in case his move did not work out.

Looking back at his Bristol career, Stoppard embroidered his memories with an ironic sense of romance. Was it a disillusioning time? 'Not at all. It was every bit as glamorous and exciting to report petty sessions in Bristol as I had always imagined it must be. A reporters room is a terrific place to be part of [but] of course the work can be an awful drag as well. One is always working to a ludicrously disproportionate ratio between effort and output.'[61]

CHAPTER 5

SWINGING LONDON

*The new dramatists have not much to show as yet to
warrant the interest they have aroused.*
The British Imagination, 1961

Stoppard had been running up and down to London since he stopped
writing regularly for the *Bristol Evening Post*. He would go up for a day,
review a play, write a feature or do an interview and rush back on the
midnight train from Paddington. Occasionally, he stayed overnight if
a friend invited him. By August 1962, he decided that the opportunities
would be greater and the freedom to write vastly improved if he lived
in the city, though he arrived without money or a place to stay. London
was embarking on a decade as the international scene for Pop culture
in music and fashion.

Trendy Chelsea, fashionable Kensington and mod Carnaby Street
greeted Stoppard on his arrival. A month after Stoppard settled, the
Beatles were recording their first hit and 'Love me Do' soon made its
way up the charts to number 17. Earlier, in July, the Rolling Stones had
given their first performance at London's Marquee Club. In the
summer of 1962, Arnold Wesker's *Chips with Everything* was at
the Royal Court, Pinter's *The Collection*, directed by Peter Hall, at the
Aldwych. Peter O'Toole became an international star in David Lean's
epic *Lawrence of Arabia*, and the first James Bond film, *Dr No*, was
released. David Hockney received the Royal College of Art Gold
Medal, wearing a gold lamé jacket. Satire was the new mode: the first
issue of *Private Eye* appeared in February and by November, the BBC
broadcast the first edition of its weekly satire, *That Was the Week that
Was.*

The social changes in London were as galvanizing as they were cataclysmic and underground culture exploded. *Time* wouldn't feature 'Swinging London' until its April 1966 cover, but meanwhile boutiques sprang up on the King's Road, Chelsea, led by Mary Quant's Bazaar, followed by Biba, with its black-and-gold interior, in Kensington; Carnaby Street's glam look also became fashionable. 'Dolly birds' with long fringes and spiky eyes wore shifts made from upholstery fabrics – when they weren't wearing miniskirts with tights or patterned stockings under maxi coats with suede boots, or slithery gowns of satin with platform shoes. Tie-dyed T-shirts in psychedelic patterns became the rage, and drugs the route to excess, although Stoppard resisted, declaring that he never did 'that 60s drug thing – always too much of a coward – I still am'.[1]

The clothes, however, did affect him. Accused by some, and praised by others, as sartorially challenged, Stoppard paid attention to the changing fashions, and when he could afford it, he began to adopt the new look, with a loosely flowing scarf, patterned shirt, shapely cut jacket (velvet if possible) and boots. Sometimes a colourful sweater would offset his long jaw, full lips and unruly hair, prompting one journalist to describe him as 'a sort of Mod Pre-Raphaelite'. In preparation for his post at the magazine *Scene,* he secured a £30 loan from 'the bank to get some critical clothes' – either to look the part of a critic or to supplement his shop-worn Bristol wardrobe. He had also been writing that summer, telling Smith he had completed two short stories and was reading Henry Miller.[2]

His stylized, costumed look radiated theatrical presence. His green suit and black-and-white checked sweater caught the eye when he lunched in the 1970s. In the mid-eighties, he was outfitted in varieties of buff and dull green, climaxing in 'a complicated camel coat with myrtle green lapels which he earlier removed and placed across the back of a chair in a movement of fastidious nonchalance'.[3] A richly woven wool scarf dramatically draped around his neck defined his pose for a photo accompanying a 1990 article, when the casually elegant look dominated. Such an image underlined his rejection of sartorial order. A certain insouciant, louche manner defined his dress, as the peacock replaced the dandy in men's fashion and Stoppard's closet.

Culturally, the 1960s were a time of free expression, partly initiated by the 1960 victory for *Lady Chatterley's Lover* in the courts and the

West End hit of May 1961, *Beyond the Fringe*. The revue became an instant favourite with its series of hilarious set pieces: Jonathan Miller's Shakespearean parody, 'So That's the Way You Like It', Peter Cook and Miller's 'Man Bites God', attacking trendy vicars, and a hilarious account of the lost trouser room. Anticipating the new range of comedy and satire, Tynan praised *Beyond the Fringe* for signalling a moment when English comedy took its first 'decisive step into the second half of the twentieth century'.[4] The sensational audacity of the revue, its display of verbal wit and high level of intelligence outlined a new direction in British theatrical comedy. The papers soon referred to 'a satire boom' in which the anarchic, subversive and outspoken took on numerous forms, as in this excerpt from a satirical column in the *Observer* written by Peter Cook: two bowler-hatted, pinstriped men complain about the state of the theatre *c.* 1962, one explaining to the other in a deadpan manner, 'You know, I go to the theatre to be entertained. I don't want to see plays about rape, sodomy and drug addiction. I can get all that at home.'[5]

Repudiation of the old order, theatrical or otherwise, was endemic. John Osborne, in a March 1959 letter, set the tone, indicting the middle class and the London theatrical establishment for neglecting the innovations introduced by the English Stage Company at the Royal Court – or worse, patronizing them as 'fashionable'. Others argued that agencies like H. M. Tennent, under the control of Hugh 'Binkie' Beaumont, paralysed creativity through their control over theatres which mounted only mediocre, inoffensive plays with key parts for known stars. Challenging such stultifying drama was the work of Joan Littlewood and the Theatre Workshop in East End London, as well as that of George Devine and the English Stage Company. Inventiveness was catching on with the public. Playwrights like Shelagh Delaney and Brendan Behan, and Littlewood's 1963 staging of *Oh What A Lovely War* which presented the carnage of the First World War in terms of a *pierrot* show, garnered widespread interest. Devine's English Stage Company continued to startle, following its 1956 production of Osborne's *Look Back in Anger*, with work by N. F. Simpson, John Arden and Ann Jellicoe. These innovative plays and productions would soon be extended by Charles Marowitz's In-Stage experimental theatre (1962), Peter Brook's production of *Lear* (1962) and their radical Theatre of Cruelty workshop with the RSC (1963) and the revolutionary *Marat/Sade* (1964).[6] For Stoppard, the theatre was clearly the most thrilling arena for a writer.

The plot gets curiouser and curiouser, never more so or more
suddenly [than] in the nearly fatal second act . . .
Stoppard, 1962

The theatricality, dandyism, glamour and spectacle of sixties London found expression in the magazine *Scene*. Nick Luard and Colin Bell persuaded Peter Cook, one of the original cast of *Beyond the Fringe*, to develop a publication based on The Establishment's cinema club newsletter, a glossy weekly magazine with up-to-the minute reports on the arts. The project was announced in May and the first issue appeared in September 1962 with two official – and several unofficial – pieces by Tom Stoppard.

Stoppard had heard rumours of *Scene* while in Bristol and had applied for the job of theatre critic during one of his lightning visits to the city. The interview itself was more Stoppardian than professional, as he reported to Anthony Smith: 'I discovered SCENE at 69 Fleet Street to be a subterranean hive of inactivity. My arrival took everyone by surprise – my appt. was not in the appt. book.' The editor, exploring Stoppard's supposed theatre connections, asked him whether he knew if O'Toole was back in England yet. Stoppard immediately picked up a phone, called O'Toole's girlfriend, Sian Phillips, and located O'Toole in Hampstead: 'I did it all deadpan and barely refrained from adding "Oh, by the way, Albee sends his love" ' to the editor. (Edward Albee's *Who's Afraid of Virginia Woolf?* premièred that year.) Although he did have to write two sample pieces, Stoppard was almost hired on the spot. He closed his note to Smith by saying he was off to review Christopher Hampton's *The Pessimist*, actually 'my sly suggestion'.[7]

The editor, in fact, wanted a critic who could also write news features. Stoppard did a dummy review which was vetted in competition with another writer. Stoppard got the job when the adjudicator (who, it turned out, was a friend of O'Toole's) said his piece was brilliant. But Stoppard also had the back-up of Richard Hawkins' invitation to be the *Western Daily Press*'s theatre critic and features writer in London. Hawkins had told him that he 'would pay me more than *Scene* to write features part-time from London . . . so if *Scene* folds, I'll be okay'. His early optimism for the magazine would dissipate, however, when he discovered that *Scene* wasn't up to his standards: 'it is a bit pop, and I keep having to write down, which is a disappointment. Much lower standard than the arts page.'[8]

After kicking about London looking for accommodation, staying briefly with O'Toole and then some friends in Wimbledon, Stoppard settled in a dilapidated Notting Hill Gate basement bedsitter at 48 Blenheim Crescent that was also home to the writer Derek Marlowe. The four-storey terrace house, on a curving street in a modest residential area, was on the northern edge of Notting Hill, close to Ladbroke Grove and the North Kensington Library. Roger Jones, an actor at the Royal Shakespeare Company, actually rented the room, which Stoppard sublet. The space was dark, and sparely furnished. Each night, Stoppard smoked and wrote: reviews, features, short stories, radio plays, dramas and letters to his friends in Bristol. He would lay out a row of matches and say, 'Tonight I shall write twelve matches' – 'meaning as much as he could churn out on twelve cigarettes,' Marlowe recalled.[9] His letters to Isabel Dunjohn and Anthony Smith detailed his insecure life and constant financial disarray.

In London, Stoppard maintained his friendship with O'Toole and often went to visit him. O'Toole was delighted that Stoppard had found work and partly celebrated by taking him to The Establishment to see the comedian, Frankie Howerd. Sian Phillips, O'Toole's girlfriend and later his wife, joined them, although Stoppard felt she was somewhat cold towards him. On one occasion, O'Toole asked Stoppard to come back a few days later to help him with a film script of *Godot* which he was writing and planning to film in Ireland with Jack MacGowran and José Ferrer. Stoppard thought O'Toole had done a fabulous job with the script, 'not changing dialogue of course, but working out the shots. We're doing Lucky's speech tomorrow, big problem.'[10]

The pair were close friends, O'Toole confiding in Stoppard that he was unsure of what the success or failure of *Lawrence of Arabia* would do for him: 'It's worse than a first night, waiting for *Lawrence*. I mean, it's all out of my control – [I] just sit there and look at it.'

Paradoxically, the anxiety over *Lawrence* made O'Toole want to return to the stage and he chose Brecht's *Baal* as his vehicle, describing the extraordinary range of the play to Stoppard and telling him it was 'pre-Marxist Brecht so it has nothing to sell'. Furthermore, it was 'the only way I know to get back in touch with what I know I am about. That is, the theatre . . . it will also be a great skylark. With me, fun is a deep philosophical attitude.' O'Toole proudly remarked of the sleazy womanizer in the work: 'It makes Jimmy Porter [of *Look Back in Anger*] and *The Ginger Man* look like *Mrs Dale's Diary.*'[11]

It takes a trained mind to relish a non sequitur.
N. F. Simpson, *A Resounding Tinkle*

Stoppard's early enthusiasm for *Scene* and the extra effort he made regarding layout, writing and production impressed his editor. But it wasn't just wanting to impress his editor; Stoppard was genuinely excited to be doing such work: 'I do feel bound up with it and excited because it IS an exciting thing, being in at the beginning of a new publication. I'd hate to just drop my copy in and never be there.'[12] His later involvement with rehearsals for his plays duplicates his early desire to be part of the process of the publication or performance of his work, as witnessed by his labour on the Arts Page with Anthony Smith. For the first issue of *Scene,* he had 'one review, two fake reviews, one feature, two news stories, some gossip pars and a fake letter to the editor; not bad for a drama critic', he told Isabel. He was upset about the feature article, however, since it was ineptly cut. He feared that readers of the first issue, especially editors who could offer him future assignments, might find his work weak.[13]

Stoppard worked for *Scene* for seven months, until April 1963, when it folded; his pay was £20 a week. But he was often frustrated by the limitations of space and time allotted to complete the writing. Nevertheless, he persisted in his own perfectionism and conscientiousness. His first assignment was to do two short pieces:

I was up all night in agony . . . and by 10 o'clock the next morning I had succeeded in doing one of them badly. It was strangulated with tension. I bluffed about the second one and said I would do it by lunchtime and by then I'd begun to realise . . . It wasn't until I had been there and looked about that I realised that people weren't actually that good.[14]

The demands of journalism contrasted with his goal of writing well. He felt the magazine could make it if it allowed him more control and he soon came to write articles and features (including interviews with actors and playwrights) for the understaffed journal, reviewing 132 shows before the magazine closed. Stoppard also took a keen interest in layout and design and criticized those assigned that duty whom he found incompetent.

Stoppard's first piece for *Scene* was a review of *Brecht on Brecht* at the Royal Court, a production noted for its sparse but dramatic design and revolutionary, if spare, presentation. This, his first contribution – 14 September 1962 – makes the prescient point that Brecht used all kinds of tricks to alienate the play's doctrine from the audience's self-identification with the situation. Brecht had 'to remind the audience that they were watching actors, mere puppets to his argument', a point Stoppard would elaborate with *Rosencrantz and Guildenstern*. His second contribution to the first issue was a review of an all-black musical, subtitled 'The Black Alcestis', in which he wrote that 'this allusion to a rival version by Euripides should not deter the hoi polloi'.[15] One problem he faced, however, was that the printer's deadline meant an advanced copy-date: it was always a week before publication, so he either had to review shows a week late or a week before they opened.

In *Scene*, Stoppard's writing became increasingly confident, self-critical and unafraid to offer generalizations, as in his summary of American drama, much of which he says 'is a celebration of the failed tightrope-walker'. But he was also mimicking the popular self-conscious style of the time: 'having thus paragraphed the Contemporary American Drama scene into a triumph of the tidy mind and forbearing to trot out the dozen examples that have unaccountably failed to spring to it, I remain unembarrassed'. He then provides a judicious review of Hugh Wheeler's *Big Fish Little Fish* and admires the direction of Frith Banbury and the acting of Hume Cronyn. Perceptively, he notes that the ending is the ultimate 'compromise with the real thing – defeat put over as triumph'.[16]

From Ibsen to Muriel Spark, from Beckett to Shakespeare, Stoppard surveyed the theatre scene in London and elsewhere. His comments on Paul Scofield's *King Lear* at Stratford are revealing, noting that 'Peter Brook [is] the only director between Guthrie and nobody to have his own audience.' Aware of the structural imperfections of the play – Lear only cast as a shadow over the fourth and fifth acts – Stoppard none the less praises the production because Brook takes this problem and exploits it. However, he admires the performance and production more 'for their good sense and ideas than for their emotional effect. It is a text more brilliantly plumbed but not often moving.'[17] Soon, other actors received attention, with Peter O'Toole becoming the subject of an extended column in which Stoppard expatiated on the actor's generosity and driving ability, the latter well recognized throughout Bristol:

> As a driver O'Toole is better on a camel. He drives as if auditioning for *Ben Hur* . . . for the loser. Not counting minor incidents – and nobody has – he has written off two cars, a Riley on the M1 (he fell asleep, and never returned to claim the wreckage) and an M.G.

The point of Stoppard's column was that while filming *Lawrence*, O'Toole was frequently in greater danger.[18]

As a theatre critic, Stoppard was himself open to criticism, as a letter from one reader which appeared in *Scene* 15 (27 December 1962) made clear. It took him to task for not knowing that Paul Scofield was a CBE and that John Gielgud had appeared in contemporary dress on the stage more than three times in the last twenty years. It ends with this admonishment: 'if he [Stoppard] is to be the regular theatre reviewer (I cannot possibly refer to him as a drama critic), I suggest he takes a little more time and care over his writing.'

The first of two important columns by Stoppard on contemporary theatre is on James Saunders's *Next Time I'll Sing to You* which appeared on 9 February 1963. The second is an account of Stoppard's participation in a discussion with Michael Codron, William Gaskill and James Saunders, headlined 'Theatre Now' for *Scene,* 23 March 1963. The Saunders review is a laudatory account of the 1963 hit featuring four actors and a director who have assembled to do a play about a hermit in the theatre we are sitting in during the time we are present: ironically, 'the play never begins. It never begins every night,' writes Stoppard.[19] Stoppard's own aesthetic is expressed in his praise of elements that will later define his own work. Saunders, for example, is not concerned with reality: 'he is a man who leaves no stone unturned expecting to find the truth not beneath any one of them but in what the stones look like the wrong way up.' Of his language and style, Stoppard explains that Saunders 'enlists the cadences of Beckett in the service of the comic surrealism and maniacal logic of Ionesco and Simpson'. This tendency also brings criticism: 'some of his dialogue is so Beckettian as to be pastiche', a comment to be repeated in the 1970s of Stoppard's own plays. But Stoppard finds in Saunders a crucial feature which his own work will elaborate: 'Mr. Saunders has a way of investing significance on small verbal jokes, without either conveying their significance or admitting that he *is* merely having fun with words.'

The explorations of identity in the play anticipate many of the questions Rosencrantz and Guildenstern will ask, summarized by this query by the actor playing the hermit: 'I want to know the kind of person I'm supposed to be.' Guildenstern says, 'we don't know what's going on, or what to do with ourselves'.[20] Dust, a character in Saunders' play, has a response:

> You have a part to play and naturally you wish to know what is the part and what is the essential you which is to play the part. So do they [the other actors], of course. That's why they're sitting there so patiently.

In *Rosencrantz and Guildenstern*, when Guildenstern asks the Player who decides when and how events play themselves out to their logical conclusion, the Player sharply responds, '*Decides?* It is *written.*'[21] Lines in Saunders frequently anticipate Stoppard; at one point the Hermit says, 'After all, I'm only an actor, and it goes without saying that an actor's the last person to have any conception of what a play's about'.[22] Guildenstern declares, 'we don't know how to *act* . . . We only know what we're told, and that's little enough'.[23] And in a line that Stoppard almost borrows directly, Meff tells Dust that life boils down to only three things: 'making an entrance, making an exit, and filling in the time in-between. As for *what* you fill it *with*, that's the least of it.'[24] In *Rosencrantz and Guildenstern*, the Player says: 'Every exit . . . [is] an entrance somewhere else'.[25] Stoppard would not begin to draft his play for another year, when he attended a Ford Foundation seminar for five months in Berlin where his principal mentor was James Saunders.

The illogical sense of logic in *Next Time I'll Sing to You* would also distinguish such early Stoppard plays as *The Dissolution of Dominic Boot, The Real Inspector Hound* and *After Magritte*. In Saunders's play, Lizzie warns Meff that she is 'not dead certain about premarital intercourse . . .':

Meff   Who said anything about marriage?

Lizzie   It's the same thing.

Meff   How can it be the same thing? If we're not going to get married it can't be premarital, can it? Let's be logical.[26]

This exchange would appeal strongly to Stoppard's developing comic sense, as would Meff's lament at the opening of Act Two:

Any Venusians present? Any seducers? Cat thieves? Pathological liars? Kleptomaniacs? Are there *any* exceptional persons present at all? Anyone who feels he is absolutely *normal*?[27]

Stoppard would have also likely noticed an important principle about comedy expressed by Dust: why, he asks, is the audience made to laugh? He answers, 'To enable them to shift their bottoms on their seats without their knowing it . . . because if they *do* know it, if they do it on purpose, they realize what a fraud it all is.'[28] This, too, would become one of Stoppard's goals: to use comedy as a technique to create full belief in his work.

Stoppard sensed in Saunders the seriousness that gives comedy authenticity. The truth about the Hermit is not to be approached from the outside but the reverse: 'that is the point, and ultimately all the dazzling divisions, cross-indexed and self-cancelling are beside it'.[29] Stoppard's own sense of humour was suited to the times and very English: droll about serious matters, yet conscious, in its undercurrent, of the cynical and the sublime. He recalled that when he was fourteen, he heard a line from *The Goon Show*: 'And then the monsoons came, and they couldn't have come at a worse time, bang in the middle of the rainy season.'[30] Twenty-five years later, he still thought this funny, largely because of its tautology, a mixed-up trope which infiltrates much of his own work, as in the phrase used by Moon to codify the whodunnit he watches in *The Real Inspector Hound*: '*Je suis*, it seems to be saying, *ergo sum*.'[31]

Stoppard's article 'Theatre Now', a report on a theatre round-table, focuses on the uncommercial nature of certain West End productions, beginning with Saunders' work. Questioning the producer Michael Codron, who had had a hit with Pinter's *The Caretaker* and had transferred *Next Time I'll Sing to You* to the West End, Stoppard follows the many false steps preceding a play's arrival. He notes that *Next Time* failed when it moved from Ealing and the Questors Theatre to the New Arts Theatre until Harold Hobson's two notices saved it and Codron cast the actor Donald Albery for its run at the Criterion.[32] Further discussion pits the audiences of the Royal Court against those of the West End and the success of Pinter – 'something absolutely new and [his] success is completely inexplicable' – against Osborne and Wesker.[33]

William Gaskill, Peter O'Toole's director in Brecht's *Baal*, then explains that the combination of Brecht and O'Toole has pulled in reasonable audiences. Codron adds that the success of a play in the West End often has little to do with the quality of the work and a great deal to do with its publicity, star power and belief that it is something that must be seen. In a remark Stoppard must have taken to heart, Codron observed that when novelists write plays, or 'play around with' the theatre, they do so from their study and not the theatre directly: 'That is why those sort of plays don't make their mark.' Saunders offers a comment that will again resonate in the treatment of Stoppard's *Rosencrantz and Guildenstern*: 'I could write a one-act play for my own amusement. I don't think I could write a full-length play for my own amusement. It [*Next Time I'll Sing to You*] was in a sense a chapter of accidents.'[34] The evolution of *Rosencrantz and Guildenstern* from the one-act 1966 Edinburgh student production to the three-act play staged by the National Theatre in 1967 at the behest of Olivier and Tynan follows this pattern.

In his discussion for *Scene,* Stoppard reveals his own view of theatre management, the differences between those plays written for non-commercial and those for commercial venues and the compromises playwrights must make in order to have their works performed. A seminar for the aspiring dramatist with a popular playwright, distinguished director and successful producer, 'Theatre Now' is an important register of what Stoppard was learning.

One thing he found difficult to do as a critic, however, was to criticize the work of people he knew. 'I never had the moral character to pan a friend,' he said in 1972. 'I'll rephrase that. I had the moral character never to pan a friend.'[35]

> *What an Exchange had this been, without Boot?*
> *What a Boot is here, with this Exchange?*
> Shakespeare, *The Winter's Tale*

Stoppard became his own double in *Scene*, repeating his habit from the Arts Page of using a pseudonym and anticipating the numerous doubles or twins that populate his work:

> Being short of money, the magazine had this critic Tom Stoppard and a man named William Boot who wrote about the theatre. I was both of them, which embarrassed me because I had this feeling that critics shouldn't meet anybody in the theatre in case the pure platinum of the response would get corrupted. This is about as wrong an attitude as one could have.[36]

He later corrected his view that reviewing and interviewing should not be done by the same person, 'which I now no longer believe – I think it *ought* to be done by the same person'. Believing at the time that critics 'ought to come down on pulleys from the cumulus and review a play and go back', however, he decided that his dual role required a new sobriquet. Boot was his choice, derived from the character in Waugh's novel *Scoop*.[37] 'I've always been attracted to the incompetence of William Boot,' he wrote: 'he was a journalist who brought a kind of innocent incompetence and contempt to what he was doing'. As Stoppard later wrote in *The Real Inspector Hound*, 'I have been leading a double life – *at least!*'[38]

William Boot took in culture as well as the theatre, beginning with a seminar on the theatre sponsored by the *Sunday Times*, reported in a slightly satirical tone. For a later piece, he interviewed Vincent Tilsely, the BBC Television Script supervisor, who explained the extraordinary exposure of television material and the opportunities for original drama – significant information for Stoppard, who would soon be offering various scripts to television studios. He also reported on the role of script editors in occasionally doctoring a submission.

Another column, on the thriller boom, parodied an Agatha Christie play, distinctly anticipating the setting and style of *The Real Inspector Hound*, of which Stoppard had already written an ur-version. The protagonist in the column murders a producer (keen to stage more thrillers) with 'a blunt instrument, the quarto hide-bound edition of Agatha Christie's Works'. Slurp, our supposed hero, shouts 'You'll never get me alive', and promptly and literally eats his words – those of an essay he's been writing – and falls dead.[39] Further columns by Boot report on the newest, high-tech developments in theatre design aimed to provide a new versatility; the efforts of the designer Sean Kenny to plan a theatre for the Dunes Hotel in Las Vegas; an interview with John Antrobus, who co-authored his first play with Spike Milligan about a man who turns into a bedsitting-room; the increasing popularity of British cartoons; and the value-added element of theatre-going. In this last, Boot asks, 'how many minutes do you get for your money? Who's charging what for the programme? Is the convenience convenient?' This marvellous survey, complete with a comparison chart of lavatories, bars, programmes and cloakrooms, has one flaw in its effort to determine minutes-per-shilling value: 'Pedants will observe that this survey has taken no note of whatever play happens to be on at a theatre.'[40] The results? The Old Vic offers the best-value evening out, with nineteen minutes of theatre per shilling with reasonable facilities. The Palladium beats the Aldwych because of its exemplary toilets.

Scene provided Stoppard with a position from which to observe, criticize and learn about London theatre. From playwrights to producers, he was able to test his own notions about dramatic structure, production and acting, and express them through his columns. Concentrating increasingly on the theatre allowed him to develop his own ideas on the craft which he was beginning, with encouragement from his agent Kenneth Ewing, to develop. The end of his stint as a critic at *Scene* forced him to become more productive in his own work, overcoming a certain inertia, as he realized that he had little choice but to start earning money from his playwriting. A few years later, when his then wife, Jose, quit her job at the consumer magazine *Which?*, it would force him to get on with playwriting in order to support them both.

Scene folded in April 1963, partly because Cook & Luard Productions had purchased a majority interest in *Private Eye* in the summer of 1962 (the shares were actually all under Luard's name). *Scene* remained in its Fleet Street offices, while *Private Eye* moved into cramped quarters in The Establishment. But soon, Cook and company were more creatively involved with the successful *Private Eye*, while *Scene* lost its readership. The Establishment was losing money, and *Scene*, a financial liability, declared bankruptcy on 28 June 1963. But a biographical sketch Stoppard wrote of himself at this time, possibly in hope of finding new employment, reflects the confidence, panache and parodic style of the young writer:

> Tom Stoppard, who is 25, is of course the well-known playwright. ('Young British playwright' – Village Voice; 'up and coming young playwright' – Scene) and he hopes to finish his first play this year, though he has already, of course, been published by the Village Voice and Scene. Mr. Stoppard has travelled widely to New York (where he quickly established a reputation as a Hemingway parodist on the Village Voice) and is now a theatre critic for Scene while awaiting the completion of his first play. He is 25.[41]

After *Scene* closed, Stoppard entered 'panic straits' in search of work: 'I'm jobless and sinking,' he reported to Smith in the spring of 1963, explaining that he almost got on the *Daily Express*: the showbiz editor Peter Evans wanted an assistant; Stoppard fitted the bill, but the paper wouldn't let Evans hire a showbiz reporter. The shock of the rejection letter sent Stoppard to his bed, where he lay 'to save cigarettes till teatime in a slough of hopelessness, sorting out my despair like playing cards into suits: no money, debts. Stuck on play, listless, cigless, starving, rent overdue . . . and mainly the awful too-late feeling of having missed the bus somewhere, leaving me stranded in limbo with the ghosts of the unwritten books and plays to haunt me . . . very dramatic.'[42] A post at *TV Times* seemed the only recourse, while Ewing kept asking him about 'the play which (I lie) I am progressing with' and the BBC expected ideas from him for possible commissions. His determination shines through, however: 'I've decided I don't give a fuck about anything except to write a full length stage play and at least one TV this winter but find myself incapable of thought until my grotesque finances are bolstered into at least an illusion of security.'[43] Only the taping of *Walk on the Water* for television consoled him.

Despite his London activities, Stoppard increasingly missed Isabel Dunjohn. In many letters to her, he constantly thought up ways to get back to Bristol or for her to come and stay with him in London, while he reported on life in the city, from a new Beckett play (*Happy Days* at the Royal Court, which he disliked) to what he was reading: F. Scott Fitzgerald's *The Crack-up* and Cyril Connolly's *The Rock Pool*, a work stuck between 'being mandarin – Henry James – and tough cooky'.[44] He also sent her cartoons and even his own poems. And he revealed emotions that his public writing often hid. Citing what he believed to be a particularly strong image referring to the break-up of a minor relationship – 'thank god for an unmessy break which does not leave glass splinters lying around so that you cut your feet every time you approach the scene of the accident' – he adds with a tone of unusual self-congratulation,

> I'm good in letters, sometimes when I'm lucky or in desperation, because you're my only true and loved audience, the only one I can take risks with, write things closer to the emotion that dropped me into them, and know it doesn't matter too much if it reads sick or cynical . . . or simply bad English and bad thinking. I can come clean with you, don't have to pose and scrutinize and pass my thoughts before committing them and myself . . . There isn't much work waiting for me in the next fortnight. I must earn. I am in debt to my friends and my brother and my bank and my government and no one owes me a cent. I'm going to work all night; when the sun comes maybe there will be something good.[45]

His working method, however, remained the same: 'ineffectual inefficiency' as he explained in another note from his 'basement retreat' with its 'warped table and wonky anglepoise [desk lamp], more angles than poise, a fair imitation of an impoverished writer's workspace and a fair imitation of an impoverished writer, me, Tuesday'. Attempting to finish a piece on the little theatres in London, he predicts that on Thursday, he'll 'have one of my panic sessions to wrap it all up, using myself and two other writers'. But occasionally, things went well:

Tonight I feel cool and objective and no knot in me. . . as the sordid tale of Tom Stoppard unfolds on the screen. Bad script it is too. I think I'll walk out. Oh, what I mean to say about me writing was – probably there was a period when my letters were widely spaced and short and prosaic. They mean I think, that my work is going well. That fills a need and a vacuum, temporarily. Everything is temporary, but some of them last longer than others, like the world lasts longer than a snow-flake, both degrees of temporariness.[46]

His spirit, during this period between the end of his employment at *Scene* and taking off for a seminar in Berlin, remained generally buoyant and his writing comic, as in this pastiche from what he called his new play which anticipates later refinements in *Rosencrantz and Guildenstern* and his film script, *Shakespeare in Love*:

Scene is a coffee cellar in Montmartre. Enter Lord Byron reading Eliot.
Lord B.   Now is the winter of our discontent (poor booby has not realised that someone put the wrong dust jacket on his book.)
Dalmation: That's Shakespeare, you nit.
Lord B: Where?
As the light strengthens, we see that Shakespeare is, indeed, sitting in the corner.
Dalmation: There.[47]

In the early spring of 1963, Stoppard had joined his mother and stepfather in Scotland in a rented house near the Spey, borrowing money from friends to get there since *Scene*, now closed, had not yet paid its writers. This pattern of short-term borrowing but little restraint from taking holidays or taxis would persist for the next four years, a period he characterized as being 'mainly self-unemployed'. In Scotland, he fished and felt a little dislocated: 'Everyone dead by eleven, except me, and snoring by midnight, except me, and up at eight, except me.' An addendum comically reveals his journalist habits: 'as soon as I have to write in longhand – no typewriter – I seem to lose all sense of criticism and style. I *almost* hope the magazine [*Scene*] has failed before it appears.'[48]

During this period, Stoppard also wrote short stories, many of them based on his journalistic experiences in Bristol. Through Anthony

Smith, he soon learned of a young editor at Faber named Frank Pike, whom Smith had known at Cambridge. Pike was putting together a series on new writing called *Introduction* and in 1962 wrote to Smith in Bristol to ask if he knew of any promising young writers. Smith suggested two: Zulfikar Ghose, who was appearing in the Arts Page, and Stoppard. Smith urged Stoppard, whose writing agenda was fragmented into plays, short stories and thoughts about a novel, to contribute. He put together several pieces and sent them off to Pike, who accepted three of them in June 1963. They would appear in *Introduction 2* (1964) with work by Frances Hope, Sheila McLeod, Angus Stewart and Garth St Omer.

Not surprisingly, Stoppard drew on his journalistic experiences for his three contributions, 'Reunion', 'Life, Times: Fragments' and 'The Story'. They all share an ironic vision and reflect his attempt to test various genres and outline possible avenues for a longer work of fiction. Interestingly, the author's note, probably written by Stoppard, stresses his exotic background, the first sentence reading: 'Born in Czechoslovakia in 1937 and came to Britain in 1946 after six years in Singapore and India'. Stoppard's humour is evident in his summary of his journalistic career, noting that for eight years he was a 'news reporter, feature writer, theatre critic, film critic, gossip columnist and, for six weeks, the only motoring correspondent in the country who couldn't drive'. 'During the last two of those years', he was a 'desultory free-lance'. Statistics play a key role: 'within seven months he had seen 132 plays and completed these three short stories'.[49]

The stories' various themes would unite Stoppard's later work. 'Reunion' is a carefully constructed meeting between two old lovers, gingerly exploring their past feelings in sensitive language, one passage prefiguring the speech on language using the metaphor of the cricket bat in *The Real Thing* (1982). The protagonist in 'Reunion' says:

> There is a certain word which if shouted at the right pitch and in a silence worthy of it, would nudge the universe into gear. You under-stand me, it would have to be shouted in some public place dedicated to silence, like the reading room at the British Museum . . . He [the speaker] will have shuddered into a great and marvellous calm in which books will be written and flowers picked and loves comple-mented. No one knows what the word is.[50]

Anticipating the word games of *Dogg's Our Pet*, Stoppard suggests that the word might be a marvellous mixture of phonetics and chance, like 'Pafflid' or 'culp, matrap, drinnop, quelp'.[51] A realistic story about separation and loss, it nevertheless shows an absorption with words and the way they unite us.

'Life, Times: Fragments' deals with life as a reporter and the cavalier treatment of lives, which sometimes has severe consequences. Stoppard fictionalizes the *Evening Standard* interview in London at which he could not remember the name of the then Home Secretary (for the purposes of the story, he switches it to the Foreign Secretary): 'he had only admitted an interest in politics, he had not said he was obsessed with the subject. I'll have a shot at a novel, he thought. Then I can make the Foreign Secretary anybody I bloody well like'.[52] Other incidents from Stoppard's life add to the fragments of his story: a vacation in Spain, and his realization that, at twenty-seven, he was not much of a writer yet. Outwardly imitating T. S. Eliot, 'I read, much of the night, and if I don't complain about the others she'll take me south in the winter',[53] the story exhibits his reading while listing his literary heroes: Wilde, Flaubert, James, Thackeray, Proust, Turgenev, Joyce, Lawrence, Edmund Wilson, H. L. Mencken and Hemingway, all parodied in the narrator's comic cry to his lover, '*I am – I feel – seminal!*'[54] The narrator here is aged thirty-four. The next section has him at fifty, a sub-reporter in London, slightly embarrassed at his constant intrusion into people's lives. The story ends allegorically, with the writer confessing he'd rather be accepted by a publisher than God: 'he was not sure whether he believed in God, and for a long time he compromised by praying at his typewriter'.[55] Following his suicide, a critic discovers the body of his work, finally affording the writer fame.

'The Story' is the most affecting of these works and the most emotional. An account of how a young reporter accidentally reveals the name of a possible child molester, a master at a top school who pleads guilty to the charge and pays his fine, it documents the devastating consequences of such public knowledge through the suicide of the schoolmaster, who jumps in front of an underground train. In the story, Stoppard displays his journalistic virtuosity by writing three versions of the incident, each with a different slant. It concludes with an ironic tally of the money the story earned for the reporter and an awareness that, while a man has been killed, the money is squandered. This critique of journalism is Stoppard's cynical look at what can, and sometimes did, happen with stories that were distorted in the press. It also suggests something of his leery attitude towards interviews and later examination of the press in *Night and Day* (1978). Stoppard earned £20 for the three stories in *Introduction 2* but, more importantly, gained the support of Frank Pike at Faber, who would remain his editor until he retired, thirty-seven years later.

While he missed Isabel Dunjohn during this period, another woman began to capture his interest, although as he admitted, at first it was platonic. Throughout 1963, Stoppard continued to see Isabel Dunjohn and, for a time, the daughter of the ex-President of Guatemala. But late in the year, he began to pay increasing attention to Jose Ingle, a short, 'svelte and sun-tanned' young woman three years younger than himself who also had a room at Blenheim Crescent. With her boyish figure and dark hair cut in a straight bob, she was fashionable and attractive. For the first six months, Stoppard and Jose ignored each other, as merely co-tenants in the same building: 'Good friends for a long time before anything else, which in retrospect is a rather good arrangement.'[56] But gradually, things changed.

Jose was from Rubery, a suburb of Birmingham, an area Stoppard vaguely knew from having lived briefly in Ockbrook, just south of Nottingham. Like his mother, she had a background in nursing, although at the time they met, Jose was working as a researcher for the consumer magazine *Which?*, where she did product assessment. Stylish in her miniskirts and maxi coats, she was friendly with two of Carnaby Street's best designers, Marion Foale and Sally Tuffin, but felt comfortable as a 'Biba bird', from which store Stoppard bought her two silk scarves. She became quite serious about Stoppard who helped her find a new flat in the spring of 1964, before he travelled to Germany for five months on a Ford Fellowship. Jose objected to his departure, although their courtship would continue during his absence in Berlin from 2 May to the beginning of October, and intensify when he returned.

I'm not plot-headed about things as you know.

Stoppard to Anthony Smith, 1963

In November 1963, Anthony Smith married Alison Kennedy, a drama student, with Stoppard as the best man. The preceding September, Stoppard had accompanied Smith, his fiancée and a student drama group headed by George Brandt from Bristol University to an international student drama festival in Zagreb where nine European and various Eastern Bloc countries competed. The contribution of the Bristolians was Alfred Jarry's *Ubu Roi*, an adventurous choice for a festival in a Communist country. The play had, in fact, never been produced in England because the Lord Chamberlain objected to the language; the text had to be modified for the university's production. Daily criticism of productions took place and it was often necessary to wear headphones in order to hear simultaneous translations in four languages. The Russian and Czech students were apparently the most accomplished technically but the least successful emotionally. A report dated 24 September 1963 in the *Bristol Evening Post* detailed the success of the Bristol University production. For Stoppard, attending the conference meant exposure to European theatre at the same time as a reconnection with central European culture.

The adventure in Zagreb included an unexpected encounter with Montgomery Clift shooting a Nazi war film and practising his 'Heil Hitler', which Stoppard 'found hilarious'.[57] At this time, Stoppard gave some comic thought to his first book, described in a letter to Isabel:

> I've just thought of a title for my first book, having rejected The Complete Tom Stoppard; Tom Stoppard – Works; The Pocket Tom Stoppard; The Essential Tom Stoppard; and The Tom Stoppard Yearbook – I've decided on The Bedside Tom Stoppard. Smith says I can't lose.

In a summary of the trip, he adapted Verdi's remark on Wagner: 'we had some bad moments but some good quarters of an hour'.[58] Following the conference, Stoppard travelled to Athens, Gibraltar and Malta. Peter Stoppard became agitated, believing his brother had gone missing, and thought the KGB might have grabbed him. While he conveyed this worry to Smith, now back in Bristol, Smith nonchalantly practised his bowling.

Funny Man, a sixty-minute television play about a professional gag-writer going through a comedic crisis, 'a joke factory drowning in tears', was one of Stoppard's efforts from this period. The plot involves the personal and professional dilemmas of Martin Bush, a gag-writer for the 'Diamond is Trumps' show, who is called in to revise new scripts for additional humour. The star, Danny Diamond, has Bush 'put stuff in, take stuff out and fill in the gaps' so that he can appear to be even funnier. He calls it 'watching his style'.[59] Longing to be a novelist, Bush is unhappy as a gag-writer; his wife, an actress, is a would-be poet who is having an affair with her agent. If life is always a joke, then 'plain ordinary dull jokeless living begins to look like a holiday', the wife laments to her husband. He doesn't get it. Interestingly, the wife, Angie, is the most fully developed female Stoppard created until *Night and Day* in 1978. Stoppard wrote *Funny Man* in a week, working from 6 p.m. to 7 a.m., using himself and Smith as models. But despite his enthusiasm for the work, Arthur Rank and the BBC both rejected it. A second draft dated 1964 was similarly turned down by Rank and Associated Television.

John F. Kennedy was assassinated on 22 November 1963. The national and international reaction entailed a scheduling shift at ITV in London, which quickly rejigged its programming to postpone the planned broadcast on 25 November of John Whiting's *Marching Song* with Derek Godfrey and Judi Dench. (Whiting's *The Devils* was a controversial if somewhat brutal success at the RSC in 1961, in a production noted for its rituals and tortures.) *Marching Song* dealt with the dilemma of a defeated general who must kill himself for the good of the country. The topic was considered inappropriate so soon after Kennedy's death and the network replaced it with something less sensational, *A Walk on the Water,* Stoppard's 1960 play, rewritten for television, which had been sold to ITV in the summer of 1963. Ralph Richardson had considered the work seriously during the year Tennent's held an option on it, and had sent it on to Peter Brook, but little came of it, other than Richardson suggesting to Stoppard that it wasn't long enough. Stoppard had worked frantically to extend the work during August 1962, resulting in an hour-and-a-half-long play, which then had forty-two minutes cut when it was filmed for television: 'I'm thinking of calling it "Walk on the" or "Walk on the Wa",' Stoppard joked in a letter to Smith, adding that the only saving grace was that the cast loved the play; he was pleased with the sale in the summer of 1963, although he made it clear some years later that he preferred to write for the stage and that his television work was to be thought of as 'stepping stones towards getting a play on the boards'.[60]

Filming was to begin that summer, in the hope that Richardson would play the lead; production was delayed until autumn, but Richardson was still unavailable. The first rehearsal was difficult and further cuts had to be made. Filming actually began in November, for a scheduled March broadcast. However, one morning in November, the producers suddenly told Stoppard that the play would be aired that night, because of the rescheduling following the Kennedy assassination. He just had time to call a few close friends, beginning with Val Lorraine who was in turn to call Anthony Smith. There could be no advance notice for either critics or the public and there was no time for *TV Times* to run a notice in its 'Playbill' section, as it had done for Whiting's work, pulled at the last minute. Stoppard had mixed emotions about the broadcast: on the one hand, it meant that there would be no publicity for the show; on the other, the 'fewer people who connect me with it, the better'. The production, made for Rediffusion, depressed him. None the less, the airing had two benefits: praise from Charles Marowitz, the critic and theatre personality who would shortly recommend Stoppard for a Ford Foundation fellowship in Berlin, and the sale of the work in its stage form to Doris Cole Abrahams, who bought a financially welcome two-year option on the play.[61]

Stoppard survived on his freelance work, while earning only a minimal living from his television and radio writing. A series of unproduced scripts soon emerged, underlining his ambition. Scriptwriting for radio and television had become his new trade, while he began to rewrite *The Gamblers* and had plans to finish revising 'The Critics'. Working mostly at night, and smoking excessively, he persisted, although he had no guarantee of publication or performance.

Bristol's cultural effervescence was, in part, owing to the BBC's new television facility there. Patrick Dromgoole was radio drama producer and television producers Michael Croucher and John Boorman, later a film director, had the funds to make documentary films. In 1963, Boorman had contacted Smith regarding Arnold Wesker's Centre 42, a crusade to disseminate the arts through the trade unions. Boorman had read some of Smith's material on the project in the Arts Pages. When Smith went to see him, Boorman asked him to be the on-air presenter. He nervously agreed and, despite one on-air gaffe, their friendship flourished.

At about this time (June 1963), through Smith, Boorman commissioned a script from Stoppard and Smith for a documentary series. Stoppard's topic was surrealism. Boorman thought the two young writers talented and encouraged them to produce television scripts and ideas for films. At lunch one day, Boorman introduced the idea of adding visual surrealism to the television scripts Stoppard was writing. Boorman liked the dialogue, mood and cutting, 'but it was all embedded in a traditional *form* of documentary and his interest is in a new *form*,' Stoppard complained to Anthony Smith. 'I got it,' he then exclaimed, and gave as an example a man looking at a watch-face showing three-fifteen while a voice-over said: 'It's two o'clock, I'm late', at which the watch-face is seen to be a church clock in close-up.[62] The cut-away is to his late arrival for his wedding, standing at the church door when his bride comes out with another bridegroom.

These experiments and further attempts to write for Boorman soon influenced how Stoppard conceived his own early drama, especially the radio plays, which reflect a good deal of surrealistic action and quick cuts from scene to scene. Indeed, his work for Boorman spurred on his own efforts, which included a new piece on O'Toole which he sold to the *New York Post*. Alternating bouts of intense work and prolonged exhaustion, which encouraged a certain lackadaisical attitude towards his work, soon became his pattern. Stoppard was in reasonable financial shape by the end of the summer of 1963: he had earned £350 for the television rights to *Walk on the Water* and $50 for the *New York Post* article. He promptly spent most of it, however, on a ten-week holiday in the Mediterranean with Isabel and again faced penury when he returned to London that autumn.

In order to launch BBC2 in 1964, Boorman proposed a six-part quasi-documentary series which Smith would write. It would be the story of a young couple expecting their first child and seeing Bristol through their eyes. Smith and his new wife were suddenly in the centre of the series which would also record the social and cultural life of the young and restless of Bristol and how they saw the new era of government. Stoppard would also have a small role. Originally titled 'The Smiths', it was retitled 'The Newcomers'. Filming took place in January and February 1964 and Stoppard made various trips to Bristol for the shooting, receiving six guineas for each day's attendance.

Episode one has a wonderful scene of Stoppard and friends, including Smith, at dinner in Marco's restaurant, Stoppard telling a comic story about a man visiting a shop for a pair of blue trousers. A cut-away then shows Stoppard with Smith and Derek Balmer planning a new photo magazine. A brief shot shows Stoppard playing the cords from which a bookcase is suspended with a violin bow. Next is a scene at a night-club, where Stoppard chats up a young woman and then dances with her. Thin but attractive, Stoppard seems quite at home in front of the camera.

The episodes were unscripted, although Boorman worked hard to set up the scenes; for a final party to celebrate the free spirit of Bristol youth, Boorman provided unlimited wine and beer; the waiters were actually members of his BBC crew. The pregnancy of Alison, Smith's wife, was one of the continuing stories in the film. Contrasted with the documentary element of the film was an attempt to be 'arty' or at least cinematically sophisticated. The broadcast, in April and May 1964, gained notoriety for the Smiths and attention for Boorman. It was common for Bristolians to approach Smith and his wife in the street to comment on the series.

Versatile, that's me.

Stoppard, 1963

In 1961, Stoppard outlined how he would earn nearly £40 one week by covering a West Country tennis match for the *Western Daily Press* while simultaneously writing and editing for the Arts Page, completing two 'Brennus' columns and another regular column. Two years later in London, nothing had very much changed, his habit of procrastination not much help. Typically writing late into the night, he described his efforts to write a play in June 1963. Two weeks before he went off to Spain, he reports that he had begun serious work on the play only a week previously: 'worked all night for five nights, and discovered to my surprise and suspicion that I had reached the end, at

6 a.m. yesterday morning. Now I am more or less re-writing from the beginning to put some guts in and kick the shit out, make it conform to my post-rationalisation and generally turn the discursive aphoristic ramble into something tighter, deep and theatrical.' His working habits remained unconventional, however:

> the sun shines, enthusiastically every day, and most of it I miss because it is just showing when I go to bed, and well past the top when I unglue my eyes and my body and my tongue and knock the 16mm surrealistic home movies out of my head – I dream, every night, six dreams a night and all of them the weirdies.[63]

In these and earlier letters, Stoppard revealed a strong sense of himself, alongside a need for public approval. Such a requirement would soon be parlayed into his determination to include a joke in the first thirty seconds of every work in order to keep the audience attentive and sympathetic, on account of what he believed to be an original weakness in the opening lines of his first hit, *Rosencrantz and Guildenstern*. In a letter, he gives a few samples of his comic dialogue: 'How long have you been a pedestrian? Ever since I could walk' or 'critic: With an uncanny ear that might have belonged to Van Gogh'. 'Well, you can see it has a certain madness, but I haven't convinced myself that it is a *play*,' he concludes.[64]

> *The first duty of the artist is to capture the radio station.*
> Stoppard, *Artist Descending a Staircase*

Radio plays soon became a more effective creative and commercial outlet for the young writer repeatedly short of funds. What little money he had, he spent; Kenneth Ewing recalled that Stoppard would often take a taxi to his office rather than the tube to receive any of his advances. 'When I first met Tom he had just given up his regular work as a journalist in Bristol and he was broke. But I noticed that even then he always travelled by taxi, never by bus. It was as if he knew that his time would come.'[65] In late 1965, when Ewing arranged for Stoppard to write a BBC radio series about an Arab student in England, Stoppard, broke and wanting to go home, borrowed £40 from Ewing: 'Well, he turned right around and hailed a taxi. I went home on a bus.'[66] On one earlier occasion, Stoppard donned a disguise in order to gain some cash. In autumn 1963, he reported to Smith that he entered his bank wearing a false beard, 'rushed up . . . to the newest young clerk, whipped out self-cash cheque for ten quid. He caught it second bounce and I dashed out with the tenner, so am back in fags [cigarettes] again.'[67]

His first success led to a second attempt that went awry when he overslept, but the misadventure became the foundation of *Dominic Boot*.

> I formulated a plan to make another incognito raid on my bank. Unfortunately I slept through alarm and woke up at 2.30 (from 8 a.m.); sailed out, waited for bus, in desperation hailed a taxi which arrived at the bank at 3.1[0] p.m., leaving me with a taxi and the aforementioned 1.s 7d, with 2s 3d on the clock. There was a slight altercation, which ended with me giving him aforesaid 1s 7d and a promissory note. Walked back home reflecting on my ruined day, which was to have been pleasant: look in on rehearsal of Walk, wander over to Old Vickers [the Old Vic] and see O'T and perhaps even get into Hamlet. Got home . . . and happily remembered 2s in the gas meter which was swiftly converted into Woodbines. And here I am. Tomorrow I shall attempt the bank once more.

In the same letter as he narrates this adventure to Smith, he hastily writes in longhand that he is 'now writing a 15 minute play about a man who takes a taxi, broke to the Bank . . . and keeps on the taxi, going from place to place trying to borrow the money to pay . . . and never *quite* catching up the clock'. Stoppard quickly seized on his own adventure as a source for his art, another mark of the double life. And all was not lost. With some rescued cash, Stoppard set off to the Dorchester in a cab 'to renew acquaintance with the blonde daughter of the ex-President of Guatemala'. He also reports that O'Toole, discovering that he was broke, immediately gave him £10 of the £100 'I had just seen him win at chemin, and wrote out a check for £100 . . . Taking O'Toole and my presidential lady to see my Walk recording,' he triumphantly concludes.[68]

With its revamped programming, the BBC sought new dramatic works. Ewing took advantage of the situation and offered two plays for *Just before Midnight*, a fifteen-minute drama spot at 11.45 p.m. *The Dissolution of Dominic Boot*, broadcast on 20 February 1964, 'was the first and last self-propelled idea I ever had, and I think I wrote the play in a day'.[69] It was an embroidered account of his failed attempt to get to his bank before it closed.

With its comic turns and increasing anxiety, not to mention the frantic state of the hero, the play was a comic hit, becoming the basis of a 1970 television play of Stoppard's, *The Engagement*. And in response to early criticism that his characters didn't behave coherently, he replied 'neither do people'.[70] This was the beginning of Stoppard treating reality as a premise, not a thesis, and recognition that order may lack meaning.

The success of *Dominic Boot* led to work on another script based on a rejected story for the Faber collection. This became *M is for Moon among Other Things*, produced by the BBC on 6 April 1964. Situation rather than plot defines the work as dialogue competes with the interior monologues of two characters, the male fantasizing about the death of Marilyn Monroe and how he might have comforted the misunderstood star. The tightly constructed work suited the radio format, as did *Dominic Boot*. Or, to be more accurate, the format forced Stoppard to tighten his structure and focus his characters.

Stoppard also worked on a longer script during this time, a sixty-minute television play finished in late 1963 entitled *I Can't Give You Anything But Love, Baby*. The unproduced and unpublished play deals with two brothers, the younger mentally deficient and sheltered from society by the older. The younger compulsively buys items on instalment plans from door-to-door salesmen; his older brother berates him but the younger poignantly explains that the older doesn't need things, he's got people. The fiancée of Arthur, the older brother, complicates the plot. While sibling bonds and the presence of an 'idiot' character are new for Stoppard, the theme of mistaken identity and surrealistic images are not. The play was never produced but it was on the ride back from a meeting at a television studio where the script was rejected that Kenneth Ewing first suggested that Stoppard might write a play about the two supernumeraries in *Hamlet*, Rosencrantz and Guildenstern. Stoppard had never considered the subject before and had only a partial grasp of Shakespeare's drama, yet the suggestion would prove to be monumental in defining his career some three years – and many drafts – later.

Portland Place, home of the BBC, became a welcoming source of both exposure and income for Stoppard. One of the key figures there was Richard Imison, Script Editor. Imison nurtured writers for the BBC drama department, a unique figure who encouraged new talent and programming innovation. As editor of Radio Drama from 1963–91, he understood the important role of the BBC as a patron of original, dramatic writing in Britain and he fulfilled that mandate by commissioning works from known and unknown writers. Among his contributors were John Arden, Harold Pinter and Stoppard. *Lord of the Rings* and *War and Peace* were among his most important series. Along with John Tydeman (originally a radio producer trainee when Stoppard first met him and later Head of Radio Drama), Imison was instrumental in supporting and extending Stoppard's radio career which at this stage was crucial for his continued stay in London and commitment to stage writing.

In February 1966, *If You're Glad I'll be Frank* was broadcast, the result of Imison pouncing on Stoppard, 'Tigger-like with news of a series of short plays about people in imaginary jobs. There and then I proposed the Speaking Clock', formerly a fixture in British life.[71] Exposure on the BBC assisted in establishing Stoppard's name, Michael Billington of the *Guardian* noting that he first heard of Stoppard's work when he reviewed two of his early radio plays for a Radio 3 arts magazine. However, only persistent cajoling of Stoppard by Imison and Tydeman – by letter, phone and postcard – to complete commissioned work saw his various radio plays finished and broadcast. But not everyone appreciated this new voice, nor thought of Stoppard as a coming man in the theatre: mentioning Stoppard's work at the time to a now distinguished opera producer brought an immediate and disdainful reaction: 'I know Tom Stoppard – he's a punk journalist from Bristol.'[72]

CHAPTER 6

BERLIN COWBOY

You might as well know that I, wearing black trousers,
pink shirt, black cowboy hat, gunbelt, sixguns and spurs,
did a high noon walk . . . to the Brandenburg gate,
for the cameras.
Stoppard, June 1964

Stoppard was ambivalent about visiting Berlin in May 1964 when he won a Ford Foundation fellowship. On the one hand, it would distract him from his financial difficulties, eliminate the pressure to write more television or radio scripts and allow him to concentrate on playwriting. But time in Berlin would also remove him from the literary scene in London and his new relationship with Jose Ingle. She opposed his departure, but to pacify her objections, he agreed to visit her in the middle of his stay: 'I left Jose wet-eyed but brave, and Blen Cres without regret,' he admitted to Smith – yet he also knew that once the seminar was over, he'd have to face some important decisions.[1]

Stoppard understood that Berlin might refine his talent as a playwright, especially because Saunders, a dramatist he much admired, would be the senior consultant for the youthful playwrights invited to the Literarisches Colloquium. But it would also mean a five-month absence from London just as he was making a name for himself. His radio dramas were being broadcast steadily on the BBC; his career as a television dramatist was slowly taking shape; three of his short stories had recently been accepted for the Faber collection. He set off with a mingled sense of escape and excitement, a passage from his short story 'Life, Times: Fragments' self-consciously suggesting what he left behind: 'You should see me. I am drowning with the panache of someone walking on the water. That's not bad. I could slip it in somewhere. When people ask me what I do, I say I'm a writer.'[2]

In an effort to renew the culture of post-war Germany, the Ford Foundation had organized a seminar for young and talented artists: half would be from Germany and half from the west. The critic, director and playwright Charles Marowitz was asked to suggest one or two candidates who might benefit from the cultural exchange and, on the strength of the televised *A Walk on the Water* plus a favourable impression of Stoppard's writing in *Scene,* he nominated Stoppard, who agreed to attend not only because of the experience and chance to write unencumbered but also because of the money. Marowitz had actually known Stoppard since 1962, when Stoppard wrote a praiseworthy account of alternative theatre in London, emphasizing the originality of 'London's only truly professional (unpaid) and truly experimental theatre' founded by Marowitz, the In-Stage.[3]

Until this point, Stoppard had been exploring numerous genres in addition to journalism: television plays, radio scripts, the short story, experimental documentaries and plays. Berlin would be a chance to concentrate on one genre in sumptuous, almost unreal, surroundings. Indeed, with all expenses paid, plus a small stipend and the chance to write, Stoppard could hardly turn down the opportunity, although he hesitated. He went, discovering that the two other English participants were Derek Marlowe and Piers Paul Read. Two Americans also joined their group: Peter Bergman and Tom Cullinan.

A Converter of Manuscripts.
Stoppard, 1964

Introduction 2, the short-story collection, appeared just before his departure for Berlin and encouraged two publishers, Collins and Anthony Blond, to approach Stoppard to write a novel. Blond felt more confident and commissioned a work in 1964. During his Bristol days, Stoppard, like Smith, thought he would first succeed in the literary world as a novelist, despite the attention paid to dramatists; as late as August 1966, Stoppard expected to make his name not with *Rosencrantz and Guildenstern,* which had premièred that month at the Edinburgh Fringe, but with his novel which appeared the same week. Although he was writing television and radio drama, Stoppard kept the map to literary fame unfolded. Smith also alternated between drama and fiction, publishing his first novel, *The Crowd*, in 1965 and his latest, *The Dangerous Memoir of Citizen Sade*, in 2000. Smith has since written more than twenty plays for the stage and screen, his most recent an adaptation of Stoppard's radio play *Albert's Bridge* as an operetta.

When Stoppard signed the contract for his novel in Ewing's office, he had to fill in a blank for the title: 'Provisionally and sentimentally, and thoughtlessly,' he told Smith, 'I wrote down "Jose". Now I'm told that Blond has issued his list of forthcoming novels, including "Jose" by Tom Stoppard. Ewing is busy trying to flog the film rights while I'm busy trying to think of a subject. I suppose some daemonic force will take over and the damn thing will be about Jose . . .' Stoppard refers to the woman he would marry a year later.[4]

Stoppard took a liking to Blond, despite needing to revise his image of a publisher:

> that is to say that I had to ditch my fond hopes of ever having a patrician publisher who took me to dinner with the remaining Sitwells to discuss my stylistic nuances, and having also rationalised the practicality of the image, I took to Blond as the polar opposite. He described himself as a Converter of Manuscripts. 'I convert them into as many different forms as I can, with a price for each form, and I take my cut for doing it.'[5]

Contractually, Stoppard had to deliver the novel in May 1965 [it would actually be done in August 1965, but was started only a few months – although Stoppard prefers to claim a few days – before the deadline]. Later, however, Stoppard told Smith that Blond was hesitant about publishing his unusual work when the manuscript finally appeared, confessing to him that 'much as he admired my book, people were not buying novels at all, short novels even less and funny novels even less than that . . . and I had written a short funny novel . . . However, he said, "I always back passion" and having had two favourable readings of the novel, he was going ahead, although he wanted to hold it back until June 1965 or possibly September.'[6]

At this moment in his career, Stoppard remained unsettled about which genre would be his. He was testing them all: short stories, fiction and drama, even poetry, although that was private and included only in letters to such intimates as Isabel. He still felt it more likely that he would be a novelist rather than a dramatist; Smith and others thought the same. Early London days, writing for hire and needing money meant trying every form.

As his two radio plays were going into production, Stoppard worked on other projects. The Arthur Rank organization commissioned him to adapt 'The Story' from the Faber collection into a television play. He was looking for a breakthrough on many fronts and was upbeat as long as he was busy. BBC Radio 4 then commissioned him to write, as a trial run, five fifteen-minute episodes of the popular daily soap opera *Mrs Dale's Diary*. He accepted the assignment but his sample scripts were rejected as too sophisticated. In a January 1964 letter to Smith, he cavalierly summarized his long list of prospects and writing assignments, which included an adaptation of *Walk on the Water*, work for Boorman and what he casually refers to as 'Rosencrantz and Guildenstern', plus 'a novel for Blond or Faber'.[7]

Commitments accumulated, as was customary with him, but at this point in his career, spreading his talents in so many directions, he was both confident and uncertain, making him feel 'a bag of nerves, contemplating jobs in hand. In my mind's eye is the Mona Lisa, while in front of me is a block of marble and I keep daring myself to pick up the chisel.' This would be a constant hymn throughout his writing career: the challenge of getting started. Or, as he explained in relation to *Hapgood* (1988), 'My refrain is that the long uphill struggle in playwriting is getting to the top of page one. Once I know roughly what I'm supposed to be doing, I find dialogue much easier to write.'[8]

But his money worries persisted and propelled his writing, his only means of income. Occasionally, he would become depressed over his situation, although encouraging letters from Anthony Smith would pull him up: 'I think you're right, the only really important thing, the only thing one can't do without is writing the masterpieces. Everything else is masks and subterfuge and bribing of sentries; only the princess's bedroom, the writing, is reality.'[9]

One of the scripts Stoppard had difficulty starting was *This Way Out with Samuel Boot*, a work for television which remains unproduced and unpublished. In it, he attempts to salvage some of the ideas from the earlier *I Can't Give You*. The new work, written in late April or early May 1964, around the time Stoppard arrived in Berlin for the seminar, also deals with two brothers: one, Samuel Boot, preaches the total rejection of property, the other, Jonathan Boot, compulsively buys on credit only to have these items repossessed. Tynan, who read the script, referred to it as a patchy blend of 'absurdist comedy and radical melodrama'.[10]

> *I think too much of artistic matters, of what might be good*
> *for the theatre, ever to be completely serious.*
> Brecht to Walter Benjamin, 1934

In Berlin, Stoppard joined Marlowe, Read, Bergman, Cullinan and Saunders at a luxurious villa on Lake Wannsee, a Berlin suburb and the location for the symposium. Derek Marlowe, at twenty-six, had just won the Foyle Award for the best play of 1961–2, *The Scarecrow*, produced at the Royal Court. Four years later, he would draw on his observations of Communism in his popular novel, *A Dandy in Aspic*, which dealt with a Russian agent who wants to quit but is not allowed to do so; he later turned it into a successful screenplay.

Piers Paul Read, twenty-three, son of Sir Herbert Read (who would visit the young writers during their tenure in Berlin), had graduated from Cambridge in 1962, worked for a year in Munich for a publisher and stayed on in Germany as Ford Fellow in Berlin, first to write fiction and then to join the group of dramatists at Wannsee. When he returned to England in 1964, he became a sub-editor on the *Times Literary Supplement*. In 1968 he published *The Junkers*, a novel about Nazi Germany through the eyes of a British attaché serving in Berlin in 1963. From the cafés on the Kurfürstendamm to Alexanderplatz, Berlin is well-drawn; the novel won several awards and Read continued to write fiction as well as the non-fiction bestseller *Alive: The Story of the Andes Survivors* (1974), which was later filmed. Peter Bergman and Tom Cullinan were Americans who began their careers as playwrights. Bergman would return to New York to start the Firesign Theatre; Cullinan would become a novelist. His 1966 work, *The Beguiled,* about a wounded soldier in the US Civil War, became a 1971 film starring Clint Eastwood.

At thirty-nine, James Saunders was the slightly elder statesman of the group and the most experienced writer whose recent hit, *Next*

Time I'll Sing to You, had been produced in London and New York in 1963. Stoppard attended the West End opening and praised the work in a review in *Scene*. He would later call this experimental text about rehearsing a play dealing with the discovery of an Essex hermit 'one of the best plays written since the war, simply because it's written like music' (and he would borrow something of the hermit motif for *Arcadia*).[11] The self-conscious theatricality, stylized dialogue, audience involvement, existential–intellectual humour and satire, supported by verbal wit, appealed to Stoppard who worked under Saunders' guidance. Indeed, it was Saunders who advised Stoppard to expand *Rosencrantz and Guildenstern meet King Lear* after a Berlin presentation and who commented at length on the play following a reading of the text at the Questors Theatre in Ealing shortly after their return from Germany.[12]

The seminar was organized by Walter Hasenclever, a German bureaucrat from the Ford Foundation who was not entirely liked by the Germans because his name was the same as a well-known German playwright, actually his uncle, and many thought it devalued the name of the playwright to be associated with an administrator. Yet Hasenclever carried out his duties precisely, welcoming the writers by telling them that 'here, everything is free, you can do exactly what you want – but don't touch that painting! And don't move that chair! You can come to breakfast whenever you wish; it is served between 8 a.m. and 8.30!' This kind of contradictory behaviour was best illustrated by the library in the villa. It contained no books but had a double lock. If you wanted to visit it, you had to ask the porter to unlock a glass-fronted case to remove the two keys which then had to be taken carefully to the double-locked doors, which were ceremoniously unlocked before one could enter the empty but grandly furnished room.[13]

But Berlin also bred experimentation and playfulness, opening up the unexpected and outrageous for Stoppard. In his punning and sarcastic style, Stoppard reported to Anthony Smith on life in the German city under the salubrious guidance of the Ford Foundation in the mansion set aside for the visiting writers. Told by the resident Ford director – whom he described as 'a convertible two-tone named Hasenclever' – that he could redecorate his room any way he wanted because he was among individuals, Stoppard confided to Smith that

I didn't want to tell him I was just a middle class boy who wouldn't get a job and liked the atmosphere fine. Perhaps I will roll up the carpet and hang it on the wall in case he thinks I am a fake.

What he did hang were pictures of the Smiths, one of himself with James Saunders and a few more. He added that the 'cultural picnic' sponsored by the Ford Foundation meant they were 'fed and housed in great comfort', noting 'of course, it was quite incapacitating'. He headed one letter, 'Lit City, Monday'.[14]

Stoppard read eclectically: Camus's *The Outsider*, William Styron's *Lie Down in Darkness* (which he gave up after 100 pages), a collection of H. L. Mencken's essays and Hemingway's *A Moveable Feast*, read in two hours. Earlier, he had studied *Tristram Shandy*, explaining to Smith that he could 'detect no connection between it and *Travelling People*, except that Sterne does certain things as marvellous, irrelevant and irreverent jokes (in 1728) which [B. S.] Johnson does in grim meaningful earnestness'. But a certain dismalness marked his own literary output: 'In my spare sink I have a bottle of cinzano and of scotch and of beer. On my table a yellow rose. The sun is on my balcony. If I had a play working, life would be good,' he tells Smith, adding that James Saunders has been moderately helpful with his work – which has been terrible: 'I have thrown away everything I've managed to write (pitifully little),' he confesses. Life was relaxed: 'Marlowe, Read and I sit in each other's rooms chatting and re-arranging the furniture.' He and Marlowe shared their ambitions while drinking wine and occasionally smoking grass.

In Berlin, Stoppard found himself playing new roles, acting as a cowboy in a film based on a Borges story, and horse-riding in the Tiergarten. For the Dutch director of the Borges story (most likely 'Streetcorner Man'), Stoppard, in full cowboy regalia, swaggered to the Brandenburg Gate for the cameras. He loved doing it – 'but is it art?' he questioned.[15] His role – and pleasure – may have suggested the satiric cowboy characters that emerge in *Lord Malquist*, his first and only novel, which would appear two years later, and for which he was making notes (although he could not come up with a plot). In the book, several cowboy figures vie to become 'the Hungriest Gun in the West man with the porkiest beans straight out of the can'.[16] And when they remember, his characters talk with an excruciating Texas drawl.

Sensing Stoppard's potential as an actor, an American writer, George Moorse, thought Stoppard would be great in a feature to play a bit part with Ben Carruthers. 'It might be a giggle,' Stoppard told Smith, but the film did not come off.[17]

He did take to riding: 'Yesterday I went riding (a horse). 50 minutes of Stoppard on an animal within which he damn near ended up.' The stable was close to the East German border so one rode alongside 'concrete posts, 15 yards-deep barbed wire, Vopo-manned machine gun turrets and Alsatians'. The group also accidentally rode through groups of American soldiers on manœuvres. It was frightening, he admitted, to come upon camouflaged figures with guns or 'motionless groups of tin-hatted troops, sometimes lying prone behind wicked machine guns, sometimes wirelessing'. He was positive that if someone fired even blanks, 'it would be a case of WRITERS IN RUNAWAY HORSE HORROR. Today I am stiff saddle-sored (DARK HORSE GETS HIS),' he concluded.[18]

> *That future historians of English drama will describe*
> *the period since 1956 as an era of Brechtian influence is*
> *quite possible.*
> Martin Esslin, 1966

The political and diplomatically tense world of Berlin at this time was criticized, if not ridiculed, in the city's theatres, with their tradition of satire, class conflict and expressionism initiated by Max Reinhardt, the Dadaists and Brecht. The cabarets elaborated elements of the theatrical avant-garde. Brecht and Kurt Weill incorporated the underworld into their 1928 hit, *The Threepenny Opera,* and two years later, Marlene Dietrich captured Berlin's eroticism in *Der blaue Engel.* The women on display in clubs like Die weisse Maus, where tableaux of naked girls made up the show, led Klaus Mann, son of Thomas Mann, to exclaim 'we used to have a first class army; now we have first class perversions! Vice galore! A choice!'[19]

While Berlin stood divided in the early sixties, experimentation in the theatre still united East and West. The best-known theatre group was the Berliner Ensemble, the East German company Brecht had formed the day Communist East Germany was established in 1949. Its first production was *Mother Courage and Her Children*. The company was noted for its clarity of presentation, with every detail of a production contributing to what Brecht labelled the *Fabel*, the plot of the play told in a sequence of actions, each event dialectically recounted. The acting, music and staging had to contribute to the storytelling in order to make it lucid and entertaining. Brecht put great emphasis on 'blocking' and gave the entire cast notes, regardless of their importance in the scene.[20]

Politics prevented Stoppard from seeing the key Berliner Ensemble production of 1964, *Coriolan*, although he read and heard much about it and other offerings from his fellow writers and artists. His Czech origins made him wary of entering East Berlin during the Cold War and he even visited the British consul to clarify the political situation. He met curious ignorance: 'he [the Consul] replied that he thought the Germans and Russians had settled the Czech Question years ago; no, no, I said.'[21] Although his passport stated that he was British, it listed his birthplace as Czechoslovakia. He was nervous about jeopardizing his freedom, although in the summer he did once cross to East Berlin to see Brecht's company: 'Went to East Berlin, 3d opera, didn't like it much,' he curtly told Smith [the reference is to Brecht's *Threepenny Opera*]. What he did find fascinating was Checkpoint Charlie: 'must write Absurd play about Checkpoint Charlie. Unbelievable – the zone-situation here is like some giant Waddington game (all the country can play!, complete with printed Rules).'[22] His efforts in working out his version of Shakespeare during his Berlin sojourn may have been encouraged by what he heard about the original version and imaginative production of *Coriolan*. It is more likely, however, that Stoppard saw the Ensemble's production during their second visit to London in 1965, when it was part of their repertory.

Two other plays of the 1963–4 Berlin season quickly gained world attention: Rolf Hochhuth's *The Representative* (retitled *The Deputy* in the States) and Peter Weiss's *Marat/Sade*. Both premièred in Berlin. Hochhuth's play, which opened at the new Freie Volksbühne in 1963, dealt with accusations that Pope Pius XII did not intervene to prevent the arrest and extermination of the Jews. Extending the tradition of Schiller's historical drama, forcing individual responsibility for moral actions, the play also confronted history, although Hochhuth chose not documentary naturalism but an elevated, literary style, similar to that which Stoppard would follow. Erudition, history and individual moral decisions – all qualities that would later mark such Stoppard plays as *Rosencrantz and Guildenstern, Jumpers, Professional Foul* and *Arcadia* – defined Hochhuth's challenging documentary drama.

Marat/Sade by Weiss was equally innovative. Opening at the Schiller Theatre in Berlin in April 1964, the play, in the words of its English director, Peter Brook, was revolutionary: 'Starting with its title, everything about this play is designed to crack the spectator on the jaw, then douse him with ice-cold water, then force him to assess intelligently what has happened to him, then give him a kick in the balls, then bring him back to his senses again.'[23] With its emotional shocks drawn from Artaud and its social relevance from Brecht, *Marat/Sade* shattered theatrical conventions, with the Marquis de Sade directing the inmates of a lunatic asylum in an 1808 play about Marat's murder by Charlotte Corday. Stoppard set *Arcadia*, with its play within a play, in 1809. *The Real Inspector Hound*, as well as *Rosencrantz and Guildenstern, Travesties* and *The Real Thing*, also use the play-within-a-play convention. Revolution and individualism are the themes Weiss examines, as Stoppard would in his political plays of the late seventies, such as *Professional Foul*. Weiss and Stoppard also share a similar conception of playwriting as discovery: 'I write to find out where I stand, and so each time I have to bring in all my doubts,' Weiss explained.[24] The documentary dramatists of Berlin in the mid-sixties shaped the method of many of Stoppard's plays. Like them, he constructs his plays on research, reading and revising works from the past, whether the subject is moral philosophy (*Jumpers*), literary history (*Travesties*), chaos theory (*Arcadia*) or Shakespeare (*Rosencrantz and Guildenstern*).

Blocked on Rosencrantz and Guil.
Stoppard, 1964

Saunders actually interfered rather than helped. He had a tendency to treat each play by the participants as if he had written it himself, 'so I find little help and quite a lot of off-put in the discussions. We are doing less and less together, theoretically so that we may do more and more separately.' Saunders was also distracted because he was committed to two one-acters for the Questors Theatre by the middle of August and couldn't make a start. He also had a new, full-length play opening in London that month (*A Scent of Flowers*) but the script departed from his usual humour: 'he says he can't write like that any more, it comes out too mechanical'.[25]

Stoppard's principal effort in Berlin was writing *Rosencrantz and Guildenstern meet King Lear*, a one-acter, popularly thought to be a verse burlesque. The surviving text shows it is neither in verse nor a burlesque, but a pastiche. The idea originated from Kenneth Ewing's suggestion on the way back from a meeting at which they had offered ITV *I Can't Give you Anything But Love, Baby*. Stoppard and his agent had been told the writing was too downbeat and Ewing advised Stoppard to 'stick to theatre. Your work can't be contained on television.'[26] During the taxi ride home, they discussed the National Theatre at the Old Vic's inaugural production of *Hamlet*. Ewing had recently seen the production in which Olivier had cast Peter O'Toole in the title role, capitalizing on his success as Lawrence of Arabia, to the dismay of his assistant directors, John Dexter and William Gaskill, to whom it looked like window-dressing. Other members of the cast included John Stride as Fortinbras – he would later become the first Guildenstern – Derek Jacobi as Laertes, Michael Redgrave as Claudius and Michael Gambon as one of the Elsinore sentries.

Ewing's suggestion was the first and only one Stoppard followed up: to do something with the supernumeraries in *Hamlet*. Ewing thought the project might amuse Stoppard, and mentioned that the king of England who receives the sealed message ordering the execution of Hamlet's two student friends would most likely have been King Lear. The seed was planted. Stoppard said he found the idea appealing and despite other projects, which included an adaptation of his short work 'The Story' for television and another offer to write a novel, he began to research his *Hamlet* project.[27]

Vacationing in Scotland in January 1964, Stoppard re-read *Hamlet*, *Lear* and criticism such as J. Dover Wilson's *What Happens in Hamlet*. In late 1963, John Barton's new adaptation of Shakespeare's history plays, *The Wars of the Roses*, opened at Stratford-upon-Avon to favourable reviews, confirming the possibility of integrating, restructuring and possibly rewriting Shakespeare. Peter Hall's production mixed *Henry VI*, *Parts One*, *Two*, and *Three* with *Richard III*, legitimizing for Stoppard the enterprise of revising Shakespeare. In 1964, the production became a seven-and-a-half-hour television drama for the BBC.

By June, however, Stoppard was far enough along with his first version of *Rosencrantz and Guildenstern* to write a long description to Smith from Berlin. He describes it as a

> one-acter, char: Fortinbras, Captain, Rosencrantz, Guildenstern, Player, King Lear and Horatio, not forgetting Hamlet . . . It lasts anything from 40 min. to an hour (I really don't know) . . . my whimsical contr. to quartercentenary . . . The gist is that Ros, Guil and Ham are joined on the boat by the Player from the play-in-Hamlet, i.e. 'Lucianus nephew to the King'; i.e. the Player who represents Hamlet-figure in the play-in-Hamlet and is therefore madeup to look rather like Hamlet. So Hamlet and Player change identities on boat; the Player is captured by Pirates and goes off to fulfill Hamlet's role in the rest of Shakespeare's play. Hamlet goes on to England, witnesses execution of Ros and Guil, returning to Elsinore just too late to take over, i.e. just in time for the final tableau of carnage; and so he is stuck in space, a man 'caught out of the action'. Sounds a bit screwy but it could be fun and is written as fun. So I'm at the moment pleased about having done that; if I didn't have to write a television play in 7 days (which I will make a gallant failure at), I would be content.[28]

Stoppard's account focuses on the boat voyage to England, outlined at the end of Act Four, scene three of the original, which, three years later, would become the third act of his finished play. In the original draft, Rosencrantz and Guildenstern's contact with King Lear is limited to only four of the forty-four pages. And despite Stoppard's reference to the play as unspeakably bad, he actually incorporated a number of pages from the first half of the Berlin version into the final version of *Rosencrantz and Guildenstern*.

Ewing, kept informed of Stoppard's progress, commented on its evolution in several letters. In May 1964 he tried to deter Stoppard from the project: 'the idea of modernising Hamlet and R&G seems to me to defeat the whole idea', adding that 'perhaps it is just a late-night brainstorm of yours, I hope'. By July, however, he offers a more substantial critique, having received a copy of the one-act version (a second copy went to the Schiller theatre in Berlin since the dramaturg asked for copies of any work the young writers produced):

> As regards Rosencrantz, I very much like the characters of R and G and their cross talk, but I am not so happy about the fact that in the end this becomes a play about Hamlet, whom you have found much easier to cope with than Lear . . . but I am not sure that it justified the original idea, especially as the Lear bits resolve into a rather esoteric parody of the old man . . . In short, there seems to be a danger that the play drops to a parody of Shakespearian style rather than a flight of fancy which should soar out of our bizarre view of a Shakespearian plot. This latter would seem to me to have more scope for romping entertainment and less danger in it than the first.[29]

The exchanges indicate Ewing's important role in shaping the thoughts of the young playwright and his development of the play.

Rosencrantz and Guildenstern meet King Lear was completed before 22 June 1964. A twenty-five-minute, one-act version was produced at the Forum Theatre on the Ku'damm in Berlin in September 1964 as part of a presentation of the colloquium's work: the evening was called 'Colloquialisms' and had five short pieces by the young dramatists. Stoppard directed his production 'as a "work in progress" (work in regress, work in digress). I hope to turn it into a full length play, I hope while I am here,' he told Smith. With an amateur actor from the RAF security branch stationed in Berlin and four actors from the Questors Theatre, Ealing, he directed his first show, although the military man was 'a total amnesiac when it came to lines, and all is in panic'. Stoppard did remark, however, that he thought himself a 'very good director, though possibly only of my own work':

> You should see me doing my Guthrie, striding about chain-smoking and revelling in the unquestioning if uncomprehending obedience which all actors seem to pay to anyone who calls himself their director . . . It's lucky I go to the films a lot otherwise I wouldn't know what to do.[30]

The twenty-five-minute version focused more on role-playing than what he would later stress: the uncertainty and anxiety of Rosencrantz and Guildenstern. Charles Marowitz and Martin Esslin informally adjudicated the Berlin evening, Marowitz reporting in *The Times* that

Stoppard's play was 'a lot of academic twaddle'. Esslin was less dismissive, although Saunders remembers that he was always creatively critical in his complaints of plays he disliked.[31]

Stoppard lost enthusiasm for *Rosencrantz and Guildenstern meet King Lear* after the Berlin performance, deciding it was awful. A subsequent reading, actually a studio performance, did occur, however, at the Questors Theatre on 4 October 1964, arranged by the actors who had performed it in Berlin. Stoppard directed, and for this production added some new dialogue and shortened, as well as reversed, the title to *Guildenstern and Rosencrantz.* The text is similar to the opening section of the Berlin version, the part that Stoppard would maintain for the third act of the finished play. Opening this version are the two characters playing 'a recurrent game of how-much-did-the-King-give-you' (reduced to a single short passage in the final play), rather than the better known, yet-to-be written coin-tossing scene with which the finished text begins. Following the Questors presentation, which he did not like, Stoppard scrapped the original and started again, developing interest in 'the characters as existential immortals'.[32]

The new work was not set in England but backed into the frame of *Hamlet.* Stoppard explained the reason for the transition as

> the attempt to find a solution to a practical problem – that if you write a play about Rosencrantz and Guildenstern in England, you can't count on people knowing who they are and how they got there. So one tended to get back into the end of *Hamlet* a bit. But the explanations were always partial and ambiguous so one went back a bit further into the plot and as soon as I started doing this, I totally lost interest in England. The interesting thing was Elsinore.[33]

The new, full-length play would end where the short one began, with Rosencrantz and Guildenstern waiting to board the boat to England, providing a summary of the action of *Hamlet* and arguing over how much Claudius had paid them to accompany Hamlet.

In the original version, when Rosencrantz and Guildenstern, Hamlet and the Player arrive in England, they meet a mad King Lear running off on the heath.

Hamlet	Who is that so fantastically garlanded in flowers?
Guildenstern	A mad man.

Rosencrantz	They are all mad here: it is well known in Denmark.
Hamlet	That is why you were taking the mad prince here?
Guildenstern	He would not have been noticed among such loons.[34]

Hamlet has exchanged costumes with the Player on board the ship and is now mistakenly thought to be him.

When the three re-encounter the King, Lear warmly greets Hamlet since he recognizes him through his disguise and knew Hamlet's father; he is then given Claudius's letter. Lear can't read, however, and has Guildenstern read the note which reveals their imminent execution. Rosencrantz draws his sword, Hamlet orders Lear's men to seize them, Lear cries 'Kill! Kill! Kill!' and they are stabbed. A blackout ends the scene. When the lights return, Hamlet is back in Elsinore, but *after* the main action of Shakespeare's play. Bodies lie about the stage and Fortinbras is about to take command (interestingly, the play began with Fortinbras's speech on the plain of Denmark). Hamlet's role has been played out, his identity erased; his fate, as he tells Fortinbras's Captain, is to 'walk the earth . . . I have time. The sun is going down. It will be night soon. Do you think so? I was just making conversation. I have a lot of time,' he concludes.[35] Hamlet's character has been removed from the stage, as have been the bodies.

Stoppard completed the revised play in the spring of 1965, but where the original focused on role-playing (masks are crucial, the Player wearing a mask of Hamlet throughout the last portion of the work), the final, retitled version explores the existential situation of Rosencrantz and Guildenstern.[36] What the original illustrates is not only the groundwork, and the conceptual shift in the more polished, finished version to be written in London, but Stoppard's practice of adapting an earlier, shorter form into a lengthier final piece. The forerunner of *Jumpers* (1972) was his thirty-minute television play *Another Moon Called Earth* (1967), while the antecedent of *Travesties* (1974) is, in part, the radio play *Artist Descending a Staircase*. The challenge in revising *Rosencrantz* was, in Stoppard's words, trying to 'prise loose Guildenstern from [Stoppard's] own character'.[37]

Shall I be the new Terence Rattigan?
Stoppard, 1964

While working on *Rosencrantz and Guildenstern meet King Lear* in Berlin, Stoppard went to Hamburg to oversee a production of *A Walk on the Water* on 30 June 1964, the first full staging of one of his plays. This had been planned for some time; in fact, he had already been interviewed by a German theatre magazine in advance of the opening. Translated into German, the production of *A Walk* at the Thalia Theatre benefited from Stoppard's revision of the script before the première, although he confessed misgivings to Smith over the process and the leading man:

> My guess is that the venerable (i.e. senile) star of Stoppard's Follies (1960-64 inc) doesn't reckon on lasting out till August and wants to get his farewell performance in with the critics there. I'm having a private bet that in the six week break [because of an obligatory vacation; his Riley play would open 30 June for one performance and then begin a proper run six weeks later] he'll decide to pull out (having had his first-night last-night glory). It may be that he has decided the play is a lemon and wants out. I don't know. Nor, believe me, do I care.[38]

His rewrites altered the original play, cutting out a flashback and providing a new beginning, first-act curtain and title, which by the time of the opening became *Der Spleen des George Riley*. Stoppard later joked that the title made the play sound like 'an episode of *Emergency Ward Ten* [a British television show]'.[39]

Reporting on his first production meeting with the theatre company, Stoppard expressed embarrassment at their enthusiasm, the size of the theatre (1,000 seats), the earnest discussion of psychological motivation, the fame of the leading actor and his own anxiety. There was also the strange rehearsal and performance schedule. By the time of the opening in August, Stoppard was dismayed at the play's new form and his lack of identity with the work.

The play received mixed notices, students in the gallery on opening night hissing at the conventional domestic comedy while the middle-class members of the audience seated below offered polite applause. The Hamburg papers had billed it as the work of one of Britain's most innovative dramatists and the public was disappointed; as Stoppard comically reported to Anthony Smith, the papers made him out to be

> a combination of Absurdist (admiration for Beckett, Pinter) Beatle (hair, long), and Angry Young Man (furious, 26, male). Following this beautifully spurious image what should roll up but a somewhat tedious 1933 play (a good year for some, like Hitler, but not for plays).[40]

Just who Stoppard was remained a mystery, though the public's need to invent a persona had been satisfied by the journalists. However, Stoppard had yet to invent his own.

At the urging of his German agent, Stoppard took a bow with the actors, who would have been offended if he didn't join them. Showing indifference to the audience, he flaunted a cigarette in his mouth, echoing Oscar Wilde's show of indifference to the audience at *his* first play, *Lady Windermere's Fan*.[41] Boos from the gallery and cheers from the stalls greeted Stoppard: 'robotlike and blank I allowed myself to be guided by the cast and director not once but twice more back onto the stage to witness the riot, which grew hilariously with my every reappearance'.

Hamburg would be the only time Stoppard was ever booed off a stage, although he admitted to Anthony Smith that the play was thin and repetitive. But at an after-show party, he found solace in the presence of Derek Marlowe and Ewing, who had flown in for the first night from Cannes, where he had been on holiday: 'Actually it was a good evening with me chatting up one bird (Florence Lawrence) and Marlowe the other (Linda).'[42]

A few days after the opening, Stoppard told Smith that he felt 'partly fed up and partly furious that I let WOTW, whatever its virtues, represent me as a writer first time out.' He vowed never to have it produced in England and said that if Ewing tried to get it put on in London, he'd fire him on the spot. The only exception would be financial:

> If I ever really run short of cash I may sanction a production in Lima or Fiji; but otherwise may it only be performed after my death as a historical curiosity, assuming, of course, that I arouse any posthumous curiosity, which, by the way I feel now, is a large assumption.[43]

Ironically, he did receive a sizeable amount for the Hamburg production and the play would be put on in London by Doris Cole Abrahams, following the success of *Rosencrantz and Guildenstern*, much to Stoppard's consternation.

After his return to Berlin and further work on *Rosencrantz and Guildenstern,* he found the colloquium boring but did admit it was 'worth it for doing work in'. The composition was helped by repeatedly listening to two Dylan songs, 'Like a Rolling Stone' and 'Subterranean Homesick Blues'.[44] The meals, however, were 'regularly appalling'. As the colloquium wound down, Read prepared for a motor trip down the Dalmation coast. He would be driving through Czechoslovakia, not far from Zlín, and if Stoppard agreed to join him, he would stop in the town. 'Naturally, I am very keen to do it,' he told Smith, but he hesitated, partly because of the possible commitment of a television script for Boorman and partly because of his fear that once he had returned, the Czechs might not let him leave and would require him to do military service. In the end, the trip was cancelled. He also tells Smith that he needs the time to work on 'Rosguil'. An imminent visit to Berlin by Sir Herbert and Lady Read also meant that he and Piers had to be *in situ*.[45]

Stoppard returned to England in autumn 1964, filled with ambition and plans. He listed his 'aforesaid inactivity' to Smith:

Rejected AR [Arthur Rank] play gone to BBC
  Rejected ABC play gone to AR
  Gamblers to rewrite
  Rosenguild to rewrite
  Novel to start. I have returned with a notebook of ideas and bon mots. I itch to begin. Which I shall very soon, but simultaneously I require one television sale to give me the security till April . . . All in all, I long just to find a nice cheap desk and a good chair, an anglepoise lamp and a new typewriter . . . . Thanks to the socking overdraft built on the sands of the deutschemark, I'll just about get straight in time to write a television play and a letter of apology to Anthony Blond.

He was happy to tell Smith, however, that Ewing was able to get £481 net for the Hamburg production of *Walk on the Water*: 'I figure we must have played 39 complete performances and folded shortly before the need of the second act of the fortieth. So I'm a capitalist now.'[46] He was eager to get under way with new work, however, and did so by trying to sell a television play, revise his early sketch, *The Gamblers*, into a full-length play (which the Bristol Old Vic Theatre School would mount in May 1965) and rewrite *Rosencrantz and Guildenstern*, a work that within several years would bring him international fame.

Hoping to return to Bristol, where he could accomplish more writing, he was under pressure from Jose to return to London, where she was working. He faced a conflict between wanting to 'get away by myself to write like some madman till April, and placating Jose'. He frankly could not afford to support both of them and did not want to write a television play while he needed to finish his novel, for which he had notes but not a plot. Displeasure with the cuts, changes and modifications required by television made him resistant to such writing. To Smith, he confided that he was feeling 'rather desperate about the work/money situation and feeling rather selfish about the Posy [Jose] situation which somehow has developed much more in her mind than in mine . . . I really must stop being flippant about things which are not flippant.'[47]

But instead of Bristol and his wish to be taken roughly aside by the Smiths and be 'belaboured about the head with a willow bat by the one, while being given a short course in the Female Mind by the other', he returned to London, taking rooms with Derek Marlowe and Piers Paul Read at 11 Vincent Square Mansions on Walcott Street, Pimlico, across the street from the Westminster School playing field with its large cricket pitch and a short distance from Victoria Station. Stoppard found the process of setting up the flat, which was rented in his name, with the other two subletting from him, expensive. He and Marlowe painted it and bought furniture. To Smith, he expressed admiration at his 'elan as a family man living on sheer optimism' when 'as a footloose bachelor am juggling financial promises against negotiated overdrafts simply to get a flat established'.[48]

As a distraction one weekend during this period, Stoppard accompanied Piers Paul Read to the Yorkshire home of his father, Sir Herbert Read, and was startled to see Sir Herbert's huge library. Stoppard admired the grand home which seemed to have books everywhere and never forgot the impression made on him by the 'bookish' household.[49] From the moment he could afford them, Stoppard bought – and continues to buy – books: bestsellers, new titles, second-hand works and rare first editions. At one point, he had a distinguished Hemingway collection; at another, the works of Oscar Wilde. As an author, he also felt it was important to support the work of fellow writers and he often walked out of his favourite Chelsea bookshop, Sandoe, with shopping bags full of books.

Stoppard began to model himself on his new idol, Mick Jagger, whose look, insouciance, louche behaviour and rebellious attitude was beginning to makes its impression on pop culture. Physically, they shared the same rubbery lips, lank frame and untutored hair; journalists soon began to draw parallels between the two. By 1964 – the Rolling Stones' first album appeared in April that year – Jagger's theatricality, on and off the stage, sanctioned a certain unorthodoxy that Stoppard was attempting in the theatre. And as Stoppard would later discover through his friendship with Jagger, both took books seriously, although Jagger kept this aspect of his life out of the spotlight. A kind of cultivated arrogance and 'primitive cool' were his preferred poses. Stoppard found the Jagger image alluring and in his own quiet way imitated his dress and manner.[50]

Countering this rebelliousness, however, was Stoppard's pull to the conservative ritual of marriage, which he understood as offering him a degree of stability, allowing him to concentrate on his writing. Despite some early qualms about his relationship with Jose (defined largely by her pursuit of him), Stoppard married her on 26 March 1965 at a small ceremony in St Norman's Church in the district of Troon in the county of Ayr, Scotland. It was 'a groom's wedding', meaning that it took place where the groom's parents resided; at the time, Stoppard's parents lived in Milngavie, outside Glasgow. Stoppard and Jose returned to live in Stoppard's Pimlico flat. Read had already moved out, having taken a job at the *Times Literary Supplement*. Derek Marlowe remained for a short while with Stoppard and Jose, but soon left the large mansion apartment at Vincent Square, which was now dominated by their favourite possession: a huge Edwardian sofa: 'We bought it instead of having a honeymoon and spent what should have been our honeymoon on it,' Jose explained.[51]

Soon frustrated by her husband's lackadaisical manner towards writing and his preference for sleeping most of the day and writing most of the night, however, Jose threatened to quit her job at *Which?* in order to force Stoppard to write and earn enough money for them to live on. 'I'm going to give up my job and you'll have to keep me,' she threatened. Eventually, she did, partly compelled by her pregnancy in the late summer of 1965. Stoppard didn't panic, although he was anxious: he had only freelance work to rely on, mostly in television and radio. But writing remained his obsession, Jose conceding that it was the centre of his life. Stoppard concurred; his true love *was* writing. 'I've been married to it for longer,' he joked.[52] But writing was also his only weapon to combat the uncertainty of the future and achieve some degree of financial order.

CHAPTER 7

ROSENCRANTZ ON THE ROYAL MILE

*I got a bigger thrill from seeing my first byline . . . than from
having my first play on at the National.*

Stoppard, 1995

There is something at best comic and at worse facetious in Stoppard's
declaration which denies his excitement at being the youngest
playwright ever to be produced at the National Theatre, of suddenly
dealing with the most influential figures in the theatre of the day –
Kenneth Tynan and Laurence Olivier – and of becoming an overnight
theatrical sensation. One anecdote illustrates Stoppard's bewilderment: recounting his first meeting with the powers at the National, he
recalled that 'after about an hour Olivier went out. I said to Tynan:
"What the hell's all this?" Tynan said: "Didn't anyone tell you? We're
doing it in April" – "it" being "R& G Are Dead".'

After returning from Berlin in October 1964, Stoppard had attended
a brief reading of the play at the Questors Theatre, Ealing, but was still
dissatisfied with the one-act work, which emphasized role-playing and
identity rather than the title characters. He needed to explain more
about Rosencrantz and Guildenstern before they arrived in England,
which meant moving the characters back into *Hamlet*. He shifted the
perspective and wrote the first two acts of what would be the three-act
play. The cause for the change was pragmatic: 'it was only [by] the
necessity of explaining how they came to be in England that little by
little I was drawn back into the action of Shakespeare's play in order to
give them some kind of world to grow out of. Well, the tail began
wagging the dog with a vengeance. Finally, I became much more
interested in their position in Hamlet than after they left.'[1]

Stoppard submitted the revised, two-act version to Questors' New

Play Festival in March 1965. The response was cool: the unfinished work was too late for consideration in that year's competition, although the director of the theatre, Alfred Emmet, passed the script on to James Saunders who, of course, knew Stoppard from Berlin. In April, Saunders wrote a lengthy critique, beginning with the remark that the play could do with some cutting. The original version worked better, he suggested: 'I get the feeling of a certain amount of self-indulgence in this script . . . [and] I have an idea that some of the dialogue would be too obscure at the pace at which it needs to be played.' The biggest complaint was that in the original version, 'Ros and Guil' were conscious of their function as characters and already suspect that 'they are already *determined*'. The present version didn't make this clear enough at the outset: 'I think you have to postulate predetermination of their plot before they can begin in an apparently random way, otherwise the randomness will be connected with nothing but the play *you* are writing.' 'Two courtiers on a road can kill time, but not waste it,' he continued. 'One game, but not two, unless they explain. I think the *theatricality* of their characters as *characters* could come out earlier,' he concluded.[2]

Stoppard was unwilling to wait a year to resubmit the play for the Questors competition and did not agree fully with Saunders' criticisms, so in the spring of 1965 he sent his new version to the Royal Shakespeare Company. He did not know at the time that the Literary Manager of the RSC, Jeremy Brooks, had a certain aversion to plays dealing with secondary characters in Shakespeare, which he believed was 'a favoured device of unperformed playwrights'.[3] Nevertheless, Brooks responded to Stoppard's work with enthusiasm. In May 1965, he wrote: 'it is a long time since I have actually had to suppress laughter when reading a play in order not to annoy the other people in the room'. 'Peter Hall has also read it,' he continued, 'and is very keen and I would like to talk to you now about the possibility of our commissioning the third act.'[4] Their eagerness led to a one-year option on the play. By late June, Stoppard completed the third act, although Brooks reacted cautiously to the new material, noting in a letter that he had, as Stoppard requested, sent a copy of the play on to Richard Imison at the BBC but that while the RSC option remained in place, they had control. Brooks added that 'a lot of the double-talk, amusing and stimulating as it all is, needs cutting; and that the acting of the present third act needs to be resolved, somehow, in a more positive way'.[5] Early response favoured a two-act play.

Before Brooks could reply in greater detail, Stoppard had good news from Richard Imison and the BBC on another project: after discussion with Martin Esslin, then Head of Radio Drama, Imison and others approved Stoppard's synopsis of *Albert's Bridge* and would like to commission it, although they would prefer a forty-five-minute rather than a sixty-minute version. Imison also suggested some structural improvements. This development eased Stoppard's financial difficulties. At the same time, Stoppard felt under mounting pressure to complete the novel he had contracted with Anthony Blond.

Although other work preoccupied him, the pattern of debt and doubt continued. Following a vacation in France with Jose, he confided to Smith that for the previous two months he hadn't been able to apply himself to his work. He had only a month to write *Albert's Bridge* and do a rewrite of *Rosencrantz and Guildenstern*. Debt, competing with demands on his time, generated paralysis. But he forged ahead, propelled as much by fear as by financial need, and gradually regained his financial footing through new work at the BBC, the sale of a radio play, *If You're Glad I'll be Frank*, some script rewrites for the RSC and advances for various television projects. His novel, however, loomed largest on his cluttered horizon.

On the strength of the three short stories that appeared in Faber's *Introduction 2*, Anthony Blond had commissioned Stoppard to write a novel and, needing the money – the advance was for £150, £75 on signing and £75 on delivery – and sensing that perhaps fiction rather than drama might be his *métier*, Stoppard had leapt at the chance but wrote less energetically. Only a deadline of 1 May 1965 prompted him to get going. In 1965 he began to write the novel but couldn't get anywhere. He finally started it, in a panic, two days before it was due: 'I worked out that if I wrote 30,000 words a day, I could still get it done in time.' He completed the novel in August 1965 and believed that his reputation would be made by the book: 'I believed the play would be of little consequence.'[6] It was, and the novel wasn't. But the pressure to finish grew, Jose Stoppard recalling that 'he sits up all night smoking endless cigarettes when he realises that it's *got* to be done'. Jose read the newly typed pages out loud each night in bed while Stoppard revised. She also commented freely on the story, contributing to its development.[7]

The novel was unorthodox and, at first, Blond hesitated to publish. But in September 1965, Ewing gave Stoppard some good news: Blond and his editor were no longer criticizing the novel but 'as a book, they just don't think that there is going to be a reading audience which will understand it, and felt ten days ago that they could not publish it'. A formal notice to that effect was sent to Ewing, who assured Stoppard that if this did indeed occur, Stoppard would not have to repay the portion of the advance he had already received. However, the manuscript had been sent to a female reader who reported that the work 'is the most brilliant book they have ever given her to read'. 'It has now gone to an even more distinguished reader and if he, too, approves the ms. the work will surely be published.'[8] The next day, a telegram from Ewing ended the suspense: Blond would definitively publish, although the book would not appear for nearly eleven months.

Incidents! All we get are incidents! Dear God, is it too much
to expect a little sustained action?
Stoppard, *Rosencrantz and Guildenstern are Dead*

The revised three-act version of 'Rosguil' (as Stoppard came to refer to the work) was not selected by the RSC, although they maintained their option for a year. The original idea was that the play would alternate with David Warner's *Hamlet*, which was bringing in crowds at Stratford. Warner appealed to the younger generation as a slightly bewildered young man upset at the way his elders let down the young – but who also rebelled against the Establishment, which did not overwhelm him. A new play by a youthful playwright about the two university friends of Hamlet would complement Warner's performance. Instead of *Rosencrantz and Guildenstern*, however, the RSC chose David Wright's *Strike*, which Peter Hall subsequently cancelled after he returned from holiday to discover that the script was not finalized and rehearsals were a mess.

But in July 1965, there was still hope. Jeremy Brooks wrote to Stoppard with suggestions after re-reading the new three-act *Rosencrantz and Guildenstern* three times and canvassing the opinions of others. First, he recommended that the play be in two, not three acts; second, the double talk needed cutting; and, third, the action in the final act had to be resolved more positively. But, he added, he was still 'dead keen on the play and very much hope we can find a way of presenting it. But I do think more work needs doing before I show it to Peter Hall again (he hasn't read the third act yet).' Trevor Nunn had read it over and was also still eager to do the work, Brooks concluded.[9]

Stoppard had other projects on the go, in an effort to earn a living. One was a ghost-written piece on John Boorman for the *Observer*. Richard Findlater, editor of the arts pages, explained to Stoppard that he wanted to give him a byline on the essay to which he had contributed – Anthony Smith got the credit – but 'I am afraid that it was really too difficult to get acknowledgement of your Boswellising into the intro or bye line'.[10] Where he did receive credit, however, was for a series of actor profiles for the Royal Shakespeare Company inserted in the programmes for various productions in 1965, partly the result of Anthony Smith writing programme notes for RSC productions during this time. Among those Stoppard interviewed were Timothy West, Jeffery Dench, John Normington and, most interestingly, David Warner. This profile opens with the prescient comment that 'the character of Hamlet has the mystique of being at least paradoxical and perhaps an insoluble mystery; a production of the play tends therefore to be identified with its interpreters more closely than is the case with any other Shakespeare play.' Stoppard, of course, was himself one of those interpreters. He also includes various comic details that reflect his deft touch. Warner, commenting on his lack of athletic prowess, reports that he recently played cricket for the RSC team: 'I scored four and was then hit on my dagger hand!'[11]

Stoppard's most lucrative projects during this time were what he fondly called his 'Arabs', a series of scripts for the BBC Arabic service. Richard Imison, the Script Editor for BBC Radio Drama, considered a number of writers he came across in the summer of 1965, and conveyed his list to an assistant, Hope Alexander, in a poem:

> *Unmemorable faces*
> *Turn up in unexpected places;*
> *However long I fail to cope,*
> *There is always Hope .. .. ..*
> *Arnold Yarrow, Jon Rollason, Sheila Hodgson, Tom Stoppard –*

For addresses apply next door;
In difficulty
Try me!
 Free verse![12]

It was not until October, however, that Imison and the Arabic producer, Mr Rizq, selected Stoppard and Peter Hoar. Kenneth Ewing recalled the absurdity of the contract: 'I got him a job writing a BBC radio series about an Arab student – it was ridiculous really, because everything he wrote was translated into Arabic for broadcast overseas.'[13]

But Stoppard was thrilled to write *A Student's Diary* for the BBC, a series of scripts about a young Arab arriving in London to study medicine. A letter of 12 October 1965 to Smith reports that 'half an hour ago: a phone call from the Arab Man Bush House to say they want me for Ali in Wonderland, to which my reactions are Whoopeee (£30 a week) and Oh Christ (Who? In where?), not necessarily in that order. One more thing to fit into this impossibly short month.'[14] In the same letter, he confesses that he will have to go to the library 'and get a few books about the Arab World of which I know nothing except such tales as have reached me concerning the available experiences in Alexandrian brothels (which may well come in handy when the serial has got under way a bit)'.

The first script in the series – recorded on 24 March and transmitted on 3 April 1966 on the Arabic World Service, lasting 14 minutes, 17 seconds (Stoppard worked out the length to equal 6.5 typed foolscap pages) – describes the Channel crossing of Amin Osman and his first encounter with an Englishman who plants some cocaine in the pocket of a coat he gives the naïve student. A run-in with the law follows. Suspicions of Amin's intent in coming to England develop in the second episode, which focuses on an extended interview with officials, the Chief of Customs adding, 'I think I believed you before, but frankly a little bit of corroborative evidence is worth a lot of character-reading.' A plan is afoot: to capture Blake, the Englishman, through a news story the police will put in the papers about Amin's delay. The first inspector in Stoppard's work then appears, Inspector Symes. By episode four, Amin is in London and is greeted at Victoria Station by his friend Karim; on the No. 53 bus, observing the sights and the people, they comment on immigration, the London papers and British manners, all subjects Stoppard treats with amused concern. Amin remarks that at home in Jordan, the bus would be resounding with arguments and conversations, but in London, as Karim interjects, 'the British are the world's greatest exponents of the art of mind one's own business'. Amin: 'It's like a busload of spies all waiting for someone to say the password.'[15]

These early episodes of the series show Stoppard's comic presentation of the clichés and stereotypes of England for the Arabic world but also emphasize an undercurrent of deception and trickery. In many ways, Stoppard makes his tale a warning for immigrants and a very sixties story: drugs, sex and rebellion soon dominate the series. Episode five, the end of Stoppard's first set of scripts, concludes with Amin's interview at the teaching hospital where he hopes to be accepted as a medical student. But the conversation comically focuses not on his training but his ability as a goalkeeper; the episode concludes with the news that the criminal, Mr Blake, has called.

Peter Hoar wrote episodes six to ten of *A Student's Diary*. Stoppard began again with number eleven. They alternated in sets of five scripts throughout the series, until Stoppard withdrew because of the sudden success of *Rosencrantz and Guildenstern*. Throughout the first half of Stoppard's contributions, the writing is clear, direct and unadorned. The introduction of an attractive woman, Annabel Franklyn, who may or may not be in league with Blake, increases the tension and suggests some of the complications with spies and agents Stoppard would later elaborate in *The Dog it Was that Died* and *Hapgood*. But while the plot's complexity increased, the dialogue remained relatively flat and unimaginative. If anything, the dialogue and narrative display Stoppard's parodic skill as he piles clichéd syntax and tone on to his story, borrowed from typical whodunnits and mysteries. In episode fourteen, for example, on the prosecution of the arrested Blake, Inspector Symes parodies a B-movie detective: we must 'catch him out on a lie somewhere, then that might be the thin edge of the wedge that would crack history wide open. So I want you to think very carefully and see if you can remember anything – anything at all which you haven't told me about the events leading to Blake's arrest.'[16] This is only a few typing strokes away from Stoppard's tone in *The Real Inspector Hound*.

Further episodes involve a pickpocket and Amin's first day at medical school, St Mark's, where he meets a fellow student, Peter, whose devotion to medicine is less than complete. His aunt left him £10,000 on condition he become a doctor: 'I was at Cambridge studying classics when that happened. It took me about three tenths of a second to decide that deep down I had an urge to be a doctor! So here I am.'[17] In this, the twenty-third episode, Stoppard also includes the first of a series of lectures in his plays, later illustrated by George in *Jumpers*, Cecily and Lenin in *Travesties* and Housman in *The Invention of Love*. Here, the dean of medicine provides a pompous and sententious lecture, satirized, of course, by Stoppard, on the import- ance of commitment and study, adding with a deft, Stoppardian touch that there are also numerous clubs that the students should join, from judo to motoring, mountaineering, music and chess: 'Mind you the clubs exist to enrich your leisure hours, not to tempt you away from your studies. There have been one or two students who after five years at St Mark's have gone out into the world with a nodding acquaintance with medicine and absolute genius for ping-pong.'[18] One can only imagine how it would sound in Arabic.

Other issues dominate the remaining scripts: where to live, lack of money, a jewellery theft and science. This last, of course, would become a crucial Stoppard theme, as Amin forecasts: 'I'm fascinated by science, by the sort of things I'm learning here, but when I try and imagine myself trying to apply it all to an actual human case – a patient who is depending on me, well, frankly the thought just terrifies me.'[19] One of the preceding episodes contains an important speech on the heart as an emotional and biological organ. Amin, distracted by a dream, cuts too deep on a cadaver, severing the aorta; when he witnesses an actual operation, he faints.[20] A later episode, however, shows Amin applying his skill, saving the life of a young woman who is choking.

Other adventures follow, including summer work as a waiter on the south coast of England and an encounter with a child psychiatrist who is his new landlord. Journalists are again shown to be unfair: a semi- confidential discussion about a new treatment for children accident- ally gets into the papers through Amin's unguarded remarks to a journalist. The politics of hospitals, the diagnosis of illness and the element of the absurd all appear:[21] 'Minnie, Mrs Martin's dog, is in the hands of the police, following the death of Mr Cook who had a heart attack during a private argument with another man. Minnie had been on the scene and added to the excitement, jumping around, and as a result it was left to the magistrates to decide whether Minnie had attacked Mr Cook or not.'[22]

Later scripts show more inventiveness and flexibility than the earlier episodes. They also became more English in their comedy and orientation, experiencing rather than merely talking about English situations.[23] The clichés disappeared in favour of slightly absurd, if not surrealistic, moments, anticipating the playfulness of *The Real Inspector Hound* and the originality of *After Magritte*. Dialogue is looser, faster and sharper in Stoppard's last script, episode 138, recorded on 30 May 1967. *Rosencrantz and Guildenstern* had opened at the National Theatre's Old Vic six weeks previously. Although Stoppard left *A Student's Diary*, the series continued until episode 397, broadcast on 10 February 1969. The experience taught Stoppard how to make his style more inventive and to sharpen his dialogue, although his plots remained borrowed and predictable. But until the production of *Rosencrantz and Guildenstern* was assured, Stoppard committed himself to another BBC soap-opera series, this time for Africa.

Nevertheless, insecurity dominated his life. While the National reviewed *Rosencrantz and Guildenstern*, he had doubts about their commitment. To Smith he explained that while Tynan, Olivier and John Dexter, who was eager to direct it, were all enthusiastic, there was a problem as to when they could produce it. October 1967 was the first choice if Stoppard could wait that long, but they assumed that he wouldn't. They needed more time and bought a six-month option. Stoppard consulted O'Toole on the matter of leaving the play with the National for an October production; he advised against it, citing other plays that had been dead certs until the mail brought newer ones. Stoppard agreed and offered the view that 'plays go off, like fruit. Somehow, in a year's time the play won't be as good a play. It's not as good now as it was a year ago when I wrote it.'[24] While he waited, he fielded requests for the work from foreign and North American publishers and producers. But until the National made up its mind, he was virtually penniless.

Although Stoppard was just beginning his career, he was determined to have a say in the rehearsal and production of his work. An incident from 1965 involving the filming of his short television play *A Paragraph for Mr Blake* is one example. The show was to be taped at the Elstree studios in the presence of the producer, Lord Willis. Stoppard suggested to Smith that he read the final script 'as an illustration and a warning of what is liable to happen to a play if the author is fool enough to go abroad at the critical time'.[25] Stoppard went on a short summer vacation with Jose to France and, in his absence, Willis made numerous changes to the text, which essentially dealt with a reporter stealing from a supermarket. Willis cut the subplot focusing on the reporter's home life and inserted pages of 'corny' dialogue. When he read it, Stoppard wanted his name removed from the text, 'but things had gone too far – I had already been interviewed by the TV Times and Post, so I resigned myself to Lord Willis's fate (accompli)'. Attending a walk-through at a church hall, he realized it was impossible 'to even murmur my misgivings – the production was so far advanced, and everyone ws so terribly NICE that to say anything adverse would have been to hit a child. So. I curl at the thought of it being WATCHED, but rationalise that the curling is a fair swap for a holiday in France.' The ironic epitome of Lord Willis's role occurred when his title credit appeared on the camera-script, 'namely, The Creator'.[26]

Despite his cynical amusement, Stoppard shows here a tolerance to changes in his work (compromised, perhaps, by his payment for the play), but underneath there is a resolve not to let such abuse occur in the future, as a 1968 interview makes clear. Explaining the importance of attending rehearsals – which he continues to do when his plays are mounted, remounted or even recast – he explains that:

> what one is there for is to prevent oneself from being misrepresented, because the first and real truth about having a play put on is that with the most intelligent and sympathetic director possible and the most accomplished and intelligent actors available you will only actually get about 70% of what you meant, because a script turns out to be a great deal more obscure in its intentions than one could possibly imagine oneself. . . .
>
> I write with a very dominant sense of rhythm in the dialogue, and to me the orchestration of that dialogue has a kind of inevitability . . . [but] there are other ways which often work better which one hadn't even thought of.[27]

The stance of clarity and confidence, contrasting with an openness to other interpretations, characterizes Stoppard's attitude towards the staging of his plays, which would be brought into focus during rehearsals for *Rosencrantz and Guildenstern* at the National in the spring of 1967.

Another event during this period accelerated the need for money: the birth of his son Oliver on 4 May 1966. The baby, who had to spend several weeks in hospital because of his low weight before coming home, gave him a new outlook on life: 'Jose is sleepless, and I am alternately sym-pathetic. Have yet to change a nappy, can't conquer my tendency to stab myself with the pin to make sure I'm not stabbing him,' he wrote to Smith in June. Stoppard had been impatient to become a father, telling Smith in 1964 that he had had tea with Mrs Wilders and her three 'super' children; and when the Smiths had twins that same year, Stoppard declared to his friend that 'I must get myself a baby. I think I'm going to be attracted when I see yours.'[28] Children, as a symbol of family and stability (psychological as much as social), would become a persistent theme in his later work and especially important in *The Real Thing, Hapgood* and *Arcadia*. Although his first commitment was to writing, Stoppard secretly longed for a family and, once he had children, valued family above all else. He constantly involved himself in the active life of his four sons (two by Jose and two by his second wife, Miriam). In the seventies, he would repeatedly credit family life with providing the security he needed for his writing.

In late 1965 and throughout 1966, Stoppard began to be well paid by the BBC. In November 1965, John Tydeman produced *A Walk on the Water* for radio. In December 1965, he received a fee of £150, fifty per cent of his payment for a commissioned drama-documentary project: a thirty-minute original television play united with a documentary to be delivered by 31 March 1966. Stoppard was, as always, eager to pick up the needed funds. Memos indicate that he collected the advance a few days after he signed the contract, one letter to Ewing reporting that 'Tom Stoppard finally found us last Friday and signed his contract for the 30 minute play at the fee you and I agreed. . . . I hope Mr Stoppard managed to pick up the cheque from Television accounts all right.' August the next year saw equal effort in securing payment for various *Student's Diary* accounts, with Stoppard pleading to the administrative assistant to 'short-cut the System so that by Friday I'll be able to emerge from that skyscraper clutching my cheque'.[29]

But not every piece of work was accepted. He had been gaining attention through his radio plays and had a few television scripts aired, yet he remained largely unknown to the wider public and, because of his originality, largely unproduced. Five proposed scripts for the popular radio soap *Mrs Dale's Diary* were turned down because the writing was too unique. As the script editor and producer Keith Williams explained, 'your style and treatment are too individual for this particular purpose'. It would be difficult for other writers to maintain continuity of character and the general style of the episodes; similarly, it would be equally difficult 'to expect you to adapt yourself to a style so obviously not your own'.[30] A memo of 31 March 1966 reports another rejection. A proposed television play, to be linked to a documentary, was delivered on time for the series *Pursuit of Happiness*, but, while noting its competence, it was returned, although he was asked to write a completely new work. His fee was also increased by another £100. *A Separate Peace* was the result, a comic account of a man who checks himself into a hospital for the pleasure of its service: 'the point is not breakfast in bed, but breakfast in bed without guilt – if you're not ill'. Lunch is more problematic and 'to stay in bed for tea is almost impossible in decent society . . . but in a hospital it's not only understood, – it's expected'. Linked to the play was a documentary he made with Christopher Martin on chess, although Stoppard later doubted 'that chess and the desire to escape from the world are good metaphors for each other'.[31] The play and documentary were broadcast in August 1966.

In September 1966, Stoppard delivered *Albert's Bridge*, which went fifteen minutes over the contracted time of forty-five minutes. They adjusted his fee. In November, there was a new contract for what would become the television play *Teeth*, the first of his works to involve the actor John Wood. In December 1966 he received another commission to write a thirty-minute pilot episode with Gordon Williams for a proposed light programme entitled 'Tales of Doctor Masopust'. That was a quick forty-five guineas. Alternating between radio dramas and television plays, while also writing his novel (another useful advance), Stoppard eked out a living, at least enough to meet his expenses with his wife and infant son. The success of

Rosencrantz and Guildenstern, however, would dramatically alter that situation.

> *Nevertheless, I suppose one might say that this was a chance.*
>
> Stoppard, *Rosencrantz and Guildenstern are Dead*

As Jeremy Brooks had told Stoppard, Trevor Nunn wanted to put on *Rosencrantz and Guildenstern* in a studio series of three plays by new playwrights produced by the RSC and financed by an American socialite. This satellite season at the Jeannetta Cochrane Theatre at the Central School of Art and Design ended abruptly, however, when the money dried up; it was needed to keep the Aldwych alive. Nunn could not proceed, but he recalled that by then he had persuaded Stoppard to rewrite some of the third act and that he was planning to cast it with actors playing the same roles in the David Warner *Hamlet* at Stratford.[32]

The RSC option expired in May 1966, however, and Stoppard began to shop around for a new home for the play. Even the Royal Court was sent a copy.[33] But the play's linguistic flamboyance, canonical source and elegant, complicated structure, requiring a quasi-Elizabethan setting, meant that *Rosencrantz and Guildenstern* was, at least on the surface, foreign to the goals and production values of the Royal Court, which featured sparsely designed, socially realistic drama, often of working-class life. For the Royal Court, the role of the director was to locate the production that was already in the text rather than translate a text into a performance – the very essence of a Stoppard work. Resistance to theatricality characterized the Royal Court's productions at this time, whereas Stoppard's text thrived on it.[34] William Gaskill, then artistic director of the Royal Court, viewed the stage as a neutral means of revealing a play, an attitude very different from either the RSC, who thought in terms of large-scale treatment of large-scale works, or the National, which was thriving on productions like Olivier's *Othello,* Noël Coward's *Hay Fever* (which he directed) and Peter Shaffer's epic, *The Royal Hunt of the Sun.* Productions at the 878-seat Old Vic theatre played to near-capacity houses throughout the 1964 season.[35]

Although the RSC option expired, Nunn encouraged Stoppard to wait for the following season, when the studio programme might be revived. In the meantime, Nunn offered Stoppard the chance to revise a literal translation by Nicholas Bethell of the Polish playwright Slawomir Mrozek's *Tango*, which was to open the RSC's spring season at the Aldwych. About two weeks before the play was due to open, Nunn called on Stoppard to improve the dialogue: 'Bethell's [the translator's] advantage was that he could read Polish and mine was supposed to be that I could write dialogue.' Stoppard hesitated, telling Nunn that he didn't know any Polish. 'Never mind,' Nunn replied, 'we can buy Poles.'[36] And so he did, hiring a native Polish speaker to assist Stoppard in smoothing out the script.

The play opened at the Aldwych in London on 25 May 1966, Stoppard's first professional appearance in the West End. The leading man, Dudley Sutton, was in hospital and Nunn had to take on the role of Arthur for the first few nights. The papers commended his performance. Nunn, who joined the RSC in 1965, had his first directorial success with *The Revenger's Tragedy*, starring Ian Holm, Diana Rigg, Ian Richardson and Alan Howard. The production was hailed as revolutionary in terms of its acting, design and staging which was flamboyantly theatrical and anti-naturalistic.

Tango, a philosophical comedy, opens with a curious foreshadowing of Stoppard's later work, as Eugenia declares '(*with exaggerated flourish, throw[ing] a card on to the table)* There's my trumper, stick it up your jumper!'[37] In *Jumpers*, George's pet hare is named Thumper, and, of course, jumpers abound in the play, a curious connection with this early effort at adaptation. A rhyming game follows the card game, anticipating several moments in *Travesties*; interestingly, the game in *Tango* emphasizes the word 'boot', an important term for Stoppard. The ensuing repartee mixes philosophical, political and naturalistic detail, which would soon be evident in his own work. *After Magritte*, for example, replicates the bedlam and anarchy of the house in the play.

Stoppard was impatient to get *Rosencrantz and Guildenstern* produced, partly because a vogue for redefining and restructuring Shakespeare was in the theatrical air. Peter Brook's 1962 production of *Lear* with Paul Scofield drew on concepts outlined by Jan Kott in *Shakespeare Our Contemporary*, linking Shakespeare with Beckett. *The Wars of the Roses*, a seamless linking of a series of Shakespeare's history plays directed by

Peter Hall and others, including Peter Wood, was staged in 1964 by the Royal Shakespeare Company. Charles Marowitz's *Collage Hamlet* was the first work in Peter Brook and Marowitz's 'Theatre of Cruelty' season at LAMDA, part of the RSC's experimental season of 1963–4, and applied the ideas of Artaud on stagecraft and writing in which 'the play, the event itself, stands in place of a text'.[38] The July 1966 avant-garde production of Alfred Jarry's *Ubu Roi* at the Royal Court, with its brief Shakespearean parodies, further prefigured Stoppard's restructuring of Shakespeare. The slightly daft *MacBird*, a rewrite of *Macbeth* in terms of the Vietnam War by Barbara Garson, was also on in London at the time and drawing curious audiences; it opened on 3 April, eight days before *Rosencrantz and Guildenstern*'s première.

All these modern reworkings of Shakespeare were preceded by W. S. Gilbert's *Rosencrantz and Guildenstern, A Play*, which first appeared in the periodical *Fun* in 1874 but was not performed until 1891. An amateur performance in 1900 featured P. G. Wodehouse as Guildenstern; a benefit performance of 1904 included Gilbert, G. B. Shaw and Anthony Hope, the author of *The Prisoner of Zenda*, in the cast.[39] Oscar Wilde praised Rosencrantz and Guildenstern in *De Profundis* (1905) as an example of Shakespeare's subtlety of observation in the irony of their lack of knowledge yet participation in the action: 'they are what modern life has contributed to the antique idea of friendship . . . they are types fixed for all time. To censure them would show a lack of appreciation. They are merely out of their sphere: that is all.'[40] Although he did not directly draw on these sources, Stoppard was aware of this tradition.

When the studio season of the RSC was cancelled, Nunn passed *Rosencrantz and Guildenstern* on to the Oxford Playhouse, run by Frank Hauser. Hauser couldn't do it, but contacted a student group, the Oxford Players, who, under the auspices of the Oxford Theatre Group Productions, Ltd, presented the play at the Edinburgh Fringe Festival at the Cranston Street Hall on the Royal Mile from 24 August to 10 September 1966. The students, eager for a new work, took on the project, although their contract with Stoppard contained a crucial clause: ten per cent of all gross receipts from future productions of the play in English would be payable to the Oxford Theatre Group for a period of five years. It also stipulated that the author would complete certain revisions to the play 'which we have indicated' and deliver the revised text to them before 31 July 1966. Also outlined in the agreement was permission for Stoppard to attend rehearsals, the provision of free board and lodging while in Edinburgh and a first-class return train ticket from London to Edinburgh. Stoppard received no payment from the production. By contrast, when the National Theatre purchased the play the following year, he would receive a £250 advance on royalties and a licence fee from the National allowing them to perform the play for nine months.

The unknown playwright preparing for the opening of his unfinished play continued his practice of attending rehearsals, although when he arrived at the Cranston Street Hall on the Royal Mile he found chaos. The director and his leading lady/girlfriend had quarrelled and dropped out, followed by some of their supporters. The stage manager, Diana Cornforth, took over, although the remaining actors were mutinous. A few RADA students were rounded up to fill the gaps in the cast, but everyone was bewildered by the text, which seemed to have massive amounts of repetition and *non sequiturs* which Stoppard soon dismissed as a 'massive typing error'. It turned out that they *were* typing errors: a substitute typist had inadvertently copied over the same lines and pages several times and handed them round to the actors, who gamely worked over the script without questioning the logic. Ophelia, for example, had one line and one scream.[41]

When Stoppard arrived for a two-day visit, he made an immediate impression. Janet Watts, the original Ophelia, recalled that

> the company was camping in an old Freemasons Hall just below Edinburgh Castle. Here, early one morning, the unknown author showed up. As we descended blearily to breakfast, which was served in a dungeon, there he was: a thin, smiling man in a dark corner, already deep in conversation. He wore a grey tweed suit of a sort we had never seen. There wasn't a man or woman who didn't like that suit.[42]

Stoppard immediately sized up the situation and took control, more amused than annoyed to find that his script had been mistyped. He revised the two acts and 'was very light-hearted about the whole thing because I had a novel published in the same week that the play opened': he believed it was the novel that would make his reputation, and that the play would be 'of little consequence'.

When an actor queried a speech, Stoppard lyrically explained:

'that's poetry, man'. And it was, Janet Watts remembers, Stoppard's remark anticipating what David Mamet would later describe as the 'dirty secret of drama': 'the deep-down dirty secret of dramatic writing is that it's poetry, dramatic poetry. That's what makes a play work, in addition to the plot.'[43] Another actor in the production remembers that Stoppard was pretty determined 'to get the thing through. We went through several sleepless nights with him, trying to get it to sound the way he heard it in his head. He smoked Guards, chewed Hollywood gum, used a lot of curious expressions like "tough beans".' The minuscule stage and small number of actors, however, prevented them from even attempting the final scene.[44]

Stoppard's 1981 'Programme Note' for the Edinburgh Festival opening of *On the Razzle* recounted the circumstances of the 1966 world première:

> *Rosencrantz and Guildenstern Are Dead* received its first performance in the Cranston Street Hall on August 24th 1966. I had arrived in Edinburgh a few days previously to be shown the fruits of rehearsal. The Oxford Theatre Group had been labouring under certain disadvantages. The director had abandoned ship before we had left port. The actors were using scripts typed by somebody who knew somebody who could type. And the first thing that struck me was that there were a few unfamiliar cadences and some curious repetitions in the text they were using. For example Rosencrantz (now a solicitor in the north of England) might say, 'Well I can tell you I am sick to death of it. I don't care one way or another so why don't you make up your mind'. It turned out that such was the Oxford Theatre Group's touching faith in my play that they were faithfully rehearsing the typographical errors. The authentic Shakespearean phrase 'Glean what afflicts him' was coming out as 'Clean what afflicts him'. So we stopped and tidied all that up. At this point I discovered in myself my latent desire to stick my oar in a every five minutes during the rehearsals of my plays. Ever since Edinburgh in '66 I have always enjoyed most the business of the rehearsal room. This is not the same thing as wishing to direct my own plays. When it comes to the transfer from rehearsal room to theatre, the infamous technical weekend, I am invariably relieved not to have the responsibility. In Cranston Street in 1966, however, with an absent director, I suppose I must have done rather more in the final stages than

I have ever done since I can remember the extent to which I kept my oar in but anyone interested might get better information from Ophelia who now writes for the *Guardian* under the name of Janet Watts.

I think a couple of dozen people attended the first night. At any rate, there were not so many that the difficulty of seeing the stage from a flat-floored auditorium was very great. I had been insistent upon the play's being a comedy first and foremost, rather than a Comment on the Human Predicament. The amount of laughter which the play generated hardly justified my insistence. (I was vindicated in a backhanded way a couple of years later when the Paris production of which I had attended a slow and deeply serious final rehearsal turned out to be the play's first professional failure.)

Nothing very much seemed to be riding on the play's success on this occasion. I had a novel coming in the same week and was rather more concerned with the reception of that. So, for the first and last time, I attended my own first night without being in a state of great anxiety.[45]

The playbill for the production at the Cranston Street Hall listed Brian Daubney as director (a poster listed Andrew Snell, the director who decamped), David Marks as Rosencrantz and Clive Cable as Guildenstern. An author's note summarized Stoppard's career to date and stated that an adaptation of the play was planned for the London stage at the end of the year. The final lines from a paragraph headed 'The Play' in the playbill underscore the existential situation of the two protagonists: 'they have been thrust into a situation which is nothing to do with them and which they hardly understand.'[46]

As Stoppard recalled, Ronald Bryden was in the audience for an early performance because he slightly knew him:

He had bought a short story of mine when he had been editor of a swinging sixties magazine called *About Town*. I remember seeing Bryden walking up the pavement outside the hall after the play. He glanced at me and gave me what I thought was a rueful and perhaps quizzical look. This seems to fit in with the general bemusement which was the most common reaction to the play. 'What's it all about Tom?' was the headline over the review in the *Scottish Daily Express* the next morning. The *Glasgow Herald* had a piece the gist of which was that every year the Oxford Theatre Group brought something worth seeing to the Festival but on this occasion someone had blundered. I kept a stiff upper lip, after all my novel was published that morning and I thought rather well of it.[47]

> *– What were you doing?*
> *'Nothing' said Moon. 'I was trying to face one way or the*
> *other and I got confused and fell over.'*
> Stoppard, *Lord Malquist and Mr. Moon*

Stoppard's 192-page novel – the work he thought would make his name – appeared on 22 August 1966 in red boards with a sensational cover: against a black-and-white backdrop of modern London are two colourful characters in an elegant yellow coach, the driver, in a dramatic red outfit, and Lord Malquist, who leans from the coach door over his coat of arms. The rear jacket reveals that they are leading a procession which includes a gun-toting cowboy in yellow trousers on a black-and-white horse and, behind him, wearing a yellow robe and sandals and riding a donkey, an Irishman as the Risen Christ. This unusual procession appears to be moving through central London, perhaps towards a funeral; a Union Jack is at half mast. The jacket flap only partially illuminates these enigmatic figures, describing Lord Malquist as 'a dandy figure whose self-imposed role it is to live out in the 1960s the last flourish of a redundant aristocracy – which he does with the aid of a liveried equipage, a pet lion, numerous creditors and the philosophy that there is nothing to be done except to survive in whatever comfort one can command'. Or, as Malquist announces in the novel, he is withdrawing 'with style from the chaos'. In one sentence, Stoppard summarized the novel: it's about '24 hours in the day of Churchill's funeral and a quartet of characters who do a crazy quadrille through London and an Irish risen Christ – say no more . . .'[48] Stoppard's imagination was clearly running at high speed, which simultaneously challenged and threatened the publisher and reader alike.

The original press release prepared for the London papers by Stoppard's agents emphasized the productivity of the author: 'Writer TOM STOPPARD has a novel, a television play, a film documentary and a stage play all coming out within three days of each other this month', and then cites the appearance of the novel on 22 August, the

same day BBC2 was to show *A Separate Peace*, 'a 60-minute programme consisting of a film which explores grandmaster chess as the
pursuit of happiness and a play which treats the same theme'. On the
24th, the press release notes, the first production of his play
Rosencrantz and Guildenstern are Dead would première at the
Edinburgh Festival. The biographical details are brief: 'Tom Stoppard
is 29, married, with one child, and lives in London.'[49]

The novel's success was limited. Stoppard would comically say
that it was a bestseller in Venezuela and that some 681 copies were
sold. The statement of royalties dated 31 December 1966, however,
reveals that home sales were 481, export sales 207. The total is 688. He
was to receive an additional £100 on the basis of these sales, although
even after the success of *Rosencrantz and Guildenstern* sales did not
increase. A royalty statement for the six months ending 31 December
1968 indicates that only fourteen copies were sold in the UK and
thirty-five copies abroad. In June 1967, however, Blond managed to
sell the novel to Alfred Knopf in New York for $1,000, adding that
'your editor is a rather serious, quivery, sandy-haired, intense,
honourable young man and you should visit him when you are
there'.[50] The novel appeared in New York in April 1968.

Lord Malquist and Mr. Moon is a disjointed, comic work, theatrical,
dramatic, and even cinematic. No matter how outlandish, the novel
suggests that 'there is an explanation for everything', implausible as
things might first seem, an idea Stoppard would develop in his plays.[51]
Yet 'How can one be consistent about anything, since all the absolutes
discredit each other?' Moon asks.[52] This is the typical Stoppardian
position not of doubt, but the dilemma of being caught between
equally plausible reasons, which he would outline most famously in
the 1972 interview in which he explained that

> I write plays because writing dialogue is the only respectable way of
> contradicting yourself. I'm the kind of person who embarks on an
> endless leapfrog down the great moral issues. I put a position, rebut it,
> refute the rebuttal and rebut the refutation. Forever. Endlessly.

Two years earlier, Christopher Hampton had expressed this view on
stage in *The Philanthropist*, when the writer Braham explained that the
quality needed by a writer is 'self-obsession combined with the ability
to hold opposite points of view with equal conviction. The marvellous

thing is that if the internal logic is coherent, I know that even if I'm wrong, I'm right. Makes me what you might call an existentialist's nightmare.'[53]

Stoppard's novel offered the first statement of this position, which he would constantly reiterate:

> I distrust attitudes because they claim to have appropriated the whole truth and pose as absolutes. And I distrust the opposite attitude for the same reason . . . I take both parts . . . leapfrogging myself along the great moral issues, refuting myself and rebutting the refutation towards a truth that must be a compound of two opposite half-truths.[54]

Rosencrantz and Guildenstern embodied this attitude. The opportunity to argue both sides of a situation persuasively from both points of view was, he later claimed, the very reason he chose to write drama. 'I cannot commit myself to either side of a question,' Moon summarizes, 'because if you attach yourself to one or the other you disappear into it.'[55] This is both a fear and a strategy for Stoppard: the danger that he may be penalized for holding a direct opinion is mitigated by means of holding two positions, a form of survival. It is the core of his double act. He realized that it could be achieved through comedy because comedy enabled him to hold contradictory positions with a panache that elided any conflict. 'Camouflaged by display', a phrase Stoppard used in 1997, might best summarize this position which *Lord Malquist* first presents.[56]

Stoppard, who had studied classics at Pocklington, may have been aware of the classical roots of this technique: Aristotle's *Rhetoric* emphasizes the positive strategy of arguing both sides of a question because in this manner one will know the truth more clearly. Cicero linked this approach to epistemology: arguing both sides of a question (*disputatio in utramque partem*) helps to acknowledge the difficulty of arriving at a single truth.[57] Stoppard may not have recalled these sources, but the roots of his stance, which have characterized so much of his work, have ancient origins.

Moon, the pseudo-biographer, is also the prototype for several biographers in Stoppard's work, repeatedly taking everything down and getting it all wrong. Bernard in *Arcadia* and Eldon Pike in *Indian Ink* are later embodiments of this well-meaning but wrong-headed recorder. The opening scene of the novel makes this clear as Moon distorts, fragments and divides Lord Malquist's polished phrases; in the opening sequence, he tries to write down the words of Lord Malquist as the two travel in a coach and four, but gets them all wrong. (The scene is a parody of Oscar Wilde, who, in 1895, was driven to his trial in a two-horse carriage equipped with a brilliantly outfitted coachman and a powdered page.) Stoppard begins the novel by showing how inept biographers can be, even as secretaries. The comic adventures of the pair during their carriage ride, which includes a woman hurling herself under the carriage wheels, also burlesques St Evremonde's coach ride in Dickens's *A Tale of Two Cities*.

Lord Malquist and Mr. Moon contains a surprising number of passages that express attitudes Stoppard would expand throughout his work, especially in the first decade and a half of his career. As if outlining Stoppard's reaction to events, the narrator at one moment writes that every response to action gave Moon the feeling that 'reality was just outside his perception. If he made a certain move, changed the angle of his existence to the common ground, logic and absurdity would separate. As it was he couldn't pin them down.' 'Everything reaches me at slightly the wrong angle,' Moon laments, a remark that might be applied to Stoppard's early dramatic vision.[58] Happiness, Stoppard would later claim, using another physical analogy, is 'equilibrium' achieved by 'shifting your weight'. Stoppard himself referred to the characters in *Lord Malquist* as having 'a sort of eccentricity that moves them into a Surrealistic context, but the book isn't in the least Surrealistic. Nothing in it is unreal or distorted, although some of it is heightened to a degree of absurdity. I think that realism has room for absurdity.'[59] Again, the double act: the novel is and is not surreal.

The position is complicated by the belief that

> hardly anyone behaves naturally any more, they all behave the way they think they are supposed to be, as if they'd read about themselves or seen themselves at the pictures . . . It's even impossible to think naturally because opinion has been set out for you to read back. Originality has been used up. And yet faith in one's uniqueness dies hard.[60]

This condition is something Stoppard would challenge, criticize and revise throughout his writing life, comically summarized as 'a lifetime in the cause of ambivalence'.[61]

The view of biography contained in the novel outlines a position consistent with Stoppard's later writing. Essentially, it is the conviction that biography can never accurately recover the past, that facts are as elusive as atmosphere. Therefore, if you forget or misinterpret facts, you should not panic. When Moon loses his notebook, Malquist explains to him that such facts are mere 'technicalities': 'the secret of biography is to let your imagination flourish in key with your subject's. In this way you will have a poetic truth that is the jewel for which facts are merely the setting.' All one can hope for, as Moon tries to write down what Malquist has just said to him in the opening paragraph of the novel, are 'the tail-ends of recollection ... [reproducing] *the comic inaccuracy of his remark*'. But biographers, too, can become frustrated: 'Moon had relapsed into interviewing himself,' just as Stoppard often did during the early days of his journalistic and dramatic career.[62]

The novel introduced the names Moon and Birdboot, a liveried butler,[63] both of which names came to prominence in subsequent texts such as the radio play *M is for Moon*, the television script *Another Moon called Earth* and *The Real Inspector Hound*. Stoppard's fascination with the name Moon originated in Bristol when he saw Paul Newman in *Left-Handed Gun*. At one moment in the film, the moon is reflected in a horse trough. The drunken cowboys start shooting at the reflection and Newman shouts the word 'Moon', also the name of one of the characters. At the time, Stoppard was writing the first draft of *The Real Inspector Hound* (which at one stage went under the working title 'Moon's Dream Murder of Higgs') and the name seemed to fit one of the critics.[64] In *Jumpers*, a few years later, the moon becomes an elaborate conceit and the constant musical fixation of Dotty.

Birdboot is a variation of William Boot, the pseudonym Stoppard used for some of his articles for *Scene*, borrowed from the disoriented journalist of Waugh's *Scoop*. Boot had already appeared in the comic radio play *The Dissolution of Dominic Boot*. Stoppard himself distinguished between the two recurring names: Moon characters are acted upon and suffer from inner conflicts. Boot characters act and are more aggressive. These divisions later developed into the 'Who' and 'Whom' established by Lenin in *Travesties*: again, the difference is between those who do and those to whom it is done. Occasionally, however, the two fuse: 'I'm a Moon, myself,' Stoppard has said. 'Confusingly, I used the name Boot, from Evelyn Waugh, as a pseudonym in journalism, but that was because Waugh's Boot is really a Moon, too.'[65]

About a year after *Lord Malquist* appeared, Stoppard prepared an on-spec screenplay version. In the draft, Stoppard parodied his own efforts with Shakespeare as Malquist describes the book *he* is trying to write:

> a monograph really – on *Hamlet* as a source book of titles, a subject which does not interest me in the slightest but it is the duty of an artist to leave the world decorated by some trifling ornament.

Another passage expresses every writer's frustration and hope, especially that of the young Stoppard: Moon deflects Jane's question as to how much he had written of his history of the world by explaining that 'sometimes I feel that if you got it really sorted out, and saw it all, from the right angle, then you could get it all into one paragraph, if you could just get it right'. Declaring that he did not mean to write a history of the world – at the beginning, it was to be only of himself – he admits, in a characteristic Stoppardian reflection, that 'the rest of the world, and all time, bit by bit connected itself. I was always looking for the explanation of the explanation. And one day I suddenly realised that without taking it all in, the whole of it, there was no explanation for me.'[66]

Stoppard's cavalier claim that his novel would make his reputation was misleading. His desire to become a novelist was secondary to his hopes of being a dramatist, although a novel published in London was more likely to gain attention than a complex play staged in a church basement at a fringe festival in Scotland. Yet his publisher's lack of enthusiasm for the work, plus disappointment over its initial rejection by German and US publishers, did not provide much encouragement. By contrast, drama seemed to offer more hope.

Beyond the wrinkled tights
Michael Codron, 1966

Initial response to *Rosencrantz and Guildenstern* in Edinburgh was unequivocal: the local papers and some of the London dailies hated it. Allan Wright in *The Scotsman* called it 'no more than a clever revue sketch which has got out of hand'. Stoppard fails to enlighten; the 'play is peppered with incriminating phrases that could be taken down and used in evidence against it'. Douglas F. Blake in *Stage and Television*

Today felt that the 'basic idea was stretched beyond its limits by the large amount of verbal padding and repetition'.[67] Harold Hobson in the *Sunday Times* thought that 'the result is perhaps merely a literary and theatrical curiosity, offering neither guarantee nor bar to Mr. Stoppard's future as a dramatist'. Michael Codron, who would later produce most of Stoppard's West End work, recalled that 'it was difficult to see beyond the wrinkled tights'.[68]

Stoppard, however, didn't mind such barbs: he still pinned his hopes and future reputation on his novel:

> So when I got on the train to come south on Sunday morning, and opened the *Observer* and saw a photograph of myself captioned 'Most promising debut since Arden' my first thought after the shock of pleasure was – how very odd, never knew Arden had written a novel. But the photograph was not in the fiction page, it was in Bryden's column. There were two immediate consequences to Bryden's review. The Cranston Street Hall started packing out – alas I never saw the production in those happy conditions - and the next day there was a telegram from Kenneth Tynan at the National Theatre asking to read the play.[69]

Bryden recalled that his decision to view the play stemmed more from curiosity than an assignment. He also reasserted that he certainly did not discover Stoppard. He had known him from London as a contributor to *About Town* and *Scene*. He knew he was a 'clever fellow' and something of a playwright, since he had had a number of television shows produced. He had popped in to see what the ingenious Stoppard might be up to, and he still remembered the discomfort and dampness of the space – plus the jokes. The review stressed the originality of the play and the marvellous word play.[70]

Entitled 'Wyndy Excitements', Bryden's comments in the *Observer* – actually only the final three paragraphs of a general survey – featured a photo of a youthful and slightly bemused Stoppard, head bent to the right with his hand touching his forehead as he smiles at the camera. The caption actually reads 'Tom Stoppard: the most brilliant debut since John Arden's', which is also the final line of the review. Bryden summarized the Festival's various offerings, noting that 'the real action was up the wynd and down the stair, in church halls and school cellars' as agents, critics, drama teachers tried to spot next year's talent. The most expensive production was Frank Dunlop's 'pop theatre production of *The Winter's Tale* at the Assembly Hall' with Laurence Harvey as a disappointing Leontes. Equally unsuccessful was the Scottish adaptation of Aristophanes' *The Birds*, performed in a Scots brogue. A programme by a group from the University of Southern California fared no better: 'their material is unequal but their confidence is magnificent and their professionalism formidable'. Finally, Bryden turned to Stoppard.

He began by declaring *Rosencrantz and Guildenstern* 'the best thing at Edinburgh so far': 'Mr Stoppard has taken up the vestigial lives of Hamlet's two Wittenberg cronies and made out of them an existentialist fable unabashedly indebted to "Waiting for Godot", but as witty and vaulting as Beckett's original is despairing.' The remaining two paragraphs of the review, because it was so influential, should be quoted in full:

> The play does not pretend to know more of the pair's lives than Shakespeare: its point is, neither do they. While the violent drama at Elsinore unrolls off-stage, occasionally sucking them into its fury, they spin coins endlessly in ante-rooms, wondering what is going on, what will happen next, what will become of them? They sense that they should escape, but what to? The tragedy of Denmark offers them the only significance, the only identity life has held out to them – it offers them roles.
>
> Behind the fantastic comedy, you feel allegoric purposes move: is this our relation to our century, to the idea of death, to war? But while the tragedy unfurls in this comic looking-glass, you're too busy with its stream of ironic invention, metaphysical jokes and linguistic acrobatics to pursue them. Like *Love's Labour's Lost* this is erudite comedy, punning, far-fetched, leaping from depth to dizziness. It's the most brilliant debut by a young playwright since John Arden.[71]

Stoppard suddenly found he needed to reinvent himself as a dramatist, not a novelist. He recalled that the audience received the play politely 'rather than with hilarity', but that after the Bryden review appeared, 'people tended to laugh at it rather more'.[72] David Marks, playing Rosencrantz, was awakened on his camp bed that Sunday morning by someone with the *Observer* review: 'We all just gaped at it in disbelief. We knew, some of us, what a good play it was. We didn't expect anyone else to realise that, though.'[73]

CHAPTER 8

THE OLD VIC AND A NEW PLAYWRIGHT

Je suis, *it seems to be saying*, ergo sum. *But is that enough?*
Stoppard, *The Real Inspector Hound*

Stoppard was not the only reader of Ronald Bryden's Edinburgh review. In London, Kenneth Tynan, literary manager at the National, sent a telegram to Stoppard at Vincent Square Mansions. When Stoppard returned, he found the message requesting a copy of the play: 'I came back to London and there was the telegram from Tynan to my delight and amazement. I had never met him so I was thrilled just to go and see him.'[1] Uplifted by the telegram, Stoppard sent another script to Tynan and was shortly summoned to a meeting with him and Laurence Olivier, who was at first less enthusiastic than Tynan.[2]

Recalling his first meeting with Tynan in his tiny office in the temporary quarters of the National, wooden huts off Aquinas Street, Stoppard remembered that he was quite awed and that Tynan had 'an endearing stutter. I was so nervous about meeting him that I found to my horror that I was mimicking it! . . . We sat stuttering at each other, mainly about his shirt which was pale lemon and came from Turnbull and Asser in Jermyn Street. This was in the late summer of 1966 when we wore roll-neck shirts.'[3] Tynan had been literary manager of the National Theatre since its establishment in 1963, following a striking career as a precocious, knife-sharp theatre critic. 'Rouse tempers, goad and lacerate, raise whirlwinds' was the quotation – Tynan's own – pinned above his writing desk. His tart views of actors and plays earned him a reputation as uncompromising, John Mortimer referring to him as an 'immaculate left wing hedonist'. He championed Brecht, Beckett and Czech playwrights, notably Havel.[4]

At the National, Tynan was responsible for recommending,

commissioning, and adapting plays and referred to himself as 'house critic'. He articulated his vision for the National, which he summarized as the presentation of 'the widest possible selection of good plays from all periods and places'.[5] The theatre, he emphasized, would resist specialization. However, Tynan also recognized the shortcomings of the National, telling Laurence Olivier in August 1966 that 'in three years we haven't had a single top-level (*your* level) discovery with a single new author'. They had an obligation, Tynan argued, to 'make the theatre a place of contemporary excitement'. A year earlier, he had pleaded with Olivier to seek something 'experimental' and 'mainly verbal in its appeal. If possible, it should be an English-speaking premiere.'[6] *Rosencrantz and Guildenstern* fit the bill exactly.

Stoppard had long admired Tynan's writing and a friendship quickly formed between the two, one point of contact being their mutual love of theatrical self-presentation and the flamboyant. Tynan was impressed with Stoppard and immediately after the success of *Rosencrantz and Guildenstern*, asked him to prepare an English adaptation of Ibsen's *The Pretenders* for a production proposed to Ingmar Bergman in June 1967 (it didn't happen). The following year, Tynan asked Stoppard for some last-minute rewriting on the controversial production of Rolf Hochhuth's *Soldiers* which Lord Chandos, chairman of the National's Board, vetoed but which Tynan finally produced in the West End in 1968 after it had played in Berlin, Toronto and New York. Stoppard would often visit Tynan at home, sometimes joining him in his bedroom for coffee, perched on the end of the bed. Tynan, in turn, wrote one of the most influential and revealing profiles of Stoppard, which appeared in the *New Yorker* in December 1977. Three years later, Tynan died at age fifty-three and Stoppard, the final speaker at the memorial service in St Paul's Church, Covent Garden, celebrated Tynan's wit, intelligence, toughness of mind and style: 'his paragraphs – paragraphs were the units of his prose, not sentences – were written to outlast the witness'.[7]

Stoppard's relationship with Olivier was more distant, as one might expect. As the most distinguished actor in England and one of the last actor-managers, Olivier lent lustre and gravitas to the National. But he could be imperious. Peter Nichols, among others, referred to him as an 'autocrat', who, without Tynan, would probably produce only 'high-toned revivals'. Olivier and Tynan did not always see eye to eye, partly because the actor was jealous of Tynan's intelligence and erudition. Olivier called him 'his reference book and his education'. Yet Olivier knew Tynan admired him. When Tynan proposed himself to be the literary manager of the National, Olivier at first boiled over at the idea. His wife, Joan Plowright, however, told him to reconsider: the combination of great actor and rebellious critic would have immense appeal. When he agreed to Tynan's suggestion, Olivier appended the note: 'GOD ANYthing to get you off that *Observer!*'[8] But at times Tynan seemed too blunt in his criticisms, as when he complained to George Devine about his production of Beckett's *Play*. Olivier intervened, telling Tynan

> I like you, I like having you with me, apart from it rather tickling me to have you with me, but you can be too fucking tactless for words. . . . you should realise your gifts for what they are and your position for what it is and like a wise jockey not always let these things have their head.

But Tynan could also be self-deprecating. When a fan told him he read his work religiously, Tynan expressed the wish that he would read him more 'agnostically'.[9]

Tynan's and Olivier's temperaments were complementary: Olivier's pragmatic, empirical views, shaped by expediency, balanced Tynan's visionary and encompassing sense of world theatre. Often referred to as 'Sir', Olivier was the centre of the company and admired and feared by actors for his obsession with technical detail as much as his acting ability. The company thought Tynan aloof. John Stride, soon to be the National's first Rosencrantz, reported that everyone respected Tynan's critical ability but there never seemed to be any personal gossip about him. He didn't invite friendship and was less comfortable than Olivier in the rehearsal hall. Stoppard told Nichols that he valued only Tynan's opinion, not Olivier's.[10]

But if Tynan praised, Olivier criticized. It was Olivier who told Stoppard that he had omitted a key scene in *Hamlet*, the one where Rosencrantz and Guildenstern accost Hamlet after he has hidden Polonius's body:

> It arose because Olivier pointed out that when Claudius came on and instructed them to find Hamlet, who happened to have killed

Polonius, it was the one time in the play when they were given an actual specific duty to fulfil, and it was a pity that it had been lost in the sort of cinematic cut we had then. So I wrote that scene. It's there, and I'm glad it's there.

Stoppard also recalled one meeting with Olivier and Tynan that went on until 5 a.m., where quite a lot of things were cut from the play. 'Mind you, I put a lot of them back later,' he confessed.[11] In subsequent years, their relationship remained polite but perfunctory, Olivier congratulating Stoppard on his hits while making occasional requests for new work. Stoppard would feel a greater connection with Olivier's successor, Peter Hall.

How and why did the National choose *Rosencrantz and Guildenstern*? Excitement over the play and its comic link with Shakespeare's great tragedy was one reason. The cancellation of the all-male *As You Like It*, which was to have been directed by John Dexter, was another. The production ran into trouble and was cut, to Dexter's great disappointment. There was suddenly a gap in the schedule from April, and the Stoppard play neatly filled it.

Apart from the practical exigency, there was the realization by Tynan, and latterly Olivier, that they had neglected their mandate to find younger playwrights and bring new voices to the National. Comedies had also been absent from their early seasons. The National lacked a young audience and a reputation for experimentation, unlike the RSC. Now, the timing was right and, at the urging of Tynan, Olivier agreed to do the play. Suddenly, the untried Stoppard became the first unknown playwright to be produced by the National and he unexpectedly found himself sandwiched between Strindberg and Chekhov: the former's *The Dance of Death* was to precede and the latter's *Three Sisters* was to follow *Rosencrantz and Guildenstern* in the spring of 1967. Stoppard's loyalty to the RSC was not forgotten. Stoppard promised his next play to Trevor Nunn; contractual arrangements with the National, however, meant it would actually be the one after next, which turned out to be *Travesties*.

Unlike the Strindberg, which starred Olivier, and the Chekhov, which featured Joan Plowright, the principal actors for *Rosencrantz and Guildenstern* were relatively unknown. John Stride, a proven member of the National's company who had recently been cast in the cancelled production of *As You Like It*, was now reassigned as Rosencrantz, and the lesser-known Edward Petherbridge was Guildenstern. Petherbridge had been a hit as Ferdinand Gadd in Pinero's *Trelawny of the Wells* at the National in 1965. The director of *Rosencrantz and Guildenstern* would be Derek Goldby, a young assistant director in the company, recommended by John Dexter to Olivier, although Goldby had never before directed a major production. Educated at Cambridge, Goldby had invited Arnold Wesker to his university production of *The Kitchen*; Wesker, impressed, recommended him to John Dexter, who was then at the English Stage Company, so Goldby went to the Royal Court as Dexter's assistant for a year. Work in repertory theatre and freelancing followed, until he rejoined Dexter at the National.

Assistant directors usually took understudy rehearsals or occasionally rehearsed a second cast or revival, but when he heard that the National was going to do *Rosencrantz and Guildenstern*, Goldby wrote to Olivier to ask if he could direct. Olivier called him in and scathingly demanded to know 'how I dared to write to him then threw a copy of the play at me and told me to get on with it'.[12] Goldby worked for six weeks on the play alone and then for eight with the cast. This was a big step for the fledgling director, although his selection suggested that the play was to be seen as a 'stop-gap' production with a youthful team filling in for the postponed *As You Like It*. Stoppard was twenty-nine, Petherbridge and Stride were both thirty-one, while Goldby was the youngest, at twenty-six.

Olivier's casting decisions reflected a view of the play that stressed relative unknowns to play the parts of unknowns. No stars were to be in it, although Stride was a recognized name at the National. But *two* unknowns would be simply too risky, Olivier told Petherbridge. At the casting of *Rosencrantz and Guildenstern*, Olivier asked Stoppard about the Player. Stoppard told him he should be sneaky, snake-like. Olivier looked dubious, disregarded Stoppard's wishes and assigned the part to the six-foot-four Graham Crowden who 'roars like a lion'. It was the right decision, Stoppard later realized.[13]

Stride recalled that they 'started rehearsing as a sort of cheap production thrown on at the National Theatre'. To keep expenses to a minimum, the production used costumes pulled from storage – the elaborate, romantic though partially faded Victorian–Jacobean outfits used in Peter O'Toole's 1963 *Hamlet*. The fadedness appealed to Goldby, who wanted to create a mysterious, dream-like aura. The set was equally spare: outlining the action were the walls (three flies with a raised platform in the middle) of a cobwebbed, weed-choked Gothic palace which descended around the two principals after the opening scene. Goldby remembered the detailed attention to individual lines expressed by Olivier when Stoppard, Olivier, Tynan and Goldby reviewed the script: 'anytime anybody was bothered, quite often it was Olivier; he'd say, what about that line, or what did that line mean . . . and so we solved various problems'.[14]

Olivier occasionally dropped in unexpectedly at rehearsals, which took place in the temporary quarters of the National on the South Bank behind Stamford Street, not far from the company's future home. In a large rehearsal hall with pillars in the middle of the space, the cast ran through its lines. On one occasion, when Olivier – whose presence always altered the atmosphere – was leaving the rehearsal after about fifteen minutes, he stopped at the door and handed a note to Derek Goldby, then, with a flourish and a dramatic pause, declaimed in a clarion voice: 'Just the odd pearl', and swept out.[15]

Few in the cast doubted the brilliance of *Rosencrantz and Guildenstern*, although there was frequent disagreement over interpretation. Goldby, for example, wanted Guildenstern to be portrayed in the long first scene before the players' entrance as a rabbit, lost in a warren, 'feverishly exploring each cul-de-sac'. Petherbridge felt he should be presented more as an ominous ground-swell with an undertow of anxiety beneath a rapid 'top text' presented with verbal skill.[16] The aim was to represent the gesture of thought. Petherbridge, explaining his role to a young actor preparing a school performance of the part, described the characters as being in 'a prolonged stand up comic double act – shot through with shafts of something poetic (a wonderfully heady combination)'. However, Guildenstern's 'petty impatience or long suffering "patience" or dead pan irritation with Rosencrantz is always the comic pin prick in the bubble of this attempted intellectual or philosophical quest for explanations and solutions'.[17]

A conflict did emerge, however, between the director's vision and the actors'. In rehearsal, it became apparent that Goldby's framework for moves and scenes was not working, but the director wasn't adapting. Stride and Petherbridge returned to the text and its stage directions, 'not only for physical movements, [but] for pauses, timing'. They also turned more and more 'from the director to Tom Stoppard'. They found that Stoppard actually visualized a scene and heard it from the actor's perspective: he has 'a tremendous instinct for what works in the theatre', Stride stated. When the meaning of passages still eluded the actors, Stoppard could explain them, and when he altered the ending, he actually consulted the actors, which was a rare example of 'artistic intercourse', according to Stride.

Petherbridge confirmed the actor director dichotomy. Goldby pressured the actors 'into all kinds of timing and ways of doing it that were not within the spirt of the score that has been written, so to speak'. Stoppard, however, combined a sense of the problems 'with a knowledge of how those characters ought to be played'. Goldby himself admitted that he was more concerned with the staging aspect of the production than with the 'score'. His approach was entirely from a theatrical point of view, the fantasy side of the work, not its meaning or themes. 'I approached the play basically from a kind of dream point of view . . . the overall visual interpretation of the play was . . . more my contribution than the interpretation and word side.'[18] He thought in terms of interlocking themes rather than arguments, the way Stoppard understood the work. This early split between directors and actors who failed to share the same interpretative vision of a Stoppard work meant that the directors of early Stoppard became 'scenographers', while Stoppard worked directly with the actors in the major roles. This division continued until Stoppard and Peter Wood joined forces in 1972 for *Jumpers*, and the two quickly discovered a synergy that led to a long-standing textual and theatrical collaboration.

Part of the challenge of *Rosencrantz and Guildenstern* is one shared by both actors: 'It's an extended game of table tennis which you help each other to win. You must *both* win, and be sensitive to the rhythm of each other's play.' Act Three, Petherbridge warns, might be the same old routine all over again but there is a new character, the boat: 'With the boat comes a new dramatic suspense for them [the audience] as to what will now happen to you.'[19] Yet difficulties with the text remained; not the least, the ending.

How to conclude the play remained problematic and a great deal of work was done on it during the last two or three weeks of rehearsals. Tynan himself proposed several alternative endings for the text. On a sheet dated 9 March 1967, he wrote:

1. Blackout after Guil last speech; he exits. End with Horatio still speaking after scene at court

2. Blackout after Guilds speech lights come up with Ros and Guild trapped on stage in court scene as members of Ambassadors retinue. We play through the end of Hamlet. Afterward new dialogue between Ros and Guild covering the following points:
'terrible business, casual slaughters, deaths put on by cunning'
How many deaths? At least 8; they pile up in conversation.
Let's go then. Where? Home to England. Something to suggest that they can barely remember where they are from[20]

Another version, the one that actually appears in the first edition of the play published in May 1967, but which was dropped in rehearsal and performances, had the Ambassadors comically totalling up the dead, interrupted by a distant knocking. Someone, banging on a shutter, indistinctly calls out two names that *could* be Rosencrantz or Guildenstern. One of the Ambassadors ends the play by mysteriously remarking, 'better go and see what it's all about'.[21] This circular ending appeared to restart the play, but late in rehearsal, Stoppard cut it and eliminated the scene from all subsequent performances and editions, allowing Shakespeare, through the speech of Horatio ending with 'all this can I/truly deliver', the last word. A gradual fade into darkness (rather than light as the original ending had it) follows and the music comes up. At the Old Vic, the effect was dramatic since the stage was lit in a manner to stress indeterminate distances, with an asymmetrical rostrum buttressed by a flight of steps at either end. Blackness surrounded all at the end, visually reminding the audience of Guildenstern's final words: 'Well, we'll know better next time. Now you see me, now you – (*and he disappears*)'.[22]

Despite his inexperience, Goldby made some wonderful decisions with the production, from the simplicity of the stage with its minimal props – those who saw it also recalled the haunting music by Marc Williamson and the large barrels at the end – as well as the marvellous mime work initiated by the Associate Director, Claude Chagrin. The hints of a spare, Gothic set to suggest Elsinore equalled the sense of lost terrain that enfolded Rosencrantz and Guildenstern in a dark, nebulous nowhere. This was set off against what Petherbridge called the 'champagne impact' of the language, especially in the opening scene, which required the actors to balance the comic style of vaudevillians with that of period Shakespeare actors from the 1950s in doublet and hose, and the humorous manner of Morecambe and Wise, the popular television comedy duo. Stoppard, at one point, thought the latter would have been well cast in the play.

Stride and Petherbridge, however, possessed an innate sense of deportment, a certain idiom and style of utterance that embodied Shakespearean traditions but at the same time the talent to segue in and out of that world and Stoppard's with differences in syntax, diction and rhythm. An existential unicorn might be one way of imagining the yoking of dissimilar but not contrasting worlds. The question the actors constantly faced was: 'how would we make all of this *part* of the same thing?' Petherbridge knew this would be the challenge from the moment Olivier, with his car and driver waiting outside his tiny Aquinas Street office, personally handed him the script in February 1967, murmuring 'marvellous part, marvellous play'. Olivier departed and Petherbridge read it through on the bus back to Peckham, where he was then living.[23] The world of the clown, gagster, variety theatre, costume Shakespeare and modern drama had some-how to make sense to the actors and the audience.

The six-week rehearsal period divided itself between the temporary rehearsal hall, part of the dreary Aquinas Street complex, once the headquarters of the Coal Board, and the rehearsal hall above the theatre in the Old Vic, where several large windows provided strong natural light. Two weeks before opening, a run-through of Acts One and Two without the book resulted in a large number of cuts as Olivier and Tynan watched; Act Three had not yet been finalised, although Stoppard showed no panic. Because the National was a repertory company, the cast was not allowed on to the actual stage until the weekend preceding the final week of rehearsal – and then only for one day. On the Sunday before the Tuesday opening, the cast had a full run-through on the nearly completed set. On the Monday, a full dress rehearsal took place before an invited audience, filling all 880 seats in the Old Vic. And on Tuesday, 11 April 1967, the play opened. There were no previews which would have permitted the cast a week or so to work out last-minute details. They would come about only with Michael Codron's production of *The Real Inspector Hound* in 1968.

Two days before the opening, Stoppard gave an interview to the *Observer*, outlining the background to the play and his view of theatre. He explained that the work began as a burlesque, 'Saturday-night-in-the-green-room stuff', and even though its original conception changed, it was still a comedy. This, he stated, no doubt resulted from 'a certain insecurity in me. I'm afraid of losing the audience if I say something serious. I don't trust my credentials – and humour is a universal cement.' Stoppard would maintain this view and insisted on the need for comedy at the beginning of each of his works throughout his career. He also revealed that his 'disbelief is never suspended in the theatre . . . but when a thing is funny it's easier to accept'. When asked about his work habits, he also admitted that his chief 'discipline is a cross pollination of poverty, deadlines and the guilt of *not* writing'.[24]

In a much later commentary, Stoppard revealed that he wanted to call the play 'Exit Rosencrantz and Guildenstern'. 'But I couldn't expose myself to the danger of anybody thinking that I'd thought that a plural subject would take a singular verb. And try as I might, I could not bring myself to believe that "Exeunt Rosencrantz and Guildenstern" would be universally understood.'[25] The original title from the Edinburgh production stayed.

If this is a masterpiece, my name is Rosenbaum.
Lord Chandos

The scepticism of Lord Chandos, Chairman of the Board of the National Theatre, was not directed at Stoppard.[26] But *Rosencrantz and Guildenstern* had its detractors and several first-night reviews complained of its intellectual chatter, lack of action and tendency to plagiarize. But most reviewers were ecstatic; one of the reasons was the play's contrast with the lacklustre productions that had plagued the National. *Rosencrantz and Guildenstern* was a hit, 'a very palpable hit', as Osric declares in *Hamlet*. The verve of the actors, the liveliness of the direction and the fireworks of the script made the work an instant success. Peter Lewis praised the National for pulling off 'its biggest gamble to date – a winner at 66 to 1'.[27] Harold Hobson (echoing Ronald Bryden's review from the previous August) made this absolutely clear in his opening paragraph from the *Sunday Times*:

> If the history of drama is chiefly the history of dramatists – and it is – then the National Theatre's production of *Rosencrantz and Guildenstern are Dead* by Tom Stoppard is the most important event in the British professional theatre of the last nine years.

He elaborates in paragraph two, calling the work 'the best first London-produced play written by a British author since Harold Pinter's *The Birthday Party* in 1958'. Stressing the ingenuity, complexity and theatrical mastery, Hobson celebrates the work on every level and compares Stoppard favourably to Beckett and Feydeau. But there was still a tendency to see Stoppard as an overnight sensation. He countered this by recalling his long apprenticeship and the fact that he was nearly thirty: 'I didn't feel young, actually. I felt behind schedule.'[28]

Ronald Bryden, revisiting the play in its London incarnation, exceeded his previous praise, now calling the work 'the most brilliant dramatic debut of the sixties. It's an undergraduate joke carried to the exhilarating power of poetry':

> the shortest cut to grasping its quality is to imagine the inspired quartet of 'Beyond the Fringe' pushing their Shakespeare parody on to the bleak metaphysical uplands of Samuel Beckett.

The Edinburgh production dazzled 'with its verbal fireworks and unashamedly literary university wit . . . At the Old Vic, the power of imagination behind it flowers in Derek Goldby's inventive production.' The movement of the court, swirling on and off the stage for their bits of Shakespeare, contrasted physically with the stationary postures of Rosencrantz and Guildenstern. Stride and Petherbridge played their roles with less of a Laurel and Hardy knockabout manner than their Edinburgh equivalents but with a far more haunting quality. Bryden now saw Stoppard's contribution as broader than rewriting Shakespeare: it was the importation of 'the Continental genre of modernised myth, on the lines of "Ondine" and "Electra", Sartre's "Flies" and Cocteau's "Infernal Machine".'[29]

Emphasizing the contrast between the preciseness of the language and the indistinct setting were the costumes. Guildenstern was in peacock blue, Rosencrantz in brown velvet and wrinkled woollen stockings. The members of the court, in silvers and brocades, looked magisterial. Graham Crowden, as the Player, was striking in his tongued orange and scarlet flashing out of the darkness. The contrast between the 'sunny acceptance' of Rosencrantz and the anxiety of Guildenstern, who finds his cerebral concepts tested against experience, was dramatically visualised.

Some theatre-goers, however, dissented. Petherbridge offered an explanation:

> If you're not up on the high wire with him [Stoppard] thinking I might fall off but for the moment I think I understand this terrain up here and I'm very glad to have this view, dizzy as it is, but if one minute you do fall off, well then you've had it with him.

Stoppard witnessed such a fall on the first night: 'early in the first act, a man sitting in front of me turned to his companion and said "I do wish they would get *on* with it".That finished it for me. I went to the pub and never came back.' At the interval, Anthony Smith found him drinking brandy at the bar. 'Why are you getting drunk?' 'The play's not working. They're not laughing. I never again will write a play without a guaranteed laugh in the first 30 seconds!'[30] However, after a first-night party, Stoppard read the universally favourable press notices by dashing up and down Fleet Street from one machine-room to the next.

Joe Orton attended the dress rehearsal with his companion, Kenneth Halliwell:

> V. interesting. A wonderful idea. I'd give anything to have such an original idea. Unfortunately the only drama in the play is by Shakespeare. There kept being the usual dialogue between two bored people waiting for something to happen and playing games to while away the time. This derived from *Look Back in Anger* and *Waiting for Godot* in equal parts . . . The interest in this play was that the two who have the duologues are Rosencrantz and Guildenstern . . . Knowing nothing of the plot of *Hamlet*, they have to discover the situation for themselves. This is fascinating and terribly funny until the end of the second act . . . the third act is the modern author's invention (apart

from the pirate episode) and it isn't good enough. In fact it isn't there. What a wonderful idea, though. How I wish I'd stumbled onto it.[31]

Four months later, on 9 August 1967, Orton would be murdered by Kenneth Halliwell. The year before, his play *Loot* won the 1966 Evening Standard Award for best play. *Rosencrantz and Guildenstern* would win in 1967.

Another early audience member was the comic actor Kenneth Williams. He attended in autumn 1967 with Maggie Smith and was equally disgruntled, as his diary for 30 November records:

> Maggie S. came at 6.30 & drove me to the Old Vic where we saw Rosencrantz and Guildenstern are Dead. I have never sat through such tedious boredom. I felt the anger rising within me. By the interval I was furious. Maggie asked me if I was enjoying it & I said I was bored to tears. She said, 'Well, it's a free country, you can leave right now, if you want to . . .' which I thought was awful.

Was what she said awful, or the idea of leaving the play after the interval? Three days later, Williams vowed never to visit the Old Vic again.[32]

> Rosencrantz and Guildenstern *is about Hamlet as seen by*
> *two people driving past Elsinore.*
> Stoppard, 1972

Despite his rave reviews and sudden celebrity, Stoppard sought some balance and perspective:

> it wasn't the overnight event it might sound. I'd been writing plays for five or six years before. Had one optioned but not produced, another given a student production and one or two on radio. I'd also just written my one and only novel and I think I had greater expectations of that than anything else.[33]

After *Rosencrantz and Guildenstern* opened, Stoppard realized its overall similarity to the situation of the writer. The predicament of the characters coincides with that of a playwright who faces the unknown every time he writes. This was one of the reasons the play worked so well, he believed: 'Two guys in there and there's no plot . . . they have to fill three pages and I have to fill three pages' and there's nothing – 'so they end up playing word games, spinning coins, speculating on eternals as well as the immediate situation. Instantly, an empathy is built up between the audience and someone killing time watching somebody trying to kill time.'[34]

The published text posed problems of its own. The first edition contained the ending Stoppard cut. The next issue of the work contained the revised version, with several other alterations. A note by Stoppard published in the Samuel French acting edition of the play explains the confusions: 'This play-text is perhaps unusual in that it incorporates a good many speeches and passages enclosed in square brackets, and the material thus bracketed consists of optional cuts.' In his note to French, only part of which appears in the acting edition, Stoppard writes that 'there is no definitive text of "Rosencrantz and Guildenstern are Dead". This is not an omission but a principle . . . I don't think of the play-text as being of the order of Holy Writ'.[35]

Such a view of texts versus performance would define all the printed versions of his plays. As he would often repeat, a play is to be performed, not studied.

Stoppard suddenly found himself ranked with Shakespeare, Chekhov, Molière and Strindberg, the other playwrights featured in the 1967 season at the National.[36] They collectively appeared on the same poster in front of the National Theatre, Stoppard's, of course, being the only *new* play of the season. When asked how it felt to be listed with these greats, Stoppard answered, 'I am rather neurotic and this makes me somewhat more neurotic.'[37] To escape some of the public attention, he and Jose rented a cluttered cottage tucked under the lee of Coombe Hill in the Chilterns with two outstanding features: country air and a public telephone-box a fair way down the lane from which he could call out but no one could call him. He was dealing with publicity and the news that his earnings might total £20,000. In an interview from May 1967 he admitted that he was 'very well prepared for interviews. I'm always interviewing myself.'

'The trouble is,' he continued, 'I can always see either point of view . . . and see how plausible each of them is. So I proceed by arguing dialectically with myself because I suspect neither is the truth.' Denying that he identified with either Rosencrantz or Guildenstern brought a quick riposte from his wife: 'Oh, but they're very much him,' she declared, a reporter confirming that Stoppard 'has an uncanny physical resemblance to Guildenstern, pale, desperate and obsessed by the feeling of doom closing in illogically'.[38]

The play, in repertoire over the next four years, soon went on tour to Leeds, Oxford and other cities. When interviewed about the play's success in Oxford, John Stride suggested that an increased knowledge of *Hamlet* alone would improve appreciation of the play and that the subtleties of the text should be more appreciated: 'I'm sure the camp element will be particularly well received and I hope that there will be more open-mindedness about this *type* of play; we are tired of people who say that they started to understand it during the last act.' The two lead actors also revealed that in one performance they had actually exchanged parts, with Stride saying Petherbridge's lines and vice versa: 'we carried on like that for five or six exchanges without even realising . . .'[39]

The play's success was meteoric. Ticket sales were astonishing, and many were disappointed when unable to find seats. One day, a woman called for a matinée ticket but had difficulty remembering the name of the play. 'Ros, Ros, Ros, something,' she stammered into the phone. The box-office agent helpfully replied with 'Rosencrantz and Guildenstern are Dead, madame.' A pause – and then this reply: 'In that case, I guess there won't be a matinée. Is there anything else on?'[40] By autumn 1967, the play had opened in ten European cities, the British Council sent a company on tour to India and Pakistan, and Stoppard negotiated with Columbia Pictures for film rights.

Stoppard's reaction to his unexpected fame was whimsical: he was eager to be rich but said he wouldn't be corrupted, according to an interview in the *Sunday Times*:

> I'll sit there in my Rolls uncorrupted and tell my chauffeur, uncorruptedly, where to go. No, that's a lie. I hate driving. I hate cars. I'm frightened of being killed. I wonder if they could do Rolls-Royces with water-filled bumpers? What I want is a lovely place in the country. If someone says to me write this screen play about Abbott and Costello meet Tarzan and here's a Georgian house in the country, I'm worried that I'll say no, I couldn't possibly; when do I start?[41]

Ironically, within ten years, he'd have his house in the country – Queen

Anne, not Georgian – with nearly seventeen acres, in Buckinghamshire.

One sign of Stoppard's success was his monthly 'Three Musketeer' luncheons at the Café Royal Grill on Regent Street, where Oscar Wilde took Bosie. The two other musketeers were Derek Marlowe, whose novel *A Dandy in Aspic* had been published and was being made into a movie, and Piers Paul Read, whose novels were gaining respectable reviews and accolades, Graham Greene announcing that Read was the next important English novelist. Ronald Bryden remembered the delight of the three in hosting such elegant, expensive events in the gilded and ornate dining-room. A luncheon on 28 April 1969, for example, included Stoppard, Bryden and Michael Frayn among others. Some thirty years later, the waiters still greeted Stoppard enthusiastically when he walked through the door of the Café Royal with a friend.

But even if he had become a theatrical sensation, Stoppard was still challenged by domestic matters. Sent down to the dustbin in the backyard one morning, his wife recalled, he disappeared: 'I found myself at some traffic lights, with my slippers on and a bag of rubbish in one hand.' The previous day, he had found himself in the laundry, handing over a pair of his wife's shoes to be repaired.[42] Equally amusing is the story of his efforts at television repair: according to Jose, he got underneath a television set, unscrewed the four legs and was surprised when it came down on top of him. 'Another promising writer crushed by TV,' he said, writing the headline.[43]

Soon, *Rosencrantz and Guildenstern* began to earn various awards: on 6 June 1967, the Arts Council of Great Britain awarded Stoppard, jointly with Wole Soyinka, the inaugural John Whiting Award for 1966–7. The honour was for British or Commonwealth playwrights whose work showed new and distinctive development in dramatic writing. Soyinka received it for two plays produced in Britain: *The Lion and the Jewel* at the Royal Court and *The Trials of Brother Jero*. With David Storey, Stoppard shared the *Evening Standard* Award for the Most Promising Playwright. Productions began to appear around the world, one of the most remarkable in Milan. Directed by Franco Enriquez, this staging had a woman play Rosencrantz. But the critics loved it, praising Valeria Moriconi's acting but criticizing the Italian translation as dry and literal, although the theatricality of the production was first-rate. Other international versions received similar praise and Stoppard 'wore success with an elegant lack of surprise'.[44]

One of the explanations for the great appeal of *Rosencrantz and Guildenstern* was Stoppard's imaginative decision to attach his play to the best-known work in the canon. He later explained this as 'actually using an extant concept whether an Agatha Christie play or *Hamlet* or a certain kind of style of talking or writing. So what you do is actually set up this sort of totem thinking over there and then you write your play over here but what you say is watch that; keep my play in mind because it's actually bouncing off that, something somebody else wrote.'[45] This provided all sorts of freedom, since there was always the other text to rein in for the audience the extreme dimension of either language or character in the Stoppard work. This became, of course, a critical commonplace in evaluating his plays, so that a host of other works became a kind of benchmark for evaluating his own work and range, from Wilde's *The Importance of Being Earnest* for *Travesties* to even his own work, *Another Moon called Earth*, for *Jumpers*. The internal restructuring of his own plays through the work of others mitigates the pressure of coming up with original plots or situations for Stoppard, which he has always found difficult. It also expands the persistent theme of the double as a subject and a method, linked with the idea of self-invention. Linda explains in the revised *Walk on the Water*, called *Enter a Free Man*: 'there's two of everyone. You see you need that and if the two of him's the same, I mean if he's [her father] the same in the pub as he is with us, then he's had it'.[46] There must be difference as well as similarity. The linked time frames of *Arcadia* make this point clearly.

Rosencrantz and Guildenstern became the first play at the National to transfer to New York, opening on 16 October 1967 with Brian Murray as Rosencrantz and John Wood, who would become Stoppard's favourite actor, as Guildenstern; Derek Goldby again directed. Its transfer occurred as rapidly as its London success. Reading about the play's triumph in London, David Merrick immediately contacted Stoppard and arranged to meet him in May, when he bought the New York rights. To ensure its success and head off any charges concerning the play's difficulty, Merrick had copies of the script sent to New York drama critics before the first night. Stoppard was intensely nervous about the New York production, imagining a newspaper review of the play with this statement: 'at the conclusion the entire audience rose as one man and cried "MONEY BACK!" Lynda Bird Johnson, daughter of the President, attended one of the Washington tryouts, although her reaction is unrecorded.[47]

That same month, the play opened in Paris, where it was a disaster because of the translation which was either too literal 'so that the audience cannot follow it clearly or too simplified so that Stoppard's ambiguous dexterity is trod underfoot'.[48]

For the US production, the script was altered, mostly through cutting. Almost forty-five minutes were gone from the three-hour running time in London. Goldby, again: 'the basic difference was that it [the play] got flashier . . . the audiences demanded a kind of slapstick quality . . . less like ordinary people, more like two clowns'.[49] On opening night in New York, Stoppard refused to watch. With Jose, a writer from *Look* magazine and a photographer, they waited it out at a bar next door to the theatre. But Stoppard could not stay away: at one point, he entered the theatre lobby to stand with his head bent and ear cupped against the auditorium doors to listen to what he hoped was laughter. But not until Clive Barnes's review was read out at the post-première party at Sardi's did Stoppard's mood change from anxiety to elation. Ironically, the headline of Barnes's review had a Stoppardian misprint suggesting a Germanic origin for the work; it read, 'Theatre: Rosenkrantz and Guildenstern are Dead'.

Barnes called the play 'very funny, very brilliant, very chilling; it has the dust of thought about it and the particles glitter excitingly in the theatrical air'. The work is one of 'fascinating distinction'. Another reporter noted, however, that in 1966 a playwright named Michael Stewart wrote *Those that Play the Clown*, about what might have happened at an inn to a company of players on their way to perform at Elsinore. It was a disaster.[50] But lines around the block at the Alvin Theater on 52nd Street meant that the play had to transfer to a larger theatre for its extended run. In 1968, there was no Pulitzer Prize awarded for drama, although the committee unanimously agreed that if either *Rosencrantz and Guildenstern* or Peter Nichols's *A Day in the Death of Joe Egg* had been written by an American playwright, they 'would have had no hesitancy in recommending either of them for the Pulitzer Prize'.[51]

Stoppard continued to enjoy his success. He travelled to New York on the *Queen Mary* with his wife Jose, fifteen-month-old Oliver and a nanny named Kim. Merrick arranged for their passage but Stoppard, in his own words, 'didn't have the courage to go first-class and dress for dinner'. Merrick also arranged for them to borrow the ten-room Riverside Drive apartment belonging to the actor Ben Gazzara; photographs from their stay show a youthful Stoppard mugging for his son and the camera, clearly enjoying himself. One reason was that, according to Merrick, Stoppard was likely to pull in $6,000 a week during the run of *Rosencrantz and Guildenstern*. It was in New York, some days after the opening, that Stoppard made one of his flippant remarks that would reappear for more than thirty years. Asked by a woman in front of the theatre after a performance what the play was about, he sharply replied: 'it's about to make me rich'. Somehow the quip made it to the papers the next day.[52]

But America took to Stoppard as he had taken to New York, seeming to fill a cultural gap and becoming 'the "intellectuals'" answer to the British Invasion'. His rakish good looks and mod dress suited the times, despite his conservative nature and the traditionalist outlook of many theatre-goers. Everyone wanted to see and talk to the young man elegantly slouched in a corner with a cigarette between his fingers, as Diana Rigg once described him. His agent Kenneth Ewing explained that 'the press loved him because he was lucid and good-looking and his look fitted in very well with the sixties. It was not the well-dressed, well-turned-out look of the fifties; it was a sort of challenging look.'[53] The resemblance to Mick Jagger did not hurt, enhancing his appeal to the young.

In April 1968, *Rosencrantz and Guildenstern* won the Tony Award for the best play of the season and a few days later was named best play of the year by the New York Drama Critics' Circle. Stoppard was in New York again for the ceremony, staying at the Algonquin and being interviewed for the *New Yorker* – dressed in a brightly-coloured flowered shirt, a flowing black silk tie and light-brown tweed trousers. Recounting his career, he mentioned that his earliest 'ambitions were exclusively journalistic. I wanted to end up God knows what – a correspondent under fire in some foreign field, perhaps.' He also reported amusingly that since he would not be in New York for the actual awards ceremony, he was to tape an acceptance speech in case he won: 'It's rather ghostly, isn't it, talking to a nonexistent audience about a nonexistent award?'[54] He was actually in New York to look in on his play and be on hand for the publication of *Lord Malquist and Mr. Moon*. Years later, after major productions of *Rosencrantz and Guildenstern* at the Young Vic in 1973, in the West End in 1987 and most recently at the National in 1995, the play still earned recognition: in an August 1998 poll held by the National Theatre in which play-wrights, actors, directors, journalists and other theatre professionals were asked to nominate ten English-language, twentieth-century plays they considered significant, part of the NT 2000 project, *Rosencrantz and Guildenstern* ranked seventh out of the top 100, tying with Noel Coward's *Private Lives*.

Shortly after the success of *Rosencrantz and Guildenstern*, Stoppard's television play *Another Moon called Earth* was broadcast on BBC. The June 1967 show refined a number of themes he would later elaborate in *Jumpers*, but which had already appeared in his novel. Bone (later transformed into Inspector Bones in *Jumpers*), an occasional philosopher, expresses perhaps the most important theme in the work when he explains how he constructs human history: 'I dissect it – lay bare the logic which other men have taken to be an arbitrary sequence of accidents.'[55] This method effectively became Stoppard's *modus operandi* which he had previously expressed in *Lord Malquist*: there, Moon feels 'that reality was just outside his perception. If he made a certain move, changed the angle of his existence to the common ground, logic and absurdity would separate. As it was, he couldn't pin them down.'[56] This view hovers over Stoppard's work in a variety of forms, beginning with *Rosencrantz and Guildenstern*'s search for meaning, continuing with *Hapgood*'s anatomy of experience via quantum physics, and then expanding to the chaos theory of *Arcadia* and the problematics of translation in *The Invention of Love*. But it also has an emotional component which *The Real Thing* and the Housman play, in particular, explore.

Another Moon also reflects Stoppard's fascination with the moon, not only its name, which keeps reappearing in his early work, but in its translation from romantic symbol to scientific laboratory subject. Constance in the radio play *M is for Moon* explains the frustration with the symbol: 'I don't want the moon, Alfred, all I want is the possibility of an alternative, so that I know I'm doing this because I want to instead of because there's nothing else.' Stoppard even proposed a lengthy study of the moon to Anthony Blond. In October 1965, he outlined a 'Moon Book', one which 'concerned the psychological effect on man when his moon is taken away as a symbol; [but] his idea is a book about astronauts'. Stoppard rejected that and moved on to his second idea: 'a non-fiction book . . . an anthology of the Moon on Earth, i.e., the Moon in literature and man's minds so far'. He explained this concern in a 1967 interview: 'the day they land on the Moon and look down at the Earth worries me a lot. For the first time man will see that the Earth is only that big and all his absolutes, right and wrong . . . are only local customs'.[57] *Another Moon called Earth* presents Stoppard's worry about the loss of the moon, which entirely distracts Bone from his wife Penelope, in much the same way as the philosophical worries of George in *Jumpers* distract him from Dolly's situation. The return to earth of the first man on the moon, the focus of the play, means loss, not gain, to Bone. His wife, however, sees it as a triumph. The theme continues with Dotty in *Jumpers*, which opens with her singing 'Shine on Harvest Moon'.

One measure of the triumph of *Rosencrantz and Guildenstern* was a new flat for the Stoppards. Leaving 11 Vincent Square Mansions, they rented suite number 4 at 5 Queen's Gate Place, South Kensington from December 1967 until April 1968. A previous tenant of the spacious apartment in a handsome building – described by one journalist as looking like 'a minor Ruritanian embassy in South Kensington' – was Harold Pinter.[58] The antique reproductions and Regency stripes of the wallpaper matched the upholstery and reflected Stoppard's new status.

Nearby was the Imperial College of Science, Technology and Medicine, and dominating the skyline was the Queen's Tower, built to honour Queen Victoria, one of two original granite towers constructed in an Italian style for the original Imperial Institute of Science and saved when the site was rebuilt in 1956 for a new campus. Looking more like a church spire than a monument to technology, it stood as a symbol for the new and the scientific rather than the old and the spiritual. It may have served as a constant reminder to Stoppard of the possibility of linking science with art, while encouraging the role of science in his writing. The neighbourhood itself blended science and the arts: adjacent to Imperial College is the Royal College of Music and the Royal Albert Hall. A neighbourhood park across from 5 Queen's Gate Place meant space and a patch of green in the middle of the city. In this stimulating environment, Stoppard worked on *The Real*

Inspector Hound and accepted occasional speaking requests, addressing, for example, the National Union of Students' thirteenth National Student Drama Festival in Bradford with a talk entitled 'On the Other Side of Hamlet' on 30 December 1967.

After almost eight months at Queen's Gate, Stoppard and his family made the leap to the suburbs, moving to River Thatch, Abbotsbrook, in Bourne End in April, the first of several locales in Buckinghamshire that Stoppard would, over the next twenty years or so, make his home. This was his and Jose's first substantial house, situated beyond Slough in the well-appointed middle-class belt of homes around London with a tiny stream running next to the house. The thatched house had a small drive, and a carefully cut front lawn doubled as a croquet lawn. A magnificent tree stood to the left of the house, shading a sitting-room that faced the stream. Stoppard, however, was hesitant about making the move because the house

> is on a sort of snobby private estate down a private road; it's pink and everyone around owns a large dog which votes Conservative. It screams Comfortable Middle Class. Backbone of Traditional Values, etc. *However*, it became a choice between splendid isolation and practicalities – ie 5 minutes walk from railway station to London . . . What I really wanted was either distant and damp and impossible or £60,000 (central heated Georgian with croquet lawn going to Thames at Hampton Court).[59]

In a thank-you note following a visit in July 1969, Trevor Nunn wrote: 'I didn't think that thatched houses with the croquet green and the small river running at the bottom of the garden, really existed but now that I have seen one with my own eyes, I suppose all I can say is that I want one.' He then added that 'there is nothing I would like more than that there should be some relationship between yourself and the RSC'.[60]

In a short piece for an architectural magazine, Stoppard described where he now wrote, a Victorian boathouse, explaining that as 'an office to write in, it appeals to my sense of security and my sense of humour'. The sixty-year-old, double-decked wooden building with balconies at each end and a heavily thatched roof stood on a tiny island reached by a narrow bridge: 'from certain angles it looks like the Ark, with the Flood just beginning to subside; from others, it looks like a large dog, not a very bright dog, but very friendly. It's the only building I know which doesn't try to be somehow better than itself; it does not aspire, neither does it impose.' 'Between paragraphs', he even managed to catch 'a few small dace on a dry fly'. From the opposite balcony, he 'watched a snake swimming, a kingfisher fishing and (though I may have been dozing off in the sun) a rat rowing about in a little boat'.[61]

River Thatch was a clear sign of success and considerably more substantial than either of the two preceding flats. Stoppard, seeking domestic stability (long a goal and probably a response to his own nomadic youth and disjointed family life), found somewhere where he could write and bring up his family – his second son, Barnaby, would be born there on 20 September 1969. But signs of the domestic stress that began after the success of *Rosencrantz and Guildenstern* were growing. In contrast to the appearance of middle-class comfort, there were personal difficulties. Stoppard's hectic scheduling and the sudden change in his way of life were difficult for Jose to cope with. Tynan, in his profile of Stoppard, quotes a friend: 'Jose was a feminist before her time, and she got bloody-minded about being overshadowed by Tom.'[62] Her sense of independence in seeking a career, determination to be understood on her own terms and refusal to be known only as 'Mrs Stoppard' confirmed her self-reliance. But soon, signs of a nervous breakdown appeared: she had difficulty dealing with her child, suffered from anxiety, became irritable and experienced excessive tension. An irrational jealousy emerged, an acquaintance reporting that Jose even began to tell friends that she had really written *Rosencrantz and Guildenstern*. Despite an aversion to theatre people and theatre talk, she became competitive and sought acknowledgement as a contributor to her husband's work. Peter Nichols recorded her odd behaviour on several occasions. At a 1969 dinner at his home with the Frayns and Stoppards, Jose dramatically threatened to leave because of a cold that made her sniffle. On a visit, later that year, to the Stoppards at Bourne End, idyllic and like 'the first-scene setting for a pantomime, The Village Green', a pregnant Jose 'burnt the roast and slept much of the afternoon', wrote Nichols.[63]

During this period, Stoppard drafted no major plays, limiting himself to short entertainments and screenplays. The birth of their second son did not help; in fact, it only intensified Jose's difficulties in coping. Stoppard's energy was preoccupied in trying to keep the family together: while 'Tom was behaving with chivalric constancy', according to one friend, others 'were throwing up their hands because he was spending all his time looking after the children and doing the washing up'.[64] Tellingly, between the five years that separated *Rosencrantz and Guildenstern* and his next major work, *Jumpers*, Stoppard worked principally on four unproduced screenplays. The money was necessary to meet his mounting financial responsibilities.

Stoppard's popularity in 1967–8 meant that his views were eagerly sought – on subjects from the state of contemporary theatre to influences on his work. Of the latter, he was characteristically unsure, or at any rate maintained a façade of indefiniteness; of the former, he put on a journalistic face and offered his tentative opinions, although always uncertain of his views, something captured in a BBC television programme of the early seventies called *Tom Stoppard Doesn't Know*. The influences question perplexed interviewers more than Stoppard and he frequently took note of the 'influences that have been invoked on my behalf', citing Beckett, Kafka and Pirandello. Beckett was the most important, he acknowledged, but Beckett's novels, as much as his plays, because of the *way* he expressed himself, and his humour: 'I find Beckett deliciously funny in the way that he qualifies everything as he goes along, reduces, refines, and dismantles. When I read it I love it.'[65] In an essay for the *Sunday Times*, Stoppard explained further his love of Beckett because 'he always ends up with a man surrounded by the wreckage of a proposition he had made in confidence only two minutes before'. He also remarks that when others find elements of the subconscious or symbolic in his work, he's shocked: it's much like 'a duped smuggler when confronted by a customs officer'. As he goes through his luggage and discovers a variety of 'exotic contraband like truth and illusion . . . I have to admit that the stuff is there but I can't for the life of me remember packing it.'

In the same essay, Stoppard reveals that when his mother remarried and his name changed, he didn't much care, 'but then it occurred to me that in practically everything I had written there was something about people getting each other's names wrong'. And finally, as a corrective to language becoming an end in itself, he recalls Peter Brook's production of *US*: at the end, a series of white butterflies were released in the auditorium, the last set aflame. The impact was astonishing, the theatricality overshadowing any words. He ends by admitting some guilt over being a writer and that he is rarely moved by social events, although he wanted to write a play commemorating 'rather sceptically' the fiftieth anniversary of the Russian Revolution but it hadn't been done. No, he didn't write out of social or historical causes, but simply because he loved writing.[66]

Soon, other events in 1968 capitalized on the success of *Rosencrantz and Guildenstern*, namely a staging of his first play, retitled *Enter a Free Man* (March 1968), and the West End performance of the more successful *The Real Inspector Hound* (June 1968). *Enter a Free Man*, produced by Doris Cole Abrahams, was greeted with disappointment. The production opened on 28 March in the West End's St Martin's Theatre, with Michael Hordern as George and Megs Jenkins as Persephone. Frith Banbury directed. Cole Abrahams had bought a two-year option on the play and produced it after Stoppard made further revisions to the text. Stoppard's own view of the work was mixed: there was 'gratitude and affection, and a certain amount of embarrassment' because 'I don't think it's a very true play, in the sense that I feel no intimacy with the people I was writing about . . . it's actually phoney because it's a play written about other people's characters'.[67] The production in the West End tried to capitalize on Stoppard's success with *Rosencrantz and Guildenstern*, but the work lacked the energy of the National Theatre hit. Despite strong notices for the acting, especially Hordern, who would soon star in the very popular *Jumpers*, the play excited little interest from the public or Stoppard. He was gaining further recognition, however: that May, he won a prize in the fifth international festival of radio plays organized by Czech radio for *Albert's Bridge*. The winner was to spend two weeks in Czechoslovakia; he accepted the prize, but declined the invitation. That July, he was also invited to visit Prague for the International Drama Festival or to première a new play the following spring at the Theatre on the Balustrade. This was during the Prague Spring; by August 1968, however, Soviet-led armies invaded the country and eliminated such activities.

Sudden fame also meant an onslaught of approaches to the young playwright for new projects. In May 1968, for example, he was thinking about a possible play on the Romantics. The savvy producer Michael Codron, former artistic director of the New Arts Theatre, London, and the original producer of Pinter's *The Birthday Party* (and who would soon stage Joe Orton's *Entertaining Mr Sloane*), wrote to Stoppard before Easter to say that Peggy Ramsay 'feels strongly that you would do a wonderful play about Keats and that John Hurt would be splendid as the poet'. Ramsay had earlier sent Stoppard a biography of Shelley.[68] But Stoppard had a different work in mind for Codron, who had lost the rights to *Enter a Free Man*. It took the form of an unorthodox comedy satirizing the critical practice of drama criticism itself. And when Codron read the finished script, he sent Stoppard a one-word telegram via his agent: 'Dazzling'.[69]

The Real Inspector Hound opened at the Criterion Theatre on 17 June 1968 and ran for six months. This was a new Stoppard work, shorter and more structured than *Enter a Free Man*. It also marked a departure in West End theatre practice, since it began the custom of previews. Until then, dress rehearsals (with the last usually before an invited audience) were followed directly by first night, marking the début of a new work. Out-of-town performances were used to refine or restructure shows. Michael Codron, however, had another idea, borrowed from Broadway: that of allowing a London audience to see a show before it opened, permitting the actors to get accustomed to the audience and the theatre while allowing the writer to make changes and the technical staff to overcome any unexpected problems. It also made a pre-London tour unnecessary, saving producers out-of-town costs. Finally, the preview gave the producer a chance to limit the access of critics until the play was ready, while building up public interest.

Stoppard found previews invaluable:

> Previews are essential. The idea of going straight from a dress-rehearsal to a first night is frightening. It happened with R&G and we got away with it, but for *Jumpers* we had several previews by the end of which I had taken fifteen minutes out of the play. I hate first nights. I attend out of courtesy for the actors and afterwards we all have a drink and go home.

The Real Inspector Hound was a plot-driven contrivance that immediately struck sympathetic chords with reviewers, although the play was initially not about theatre critics:

I originally conceived a play, exactly the same play, with simply two members of an audience getting involved in the play-within-the play. But when it comes actually to writing something down which has integral entertainment value . . . it very quickly occurred to me that it would be a lot easier to do it with critics, because you've got something known and defined to parody.[70]

'Rival witnesses to an incongruous event' became a favoured Stoppardian device, from *Rosencrantz and Guildenstern* to *The Invention of Love*, where the older and younger Housman simultaneously observe certain actions. This is also the ultimate role of the audience in a Stoppard play. About *Hound,* Stoppard added that: 'I'm very fond of the play because I didn't know how to do it. I just got into it, and I knew that I wanted it somehow to resolve itself in a breathtakingly neat, complex but utterly comprehensible way.'[71]

Originally, there was a sort of 'goon-show version of it, which had no kind of structure – it was just a situation of two people watching a whodunnit and getting involved in it'. This was 'The Critics' – also variously titled 'The Stand-Ins' and 'Murder at Mousetrap Manor' – in its earliest form, a Bristol manuscript of several pages written in 1960 after *The Gamblers*. Later, in 1962, while a drama critic at *Scene*, Stoppard had written a caustic review in dialogue form spoofing the then-current proliferation of Agatha Christie-style thrillers. Slurp, a 'suave drama critic', is interrupted by a Detective Inspector Rafferty and Constable Wilkins, who accuse the hapless critic of the murder of a London producer who had recently mounted three Agatha Christie plays. He has been found bludgeoned to death with a hide-bound quarto edition of her works. Bits of the dialogue from the review actually found their way into *The Real Inspector Hound*.[72] The text remained unfinished until 1967, however, when Stoppard revised it, giving Higgs, Moon's first-string senior theatre critic, a major role. Stoppard explained how his characters took over his writing, with Moon and Birdboot telling him that Higgs is the corpse under the sofa.

The play itself is a wonderful parody of the formulaic Agatha Christie work *The Mousetrap*. His play, Stoppard has said, was an attempt 'to bring off a sort of comic coup in pure mechanistic terms'.[73] Stoppard here outlines something that he would repeat in many of his plays: the setting-up of complications followed by their working out in carefully constructed resolutions. This is theatre as problem-solving, one of its great attractions for him. However, when ideas prevail over plot, as they so often do in a Stoppard play, 'the nuts and bolts [of plot] become metaphoric girders for his intellectual debates', as in *Rosencrantz and Guildenstern, Jumpers* and *Travesties*.[74]

The Real Inspector Hound benefits from this structure through its conscious parody of the Christie play, the entire work summarized by one critic as 'a Chinese puzzle of intersecting parodies'.[75] The isolated, fog-shrouded Muldoon Manor, the stock characters, right down to the housekeeper, Mrs Drudge, the entrance of a seemingly paralysed figure who possesses not one but two double identities, all tied to the competitiveness of provincial theatre critics, links the world of the theatre to that of mystery through the plot of detection, a Stoppardian feature. Higgs (first string), Moon (second string) and Puckeridge (third string) are theatre critics who vie for prominence, with Moon, substituting for Higgs, sitting next to Birdboot, a critic from another paper. Formulating their view of the play they watch as it opens – 'Let me at once say that it has *élan* while at the same time avoiding *éclat*. Having said that, and I think it must be said, I am bound to ask – does this play know where it is going?' asks Moon – they both, for different reasons, become involved in the action: Birdboot because of his obsession with the leading lady, Moon because of his hatred of the first string (ironically, he will be shot by the third string disguised as one of the characters in the play).[76]

The plot of the Christie parody involves the discovery of a body beneath a sofa and the arrival of Inspector Hound (who turns out to be Lady Muldoon's allegedly deceased husband, disguised as his wheelchair-ridden brother). This complicates matters, since Hound is also the third-string critic, Puckeridge, as well as the detective. Moon jumps on to the stage to answer a ringing phone, only to discover the call is for Birdboot, a device which suddenly brings the latter into the action. Now face to face with the actresses he admires, Felicity and Cynthia, Birdboot acts his part which results in his being shot. Moon, in response, leaps to the stage again, exclaiming to the actors, 'He's dead . . . That's a bit rough, isn't it? – a bit extreme! – He may have had his faults – I admit he was a fickle old . . . Who did this, and why?'[77] Reality and stage life have united, but the final unravelling of the plot begins only when Moon turns director: 'All right! I'm going to find out who did this! I want everyone to go to the positions they occupied when the shot was fired.[78] At an October 1975 performance of the play in West Dorset, the acting was so convincing that one member of the audience found himself incapable of remaining in his seat. Reacting to the shooting, a clergyman jumped up while the bodies were being removed, addressed the crowd with the words, 'I think somebody needs a clergyman back there', vaulted on to the stage and took off into the wings, to everyone's applause.[79] The cast reacted with surprise, while the audience waited for more.

The Real Inspector Hound showed Stoppard's public how parody could convey complex ideas at the same time as he was exploring ways to dramatize a growing interest in philosophy. He told Smith he was reading Wittgenstein at the time. With lines like '*Je suis*, it seems to be saying, *ergo sum*. But is that enough?'[80] Descartes collides with comedy, anticipating the action of *Jumpers*. 'I think we are entitled to ask – and here one is irresistibly reminded of Voltaire's cry, "*Voilà!*" – I think we are entitled to ask – *Where is God?*' Moon implores.[81] *Jumpers* would provide part of the answer, in 'a serious play dealt with in the farcical terms which in *Hound* actually *constitute* the play' – what he would shortly describe as marrying 'the play of ideas to comedy or farce'.[82] And through his play with identity – Magnus, who is Puckeridge in disguise *and* the real Inspector Hound, exclaims at the end 'I have been leading a double life – at *least!*'[83]– Stoppard again engages the question of self-invention, a persistent theme in his work.

Critics loved the new play, finding themselves both the subjects of, and commentators on, the satire. They argued that Stoppard was much more than a one-play wonder. Exploring the fantasy of critics wanting to cross the footlights and showing what might happen if, in fact, they did so, Stoppard confronted their dreams with theatrical reality. The result is 'piercingly and dazzlingly funny'. One reviewer encapsulated the action as the product of enthralled critics who burst out of their seats and begin acting the principal parts but 'get shot dead' for their enthusiasm. Poetic justice? Perhaps. Melodrama, mystery, parody and farce successfully mix together, although one critic demurred. Irving Wardle opposed Stoppard's 'detachment from life' and portrayal only of masks, not characters. 'His mirrors reflect nothing but themselves'; his plays suggest only 'the logical working-out of an arithmetical problem', with Lewis Carroll rather than Beckett his model. Others, however, thrilled to the play and even found Stoppard parodying himself: the two critics disappear into the murky happenings of Muldoon Manor as Rosencrantz and Guildenstern disappear into the enigmatic events of Elsinore.[84]

But while Stoppard's art was taking new form, his life was falling apart. His relationship with Jose was shattering. In one sense, he outgrew her; in another, she may have found his success and response to it too difficult to accept. Several friends from this period recall how she would isolate herself and display no interest in theatre talk. Domestic matters took up her energy, though she increasingly despaired. She found it difficult to deal with her two infant sons, while suburban life at River Thatch intensified her isolation and loneliness. Anxiety, nervousness and sometimes depression resulted. A comment she made in May 1967 illustrates with chilling foresight the nature of her difficulty with the relationship: 'The hardest thing I've had to accept is that if I died or disappeared, he'd be upset but in the end his life wouldn't be all that different. Writing is the core of his existence.'[85]

What saved Stoppard was meeting Dr Miriam Moore-Robinson, in France.

CHAPTER 9

SWINGING FROM AN EPIGRAM

Show business is my main interest, closely followed by
crime detection.
Stoppard, *Jumpers*

Anthony Smith and his wife Alison first met Miriam and Peter Moore-Robinson at the movies. The Moore-Robinsons, recognizing the Smiths from Boorman's six-part feature 'The Newcomers', introduced themselves as they left a Bristol cinema. They were an attractive pair, a doctor and a vet, who had recently moved to Keynsham, just south of Bristol. The two couples quickly discovered similar interests, one of them cricket, and soon began to socialize.

Born in Newcastle in 1937, Miriam Stern was the granddaughter of a Czech–Hungarian Jewish immigrant. Her father, originally a tailor, became a nurse in the army and followed this career after the war. He was fascinated by medicine and determined that his first-born, whether male or female, would become a doctor. Miriam's energetic, Scots–Irish mother concurred. Winning a medical scholarship to the Royal Free Hospital in London, Miriam began her medical studies at eighteen and qualified in 1961. After graduation, she began to specialize in dermatology. In 1963, she went to King's College, University of Durham and then to the University of Bristol as a research fellow. Between 1966 and 1968, she specialized in dermatology at the university hospital. Petite, with dark-brown hair and large blue-grey eyes, she managed to be both accomplished and feminine, capitalizing on her independence and self-sufficiency. She married Peter Moore-Robinson on 23 September 1962. The couple later moved from Bristol to Marlow in Buckinghamshire when, after being passed over for a promotion at her hospital, she joined Syntex, a multinational pharmaceutical firm, in 1968.

In September 1965, the Moore-Robinsons unexpectedly dropped in on Anthony and Alison Smith at St Céré in the Dordogne. France had been a favourite vacation spot for the Smiths since the early sixties, Stoppard joining them on one occasion in 1962 with his then girl-friend, Isabel Dunjohn. Stoppard himself had long enjoyed visiting France: in 1961, he and several Bristol journalist friends, including Anthony Smith, Richard Hawkins and Derek Balmer, a photographer, visited Blauvac in Provence. One photo from the trip shows the dark-haired, youthful writer artistically poised on the edge of an ancient well with pen and paper in hand, oblivious to the conversation of two friends in the background. Smith used the experience of Provence in his 1971 novel, *Zero Summer*.

Miriam and Peter Moore-Robinson arrived at St Céré when Stoppard, Jose, Alison and Anthony Smith were in the kitchen of their rented house, attempting a Hollandaise sauce. Smith introduced Miriam to Stoppard, their first meeting. They spoke but nothing much happened, the Moore-Robinsons moving on to their own rented home. The Stoppards soon found their own holiday home: Jose, finding it difficult to deal with the domestic chaos caused by the Smiths' infant twins, suggested that she and Stoppard would be happier staying nearby.

In the years following that first meeting, Stoppard was caught up in family life and the activities of his two young sons. He and Miriam had only occasional contact, often at the sporadic cricket matches organized by Smith, who frequently invited Peter Moore-Robinson and Miriam to attend.[1] As Stoppard's relationship with Jose became more untenable, he found a sympathetic and appealing audience in the understanding Miriam, whose own marriage was in difficulty. Stoppard soon discovered that he shared with her similarities of age, background and the importance of family life. He found her Jewish-ness compatible, even though his own connection to the religion was tenuous at best; and many would later remark that Miriam's physical appearance and behaviour were similar to those of Stoppard's mother. He was also attracted to her independence; indeed, all three women central to Stoppard's personal life – Jose, Miriam and, later, Felicity Kendal – have had professional careers, the last two sustaining them during their relationship with the playwright. Stoppard constantly encouraged their independence.

Stoppard felt guilty over his divided loyalties during this period: on the one hand, he sought to make the relationship with Jose work, but on the other, he needed an understanding woman who could share his changing life and would not shy away from success. Stoppard felt constant anxiety over Jose's condition, remaining aware that his ideal of a stable family life was disintegrating. His own fragmented past – defined by his displacement from Zlín, relocation to Singapore, loss of his father, resettlement in India, his mother's unexpected remarriage and removal to England – only intensified his need for domestic security. Throughout 1968 and 1969, he struggled to provide it.

As he assumed more domestic duties, Stoppard found increasing support in Miriam, whose own marriage was unravelling because of a growing gulf between her own ambition and her husband's placidity. Jose was becoming increasingly withdrawn – not only from Stoppard but from her children. As the problems multiplied – at one point she angrily threatened to harm the two boys – Stoppard found he was more and more incapable of helping her. The absence of domestic stability troubled him intensely and the situation prevented him from working. Frustrated and unhappy, Stoppard realized what had to be done and acted with frightening clarity: he left Jose in December 1969, taking the children. River Thatch had unhappy associations; that month, he wrote to Smith, 'River Thatch sold today – I cross out the letter-head with special relish.'[2] Divorce and custody proceedings began in early 1970, although they would take two years to finalize. By late 1969, however, Stoppard was deeply involved with Miriam, finding her sympathy and understanding essential to his own well-being. By August 1970, he and his two young sons had moved in with her. Peter Moore-Robinson petitioned for divorce in October 1970, naming Stoppard as the co-respondent.

Albert's Bridge, Stoppard's 1967 radio play, may be understood as an early expression of his dilemma and increasing anxiety over his inability to help Jose; it also suggests that he could no longer live in that situation. The play introduces the persistent but complicated Stoppardian subject of distance and isolation: only from a distance can one understand the whole, but to do so is isolating. Mathematics, philosophy and order also appear as subjects. In the work, city councillor Fitch proves by algebraic formula the virtue of eliminating three of the four painters of the Clufton Bay Bridge, leaving philosophy student Albert, who celebrates order and a sense of completeness, to do the work. But this hero, happy only on the dizzying heights of the bridge, experiences frustration in his marriage to Kate, a former housemaid whom he has made pregnant. Imprisoned domestically, Albert escapes to the physical and mental freedom of his bridge.

Parallels with Stoppard's life begin with the bridge itself, linked by name to Brunel's famous Clifton Suspension Bridge in Bristol, which stands 264 feet over the River Avon. For a short time, Stoppard had lived below the bridge, in Hotwells. In the play, Albert's father is a successful businessman, founder of Metal Alloys and Allied Metals; Stoppard's stepfather was a successful businessman with F. B. Tools. Albert, of course, rejects the course of following in his father's footsteps and at one point unexpectedly sings a song with the line 'the sun was shi-ning . . . on my Yiddisher Mama', possibly an allusion by Stoppard to his Jewish origins and his mother's manner.[3]

Albert also exhibits a number of Stoppardian traits, one of the most important being a welcome sense of moral responsibility. When Fitch asks him if it is 'the open air life that attracts you' to painting the bridge, Albert replies:

> No. It's the work, the whole thing . . . being responsible for so much
> that is visible . . . I like it because I was happy up there, doing some-
> thing simple but so grand, without end. It doesn't get away from you.[4]

This might be an early definition of playwriting for Stoppard: creating works of art for public display on the stage, he recognizes that he is 'responsible for so much that is visible'. And each time, he, like Albert and another character, Fraser, flirts with self-destruction (failure) as well as fame. But playwriting (or bridge painting) is also something Stoppard could control and make visible. Playwriting gave Stoppard an important artistic purpose, transforming his life into a pattern of grand undertakings designed to achieve public approval, similar to Albert's work.

Kate, however, like Jose, cannot grasp Albert's purpose and repeatedly cites his education as a divide between the two of them. In turn, Albert has difficulty relating to her, preferring to paint his bridge rather than spend any time with her. Only when he is alone above the city does Albert gain perspective and feel fulfilled. He also experiences a sense of order, since the structure of the bridge is complete; his job, however, is to improve it through painting (an act that parallels Stoppard's locating his work on the superstructures of such pre-existing texts as *Hamlet* or *The Importance of Being Earnest*). But the job for Albert is never done; once he finishes, he must immediately start again. This might be analogous to Stoppard's realization that once he completes a play, the process of rehearsal and performance immediately initiates changes to the work. He must in a sense start again, just as when he begins a new work. What Albert has difficulty accepting is Kate's realism. Told by her that 'life is all close up, isn't it', he reluctantly admits, 'Yes, it hits you, when you come back down. How close it all is. You can't stand back to look at it'[5] – unless you are high on a bridge or struggling to write a play. The line may also suggest, or at the least prefigure, the conflict Stoppard sensed between the reality of his marriage and the distance or height he experienced with his sudden fame.

In a further passage, Albert recalls how he became involved with Kate; what he had hoped for her reflects Stoppard's initial feelings for Jose, which became tinged with guilt over her isolation: 'I never had any regrets, but I did want her to be happy too,' Albert remarks.[6] Penelope, neglected wife of Bone in *Another Moon called Earth*, Dotty, the overlooked wife of the moral philosopher George in Stoppard's next major play, *Jumpers*, and even Ruth, the 'discarded' wife of Geoffrey Carson in *Night and Day*, similarly reflect this situation. This is not entirely a surprise, since Stoppard was conscious of his growing distance from Jose when he began an early version of *Jumpers* in the summer of 1968.[7]

Albert's Bridge contains two Stoppards: one is Albert, who seeks to escape from the domestic, everyday world into his elevated work via the isolated beauty and height of the bridge; the other is Fraser, a more intellectually mature figure who, in his effort to escape life by jumping off the bridge, understands that below him is a world that only *seems* to function: 'All is quite ordered, seen from above,' he offers. But he also knows that he is 'a victim of perspective' and although he fails to jump (preferring order to chaos), he understands that he cannot escape the disorder and confusion below him.[8] This is the Stoppard who knows he cannot escape the messiness of his life, as Henry will later acknowledge in *The Real Thing*.[9]

The collapse of the bridge from the weight of the massed painters marching to finish the repainting in one day is the expression of the disorder that finally overtakes the physical and mental universe of the characters. One cannot escape it, no matter how high. The effort to get free of the disorder and chaos leads to implosion, as the effort of Stoppard to free himself through his art would lead to his inevitable break-up with Jose, who became jealous of his commitment to his writing and the success it engendered. *Albert's Bridge* suggests many of these issues through its well-constructed treatment of a seemingly empty, repetitive activity. But the simple always masks the philosophical for Stoppard, a key idea and ideal in his work. *Albert's Bridge* was an international hit, winning the Prix Italia in 1968 and an award from Czech Radio International.

Get me someone unbelievable!
Stoppard, *Jumpers*

Stoppard's divorce decree was handed down on 31 January and made absolute on 8 February 1972. He was thirty-four, Jose thirty-one. Normally, a decree would not be made absolute for three months but in this instance the President of the Court shortened the time to one week to allow Stoppard to marry Miriam before their own child was born in March. Stoppard was to pay Jose £3,000 per year until 1976 when, anticipating a larger income, the sum was increased to nearly £6,000. At the time of the divorce, Stoppard, Miriam and his two sons were living in the country at High Barn, near Maidenhead, Berkshire. Stoppard and Miriam married on 11 February 1972 at Maidenhead Register Office, three days after the divorce was granted. Their son William was born on 7 March.

This was a thrilling time for Stoppard: his remarriage and the imminent birth of another child was topped only by the successful opening of *Jumpers* on 2 February 1972 (nine days before his wedding), his first major play since *Rosencrantz and Guildenstern*. The sequence and compression of events contained a momentum that seemed positively Stoppardian, since all of these changes, which, of course, had accumulated over time, seemed to have been condensed into two weeks. He took them in his stride.

In 1968, Miriam had joined Syntex Pharmaceuticals, an American multinational specializing in birth-control research; by the time she and Stoppard began their relationship, she was moving quickly up the executive ladder. Her early investigations of an oral contraceptive for the company soon made her a sought-after commentator on television, which gradually led to her role as a panellist on the popular television show *Call My Bluff* (on which Stoppard would appear twice). She was also one of the presenters on Yorkshire Television's *Don't Ask Me*, beginning in 1973. She auditioned for the job while five months pregnant. The media soon portrayed her as a career woman who could do it all: lead a professional life, be a mother, have a successful marriage to a talented writer – and grow her own vegetables.

Miriam also became a health-and-beauty and self-help expert, with a series of immensely successful books such as *Miriam's Book of Health Care* and *Everywoman's Lifeguide*. Interviews emphasized her ability to organize her time, run an efficient home and sustain a loving marriage. The one-word headline for a *Sunday Times* article about her, dated 5 June 1977, is 'Supermum'. Her popularity soon outstripped her husband's, although she credited Stoppard for expanding her career: 'without his encouragement, I wouldn't have done television, I wouldn't have written books . . . the more I did, the more he approved and the happier he was.' She explained, 'Tom likes women who are independent, who can take care of themselves and have lives of their own. He *likes* working women. He likes to be left alone.' During their eighteen years of marriage, as one of Britain's most notable and noticeable celebrity couples, she also transformed herself from 'a rosy English pudge-bunny all moonfaced and brighteyed. . . [to] a lithe and gravely beautiful woman with a murmuring voice and a brunette sheen that reminds one of Elizabeth Taylor'.[10]

But there was also controversy and a backlash to her 'supermum' image. When she revealed in 1975 during an on-air introduction to a television programme on the right to live and the right to die that, as a young doctor in Newcastle in the sixties, she had turned off the life-support machine of a twenty-seven-year-old who had had a cardiac arrest, a furore erupted. The patient was medically dead, she explained, but it was still 'the most upsetting experience of my medical career'.[11] Her later prominence, with television programmes like *The Health Show* for the BBC (1977), *Baby and Co.* for Yorkshire Television (1984–7) and, most recently, the *Health Circuit* for Sky News, increased her profile; she was soon known to a wider audience than her play-wright husband. Before she achieved fame on television, she had published her first book, *The Book of Babycare*. By 1991, aged fifty-four, she had published twenty-four books, including *The Magic of Sex*. Even recently, her profile in certain circles still exceeded Stoppard's. Stoppard found proof of this when he hosted a supper for cast members at the end of the 1998 revival of *The Real Inspector Hound* at the Comedy Theatre in London. He entered an Italian restaurant, claiming to have booked a table in the name of 'Stoppard'. The waiter tried unsuccess-fully to pronounce the name several times. The playwright enunciated helpfully. After a pause, the waiter smiled and said, 'Ah. Stoppard. Of course. As in Dr Miriam.' The playwright reportedly beamed.[12]

With Miriam, Stoppard found the security of domestic life with a woman who could nurture and support his talent. Her dark beauty evoked his mother's looks, while her concern for her family's well-being duplicated his own mother's constant efforts. Miriam also came from an Orthodox Jewish family and affixed a mezuzah to the doorposts of their family homes. This was a connection with the past that would become increasingly meaningful for Stoppard. By the time their second child, Edmund, was born in September 1974 (they collectively had four, now, since his first two sons had remained with them), he thrilled to his life as a father on a country estate of four acres, Fernleigh, in Buckinghamshire, which they acquired in 1972. Domesticity reinforced his creativity: 'I absolutely prefer being at home. I'm much more prolific now with my second marriage . . . I hate being away from my wife and children for more than about two days. I'm quite insecure if I leave my immediate sort of blanket where I can just write and see my own family.'[13] For Stoppard, writing and family were at last united.

Fernleigh, in Iver Heath, Buckinghamshire, 'the first house on the left from the Crooked Billet Pub', did not at first interest Stoppard at all:

> We pulled up there, and I wasn't even going to get out of the car. Happily I did, and happily that's where we now live, and it's also the first house I ever lived in where the best room is going to be the room where I work. Miriam has this exaggerated respect for what I do

he told a reporter in August 1972, just before they moved in. The

location in Maidenhead was ideal, although what he really wanted was
'1815 red brick, six bedrooms, three bathrooms, billiard room, tennis
court. All this.'[14] Ironically, within seven years he would own a home
that came extraordinarily close to this description.

Fernleigh had a stone unicorn beside the small front door, a curious
reminder of the unicorn that was cut from and then restored to the
text of *Rosencrantz and Guildenstern* and which appears in *Jumpers*
when Dotty relates her impression of seeing the first men land on the
moon: 'it was as though I'd seen a unicorn on the television news . . .
It was very interesting, of course. But it certainly spoiled unicorns.'[15]
The large house with its paved front area was not at first glance
attractive, although the grounds at the back led to a tennis court and,
on the side, to a paddock. Through the leaded glass windows of his
study, Stoppard looked out on a green lawn. The lawn and trees
provided inspiration, Stoppard told the family who would purchase
the home in 1979, noting that in the seven years they had lived there,
he and Miriam had added a sun room and garage. Iver was the nearest
village, noted in the Domesday Book: King Alfred's struggle with
Danish invaders in the region was recorded in 893. More recently, its
residents included HRH Princess Victoria and the publisher Martin
Secker.[16]

Fernleigh had a modest, double-columned entrance gate close to
the road which led to a two-storey, white Victorian building and a
variety of spacious rooms awkwardly added at various times. Past the
kitchen and a small room decorated in fuchsia pink by Miriam, was a
large addition, with high ceilings and tall windows, that looked out on
to the quiet back lawn. This was where Stoppard had his desk, facing
the garden. The room had once been divided into a small billiard-
room accommodating only a three-quarter-size table and a study.
There were two partners' desks, one of them Miriam's. An oriental
carpet covered the floor; a comfortable couch was on Stoppard's left,
where a prominent cushion read 'JUMPERS'.

The two often worked together, an idealistic bond. Since he worked
best at night, after the children had gone to bed, she, too, did her work
at that time, silent together in the same room. She referred to it as 'that
team spirit which was absolutely unspoken and never declared . . . I
very much have that feeling when we work together at night and it's
dark. We're supportive of one another. It's unique,' she said in 1980.

Such a portrait, however, lent itself to satire, and three years later Clive James, in *Brilliant Creatures*, couldn't resist referring to Miriam, as Naomi, as no less than an 'interdisciplinary dynamo engaged in a perpetual attempt, successful every second day, to be even more impressive than her husband'.[17]

Stoppard's portion of the study was furnished for work. To the right of his large, leather-topped Victorian desk was a lectern which variously held a dictionary, books or notes; next to this was an ashtray, elevated on its own pedestal. An ungainly rubber plant stood to his left. A phone complemented the pads of paper, pencils and pens on the desk. Left-handed, Stoppard wrote with a fountain pen, often on unlined paper, then dictated the text into a tape recorder, sometimes acting the various parts. The tapes would be sent for transcription to his secretary, and typescripts would be returned to Stoppard, who would then make longhand corrections and alterations before sending them back for retyping. His first secretary was Frances Whitley, originally employed by an estate agent; later on, the energetic, organized and remarkably capable Jacky Chamberlain, who had originally worked for Miriam at Syntex, joined him. She has remained his secretary for more than twenty-five years.

Fernleigh, reflecting Miriam's taste for bright colours and her preference for doing things in a big way, as one friend remarked, became a welcoming home for the young family. Breakfast, for example, was always a formal, family affair in the dining-room: a photograph from the late seventies shows four young boys at the table with Miriam in charge, a nanny ready to help and Stoppard completely distracted by a newspaper. Miriam's increasing success at Syntex culminated in her becoming deputy managing director in 1976, which satisfied her dual ambition of medicine and management. They had decided to live in Iver Heath largely because Stoppard insisted they be closer to her job. Family life gave him a foundation, an anchor which made his brief departures for rehearsals, new productions or lectures always unsatisfactory. 'I'm a very domestic person. The idea of doing glam things just fills me with deep depression. I absolutely prefer being at home,' he proudly told a reporter in 1973.[18]

Too ill to work. Writing play.
George Bernard Shaw, postcard to a friend

Between 1968 and 1972, Stoppard had little time to write, although he was under financial pressure again because of his separation and divorce. Marital difficulties curtailed his efforts, although the success of *Rosencrantz and Guildenstern* had made him a hot property. In 1968, he had three new plays produced in London: *Rosencrantz and Guildenstern*, *The Real Inspector Hound* and *Enter a Free Man*. The film industry was also pursuing him: within a month of the success of *Rosencrantz and Guildenstern*, Stoppard was offered and rejected four film projects. By the end of the year, however, he had sold the rights to *Rosencrantz and Guildenstern* to MGM, along with the rights to his novel *Lord Malquist and Mr. Moon*. He wrote screenplays for both works in 1968, but privately questioned their viability as films. Neither was produced. In 1969, he and Anthony Smith rewrote *Albert's Bridge* as a film script for Al Brodax, the producer of the Beatles' *Yellow Submarine*. That, too, went nowhere.

But Stoppard was becoming better known in theatrical circles. In an August 1969 note, Harold Pinter confessed that 'I didn't know it was *you* at the [Michael] Hordern party. How stupid of me – but you didn't introduce yourself! I *knew* I knew your face – from television – how ridiculous. My son (eleven) knows Rosencrantz & G. almost by heart. I hope you play in the cricket match at Stratford and that we at least meet there.'[19] Previously, Stoppard had tried unsuccessfully to meet Pinter. As a journalist in Bristol, Stoppard attended a student production of *The Birthday Party* and realized that Pinter was seated in front of him. Intimidated, he spent most of the evening thinking of how to approach him. 'Finally, I tapped him on the shoulder and said, "Are you Harold Pinter or do you just look like him?" He said, "What?" So that was the end of that.' In 1967, a congratulatory telegram for *Rosencrantz and Guildenstern* arrived, signed 'PINTA'. 'I thought that in some curious way it was connected with the Milk Marketing Board.'[20]

By 1969, however, their friendship flourished, Pinter characterizing his relationship to Stoppard as avuncular in a 1985 introduction to Stoppard's lecture 'Direct Experience'. 'I'm now going to pass you over to my nephew,' Pinter quipped.[21] In the 1970s, Stoppard's prowess as a wicket-keeper was constantly tested, playing for Pinter's team.[22] Years later, Pinter praised Stoppard's independence: 'He writes what he likes – not what others might like him to write, and manages to write serious plays that are immensely popular.' Stoppard returned the praise in 1990, providing an encomium to Pinter in the *Sunday Times* to mark his sixtieth birthday, celebrating Pinter's ability to break and then redefine the contract between audience and playwright.[23]

Paradoxically, Stoppard's security – through his marriage and family – encouraged greater experimentation in his work. He now had the time and freedom for the 'background reading', as he called it, rather than research, for his new plays.[24] The result? A series of short works and then *Jumpers,* possibly his most ambitious play, bursting with action and ideas. But as he explained to his close friend and neighbour at the time, Paul Johnson (former editor of the *New Statesman* and by 1970 a freelance author), the writing was slow because he always began with a scene or a dramatic incident and then expanded it in all directions. He never started with a fully formed plot or character. Beginning with a particularly effective dramatic moment, analogous to a great portrait painter beginning with the eyes and then establishing the form of the face, Stoppard would find a play to suit his situation.

Although he never read his work-in-progress to friends, Stoppard would take almost daily late-afternoon drives to visit Johnson, who lived nearby in Iver, to discuss aspects of his writing. One of his most remarkable features, Johnson reported, was Stoppard's ability to be self-critical and to accept the criticism of others. He was always intellectually secure enough to do this and never felt intimidated by the advice of others. The physical composition of the play would go quickly once he worked out what the originating scene or incident represented. As he often told Johnson, 'there aren't actually many words in a play'.[25]

One of Stoppard's more intriguing but unsuccessful experiments at this time was a reworking of Brecht's *Life of Galileo* as a film script, his fourth attempt at a screenplay during 1969–70. Stoppard believed that Brecht's play would make an excellent movie. His ambitious script, however, had twenty-seven speaking roles and lacked formal scene divisions, flowing freely among events and locations. He sent the script first to John Boorman at Warner Brothers in April 1971, but found resistance. Boorman told him it was more informed than Brecht, but questioned its lack of cinematic structure. A letter from Stoppard to Peter Bart at Paramount Pictures the following month defended his 115-page screenplay by claiming he would be 'writing a Galileo which would be essentially faithful to history'. He was not interested in writing a tract and argued that 'it is a drama of general appeal'.[26] Stoppard actually visited California to present the script to Paramount following the failure of MGM to 'green light' the project. Stoppard's letter shows him energetically sticking up for his work, determined to protect what he had written. But after two drafts, the script was finally rejected, partly because Paramount felt it lacked a sense of growing jeopardy for Galileo. The movie was not made, although Stoppard still thought it was an important work. Then he lit upon the idea of reshaping it as a stage play for production at the London Planetarium.

By early 1973, the London papers reported the script ready for the Planetarium, with Michael White producing. It soon became evident, however, that technical difficulties made the production too difficult. The new National Theatre building, the RSC and the Young Vic were proposed as alternative sites, but none of these possibilities worked out. As a result, Stoppard withdrew the playscript, although the screenplay resurfaced as recently as 1993 when Michael Eisner of Disney asked Stoppard if he would be interested in reviving the project and possibly directing it. Stoppard explained why it wouldn't work in a June 1993 fax, emphasizing the witty, well-researched character of the play, although it 'does not wear its research lightly'. It hardly resembles a film script, however, because it has long scenes, long speeches and little movement. 'It's much more like a free-form play,' he adds, reflecting the influence of *A Man for All Seasons* by Robert Bolt.[27] He was not interested in directing, but would do a script polish if a director were found. But for *Galileo* to be commercial, it would require a major rewrite which he was not prepared to do, partly because of other commitments.

Despite all this activity, the period after the summer of 1968 when he wrote *The Real Inspector Hound* was unproductive. Stoppard had spent nearly three months in America with *Rosencrantz and Guildenstern* and then was involved with another production of the play and a mini-film based on one of his radio plays. Two years went by before he wrote *After Magritte* 'and then I had a very big hang-up over writing *Jumpers* which I began a couple of years before I finished it'.[28] Discounting his personal problems, Stoppard's distractions with success and general lassitude – he has often admitted that without a deadline or sense of moral commitment, he finds it hard to write – contributed to the slowdown.

One of the important figures for Stoppard's work at this time was and old friend from Bristol, Geoffrey Reeves. Reeves directed the world première of *Dingo* by the Bristol-born playwright Charles Wood, which transferred to London's Royal Court in 1967. Reeves then became an assistant to Peter Brook on *US*, Seneca's *Oedipus* and Ted Hughes's *Orghast* and in 1970–1 was co-director of Brook's Centre for International Theatre Research in Paris.

Stoppard was experimenting with form at this time and writing smaller works for smaller venues. His friendship with Reeves led to the production of *After Magritte* (1970), which Reeves directed for Ed Berman's Ambiance Lunch-Hour Theatre Club in London. Berman was an American who had come to England as a Rhodes Scholar at Oxford. He stayed on to found an unusual educational and theatrical cooperative called Inter-Action in 1968 which began to feature short, lunch-hour plays. They began in the Ambiance Theatre Club, moved to the Green Banana Restaurant and then, in 1971, established the Almost Free Theatre on Rupert Street in London. The name Almost Free derived from the box-office policy of paying only what you could afford. Dogg's Troupe, their children's theatre group, was named after the comic pseudonym of Berman, Professor R. L. Dogg, adopted so that in card catalogues he would appear as Dogg, R. L. (Stoppard said: 'anyone who could wait that long for a bad pun to explode deserved better' and so wrote *Dogg's Our Pet*, an anagram of Dogg's Troupe, itself an imperfect homonym.) This wing of Inter-Action Productions often took productions out into the community on the Fun Art Bus, a double-decker converted with what Berman called 'the smallest proscenium arch theatre in the world installed on the upper deck', which required 'smallish plays'.[29]

Early success for Berman and his troupe came about because of a scandal with their first production: Jennie Lee, an actress, appeared nude for some three seconds in John Arden's *Squire Jonathan*. As an unlicensed theatre club, Inter-Action escaped the censure of the Lord Chamberlain, who still had control over the theatres; the nude scene went on, filling the house. High attendance at other plays meant receipt of a small Arts Council grant in 1968 and the appearance, at least, of legitimacy. Top playwrights and actors began to lend their talent.

Soon, experimental use of the audience balanced the experimental nature of the plays at Inter-Action as the audience became virtually a structural element of the set. And when necessary, Berman took his plays to the street, as when he performed James Saunders' *Dog Accident*, which is itself set in a busy street at lunch-time. At the time, the Ambiance Restaurant had gone bankrupt so it was both necessary and useful for Inter-Action to perform outside. From the bankrupt restaurant, the ensemble moved to the Green Banana Restaurant on Frith Street in Soho, where *After Magritte* premièred in April 1970. The small basement restaurant, with a pillar in the middle, was in constant turmoil and every morning at about 5.00 a.m. during the run of *Magritte*, a truck would pull up outside and unload the box set of the play. The contents of the basement night-club – the Green Banana's other incarnation – would be carried up to the street and loaded into the truck. The set was then carried down the narrow, winding stair by two stage managers who were able to dress 'the stage' for the 11.00 a.m. lunch-time opening. By 2.15 p.m., the truck would return with the restaurant props – tables, chairs, chandeliers – and change the restaurant back into a night-club for the dinner-time clientele. The whole switch-over seemed positively Stoppardian.

There's no need to use language. That's what I always say.
Stoppard, *After Magritte*

Partly based on a Magritte painting, *The Menaced Assassin*, exhibited at a 1969 London show – the painting depicted a murdered woman naked on a couch and a man dressed in a black suit looking into the horn of an old-fashioned Victrola while the heads of three men look in through a window – *After Magritte* opens with a policeman looking through a window into a disordered room where a female is lying on an ironing board, a woman in a ball gown is crawling on the floor and a man in rubber waders and black evening-dress trousers is blowing into a lampshade. By the end of the play, there is a logical explanation for all of these actions.

The events that prompted the play were related to Stoppard by the film producer George Brown. As a birthday present, Brown was given a brace of peacocks, which he put in his garden surrounding his 400-year-old home in Marlow, Buckinghamshire. One morning, while shaving, he was surprised to see one of them take off. He rushed into the garden in his pyjamas, shaving cream on his face. A second bird began to take flight, both landing on a strip of grass across the road. Brown dashed across and caught them. Waiting to return across the road with the birds under each arm, his pyjama bottoms reacted to the gravity of the situation and began to slip. Not one of the passing motorists stopped or even noticed the scene. Stoppard, amused by the situation, thought of including it in the BBC television show *One Pair of Eyes*, which aired in July 1972. Instead, it became part of the origin of the surreal *Magritte*: 'I tend to write plays about people who drive by in a car just at that moment,' Stoppard explained.[30] The surrealistic farce which resulted has become one of his most frequently staged works.

By December 1971, the Almost Free Theatre opened on Rupert Street: the inaugural double-bill was *Dogg's Our Pet* and Michael Stevens' *Have You Met Our Rabbit?*. The artistic policy was new plays only and then a seasonal theme was introduced, such as Rights and Campaigns and Black and White Power Plays. Partly to celebrate this development and acknowledge the influence of Berman, Stoppard published 'Yes, we have no bananas' in the *Guardian*. Recalling Berman's insistence that he write a new play, since his lengthy new work, *Jumpers*, was supposedly completed and going into rehearsal, Stoppard provides a humorous and sympathetic account of Berman's career, noting his successful Human Flea Circus in Camden Town, a children's theatre hit.

Recounting an early meeting with Berman in the Green Banana, Stoppard recalled the set of *After Magritte*, 'a living room play with lots of furniture . . . mounted in a space measuring twelve feet by twelve with a ceiling of eight'.[31] He also recalled how he received an author's fee from the Arts Council of £50, which he put towards Berman's expenses – so that it seemed as if he was paying Berman to put on his play. But Stoppard admiringly summarized Berman's activities, from his four theatre groups under the Inter-Action umbrella to the playgroups, art projects, advising councils and visits to schools, mental homes, remand homes and the streets: 'Berman makes it happen, raises money, works 100 hours a week, writes, directs, sings, acts, sweeps the floor and negotiates for more money.' In 1970, he was described in the Council of Europe report as 'the most dynamic phenomenon in the British community arts scene'.[32]

In his article, Stoppard outlines his idea for what would become *Dogg's Our Pet*, interspersed with details from Kenneth Tynan on problems with *Jumpers*. The result is a kind of Stoppardian cross-talk between the creation of one play and working out the details of another as he itemizes his preparation for the alternative theatre group alongside the preliminary stages in readying *Jumpers* for the National. Both are subject to similar advice from directors and producers concerning speeches that are too long, the immediate need for revisions and the way actors and directors behave, especially when trying to open a new theatre. Stoppard ends the piece with his own cross-cutting: on the first day of rehearsals for *Jumpers*, he realizes he should cut a speech by Geoff in *Dogg's Our Pet*, rushing over to Rupert Street during the break to inform Berman. But Berman is all questions: 'How about doing a bus play for us?' 'You mean a play about a bus?' Stoppard replies. 'No, no, a play *in* a bus.' And so his next Berman project got under way.[33]

Dogg's Our Pet, which opened at the Almost Free Theatre in December 1971, originated in a section of Wittgenstein's philosophical investigations which Stoppard read as background for *Jumpers*. The play explores the arbitrariness of language by showing how two individuals working together can unite without a shared language. The appeal to Stoppard 'consisted in the possibility of writing a play which had to teach the audience the language the play was written in'.[34] The work combines his revisionist thinking about language and his observations of Hughes's *Orghast*. In the published text, as a concession to readers, Stoppard provides a translation from 'Dogg' language to English which opens in this way:

Baker (*offstage*) Brick! [Here!] Cube. [Thanks]
Able (*into a microphone*) Breakfast, breakfast . . . sun-dock-trog . . .
[Testing, testing . . . one-two-three . . .]

Comically and ironically, words like 'Slab'[Okay] and 'Vanilla Squire' [Rotten bastard] are soon comprehended by the audience, but through the actions of the characters who are building a wall rather than by the direct meaning of the words themselves. When Dogg asks 'Upside artichoke almost Leamington Spa?', he is actually saying 'Have you seen the lorry from Leamington Spa?'[35] Such an investigation of words is a prelude to the more intense examination of terms by the philosopher George Moore in *Jumpers*.

By 1972, the Fun Art Bus was a reality, but Berman needed theatrical, artistic and musical works to fill it as it travelled about London. Stoppard responded by drafting *The (15 Minute) Dogg's Troupe Hamlet* for a cast of seven. However, the script was misplaced for four years and was not performed until 1976 and then only on the grey terraces of the new National Theatre. Beginning on 24 August 1976 – the Official First Night of the new National Theatre building would not come until October 1976, with the opening production, *Hamlet*, directed by Peter Hall and transferred from the Old Vic – *The (15 Minute) Dogg's Troupe Hamlet* was performed twice a day.

Stoppard found in Berman a supportive and innovative 'impresario' who wanted to sponsor experimental works and one-act plays for audiences in informal settings at an affordable price. Throughout the seventies, Stoppard would write further works for Berman, notably *Dirty Linen*, *New-Found-Land* and *Cahoot's Macbeth*. The first two works premièred on 5 April 1976, marking the date when Berman became a British subject; the third on 21 May 1979. Berman's venue and comic sense of theatre provided an alternative for Stoppard from the more rigid, institutionalized National Theatre or RSC, although only such companies could put on large-scale productions like *Jumpers*.

Stoppard had written *Dogg's Our Pet* while waiting for rehearsals to begin for *Jumpers*, and divided his time between the productions. *Jumpers*, however, which he redrafted in 1970 from a brief attempt in 1968, took more energy and time and even required an interlude in the desert.

Tell me something – Who are these acrobats?
Stoppard, *Jumpers*

The conception of *Jumpers* may have occurred in the exchange in *Rosencrantz and Guildenstern* when Rosencrantz asks, 'Shouldn't we be doing something – constructive?' and Guildenstern replies, 'What did you have in mind? . . . A short, blunt human pyramid . . . ?'[36] Stoppard loved the image of a pyramid as a theatrical event, especially with one member of the pyramid blown out of it with a gunshot. Philosophy also attracted him at this time, as he wrote to Anthony Smith in July 1968:

> I'm on a ridiculous philosophy/logic/maths kick. I don't know how I got into it, but you should see me trying to work out integral calculus with one hand, while following Wittgenstein through 'Tractatus Logico-philosophicus' with the other. I shall end up writing an unsatisfactory play by preparing just enough ground to reveal the virgin and impenetrable tract(atus). However.[37]

In the same letter, Stoppard reflects on his new-found riches, reporting on an afternoon visit to Sotheby's where a range of literary first editions were on view for a forthcoming auction. Included were 'firsts' of *The Waste Land, Prufrock, Ulysses*, 'signed copies of about two dozen Eliots, [and] a couple of Beckett, Waugh, Hemingway[s]'. Parodying Beckett in the letter, Stoppard adds 'I can't go on. I must.' What appealed most to him was the manuscript of Waugh's novel *Scoop*, one of Stoppard's favourite books. He left 'forlorn bids' on the manuscript and on a letter by Wilde rebuking a forward solicitation which read: 'Sir, I see that to the brazen everything is brass. Your obedient servant, Oscar Wilde.' John Wood later commented that such acquisitions were the only signs of Stoppard's wealth.[38]

Jumpers, begun two or more years before, was a difficult work to finish, the more so because he didn't know anything about the subject: 'I wanted to write a play about an ethical question in terms of academics. But I didn't know any philosophers and hardly any academics.' He set himself a huge reading programme, 'to make sure that what I thought were my penetrating insights weren't simply the average conclusions of a first-year philosophy student, which they invariably turned out to be.'[39] He later explained that the original impulse for the play was the image of a troupe of gymnasts making a pyramid, followed by a gunshot blowing one gymnast out, causing the pyramid to collapse: 'I had this piece of paper with this dead acrobat on the floor and I didn't know who he was, who shot him or why.' Soon, he linked the image to the idea of moral values as social conventions and 'jumpers' quickly signified acrobats as well as 'jumping to conclusions'.[40]

Stoppard was under pressure to top *Rosencrantz and Guildenstern*, to show that he was more than a one-play writer. His success made him alternately less ambitious and equally determined to prove himself. He explained that the time it took him to write a play derived partly from his need to make the underlying logic of the work unshakeable.[41]

The National, which was to stage *Jumpers*, was going through a difficult period. *Long Day's Journey into Night*, the preceding play, directed by Michael Blakemore, was a critical and box-office hit, with Olivier in his last major role for the company. But a single hit contrasted with the constant successes of the RSC, which was flourishing internationally with Peter Brook's acclaimed production of *A Midsummer Night's Dream*. The play had opened towards the end of the 1970 season in Stratford and transferred to the Aldwych via Broadway in 1971–2. The RSC was the talk of the country, the National the butt of criticism and attacks in the press for its lack of exciting drama. Brook's acrobatic production of Shakespeare's comedy, staged in a white circus ring, convinced many that the National was creatively depleted. *Jumpers* might be understood as 'the National's gymnastic riposte to the RSC'.[42] Tynan tartly summarized the rivalry between the two companies: 'our delight at their successes is slightly greater than our delight at their flops'. With a growing financial debt – £140,000 for 1971 and 1972 – the National had to restructure, and reduced the company from seventy to forty members. Yet Stoppard admitted that he probably wouldn't have written *Jumpers* if he hadn't known it would be shown at the National 'where they wouldn't recoil from a large play with acrobats'.[43]

In the early stages of writing his play, Stoppard had no idea who the shot gymnast was, or who had shot him or why – in much the same way as he did not know who the corpse was under the sofa when he began *The Real Inspector Hound,* only that a corpse was there. Yet he knew the gymnasts opened the play, just as he knew he wanted to write a play about a moral philosopher. The visual and the intellectual had to come together. His reading of academic philosophy led to his wish to parody its language, interests and values. 'Dons talk like they write. I read it [philosophy] with great enjoyment. It was really very stimulating as well as absurd,' adding the characteristic Stoppardian double-take which he exploits in the play.[44]

Stoppard had two prototypes for *Jumpers.* The first was his own work, *Another Moon called Earth,* a television comedy of manners from 1967 in which Penelope, the neurotic wife of Professor Bone, distraught over man's landing on the moon, receives visits from a dapper Albert Pearce. Stoppard returned to the outline of the play for the bare structure of *Jumpers,* with Archibald Jumper visiting the semi-retired, former musical comedy star Dotty while her husband, the distracted professor of moral philosophy, George Moore, prepares a lecture. The second prototype was Václav Havel's play *The Increased Difficulty of Concentration* (1968), about an academic dictating an incompetent lecture on moral values which goes against the nature of his society. An additional, if indirect influence may have been Christopher Hampton's 1970 work, *The Philanthropist,* premièred at the Royal Court, about an emotionally detached lecturer in philology.[45] The play opens with a device Stoppard would use at the beginning of *The Real Thing*: a character speaking lines that are actually from a play written by the protagonist but which the audience believes to be part of the drama they are watching.

> *The truths that have been taken on trust, they've never had*
> *edges before.*
> Stoppard, *Jumpers*

Stoppard's confusion over his initial ideas for *Jumpers* equalled that surrounding his initial presentation of the work to the National. In December 1970, Stoppard told Kenneth Tynan that the new work would not be ready until the following autumn. In late summer 1971, Tynan pleaded with him to give the National some idea of its content: within weeks they would have to fix their plans for the forthcoming season. Stoppard replied that the first draft was nearly done but he had no time to type it. Could he read it to Tynan and Olivier? Tynan arranged an unusual audition at his Kensington home; Olivier, John Dexter and Tynan would listen to Stoppard, who arrived at the late-afternoon meeting with 'the text and a sheaf of large white cards, each bearing the name of one of the characters'.[46] Olivier had come directly from an exhausting rehearsal. After they had all had some wine, Stoppard announced he would read the play, 'standing at a table, holding up the appropriate card to indicate who was speaking. What ensued', writes Tynan, 'was a gradual descent into chaos.'

The play, then titled 'And Now the Incredible Jasmin Jumpers' and later 'The Incredible Archibald Jumper' before finally becoming *Jumpers*, was complex, and Stoppard soon got his cards mixed. Within an hour, Olivier fell asleep, but Stoppard pressed on, although in the gathering dusk he became more desperate with the shuffling of pages and display of cards. After two hours, he had barely finished Act One. The denouement was equally out of step with the event:

> At that point, Olivier suddenly woke up. For about thirty seconds, he stared at the ceiling, where some spotlights I had recently installed were dimly gleaming. Stoppard looked expectantly in his direction: clearly, Olivier was choosing his words with care. At length, he uttered them. 'Ken,' he said to me ruminatively, 'where did you buy those lights?' Stoppard then gave up and left. Next day it took all the backslapping of which Dexter and I were capable to persuade him that the play was worth saving.[47]

Tynan may have been unaware of Stoppard's dismay at the audition (at which he remembers Michael Blakemore also being present): 'biggest mistake I ever made'. Holding up the wrong card for the speeches he was reading made the play almost incomprehensible. Afterwards, he wrote nothing for two weeks: 'I couldn't – I was stunned, in total despair. Then I got a very encouraging letter from [John Dexter] . . . and I finished the play. I'm a hideously insecure person, really. I need constant reassurance.' Nevertheless, despite the débâcle, Tynan remained enthusiastic over the play, offering memos, suggestions and comments on the text throughout the lengthy process of preparing it for the stage.[48]

After completing a first draft of *Jumpers*, Stoppard sent the play to

Geoffrey Reeves, who had directed *After Magritte* and was by then an assistant director to Peter Brook at the new Centre for International Theatre Research in Paris. In the summer of 1971, Reeves, Brook and Ted Hughes were in the Iranian desert, preparing a production of Hughes' highly unorthodox work, *Orghast*. Stoppard and Miriam, vacationing in the Middle East, decided to see the production, which was scheduled for the Shiraz Festival on the cliffs above Persepolis. They arrived to find not only Reeves but also Anthony Smith who, having done some research for Brook, was asked to join and document their Iranian expedition. The result was *Orghast at Persepolis* (1972), an account of Brook, the production and the work supported by the principles that organized Brook's ideas of the theatre at the time, summarized in a remark he made to an actor in his momentous production of *A Midsummer Night's Dream*: 'You must act as a medium for the words. If you consciously colour them, you're wasting your time. The words must be able to colour you.'[49]

Stoppard, who attended a rehearsal of *Orghast* Part I in July 1971 at the tomb of Artaxerxes and then interviewed Ted Hughes, set out the importance of the production in an article for the *Times Literary Supplement*. However, instead of focusing on the production, he concentrated on the creation of a new language by Hughes, in part a reflection of Stoppard's own current involvement with language and philosophy. While praising the effectiveness of *Orghast*, Stoppard remained puzzled by the absence of meaning in the words, falling back on Wittgenstein's remark that 'some things cannot be said but only shown'. But Hughes' premise is clear: the sound of the human voice, in contrast to language, can project complicated mental states. The ritualistic action of *Orghast* enhances this condition when sounds create recognized mental states. Hughes commented: 'I was interested in the possibilities of a language of tones and sounds without specific conceptual or perceptual meaning . . .' Stoppard quoted a passage from Peter Brook to supplement the remark: 'A word does not start as a word – it is an end product which begins as an impulse stimulated by attitude and behaviour which dictate the need for expression . . . the word is a small visible portion of a gigantic unseen formation.'[50]

Persepolis was important for Stoppard for several reasons, not least his exposure to the radical creation of a new dramatic language and narrative, set in a ritualistic world of stylized action. Encountering ideas of language and production that were revolutionary and complex prompted him to reconsider the limitations of conventional expression while reinforcing the musicality of verbal exchange. These ideas would coalesce on a small scale in the experimental *Dogg's Our Pet* and on a large scale in *Jumpers*, which required an astute as well as sympathetic director. Olivier chose Peter Wood.

Best known for his productions of Restoration drama and for the original (and not very successful) 1958 production of Pinter's *The Birthday Party* at the Lyric in Hammersmith, Wood, who had directed *Rosencrantz and Guildenstern* in Nottingham in 1971, was familiar with Stoppard's work and had a flair for witty comedies. His 1966 production of Congreve's *Love for Love* at the National was an immense hit, not least because Olivier played Tattle. But Wood was initially reluctant to become involved with *Jumpers*:

> I was a little affronted by the play. My Catholicism at first made me question its facetiousness about belief. And deep down I felt that Tom wanted a director who was at home with moral philosophy – Jonathan Miller, perhaps. When Sir Laurence Olivier insisted I should do it I would say, 'Why? We don't get on.'

In the programme for the 1976 revival of *Jumpers* at the National, Wood somewhat comically wrote 'when I first asked [Stoppard] what the play was about, he said, "It's about a man trying to write a lecture". But for me it was about a man trying to write a lecture *while his wife was stuck with a corpse in the next room.*'[51]

Wood did get involved in the production, significantly contributing to the verve of the piece with his ideas about staging, performance and music (something he would also do for *Travesties*). But he also took the initiative: at one point, when Stoppard left the rehearsal for ten minutes, Wood boldly cut a scene in two and played it backwards, reversing the two halves of the first act. (Stoppard thought it was an improvement.) Wood also learned to deal with Stoppard's seemingly endless revisions, recalling that even on opening night, Stoppard came round at 6.30 p.m. 'with a list of notes as long as this arm to take to the cast'. Realizing that they had at last become friends, Wood knew he had to tell him straight out: 'You can't do that!'[52]

Michael Hordern, who played George, was at first equally dismayed with the text. He found the work difficult to understand when he first read it in Belgrade, where he was making a movie. Nevertheless, he knew it was brilliant and accepted the part. He had already worked with Wood and admired Diana Rigg who had accepted the role of Dotty. Rehearsals began unpromisingly when Olivier walked out of the first read-through, 'finding the play unintelligible'. Hordern's first speech was a remarkable thirteen minutes in length and dealt with the existence of God, daunting to say the least. There were a number of unhappy dinners in Chinese restaurants which lasted late into the night as Stoppard, Tynan and Olivier debated the merits of the work, thought to be 'too long for its own good'. Since this was only his second major play, Stoppard told Hordern that he had 'got to the stage where he really had no idea if it was all going to be comparatively wonderful or was simply dreadful'. Hordern further reports that

> The epilogue was cut to half the length and, in a panic, lots of changes were thrown at me at the last minute. I became very cross by that time and shouted a bit, after which they backed down and left me alone to get on with it.
>
> The last dress rehearsal in front of the public was very fraught indeed as the revolve, which was crucial to the play, broke down and had to be mended, making the evening seem intolerable. [But] the first night of *Jumpers* was unbelievable, one of the highlights of my career.[53]

In his 1968 article 'Something to Declare', Stoppard explained that he thinks 'in visual terms, not in terms of colours . . . but certainly in terms of movement'.[54] This is literally the case with the opening of *Jumpers*: as the ex-musical comedy star Dotty tries to sing 'Shine on Harvest Moon', a woman, who we later learn is George's secretary, does a striptease on a trapeze. Crouch, a porter pressed into serving drinks at the opening party scene (formerly the hall porter in *Another Moon called Earth*), is hit by the swinging secretary; a blackout follows, and then, after an elaborate introduction, eight identically yellow-suited acrobats enter, 'jumping, tumbling, somersaulting'.[55] Dotty is not impressed, while her philosopher husband George is oblivious to these events – until the acrobats form a human pyramid, and a sudden, unexpected gunshot rings out. One acrobat is blown out of the pyramid which miraculously remains standing until Dotty walks through the gap. Dramatically, the dying jumper pulls himself up against Dotty's legs and crawls up her body. The pyramid then collapses.[56] Such confusions prompted Martin Esslin to remark that Stoppard thinks in terms of an improbable image 'which looks like sheer surrealism out of the wildest kind of Lewis Carroll invention, and then the rest of the play serves to actually explain what it was'. It 'was a perfectly natural event if you take certain premises', he noted.[57]

As if the opening wasn't puzzling enough, the treatment of philosophers in the play is even more complicated, with the jumpers extending the disorder by assuming competing identities. 'Who *are* these acrobats?' Inspector Bones asks. George answers:

Logical positivists, mainly, with a linguistic analyst or two, a couple of Benthamite Utilitarians . . . lapsed Kantians and empiricists generally . . . and of course the usual Behaviourists . . . a mixture of the more philosophical members of the university gymnastics team and the more gymnastic members of the Philosophy School.[58]

In the play, George acknowledges what Stoppard understands about language: 'words betray the thoughts they are supposed to express. Even the most generalized truth begins to look like special pleading as soon as you trap it in language.' In his pursuit of God, George faces a constant dilemma: 'I don't claim to *know* that God exists, I only claim that he does without my knowing it.'[59] His lecture is for the symposium 'Man – Good, Bad, or Indifferent?', where George is to debate with Professor McFee, now deceased and hanging from a closet hook in Dotty's bedroom, although George does not know it. Confronting George's theism is Sir Archibald Jumper's relativism. The Coda to the work, cut in the original production but later restored, confirms the instability of George's position when he refuses to interfere when Archbishop Clegthorpe, a former veterinarian, is shot for failing to repudiate his belief in God. One of the ironic but comic features of the play are George's animals, Thumper, the hare, and Pat, his tortoise, a forerunner of the tortoise in *Arcadia*. Philosophy and murder, fringed with musical comedy, collide in the play.

The world is a comedy to those that think, a tragedy to those that feel.

Horace Walpole

Stoppard addressed Walpole's axiom from the pulpit in March 1973 in a public dialogue on his writing at the Church of St Mary-le-Bow, London. *Jumpers* had just returned to the repertoire of the National after a six-month hiatus, while Stoppard was busy in revising his Galileo play. In his exchange with Reverend Joseph McCullouch, the vicar, Stoppard defended Walpole's apophthegm, pushing aside the ambiguities or impreciseness of the expression. Conveying the idea was what mattered. Yet earlier, Stoppard had contradicted himself, declaring that 'I'm not actually hooked on form. I'm not even hooked on content if one means message. I'm hooked on style.'[60]

Jumpers balances both positions in its self-conscious appropriation of the complexity and limitations of language. 'If you and I both know what is meant by x, then it doesn't actually matter if we express it ambiguously,' Stoppard explained to Reverend McCullouch. 'Language is an approximation of meaning and not a logical symbolism for it,' he had stated in the play.[61] And, duplicating the situation in *Rosencrantz and Guildenstern*, the characters in *Jumpers* exchange identities, Dotty at one point in the first act speaking like George as she summarizes Archie's view that 'better' is not a property but another angle of vision. The business of establishing identities is never clear-cut. Crouch, for example, is an amateur philosopher, while Inspector Bones is an unrepentant *aficionado* of the music-hall.

Archie presents the 'plain facts' of the play, but in Stoppard there are never just 'plain facts'. What Archie sees as a straightforward murder of Professor McFee 'while performing some modest acrobatics for the entertainment of Miss Moore's party guests', Inspector Bones sees in a more complex light:

> The way I had it, some raving nutter phones up the station with a lot of bizarre allegations starting off with a female person swinging naked from the chandeliers at Dorothy Moore's Mayfair residence and ending up with a professor picked off while doing hand springs for the cabaret, and as far as I'm concerned, it's got fruit-cake written all over it.[62]

Every action and word is open to interpretation, supporting Stoppard's claim that he constantly writes 'about oppositions and double acts'. Although he sympathizes with the character 'who believes that one's mode of behaviour has to be judged by absolute moral standards', Stoppard can just as easily 'shoot my argument full of holes. This conflict between one's intellectual and emotional response to questions of morality produces the tension that makes the play,' he told a reporter in 1974.[63]

In the play, excluding for the moment the range of conflicting ideas and the incomplete lecture by George, 'Is God?',[64] opposing characters and jealousies dominate, one of the most comic and ironic being that of Crouch, the hall porter who called the police to report the murder of a jumper, but who is himself an armchair philosopher of some note and gladly offers critiques of George's lecture. This parallels George's philosophic duel with the dead McFee (partly embodied in Archie, his other antagonist), while echoing earlier figures in competition with, or in the shadow of, others: Rosencrantz in the shadow of the brighter Guildenstern, Moon in the shadow of Higgs, or, later, Carr in the shadow of Joyce and even the younger Housman in the shadow of the older.

Jumpers contains a fundamental logic, although structurally it runs backwards. Diana Rigg, the original Dotty, expressed it clearly:

> Everything in this play is perfectly logical. Everything ties in, but it doesn't tie in the sequence that we, as theatre-people, are used to. More often than not the clue to the person's dilemma comes 35 minutes *before* the fact, which is a complete inversion of how it's normally done. Tom expects his audience to lean forward in their seats and take note of absolutely everything because in order to understand the play it is necessary.[65]

Jumpers is the logical world of the illogical: a dead jumper, Aesop's fable and Zeno's paradox do not so much integrate, however, as intersect by the play's end. 'Firstly, is God?' does not seem such an outrageous question if one is following the process by which Stoppard tries to test the proposition that 'moral values are purely social conventions or, alternately, they refer to some absolute divinity'.[66]

*I belong to a school which regards all sudden movements as
ill-bred.*

Stoppard, *Jumpers*

Ten days before the première, the text of *Jumpers* was still in flux and
overlong at four hours' running time. Tynan, in an apocryphal
account, begged Olivier for permission to cut; Olivier told him to
approach the director, but Peter Wood would not allow any changes
unless Stoppard approved. The author actually felt that any alterations
at this stage would upset the actors. Tynan, seeing this impasse, took
singular action, the next day dictating to the actors a series of cuts and
transpositions to reduce the text. They were accepted.[67]

The response to the play was exuberant: Irving Wardle wrote in *The
Times* that *Jumpers* 'contains more good lines a minute than any other
modern comedy now on show', adding that Peter Wood's production
confirmed the recovery of the National which had begun with Olivier
in *Long Day's Journey into Night*. Stoppard, for the second time,
restored the National's popularity and reputation for original and
stimulating productions. Milton Shulman, in the *Evening Standard*,
admired the parallels between Diana Rigg's character and Marilyn
Monroe and celebrated the play as one that 'will make the cognoscenti
squeal with laughter and leave those who think Wittgenstein is a lager
beer not very amused'.[68] Peter Nichols enjoyed it more than any other
Stoppard work, although Michael Frayn, who had read philosophy at
Cambridge, thought it shallow, an 'unusually positive' opinion, says
Nichols. Frayn, he adds, 'always leans over backwards to see the other
point of view'.[69] Each night, as many as sixty copies of the play were
sold from the bookstall in the foyer of the Old Vic. Faber reported that
nearly 1,500 copies had been sold at the theatre within the first month
of its run, the only play to have done so well, they trumpeted, since
Christopher Hampton's *The Philanthropist* played at the Mayfair.
However, one curious aftershock relating to *Jumpers* occurred in 1979,
when Stoppard learned that a letter he had written to the widow of
George Moore, the Cambridge philosopher, apologizing for the use of
his name in the play, was to be auctioned by Sotheby's. The two-page
letter was expected to fetch between £100 and £150, which surprised the
playwright.[70]

The Oxford philosopher A. J. Ayer weighed in with academic praise in his frequently cited article, 'Love among the logical positivists'. Not only did Ayer enjoy the play, but he admitted that some of the actor Michael Hordern's mannerisms in playing George were not unlike his own: 'the mishearing of "logician" as "magician" is part of my family saga,' he admitted. Hordern was a friend of Jonathan Miller, who was, in turn, a close friend of Ayer's. 'I think perhaps Michael Hordern did Freddie Ayer twice removed,' Stoppard offered.[71] Ayer emphasized that George, though sometimes absurd, is never pathetic. Summarizing the argument of the play as that between 'those who believe in absolute values, for which they seek a religious sanction' and those who uphold values more frequently found among contemporary philosophers who are relativists or subjectivists in morals, Ayer praises the parodic power of the work and its world, where churches have become gymnasiums and the former Minister of Agriculture has become the Archbishop of Canterbury. The dichotomy is clear when Archie tells Crouch that 'truth to us philosophers . . . is always an interim judgment'; this is countered by George's statement that 'there are many things I know which are not verifiable but nobody can tell me I don't know them'.[72] Altruism vanishes when belief in absolutes disappears, Ayer writes.

An exchange of letters between Stoppard and Ayer following the publication of the article led to a friendship that saw the philosopher offer advice and commentary to the dramatist. Tynan described a visit Stoppard and he made to Ayer at his Oxford college in *Show People*. Ayer was soon invited to Fernleigh and, later, Iver Grove; on several occasions, he joined the Stoppards for New Year's Eve, when he always won the parlour games, according to Paul Johnson. In the 1976 revival of *Jumpers*, with Julian Glover as Archie, Julie Covington as Dorothy and Michael Hordern repeating his success as George, excerpts from Ayer's review appeared in the programme.

Jumpers continued to bring audiences to the National, during its second run in repertory from February 1973. Stoppard slightly altered the work in response to improvements suggested by Peter Wood. One change in the 1973 revival was the disappearance of Scott, the astronaut, from the Coda, 'a more difficult decision but I think on balance the right one; he added little and delayed much,' Stoppard explained.[73] Later changes to a 1985 West End production, which starred Felicity Kendal as Dotty and Paul Eddington as George, included a tighter opening and a re-ordering and editing of some of the speeches to clarify what was happening at the outset, including Dotty now clearly shouting 'there's a corpse in the cupboard'. The most dramatic change was the restoration of Scott and Tarzan (Lord Greystoke) to the Coda. Tarzan disappeared in the 1972 and 1973 performances, as well as its revival for the Royal Opening of the new National in October 1976 .[74]

The gala organized for the Royal Opening mixed royalty with theatre history. The rainy night's festivities began with 'Richardson's Rocket', an instant tradition invented by Sir Ralph Richardson: setting off a firework on the roof before every first night to let London know that the curtain at the National was going up. After the Queen and her party had arrived and the obligatory speeches had been offered, the royal party divided, the Queen and Prince Philip visiting the Olivier Theatre to see Goldoni's Venetian comedy *Il Campiello,* and Princess Margaret attending a performance of *Jumpers* in the Lyttelton. Her presence and delight in the play prompted a long fascination with Stoppard's work, which grew into a friendship. The selection of *Jumpers* for the gala marked its prestige and, at last, Stoppard's ascendance.

With the achievement of long-sought domestic stability through his new marriage, Stoppard felt secure enough to experiment with structure, language and action. This initiated a new phase in his writing which his next major play, *Travesties,* would consolidate. Stoppard had developed from an ingenious playwright who inventively rewrote Shakespeare into an original dramatist who could enthral audiences, royal and otherwise, with his intellectual fun.

CHAPTER 10

ARTIST ASCENDING A STAIRCASE

*It is only when the imagination is dragged away from what
the eye sees that a picture becomes interesting.*
Stoppard, 1972

Jumpers' success magnified Stoppard's popularity, while intensifying demands on his time. Requests for screenplays, television scripts and even television appearances multiplied. In July 1972, for example, he was the focus of BBC Television's *One Pair of Eyes*, a programme that encouraged guests to express their views on a series of topics. Stoppard, disturbed by the apparently fixed opinions of so many on television, took a different tack, arguing with refreshing scepticism that, frankly, he didn't know about anything. Emphasizing the absence of certainty in the Church, the arts or himself, he expressed proud delight when the Department of Weights and Measures admitted to him on screen that even *they* dealt in approximations. There was an on-camera, split-screen dispute between two Stoppards, an extension of his propensity to argue either side of a proposition equally and his early habit of interviewing himself.[1] Stoppard, in a spirit of self-confrontation, recorded his own double act.

The question of aesthetics and the shaping of his plays absorbed him throughout the post-*Jumpers* period. His concern with form – and his growing reputation for being a verbal rather than a visceral playwright – found further expression in his November 1972 radio play, later adapted for the stage, *Artist Descending a Staircase*. In this work, the artist Martello complains that he has 'achieved nothing but mental acrobatics – *nothing*', Stoppard voicing his detractors' complaint against himself.[2] Yet the work displays his continued engagement with modern art, first presented in *After Magritte*; in this case, Magritte's

The Menaced Assassin is replaced by Marcel Duchamp's 1912 painting, *Nude Descending a Staircase*. The reworked title of the play signifies its new subject: three ageing artists and a young, beautiful but blind model who tragically jumps from a window. 'The reasons *for* art' and its different perceptions are at the centre of the play, although Stoppard admits that he 'didn't go into Duchamp too much'. However, one critic suggested that the temporal, accordion structure of the play echoes Duchamp's pictorial segmentation in *Nude Descending*.[3] The play was fundamentally a love story, Stoppard said, focusing first on the friendship of the three artists and then on Sophie, the woman they all loved and portrayed. Her blindness makes it impossible for her to see how they represent her. This is a typical Stoppard touch, as is the artist who moulds sugar, giving 'cubism a new lease of life' as one character facetiously observes.[4]

Time, not art, is the most intriguing element in the play. The work is a ninety-minute geometric puzzle that weaves back and forth from 1972 to 1914 and then back again, trying to determine how Donner, the artist in the first scene, died. Was it suicide, accident or murder? Detection motivates the plot, which opens in the present, each of the following five scenes being a flashback from the previous scene; the last five scenes continue the fifth, fourth, third, second and first. 'I'm telling everything back to front,' says Sophie at one point, summarizing the technique. What Stoppard calls the 'sequential hijinks' allow him to get at the emotions more effectively, involving a tape loop which replays the final moments of Donner which need to be deciphered.[5] Structuring a play through the repetition or recall of a past action would become a basic technique which Stoppard would elaborate in *In the Native State*, *Arcadia* and *The Invention of Love*. And in working out the seemingly inexplicable – how did Donner die? – he repeats the pattern of *After Magritte* and provides a solution at the same time as he explains the odd behaviour of the group.

But if Stoppard can unravel the artful structure of the play, he has greater difficulty in unravelling what is art. His three artists debate the question, posing alternate yet complementary ideas. Beauchamp defends his inclusive, unfiltered soundscapes of the everyday. Donner, a sculptor, tries to adapt traditional values to modern conditions, while Martello, the painter, employs a unique reassembly of found objects to express content metaphorically. Stoppard gives Donner the most direct critique of modern art, anticipating Stoppard's own attack on conceptual art some twenty-nine years later, at the opening of the Royal Academy's Summer Exhibition in June 2001.[6] In the play, Donner alleges that

> skill without imagination is craftsmanship and gives us many useful objects such as wickerwork picnic baskets. Imagination without skill gives us modern art.[7]

There are immediate objections: Beauchamp declares that 'at our age, *any*thing we do is faintly ludicrous. Our best hope as artists is to transcend our limitations and become *utterly* ludicrous.'[8]

For more than a decade, Stoppard resisted efforts to stage *Artist*, preferring it as a radio drama. Indeed, an incident a few years later demonstrated Stoppard's commitment to radio work: 'Stoppard was telephoned by a Hollywood mogul who offered him a fortune to drop everything and write a film script. "I'm sorry," replied Stoppard, "I'm committed to the BBC." "Forget television," said the mogul scornfully. "What do you mean, television? I'm writing a radio play," Stoppard answered.'[9]

In 1988, however, a fringe theatre group housed in a north London pub made a plea to stage *Artist*. Stoppard agreed and the production by the King's Head Company was a hit, transferring to the Duke of York Theatre in the West End. A production followed in New York in November 1989, with Paxton Whitehead and Harold Gould starring. *Playbill*, the New York theatre programme offered to all theatre-goers, anticipated audience confusion and included a schematic breakdown of the V-shaped time-frame of the play for its patrons. But the play was not a hit, closing in New York after thirty-seven performances.

Artist continued Stoppard's debate with modern art, which his next work, *Travesties*, would elaborate. Several conversations in *Artist*, in fact, anticipate dialogue in the later play, especially in reference to misunderstood historical and cultural events. At one point, Donner and Beauchamp argue over Wyndham Lewis, Edith Sitwell and Nancy Cunard. Beauchamp, in frustration at Donner's confusion, sharply tells him that his mind 'keeps wandering about in a senile chaos'. This is exactly the charge Carr brings against himself in *Travesties*, defending his digressions as 'the saving grace of senile reminiscence'.[10] Labels, while meaningless, are necessary categories in both plays:

Beauchamp, for example, criticizing Donner's portrait of Sophie, says 'surely you can see that a post-Pop pre-Raphaelite is pure dada brought up to date –', while Carr, in his monologue, asks:

'Whatsisay Dada?? You remember Dada! – historical halfway house between Futurism and Surrealism, twixt Marinetti and André Breton, 'tween the before-the-war-to-end-all-wars years and the between-the-wars years – *Dada!* – down with reason, logic, causality, coherence, tradition, proportion . . . my art belongs to Dada 'cos Dada 'e treats me so – [11]

Throughout *Artist*, Stoppard mediates between the avant-gardism of Beauchamp and Sophie's traditionalism. In a passage Stoppard has frequently cited as expressing the accidental fortune of the playwright, Beauchamp justifies the artist to himself by saying

The artist is a lucky dog. That is all there is to say about him. In any community of a thousand souls there will be nine hundred doing the work, ninety doing well, nine doing good, and one lucky dog painting or writing about the other nine hundred and ninety-nine. [12]

Yet, with the First World War as a backdrop to several of the flashbacks, Stoppard tests the role of the artist and his value in a society and culture that is being destroyed, anticipating issues that would be addressed in *Travesties*.

Stoppard dedicated *Artist* to his mother and father, an acknowledgement of their efforts to survive the war and struggle to maintain some awareness of culture despite their dislocations. It may also be an indirect expression of thanks for their implicit encouragement of the value of art. Stoppard's dedications, in fact, reflect his close attachment to his family and inner circle: *Jumpers* was dedicated to Miriam; *Travesties* to his four sons, Oliver, Barnaby, William and Edmund; *Dogg's Hamlet* to 'Professor Dogg and the Dogg's Troupe of Inter-Action'; *Cahoot's Macbeth* to Pavel Kohout, the dissident Czech playwright; *Dirty Linen* to Ed Berman; *Professional Foul* to Václav Havel; *Night and Day* to Paul Johnson; his adaptation of *Dalliance* to Peter Wood; *The Real Thing* to Miriam again; *Hapgood* to his son Oliver, the only dedication which includes the words 'with love and thanks'. *In the Native State* is dedicated to Felicity Kendal; *Indian Ink* to Laura Kendal, Felicity Kendal's late mother. *Rosencrantz and Guildenstern are Dead, Arcadia* and *The Invention of Love,* as well as his novel *Lord Malquist and Mr. Moon,* all lack dedicatees. No work has been dedicated to Jose Stoppard, Kenneth Ewing or Anthony Smith, all of whom have been close to Stoppard at various stages in his life. Again, he may be waiting for the right play – or masking his feelings, hesitant to declare publicly the role of these figures in his life.

> *Even in the most respectable salons to try and follow*
> *a conversation nowadays is like reading every other line*
> *of a sonnet.*
>
> Stoppard, *Travesties*

The identity of the artist and his role in society soon took on another form in Stoppard's next major work, *Travesties,* a dazzling play that elaborated the value of art and its connection to politics. The play went to the Royal Shakespeare Company because of an obligation not yet met: Trevor Nunn had promised Stoppard that he would stage a work of his after the early option for *Rosencrantz and Guildenstern* had expired. Stoppard felt he wanted to do something for the company – and in particular for Nunn, who had also given him the early job of adapting *Tango* – but only after an earlier commitment to the National had also been met: they, of course, had given him his first big break. *Jumpers* fulfilled that obligation, and so, with John Wood in the RSC company, Stoppard delivered *Travesties* to the RSC. When, in the spring of 1973, Olivier and Hall had written to ask for a new work for the National, they were politely rebuffed. Peter Hall expressed his disappointment at losing *Travesties* to the RSC. He acknowledged the significance of John Wood, 'one of his [Stoppard's] favourite actors', being in the company. 'I am torn between being furious that we didn't have the play . . . and relief that the Aldwych has at last had a substantial hit. The relief has it.'[13] Hall was absolutely right on both accounts: Stoppard stated that 'in a way I wrote the play for John Wood . . . I've always thought he was one of the best six actors in captivity', and the popularity of the play would put the RSC back on the map.[14]

Stoppard was to present the play in July 1973, but that shifted to September and, finally, to December. The play actually arrived in

January 1974. The movable deadlines were typical, like the promises that went with them, the conventional mode of spurring on his work: 'It's as good a way as any of getting a play done. It gives me a moral obligation at best, a deadline at worst.' However, 'I always end up being impossibly behind the time. Only once I'm really in trouble do I get started. It takes a very long time to get any words down.'[15] Nevertheless, Trevor Nunn was thrilled with the new work and suggested Jonathan Miller and Diana Rigg for leading roles.

The RSC at the Aldwych desperately needed a hit. Although its productions were more successful than those at Stratford, where work was split between two different companies and new directors and actors were imported, the diluted policies at the Aldwych created confusion. *Sherlock Holmes*, starring John Wood, brought back audiences, as did their 1973 success *The Romans*, Shakespeare's four Roman plays. But a single working ensemble of actors had vanished. Stoppard's *Travesties*, soon to be the hit of the 1974 season, was essentially a West End production inserted into the repertoire of the RSC. John Wood was in his fourth year with the RSC, but the director, Peter Wood, the designer, Carl Toms (who would go on to design a number of other important Stoppard works), and the rest of the cast, came from outside the company.[16] The production would earn substantial revenue and high praise, but had no connection with the RSC's principles of company work.

Stoppard had begun to think about the play as early as 1969, when he read Wittgenstein. Earlier, in 1960, Anthony Smith had mentioned to him that Tristan Tzara and Lenin were in Zurich at the same time; reading Richard Ellmann's biography of Joyce, Stoppard discovered that Joyce was there as well, a point Smith repeated in a passage from his 1971 novel, *Zero Summer*. In that work, an English photographer who has decamped for Provence says that 'I once imagined that Lenin, Tzara, Joyce and Jung all lunched on the same day, in 1916, in the Café Voltaire at separate tables, four bacilli shortly to be dispersed throughout Europe.'[17] A good deal of Stoppard's background reading for the play took place during his commute between Iver Heath and the Greenwich Theatre, where he was directing *Born Yesterday* by Garson Kanin. The tube trip alone required three changes, allowing him a great deal of time to read.

Artist contains a clue to Stoppard's interest in the period:

Beauchamp playfully recalls some of Donner's antics in Zurich in 1915, when 'you told Tarzan he was too conservative'.[18] The reference is a comic error for Tristan Tzara – to appear in *Travesties* – but also leaps back to the uncut Coda of *Jumpers*, with the appearance of Tarzan (Lenin is also cited at several moments in *Artist*). The incident with Tarzan/Tzara in *Artist* also anticipates the confusion of names and memory that characterizes *Travesties*, a feature Stoppard had developed from the first meeting of Rosencrantz and Guildenstern with the Player in the opening act through to *Jumpers*, where Inspector Bones never gets George's name right. This habit would shortly distinguish the behaviour of Henry Carr in *Travesties*.

Stoppard had started work on *Travesties* in 1969, before *Artist*, and its influence on the radio play is evident in a passage on the absence of lemons in Zurich during the war:

> Good God, I said, is Switzerland at war? – things have come to a pretty pass, is it the St Bernard? – Not a smile. Man at the next table laughed out loud and offered me a glass of squash made from lemon powder, remarking, 'If lemons don't exist, it is necessary to invent them.' It seemed wittier at the time, I don't know why.[19]

In *Travesties*, remarks on Switzerland, cafés and the impact of the war, underscored by the absence of certain luxury foods, parallel this passage, turned up a few cultural degrees.

A new, fresh aesthetic emerged in *Artist* which would in turn shape the freedom and playfulness of *Travesties*: the idea that one way of becoming an artist 'is to make art mean the things you do'. Great questions are comically but not frivolously addressed in *Artist*, despite the outbreaks of humour, as in the discussion of Donner's sugar statue of Sophie requiring one either to break off a nipple for sugar in one's coffee or to tilt the statue so that the nipple swirls in the cup. 'How can one justify a work of art to a man with an empty belly?' Donner then asks. His answer: 'make it edible', leading to the new, comic cry, 'let them eat art!'[20] Art certainly *was* allowing Stoppard to eat. His plays were being produced worldwide and he was much in demand.

My memoirs, is it, then? Life and times, friend of the
famous. Memories of James Joyce. James Joyce As I Knew
Him. The James Joyce I Knew.
Stoppard, *Travesties*

History rewritten as fiction is the motif of *Travesties,* a work that
exploits the coincidence of Joyce, Lenin and Tzara being in Zurich in
1918.[21] Factually, they never met, but Stoppard links them through
Henry Carr (a minor official at the British Consulate who had a
dispute with Joyce) and his involvement with Joyce's English Players
in their attempt to produce Wilde's *The Importance of Being Earnest.*
Stoppard treats factual events fictionally, creating a sparkling work
that uses and misuses history: 'scenes which are self-evidently documentary mingle with others which are just as evidently fantastical,' he
wrote in the programme note.[22] He again uses a base-text, Wilde's
play, against which his own work is set. Much of the action is presented
through the unreliable mind and narrative of Henry Carr, who is
alternately an old figure looking back and a young man participating
in the events. A working title for the work was *Prism,* both a
description of the processes of Carr's mind and a reference to Miss
Prism in *The Importance of Being Earnest.*[23]

Events separated by months or even years are made simultaneous
as Carr addresses the issue of 'whether the words "revolutionary"
and "artist" are capable of being synonymous, or whether they are
mutually exclusive, or something in between'. The style of the play
amalgamates Wilde and Shaw through Stoppard's effort 'to marry
the play of ideas to comedy and farce'.[24] This is pastiche, a favourite
Stoppardian technique which flatters earlier works through
imitation rather than mockery of their style. Its repeated use may be
explained as the way Stoppard solved what he claimed to be the
deficit of original ideas for his plays, a remark he has often made in
interviews.

In *Travesties,* ideas of art and the artist flit with immense speed across
the stage, especially as Tzara and Joyce debate their respective aesthetics.
Carr intervenes with various Wildean *aperçus* which recall Vivian in
Wilde's 'The Decay of Lying': 'To art's subject-matter we should be
more or less indifferent,' Vivian declares, a statement echoed by Joyce in

the play. Carr, sounding like Wilde himself, announces at one point that 'art is absurdly overrated by artists, which is understandable, but what is strange is that it is absurdly overrated by everyone else'.[25] In a line parallel to the passage in *Artist* about the artist as 'a lucky dog', Carr challenges Tzara with the question 'What is an artist?' and answers: 'For every thousand people there's nine hundred doing the work, ninety doing well, nine doing good, and one lucky bastard who's the artist.'[26] Tzara responds with 'the difference between being a man and being a coffee-mill is art. But that difference has become smaller and smaller and smaller . . . without art man was a coffee-mill: but *with* art, man – is a coffee-mill! That is the message of Dada.'[27]

Joyce views the artist as apolitical and transcendent: 'An artist is the magician put among men to gratify – capriciously – their urge for immortality.'[28] Genius, not being a run-of-the-mill figure with some talent, defines the artist who creates for art's sake – unlike Lenin, who believes that art is an instrument of the state. But it is Joyce who literally pulls a rabbit out of a hat at one moment in the play.

The historical element of Carr's contretemps with Joyce over the price of a pair of trousers for the production of *Earnest* and Joyce's demand for repayment for the cost of tickets to be sold by Carr for the English Players production provided Stoppard with the pretext for the invented meeting of the characters of Wilde's play: Carr is Algernon, Tzara is Jack; Gwendolen is Carr's sister and Cecily an attractive single woman. Joyce, with his interrogations, echoes Lady Bracknell. Confusions abound, including Cecily's belief that Carr is Tzara and that Tzara is Jack. Late in the play, Cecily exclaims, 'Ever since Jack [Tzara] told me that he had a younger brother who was a decadent nihilist it has been my girlish dream to reform you and to love you.'[29] At another point, Joyce quotes directly from *Earnest*. When he offers Carr the part of Algernon, he cites Jack Worthing's line: 'I may occasionally be a little overdressed but I make up for it by being immensely over-educated.' Carr parodies this statement in Act Two when discussing the function of art, implicitly paralleling Joyce's neutrality towards politics and Wilde's play: 'Wilde was indifferent to politics. He may occasionally have been a little overdressed but he made up for it by being immensely uncommitted.'[30] *Earnest* is the audacious conceit piggybacking on the fictitious encounters of the principals in Stoppard's play.

As a fiction piled on another fiction and exploited for its thematic as well as theatrical importance, *Travesties'* mix of styles and allusions echoes his earliest version of *Rosencrantz and Guildenstern*, which was a 'pure farce with some regrettable pastiche-Shakespeare blank verse'.[31] Audience familiarity with Wilde permitted Stoppard to depart radically from the structure of that work: the comedy of the first act ends with Carr comically misremembering the details of the lawsuit between Joyce and himself, with frequent asides to the audience – 'anybody hanging on just for the cheap comedy of senile confusion might as well go because now I'm on to how I met Lenin and could have changed the course of history et cetera' and his cross-examination of Joyce – 'case practically won, admitted it all, the whole thing, the trousers everything, and I *flung* at him –'.[32] Stoppard constantly parodies, burlesques, criticizes and rewrites the story of Joyce and company in Zurich. Overstatement and understatement alternate wildly in the play: disdainfully, Carr asks Joyce, 'And what did you do in the Great War?' 'I wrote *Ulysses*,' he says. 'What did you do?' Bloody nerve,' Carr mutters. This imaginary repartee ends Act One.

Act Two begins with Stoppard reversing the lingering humour with an attractive girl (Cecily) lecturing on Marxism. The length of this speech, however, presented constant problems for Stoppard and was variously cut or altered; his stage directions read: '*the performance of the whole of this lecture is not a requirement, but is an option.*'[33] Only in a Paris production was it fully restored and dramatically successful, holding the full attention of the audience – largely because the actress delivering it was naked. In a 1994 lecture referring to the incident, Stoppard actually worked out an equation to represent the satisfaction rate established by this change in presentation. Whimsically, he showed that $n(t) = S - (co)$, where n is the scene, t is fifteen minutes, the approximate timing of the lecture, S is satisfaction and (co) is the clothes-off factor. 'By adding clothes off to each side of the equation the Parisian director achieved satisfaction,' Stoppard explained.[34] In the original draft of the play, Stoppard wanted to end the first act with a lengthy exposition of Dada and begin the second with a corresponding exposition of Lenin's trip to Zurich. That altered with the shift in sympathy for Lenin.

Stoppard recognized the structural similarities between *Jumpers* and *Travesties*. Both, he explained to Ronald Hayman, start with a prologue which is slightly strange. Then you have an interminable monologue which is rather funny. Then you have scenes. Then you end up with another monologue. And you have unexpected bits of music and dance, and at the same time people are playing ping-pong with various intellectual arguments.[35]

At the same time, Stoppard acknowledged that his plays

are actually constructed out of people deflating each other. I am a very hedgy sort of writer. What I think of as being my distinguishing mark is an absolute lack of certainty about almost anything. So I tend to write about oppositions, rather than heroes . . . I don't feel certain enough about anything to put up a hero to say it for me.

Summing up the entire issue of *Travesties* for Stoppard is the question, 'how does one justify *Ulysses* to Lenin? Is it possible?'[36]

Peter Wood added new elements of theatricality to the production. Although Stoppard counts on certain theatrical effects, it was Wood who drew them out and often refined them. When Tzara enters, for example, to the noise of an orchestra, the song is 'Every Little Breeze Seems to Whisper Louise', an idea of Wood's that absolutely works, as does the fluttering of Bennett's hands in the dance scene at the end – 'one of my favourite moments in all of theatre!' Stoppard exclaimed. 'We work together well,' Stoppard added: 'he [Wood] sort of saves the play from the author and I save it from the director. He has a way of being totally unimpressed, then ludicrously flattering.'[37] But challenges persisted throughout rehearsals, which took place largely on the top floor of an ex-warehouse in Covent Garden, not far from the Aldwych Theatre, the RSC's London home.

Three long skylights illuminated a canvas-covered floor with markings for the outlines of the stage set. Tables, chairs and bookcases stood about, while along one wall there was a long table where Stoppard, Peter Wood and a couple of assistants sat. An edginess pervaded the rehearsals the week before the Monday first night, since various scenes, including the opening, still needed to be finalized. At one rehearsal, according to Hugh Herbert, Peter Wood began with a list of the sound effects that would precede the play's opening: 'Gunfire. Machine-gun fire. Army boots clumping on duckboards . . .', but each time it varied slightly. The play commenced: Tzara begins to snip up sheets of paper; Joyce dictates part of the 'Oxen of the Sun' episode from *Ulysses*; Lenin begins to write, but the action does not begin until he hands the papers on which he is writing to Cecily. Wood wanted him to blot the papers, although we wouldn't understand why until later: it is a scene 'of vital secret words on a blotter that can be read in a mirror'. The four-minute scene was anything but naturalistic, however: 'it's several days capsulated into this moment, showing that several groups were at work in this library,' Wood explains.[38]

An essential piece of business for the scene is the exchange of two identical brown cardboard folders, Gwendolen's containing a chunk of *Ulysses*, Cecily's a piece of prose by Lenin. They must be accidentally swapped, as the famous handbags were swapped in Wilde's *Importance of Being Earnest*. Wood explained that the scene has 'a lot to do with a spy story. The whole audience has to be alerted to that Hitchcock moment when they swap folders' and has to store this information until the end of Act Two. In the original production, the accidental exchange is prompted by Gwendolyn dropping a glove, although in later stage directions Stoppard wrote: 'it is not important how this transference is achieved, only that it is seen to occur.'[39] Crucially, 'the detective instinct is alerted', as Wood noted, echoing Stoppard's lasting fascination with detection, from *Rosencrantz and Guildenstern* and *The Real Inspector Hound* to *Jumpers*. Spying in *Hapgood*, academic sleuthing in *Arcadia* and textual detection in *The Invention of Love* are further examples of Stoppard's absorption with discovering.[40]

On the Friday before the opening, Wood wanted a first run-through of the whole play. He tried to relax the cast by telling them he wouldn't even listen; he'd brought a good book and magnetic Scrabble. Some of the actors dried, however, and were upset with themselves. John Wood pleaded sharply with the prompter to stay with him, expecting instant aid. John Hurt, playing Tzara, on the other hand, was affronted when the prompter came to his aid, rejecting his help. Hurt, at a break, expressed the inevitable frustration at the first run-through: 'You know perfectly well that it always falls apart the first time you put it together, but you never seem able to prepare yourself for it. It's still shattering when it happens.'[41] Fortunately, the second part of the rehearsal went well, the comedy worked and the cast laughed, which they couldn't do on stage.

Some great lines, however, had to be cut, including a long speech by

Joyce beginning with a failed limerick and then outlining his early life, the behaviour of his father and their many moves around Dublin, before moving on to a litany of those who wore monocles. There is also a compressed survey of the Joyce fortunes, or lack thereof: 'between 1882, when I was born, and 1894, four sons, six daughters and eleven mortgages brought him [Joyce's father] back to Cork to sell all that was left'. The monocle remains a wonderful motif, wittily summarized by the final sentence: 'All in all, I am no stranger to monocularity, Mr Tzara, but I have yet to meet a man to touch you for two-dimensional vision.'[42] In the final text, Stoppard pared down the speech to Joyce's comment that 'Tzara's disability is monocular, and, by rumour, affected, whereas I have certificates for conjunctivitis, iritis, and synechia, and am something of an international eyesore.'[43]

At this point in his career, Stoppard had informally organized a 'company' of his own to execute his plays: the principals were Peter Wood, director; John Wood, actor; and Carl Toms, designer. Michael Codron and either Peter Hall, Trevor Nunn or John Tydeman (of BBC Radio) were his favourite producer/directors. This circle, which would later include Felicity Kendal as his leading lady on and off the stage, worked together on a series of plays from the early seventies through the nineties, offering Stoppard a team whose vision was consistent with his own.

> *Whatever did they do before they invented you?*
>
> Mrs Henry Carr to Stoppard

Travesties was a hit: Michael Billington in the *Guardian* could not contain his pleasure: 'I find it difficult to write in calm, measured tones about Tom Stoppard's *Travesties*: a dazzling pyrotechnical feat that combines Wildean pastiche, political history, artistic debate, spoof-reminiscence, and song-and-dance in marvellously judicious proportions.' Benedict Nightingale wrote in the *New Statesman* that 'Stoppard's great gift is to treat solemn subjects with a gaiety that enlightens without trivialising'. But after praising his technique, he admits his less-than-enthusiastic response to the 'amusement-arcade style', partly because 'we've grown so accustomed to it'. But the songs, puns, sparkling monologues, limericks, disguises and misunderstandings pack 'the action like pinball machines in a debating chamber': Stoppard seems carried away by his own energy and wit. Michael Coveney drew parallels with Alan Bennett's *Forty Years On* with its fatuous aesthete remembering the heroes of Bloomsbury. Clive James, however, said that seeing *Travesties* was 'like drinking champagne' – but it wasn't just effervescent. It was wildly intelligent, presenting an elegant 'plurality of contexts' that gave the play its meaning. His serious games remain 'unparalleled in the theatre'.[44]

While most were overjoyed, some were overtaxed, reacting negatively to the showy demonstration of wit. Was it necessary for an entire scene to be written in limericks or to hijack *The Importance of Being Earnest* into the text? Were the aria-like debates required? Stoppard's defence was clear, explaining that the

> work consists of serious propositions compromised by my personal frivolity . . . that's where it misses the people it misses. The serious people find the whole thing hopelessly frivolous, and people who really think they are going to see an empty comedy find the whole thing impossibly intellectual. And my object is to perform a marriage between the play of ideas and farce.[45]

Compounding the blend was his love of jokes and his habit of inverting a cliché to coin an epigram. The ending of the play, which employs a dance sequence, expresses his union of ideas and farce clearly: Tzara dances with Gwendolen, Carr with Cecily; Joyce and Bennett dance independently; Carr and Gwendolen then transform themselves into older characters. The scene functions to blend time and character and echoes the end of Stoppard's adaptation of *Tango*, while anticipating the conclusion of *Arcadia*.

Among the more unusual responses to the play was a letter Stoppard received ten days after the opening from the seventy-three-year-old Mrs Henry Carr. Surprised and taken aback, Stoppard replied and a friendship ensued, highlighted by Stoppard's arranging for her to attend a matinée in mid-August. 'So much oddity & so much sharpness & wit,' she wrote in a thank-you note: 'I admit that I was a bit bedazzled by the speed; my ears heard, but my mind lagged behind at times.' Almost a month later, she tells him that she 'can't open a magazine or an *Observer* without reading something you have written on different subjects – whatever did they do before they invented you?'[46] Two years later, at Stoppard's suggestion, she sent John Wood a souvenir of Henry Carr's, a bronze cigarette case with Carr's initials on the inside. Stoppard and Mrs Carr continued their friendship for several years, Stoppard frequently sending her gifts, including an inscribed copy of the play.

Travesties opened in New York at the Ethel Barrymore Theater on 30 October 1975. David Merrick produced the RSC production, which was a smash, arriving with a glittering reputation as being erudite, witty and clever, with Stoppard remembered as the *wunderkind* who wrote *Rosencrantz and Guildenstern* which had played on Broadway for over a year. For New York, Stoppard modified the script of *Travesties*, making cuts and sharpening the dialogue.[47] The public took to the play – for the first few months. By February, attendance had fallen off, except for weekends; in fact, business had been sliding since just before Christmas. Receipts for the week of 26 January were the lowest ever, at $47,000. A new advertising campaign began in an effort to hold on until the Tony nominations. In London, *Travesties* ran for 130 performances; in New York, the prospects looked dim. Stoppard, setting an example, told the production company to deduct ten per cent from all sums due to him from the US production and remit them to the company to help meet expenses. Advance sales were also down, although as one producer wrote, 'the play is playing beautifully, and very much more exuberantly than when you last saw it. We have had some marvellous audiences who have brought the cast up to their finest.'[48]

But not everyone felt so happy. Audiences were becoming less sophisticated after the *aficionados* and 'intellectuals' had seen it early in its run. John Wood actually suggested to his agent that there was a 'backlash' developing towards the play as audiences became irritated because they believed the show had been oversold to them. Letters in the *New York Times* first signalled this reaction. Soon, there were walkouts at every performance, partly during the first act and then during the intermission. Wood also reported that where he had had enormous laughter in Act One, there was now silence, because these less sophisticated audiences had become 'hostile to a lot of talk that is too fast, too clipped, too remote and too lacking in any points of identification and direct reference to their own experiences of life'.[49] Even his first appearance at the piano in his crazy overcoat, which should have provoked amusement as a sign of British eccentricity, failed to raise laughs, because he looked nothing more than a Bowery bum to a New York audience.

One proposed solution was to make further cuts, especially to 'the weakest part of the evening, the whole Lenin episode' which made it impossible for the company to lift the play up again. Speeches also had to become more distinct and clearer in presentation, slowing down the delivery. If these changes were not made, January could be an extremely difficult period at the box office, it was suggested. It was essential that Stoppard made cuts to overcome the hostile word-of-mouth and ensure its continuation on Broadway, wrote one producer to Stoppard's agent, Kenneth Ewing.

The ebbing of enthusiasm worried Stoppard's agent less than it did the New York producers, although John Wood's distress was cause for concern. Nonetheless, Ewing discouraged Stoppard from making any further changes. The play held on, the Tony nominations for best play and best actor propelling sales at the box office, and when it won both awards in April, further success was assured. The triumph confirmed Stoppard as a bankable playwright in New York.

Los Angeles wanted to get in on the action and a production was assembled in 1976, Stoppard preparing a lengthy memo which reported cuts throughout the text; the two areas to benefit most from this were the first Bennett–Carr scene and the Lenin section. The postscript to the memo was vintage Stoppard: 'Needless to say any director who wishes to ignore all these cuts has my blessing.'[50] Edward Parone, Associate Director of the Mark Taper Forum in Los Angeles, remained confused: 'Which play am I doing?' he asked: the printed version, the script version from New York or a further revised version? Stoppard replied with an annotated script which Parone had sent him, plus the Faber paperback. Stoppard then confused the matter further by encouraging a restoration of sorts:

> The changes in the New York version were often to do with length per se but I hope that what is deemed to be too long in a commercial and nervous Broadway may not be so in a patient, enlightened and subsidized Los Angeles. At any rate it was not too long for the unsubsidized West End.

Stoppard went on to say that the scene between Joyce and Tzara at the end of Act One had never been performed in its full-text version because 'by the time we got to it the audience had been hit with too many things for too long'. He suggests the New York version, but prefers the Faber version for the opening Bennett–Carr scene from which he thought too much had been cut. 'You gather from all this that I'm not a believer in the principle of a definitive text. The equation (including images, music etc.) is too complicated.'[51] He then notes that he and Peter Wood never stopped tinkering with the Lenin oration, but that he finally prefers the Faber text and placement. Cecily's speech at the opening of Act Two had been performed in full at the play's first couple of previews; but he had been shortening it ever since. His own preference is to begin with the lines 'The war caught Lenin and his wife in Galicia', three-quarters into the printed speech.[52] As a warning, however, Stoppard concludes: 'you will probably find, as we did in New York, that the audience will resent the absence of jokes and parody' in the Lenin section. Clearly, Stoppard finds audience response crucial and the idea of a definitive text untenable; characteristically, he bends the work to the needs of the performance, the theatre and the decisions of the director.

One of the more absorbing as well as amusing aspects of *Travesties* is, naturally, the verbal nonsense couched in political expressions, a combination of Lewis Carroll and Lenin. Throughout the Carr–Tzara conversations, as well as those with Joyce, who prefers to speak in limericks, there is a rapid and constant exchange of puns, repartee and *doubles entendres*. When Carr tells Tzara of his pleasure in drinking a glass of hock and seltzer before lunch for his nerves when 'nerves were fashionable in good society' – this season, the fashion is for trenchfoot, he confesses – Tzara replies that Carr might have felt much better anyway. Carr then says, 'No, no – post hock, propter hock', a pun on the philosophical tag *post hoc, ergo propter hoc*. Tzara then tells Carr he speaks nonsense, prompting this answer: 'It may be nonsense, but at least it is clever nonsense.' The line not only anticipates Lady Croom telling Captain Brice, 'Do not dabble in paradox, Edward, it puts you in danger of fortuitous wit', but the subsequent conversation on chance in *Travesties* anticipates several passages from *Arcadia* – not entirely surprising since Stoppard was working on *Arcadia* at the same time as he was preparing for the RSC revival of *Travesties*.[53]

The play's revival was notable for its originality and acting: the 1993 RSC version at the Barbican starred Antony Sher. A nervous, smoking Stoppard greeted Sher at the Clapham rehearsal room; seeing him so ill at ease immediately endeared him to the actor. The director, Adrian Noble, seeking to encourage the cast, reported that Stoppard had done some rewrites, stressing that the conservative Carr and the far-left Lenin now shared a common view of art: 'a dislike for its poncy practitioners', as Sher describes it in his autobiography.[54] Stoppard told the cast at this early rehearsal that he was 'dead chuffed' about the revival, although the phrase sounded odd on his lips, 'like a foreigner speaking English. Which he both is and isn't,' Sher notes.[55]

Stoppard, however, still worried over the text: 'on the page his humour is light and effortless, in life it's serious, almost scientific. "There are just too many words in this gag," he'll say solemnly.'[56] His humility and criticism of his own text surprised Sher: 'I think I may just have been showing off here, swanking with the research,' he said on several occasions. But as Sher discovers, 'working on the Stoppardian–Wildean mix, you wake up to language'. And even the actors saved his handwritten rewrites, although they were not above doing impersonations of the playwright when he was absent, exaggerating 'the soft "r", the sideways opening of his mouth, the flapping hands going up the great coiff [of hair]'. But Stoppard's musical language – Noble actually propped his copy of the script on a music stand – triumphs: it is 'a circus of words', Sher exclaims.[57]

Stoppard, however, remained an enigma: shy and serious, Sher offers, aware of Stoppard's sensitivity to acting. After a matinée on 11 September 1993, Stoppard gave Sher 'excellent notes, about not over working the speeches, about letting *him* [Stoppard] do the work. Shakespeare would've asked actors the same thing.' At another point, Stoppard told Sher that in the two-and-a-half hours of the show, he hit only one line wrong, '"the 'Oh yes' after Joyce has corrected you about who the Prime Minister is. You hit a note that's simply not Carr. It's – how can I put it? – petulant? – not quite – um . . ." I helped him out: "Camp?" "Thank you," he said, with a rare smile.' Learning that Stoppard, like Sher, did not attend university and that he wanted to, Sher writes in near-disbelief that Stoppard *wants to be brighter.* The idea that this brilliant, intellectual playwright wants more knowledge is incomprehensible to the actor, who, at the dinner after the press night, presented Stoppard with his original drawing for his first-night card: a cartoon of Stoppard as Oscar Wilde.[58]

For the 1993 revival, changes to the text were again in order, visual as much as verbal. This was the first major British revival of the play since 1974 and Stoppard had an altered sense of the work:

> When I wrote *Travesties*, I was simply so excited by what I'd learnt in my research that I couldn't resist shovelling it all in in bucket loads. The revised version involved taking rather a lot out again.

'I'm fated', he explained, 'to write plays in which the first act is fractionally too long and, mysteriously enough, *Travesties* doesn't seem to be getting any shorter.'[59] Changes again took place, notably the reduction of Cecily's lecture on Lenin that opens Act Two, but Stoppard also added new lines, such as this declaration by Carr, with implications of his own double act:

> I don't know that I approve of these identity disorders. I realise that the split personality is all the rage in Zurich – I have known plain men with no personality whatsoever turn a salon into a sort of adoration society simply by presenting two contradictory visiting cards – but if it's going to prove impossible to get undivided attention the end can only be ruin and decay.[60]

Further revisions and additions included making Lenin's views on culture more entertaining, with Carr, in a new line, declaring 'there was nothing wrong with Lenin except his politics', matched by another new remark by Carr: 'If Lenin did not exist, it would be unnecessary to invent him.' Lenin in turn alters a line from *The Importance of Being Earnest*: 'To lose one Revolution may be regarded as a misfortune. To lose two looks like carelessness.'[61]

The huge sets by Richard Hudson for the RSC revival were surreal and overpowering, very different from the emphasis on history in the original production designs by Carl Toms. The pace was reduced, although the stage machinery was enhanced. At one point, Lenin's rather large, sealed train emerged from a huge fireplace like a Magritte painting and puffed across the stage.[62] The set was Carr's oversized white room, with a gigantic mirror and graffiti on the walls, plus a large cuckoo clock. A vast cut-out of a Soviet poster was on one wall, with the corresponding library all in red, with red shelves and red-covered books; even the folders that get mixed up by Gwendolen and Cecily were red. Projecting an Alice-in-Wonderland look, all the furniture and bookcases were tilted, offering a continuous slant. In 1974, Peter Wood merged the play with Dada by joining the play's two locations. In 1993, Noble reinstated a dark, front-stage library leading on to Carr's quarters, an all-white cavern with asymmetric doorways and furniture that appeared to be sinking into the floor. The setting was elegant enough for Wilde and surrealist enough for Lenin's train to roar out of the fireplace. The red of the library and the white of Carr's room emphasized the disjunction as well as difference between two worlds, one of politics and art, the other of memory. The successful production transferred from the Barbican to the Savoy Theatre in March 1994. That season, Stoppard achieved the unusual feat of having two major plays – *Arcadia* and *Travesties* – running simultaneously at the National Theatre and the Royal Shakespeare Company's Barbican Theatre.

Despite revisions and a modest toning down of the work, Stoppard could not shake his reputation for plays that demonstrate 'the virtuoso performance of an agile intellectual turning somersaults'. By 1993, however, he had shifted his view of the importance of wit and works that got by on fine writing alone. 'Now I realise', he told a reporter, 'that for drama . . . story-telling is the most crucial consideration. Little inserts of wit or prolonged philosophising merely jam the system – it stops the wheels going round . . . So long as the wheels were turning I could concentrate on the paintwork of the coaches. Nowadays . . . I'm more concerned with the audience's desire to know what's coming next than in transmuting what I read up into monologues . . . My conceit about *Travesties*', he concluded, 'was that it was an anthology of styles.'[63]

But if Stoppard would qualify and confront some questions about his reputation in the theatre in the nineties, throughout the early seventies he was expanding his relationships in the theatrical world. In August 1974, for example, he and Miriam attended *Pygmalion* at the National with Peter Hall, who thought that Shaw had 'carpentered' his works 'to spell out their themes with a care which amounts almost to contempt for the audience. The play-making is so evident.'[64] Stoppard, occasionally compared to Shaw, worked energetically to befriend the audience through laughter or wit, or both. The practicalities of making his plays work from the perspective of the audience, actors and directors remained uppermost in his vision of drama.

During the seventies, Stoppard also undertook other forms of theatrical expression, notably adaptations. These began with *Tango* in 1966 and shifted in 1973 to Lorca. Suggested to Robin Phillips, director of the Greenwich Theatre, by Patience Collier, Stoppard adapted a translation from the 1940s Penguin edition of Lorca's *House of Bernarda Alba*, aided by a recent literal translation by a Bristol University student, Kate Kendall. The text, he hoped, should, 'by a careful choice of words . . . put into it what is *understood* in the original'. But freedom and fidelity to the text are not easily equated, he explained; they require 'a balance between passion and a detached concern for making the thing work for the actors'.[65]

Whatever the qualities of the adaptation, the production did the play no favours. Focusing on the repressed daughters of Bernarda, the design of the piece should evoke heat; instead, the set, made out of polished white vinyl, suggested ice, not fire. Sound effects were equally disquieting. One critic ambiguously praised Stoppard's language, however, noting that instead of the final '*Silence!*' that Bernarda should shout, 'in Tom Stoppard's crisp, colloquial, but overly jocular adaptation she enters saying "*Shut up!*"' The same critic complained that English performers may 'lack the fierceness and passion for Lorca' and described the young Mia Farrow as 'too ethereal and Bohemian to capture the . . . eroticism of Adela'. Irving Wardle in *The Times* also drew attention to what would become characteristic of Stoppard's style. Noting that the tone of playing varied between generalized rhetoric and 'flip near-comedy', he remarks that 'the English version is by Tom Stoppard, who has certainly achieved a more speakable and pithier translation than the previously inescapable American text'.[66]

During the same period, Stoppard was trying his hand at directing, capitalizing on another invitation from Robin Phillips, this time to oversee Garson Kanin's 1946 comedy *Born Yesterday*, which had run for three years on Broadway and won an Oscar for Judy Holliday in the 1950 film version. The plot concerns a Washington tycoon who hires a journalist to teach his ex-showbiz girlfriend to speak properly. She then challenges her boyfriend on his ethics and in the end succeeds in outsmarting him with the help of the journalist. The play was a mixture of satire and comic action, something which naturally suited

Stoppard's style. Significant statements defused by vigorous physical comedy defined the production, and Stoppard expressed his approach by his remark that 'what interests me is getting a cliché and then betraying it'.[67] The play found favour with the critics and audiences, not the least because of the performances of Lynn Redgrave and David King. Stoppard's direction, however, lacked 'whiplash precision; we get Anglo-Saxon heaviness and a Babel-like mixture of accents'.[68]

The Washington setting and the spectre of Watergate during the spring of 1973 nevertheless provided the play with additional relevance. But Stoppard did not find directing very satisfying and declined further invitations until 1985, when he directed *The Real Inspector Hound* in a double bill at the National. During the seventies, Stoppard was experimenting with new forms of theatrical experience which buttressed his recent work with experimental and fringe theatre – such as *Dogg's Our Pet* for the Almost Free Theatre – while he prepared to adjust his work to reflect the inescapable world of political action and repression.

Despite their popular success, *Jumpers* and *Travesties* sustained the view of Stoppard as an intellectual playwright more to be studied than enjoyed. His characters were bright, witty but emotionless. The complex material, sharp dialogue and elaborate development of ideas generated a reaction which saw his work in the popular press as clever but socially and politically irrelevant. His liking for 'dialogue which is slightly more brittle than life' became a hallmark of his major plays, and a quality which he would have to temper.[69] But this would happen only after a series of adaptations, short works, screenplays and politically focused works, all to be written between 1975 and 1982. Politics would dominate his work in the late seventies.

Travesties did not so much prompt but extend Stoppard's confrontation with politics, evident in *Artist* and earlier, if comically, in *Jumpers*. The tension between art and politics in *Travesties* implicitly set an agenda, or, at the very least, mapped a route Stoppard would soon travel not only through trips to Soviet Russia and Czechoslovakia, but in a series of plays distinctly political in content. Ironically, his concern with political instability occurred during the period of his most sustained domestic comfort and popular success, which saw his personal life more secure than ever and his financial status escalate. Yet Stoppard did not let that act as a buffer from the conditions of repression, intimidation and artistic discipline he witnessed in Eastern Europe. His activities in the mid-seventies reaffirmed his political as well as psychological and artistic links with Central and Eastern Europe. They also marked another stage of self-invention, where the playwright of intellectual glitter and word play became the serious writer publicly and artistically engaged with moral problems generated by political repression and control.

CHAPTER 11

MARZIPAN CLOCKS

_When Auden said his poetry didn't save a single Jew from
the gas chambers, he was dead right_
Stoppard, 1973

Stoppard's controversial opinion might express his critique of political art, yet his actions in the seventies contradicted his words. From public forums and Iron Curtain visits to plays that indict repression and human rights violations, Stoppard displayed an awareness of the political power of theatre. Peter Hall acknowledged this when he identified Stoppard as justifiably 'the only _European_ British play-wright, and a strong believer in humanitarian causes and values. It's his sense of irony, of the absurd and the ridiculous, which allows him to be both a very flippant and a very committed man, a great cynic and a passionate idealist.'[1] Such a combination permitted Stoppard to construct works that played off darkly comic behaviour against glittering political ideals, creating what he would label 'marzipan clocks', which, in the artificial language of _Dogg's Hamlet,_ is a warning: it means 'Watch it!'[2]

Stoppard's statement on art and the Jews condenses into a single sentence his scepticism of art's ability to institute political or social change. According to Stoppard, committed theatre is a bogus enter-prise, as his view of Lenin in _Travesties_ confirmed. 'I've never felt this – that art is important. That's been my secret guilt. I think it's the secret guilt of most artists,' he stated in 1973.[3] Yet his own success as an artist generated a debate within his work on the value of art and its importance. The issue first emerged in _Artist Descending a Staircase_ and then in _Travesties,_ where he questioned the nature of the artist as a revolutionary and his connection with politics. Simply put, an artist's success contrasts with his identity as a revolutionary, often causing guilt. In the seventies, the pressing context of human rights and political oppression, largely in Russia and Eastern Europe, tested Stoppard's indifference. He responded in a variety of ways, from public protests to write-in campaigns and political satire. *Dirty Linen*, *Professional Foul, Night and Day* and *Squaring the Circle* encapsulated his literary reaction to moral politics.

Stoppard did not develop a political conscience overnight, although it may have seemed that way to the public. He had embraced England fully and felt at home from the moment he arrived in February 1946, but he was also aware that he was different and that his Czech background would never allow his integration to be complete. He compensated through his determination to outdo the English at being English, as the content of his plays and his adoption of an English lifestyle proved. But at the same time, he implicitly began to address political matters in his plays, from the politics of deception at Elsinore in *Rosencrantz and Guildenstern*, to the politics of philosophy and government in *Jumpers*. References to the First World War in *Artist and Europe* and Russia in *Travesties* extended his concerns. Stoppard might, like Joyce, want to be above politics in matters artistic, but he could never insulate himself from it – not even in England, as his farce *Dirty Linen* makes devastatingly clear.

Satire had never been far from the tip of Stoppard's pen and in 1976 he pointed it at bureaucracy and the need for journalistic freedom. *Dirty Linen* was written to be part of the Almost Free Theatre's 'American Connection' season and to celebrate Ed Berman's naturalization as a British subject. *New-Found-Land*, an inset play, was written to 're-introduce the American connection' to the framing play.[4] Using comedy to drive home his political satire, Stoppard shows that even the dullest parliamentary committees can have sex appeal. Of course, sex and politics had intersected earlier in *Travesties*, when Cecily aggressively pursued Carr, pulling him down behind her library desk in Act Two. In the 1976 revival of the play, this became even more obvious as she did a slow striptease while standing on a library table.

Dirty Linen, first performed on 6 April 1976 at Inter-Action's Almost Free Theatre in Soho, is a non-political play populated by politicians – six members of parliament and a Home Secretary – who are to investigate the charges of someone who has seduced more than one hundred MPs. As the audience quickly learns, the individual responsible is the attractive secretary to the Select Committee on Promiscuity in High Places. As the play opens, Maddie Gotobed has already slept with five of the six committee members; during recess, she will complete her sweep. Crucially, she will convince the committee that the private lives of government officials are of no concern to the press. This summary gives an inadequate sense of the comedy and farce, from the comic, pin-up poses of Maddie on stage to the formal language of the committee members, which comically disguises some unexpected truths.

Cross-talk and confusions abound:

McTeazle I expect it's not every girl who proves herself as you have done, Miss Gotobed. Do you use Gregg's or do you favour the Pitman method?

Maddie   I'm on the pill.[5]

Such exchanges are constantly being topped. McTeazle, outlining the duties of the committee, says it is 'to report on rumours of sexual promiscuity by certain unspecified Members'.[6] The issue the play investigates is the power of the press to treat innuendo and rumours as truth. Has 'a sexual swathe . . . passed through Westminster'? Is someone 'going through the ranks like a lawn-mower in knickers'?[7] That is the question McTeazle presents with a straight face, while he discovers a pair of knickers in his briefcase and casually hands them over to Maddie, who puts them in her desk drawers, or rather drawer. Here, Stoppard builds on his habit of using sight gags to reinforce his comedy and, throughout the play, various undergarments will change hands.

But as the language becomes increasingly off-colour, it becomes more comic. Cocklebury-Smythe, transfixed by Maddie's cleavage, suddenly turns to McTeazle and says:

why don't you go and see if you can raise those great tits – boobs – those boobies, absolute tits, don't you agree, Malcolm and Douglas – though good men as well, of course, useful chaps, very decent, first rate, two of the best, Malcolm and Douglas, why don't you have a quick poke, peek, in the Members' Bra – or the cafeteria, they're probably guzzling coffee and Swedish panties . . .[8]

Increasingly distracted and slightly hysterical, Cocklebury-Smythe warns McTeazle that the

> Division Bell will go before we even get started and then we'll all have to go off and vote on some beastly amendment to make anyone who buys his own council house a life bishop with the right to wear a nightie on his head, mitre on his head. My God, I could do with a drink – [9]

Confusions pile upon one another with quips, jokes, *doubles entendres* in Latin and French, tongue-twisters and inverted logic flying about: 'You do speedwriting, I suppose?' asks the Chairman Withenshaw. 'Yes, if I'm given enough time,' is Maddie's reply.[10] In this play, a briefcase actually carries briefs.

As the puns and phrases fly, borrowing from football as well as gossip columns, Maddie loses various parts of her clothes in a prolonged but revealing striptease. However, she is the only one to restate the primacy of privacy and the ineffectuality of the press, which is no more than a commercial enterprise. Accusing the press of malice is admitting that 'they've got a right to poke their noses into your private life,' she claims.[11] Additionally, she pins down the real behaviour of journalists who write such gossip not for their readers but for other journalists. Only the *pictures*, she claims, are for the people. This is Stoppard the journalist exposing journalists. In a sudden chorus of restaurant names (she has been to *all* of them with the committee members, who have suddenly been called away to vote, except for a Mr French), Maddie continues to itemize her assignations until two other voices are heard. She asks to be shown to the ladies' room and exits with Mr French as two men – from the next play, *New-Found-Land* – enter.

The discussion between two Home Office officials on the suitability of an applicant for British citizenship forms the inset play. An applicant with a beard is immediately rejected. There is a comic description of Lloyd George visiting one official's mother in the afternoon. Comic misunderstandings follow, all related to the actual activities of Ed Berman, as Bernard, the senior Home Office official, puzzles over the question of 'a theatrical farmer with buses on the side, doing publishing and community work in a beard . . . are we supposed to tell the minister that he's just the sort of chap this country needs'?[12]

Bernard and Arthur, the junior Home Office official, praise America, Stoppard offering his own sympathetic view of the country through Arthur's virtuoso summary of American history in five pages of comic clichés, moving from ship to train as he imaginatively crosses the country from New York to Los Angeles, where he arrives to stare, 'like stout Cortez' in Keats's poem, silently upon the Pacific – until the return of the Select Committee members interrupts the reverie.

The Home Secretary enters and disputes the use of the room with Withenshaw, but it is evident that he is also implicated in the sex scandal. The play then leaps to a concluding flourish with a proposal by Mr French that a new, shorter and more accurate report be tabled. As the vote is tallied, 'Arsenal 5 – Newcastle nil', French inadvertently takes out his breast pocket handkerchief *which is now the pair of knickers put on by Maddie at the beginning, and wipes his brow*. Impassively, he remarks: 'Toujours l'amour.'[13] Performed for three seasons in the West End and subsequently around the world, *Dirty Linen* has been Stoppard's most successful commercial play after *The Real Thing*.

One publicity feature of the play was a contest Stoppard ran to change a reference to Mark Phillips and Princess Anne in the play, suggesting that any mention of them in the press would instantly increase circulation.[14] Audiences seemed uncomfortable with the allusion and the actor playing the role of the chairman in the play asked Stoppard for a substitute reference. He suggested the leader of the Conservative Party, Margaret Thatcher, but that did not go down well, so in a squib in the *Sunday Times* of 24 April 1977 headed 'Tom's SOS', 'Atticus' reported that Stoppard was asking the public for suggestions; meanwhile, the exchange was temporarily deleted from the script. In May, the paper announced that Stoppard had gone through more than 200 suggestions, the first choice of the public being Prince Charles, just ahead of Antonia Fraser and Margaret Trudeau. Stoppard, however, decided to dispense with the line in performance, although it still appears in the published text. When he attended a subsequent performance, however, he discovered that the Prince Charles reference had already crept into the script; he 'ordered His Royal Highness's immediate deletion', 'Atticus' reported.[15]

Dirty Linen introduced a character named Chamberlain, a slightly lecherous committee member interested in Maddie. The name would soon appear in a great number of Stoppard's plays, including *Professional Foul* (as a British sportswriter), *Night and Day* as 'the guy in the AP office . . . Ask him to print up this one – I marked it – and wire anything which looks worthwhile', *The Real Thing*, with a reference to a Mrs Chamberlain coming to clean up, and *Hapgood*, where Chamberlain remains a man in a taxi just off stage.[16]

Stoppard would also include the name in *In the Native State* and its stage version, *Indian Ink*: in both works, Joshua Chamberlain is an off-stage politician who provides Flora Crewe with letters of introduction to people in India. In *The Invention of Love*, Chamberlain is Housman's colleague in the patent office. Coincidentally, the name even appears in Stoppard's popular success, the film *Shakespeare in Love*: Richard Burbage's acting troupe was commonly known as the Lord Chamberlain's Men. All of this is a tip of the writer's hat to Stoppard's secretary, Jacky Chamberlain. He once explained that he put her name in to wake her up when she was typing his manuscripts.[17]

> *You see all the trouble writers cause. They spoil things for ordinary people.*
>
> Stoppard, *Every Good Boy Deserves Favour*

Stoppard soon found a cause close to home on which to express his political views. In September 1976, he wrote an impassioned defence of Peter Hall as director of the National Theatre. Hall had been attacked by Max Hastings in the *Evening Standard* for the seemingly foolish expenditure of money on certain productions. Stoppard came to his defence, admitting his own interest in doing so, having 'just had a play [the revival of *Jumpers*] superbly and expensively produced at the National'. But he objected most strongly to 'slipshod arguments and tatty insinuations', which forced him to speak out against the accusations.[18]

Larger issues were soon at hand: human rights and freedom in Russia and Eastern Europe. As Stoppard would soon learn in detail, his career unfolded in concert with repression and the abuse of freedom in Russia. From the mid-sixties, the forcible confinement of dissidents in psychiatric hospitals had become common. Writers and sympathizers were regularly arrested, tried, sent for mental examinations, retried and often never heard from again once they had entered the labyrinthine world of psychiatric care. A defendant under Soviet criminal law need not be told that an order calling for his psychiatric examination had been made, nor be informed of the results of the examination. Furthermore, if the sanity of the accused had been called into question, investigators were not required to inform him of the new charges. Increasingly, and frighteningly, the explanation of dissidence in terms of mental disturbance became accepted.

Gradually, the complicity of psychiatrists was documented through the efforts of Amnesty International, *Index on Censorship* and US government investigations such as the 1972 study *Abuse of Psychiatry for Political Repression in the Soviet Union*. The January 1967 arrest of four writers, including Alexander Ginzburg and A. Dobrovolsky in Moscow, the 1969 exile of Alexander Solzhenitsyn from the Writers' Union and then his restriction from receiving his Nobel Prize for Literature in 1970, exceeded only by his forced exile to the west in February 1974, were only some of the most publicized acts of Soviet repression. Many others went unreported.

Stoppard became aware of these issues through a variety of channels, not least of which was *Index on Censorship*. This journal constantly kept its readers informed of abuses of freedom of the press, human rights and repression, devoting one entire issue to Czecho-slovakia eight years after the Prague Spring (volume 5, no. 3, 1976). In it were several pieces by Václav Havel, including his new one-act play, *Conversation*, and his letter to Czech officials on police action against his 1 December 1975 production of John Gay's *The Beggar's Opera*. Articles on the state of the Czech theatre and a list of the so-called Padlock Publications, fifty banned books that circulated only in typescript, would have also kept Stoppard informed of the survival of literature under the Soviets. He became a member of the advisory board of the *Index* in autumn 1978.

It was an earlier issue of the journal, however, that prompted Stoppard to translate concern over the repressed into action. *Index on Censorship* for the summer of 1975 (volume 4, no. 2) included two pieces documenting psychiatric abuse in the USSR: Clayton Yeo's 'The abuse of psychiatry in the USSR' and Victor Fainberg's 'My five years in mental hospitals'. Yeo's piece, actually drawn from an Amnesty study which would appear in 1976, *Prisoners of Conscience in the USSR:*

Their Treatment and Condition, details the manipulation of the legal and medical systems to enforce the confinement of political dissidents to mental hospitals. Through example and documentation, from Vladimir Bukovsky to Leonid Plyushch, Yeo chillingly shows the systematic abuse of psychiatry and its role in imprisonment. One example is the reply of a psychiatrist to the wife of Vladimir Borisov, who protested at his confinement in a Leningrad psychiatric hospital: 'he is unlucky . . . what may be a symptom of opinions in a normal person is a sign of illness in your husband'. Stoppard aptly revised this remark in an exchange in his play *Cahoot's Macbeth*: in response to an Inspector asking 'what's the language he's talking', the hostess answers 'at the moment we're not sure if it's a language or a clinical condition'.[19]

Victor Fainberg's account is even more disturbing in its precision. Explaining that he was arrested and beaten by KGB agents in Red Square on 24 August 1968 for a five-minute demonstration with other members of the human rights movement protesting the invasion of Czechoslovakia, Fainberg then details the treatment, beating, abuse and constant bureaucratic tangle that kept him in various psychiatric hospitals from 1968 until his final release in November 1973. At one point, a doctor in the infamous Arsenal'naya special psychiatric hospital in Leningrad told him:

> Your discharge depends on your conduct. By your conduct we mean your opinions precisely on political questions. Your disease is dissent. As soon as you renounce your opinions and adopt the correct point of view, we'll let you out.[20]

This statement would soon find its way into *Every Good Boy Deserves Favour*, Stoppard's 1977 work about mental patients in the Soviet Union performed with the London Symphony Orchestra. Late in the play, a doctor tells Alexander, in response to his claim that he has 'no symptoms, I have opinions', that 'Your opinions are your symptoms. Your disease is dissent.'[21]

Fainberg also narrates various hunger strikes he undertook which did achieve some impact, largely because of the Soviet fear of publicity if he should die. This also figures in Stoppard's play, as do the arbitrary, whimsical and absurdist logic of appeal, denial and release which Fainberg documents. Late in his imprisonment, one commission stressed they weren't interested in his political views, a volte-face given that the first condition of a political prisoner's release is that he renounces his beliefs, agrees that he is mad and thanks the doctors for his treatment. Another commission allowed Fainberg to choose his own treatment, but they could not release him until they could report some improvement. Stoppard dramatized this absurdity in his play.

Fainberg's friendship in prison with Volodya Borisov may have sparked Stoppard's placement of two prisoners in the same cell in *Every Good Boy*. Stoppard actually met Fainberg in April 1976, during a visit to London, at a time when Stoppard was floundering for ideas. He had promised a new television play to the BBC to mark Amnesty International's 'Prisoners of Conscience' year. He had been reading about the Russian dissidents and he was aware of Fainberg's past. At the time, Fainberg's main concern was to use his new freedom to release Vladimir Bukovsky, another victim of psychiatric abuse in the USSR, whose revelations about that abuse brought him consecutive terms of prison and internal exile amounting to twelve years. Impressed by Fainberg's courage, single-mindedness and 'willingness to make a nuisance of himself outside and inside the walls of any institution', Stoppard considered that his captors must have been happy to get rid of him.[22] Shortly after his encounter with the dissident, Stoppard told André Previn, who in 1974 had asked him if he would like to write a piece for an orchestra, that his original conception was of a lunatic triangle-player (Stoppard had once played the triangle in a school percussion band in India) who thought he had an orchestra but who was now sharing a cell with a political prisoner.[23]

The hero, Alexander, is not Victor Fainberg – but his speech describing his treatment at the Leningrad Special Psychiatric Hospital is taken from Fainberg's account in volume 4 of *Index on Censorship*. Fainberg makes his own appearance in the text as one of the group Alexander identifies only by letters of the alphabet. The off-stage hero of *Every Good Boy*, referred to as 'my friend C', is Vladimir Bukovsky, who in December 1976 was released and exiled to the west.[24] In June 1977, Bukovsky actually attended a rehearsal of the work at the RSC's rehearsal rooms in Covent Garden. He offered some helpful comments with details but his presence was disturbing because there was a sense of collision between the worlds of the self-contained dramatic text and reality. At the moment he arrived, Ian McKellen (playing the part of Alexander) was rehearsing one of the more serious speeches and had to stop – not because of the discrepancy between the mood of the art and real situation which Bukovsky represented, but because of 'the discrepancy between art and life, full stop', Stoppard explained.[25]

The use of actual figures like Fainberg and Bukovsky extends Stoppard's habit of drawing from history and using personalities such as Lenin, Tzara, Joyce, Housman or Wilde in his plays. But he also upholds his right to fictionalize them. Hence his 'embarrassment' at the presence of the actual Bukovsky, which had the effect of freezing the work of the actors. The moment the artist and his source collide is also the time to pull them apart. Being so close to the 'originator' paralyses rather than frees the artist because it makes the artist realize that reality can often overpower art.

Stoppard, who has always drawn from the work or lives of others, needs imaginative distance in order to create. When he does actually identify the sources of his characters, it is separate from the texts, most often in the dedications. Victor Fainberg and Vladimir Bukovsky are the dedicatees of *Every Good Boy*. The play also embodies one of Stoppard's earliest ideas, that 'A political prisoner is a man who found himself in the wrong place when the music stopped', a line from his early work, *The Gamblers*.[26]

The unusual staging of *Every Good Boy* determined its unusual shape. The challenge for Stoppard was to make the subject of the work follow its proposed form, 'performed in conjunction with, and bound up with, a symphony orchestra'.[27] Preparing a work for the eighty-piece London Symphony Orchestra challenged Stoppard's notions of what structure such a play might have, incorporating the uniqueness of its presentation. Rehearsals meant both small gatherings – one occurred with Stoppard, Previn, Trevor Nunn and John Wood in Ian McKellen's Camberwell sitting-room – and large, with the full orchestra in the Royal Festival Hall. The one-off production of *Every Good Boy* in July 1977 (later televised) was a hit. When it was remounted in 1978, the music was rewritten for a chamber orchestra and recorded, the recording offsetting the costs of staging the work.

Stoppard understood from the first that his play had to be about an orchestra and his first thought was of a millionaire who owned one. Knowing nothing about orchestras, however, hampered the project, so Stoppard next thought of making the orchestra a delusion in the millionaire's mind. An imaginary orchestra would be the key; and he considered a lunatic triangle-player who believed he could hear an orchestra, rather than a millionaire. But that idea also got nowhere: 'Music and triangles led me into a punning diversion based on Euclid's axioms, but it didn't belong anywhere.'[28] Meeting Victor Fainberg and learning of his experiences in Russian mental hospitals, however, provided focus for Stoppard; he also decided that the triangle-player would now share his cell with a political prisoner. Alexander became the prisoner, Ivanov his triangle-playing cellmate. Stoppard completed the work in a few weeks.

The project was a first in a number of areas: it was the first time the London Symphony Orchestra had participated in such a production; it was the first time Stoppard ever wrote for an orchestra; it was the first time Trevor Nunn directed a Stoppard play and it was the first major attempt on the British stage to tackle the issue of Soviet dissidents. The combined strength of the RSC, who produced it with five of their leading actors – Ian McKellen, John Wood, Patrick Stewart, Philip Locke and Barbara Leigh-Hunt – and the London Symphony Orchestra made it a significant event. The one-off performance on the giant stage of the Royal Festival Hall with an audience of some 6,000 provided a scale for the work unlike anything the playwright had previously done. But the music, with its echoes of Prokofiev and Schoenberg, the acting, with outstanding performances from Ian McKellen and John Wood, and the text, which managed to integrate the angst of the prisoners with the power of the orchestra, made it an outstanding success.

When *Every Good Boy* was remounted for an extended run in June 1978 at the Mermaid Theatre, the music was re-scored and the final scene modified to make it clearer that the mix-up in names and truthful replies is a legitimate strategy for the decision of the colonel to release both of them – aided by the prisoners now making exaggerated but hopeless attempts to point out the mistake to the colonel. The new production, however, suffered somewhat from the cramped stage of the Mermaid in contrast to the expanse of the Festival Hall. None the less, this version had a successful American tour which played at the

Kennedy Center in Washington in 1978 and the Metropolitan Opera House in New York in July 1979.

The political focus of the text did not prevent Stoppard from displaying his wit, although it was not as pointed as that of *Jumpers* or *Travesties*. Reminiscent of the confusions in *Dirty Linen*, Ivanov at one point tells Alexander that:

> I've had clarinet players eating *at my own table*. I've had French whores, and gigolos speak to me in the *public street*, I mean horns, I mean piccolos, so don't worry about *me* maestro, I've sat down with them, *drummers* even, sharing a plate of tagliatelle Verdi and stuffed Puccini.[29]

Accompanying the constant and rapid change of scene from the hospital cell to a classroom and then doctor's office is a characteristically quick repartee, often between a character and the orchestra, usually when Ivanov denies ever having an orchestra. But the more he denies it, the more we actually see and hear it perform.[30]

Arrested because he protested over the detention of a friend for possessing a controversial book, Alexander provides a long and geometrically based explanation of his actions: 'The fifth man was my friend C, who had just got out of the mental hospital where they put him for demonstrating against the arrest of A and B.' The passage partly derives from the end of Havel's *The Garden Party*, when Hugo explains that 'the time of static and unchangeable categories is past', illustrating this shift through the geometric use of letters.[31] Earlier in Stoppard's play, Sacha, Alexander's son, has geometric axioms politically interpreted by his teacher. Alexander can only conclude, 'You see all the trouble writers cause. They spoil things for ordinary people.'[32]

Science, specifically mathematics, becomes the means of clarifying and explaining the actions of an apparently arbitrary and illogical system and offers a glimpse of the role it will increasingly play in Stoppard's later work. Earlier, his fascination with science appeared in the opening scene of *Rosencrantz and Guildenstern*, with its focus on probability in tossing a coin, and fully emerged in his treatment of ideas in his screenplay of *Galileo,* to be followed by the quantum physics of *Hapgood* and the algorithms of *Arcadia*. In *The Invention of Love*, Housman confidently declares that 'textual criticism is a science whose subject is literature, as botany is the science of flowers and zoology of animals and geology of rocks'.[33]

Every Good Boy explores the questionable divisions between patients and physicians. In the upside-down world of the play, the Colonel, also a doctor who is in charge of the case, is not trained in 'psychiatry *as such*'. Alexander asks, 'What is his speciality?' 'Semantics. He's a Doctor of Philology, whatever that means,' the Doctor answers.[34] In the world of the play, logic has disappeared in favour of a bureaucracy which tries desperately to release the inmates if only they would admit that they are insane. Or that they have been cured. Wit in the work is never far from the mad surface of the play, punctuated throughout with Previn's music, as Stoppard reminds us in the printed edition of the play when he states that the work is 'incomplete without the score composed by its co-author, André Previn'.[35]

> *The ethics of the State must be judged against the*
> *fundamental ethic of the individual.*
> Stoppard, *Professional Foul*

Stoppard's systematic political education began in earnest in 1976, when he became interested in the plight of Soviet dissidents, and it gained momentum through the next four to five years. Three years earlier, he had begun to write letters on behalf of Soviet dissidents. By August 1976, he was addressing a rally in Trafalgar Square organized by the Committee Against Psychiatric Abuse. That same month, Stoppard, along with twenty-two other European and American authors, including Iris Murdoch, Harold Pinter, Eugene Ionesco and Arthur Miller, signed a protest asking for the immediate release of Vladimir Bukovsky. Stoppard's trip to the Soviet Union in February 1977 with Peter Luff, assistant director of Amnesty International in the UK, served to intensify his views, which his article in the *Sunday Times* of 27 February 1977 detailed. And just before this account of his visit to the USSR appeared, Stoppard published 'Dirty Linen in Prague' (11 February 1977).

In this *New York Times* article, Stoppard condemns the refusal of the Czech government to permit the publication of Charter 77, the document which called attention to the absence of numerous human rights in the country, beginning with the right of free expression. The state determined that Charter 77 was 'wicked slander' and charged a group of individuals with being in the pay of 'Western reactionary forces'.[36] This should cause more than bemusement, according to Stoppard. The playwright Václav Havel, one of the three designated spokespersons for Charter 77, was arrested, and Stoppard argues that the west's reaction to this event would be 'a real test of our commitment to human rights'. A June 1977 meeting in Belgrade to review the 1975 Helsinki accords, the very basis of Charter 77, should be an opportunity to press for the freedom of the four. In Stoppard's view, the question is, 'are we going to let the Czechoslovaks off the hook?'

Stoppard refers to the following events. Around noon on 6 January 1977, Havel, plus Pavel Landovsky, an actor and playwright prevented from working, and Ludvik Vaculik, a banned journalist, were travelling in a white Saab to a post office with approximately 240 envelopes containing copies of their human rights manifesto. At an intersection, eight police cars converged on them and all three were arrested. Their copies of Charter 77 were seized; though ironically, one copy, addressed to the President's Office in Prague's castle, was delivered by the security police.

The next day, a smuggled copy was published in German in the *Frankfurter Allgemeine Zeitung* and in many other papers around the world. By June, the illegal manifesto had 750 signatures, although arrests and prosecutions increased. Pavel Kohout, a playwright who had been detained and was subsequently persecuted, and to whom Stoppard would later dedicate *Cahoot's Macbeth*, reported on how fear of harming the educational future of their children had prevented many others from signing the charter. Czechoslovakia, writes Stoppard, had become an 'upside-down country where you can find boilers stoked by economists, streets swept by men reading Henry James in English'. Millions of crowns were spent each month to 'disarm a handful of dangerous men whose only weapon is free conversation'. This information comes from a detailed report Stoppard published in the *New York Review of Books*.[37]

While the Charter 77 group faced persecution in Czechoslovakia, Stoppard visited Soviet Russia. He thought the journey would unlock the play he had promised to write for the BBC for Amnesty International's Prisoner of Conscience Year. His article, 'The Face at the Window', narrates his journey with Peter Luff. Written in the form of a journal, it begins with a visit to Yuri and Irina Orlov and her account of eight KGB men searching their flat. Throughout the piece, Stoppard presents a troubling story of the life of Soviet dissidents. Stoppard and Luff are ostensibly on an approved Cook's Tour of Russia, with side trips to meet with Amnesty's Moscow group. Stoppard is an eager witness, noting, for example, the absence of Yuri Orlov who had been arrested three days before as leader of the Helsinki Group, the unofficial agency monitoring Moscow's compliance with the Helsinki human rights provisions. Luff has brought Amnesty materials, including copies of their petition to sign for the UN in support of Amnesty's Prisoner of Conscience Year.

The wife of the jailed and ailing Sergei Kovalen, an Amnesty member, comes to see Luff and Stoppard at their hotel. Unable to receive adequate medical treatment, Kovalen is on hunger strike. They visit the small and poorly appointed kitchen of the most celebrated dissident, Andrei Sakharov, after which they go to a birthday party at Valentin Turchin's apartment. A dozen people sit about, listening to Turchin's account of his run-in with the KGB earlier that evening. Detained and driven to the KGB 'isolator', the notorious Lefortovo jail, Turchin discovered it was a trick and was soon returned to his local KGB station. Forced to sign a trumped-up confession, he wrote his own, protesting his innocence. Unexpectedly, he was allowed to leave. It was St Valentine's day, 14 February.

Luff and Stoppard next try to visit Major-General V. A. Strusov of the MVD (Ministry of Internal Affairs) who might be able to help the ailing Sergei Kovalen. The general and his staff are expecting them. This, Stoppard, realizes, is because of the electronic bugs that must have picked up their plans from their ninth-floor room in the Ukraine Hotel. The general's statuesque secretary explains that neither he nor his deputy is in. Would they like to leave a message? Peter Luff gives his prepared speech; she promises to pass it on and they formally depart.

The next day, Luff and Stoppard are in Leningrad, where Stoppard is eager to learn about Vladimir Borisov. Stoppard knew that, because of his membership on the Committee Against Psychiatric Abuse, Borisov had recently been re-arrested and was in the Third Civil

Mental Hospital. Through a friend of Borisov's, a refusenik and specialist in English literature, Ilya Levin (who can only work as a part-time lift operator), Stoppard learns of the restrictions placed on Borisov: his mother had received a letter from him in which every word had been crossed out; he was restrained in his bed so that he could not stand near a window for fear his picture might be taken. However, the chief psychiatrist for the Leningrad hospital had told Borisov's mother that he would be released by the end of the month. But the Tass news agency contradicted the doctor, saying that Borisov was mentally ill and could not be freed.

Ilya suggested that it might cheer up Borisov if he and Stoppard went to his window. Late that afternoon, the two travelled by taxi to the civil mental hospital run by the Ministry of Health, not the MVD. There was not enough light for a photo, however. Passing through a turnstile, they walked past a massive main building to a large stone house with ornate doors. No one was around. Suddenly,

> a boy about 17 comes to a large window at head-level to our left. There is no way to talk to him . . . But gradually other men come to gaze at us until we are staring back at perhaps half a dozen blank curious faces. Finally, Ilya says 'Here is Volodya.'

Expecting to see a veteran, since Borisov's name went back ten years in dissident history, including detention for five years at the Arsenal'naya hospital prison, Stoppard is shocked to see that

> the man at the window is absurdly young, a boy and beautiful, hugely pleased, even merry, smiling and waving. He's like an unsinkable toy . . . After a few minutes of sign language, we wave goodbye. Volodya claps his hands over his head and grins like the champion of the world.[38]

On their last day in Russia, back in Moscow, Stoppard and Luff arrive two hours before the return flight. The night before, they had said goodbye to Valentin, who was depressed, but Luff at least had the Amnesty petition with sixteen new names; 'later that night I copy their names down in my notebook,' Stoppard writes. Seven members of the tour group are returning home, and the other five are 'politely uninquisitive' about the occasional absences of Stoppard and Luff from museum trips and sightseeing. The first two travellers, schoolteachers, are relentlessly searched by two plain-clothes men. Then comes Stoppard and Luff's turn. Stoppard's notebook and clipboard 'excite interest' and are taken away and then returned. Luff explains that his Amnesty petition is perfectly legal since Moscow carefully avoided proscribing the Amnesty group. Loud and firm in his protest, Luff eventually retrieves the document. They manage to make it to Passport Control but they are approached again immediately afterwards.

Their wallets are now taken away and Stoppard has to empty his pockets and remove his boots. In the next booth, he suddenly hears Luff's alarmed voice: the petition has been taken out of his wallet! An argument follows, but to little avail. Stoppard writes:

> No one knows anything about a petition.
>   The petition named no countries. It was merely a generalized plea for prisoners of conscience everywhere but when it came to the point the KGB hadn't needed to embarrass the Soviet Union by officially confiscating it. They simply stole it.

The power of the institutional over the individual confronted Stoppard in Russia, revealing the repression that forced people into secrecy and the government into criminal acts.

Five months after his Soviet journey, Stoppard travelled to Prague, 'a compelling mixture of the sublime and the cynical', a city where the spirit could soar but where the smell of decay was in the atmosphere.[39] Stoppard travelled there in June 1977 to meet Václav Havel, who had been released from jail a month earlier. Havel, one of three designated spokespersons for Charter 77 – the distinguished philosopher Jan Patocka, then sixty-nine, and Jiri Hajek, a former minister from the Dubček government, were the other two – had been kept in Ruzyne prison for four months and was ultimately given a suspended sentence of fourteen months. In April, while Havel was still in jail, Stoppard was refused admission to the Czech Embassy in London when he went to present a petition on behalf of the dramatist. Stoppard and his delegation were left standing outside the locked gates on the pavement. The petition, signed by some 1,200 individuals, deplored Havel's arrest and appealed to President Husák for his release. The signatures had been gathered at fringe performances of two of Havel's plays at the Orange Tree in Richmond.

Stoppard says he first came across Havel's plays in 1967. This was likely, as that April Kenneth Tynan had published a piece on Czech theatre, featuring Havel, in the *New Yorker*. In that essay, Tynan declared that Prague 'has a strong claim to be regarded as the theatrical capital of Europe'. Martin Esslin agreed, saying that between 1960 and 1970 'the Czechoslovak theatre was without doubt, the most exciting theatre in Europe – its designers, directors, playwrights and actors led the world'.[40] With such praise, it would be hard for Stoppard to overlook the work of the leading playwright of that period, Havel.

One of the plays Stoppard read at this time, for which he would later write an introduction, was *The Memorandum*, about a bureaucracy that suddenly introduces an artificial language for greater precision in communication. The absurd attempt results in a complete breakdown in human exchange, while dramatizing the way institutions overrule individual lives and the impossible efforts of others to resist. Stoppard would explore a similar theme concerning language in *Dogg's Hamlet*.[41]

His June trip, following the May release of Havel, was Stoppard's second behind the Iron Curtain but his first to Czechoslovakia since he had left in 1939 at the age of two. Unlike his Russian journey, however, Stoppard did not publicly write about his meeting with Havel at his farmhouse, Hradecek, in the mountains of northern Bohemia. He kept his feelings private on his return, although two important pieces register his sympathy with the Charter 77 movement: the long article for the *New York Review of Books* entitled 'Prague: the Story of the Chartists' and his television drama *Professional Foul*, dedicated to Havel. It was aired in September 1977 and won the British Critics' Award as the best television drama of 1977. It also had the distinction of being shown three times in one year.

There would be no moral dilemmas if moral principles
worked in straight lines and never crossed over.
Stoppard, *Professional Foul*

Professional Foul had in fact been written before Stoppard's trip to Prague. He had finished the play in April, completing his first draft in the remarkably short time of three weeks. He had promised to deliver a work by the last day of 1976, to mark Amnesty International's Prisoner of Conscience Year (1977), but on that day he had nothing to show, despite months of trying. 'A visit to the USSR (not Czechoslovakia) finally produced a ghost of a plot, and after that the play was written in two or three weeks including turning a ballroom dancing team into the English Football squad.'[42]

By the time Stoppard left to visit Prague in June 1977, the production was in rehearsal, and when he returned, the director, Michael Lindsay Hogg, jestingly asked when he would get the rewrites. There were none, because the issues of Charter 77, Stoppard explained, were not local or particular to Czechoslovakia. He decided to make his visiting Englishman a professor of ethics 'precisely because the charter seemed to me to be not a political document but a moral one'.[43] In a further summary of the oppression in Czechoslovakia, Stoppard outlined how he met with the three key participants in the Charter 77 incident, plus others, including a historian who dug ditches and a philosopher who was a filing clerk. He also detailed the life of Jan Patocka, who insisted that the matter of human rights was *not* an internal affair of the country.

Stoppard describes *Professional Foul* as 'not a particularly sober response [to Amnesty's Prisoner of Conscience Year] but a serious response by a writer of comedies'. Its conclusion, he adds, is that

> human rights are not the gift of society, to be legitimately retracted at society's will. On the contrary, he [Anderson, the hero] asserts that concepts like freedom, fairness, justice and so on derive from a system of ethics which is the product of each man's recognition of his fellow man's rights. Society comes later.

Stoppard later explained that he wanted to write 'about the dispute between somebody who thinks that morality is an absolute and somebody who thinks that it's a convention which we have evolved like the rules of tennis, and which can be altered'.[44]

The television production absorbed Stoppard completely, largely because of his growing distrust of the medium. Stoppard had become increasingly frustrated by the writer's inability to control the frame: 'On the stage, I have a total picture in my mind about how something is going to look. But when I write for television I'm completely at sea.' The problem was that he didn't know what the director would choose to shoot; consequently, he felt it necessary to be present during the filming, 'to see what is happening to my situations and dialogue in terms of the accompanying image'.[45] Casting, rehearsals, script changes, costumes and sets all concerned him. Casting Peter Barkworth as Anderson was a last-minute decision. Stoppard had just finished revising the script, and up until then had thought of Anderson as a man of sixty. Seeing Barkworth on television one evening, he suddenly thought: 'why couldn't the character be younger?' Barkworth's performance won an award for best television actor for 1977, while the show won an award for the best television programme.[46]

Professional Foul – the title means an intentional foul committed in football to prevent a score – exposes the gap between detachment and involvement through a profound change of conscience undergone by Anderson, the professor of ethics. At first, he wants nothing to do with a former student who visits him in an effort to get his thesis about individual freedom in the state smuggled out of the country. But when he witnesses the abuses of the Czech secret police and learns of the arrest of his student, Anderson has a change of heart. The cynical betrayal of human rights is underscored not by having dissidents escape from Eastern Europe to the west, but the reverse: importing two groups of westerners to the east – the professors attending the philosophy conference and, as counterpoint, a group of English footballers.

Balancing the 'professional foul' which results in a successful penalty kick leading to the Czech victory over the English is Anderson's success (through sleight of hand) in smuggling out the thesis. An ethical triumph trumps a sports defeat. Undercutting this ethical victory, however, is Stoppard's uncanny portrayal of academic gamesmanship, the making of academic reputations and the excesses of academic language: 'There's a choice of open forums tonight – neo-Hegelians or Quinian neo-Positivists. Which do you fancy? Pity Quine couldn't be here. And Hegel for that matter,' one philosopher remarks.[47] Upon Anderson's return to his hotel from his student's apartment, the philosopher McKendrick explains to him how his belief in steadfast principles often runs into difficulty, providing Anderson with the rationale to act unethically:

there's a point – the catastrophe point – where your progress along one line of behaviour jumps you into the opposite line; the principle reverses itself at the point where a rational man would abandon it.[48]

What Anderson cannot accept is the knowledge that his principles are fictions and merely that. 'You know they're fictions but you're so hung upon them you want to treat them as if they were God-given absolutes . . . you end up using a moral principle as your excuse for acting against a moral interest,' says his opposite.[49] Anderson's experience in Prague teaches him that moral principles *do* cross lines, requiring an adjustment in behaviour.

After an encounter with Mrs Hollar and her child Sacha, Anderson's view changes, as is evident in his revised paper, which deals with rights as fictions, although they possess the force of truths 'acting as incentives to the adoption of practical values'.[50] It is Anderson's encounter with the child, Stoppard has pointed out, more than anything else, that gives him the courage to shift his position and undergo a change of conscience. Encountering the child as a victim of a repressive society cuts through all theory. Previously, in *Every Good Boy*, Alexander's son (also Sacha) had highlighted the illogical nature of the political situation through his efforts to equate the logic of geometry with the logic of Soviet repression.

In Stoppard's work, children are crucial: they are often the only intelligent observers, as will be seen in with Alastair in *Night and Day*, Debbie in *The Real Thing* and Hapgood's son in *Hapgood*. Thomasina in *Arcadia* is another sign of the genius and insight of innocence, echoed in the youthful Housman in *The Invention of Love*. The clarity of children reflects an intelligence uncorrupted by society or politics. Sacha illuminates two moralities for Anderson, one to do with systems of government and another to do with the relationships between individuals. 'The latter', Stoppard explained, 'is governed by instinctive feelings about what good and bad behaviour consist of.'[51]

While Anderson speaks, there is a cut-away to his hotel room, which is being searched. Back at his lecture, Anderson is arguing for natural justice which, as an 'ethical utterance', seems to be 'an attempt to define a sense of rightness which is not simply derived from some other utterance elsewhere'.[52] Interestingly, the text of his speech closely resembles a letter by Havel cited by Tynan in a comment on

Havel's play *The Conspirators*.[53] Anderson, as we shall soon understand, is providing a defence of his own actions which a concluding scene in a plane corroborates. As they discuss the exposure of their colleague Chetwyn for attempting to carry out letters to Amnesty International and the UN, Anderson surprises McKendrick by telling him that he placed Hollar's thesis in McKendrick's briefcase, which wasn't searched, explaining his action as a reversal of principle. In an ironic postscript, Anderson tells the shocked McKendrick, who had initiated the argument on the individuality of ethical action, that 'ethics is a very complicated business. That's why they have these congresses.'[54]

Professional Foul linked Stoppard's interests in philosophy and academics to issues of political freedom and human rights. Through Anderson's discovery that one's principles could alter in the face of shattering personal and political situations, Stoppard shows the renewed value of individually determined ethics: 'Ethics are not the inspiration of our behaviour but merely the creation of our utterances,' is Anderson's abbreviated summary of the situation. 'I cannot in all conscience start smuggling . . . It's just not ethical,' he at first tells his former student. His later actions, however, justifiably contradict this position.[55]

Stoppard, reinvented as a political playwright, managed to synthesize his concern with human rights and drama into a focused and successful work which his next major play, *Night and Day*, would expand, uniting it with his long-standing interest in journalism.

CHAPTER 12

CZECH MATES

I'm as Czech as Czech can be
Stoppard, 1978

The dedication of *Professional Foul* reads 'To Václav Havel', with whom Stoppard long felt a kinship: 'When I read *The Garden Party* about twelve years ago,' he told a journalist in 1981, 'I just thought he [Havel] was somebody who wrote like I would like to write if I was writing on the same subject.'[1] The two share a number of similarities, beginning with their age, Havel being only nine months older than Stoppard. They were also both dispossessed: Havel from property rightly owned by his family but confiscated by the Communists, Stoppard from his Czech roots, having fled the country under the Nazis. Their first works were both produced in 1963: Havel's short play *The Garden Party* and Stoppard's television production of *A Walk on the Water*. Neither playwright graduated from university, although Havel was prevented from attending, while Stoppard chose not to go. Both enjoy rock music, Havel having been an observer and critic of the 1976 trials of the Plastic People of the Universe rock band (they were indicted by the state for propagating nihilism and decadence) and Stoppard a fan of sixties pop and, later, a friend of Mick Jagger.

Early in their careers, both playwrights professed little interest in politics, although they were sharply analytical of the contradictions and moral ambiguities in their respective societies. And both linked their careers with individual theatres: Havel had many of his works premièred at Prague's Theatre on the Balustrade, while Stoppard had many of his works first performed at the National Theatre. Asked if he thought he would write the same sort of comic plays if he had stayed in Czechoslovakia with its then (1970s) Communist regime, Stoppard,

281

perhaps optimistically, replied, 'I could have written *Rosencrantz and Guildenstern are Dead*, I think. I mean *Hamlet* means a lot everywhere, so I might have done.' And when his mother died in October 1996, Stoppard felt that the 'torch has been passed on to me to be Czech'.[2]

However, many differences also exist: Havel was born into a well-to-do family of engineers and real-estate developers. But because of this bourgeois, privileged background, he was denied the right to attend university by the Communists. After four years as a lab technician, Havel studied at a technical college and then served in the army. He left and joined Group 42, a collection of artists and writers who celebrated avant-garde, anti-official writing, originally founded by an older generation of protesting writers. By the 1960s, he had found his way into the theatre, first as a stagehand, then as an assistant director and dramaturg at the avant-garde Theatre on the Balustrade. Philosophy and drama were Havel's strongest interests. For Stoppard, it was journalism: he jested at one point that playwriting had disrupted his progress towards a career on a national newspaper. Havel, of course, pursued ideological non-conformism and dissent while writing. Stoppard did not. During the 'Prague Spring' of 1968, Havel was an active spokesperson for reform; by 1969, his work was banned. He left Prague to live in the country and worked for a time in a brewery, continuing to oppose the Communist regime. Stoppard never faced such challenges or threats.

The period of so-called 'normalization' and consequent national apathy did not deter Havel from his reformist role and involvement with the Charter 77 movement. Stoppard, whose path had by then begun to cross Havel's, tells the story in 'Prague: The Story of the Chartists'.[3] But what he could not describe were the later arrests and detention of Havel, especially his house arrest in 1978–9, during which he wrote his famous essay 'The Power of the Powerless', analysing how the individual can pursue the aims of an ethical life within a totalitarian environment by rehabilitating values like trust, openness, responsibility and solidarity. In 1978, Havel joined the Committee for the Defence of the Unjustly Persecuted (VONS, in its Czech acronym), eleven members of which, including Havel, were arrested in March 1979. On his release in 1983, he was not permitted to travel; thus restricted, he asked Stoppard to stand in for him at Toulouse University to receive an honorary degree in May 1984.

Rearrested in 1989, Havel had by that time become the unofficial leader of the Czech human rights movement. The arrest depressed Stoppard, who was upset with himself because of 'my good fortune and powerlessness and things like that'.[4] But by the autumn Havel had been released and the government's power was threatened. In November 1989, he helped form a new opposition group, the Civic Forum, at the Prague Drama Academy. Using the smaller studios and alternative theatres like the Magic Lantern for its forums, the group transformed theatre into political centres, advancing new ideas and reforms to the public. Within a month of the fall of Communism in November 1989, Havel was elected President of the Czech and Slovak Federal Republic. 'When the idea first came up that I should let my name stand for president of Czechoslovakia, it seemed like an absurd joke. All my life I had opposed the powers that be,' he mused in the introduction to a series of essays from the period.[5] Nevertheless, he accepted the Forum's nomination and became president on 29 December 1989.

During the period between the Warsaw Pact invasion and Havel's election, the nature of Czech drama changed. Rooted in satire of the government through cabaret-style humour, it managed to appear harmless or comic by means of what Tynan called 'non-realistic parables'.[6] The fantastic word-worlds that characterized Havel's plays constantly outlined the need to improve man's institutions, giving a human face to absurdism. Yet for Havel, the 'best theatre has always been political . . . [having] a live, committed and penetrative relationship with the social reality of its country and its time . . . the theatre can depict politics precisely because it has no political aim'.[7] The so-called absurdism of Stoppard differs in that it confronts the absurdity of man's life and negotiates a way of going on. Havel's absurdism does not, but it contributed to the development of the so-called Authorial Theatre which, using non-text-based performance forms and original material, critiqued the period of 'normalization' (c.1968–89).[8]

Havel's impact on Stoppard was more than literary: it was political and personal – as summed up in a dream Stoppard reported to Havel in May 1984. After recounting his role as stand-in for Havel at the Toulouse awards ceremony, he reports that the previous night he had dreamt of being sent to jail without reason for three years. The dream focused on his first day in jail and his despair:

then one of my children woke me up when he was going to school and after the first moment of relief that I wasn't in jail but merely in bed I immediately thought of you and how frightful it must have been when there was no possibility of waking up and finding yourself at home. So here I am on a sunny day, half way through adapting a Molnar comedy for the National Theatre . . . dozens of silly jokes and no politics.[9]

The letter shows not only how much Havel had entered Stoppard's subconscious, but how the next phase of his writing, a series of adaptations, acted to deflect the strain of political matters. This was intensified, of course, by Stoppard's Czech origins, which, despite his claim to being English, he could never dismiss – while others would not let him forget them. 'If I had not left the country, my life would likely be like his, alternating between prison and menial work,' he has said, and his identification with Havel would become increasingly important to Stoppard on another level.

> *I'm taking this imprisonment neither as tragically as I did the one in 1977, nor as a joke, like last year's; this time I'm being more fatalistic about it.*
>
> Václav Havel, *Letters to Olga*, 19 June 1979

Havel's consistent cry for political freedom and human equality, expressed through public statements and action, functioned as a model for Stoppard's own attempts at improving the situation for human rights in Eastern Europe, particularly in Czechoslovakia. For Stoppard, this took the form of letters of protest to foreign governments, public statements in the papers, petitions, marches to the Czech and Soviet embassies and participation on the board of, and publication in, *Index of Censorship*. In February 1980, Stoppard joined Stuart Hampshire, Roland Penrose, Dan Jacobson, Mark Bonham Carter and others in signing a letter protesting at the Soviet authorities' clamp-down on human rights in Russia. The following year, he published an open letter to President Husák, ironically requesting his help in obtaining a visa to visit Czechoslovakia.

What these public actions validated for Stoppard was the importance of the Central European practice of the public expression of humanism. In 'The Power of the Powerless', Havel argued that humanism required repeated civic affirmation. Political and state censorship, however, meant that this could occur only in clandestine ways; in drama, largely through satire or black comedy. The source of this expression of humanism, providing the individual with power, originated in Masaryk's idea that morality should be an agreed basis for political activity, or, in Stoppard's words, that 'political questions resolve themselves into moral questions'. Stoppard's political plays repeatedly express this theme of the elevation of humanism to fight repression, embodying Havel's statement that 'any existential revolution should provide hope of a moral reconstitution of society'.[10] Coupled with this is the Central European sense of irony, stemming from an awareness of the paradoxes and ambiguities that always define power. Such an attitude is one of the core features of Stoppard's work and personality.

Havel's impact on Stoppard seems clear, but what of Stoppard's on Havel? It was equally intense, beginning with Havel's attempt to produce *Rosencrantz and Guildenstern* in Czech at the Theatre on the Balustrade. He had seen the play in New York in 1968, when he spent six weeks there while *The Memorandum* was performed at Joseph Papp's New York Shakespeare Festival. In a December 1980 letter to his wife Olga, Havel recalled the difficulties of getting the work on stage, beginning with a controversy over which translation would be suitable. Havel's efforts led nowhere and the play remained unproduced, not simply because there was not enough time, or adequate actors, or too many plays scheduled for the season. There were fears that it might be seen as a political critique of the regime, that it wouldn't be popular, or that the theatre manager, the influential Jan Grossman, was not enthusiastic about the work. Havel's own support of the play might have worked against it, as well as his invitation to Honza Kačer, from the rival Činoherní Klub, the rising theatrical club, to direct it.

Additionally, producing Stoppard might appear to suggest that the Balustrade needed rescuing, although the style would be vastly different than the somewhat 'intellectual tradition of our own theatre'. The different approach of the Činoherní Klub, which included 'a vigorous opening out of the actors' personalities and the themes hidden within them', would be refreshing. Havel also thought that *Rosencrantz and Guildenstern* would make an excellent companion piece for *Waiting for Godot*: 'My idea was that Rosencrantz and Guildenstern would be played by the same actors who played Estragon and Vladimir in *Godot* and our audience could then view two variations on the same principle.' Havel went on to elaborate what he believed to be the similarities between his work and Stoppard's.[11]

Not surprisingly, the relativity of truth absorbs Havel and Stoppard, who understand its complicated and multiform nature. Havel's *The Garden Party* displays this clearly. In the play, Hugo exclaims, 'no matter how one answers this sort of question, one can never encompass the whole truth, but only one of its many limited parts ... none of us entirely is and at the same time each one of us is not entirely'. Archie similarly tells Crouch in *Jumpers*, 'the truth to us philosophers is always an interim judgment', while Kerner explains in *Hapgood* that 'we're all doubles'. The misuse of language to subvert individuality is another connection between the two writers: in *The Memorandum,* Ptydepe, 'the new office language', is adopted to make communication more accurate and 'introduce precision and order into their terminology'. Of course, such language only creates greater confusion, as Stoppard showed in his own experiment with language, *Dogg's Hamlet*.[12]

In October 1977, Stoppard published 'My friends fighting for freedom', expanding on the suppression of free speech and criticism in Czechoslovakia, while detailing the 1977 detention of Havel for four and a half months, followed by a suspended sentence of fourteen months. The power of Havel's writing, as a fellow dissident wrote, 'was that he [Havel] has always written as though censorship did not exist'.[13] Stoppard supports this view in a narrative of his June visit to Havel and his trip in the same battered white Saab, driven by Pavel Landovsky, that was trapped by eight police cars when they were arrested for carrying copies of Charter 77. Stoppard describes the public's response to the arrest and the repression of the Charter, which somehow managed to increase its signatories from the initial 241 to nearly 800. Havel, who organized the original signings, was held up as a warning to others; hence his sentence. The night the trial ended, Michael Konupek called Stoppard from Prague, reporting on events and telling Stoppard that the publicity over the incident was good, despite the sentences: 'Without the attention the sentences would have been much worse. The only bad thing is to be forgotten.'[14] To make sure the English would not forget, Stoppard published 'Looking-Glass

World' in the *New Statesman* a week later, again summarizing the trial, Havel's evaluation of the proceedings, the strange lack of confidence exhibited by the court and the continued harassment of dissidents.

With only slight exaggeration, Havel may be said to have become Stoppard's political conscience. In response to Havel's October 1979 arrest and trial, Stoppard, Simone Signoret, Pavel Kohout and the German film director Volker Schlöndorff participated in a re-enactment of the trial in February 1980 for a television documentary. Filmed in a Munich tram shed, the show repeated the accusations and responses to the indictment. Stoppard, who played Havel's defence lawyer, spoke only one line but did it credibly. Pavel Kohout had the role of Havel. Simone Signoret played Otta Bednarova, a journalist arrested with Havel; Volker Schlöndorff was another defence lawyer; Yves Montand participated as a silenced relation. The audience numbered nearly one thousand. Havel himself was in Heřmanice prison in Northern Moravia, where he remained until his unexpected release in January 1983.[15]

In 1981, Stoppard continued his critique of the repressive regime by imitating Havel, who in April 1975 had sent an open letter to President Husák indicting the so called normalized conditions. Stoppard's letter, also to President Husák, requested a visa to revisit Prague, having been denied one twice, both times without reason. Ironically recounting the events and consequences of his first visit to Czechoslovakia in 1977, Stoppard politely agrees that if they don't want him, he won't complain. He writes, in fact, not to complain but to express disappointment and frustration, fuelled by a sense of craft and justice: 'the occupational prejudice of playwrights is that things only move forward through dialogue. I also retain my faith, which may be an occupational naivety, in progress through reason and reasonable discussion.' Sarcastically, Stoppard adds that 'frankly, Havel's prison sentence has been a great nuisance to me. Every week or so I have to ask myself what I can do to help him instead of being able to get on with my life and work . . .' Frustrated, he concludes that this is his final appeal. He was again refused.[16]

That same year, Stoppard wrote the introduction to a new edition of Havel's *The Memorandum* in which he stressed Havel's current (April 1980) imprisonment and his history of political dissent, including Havel's supposed statement to the judges at his sentencing. Stoppard's introduction is itself a political statement, although he tries not to detract from the inventiveness of *The Memorandum*, a play which stresses the maximum difference between words so that 'no word can be mistaken for another with the length of a word being proportional to the frequency of use (the word for wombat has 319 letters)'.[17] Language and politics: two interlinked themes essential to Stoppard and Havel.

> *I believe all political acts must be judged in moral terms . . .*
> *otherwise they are simply attempts to put the boot on the*
> *other foot.*
>
> Stoppard, 1974

Stoppard's high profile lent prominence to many causes. His role as one of Britain's leading playwrights – Pinter and Peter Shaffer being other outspoken dramatists at this time – caught the attention of a public that was at first surprised by his political actions, especially since he had previously professed non-involvement and an apolitical view of art. Many of his interviews in the first ten years of his career saw Stoppard defend himself for *not* dealing with political issues. Erudition, not politics, seemed to fascinate him. Yet it was only a matter of time before the moral issues he dealt with took on a political character.

Stoppard's increased reputation and financial security allowed him to be more forthright and outspoken on political matters. And at the same time, his private life became more public. In July 1977, he and his family were featured in *People* magazine, with flattering photographs of Stoppard and his wife at work. The article emphasizes his active involvement with his children and Miriam's ability to navigate successfully between running a home and a high-powered job.[18] They embodied the ideal, successful couple of the seventies.

In September that year, Miriam's 'superwoman' style received extended coverage in the *Observer*. Executive, mother, wife, author, media commentator, she fulfilled numerous roles while establishing her financial independence. A super organizer, Miriam nevertheless depended on help, from a live-in nanny to a housekeeper, as well as

Stoppard's secretary, to deal with home administration. She described herself as a forward-planner who plotted everything, down to shopping lists and birthday gifts in preparation for a trip. She had three sets of rollers, one at home, one at the office and one in her travelling pack; she also did all her clothes shopping in two days, finding out what was popular and then calling the shops to reserve the clothes before hitting the town. She wrote her books on planes, trains and at the kitchen table. Yet, as the article makes clear, she was torn between conflicting loyalties: businesswoman versus mother, wife versus careerist. Unhappily, she admitted that she put her job before her children.

Stoppard, she explains, encouraged her ambitions, and she praises him for allowing her to act this way: 'he likes independent, self-sufficient women and would hate it if I interfered in his life using his interests as my own. The more successful I am, the prouder and happier he is. No, he doesn't mind my going away. Tom's a very private person, who likes being left alone.'[19]

In December the same year, another glimpse of Stoppard's life appeared: Ken Tynan's lengthy profile of Stoppard in *The New Yorker*. This admiring piece combined biographical details with a reading of his plays, interspersed with recent episodes in his life, including lunch with A. J. Ayer at Oxford and a lecture in Santa Barbara, California. It displayed his wit, intelligence and fame, emphasizing his prominence as a central figure on the British, if not world, theatre scene. Tynan, who had worked feverishly on the lengthy piece, none the less felt slightly put out when he learned that Stoppard would be publishing his own piece on the Czech dissidents two weeks after Tynan turned in his profile to the *New Yorker*.[20] The month that the profile appeared, Stoppard was made a CBE.

To his credit, and the possible chagrin of those who criticized his lack of political concerns, Stoppard was now an example of how a visible public figure in the arts could use his prominence to promote issues of world importance. Unafraid to use his stature, Stoppard, like those he sought to help, did not remain silent. In 1979, he became chairman of the 'Free Mischa' campaign, the protest which reunited the Russian psychiatrist Dr Marina Voikhanskaya, who left Russia in 1975, with her thirteen-year-old son, Mischa.

It would be incorrect, however, to paint Stoppard as exclusively liberal on the issue of human rights; indeed, his own thinking on matters political occasionally became muddy, as in the issue of a cultural boycott of South Africa. In 1975, there was an outcry against the restrictive laws preventing freedom of expression in South Africa and a series of British writers objected to their works being published or performed there. A petition to this effect was signed by Edward Bond, Robert Bolt and Peter Nichols, among others. Stoppard, surprisingly, did not participate, allowing a production of *Dirty Linen* to go on in June 1977. But his position was ambiguous: he allowed *Rosencrantz and Guildenstern* to be performed there, but not *Jumpers*. Stoppard explained the dilemma:

> South African liberals say you shouldn't go. Other people say it's the only chance to have a cultural exchange. I decided to do what Athol Fugard thought was the right thing. He tipped the scales.[21]

Fugard had argued that withholding such works from South Africa would do more harm than good. However, Inter-Action, Ed Berman's company, which originally produced the play, felt uneasy. Asked to direct *Dirty Linen* in South Africa, Berman declined, saying he didn't have the time. Ironically, under a previous arrangement, a portion of Stoppard's overseas income was to go to Amnesty International. Stoppard, meanwhile, soon transferred some of his concern with human rights to the question of freedom of expression, an issue for him since his days in Bristol as a reporter.

The Wrong Hat
Stoppard, *Night and Day*

In *Night and Day*, the professional journalist Richard Wagner, of the London *Sunday Globe*, tells the President of an African country that 'even when *I* started in newspapers a proprietor could sack any reporter, who, as it were, insisted on wearing the wrong hat, but things are very different now'. Weakly, Wagner defends the advantages of the unions' closed shop and the control they exert over journalists, only to have the *femme fatale* Ruth cut in with 'now the union can sack him instead'. Her tart comment reflects Stoppard's own reaction to the power of the closed shop, which he understood to be a threat to freedom of the press as powerful as that of the owners.[22]

Stoppard and the National Union of Journalists had had a run-in as early as 1959. At that time in Bristol, he was suspended for three months over a dispute concerning his failure to support a strike against one of the leading papers. In 1977, he still opposed the union's preference for a closed shop as, to him, this meant control over the freedom of journalists. In a letter to *The Times*, he ironically explained that it was equally erroneous for newspaper owners to declare their circle a closed shop. 'Shall we spell it out for them?' he indignantly asked and then proceeded to indict the union.[23]

Interestingly, the spring 1976 issue of *Index on Censorship* contained Robert Birley's 'Freedom of the Press: an historical perspective', confirming Stoppard's concerns about the independence of the press.[24] These were the issues that found expression in *Night and Day*, Stoppard's fourth major play but the first written expressly for the West End. Michael Codron, the West End producer who had seen Stoppard's *Rosencrantz and Guildenstern* in Edinburgh in 1966 and produced *The Real Inspector Hound* at the Criterion, commissioned the work. The request, however, had a curious background: in 1977, Stoppard needed some additional income and his brother quietly approached Codron during a weekend gathering at Fernleigh, to ask if he might commission a new work. Codron did not need much convincing and offered Stoppard a £10,000 advance. The result was one of Codron's biggest financial and critical hits, *Night and Day*.

Stoppard prepared a work tailored for West End audiences: naturalistic in setting, orthodox in structure and unremarkable in dialogue. It also spoke to current issues: unions, journalism and press freedom. It made no more experimental demands on the audience than the glimpses into Ruth's mind, spoken to the audience but unheard by other characters on the stage. Its denouement was also mechanical, with the union issue becoming the cause that shuts the paper down, preventing Wagner from telexing and publishing his scoop.

Night and Day's staging, however, reflected some of the more extravagant visual and auditory effects beginning to dominate the West End at the time, as seen in such works as Tim Rice and Andrew Lloyd Webber's *Evita*, which opened that June (a week after the remounting of Stoppard's own extravaganza, *Every Good Boy*, at the Mermaid Theatre). Over the next two or three years, productions such as the eight-hour *Nicholas Nickleby* (1980), *Cats* (1981) and, later, *Les Misérables* (Paris, 1980; London, 1985) would dominate the West End with their excesses of sight and sound. Helicopter noise, machine-gun fire and a jeep, driven on to the stage at the beginning of the play with its headlights glaring directly at the audience, would create the physical rather than verbal impact of *Night and Day*, a residue, perhaps, of the scale of *Every Good Boy* and its use of the London Symphony Orchestra.

Such an extravaganza, however, posed problems: Codron had difficulty locating a West End theatre large enough to accommodate the jeep. He originally wanted the Queen's Theatre, but it was not available; he suggested Her Majesty's and, with Stoppard and Peter Wood, went to examine it. But it lacked the necessary wings space. 'Is it possible to *imagine* the jeep?' Codron asked? 'No jeep, no play,' Stoppard curtly replied.[25] The play opened, with the jeep, at the Phoenix Theatre, following tryouts in Wimbledon. Peter Wood directed the work, dedicated to Stoppard's friend, the journalist and former foreign correspondent Paul Johnson, who had spent some time in Africa.

Thematically expressing Stoppard's political and moral concern with freedom of the press, the play also draws elements from his favourite novel about journalists, Evelyn Waugh's *Scoop*. In that work, the naïve William Boot, a nature columnist best known for a controversial piece on the crested grebe, is mistakenly contracted to cover a supposed revolution in the fictitious African country Ishmaelia for the Fleet Street paper *The Beast*. Boot's adventures with the more experienced and cynical Corker in the capital of Ishmaelia, his accidental discovery of crucial news and even his love affair provide Stoppard with the essential plot and character of Jacob Milne in *Night and Day*. Milne's scoops, his near-affair with Ruth and his naïveté outshine the deceptive, self-serving Wagner. Only Milne's off-stage death in the play, something of a melodramatic necessity for the plot and its West End audience, dislodged the parallels between Waugh's novel and Stoppard's play which, even down to the detail of slightly obscure telegrams, duplicate each other.[26]

More significant is the parallel attitude towards journalism in the two works, in which mistakes are never explained, stories are always inflated and reports frequently distorted by editors. Yet the romance of journalism, which first inspired Stoppard, exists in both works, satirized by Waugh in the passage when Boot composes a dispatch on the rebel leader, Dr Benito: 'Love, patriotism, zeal for justice, and personal spite flamed within him as he sat at his typewriter and began his message. One finger was not enough; he used both hands.'[27]

Milne's accidental scoops in *Night and Day,* and what he learns about the role of fiction in reporting, parallel Boot's education in *Scoop.* Furthermore, Milne's declarations in support of freedom of the press and his critique of the closed shop reflect Stoppard's own views. 'No matter how imperfect things are, if you've got a free press everything is correctable, and without it everything is concealable,' Jacob tells Ruth, who responds with: 'I'm with you on the free press. It's the newspapers I can't stand.'[28] Milne had earlier created a controversy at his provincial paper, the *Grimsby Evening Messenger,* because he would not join the union.[29]

Ruth's retort is representative of the play's comedy: restrained but precise in its target. Unlike the wit, word-play and ingenuity in any of Stoppard's three earlier major plays, *Night and Day* is more circumspect and bounded by its realism. Its earnestness, especially in Milne's views on journalism and Wagner's cynicism – 'I don't file prose. I file facts'[30] – make the work programmatic and predictable. Laser displays of wit and surprises are absent, suggesting that the serious subject of politics and freedom requires a sober presentation. When the wit does appear, it has a residual Wildean flair. Ruth tells Wagner, for example, that 'a lady, if surprised by melancholy, might go to bed with a chap, once; or a thousand times if consumed by passion. But twice, Wagner, twice . . . a lady might think she'd been taken for a tart.'[31] *Night and Day* fulfilled Stoppard's need to write a play about journalists, just as his later works such as *Hapgood* and *Arcadia* fulfilled his desire to write plays about science – more specifically mathematics.

Night and Day also contained an embedded link to Stoppard's later work. Early in Act Two, Ruth exhibits a playful remorse over her affairs in front of Jacob, with an example of how she might renew her relationship with her husband, Geoffrey: 'Fresh start. Hello! – had a good trip? (*Pause*) I don't know. I got into a state today.'[32] This display of marriage politics is almost identical to the opening of Stoppard's next major and commercially successful play, *The Real Thing,* which, like *Night and Day,* would also incorporate popular music.

In *Night and Day,* the music expands its thematic function, which developed with changes in the script. In the original Faber edition of the play, the work ends with Ruth smashing a Scotch bottle and looking at Wagner, who is at the telex machine, as if it were a piano and she a piano-bar singer. The stage directions indicate music (*'Something fast. RUTH sings. Just a few bars'*).[33] The revised New York edition of the play is more explicit: 'The Lady is a Tramp' is heard, with a few lines sung by Ruth. The music functions as a coda to the play. During the rehearsals and previews, Peter Wood kept inserting musical clues, removing the original 'Night and Day' by Cole Porter and substituting Rodgers and Hart's 'The Lady is a Tramp' as a 'memory clue', replacing all the other musical references.[34]

One line of Ruth's, an early revision following publication of the 1978 Faber text, did not entirely make sense until it was clarified by the music:

> I was meant to be one of those women who halt the cutlery as they pass through hotel dining rooms on the first night of the holiday . . . tits first to the table through the ack-ack of teeny-weeny engagement rings (*Pause*). I'm in the wrong movie, I think.[35]

Neither Stoppard nor Wood could work in the theatrical detail of the flashing engagement rings. Stoppard finally rewrote the lines in New York, linking them to the song 'The Lady is a Tramp'. The diamond rings were gone, as well as 'tits first to the table', which, according to Wood, was 'a description of Miriam Stoppard in a hotel in the Canary islands wearing one of the first dresses without a bra', a line which never worked because it was too personal.[36] Ruth in the new version was playing Lauren Bacall, not Miriam, though the lines were included in the New York version of the play.[37]

Actors also made contributions to the development of *Night and Day.* Peter Wood described how Maggie Smith reversed the order of a line to get a bigger and better laugh, explaining that actors know instinctively 'where the audience will laugh', although they are less clear on the function of a play in its entirety. 'They make it work locally, line by line. That's the difference between their work and mine. I have to see a whole play, and they have to see one line.'[38] Other improvements included additional lines to make the audience aware that Ruth and Wagner had met each other before, put in at Peter

Wood's insistence, as well as an important exchange which has Ruth soliloquizing across the counterpoint of Carson's telephone conversation, preceded by an essential exchange dealing with their son's name tapes and the phrase 'Ruth Carson, Speakeasy Queen'.[39] Diana Rigg said that this addition became 'the pivotal scene for Ruth because having her defences down gave her a reality that was important'. Often, Diana Rigg or Maggie Smith would say: 'I can't do anything with this, Tom, you'll have to help me.' If they still couldn't do anything with it after he had rewritten it or turned the line around, they would ask, 'Well, please can we take it out?'[40]

Further alterations to the play occurred during performance, as Stoppard outlined in a lecture at Cambridge in February 1980. One of the most interesting, which represents the influence of audiences on a work, occurred at the point when Carson reads a telex from London to the reporter Wagner. The language is that of newspapermen and reads: 'Milne [the young reporter] copy blacked by subs, full chapel and machine-room support'. Even when several journalists in Washington saw the play, they didn't quite understand the references, so Stoppard made the language more explicit. But it still wasn't absolutely clear. Only after they had played a few nights in New York did he change it to read: 'Printers refuse to handle story of Jacob Milne, Grimsby scab. Hammaker won't budge. No paper this week.' The audience then understood that the paper would be on strike and that Wagner's exclusive interview with the president would not appear. The scene duplicates Boot's inability in *Scoop* to decode telegrams from his paper which only the experienced writer Corker can translate for him.[41]

Until Stoppard stopped altering it in response to the actors and director, the text of *Night and Day* was not really finished, reflecting Stoppard's view that a play 'is an event rather than a text that one is trying to convey. Text is merely an attempt to describe an event.'[42] It was Stoppard who made the alterations, though the suggestions for change more often came from Peter Wood than from Stoppard. This partly resulted from the collaborative synergy between the two and the way Wood thinks visually and aims for greater explicitness in Stoppard's work. 'This', Stoppard suggested, 'may be to do with *my* reluctance to be over explicit and *his* fear that the audience isn't being given enough information.' 'He winds up where I wind down,' Wood explained, recalling their working relationship.[43] It was the orthodox form of *Night and Day* that caused a larger than average number of alterations. Wood elaborated: 'Because Tom was trying to find a way of using conventional theatre forms to say what he wanted to say, he found this surprisingly difficult.'[44]

Night and Day was a commercial hit, partly because of its star power. Diana Rigg won the Best Performance by an Actress award from *Plays and Players* for 1978. Maggie Smith took over the role, ensuring a consistently strong box office. Despite his criticism of journalism, the attention Stoppard and the play received in the press and the timeliness of the topic turned the play into a financial success which he acknowledged with a gift to Michael Codron: a miniature ceramic bundle of papers with a headline announcing the play's triumph. It still sits in Codron's office. Critical reaction to the play, however, was less enthusiastic and praise was tempered: 'a perplexing, partial, exhaustive but unsatisfying evening which is still far better in quality than most things London's commercial theatre can offer' sums up most views.[45] Despite pulling in West End audiences, the play was thought to be a minor work. Peter Hall, after viewing the New York production, noted in his diary that Stoppard and Peter Wood had done a great deal of work on the play since its London production, but it is still 'about too many things, everything that is in Tom's head at the moment . . . somehow he has tried to make it into one play. It's four at least.'[46]

Stoppard felt that this play, more than any of his others at the time, had film potential. He wrote a draft film script that 'jealously guarded the play', being only the play 'slightly loosened up'. When enough time had passed, he rewrote the screenplay, treating the play more brutally. The results were still not right and it remained unproduced, though in the process he realized that part of what works in *Travesties* and *Jumpers* is that they happen 'in the practical physical limitations of the stage. In a medium where you can do anything you like [film], the theatricality of the play counts for practically nothing.'[47]

A week after its opening in London, *Night and Day* had competition in Pinter's first play since *No Man's Land* – *Betrayal*, a work similarly dealing with adultery – premièred at the National, directed by Peter Hall. The two most important playwrights of the day had major productions on view simultaneously. Comparisons were inevitable, and Pinter's, with its imaginative structure (the story of an affair told in reverse order), came out ahead.[48]

Night and Day was Stoppard's first play to deal with the politics of freedom, not only in the press but also in marriage, a theme he would pursue in *The Real Thing*. It was also his first to contain a serious part for a woman: in fact, Ruth Carson best embodies the irony of freedom in the work because she is the most eloquent spokesperson for freedom but also the one most enchained. Her life as the chattel of a man she adores but does not love turns her existence into that of a superfluous ornament. Her disgust over the death of Milne at the end exposes the fraudulent character of the press and the powers that shape it.

Unlike the plays focusing on dissent and Eastern Europe, which had strong liberal values, *Night and Day*, with its discussion of press freedom and the vulnerability of individuals to political pressure, was controversial. The tension between Stoppard and the dominant theatrical Left became manifest, topped by stinging criticism that in writing about European dissidents he was being both 'trendy' *and* 'popular'. For allowing his plays to tour South Africa, and for the sexism in *Dirty Linen*, he was virtually condemned. At the same time, his lampooning of the Left through his indictment of bogus journalism, political rhetoric and unions played into a certain Conservative position upholding traditional values associated with the Right which Stoppard did not deny and which the country seemed to endorse with the election of Margaret Thatcher and the Conservatives in May 1979. Stoppard defined himself at this time as 'a conservative with a small c. I'm a conservative in politics, literature, education and theatre,' stressing, however, his objection to ideological rigidity.

Stoppard succeeded in bringing his almost obsessive concern with language into the political arena, attacking the false language and distortions of journalism which he would expand in *The Real Thing*. His playful exploration of the theme in *Dirty Linen* had turned serious. As the news photographer Guthrie says at the end of *Night and Day*,

> People do awful things to each other. But it's worse in places where everybody is kept in the dark. It really is. Information is light. Information, in itself, about anything, is light. That's all you can say, really.[49]

Since certainty is unattainable, entertainment value is the
only justification for conversation.
Stoppard, *Undiscovered Country*

In spite of the criticisms of his political position at home and wavering stature as a major playwright following *Night and Day*, international recognition continued to grow. In 1979, he won the prestigious Shakespeare Prize in Germany. Previous winners included Ralph Vaughan Williams, Peter Brook, Harold Pinter and Margot Fonteyn. His acceptance speech, given at Hamburg City Hall and published in 1982 as 'Is it true what they say about Shakespeare?', summarized his quixotic relationship with Shakespeare, emphasizing that 'when we refer to Shakespeare as our greatest writer we refer to him as the author of an event and not merely of a text'.[50] This emerged as Stoppard's basic dramatic principle; for him, Shakespeare was a dramatist first and a writer second, whose talent was 'the simultaneous compression of language and expansion of meaning'.[51] But Shakespeare is also a dangerous if not challenging figure, as the inspector in *Cahoot's Macbeth* makes clear when he tells the actors that 'the fact is, when you get a unusual and timeless writer like Shakespeare, there is a strong feeling that he could be spitting in the eye of the beholder when he should be keeping his mind on Verona – hanging round the gents.'[52]

Stoppard himself embraces this lesson when he works with directors and actors to extend the possibilities of his text by translating it into an event. It is another form of doubleness in that there are always two elements to Stoppard's work: one textual, the other visual. The first, of course, remains Stoppard's territory. The second is grasped by a singular group of directors – Peter Wood, Trevor Nunn, Jack O'Brien, Richard Eyre – who have successfully understood this aspect of Stoppard's work and transferred it to the stage.

During this period, Stoppard was also developing an interest in screenplays and adaptations. His film work began in 1975, with Joseph Losey's production of *The Romantic Englishwoman* starring Glenda Jackson and Michael Caine, and continued with Rainer Werner Fassbinder's 1979 production of Vladimir Nabokov's *Despair,* starring Dirk Bogarde. He had been interested in the genre since his days as a film critic, when he had quickly understood film as a critique of culture, offering frequent jibes at the public for their rejection of its value. On the return of Olivier's *Richard III* to a Bristol screen, for example, he wrote that it's a 'crying shame and commercial fact that the word Shakespeare keeps more people out of the cinema than a hot day'.[53]

In another piece, he established an important cinematic aesthetic. In his review of *Shadows* by John Cassavetes, Stoppard wrote that the disjointed film is like life, with a reality that is not stylish but unfinished. Human speech, he adds, 'is hesitant, often thoughtless, almost always unoriginal. Never a script. . . . in technical terms, life is very bad cinema.'[54] What he disliked about cinema, however, was its moral evasiveness sustained through its unreality. He was none the less attracted to its craft, although adaptations rather than original screenplays became Stoppard's *métier*. In 1967, John Boorman had suggested Stoppard write a screenplay of *Rosencrantz and Guildenstern* for MGM. An advance from the studio assisted but the script proved unwieldy and did not make it to production. By February 1969, he published an article in *Today's Cinema* entitled 'Confessions of a Screenwriter'.[55] In 1971 he had a contract from Paramount for *Galileo*. But he did not undertake his first feature-length film, *The Romantic Englishwoman*, until four years later.

Work on the film was to last three weeks, essentially a 'doctoring job'. He did not have much interest in the project and did it more as a favour to Losey: 'he had a script which he had to shoot in a hurry and didn't like much'. The producer, Danny Angel, reviled Stoppard's effort, however, complaining about the dialogue. Losey disagreed. They compromised, and Losey worked closely with Stoppard to revise his version before sending copies of the script to the actors. If they approved, the film would go ahead with Stoppard's script. They did, and Stoppard was credited as screenwriter alongside Thomas Wiseman, who had adapted his own novel. Pauline Kael, in her *New Yorker* review of the film, complained that Stoppard's dialogue offered 'a few Noël Cowardish bitch-nifties, but not enough to keep the blood coursing'.[56]

Although *The Romantic Englishwoman* met with mixed reviews, Stoppard soon received an offer to adapt *Despair* by Vladimir Nabokov, a writer he greatly admired. Rainer Werner Fassbinder was to direct and Dirk Bogarde to star. Stoppard wanted the film, especially the dialogue, to be treated with lightness and speed. Just the reverse happened and both he and Bogarde were deeply disappointed. Stoppard, whose sense of cinematic structure and narrative had improved, repeatedly told Fassbinder what was going wrong with the film, resulting in a lack of shape and structure. The director did not listen. Nevertheless, Stoppard hoped the film might be a success. He invited a series of friends, including Harold Pinter and Antonia Fraser, to the preview. Within ninety seconds, however, he realized he had 'made a terrible social error. The first speech of the film, which I'd written as something rather ironic and cynical, was delivered as if it had been written by Milton in one of his more studious moods. I got under my seat and stayed there.'[57] He left unhappy and embarrassed and soon wrote to Bogarde that the film 'is a turkey which I believe is American for lemon. The crux of it [is that] I wanted to write the script because it was Nabokov's book and Fassbinder wanted to film the story *despite* its being Nabokov's book.'[58]

Following this unhappy experience came the chance to work on another book he admired: Graham Greene's *The Human Factor*, a 1978 bestseller. Approached by Otto Preminger after Greene himself turned down the opportunity to do the screenplay and Peter Shaffer was unavailable, Stoppard was thrilled but admitted that he was much more nervous 'of displeasing Graham Greene than I was of displeasing Otto'.[59] Throughout the process, Stoppard and Greene exchanged ideas on the script by phone and letter. Reflecting his natural sense of structure and timing, Stoppard explained that he first had to determine 'how much screen time each scene is worth. There's no point in writing a brilliant 12 minute scene that should be 4 minutes.'[60]

Although the film was a critical success on its release in 1980, Stoppard was upset and actually cried when he saw the final cut – not because of his own unhappiness at what Preminger had done to the book, but out of respect for Greene and the embarrassment the distortions must have caused.[61] The film attracted popular interest for its subject: espionage, a topic that fascinated Stoppard and that he would expand most notably in *Hapgood*, in his screenplay of John le Carré's *The Russia House* and his 1998 screenplay for Robert Harris's novel *Enigma*, about codebreaking at Bletchley Park.

*

Stoppard's theatrical adaptations originated in his earliest professional production, his reworking of Slawomir Mrozek's *Tango* for Trevor Nunn, and revisions to Lorca's *The House of Bernarda Alba*. In 1979, his first full-blown adaptation was mounted at the National, Arthur Schnitzler's *Das Weite Land*, translated as *Undiscovered Country*. Stoppard's involvement with this work was entirely accidental. One day, while rehearsing *Night and Day* in a Chelsea church hall, he noticed a copy of a translation of the Schnitzler play on Peter Wood's table. Someone who had been asked to adapt the play had pulled out after completing a literal translation. Initially, Stoppard's interest in the work was that Peter Wood was to direct and John Wood was to star, but once he read the text, he agreed with Peter Wood that this important work, entirely unknown in England, should be adapted.

Stoppard did not understand German, so he began by working with a German-speaking student. After compiling a faithful first draft, he asked himself what would he have done if *he* had written the play? He revised the literal version, shortening it and adding more dialogue. Adaptation, he has said, 'is joy time. It's a craftsman's job, not "my soul speaks through Schnitzler". You go around with a bag of tools doing jobs between personal plays.' He also remarked that 'working on the play, I often felt as if I were driving up the M1 in a Triumph Stag and finding myself overtaken by a 1922 Bentley'.[62]

The play is essentially the story of Friedrich Hofreiter, a manufacturer of light bulbs who constantly seems to be switching other people off. The play begins with a report that a Russian concert-pianist, once in love with Hofreiter's wife, has committed suicide. The plot builds towards a duel between Hofreiter and a young naval lieutenant who has casually cuckolded him. All of this is set against a background of Viennese social life, from tennis parties and summer house-parties to mountaineering in the Dolomites, civilized deceit taking place in a world of golden leisure. The transformation of the title, from *Das Weite Land* ('The Wide Country') into *Undiscovered Country*, neatly links the work with the world of dreams and sleep. Freud, in fact, admired Schnitzler's drama, which disguised its psychoses through duels, decadence and social decline.

What appealed to Stoppard in the play was the complex view of human beings and their willingness – or unwillingness – to admit their contradictions and confusions. Dr von Aigner summarizes this view when he explains why he constantly deceived his wife despite his love for her. We are contradictory beings, he argues, and 'we try to bring order into our lives as best we can; but that very order has something unnatural about it. The natural condition is chaos.'[63] Stoppard's focus is on exposing the games people play, although, unlike Schnitzler's original, he doesn't really analyse them, changing von Aigner's 'vast country' to 'uncharted' and then, a few lines later, 'undiscovered country' (the phrase is from Hamlet's 'To be or not to be' soliloquy). The reference to chaos by von Aigner anticipates the concern of Stoppard's *Arcadia*.

Undiscovered Country opened on the Olivier stage at the National Theatre on 20 June 1979 and met with general success. Stoppard deviated from the literal translation, adding a few flashes of wit. For example, instead of a laborious explanation of yearning being good for the economy of the soul in Act One, Stoppard sharpens the passage to read 'in an ideal world, more and more people would see less and less of each other'. 'You're not doing an author a favour if the adaptation is not vibrant,' he explained, 'so in the end I started "helping".'[64] The price paid was a certain simplification, not only of characterization but of atmosphere. Eliminating two speeches on death curtailed the motif, while his transposition of material enlivened the structure by breaking up long passages.[65]

The importance of language is overrated.

Stoppard, *Professional Foul*

By early July 1979, Stoppard was enjoying the unlikely triumph of four plays running in London at the same time: *Dirty Linen, Night and Day, Undiscovered Country* and the double bill of *Dogg's Hamlet* with *Cahoot's Macbeth*, performed by Ed Berman's new group, the British American Repertory Company (BARC). *Dogg's Hamlet* and *Cahoot's Macbeth* managed to join, but not integrate, the two worlds that most engaged Stoppard: the aesthetic and the political. In the first, the free-flowing style and play of theatrical devices excelled; in the second, the intense awareness of political intrigue and threat to the theatre dominated. *Cahoot's Macbeth* resulted from Ed Berman requesting a second piece for his BARC tour to pair with *Dogg's Hamlet*. Stoppard first thought he might write a play about Ernest Hemingway. Then he recalled Pavel Kohout, the Czech writer–actor who had written to Stoppard about his seventy-five-minute living-room version of *Macbeth*.

Topicality was essential to the *Dogg's Hamlet/Cahoot's Macbeth* production, and even the day before the London opening, Stoppard was making last-minute additions. Ed Berman indicated that Stoppard planned 'to update the piece – daily if necessary – to keep it current with recent developments in Prague'.[66] That process continued throughout the North American tour, with various references and updates included. The work consistently exposed repression. Informed by the Hostess that the performance is not open to the public, the Inspector in *Cahoot's Macbeth*, who arrives to investigate the actors, replies: 'I should hope not indeed. That would be acting without authority – acting without authority! – you'd never believe I make it up as I go along.' He warns them that Shakespeare is one of the most subversive writers, much disfavoured by the authorities and that language on the stage is always suspect: 'Who's to say what was meant? Words can be your friend or your enemy, depending on who's throwing the book, so watch your language.'[67]

Stoppard's own sense of playwriting was becoming clearer at this time. Explaining the motivation for *Night and Day*, he told Mel Gussow that his 'primary problem is not what the play would be about on the abstract level, but who are the people in it – their gender, their age – and where are they? . . . I write argument plays. I tend to write for two people rather than for One Voice. Rosencrantz and Guildenstern were two sides of one temperament.' As a playwright, he was 'interested in ideas and forced to invent characters to express those ideas. All my people speak the same way, with the same cadences and sentence structures. They speak as I do.' What he was also realizing was that people 'are so clever that, paradoxically, they can be persuaded to do almost anything'.[68] At the same time, from *Every Good Boy* to *Cahoot's Macbeth*, Stoppard was experimenting with new forms and testing conventional narratives, even in *Night and Day*. But despite the shift to political topics, Stoppard insisted that what was important to him was the aesthetic rather than the political: 'I'm not impressed by art *because* it's political. I believe in art being good art or bad art, not relevant art or irrelevant art.'[69]

For Stoppard, words were definitely his friends. His success at this time – the result of almost eighteen months of continuous activity – brought financial security as well as popularity, confirmed by a move in October 1979 from the four-acre Fernleigh to the seventeen-acre Iver Grove, just two and a half miles down the road but a shift in status of immense proportions. The family left a home variously described as 'slightly squirearchical' for a more baronial, Palladian-style mansion.

Iver Grove was built as a dowager's mansion for Lady Mohun, daughter of Thomas Lawrence, Chief Physician to Queen Anne, and the widow of Lord Mohun (killed in a duel in November 1712), in 1722–4 by John James, an associate of Sir Christopher Wren, though Hawksmoor was also thought to be connected. A 1933 history of Iver incorrectly attributes the building to Sir John Vanbrugh. The two-and-half-storey brick mansion, at the end of a long, semicircular drive behind two white pillars and a gate, was in a Palladian vernacular associated with Vanbrugh, which pleased Stoppard because of Vanbrugh's dramatic career as author of *The Relapse* and *The Provok'd Wife*, while Castle Howard and Blenheim Palace were two of his architectural triumphs. Stoppard preferred to think the house was a Vanbrugh because he was a playwright, although James was the actual architect.[70]

One of the more impressive homes in the Buckinghamshire hamlet of Shredding Green, Iver Grove was the subject of an 1824 print in *Ackerman's Repository of the Arts*. Despite its periods of disarray and renewal, the home had been variously featured in both *House and Garden* and *Country Life,* as well as in numerous history books on the area.[71] During the Second World War, it was a Polish refugee camp. A fire in the mid-fifties caused extensive damage, but restorations in 1956–7 returned Iver Grove to its former stature. Miriam Stoppard would renovate the large Victorian brick stable into offices, an in-law suite and a billiard-room, adding an indoor swimming-pool (a gift for Stoppard) in an adjacent building; it already had a tennis court. This country estate would be Stoppard's headquarters and retreat until late 1989, with one half of the second floor of the remarkable stable functioning as his study. One reached the imposing red-brick structure by following a path that crossed the large garden to the left of the main house. The conversion in 1984 transformed the building, its Italianate dormers looming over new glass walls with the half-curves of the roof echoing the hooped doorway. To the left on the ground floor stood the large, glass-walled billiard-room, adjacent to a modern office just beyond the entrance. Light entered Miriam's office through the impressive glass walls; her secretary worked across the hall to the right, in what were formerly horses' stalls; Stoppard's secretary worked in another office nearby.

The Stoppards introduced a striking red, wrought-iron, winding staircase at the rear of the ground-floor hall, leading to Stoppard's library-like study, featuring a music stand, cricket bat and Eames chair. The walls below the cross-beamed ceiling were lined with framed letters by Thackeray, Tennyson, Strachey, Kipling and Hemingway, plus a treasured, personally inscribed photograph of Samuel Beckett. In the middle of the room, two desks faced each other. However, Stoppard preferred to write in the kitchen 'after everyone's gone to bed', a practice that had begun at Grosvenor Lodge in Bristol.[72]

Tom and Miriam's working habits also differed, as Stoppard explained:

> Miriam is disciplined, she can do 19.5 minutes' work out of 20 at her desk. I need an empty four hours to do two hours' work. When I am into something I write in longhand with a pen until I am exhausted and then I do it again the next day. There is a compulsion. I am still nervous of the whole thing – because one doesn't know what one is coming towards. . . . Among some people I am now known as Miriam Stoppard's husband and they are quite right because I am. The others think I am Alan Ayckbourn. I hope he gets congratulated on *Jumpers* as much as I do on *The Norman Conquests*.[73]

The renovated stable overlooked the main house and, to the left, visible through a porthole window in Stoppard's second-floor study, was a formal English garden set off by low walls. Fields stretched into the distance, with a ha-ha added by Stoppard to prevent any disoriented animals from approaching the house.

The main house at Iver Grove was equally impressive, although it had been built for just one person. The dining-room was small, but the drawing-room across the hall and towards the rear of the ground floor was substantial, large and airy, done in pastels with eighteenth and nineteenth-century English watercolours on the walls and numerous bookcases, some holding leather-bound editions of Stoppard's plays, others with first editions of Dickens, Joyce and Hemingway. The owner of thousands of books, Stoppard established one rule: that the children could have and read as many books as they wanted. Floor-to-ceiling windows looked out on a lawn to the rear, used for cricket, and to the fields beyond, enjoyed by the family and their two friendly dogs. A large staircase hall greeted guests, with a painting by the Renaissance artist Guido Reni adorning one wall. The oversized canvas belonged to Paul Johnson, who had lent it to the Stoppards because he had no place to hang it.

At home, the intellectuals' playwright was something of an English country squire with his gala summer garden parties, complete with marquee. These parties quickly became one of the more important and glamorous events in the social calendar of many notables from the artistic, cultural and academic worlds. Tina Brown, Harold Evans, A. J. Ayer, Peter Hall, Harold Pinter, Antonia Fraser, Trevor Nunn and many others would appear, although the arrival of Roald Dahl with his wife Patricia Neal by helicopter remained one of the more impressive entrances.

At the end of the seventies, the Stoppards were flourishing: Stoppard's plays were being performed worldwide and his reputation was international. His adaptations were a success at the National. His movie writing, often undertaken for the practical reason of extra capital, was beginning to thrive, his name becoming known to major directors. Although he wrote unconventional plays, his life at Fernleigh and then Iver Grove was conservative in its habits and traditional in its taste. Extravagance was tempered by what he believed to be English domestic values.

The Stoppards' move to Iver Grove symbolized their achievements and status as accomplished celebrities, although Miriam's career was accelerating at an even faster pace. By mid-1980, she would resign her post as managing director of Syntex, though she remained a consultant. Her popularity would equal if not outstrip her husband's, although virtually the first question Prime Minister Margaret Thatcher asked when a guest on Miriam's popular television show *Women to Women* was: 'And tell me, *how* is Tom?'[74]

CHAPTER 13

INCURABLE SEMANTIC

Personally, I would rather have written Winnie the Pooh
than the collected works of Brecht.
Stoppard, 1972

Throughout the spring of 1980, Stoppard supported the boycott of the summer Olympics held in Moscow. The issue for him was clear: it was necessary to show that 'morality has not yet been stood on its head on planet earth'. The differences between a decent and indecent way to govern are not relative but absolute, he wrote in an article in the *Sunday Times*. Political systems must be established against 'a moral standard, a consistent idea of what constitutes good and bad'. All political acts must be 'judged in moral terms, in terms of their consequences'.[1]

Nevertheless, while continuing his involvement with human rights issues, Stoppard also sought – at least in interviews – to minimize his activism. He admitted his frequent correspondence with exiles, émigrés and Czechs, but resisted the label of activist. Opposed to ideological rigidity because it restricted individual freedom, Stoppard sought a delicate balance between political action and literary expression: 'I'm available to be asked to lend my name to something, to attend a meeting, to do this or that, but I get on with my plays, and that's my main activity.'[2]

By 1981, Stoppard had written four major plays, plus seven short works and four major adaptations, including *On the Razzle*. He had also established a set method of working, rarely deviating from it. From roughly 10 a.m. to 5 p.m., he would write, following up his efforts in the evening. He would begin by mapping something out on a single piece of paper without a line of dialogue, so I have a structure. I tend to change my mind about this map as I then write the scenes. In the actual writing, I can't bash out a rough draft. It's a slow work-through, and each bit has got to be potentially 'it' before I can go onto the next bit.[3]

An overall conception of the work came first:

I don't pick up a pen and see how things will go. By the time I pick up a pen, I've gone through so much work. Once I have the vague idea of a structure, landmark moments occur which fit into the structure. I have an idea of how a scene will end, but I don't know how to get there.[4]

He worked slowly, however: 'I don't rough things out and then re-write. I can't do the 37th line until I'm happy with the 36th – even if I turn out to be wrong about it and change it later.' A curious comfort, he explained, is that full-length plays do not involve many words: 'If you run them [the words] all together and take out the stage directions, it's 90 pages at the outside. That's a short story.'[5]

In between *Night and Day* and his next major play, *The Real Thing*, Stoppard worked on an adaptation of Johann Nestroy's *Einen Jux will er sich machen* (*He'll Have Himself a Good Time*), which he translated as *On the Razzle*. Stoppard described his method not as translation but something that might be 'compared to cross-country hiking with map and compass, where one takes a bearing on the next landmark and picks one's own way towards it'. This differed from what he did with *Undiscovered Country*, where 'the Ibsenesque undercurrents of the play made it important to establish as precisely as possible, what every phrase meant . . . and generally aim for equivalence. But with *On the Razzle* I abandoned quite early on the onus of conveying Nestroy intact into English.'[6]

The play itself had a special pedigree. It began as a one-acter called *A Day Well Spent* written by the Englishman John Oxenford in 1835. Nestroy turned it into a farce in 1842, focusing on a pompous grocer who travels to Vienna to plight his troth to a charming but easily impressed woman and prevent his niece and ward from marrying her suitor. He leaves his store in the hands of an assistant and an apprentice who take the opportunity to go on the town, where they unexpectedly encounter their superior but elude discovery. The plot builds until almost every character on stage is posing as, or is believed to be, someone else. The characteristic Stoppardian theme of mistaken identity hits its apogee in the work. Thornton Wilder had adapted *Einen Jux* in 1938 as *The Merchant of Yonkers*, moving the action to New York in the 1880s and adding the character of Dolly Levi, who wins the grocer for herself. Revised, it reappeared in 1954 on Broadway as *The Matchmaker*. Ten years later, after further revision by Michael Stewart, with songs by Jerry Herman, it became the successful musical *Hello, Dolly!*

Stoppard, urged on by Peter Wood, who knew Nestroy's work, found he could be more inventive with this adaptation than in his previous efforts, as a programme note for the original NT production made clear:

> I was struck much of the time as I am with a play of my own because there was so much more necessary invention, and declared invention at that; my inventions for *Undiscovered Country* were guilty secrets, almost admissions of failure, bits of non-Schnitzler trying not to look un-Schnitzler, put in because I couldn't make the thing bounce properly.

Stoppard's greatest adaptation, of course, has been himself, applying the habits, structures, cadences and sounds of English life to his foreign past. His complete absorption into this culture is reflected in his literary adaptations, as he makes his Viennese shopkeepers seem more like figures from Oscar Wilde than Nestroy. Each time he adapts a play – from Spanish (Lorca), German (Schnitzler), French (Molnár) or Russian (Chekhov) – he enacts his own transformation from Czech to English. His apprenticeship began at the court of Elsinore and continued in the re-creation of Zurich as a Wildean drawing-room in *Travesties*. In making these situations his own, Stoppard exhibits the chameleon skill of an adapter rather than the slavish role of translator. Not knowing the language of his source texts does not prevent him from creating works that are new, yet retain their original situation or setting. Like his own origins, the latter are evident but not prominent.

Setting the play at the end of the nineteenth century, some fifty years later than Nestroy's version, Stoppard replaces the satire with comedy. He wrote an entirely new scene to enable the character Zangler, played by Dinsdale Landen, to lose his trousers. But unlike Thornton Wilder, who was free with the plot, Stoppard made free with the language, turning the text into a minefield of outrageous puns, *doubles entendres* and comic confusions. 'One false move and we could have a farce on our hands,' cries Zangler, pursuing the wealthy widow while protecting his niece from her suitor and curbing the high spirits of his assistant Weinberl and the apprentice, Christopher. Stoppard introduces a Viennese craze for Scottish dress: 'get-ups, kilts, tam-o'-shanters, Royal Stuart pencil cases and highland flingery of every stripe since the town lost its head over the Verdi *Macbeth*'. This creates sustained laughter, underscored by the pompous Zangler spoonerisms: 'Quick, fetch me a half-witted cab you hansom fool!' and Weinberl's announcement that 'I think this tartan fad has had its fling'.[7]

Act Two, set in the Imperial Garden Café, is a *tour de force* of farcical action and mistaken identities. Felicity Kendal, as the young boy Christopher, disguised as the young woman Marie by a borrowed tartan cloak, excelled in the original production, as did Landen as Zangler and Ray Brooks as Weinberl. A randy coachman obsessed with female anatomy (Zangler: 'What sets you off?' Coachman: 'Thinking about buttocks, sir.' Zangler: 'Well, can't you keep your mind off them?' Coachman: 'I'm a coachman'),[8] aggressive waiters and distracted women all contributed to the dramatic mayhem, amidst such lines as 'Unhand my foot' and 'the wurst is yet to come'.[9] The servant Melchior's epithet 'Oh, classic!' wonderfully expresses both his frustration and criticism of the traditional elements of comedy Stoppard pulls together in this work, with its asides on journalists, economics and marriage, and even a reference to the title of his next major work, *The Real Thing*. Showing a false paper proving that Marie, Zangler's niece, is of age to marry, Sonders tell his love, 'I assure you it is indistinguishable from the real thing'. Though, as another figure responds, 'I won't feel married until we've had the consommé.'[10] Melchior's warning at the end of the play to Christopher, disguised as a woman, stands as a caution for many of the characters: 'Don't have dinner with him, miss! He'll alter you before the dessert – no – he'll desert you before the altar.' But underneath the comedy, the more serious theme of invention and disguise is expressed in the search for 'the real imposter' and the need for the restoration of order, which a coda added by Stoppard affirms.[11]

Stoppard the pragmatist prepared the play for its première. During its Edinburgh opening, a scene in a restaurant originally called for a large, flaming pudding to be brought on; fire department regulations prohibited open flames on the stage. An alternative was suggested: a great white, cardboard birthday cake with electric candles. But some-one on stage needed to have a birthday, to make it work. Stoppard chose the woman who owns the hat shop and dropped hints that her birthday was coming, rewriting where necessary. It worked, again proving Stoppard's point that 'it's the event and not the text which has to matter to the audience'.[12]

As a play moves from the rehearsal room to the stage, Stoppard is exceedingly conscious of how it is at the mercy of the technical staff, from the lighting and sound people to the raising and lowering of the flys. The entire process of staging a play he calls 'hilariously empirical' since the emotional payoff of a piece of theatre may depend on a single technical cue. The paradox, he explains, is that the metaphysical experience of the play is 'at the mercy of the physical event'. Stoppard provides the following mathematical equation: play = text + acting +sound + lighting.[13]

On the Razzle was a dazzling virtuoso work, vibrant if not 'verbally hyperactive'. Michael Billington was so uplifted that he suggested 'criticism needs a new verb: to Stoppard', meaning to retain the structure of a Viennese farce, decorate it with puns and *doubles entendres* and 'send it spinning on the stage'.[14] The work displayed a new theatre of audacity. Designed by Carl Toms, with five mobile sets on the large Lyttelton stage at the National, the play was visually stunning. The large back-projections of musical designs marking scene changes were actually applauded on the first night. Performed in the boulevard tradition, the play effortlessly slid from the grocer's shop to a restaurant to a garden with stylish fluency.

The play originally opened in Edinburgh as part of the Edinburgh Festival, the first time Stoppard had been back since the 1966 student production of *Rosencrantz and Guildenstern*. However, On the Razzle stirred some criticism because no critics from the national dailies were invited to view the show; they had to wait for the London première. Audiences in Edinburgh felt the National was treating it as a provincial run-in, not a national première. But while the Edinburgh critics celebrated the show, London critics divided into those who praised the sheer joy of the work and those who complained that Stoppard was wasting his wit. Whereas Nestroy cultivated elaborate word-play as an anti-censorship device, Stoppard did it for laughs, some argued. The lightheartedness that represented so much of his best work aroused a certain critical resentment and at first many believed that a writer who was so amusing could not possibly be serious. Realizing that he *was* serious only made it worse. But audiences were not so polarized in their reactions. They loved the fun and felt comfortable with the Stoppard they recognized in *On the Razzle*. When the play premièred at the Arena Stage in Washington, DC, there was equally exuberant praise, some critics swept up with Stoppard's own conceits: 'Stoppard has deftly laced the whipped cream with 100 proof shots of real meaning,' wrote Jack Kroll in *Newsweek*.[15]

On the Razzle confirmed the prominence of verbal, as well as visual, comic incident at the core of Stoppard's writing. Interviews headlined 'Razzle dazzle Stoppard' appeared, emphasizing the fashionable, mod aspect of his dress and manner (he wore a T-shirt with a waistcoat and tie imprinted on it plus a cardigan, casual jacket and jeans). A year later, his image projected 'the casual dandyism of a successful actor'.[16] Yet the 'Razzle dazzle Stoppard' wanted to stress something quite different: that he had become something of a bore, too much on view; he expressed frustration with the kind of play he had been concentrating on from roughly 1978 to 1981, from *Every Good Boy* to *Professional Foul*. 'I felt over-worked', he explained, 'over-exposed and over-visible. I thought I had become a bore and was in danger of boring other people. I wanted to shut up for a couple of years.'

Believing he had done too much, he just wanted 'time to fill up a bit'.[17] He laboured, instead, on a screenplay of P. D. James's *Innocent Blood*, which he delivered to Mike Nichols, although it remained unmade. But when Peter Wood brought him the Nestroy script in late 1979, he was ready to re-enter the theatre and in a style he felt comfortable with. 'If it's worth using once, it's worth using twice,' he later quipped.[18] But to avoid boring himself and his audiences after *On the Razzle*, he turned away from the verbal high-jinks and adaptations to the naturalistic manner and realistic treatment of marriage in *The Real Thing*, a move that surprised many in his audience.

As a partial break from the intensity of his writing, Stoppard spent two weeks in November 1981 as playwright-in-residence at San Diego

State University, participating in a university production of *Mackoon's Hamlet* (a retitled *Dogg's Hamlet* to honour Mack Owen, its director) and *Cahoot's Macbeth*, adjusted to include various San Diego references. He not only supervised rehearsals and conducted a seminar, but gave a lecture entitled 'The Event and the Text', which he would repeat in Florida in March 1982 and then at McMaster University in Hamilton, Ontario, in October 1988. While sharing the same title and general argument that a play is a record of an event, the content of these lectures differed slightly. In San Diego, he read out multiple versions of the telegram in *Night and Day* as he revised it for American audiences, reiterating his essential theme that a playwright crafts theatrical events to be performed rather than writing texts to be studied. Stoppard emphasized a non-academic approach to play-writing, because he had never studied it in any academic setting. 'The thing which is going on up here [on the stage] is not literature walking about,' he explained in a later lecture. 'I don't think theatre works as parable; it works as metaphor.'[19] His experience of the theatre was direct. His most important interpreters, the directors Peter Wood, Trevor Nunn, Peter Hall and Richard Eyre, as well as Mike Nichols, are all university educated, the four Englishmen at Cambridge. Ironically, it seems that only literary men can interpret Stoppard, who never attended university.

One of the important ideas that the San Diego talk elaborated, and which an interview with Stoppard at the time confirmed, was the wide range of possible interpretations a performance can elicit. He gave as an example his interpretation of one of his favourite plays, Max Frisch's *The Fire Raisers*. Stoppard originally viewed the play as a metaphor for the Nazis' climb to power before the war. He subsequently learned that Frisch intended it to be about how the Communists came to power after the war. In response, Stoppard devised the epigram 'No interpretation will be denied, and none acknowledged'.[20]

Stoppard also explained during his San Diego visit that he writes a production rather than a play: 'I really want to have a sense of how one changes the set before I can be happy about writing the first line,' he explained. 'Writing' is 'trying to write down the description of a complete production in your head'. The actual writing process he described as 'having a frame first, then swinging out and finding other things'.[21] Dialogue and action emerge from the foundation of abstract ideas which are the first catalysts of his plays. What he tries to get in balance are his abstract concepts and their potential theatricality. Add to this equation pragmatism, 'my theme for life on the subject of theatre', and one should achieve the coherence and rational sense that makes his plays stageable.[22] The theatrical and visual effects should balance the spoken word; action should suit or add dimension to the spoken word. Eighteen years later, in his lecture 'Pragmatic Theatre', Stoppard would explain that the first thing he expects from an actor in his plays is 'clarity of utterance'.[23]

To emphasize the balance of his equation, Stoppard, directing the student production of *Mackoon's Hamlet, Cahoot's Macbeth,* would drill his actors so that the actions and words moved more swiftly; he often leaped on to the stage to demonstrate proper timing, significant gesture and economy of movement. He particularly wanted the double takes to be done with absolute clarity, and he disapproved of extraneous physical actions that did not correspond to the dialogue. At one point, he substituted for Ophelia to show how she should immediately respond to Hamlet's order, 'Get thee to a nunnery!' – and gained plenty of laughs. Inflection and accentuation of the words were crucial in his drive for clarity of performance. 'The information depends on inflection and body language,' he repeated at rehearsal, adding: 'every response should have its own objective'. 'A lot of the theatre event for me,' he explained, 'has to do with adjusting instinctively, because it's not a thing one can calculate.'[24]

Enter Felicity

Felicity Kendal's first role for Tom Stoppard was as a boy, in *On the Razzle*. The imaginative and energetic stock clerk dazzled audiences with her spirit, gamine good looks and delivery in only her second season at the National. An echo of this encounter occurred years later in Stoppard's script for *Shakespeare in Love* which has the young Shakespeare falling in love with the beautiful Viola de Lesseps, disguised as a young male actor. The year before she appeared in *On the Razzle*, Kendal played Viola in the BBC Television Shakespeare's *Twelfth Night*, again in male attire.

Kendal's bubbly personality and vulnerable smile, coupled with a boyish figure, had made her a star in *The Good Life,* one of the most popular television comedies in Britain in the seventies and eighties. The forty-three episodes featured her as the slightly flighty and flirty wife of Richard Briers; feminine, and certainly not a feminist. As a child, Kendal's life was an odyssey of acting, theatre and adventure, led by her parents Geoffrey and Laura Kendal, who started a theatrical touring company bringing Shakespeare and Shaw first to India, then Malaya, Borneo and Japan. Born at Olton in England, at the age of three weeks Kendal joined the company, which had temporarily returned to England; at nine months, she set out with her parents for India, where she continued to travel, act and assist them until she was eighteen and decided – against her parents' wishes – to fly to the Berlin and then London film festivals to participate in the release of the Merchant-Ivory film about her parents, *Shakespeare Wallah,* and then pursue an acting career in England.[25]

Like Stoppard, Kendal first thought of herself as a foreigner in England and responded by proving herself more English than the English. Her otherness had to be shown as a value which made her Englishness more authentic, a situation similar to Stoppard's. Her determination to succeed as an English star, first in television and then on the stage, equalled Stoppard's eagerness to triumph in similar fields. They also shared a background in India, although Kendal's was much more thorough and lengthy. She could speak Hindi, travel knowingly throughout the country and feel comfortable in either the Bombay Breach Candy Club or the Punjab Express. And, like Stoppard, she also had a different name, her father having changed his birth name, Bragg, to the more theatrical Kendal, after the town where he was born.

In the summer of 1947, her father and mother returned to India with their thirteen-year-old daughter Jennifer and the new baby. Laura Kendal acted and looked after the girls, while Geoffrey Kendal was actor-manager; an additional troupe of four completed the touring company. Curiously, Felicity's beloved ayah, a marvellous Goan woman named Mary, at one time worked for the director of Bat'a Shoes in Bombay. The Kendals returned to England in 1948 and spent some time earning enough money to go back.

In England, at the age of five, Kendal went on stage for the second time; she had made her début as an infant, lying in a basket, as the changeling boy in *A Midsummer Night's Dream*. Her acting career began properly in India, when she was six, in 1952.[26] By the age of seven, she could recite long passages from *Othello* and at thirteen she played Viola in *Twelfth Night*. At one point, she actually performed on the stage of the boarding-school Stoppard had attended in Darjeeling, but years after he had left.

Geoffrey Kendal was the driving force of the company, a fearless man who railed at the middle-class existence, enclosing the self, that he saw in England. His strident letters to his daughter constantly criticized or challenged her and her decision to return to Britain. In one, written in the seventies and not entirely facetious, he declaimed: 'I hate my bloody family, always did, that is why I went on stage to get away from the buggers, and they have haunted me ever since.' Yet despite his rudeness, anger and energy, balanced by his love of acting and devotion to the theatre, Kendal's father supported her, although in the midst of her later accomplishments, she still felt the need to please him.[27]

As the years passed, the company, officially known as Shakespeareana, went into decline and their unique position as players of Shakespeare and Shaw in theatres, army clubs, school halls, villages and even ships altered. As travelling players, they were neither burrah sahibs nor missionaries, only an impoverished group of English actors. They slept in anything from dak bungalows to dormitories in schools or, occasionally, spare hospital beds. They toured constantly, stopping only when the bookings dried up. But as movies and television competed for their audiences and travelling became more difficult and expensive, they were less in demand.[28]

When Jennifer left the company in 1957 to marry the Indian actor Shashi Kapoor, the company went into a slump and their tour to Singapore, Malaysia, Borneo, Sarawak and back to India again was not a success. Kendal's departure to England at eighteen meant the active end of the company but the beginning of her new career. With ten years of stage experience and one film to her credit, she had never seen a live show performed by professional actors apart from her family's company and Indian actors.

She found little work in England in 1965, while feeling alienated from the morals, manners and money of the 'swinging sixties'. Her

'Victorian' upbringing in India contrasted with the frank and forward life depicted by the photographs of David Bailey, the music of the Beatles and the magazine *Queen*. But the December 1965 première of *Shakespeare Wallah* made her a star and she suddenly had an agent (Robin Fox), thanks to Ismail Merchant. Her first serious audition was for Val May at the Bristol Old Vic in the winter of 1966, but she mistakenly travelled to Bristol instead of attending the audition at the Duke of York's Theatre in London and the rescheduled audition was still a failure. Some months later, she auditioned for Olivier's 1966 season at the Old Vic for the National Theatre, also unsuccessfully, despite the presence of Kenneth Tynan, who had reviewed *Shakespeare Wallah* positively in the *Observer*. Years later, she commented that 'I have lived in a time-warp of protection, half fading British Raj, half forties theatre lore'.[29]

Lonely and isolated, Kendal constantly tried out for parts in films, plays and television. She had a part in a television series called *Love Story*, playing a Greek Cypriot waitress in a wig and no shoes. Then a role with John Gielgud in a television play called *The Mayfly and the Frog*. For this part, she had to lose half a stone, dye her hair blonde and quickly learn to ride a motorbike. She made her West End début in 1967, in *Minor Murder*. She started to go to the theatre often, writing home with enthusiasm about Peter Brook's *A Midsummer Night's Dream*, telling her father he would love it because it had no set, just a white box.

Various television and stage parts followed, and she met the actor Drewe Henley during production of a half-hour television drama in 1967; eighteen months later, they married at the Chelsea Register Office close to their flat. Slowly, however, she found herself miscast; she wanted to be an actor, not a housewife. Her ambition and commitment to acting took her out of the flat and into the theatre as frequently as possible. Her marriage came second: 'coming from a family of actors almost fanatical about the importance of work, I could not relate to a more balanced way of seeing things'. Her unusual youth as an itinerant actor made it difficult for her to feel settled anywhere: 'I don't put roots down in places. I find running a house a bit of a nuisance. I can't understand why I can't leave it all, like in a hotel.'[30]

A season at Leicester toughened her resolve to succeed, and this was topped a year later by an offer from director Richard Cottrell to play

Queen Anne opposite Ian McKellen's Richard II. To save her marriage, she turned it down. It did not work out, but soon she was invited to join the Actors' Company organized by Cottrell, McKellen and Edward Petherbridge, the original Guildenstern. The actors would run the company with directors of their own choosing, as well as cast their own productions. The company jelled and she found herself, at twenty-four, reliving the best of her experiences with Shakespeareana. Her son Charlie was born in January 1973. Further work followed, including the immensely successful *The Norman Conquests*, three plays by Alan Ayckbourn which ran for more than a year.

A casual invitation from Richard Briers to read some episodes for a new BBC series followed and almost overnight the story of Tom and Barbara Good, who decide to live off the land – actually their back yard in Surbiton – became a hit. Kendal's character, Barbara, sweet, supportive and good-humoured, was admired, although Penelope Keith as the bossy neighbour, Margot, made the greatest impact. The team of four theatre actors, Briers, Kendal, Keith and Paul Eddington, created a comic ensemble and shared the goal of wanting 'to be actors first and stars second'. Viewers became so involved that they would write in pointing out errors such as the time Kendal apparently milked a male goat. Kendal fired off a sharp reply, pointing out that she would do many things for her art but milking a billy goat was not one of them.[31]

But as the series gained even more viewers and she won such dubious accolades as 'Rear of the Year' in 1981 and was voted 'most likely bedmate', Kendal's marriage crumbled. Her career had solidified, with performances in the West End eight times a week and daytime filming of *The Good Life*; the Queen asked to attend a live recording. England, Kendal at last realized, would be her home – which became warmer and more comforting when she developed a live-in relationship with the Oscar-winning screenwriter, Robert Bolt. She returned to Drewe Henley, before finally divorcing him in 1979.

When Stoppard first met Kendal in 1981, she was a single mother with a nine-year-old son. She had a high reputation as a successful actor in both the theatre and television and had returned to the National to re-establish her status as a theatre professional, something she would not forgo for either television or movie stardom. In 1980, at the National, she had played Desdemona in *Othello* opposite Paul

Scofield, directed by Peter Hall; she had also been in the acclaimed 1979 production of Peter Shaffer's *Amadeus*. Between 1981 and 1988, she would meet, marry and separate from Michael Rudman, a Texas-born British theatre director. For her 1983 wedding, Kendal converted to Judaism. Her son Jake was born in 1988. During the run of *On the Razzle*, she was also rehearsing Pinero's *The Second Mrs Tanqueray*, directed by Rudman. Her secret for success, she claimed, was champagne, golf and exercise. She recorded a talk-through keep-fit routine of yoga and ballet that sold over 200,000 copies.

Stoppard responded to her immediately, seeing in her the prototype of his heroines, and cast her next as Annie in *The Real Thing*. She played Dotty in the 1985 revival of *Jumpers* and then Hapgood in Stoppard's 1988 West End play of the same name. Interestingly, Stoppard seemed incapable of writing a major play between *The Real Thing* and *Hapgood*, a six-year period coinciding with Kendal's absence from his life. By 1988–9, however, she began to play a greater role in Stoppard's personal life, as her marriage to Rudman was dissolving. Of the three women involved with Stoppard, Kendal was the one with the deepest involvement with the theatre. Not only did she fulfil the roles he had created for women, but she began to shape them. Her influence as a possible muse was exceeded only by her influence on the kind of women Stoppard created in his plays, including Flora Crewe in *In the Native State*, the 1991 radio play he dedicated to Kendal. Hannah Jarvis in *Arcadia* is, perhaps, the quintessential Kendal role: energetic, inquisitive, strong and possessed with a touch of *The Good Life*'s vibrant celebration of nature. The play appropriately opens with a reference to Hannah/Kendal mucking about in the garden. Kendal was also cast as Flora Crewe in *Indian Ink*. Her last role in a Stoppard play was as Irina in his 1997 adaptation of Chekhov's *The Seagull*.

Kendal joined the small circle that defined Stoppard's best work. The group included Peter Wood, John Wood and Carl Toms, supported by Michael Codron as his West End producer and figures like Trevor Nunn and Richard Eyre at the National. This core group, in its early form, also included Michael Hordern and Diana Rigg, the original George and Dotty in *Jumpers*, and was more or less responsible for a great many of Stoppard's hits from 1981 through 1997, from *On the Razzle* to *The Invention of Love*. He either wrote parts for them or trusted them with staging his work in the way he knew would best serve his conception of a play, underscoring their roles as collaborators in his productions.

Despite the popular success of *On the Razzle*, an undercurrent of worry began to surface for Stoppard, which Henry, the hero of his next play, *The Real Thing,* expresses when he muses on his reputation and his daughter crystallizes: people say they prefer the earlier stuff. The words summarize one reaction to Stoppard's writing between 1978 and 1988, from *Night and Day* through *The Real Thing* and *Hapgood*. Indeed, not only have journalists promoted this view – Sheridan Morley, to take one example, acknowledged the triumph of 'energy and eccentric invention' in *On the Razzle*, but saw no reason 'why our most distinguished comic dramatist should have been spending his recent time cobbling some new jokes into a dog-eared plot' – although academics elaborated the division into the difference between the 'aesthetics of engagement' in the early work, and the 'politics of disengagement' in the later.[32] Linked to this division was the repeated charge that women had long been the most unsatisfactory characters in his plays, and that, as a friend of his once expressed, Stoppard can be 'intimidated by women and unnerved by emotion'.[33] *The Real Thing*, with its emotional power and concentration on the politics of marriage, dispelled that view. Indeed, for some, it meant a re-evaluation of his career and the acceptance that it had taken off in a new direction.

Just three weeks before *The Real Thing* was to open, on 26 October 1982, Stoppard joined the prime minister for dinner at 29 Ladbroke Grove, the home of Hugh Thomas. In attendance was a distinguished literary crowd: Anthony Powell, V. S. Naipaul, Isaiah Berlin, V. S. Pritchett, Stephen Spender, Philip Larkin, Nicholas Mosley and Mario Vargas Llosa. At one moment during the evening, Hugh Thomas asked Mrs Thatcher a question: 'you were brought up a scientist, [but] have you ever wished you had been educated as an historian?' A general debate ensued which led, among other things, to a discussion of people's views on Russia, led by Berlin.[34] Stoppard felt at home at the table of the intelligentsia.

*It's no trick loving somebody at their best. Love is loving
them at their worst.*
Stoppard, *The Real Thing*

Staged in the West End and then on Broadway, *The Real Thing* became
one of Stoppard's most popular and longest-running plays, opening
on 16 November 1982 at the Strand with Felicity Kendal (then starring
in her television series, *Solo*) and Roger Rees (of *Nicholas Nickleby*
fame) in the lead roles. It closed after four cast changes in March 1985
– only to have a revival of *Jumpers,* also starring Kendal, open the next
month at the nearby Aldwych.

The Real Thing dissects the relationships between Henry, 'one of
your intellectual playwrights', and Annie, the actress with whom he
has an affair and then marries (dumping his own actress wife,
Charlotte) and then survives another affair, summarizing his
predicament with the Wildean remark that 'to marry one actress is
unfortunate, to marry two is simply asking for it'.[35] However, the focus
of the play is not marriage, but morality, which one critic refined into
the question of whether or not 'there can be affirmation of commitment, fidelity, trust between lovers who were themselves brought
together by infidelity, the breaking of commitments, the betrayal of
trust?' Stoppard himself said the play was 'about the difference
between someone writing about love and the real thing. It is full of felt
things, experienced things.'[36] The play was dedicated to his wife
Miriam, but in light of his relationship some six and a half years later
with its leading lady, it raises speculation of what he might have been
thinking, though not enacting.

Peter Wood again directed, and chose to border the action with grey
gauze-panelled boxes designed by Carl Toms. Seven of these panels
faced out front, rising singly or sometimes in threes or fours, to frame
the action. Projections of Islington streets, the Hammersmith Bridge
and a huge (inexplicable) crane appeared on the backlit stage. Asked
just before the opening of *The Real Thing* how their partnership
worked, Stoppard explained that 'it's very simple. He is truthful and
I'm just crafty. I know nothing about the technical side so I leave that
to Peter, though it doesn't stop me constantly blurting things out. I
think I have the best deal – power without responsibility.'[37]

The opening scene of the play makes this challenge clear, as we witness a husband's discovery of his wife's affair, only to discover in scene two that this was a scene from a play written by a playwright who is actually having an affair with the actress playing the part of the playwright's wife. Max's discovery of Charlotte's deception is a prelude to what will occur between Henry and Annie, later to be tested in Annie's relationship with the actor Billy. This was the first starring role for Kendal in an original full-length play by Stoppard and it would mark her official status as his leading actress. Her verve, voice and vision of the role gave it a depth that audiences and critics applauded. It also confirmed her move away from her television successes and established her as a legitimate stage actress. Benedict Nightingale wrote that the play put Stoppard's 'talent on the couch and subjects it to some courageous scrutiny'. At last, his characters exhibited strong personal feelings without sacrificing humour or intellect.[38]

The play treated politics not only within a marriage but also outside it, extending the political themes Stoppard had presented in *Night and Day* and *Professional Foul*. It also contains a clash between the wife who falls for a man who poses as a political victim, the jailed soldier Brodie, and Henry, who supports more élitist views of art. But Stoppard seems to be retracting some of his more liberal attitudes, expressed in his work from the seventies. There, he emphasized that political questions resolved themselves into moral questions, but here, he takes a more cynical view: political attitudes reflect purely private motives. The play also shows Stoppard relaxing the complex language games and involuted theatricality seen in works like *Jumpers* and *Travesties*. *Night and Day* had made it possible for him to bridge the gap between the extravaganza of *Jumpers* and the realism (and simplified structure) of *The Real Thing* without sacrificing his examination of moral absolutes and of the disjunction between moral abstractions and moral applications. *The Real Thing* was the first Stoppard play to focus primarily on middle-class adultery, although Dotty had a putative affair with Archie in *Jumpers* and Ruth was unfaithful to her husband in *Night and Day*.

The genesis of *The Real Thing* lay in a quotation Stoppard had read in one of W. H. Auden's commonplace books. Stoppard paraphrases it in the play as 'public postures have the configuration of private derangement'.[39] The probable passage is that under the heading of

'Commitment' in Auden's collection and the source is Ortega y Gasset: 'during periods of crisis, positions which are false or feigned are very common. Entire generations falsify themselves to themselves; that is to say, they wrap themselves up in artistic styles, in doctrines, in political movements, which are insincere and which fill the lack of genuine conviction.'[40] Stoppard turned this statement into a concise declaration expressing Henry's cynical view of political action in the behaviour of Annie and Brodie. Stoppard reiterated the theme to Mel Gussow: 'public attitudes are a kind of mirror of a private disturbance'.[41] The play explores this essentially hesitant view of political beliefs and recognition of political posturing, something which Stoppard distrusts.

> And what, after all, is the point of excellence in naturalistic
> art –?
>
> Stoppard, *Artist Descending a Staircase*

The Real Thing is by Stoppard's own admission a self-referencing work, a term Stoppard used to draw on his own experiences in the theatre and, presumably, in love. The play also takes on a strange, prescient quality, given his later relationship with Kendal. He completed the work in March 1982, changing the original protagonist from a novelist to a playwright because 'I wanted to write a play in which the first scene turns out to have been written by one of the characters in the second scene and consequently he had to be a playwright of course'.[42] All that seems real, we soon learn, is imagined, the reverse of the latter part of the play: all that we imagine turns out to be real. But what Stoppard wants to affirm is that 'the real thing', the fundamentally moral foundation of human experience, exists equally in art as well as life and makes it genuine. Furthermore, the corruption of language is the corruption of a moral vision. And yet Stoppard asserts that we can know the real thing when it happens, just as the audience can recognize at some point in the second scene that the first was part of a play.

Autobiographical parallels between the protagonist and Stoppard are undeniable but, according to Stoppard, inapplicable. To complicate the issue, however, Stoppard reported that, while writing the play, he found his character expressing some of his own ideas about writing. Shortly after finishing the play, but six months before rehearsals began, Stoppard offered Henry's statements on writing to an American audience with the explanation that he would be 'reading them out as though they are mine'.[43] But not every part was clear, especially to the director Peter Wood. He and Stoppard would argue about elements of the play on weekends at Iver Grove with 'Miriam blowing the whistle'. Stoppard was nevertheless attentive and responsive at rehearsals, teasing Wood at one point that 'the rehearsal and preview period gives me an opportunity to write the play you are willing to direct'.[44]

'The love play! I've been aware of the process that's lasted 25 years of shedding inhibition about self-revelation. I wouldn't have dreamed of writing about it 10 years ago, but as you get older, you think, who cares?'[45] *Night and Day* was Stoppard's first go at writing about love, *The Real Thing* the follow-up. Yet writing the love play is almost an impossibility, as Henry confesses when he exclaims that he does not 'know how to write love' because 'loving and being loved is unliterary'. But he can experience it; in the midst of an argument with Annie, he can turn to her and say 'I love you so'. She, too, values commitment but sees it as negotiable, failing to equate it with fidelity. However, she rejects Charlotte's view that 'there are no commitments, only bargains'. Henry, by contrast, supports wholeheartedly the idea of fidelity and commitment: 'I believe in mess, tears, pain, self-abasement, loss of self-respect, nakedness. Not caring doesn't seem much different from not loving,' he exclaims. This is not far from what A. E. Housman will tell a student in *The Invention of Love*, creating a kind of loop again in Stoppard's plays: 'life is *in* the minding'.[46] Fidelity and commitment cannot be divorced, but Henry must learn accommodation in order to continue in his love with Annie. Part of the foundation for these views was Stoppard's own committed marriage at the time, underscored by the play's dedication to Miriam and Henry's simple but positive declaration to Annie at the end: 'Don't worry. I'm your chap.' To confirm his faith, he turns up the radio which, in a pop-cultural epiphany, is playing 'I'm a Believer'.[47]

Music is an important register of change and morality in the play. One of the comic elements of the work is Henry's pronounced preference for pop rather than classical music. The so-called intellectual playwright has a fatal flaw: he prefers the sounds of Procul Harum or the Monkees to Beethoven or Verdi: 'I was taken once to Covent Garden to hear a woman called Callas in a sort of foreign musical with no dancing which people were donating kidneys to get tickets for,' he announces to Max in the play.[48] Unlike Miriam Stoppard, who is an opera lover – during one interview just before *The Real Thing* was to open, Stoppard was somewhat reluctantly preparing to accompany her to Covent Garden – he prefers Neil Sedaka, Herman's Hermits, the Hollies, the Everly Brothers, Brenda Lee and the Supremes to Puccini. While writing *Rosencrantz and Guildenstern*, he listened to Bob Dylan's 'Like a Rolling Stone' and 'Subterranean Homesick Blues'. When working on *Hapgood*, it was two or three tracks from Paul Simon's album, *Graceland*. Indeed, as he told one journalist, 'I tend to write each play to one record.' This was, in a sense, how Stoppard began, since Leadbelly's song 'Ol' Riley' became the source for his first play, *A Walk on the Water*. While he wrote *Jumpers*, he played John Lennon's 'Mother'.[49]

In the play, Annie tries to educate Henry's musical taste; Act Two opens with Verdi, which Henry guesses to be Strauss. 'How can it be Strauss?' Annie asks. 'It's in Italian.' 'Is it? So it is,' is Henry's deadpan answer. Debbie's boyfriend in the play is also a musician, although his instrument is only a steam organ at a carnival.[50] Throughout the play, music acts as a sign of the playwright's – both Stoppard's and Henry's – taste.

Desert Island Discs, on which Henry is to appear, and the conceit behind Act One, Scene Two, allowed Stoppard to express his musical interest in the collective effort of Henry and Charlotte, Max and Annie to establish Henry's list for the programme. Stoppard would himself appear on the radio show on 12 January 1985. He began his conversation with Roy Plomley, the host, with a musical reminiscence: playing the triangle in a percussion band in the main square of Darjeeling in 1944. He went on to list the eight records he would take: Bessie Smith's blues song of 1925, 'Careless Love'; the Avon Cities Jazz Band from Bristol and their performance of 'Jump for Joyce'; The Beatles' 'Love Me Do'; 'Graceful Ghost', a ragtime tune by William Balkein used in *Travesties*; 'America' from *West Side Story*; André Previn's score from *Every Good Boy*; Vaughan Williams's *Fantasia on a Theme by Thomas Tallis* – 'the most English sound one could possibly have'; and Keith Jarrett's 'Cologne Concert'. Asked to take only a single disc, Stoppard opted for the Bessie Smith, a song which always moved him emotionally. When asked to provide the title of one book he would take, he couldn't, opting instead for his usual equivocal position. He would want something that would stretch him intellectually: a book of chess problems or a history of mathematics. Eventually, he chose a book in two languages, with a dual translation from English into Italian, 'something like Dante's *Inferno*'. The text represented his characteristic pose of wanting to keep all options, especially linguistic ones, open.

Like Henry, Stoppard admitted at the beginning of the broadcast that serious music was never in the foreground of his life. He credited Peter Wood for adding music to his plays and declared that the moments he 'adores' in his work are those where 'the music affects what I've written or what is being performed'.[51] Stoppard reiterated his love of fly fishing, especially near Newbury, and his shared membership of a fishing club with Michael Hordern, for whom 'acting is a sideline', he quips. From his early introduction to fishing from his stepfather, Stoppard has enjoyed the relaxing challenges of the sport: he can alternately do nothing and wait, and then display the skills required to land a fish when necessary. Reserve and action, the modes of Stoppard's behaviour. Fishing was also one of the core sports he shared with his sons as they grew up.

Stoppard told Plomley that escape from the island would be unthinkable because death by water would be worse than death by sand and sun. And what luxury would he take? A small plastic football for him to kick repeatedly without it hitting the ground, a practice he has often followed when he has the 'delusion that a change of activity and scene would unblock me' when writing.

Ironically, Stoppard contradicted Henry's supposed ignorance of opera through his own work for the Glyndebourne Touring Opera company. In 1983, Stoppard prepared the libretto for Prokofiev's *The Love for Three Oranges,* directed by Frank Corsaro with stage and costume designs by Maurice Sendak. The opera is based on a theatrical extravaganza by the eighteenth-century Italian playwright Carlo Gozzi, about an unhappy prince who can only be cured by laughter but is cursed to fall in love with three oranges and will not rest until he finds them. After much searching, he locates them, only to discover that three princesses are hidden inside them; naturally, he falls in love with one of them and marries her, but only after much sorcery and chicanery.

The original play drew on the stylized traditions of the *commedia dell'arte*. Prokofiev worked on the opera in 1917; it had its première in Chicago in December 1921. The Corsaro/Sendak staging, originally performed in French, drew on the drawings of Tiepolo for its design and the play-within-a-play concept for its staging, opening with the performers strolling on to the stage while an easel held placards bearing the titles of the entire Glyndebourne repertoire. These were removed until the proper title appeared and the opera began. Acrobats and actors took part in the production.

The success of the 1982 production led to Stoppard's new English version in October 1983 for the Glyndebourne Touring Opera. The forty-eight-page typescript of Stoppard's libretto opens with a spirited prologue by the Philistines, who cry out, 'We want, we want a farcical burlesque! Leave in the naughty bits! We want entertainment!' The Fans of Comedy respond with: 'Give us a break, give us a laugh, high jinks and epigrams and a complicated plot! What we want, what we want, what we want is, what we want is, is a comedy!' Ending the Prologue are the Ushers, who order the Philistines and Fans of Comedy about: 'Back to your places. Off, get off the stage.'[52] The libretto, which projects at least two sides of Stoppard's own comic personality, is a spirited, ribald work. At one point, the Jester Trufaldino remarks on the coughing, vomiting King: 'He's coughing poetry! Iambics! His condition is versening!'[53] The Ushers reply with 'Well, of course! He's fed on Tennyson's Mort d'Arthur!'

An earlier draft of the opera had the Buffs of Tragedy cry out for 'lots of blood and thunder with a point of view! Oedipal sex and souls in agony', while the Opera Buffs yelled 'Give us tunes that we can hum! Romance young love! Ecstasies of passion! Love's young dream juney, moony moons!' At that point, the Fans of Comedy burst out with 'You're masochists!' The four acts of the opera are spirited, witty and amusing with lines that are distinctly Stoppardian and matched the staging. Some ten years later, in 1993, Stoppard would do another operatic adaptation, this time of Lehar's *The Merry Widow*, again for Glyndebourne, which would be presented at the Festival Hall with narration by Dirk Bogarde and performed by Felicity Lott, Thomas

Hampson and the London Philharmonic Orchestra, conducted by Franz Welser-Möst. Periodically asked by Stephen Sondheim and others to write libretti or lyrics, Stoppard has always turned them down on the curious grounds that he is tone deaf. The actual reason may be his general dislike of musicals, although in the mid-nineties he worked on a film script – unproduced – of *Cats*.

Emotionally I like to conserve.

Stoppard, December 1994

The unpolished simplicity of Stoppard's dialogue in *The Real Thing* validates the naturalistic form and uncoached emotions of his characters. The presence of wit intensifies the emotional truth of the play and satisfies his desire 'to simplify questions and take the sophistication out'. He also achieved his ambition to write what he called 'a quiet play', one that decreased his rapid-fire intellectualism.[54] It is as if he experienced a counter-reaction to his own, more flamboyant work and formed an unconscious challenge to the image Tynan presented in his 1977 profile, misrepresenting him as withdrawing from the chaos of life through style. Stoppard would argue that there was no break from disengagement to involvement, but, rather, a continuation of the same concerns with only a shift in emphasis, made evident when *The Real Thing* closed in March 1985 and a revised *Jumpers* opened the following month.

The claim that *The Real Thing* was the first play in which Stoppard dealt with the emotions is unfounded. As Michael Billington pointed out in 1988, the double identity of Stoppard as cool playwright and emotional husband are at the base of his writing. His plays are not so much intellectual conceits as they are expressions of his emotional core. In *Rosencrantz and Guildenstern*, there is the bravery of the two characters who whistle in the Elsinore dark; in *Jumpers*, a marriage is audibly splitting. In *The Real Thing*, perhaps more in the New York than London production, the audience was 'aware of the torturing self-abasement that stems from the knowledge of infidelity'.[55]

Infidelity had, in fact, recurred frequently as a theme in Stoppard's work, possibly based on personal experience. He left Jose in 1969 and shortly afterwards moved in with Miriam, divorcing Jose and marrying Miriam in 1972. As early as 1967, in *Albert's Bridge*, he had outlined a marriage coming apart, while *Jumpers* (1972) presented the alluring Dotty and her occasional lover, Archibald Jumper; *Night and Day* (1978) revealed the unhappy Ruth Carson and her casual affair with the reporter Wagner in London. *The Real Thing* (1982) expanded the matter of adultery. In 1989–90, Stoppard's marriage to Miriam ended as rumours of an affair with Kendal surfaced. *Arcadia* (1993), dealing in part with the indiscreet Lady Croom (who dallies with Septimus and possibly Byron) and the overly eager wife of the poet Ezra Chater, whose 'readiness' keeps her 'in a state of tropical humidity as would grow orchids in her drawers in January',[56] continued the theme. Although Stoppard claims repeatedly that he 'does not like very much revealing [himself]', observations deriving from his own relationships cannot be discounted.[57]

Others, however, often upped the emotional ante of his work, notably Peter Wood: 'He always bullies me and says I am stingy about this side of things.'[58] This is partly explained by Stoppard's inherently emotional reserve; not a reserve of emotions, but a desire to withhold them because it is the right thing to do. Decorum rules: 'I haven't considered revealing my other side to more than one person at a time. But I suspect the genial interviewee is a sort of cover.' When Mike Nichols accused him of being the only happy writer he knew, Stoppard responded with 'that's an insult. I'm as miserable as anyone – sometimes.'[59]

But *The Real Thing* is about counterfeit politics as much as real emotions. Brodie's protest actions were more of a dare than actual opposition to political policy, designed to impress Annie. Stoppard contrasts Brodie's behaviour to the illusion built up by Annie of what she thought he did and his causes. He was infatuated with her and wanted to perform a dramatic act to catch her attention. The celebration of language in the now-famous cricket-bat speech, with its association with dancing, distinguishes art from formless indulgence:

> This thing here which looks like a wooden club, is actually several pieces of particular wood cunningly put together in a certain way so that the whole thing is sprung, like a dance floor . . . what we're trying to do is to write cricket bats, so that when we throw up an idea and give it a little knock, it might . . . *travel.*[60]

The bat confirmed for many not only Stoppard's obsession with cricket but his obsession with words. In the Greek production of the work, the bat metamorphosed into a tennis racquet.

Reaction to *The Real Thing* was strong, Frank Rich, writing of the London production, claimed it was 'not only Stoppard's most moving play, but also the most bracing play that anyone has written about love and marriage in years'.[61] British critics were less sure. 'Distressingly like other people's plays,' said the *Observer*; *The Times* mourned that 'Tom Stoppard's play, I regret to say, concerns the sentimental education of a middle-aged playwright and his final discovery of true love'. Others began to make comparisons, Michael Coveney, for example, calling the play 'Stoppard's version of Pinter's *Betrayal*' or Peter Nichols's *Passion Play*.[62] The Brodie plot came in for harsh criticism because Stoppard set him up a little too obviously, with his specious arguments and disrespect for language. The mockery of activists in the play also led to complaints, from David Hare most forcibly, that Stoppard had come out on the right and surrendered his good-natured neutrality. Additionally, the un-English display of emotions disoriented some, while others were disappointed that Stoppard 'abandoned the trapeze for the armchair'.[63] Many continued to appreciate his characteristic wit, however, as in Henry's line that 'if Beethoven had been killed in a plane crash at twenty-two, the history of music would have been very different. As would the history of aviation'. Political references also receive their jibes, Henry reassuring Annie that Brodie's script is 'half as long as *Das Kapital* and only twice as funny'.[64]

CHAPTER 14

BROADWAY TO BRAZIL

And happiness?
Happiness is . . . equilibrium. Shift your weight.
Stoppard, *The Real Thing*

Stoppard had not had a hit on Broadway since *Rosencrantz and Guildenstern*, although *Night and Day* received positive notices when it opened at the ANTA Theater in November 1979, partly because of Maggie Smith in the role of Ruth. There was a limited audience for Stoppard plays, though directors like Mike Nichols thought otherwise. Shortly after *The Real Thing* opened in London, the New York producer Emanuel Azenberg received a call from Mike Nichols, urging him to see the play; he wanted to direct it in New York. Azenberg had already seen it and told Nichols they wouldn't do it because he didn't like the production and found the staging confusing. Nichols said he would change all that. Azenberg countered that it had just won the best play of the year award, so half a dozen American producers would want to do it and he couldn't compete with them financially. Besides, when you imported a show from England, union rules meant you had to import the show you'd seen in London. Nichols suggested that they fire the original director and change the cast, though Azenberg argued that it was a success as it stood. Then Frank Rich of the *New York Times* wrote a critical review and the fleet of Broadway producers disappeared. Azenberg and Nichols became 'the only game in town'.[1] Complications in meeting their demands to change the cast, alter the production and fire the director, however, meant numerous delays. The original royalty structure would have also closed the play 'in about 8 seconds', Michael Codron explained. However, a royalty pool, whereby a portion of the royalties would partly go to British interests, was established, and in August 1983, casting began. Azenberg suggested Jeremy Irons because he thought the on-stage combination of Roger Rees and Felicity Kendal would not ignite New York audiences. Glenn Close was selected as Kendal's replacement. The production suddenly had sparks.

Stoppard was present at rehearsals. He was not there to oversee, but to explain or rewrite if necessary: during rehearsal, he reiterated, 'you recognize every nuance of where it's sliding away from you or where it's safe as houses'.[2] His changes to the text for the New York production, which he called his 'American discoveries', included tightening and polishing dialogue, so much so that when republishing the play, Faber called the text 'The Broadway Edition'.[3]

During the New York rehearsals, Stoppard and Nichols sat at separate tables, Nichols eating vegetables, Stoppard smoking. At the end of each afternoon, the director gave the actors notes; the play-wright gave them glances. Changes meant removing some Anglicisms, or improving clarity. One detail was telling: during rehearsals, a poster on stage illustrated the Polish production of 'House of Cards', the play within the play. The designer Tony Walton wanted to know the last name of Henry, in order to complete the sign. 'Call him Boot,' said Stoppard, so the talismanic name appeared again.[4] Throughout the rehearsals and Boston try-out, Stoppard adjusted the script and offered comment when necessary. His behaviour throughout was exemplary: 'Not only was he a star writer but he behaved unlike most people in this ego-infested business,' Azenberg remarked, adding that one is 'always totally intimidated with Stoppard. I mean he says "Hello" and you say, oh shit, let me leave now.'[5] But Stoppard was pleased with the treatment of the play and the respect and care it received.

The Boston opening still had props in the wrong place, momentary lighting failures and actors occasionally missing lines. Work still needed to be done, but Stoppard was generally satisfied. In his hotel room at the Ritz in Boston, he told Gussow, 'Equilibrium is pragmatic. You have to get everything into proportion. . . . when the world shifts, you shift.'[6] He stood up and shifted his weight, to demonstrate. The exchange in *The Real Thing* echoes what a young boy says in Stoppard's 1970 radio play *Where are They Now?*, when he declares that happiness is a 'borrowed word for something else – a passing change of emphasis', illustrating again the repetition in Stoppard's work.[7] Balancing opposing viewpoints, celebrating ambiguity and self-contradiction have long been Stoppard habits.

Changes to the New York production, generally thought an improvement by critics who had also seen the show in London, included an accelerated pace and replacement of the cumbersome screens and projections. Automated sets were used on a revolve, which sped up the action. Such tricks as Max's shaking a souvenir Alpine snowstorm before the stage was engulfed in teeming white specks in the London production, seem more cute than clever, as was the sofa which duplicated the one in a Hockney style painting on Henry's wall. Stoppard commented that the London 'setting tended towards the abstract, while in New York the setting was more realistic'. But either would work, he wrote in the acting edition of the play.[8] Many thought Jeremy Irons more vulnerable as Henry and the sexual chemistry more intense between Irons and Glenn Close.

The first sentence of a *New York Times* article summarized the reaction of New York to the play: 'When the curtain falls on "The Real Thing", the talk has only begun.'[9] Critical discourse, as well as after-theatre talk, had been stimulated by the work. The issue of greatest concern was whether or not art should serve a political cause. Stoppard was clear: the writer 'has no obligation except to write well. Whether that satisfies him is a different question.' But he then raised a vexing issue: 'imagine a Nazi masterpiece, if you can. At the bottom of that pit lies some truth, about art and life. But it is an elusive truth.'[10] Such concern and honesty raised the profile of the play and increased its audience. Praise heaped on praise and, despite stiff competition, *The Real Thing* won a Tony Award for Best Play, with Mike Nichols winning for best director and Jeremy Irons and Glenn Close for best actors. With these accolades, the play ran at the Plymouth Theater until 12 May 1985, just shy of eighteen months after its opening.

Reviews for *The Real Thing* were the most ecstatic that had ever greeted a Stoppard play in the US and the public was equally thrilled. Again, the altered text proved that 'Once the event takes place, one can see what the text embodies, or is capable of embodying'.[11] And again, Stoppard used other texts within his own, extracting passages from Strindberg's *Miss Julie* and John Ford's *'Tis Pity She's a Whore* (works Annie performs in) to counterpoint the contradictory evidence provided by the characters themselves, continuing his tradition of inset plays. *The Real Thing* further celebrates the business of the theatre, a subject he initiated in *Rosencrantz and Guildenstern*, and continued in *The Real Inspector Hound*, *Jumpers* (with Dotty and George's involvement with vaudevillian and metaphysical acrobatics), and *Travesties* with its production of *The Importance of Being Earnest*. Playwrights and actors are the very core of *The Real Thing*, linked by jealousy to *Othello* (evidence of a handkerchief), and by deception to Henry's play, *House of Cards*.

The power of the play resides in its confrontation of the dilemma of love and fidelity, and how marriage can be restructured to withstand both. Stoppard was reluctant to provide any exegesis, although in an undated letter he offered an extended analysis. Explaining that Annie elects to ease herself out of the accidental relationship with Billy 'rather than kick him in the head', Stoppard notes that the difficulty in the scene is that most Annies would clearly state their choice of Henry over Billy. But in his work, he explained, her action is 'a way of Henry learning that exclusivity isn't love, it's colonisation'.[12]

The Real Thing also displayed the ability of Stoppard to write realizable characters who were not histrionic, historical or highly witty. The public could relate to it without recourse to intellectual history, literary texts or even dictionaries. And in redefining the role of the artist as valuable, different and important, the play reasserted culture and education, showing why it mattered and what it could accomplish.

The staying power and appeal of the play was demonstrated by its first, successful London revival at the Donmar Warehouse in London in May 1999, starring Stephen Dillane and Jennifer Ehle. Critics and audiences were moved by the production, which stressed the messiness of love and the confusions of sexual desires among the characters. David Leveaux's fluid production virtually parodied, through the character of Henry, the Stoppard of popular reputation: all witty badinage, political detachment, galling poise and unease when writing about unguarded emotion. Deservedly, it transferred to the West End. Stoppard, who again attended rehearsals and even called in some changes from France, made some limited updates to the script, though it still addressed the question of what exactly is meant by the real thing in terms of love. 'There are no commitments, only bargains. And they have to be made again every day,' Charlotte announces, a sardonic but

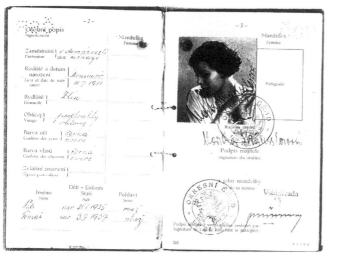

Two pages from the passport of Martha Sträussler stamped to authorize her travel with two children from Czechoslovakia to the Straits Settlements (Singapore) in 1939
(Peter Stoppard)

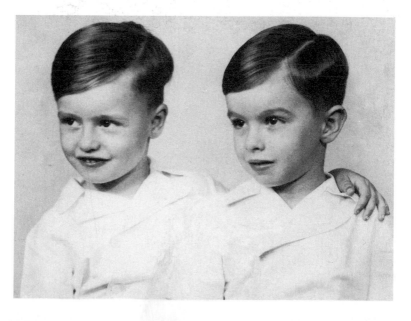

Studio shot with Tom Stoppard on the left, his brother Peter on the right, Singapore, 1939
(Yosi Studio Branch)

Tom Stoppard with
Pocklington School's
First XI Cricket team, 1954
(Pocklingtonian, 1954)

Stoppard writing at the well in the
summer of 1961 at the Château de
Blauvac in the Vaucluse. Seated is
Richard Hawkins, standing,
Anthony Smith (Derek Balmer)

Lord Snowdon's iconic photograph
of Stoppard and bicycle taken at
a playground in Rotherhithe
(Snowdon / Camera Press London)

John Stride and Edward Petherbridge tossing coins in the National Theatre production of *Rosencrantz and Guildenstern are Dead* directed by Derek Goldby, 1967 (Anthony Crickmay / V&A Picture Library)

Michael Hordern and Diana Rigg in the National Theatre production of *Jumpers* directed by Peter Wood, 1972 (Donald Cooper / Photostage)

Stoppard in a publicity shot for the 1968 US release of his novel *Lord Malquist & Mr. Moon* (New York Times)

John Wood (Henry Carr) and Tom Bell (James Joyce) in the National Theatre production of *Travesties* directed by Peter Wood, 1974 (Donald Cooper / Photostage)

Stoppard at San Diego State University in November 1981 for his production of *Cahoot's Macbeth*, re-titled in honour of the director

Dame Peggy Ashcroft's XI, at Stratford-upon-Avon, 1969. Back row: Umpire, Michael Meyer, Harold Pinter, David Bailey, Anthony Pedlay, Dame Peggy Ashcroft, Ian Carmichael, Anthony Smith, Julian Bream. Front row: unknown, Tom Courtenay, Tom Stoppard, David Warner, Morgan Sheppard (Herald Photographic Sevices)

John Cleese
Mick Ford
A. C. H. Smith
David Hare
Tony Mathews
Graham Miller
Derek Robinson
Tom Stoppard

THE PLAYWRIGHTS COMPANY

PLAY

CELEBRITY CRICKET

Playwrights Company Invitation XI
v
HTV Invitation XI

County Ground, Nevil Road:
Sunday July 12th: 2 p.m.

Admission: Adults £1
Children and Senior Citizens 50p

Tickets from: Chapter and Verse Bookshop, Park Street
Arnolfini
Gyles Brothers, Blackboy Hill
and at the gate

● In the event of bad weather, play cannot be guaranteed

Tom by Miriam
Sept. 1982

TOM STOPPARD

Flyer for a Celebrity Cricket match held in 1981 at the County Cricket Ground, Bristol; Stoppard opened the batting and scored 25 runs, including 3 boundaries

A sketch of Tom Stoppard by Miriam Stoppard, 1982.

TOP: Stoppard on a narrow gauge train travelling up to Darjeeling, India, in the Himalayan foothills in late 1990 (Karan Kapoor)

ABOVE: Stoppard at work on the terrace of the Windamere Hotel, Darjeeling, India, 1990 (Karan Kapoor)

LEFT: Stoppard at the cash register of the Bat'a shoe store his mother managed in Darjeeling, India, 1990 (Karan Kapoor)

TOP: Bill Nighy and Felicity Kendal in *Arcadia* at the National Theatre, directed by Trevor Nunn, 1993 (Donald Cooper / Photostage)

ABOVE: Paul Rhys (Housman younger), John Wood (Housman older) in *The Invention of Love* at the National Theatre, directed by Richard Eyre, 1997 (Donald Cooper / Photostage)

RIGHT: Stoppard on the film set of *Rosencrantz and Guildenstern are Dead* in studio in Zagreb, Yugoslavia (Peter Stoppard)

Stoppard receiving congratulations on his cell phone after winning an Oscar for best screenplay for *Shakespeare in Love*, 1999 (Chris Pizzello/AP Photo)

realistic view balancing the unearned romanticism of Henry.[13] Love remains exhilarating and agonizing and this was the first time Stoppard showed his characters hurting. It also confirmed that Stoppard was a romantic who uses the life of the mind to shield the heart, although the play contradicted the view that the library, rather than the diary, spawned his plays.

Among those who saw the original London production of *The Real Thing* was David Mamet. By 1982, Mamet was an emerging force in American drama, having established his name with *Sexual Perversity in Chicago* and *American Buffalo*. He was also beginning a career as a screenwriter with *The Postman Always Rings Twice* (1981). *Glengarry Glen Ross*, premièred in London in 1983 and New York in 1984, lost out to *The Real Thing* for the Tony Award as best play of 1984, but won the Pulitzer Prize for Drama that year. Stoppard first heard of Mamet in a letter from J. Handy, an actor in New York. On 9 March 1977, Handy wrote to tell Stoppard about John Wood's success in *Travesties*. He then reported going to the opening of *American Buffalo*, which his downstairs neighbour was stage-managing. 'I'm amazed it's still on! The language is befouled with harsh sounds that stick like burrs to the thighs. The performances are excellent but distort the humor of the situation by their intensity.' Then he noted seeing *Duck Variations* and *Sexual Perversity in Chicago* at the Cherry Lane Theater, 'an amusing series of skits. Some worked, some didn't.' He wanted 'to go again [to *American Buffalo*] just to listen to the play and not to get side-tracked by the production'. *American Buffalo* opened at the Cottesloc Theatre at the National Theatre on 28 June 1978, directed by Bill Bryden.

In early December 1982, Mamet wrote to Stoppard from the Athenaeum Hotel, London:

> Dear Mr. Stoppard – Saw *The Real Thing* last night.
> It is a beautiful play – moved my wife & me very much.
> We stopped going to the theatre in the US because no one seems to be writing about anything – Your deeply felt play was deeply felt by us.
> Thank you very much.
>
> David Mamet

Mamet was at that time married to the actress Lindsay Crouse and clearly responded to the parallels with Henry and Annie in the play, as did Viveca Lindfors, the Swedish-American actress who starred in

Anastasia on Broadway and in a number of American films with Errol Flynn and Ronald Reagan; in April 1984, she expressed her admiration for *The Real Thing* to Stoppard: 'It was very close to my own life. I am an actress and was married to the playwright George Tabori. Unfortunately, we did not stick it out like your couple do. Although so many of the circumstances and possibilities were the same, we did not have the faith or passion or whatever was needed.'[14]

Stoppard replied to Mamet's note in early January 1983 and a friendship began, Stoppard inviting Mamet to a celebratory lunch for the American début of *The Real Thing* a year later, where one of Stoppard's friends at the luncheon awkwardly asked Mamet, 'So, ahh, what's happening?' In his embarrassment, the friend writes, he was immediately tempted to run directly to Barnes & Noble to find a book entitled 'something like "How to Talk to Famous People" '.[15] In early April 1984, Stoppard visited Mamet at his New York apartment at 410 W. 20th Street, a brownstone on the south side of the block between 9th and 10th Avenues where Mamet lived on the top two floors. Accompanying Stoppard was Harold Pinter (a good friend of Mamet's), whose revised, three-play series, *Other Places*, directed by Alan Schneider, would shortly begin previews at the Manhattan Theatre Club. That spring, as well as a revival of *American Buffalo*, *Glengarry Glen Ross* was on Broadway, along with *The Real Thing* and Michael Frayn's *Noises Off*, the last three all being nominated for the Tony Award which *The Real Thing* won.

Stoppard did not always approve of Mamet's writing, however. His reverence for language put him at odds with Mamet's seeming disrespect for words. He could not write inarticulate or foul-mouthed characters like Mamet's, he told an interviewer in 1989: 'I love Mamet's plays, but I have no idea how to do those characters. Something happens to those plays between the page and the performance; the text goes through some interesting transformation between type and human personality. That's not really true of the kind of plays I write; you can sort of see the play and hear it just by reading it.'[16] In November that year, Stoppard went to see Mamet's *A Life in the Theatre* in New York and again visited the playwright. A year earlier, Michael Billington had drawn parallels between Stoppard and Mamet, calling *Hapgood* and its challenges 'an engrossing theatrical equivalent of David Mamet's [film] *House of Games*'.[17]

Another fan of *The Real Thing* was Leonard Bernstein. The agent Robert Lantz reported to Stoppard that at a gala honouring Bernstein at the Hotel Pierre, he stood up in response to an ovation to thank the audience but said that rather than make up his own speech and talk about music, he would quote from a play he had just read while in Munich, one he loved with a passion. He then read from Henry's speech on words (Act Two, Scene Five, line 53 in the 'Broadway Edition' of the play), beginning 'He's a lout with language' and ending with 'I don't think writers are sacred, but words are'. Bernstein asked the audience to substitute 'notes' for 'words' in the speech, adding that the work was 'remarkable' and that it had 'moved him profoundly, as well as of course amused him immensely'.[18]

> *Can you remind me, what was the gist of it? – the moral and*
> *intellectual foundation of Western society in a nutshell.*
> Stoppard, *The Dog it Was that Died*

The Real Thing ran for three years in London, from November 1982 until March 1985, and from 5 January 1984 until 12 May 1985 in New York. The play's success solidified Stoppard's bankable reputation and a new level of affluence. It also allowed him to experiment with more intractable material, namely science, quantum physics and espionage, which dominate his next major work, *Hapgood* – in many ways an extension of the calculated uncertainties that he explored in the treatment of love in *The Real Thing*. The question was one of credibility, or, as George asks in *Jumpers*, what to believe: 'How the hell do *I* know what I find incredible? Credibility is an expanding field.'[19] The irony was that while those around him seemed very certain about public situations, Stoppard never felt he quite had enough information to decide: 'I even did a television programme, "Tom Stoppard Doesn't Know",' he reminded one interviewer. (This was actually the BBC show, *One Pair of Eyes*, aired in July 1972).[20]

The prelude to *Hapgood* was the radio play, *The Dog it Was that Died* (1982), broadcast on the BBC three weeks after *The Real Thing* opened; it addressed many of the same issues, transposing them from the world of marital relations to espionage, while extending his earlier interests in uncertainty from moral philosophy (*Jumpers*) and the value of art

(*Travesties*) to science. John Tydeman, responsible for several of Stoppard's previous radio dramas including *Artist Descending a Staircase*, again directed. The title, taken from a poem by Oliver Goldsmith, introduces Blair, a chief operative, who would reappear in *Hapgood*, and the notion, to be expanded through theoretical quantum physics, that interpretation can often alter information: 'the facts', as Hogbin, a young policeman explains, 'would fit more than one set of possibilities'.[21]

The story opens with the attempted suicide, off Chelsea Bridge, of Purvis, a soon-to-retire spy. Instead of drowning, he lands on a barge and kills a dog. His having posted a letter to his superior, Blair, just before his attempt to kill himself leads to various complications, unravellings and humour: 'You're the first person to jump off a bridge on to a dog. The reverse one often used to see at the Saturday morning cinema, of course,' Blair tells him.[22] The play explores the possibility of Purvis being a double agent, set against the slightly surrealist comedy of Blair arguing with an architect about artistic juxtapositions at his home and whether or not an obelisk is centred on top of a tower (an obelisk will also appear in *Arcadia*). His wife, meanwhile, oversees the care of an injured donkey in their drawing-room. The play ends with a visit to a sanatorium on the Norfolk coast, where Blair meets a series of unusual characters, as well as the recovering Purvis.

Stoppard again displays his enjoyment of esoteric knowledge: one character, Dr Seddon, plays language games recalling those in *Dogg's Our Pet*, while another character is an expert in exotic cheeses. In the midst of the confusion, discussion of Soviet ideology, mass movements and political economy occur, until Purvis finally admits his bewilderment: 'I've forgotten who is my primary employer and who my secondary. For years I've been feeding stuff in both directions, following my instructions from either side . . .' This expresses Stoppard's own situation: seeing both sides of a question or a position equally, articulated in the view 'I hope I'm right, though I would settle for *knowing* that I'm wrong'.[23] Earlier, in *The Real Thing*, Henry had said that it was not equivocation but lack of certainty regarding Annie's relationship with Billy that troubled him.

Being a double, or even triple, agent was a major attraction of the espionage genre for Stoppard. Both *The Dog it Was* and *Hapgood* originated in an idea he had had years before: 'that was to have a double agent who wakes up in hospital after a car smash with a complete loss of memory. Both sides come to him and say "you were working for us" but he really cannot remember.'[24] He also had the idea of naming all the characters in *The Dog it Was* after one of his sons' friends on his school rugby team. He continued the tradition in *Hapgood*: Wates and Ridley are named after two other rugby-playing friends of his son.[25]

The Dog it Was anticipates precisely the situation Stoppard would elaborate in *Hapgood*, summarized in a complex speech by the Chief at the end of *The Dog it Was*: 'In other words . . . in order to keep fooling the Russians, we had to keep doing the opposite of what we really wanted to do . . . [or] in other words, Purvis was acting, in effect, as a genuine Russian spy in order to maintain his usefulness as a bogus Russian spy.'[26] This work is comically presented through Purvis's mix-ups and mistakes, even sending a second suicide note to Blair. Such loops and interweavings in Stoppard's work had begun in 1966 with *Lord Malquist* and the statement 'since we cannot hope for order let us withdraw with style from the chaos'.[27] Spies, double-dealings and espionage – all present loops within loops, in the hidden world of intrigue, not unlike that of quantum physics, where what exists we cannot see.

Between 1982 and 1986, when he began to work seriously on *Hapgood*, Stoppard continued to revise the text of his plays in production, wrote *Squaring the Circle* for television, oversaw the adaptation of Molnár's *Rough Crossing* and worked on screenplays, notably *Brazil* and *Empire of the Sun*. Four cast changes to *The Real Thing* required Stoppard's involvement with rehearsals and further tinkering with the script. The New York production then took up his time, succeeded by revisions to *Jumpers* which was revived at the Aldwych Theatre on 1 April 1985. For this production, not only did Stoppard restore Scott to the script, cut from the 'Coda' of 1975, but Tarzan reappeared, having originally been dropped during previews for the 1972 National Theatre première.

Penelope: History! Do you think history matters now?
Bone: I do not write history, I dissect it – lay bare the logic
which other men have taken to be an arbitrary sequence
of accidents.

Stoppard, *Another Moon called Earth*

Politics was still prominent in the midst of Stoppard's varied theatre work and for the first time in seven years, he completed a political drama for television, *Squaring the Circle*. Focusing on the rise and fall of the Polish Solidarity movement, it was his most historical play, overtaken, in fact, by its historical figures: Brezhnev, General Jaruzelski and Lech Walesa all appeared, limiting his inventiveness. Indeed, the need to record the events and people that shaped the Solidarity movement between August 1980 and December 1981 led to a kind of docudrama that curbed his creativity. But one element in the presentation did seem Stoppardian: the habit of freezing and repeating the action, whereby the same scene would be played two or three times in sequence, each with a slight variation. This device begins the play, with an opening scene at the Black Sea between the then First Secretary of the Polish Communist Party and Leonid Brezhnev, which is then repeated. The Narrator, a voice-over, warns us that 'everything is true except the words and the pictures', a phrase repeated at the end of the play when summarizing a special meeting held by General Jaruzelski, Archbishop Glemp and Walesa, which is itself repeated several times.[28]

The idea of looping scenes and events to emphasize different elements was, of course, not new for Stoppard, although the use of the guiding narrator and an accomplice or witness (originally there were five) who appear throughout the film, was. At one point, the Narrator is shown unsuccessfully scribbling the next scene while seated in a café, interrupted by the Witness who says 'Try the other one'. Scene 78, which follows, is a rewrite of a preceding, frozen scene 'and tears itself in half like a piece of paper with the sound of tearing paper'.[29] Such visual, narrative tricks suggest how Stoppard reacted to the limitations of events, altering history by imagination. *Squaring the Circle* is his most cinematic script.

One of the most interesting aspects of the play is its use of mathematics, as indicated by its title. Mathematics had long fascinated

Stoppard and his interest in iterated algorithms as a form of looping, or reiteration, would later dominate the world of *Arcadia*. In 1983–4, while working on his Solidarity play and reading about maths, Stoppard seized on the ancient mathematical riddle of squaring the circle, known as quadrature, as a metaphor for the political conflict in Poland between Communist control and the democratic impulse. A cliché for the reconciliation of opposites, Stoppard refreshed it by grounding it in its mathematical origins. In Scene 30, the Narrator expresses the political dilemma in mathematical terms:

> For two decades the drama of his [Kuron's] intellectual life had been the attempt to square the Communist circle inside the cornerstones of democratic socialism, and now the show had started without him.[30]

Earlier in the play, the Narrator cites the same problem when he explains how difficult it was to unite freedom and socialism:

> The attempt failed because it was impossible, in the same sense as it is impossible in geometry to turn a circle into a square with the same area – not because no one has found out how to do it, but because there is no way in which it can be done. What happened in Poland was that a number of people tried for sixteen months to change the shape of the system without changing the area covered by the original shape.[31]

Linking politics with mathematics suited Stoppard, although the two could not fully mesh. His commitment to using recent historical details limited his success with the work dramatically, despite his self-conscious reiteration of accuracy and imagination in the piece: 'there was something going on which remains true even when the words and the pictures are mostly made up'.[32] A certain solemnity overshadows the entire drama, which even *Professional Foul* managed to avoid.

These challenges were equalled by those of production. Fred Brogger, a film producer, first approached Stoppard to do a television play about Solidarity in early 1982, just after the imposition of martial law in Poland. A professional researcher provided Stoppard with details, 'although the more detailed the information the more questions were left begging'. Yet the information tempted him towards 'documentary reconstruction'.[33] His early worry was that elements of the drama would be taken as fact, not fiction, unless there was some device or disclaimer which made the fiction clear. It was the potential confusion between facts and speculation that led Stoppard to create a Narrator with 'acknowledged fallibility'.[34] Details became secondary to the principal question: 'was freedom as defined by the free trade union Solidarity reconcilable with socialism as defined by the Eastern European Communist bloc'?[35] Stoppard felt they were irreconcilable 'in the sense understood by a logician or a mathematician: a mathematician knows that certain things cannot happen, not because no one has found out how to do them but because they are internally contradictory'. Another conundrum was the identity of the fallible narrator. On the first page of the script, Stoppard put an asterisk next to 'Narrator' and at the bottom of the page wrote 'The author'.[36] While working on the script, he was both inside and out of it, though the ploy was vetoed by the American producers.

Numerous directors were suggested, accepted, left and returned, until Mike Hodges was found, a director who shared Stoppard's 'self-sceptical tone of the "documentary" and understood why the narrator and the author had fused together'.[37] Similar delays were generated by confusions over whether it would be filmed in a studio or on location, and who would star in the work. A sound stage at Pinewood Studios was eventually chosen, with an elaborately constructed set that doubled as a street, dockyard, parliamentary meeting-rooms and even an airport. Four drafts later and with more 'quirky bits' – the freeze frames, voice-overs, dialogue between the Witness and the Narrator, and the three different versions of the crucial meeting between Walesa, Jaruzelski and Archbishop Glemp – modified, the original producer went in search of more funding for the project, as the budget had ballooned to over a million pounds.

Metromedia in the US agreed to a pre-sale deal in the summer of 1983 and it seemed that the film would be made, although a series of television intermediaries now began trying to shape the outcome, starting with the idea that the Narrator should be an American. Stoppard then learned that various liberties had been taken with his script, including the addition of a scene and changes to seven pages of dialogue. His asterisk and footnote on page one had also been eliminated. A meeting with one of the studio executives in Beverly Hills in August 1983 made it clear to Stoppard that the Narrator had to be an American, a 'Famous American' at that. Richard Crenna took the part, although Stoppard regretted it, since 'what was supposed to have been a kind of personal dramatized essay turned into a kind of play about an unexplained American in Poland'.[38]

Shooting began in October 1983. Stoppard and the director believed they were making a film for Television South's Channel 4, and that Metromedia had invested $800,000 for the right to show the result in the US. They were wrong. For example, Stoppard decided the scene with Walesa, Jaruzelski and the Archbishop was stodgy and rewrote it overnight as a card game. 'Steve' from Metromedia expressed doubts, but they went ahead and Hodges finished shooting in five weeks. Then, in January 1984, Metromedia indicated its dissatisfaction with the finished print, arguing that with that version they could not successfully compete for 'advertiser support' or viewers.

Metromedia cut its own version, rearranging scenes and losing the overall shape of the film while 'dispensing with the five characters who served the crucial purpose of distancing the film from the conventional kind of docudrama which (falsely) purports to reconstruct history'.[39] The final scene, a book-end to the first, was also cut. Hodges took his name off the American version. Stoppard, upset at what he saw, also removed his name from the film. Some horse-trading quickly followed and certain elements of the film were restored, although the matter of the witnesses remained. Supported by Richard Crenna, who understood their importance, Stoppard agreed to keep the most important sections and reshoot some extra bits with Crenna and the first Witness alone. Stoppard was caught between saving the film and loyalty to the director, who had become increasingly disenchanted. Stoppard justified his defence of the film by his claim of authorship, even when the need for a commercial break in the US version caused two scenes to be transposed. When the credit titles were finally planned, Hodges suggested equal billing for Stoppard, so that it read, at least in England, 'A film by Mike Hodges and Tom Stoppard'.

It was at this time that Stoppard stood in for Václav Havel, who was not permitted to leave Czechoslovakia, at Toulouse University where he was to receive an honorary degree. On 29 May 1984, Stoppard reported to Havel that the 'ceremony itself was rather French, unfortunately not the erotic or sensual side of the French, but the political French'.[40] The formality of the occasion overshadowed its moral importance, but he was most upset over the incompetent translation of his remarks from English into French. He offered a seminar in the afternoon, although nobody bothered to inform the English and Drama departments, with an appropriately Stoppardian result: 'while I was speaking in one building there were 60 students actually rehearsing one of my plays in another building'. But he was most proud to accept Havel's degree on his behalf. In the letter to Havel, he asked about the possibility of staging his production of Gay's *Beggar's Opera*, possibly adding some refinements, allowing for both their names to appear on the same text.

Stoppard prepared an adaptation Havel's *Largo Desolato*, written in 1984. The work deals with the survival of a Prague philosopher in a repressive country and had its English première at the Bristol Old Vic in 1986. The title was taken from a movement in one of Alban Berg's compositions; Havel dedicated the play to Stoppard, who had earlier provided an introduction to the 1981 reprint of Havel's *The Memorandum*. Stoppard wrote a short essay on *Largo* for the *Bristol Old Vic Magazine*. A curious feature of the Bristol production, the first in England, was the decision to anglicize the names of the characters, something Havel approved of. Stoppard also wrote that of his many adaptations, this is 'the most faithful English version which I have written among the half dozen foreign plays I have worked on'. He concludes by declaring that 'anyone who cares for the theatre as a form, and cares for good work, should take pride in Havel who has kept his head and his humour in circumstances in which, as Bertram says to Leopold, "any of us would have cracked".'[41] Of Havel's *The Garden Party* and *The Memorandum*, Stoppard would later enthusiastically claim, 'these are my plays!'[42] In 1984, Stoppard was also considering various new projects, including an English adaptation of Havel's *The Conspirators*.

His most challenging new project, however, was his attempt at an original screenplay, entitled *AOP*, a Secret Service acronym for 'Assault on the Principal', referring to an assassination attempt on the US president. He produced a formal outline of the film in 1984. It was to focus on a presidential bodyguard who becomes disillusioned with the values he is supposed to protect. Set in the sixties, this figure questions the length the government goes to in order to prevent demonstrations at the president's public appearances. As a consequence, he leaves the service and becomes a bodyguard for a major rock star; the plot then threads back on itself when the rock star performs for the president and the bodyguard is present. Stoppard provided no resolution for the film, although he knew he did not want an assassination at the end. As part of his research for the project, Stoppard interviewed the Head of the Washington Field Office of the US Secret Service and talked to several agents; at one point, he was even allowed to observe an anti-assassination training exercise. Stoppard's interest in the film grew out of his fascination with the agent who leaped out in front of President Reagan to take a bullet during an aborted assassination attempt, as well as his generation's continued absorption with Americanism. As early as 1981, he began to make notes for the project, revising them in 1983; he completed an outline in 1984, but could not interest a producer in the project.

He can't write but he has a certain gift for construction and absolutely no original ideas of any kind.
Stoppard, *Rough Crossing*

According to Stoppard, every time Cole Porter had a Broadway première, he set sail on a world cruise.[43] Stoppard went one better, setting Ferenc Molnár's farce, *Play at the Castle*, about salvaging a script and the actors' private lives, on a ship crossing to New York, retitling the work *Rough Crossing*. In 1928, P. G. Wodehouse had written a version called *The Play's the Thing*, starring Alfred Lunt and Lynn Fontaine in New York. Music, the dominant feature of *Rough Crossing*, reunited Stoppard with André Previn. The play continued the Stoppard–Peter Wood collaboration, which would be renewed less than six months later when they worked together on a West End revival of *Jumpers*. *Rough Crossing* became a rollicking, if slightly vaudevillean, pastiche of Pirandello and *Dames at Sea*.

Stoppard had returned exhausted from New York and Mike Nichols's version of *The Real Thing*: 'I came back from New York battered like a beaten-out pewter plate. . . . when I got home I virtually wasted three months before I started writing again', but the Molnár project appealed to him.[44] Based on the Hungarian playwright Ferenc Molnár's 1924 work, the play required five songs. Stoppard bought *Walker's Rhyming Dictionary* – with supplement – but it didn't help him. André Previn did, however, and the songs were included, with

Stoppard's revised lyrics. Stoppard updated the play to the 1930s and shifted the locale from a castle to a ship as two co-authors, two actors and a composer try to work out the new material before the ship docks in New York. The play turns on a conversation overheard by Adam, the composer, between his lover Natasha and an actor (they are actually rehearsing, but he does not realize), which gave Stoppard his reason for transferring the action from a castle to a ship: 'as the walls of a castle are likely to be four feet thick, it presented something of a problem. I had to find another enclosed space where a conversation was more likely to be overheard.'[45]

The characters remained Hungarian, although the male lead was now English and the composer French, reflecting the movement between Europe and America of various continental stage and film stars such as Marlene Dietrich and Greta Garbo. Molnár, however, was not particularly witty, so Stoppard's task was to bring some zip to the lines with various puns, although Peter Wood eliminated 'premadonna'.[46] Wood had introduced the play to Stoppard (he brought it back from one of his periodic directing visits to a theatre in Vienna), though it did not at first impress him. However, since Peter 'was going to do it anyway, I thought I might as well be part of the challenge'. 'It was only much later,' he added, 'I discovered there was a perfectly faithful adaptation by P. G. Wodehouse or I would not have bothered at all, but by that time, I already had some notions about it.'[47] The subject of the theatre strongly appealed to Stoppard and the idea of a play about writing and rehearsing a play was irresistible. He transformed the subtitle, 'Anecdote in three acts', into a complete farce, or what one critic called 'an enormous hyping error' where playwrights turn truth into illusion (the actors' lovemaking) and illusion into truth (the actors' rehearsal).[48]

'Not more than a dozen lines of *Rough Crossing* will compare with the original dialogue,' Stoppard soon announced: 'I'd work a couple of days and arrive at André's home panting with ten rhymed lines. He'd sit down at the piano and in about ten minutes say, "How about this?" It seemed wonderful to me.'[49] Positive notices greeted the play, although there was, again, that lingering complaint that such a talent as Stoppard's would be better spent on his original work rather than adaptations. Many, however, found the comedy, the Art Deco sets (by Carl Toms) and sea effects successful. The comments on the challenges of playwriting expressed by the character Turai in the play were also understood as Stoppard extending the concerns of Henry from *The Real Thing*. But others were less pleased. Sheridan Morley in *Punch* wrote that 'if you're interested in musicals in trouble, *Rough Crossing* has the unique distinction of being one about one'.[50] What he didn't see was its blend of Michael Frayn's *Noises Off* with Noel Coward's *Private Lives*.

Stoppard's humour was everywhere:

Gal   We'll need costume fittings. What is your hat size?
Adam   It varies according to my state of mind.[51]

Turai, the consummate man of the theatre, interrupted in rehearsal by information that the boat is sinking, replies, 'a boat like this can take *hours* to go down'. And, believing the life rafts may be overcrowded, Turai's assistant Gal tells him: 'I thought I'd book a table.'[52] On this ship, every member of the crew, including the Captain, is a would-be playwright with a script for Turai to read (like the boatman in Stoppard's screenplay, *Shakespeare in Love*, who offers up his own script to Will Shakespeare) and the Captain alters course in order to provide Turai with a stable rehearsal room.

Names are also comically mixed up in the play: Dvornichek is called Murphy and often misunderstood. He constantly drinks cognacs ordered by others, and he is also a critic, reporting that the Captain, whose manuscript *is* actually a decent story, 'can't write but he has a certain gift for construction and absolutely no original ideas of any kind', to which Turai responds, 'he sounds like a natural'. But no word game is above Stoppard or Turai. Castigating his actors, Turai exclaims that I have 'given you a misplaced air of indispensability, what I like to call a sine-qua-nonchalance'. When Murphy, aka Dvornichek, says he's a bit rusty playing the piano, Turai quips, 'serves you right for getting wet'.[53] Turai's play is a physical production, with a replica of the Tower of Pisa in the rehearsal room that straightens up during a storm while a large chandelier remains resolutely fixed, despite furniture and the cast sliding from side to side. In the end the confusions between the lovers are resolved, with Turai the playwright shaping all, like Prospero in *The Tempest*.

Such verbal and visual humour, while delighting audiences, was difficult for some critics to fathom. One reviewer referred to the evening as 'a meringue treated as suet pudding with extended gags and conventional characters', while another castigated Stoppard for low-level wit and slovenliness with phrases like '"*festine lente*" – Every Lent a festival?' when Stoppard should have known that the Latin for 'hurry slowly' is '*festina lente*'.[54] Other critics lamented the absence of Molnár's melancholy and the substitution of a witty ending for the lugubrious one in the original. The leading actress, Sheila Gish, was miscast: she lacked the comedic talent to carry the temperamental Hungarian star, Natasha, and didn't work well with Peter Wood. The adaptation was hardly a translation, a difference Michael Billington neatly clarified in a piece on the play: 'A translation is necessarily a compromise between what is literally accurate and what is theatrically speakable'. Adaptation is a hybrid in-between. '*Rough Crossing* must surely be the worst play ever written by a good writer about bad writing,' summarized Michael Ratcliffe in the *Observer*.[55] But despite such criticisms, the previews were sell-outs and *Rough Crossing* went into the National's repertory; Stoppard had another success.

The summer of 1984 held another challenge. In late August, Iver Grove was robbed, an event that made the London papers, although they inflated the value of what had been stolen to £750,000-worth of jewellery. The *Evening Standard* went on to estimate Stoppard's income from his various plays in the high six figures and suggested that the conversion of the Victorian stable block and installation of a heated indoor swimming-pool had only recently been completed. Reported cost 'in the village': £500,000. The newspaper account ended with an odd and comical reference to 'Tom's inherent Czech modernism [which] may be spotted in chrome fittings and a curious purple loo seat'.[56]

Soon, screenwriting and directing began to absorb Stoppard, the first involving *Brazil* for Terry Gilliam, the second his efforts to prepare a production of *The Real Inspector Hound* for the National Theatre. *Brazil* challenged Stoppard's sense of multiple perspectives and originality, since Gilliam, the American animator responsible for *Monty Python*'s cut-out animations, was after an extravagant, surrealist film of immense space and astonishing futuristic sets, blending dream sequences with absurd, futuristic reality. Mental and physical reality are at odds in the movie, which begins with a trademark mix-up of names. Stoppard originated the idea of a dead beetle, swatted on the ceiling, dropping into a typewriting machine spitting out names on a series of forms with the heading 'Information Retrieval, Subjects for Detention & Interview'. The machine mistakenly types Buttle instead of Tuttle, and the next scene shows the innocent Mr Buttle arrested by security troops who storm his apartment, dropping down from a hole cut through the ceiling, thinking he is a radical offending the conformity and work ethic of the controlling regime. This will eventually lead to the innocent man's death. The theme of oppression breeding revolt, or totalitarianism prompting freedom, reflects Stoppard's long-standing concern over political persecution and human rights.

Stoppard joined the project in 1982 after Gilliam had completed a first draft in 1979 and Charles Alverson, a journalist and screenwriter, had done a first rewrite. Gilliam and Stoppard met and started to pull things together.[57] Gilliam then referred Stoppard to the Israeli entrepreneur and film financier, Arnon Milchan. He was shocked at Stoppard's fee, in the region of $100,000. And when Stoppard's first version came in, Gilliam urged Milchan *not* to read it because it lacked Gilliam's input. At the same time, he wanted more money to be sent to Stoppard for a second draft. A sceptical Milchan reluctantly agreed. In the end, Stoppard did four rewrites over six months, but was not allowed to work on the fantasy sequences which were originally going to take up half the film. Stoppard's script was then reworked by Gilliam and, to his surprise, Charles McKeown (who plays the part of Sam Lowry's slimy associate, Lime, in the film and whose major contribution to the script was the many posters and billboards with government slogans seen in the movie).

Gilliam approached McKeown because he thought the script was too tidy. He believed the texture of the film had been sacrificed to the story. Stoppard was upset at this development: to be supplanted by a Hollywood writer *after* completing his rewrites was an affront. In fact, Gilliam felt isolated by the writing process, since it was Stoppard's habit (and still is) to work alone. Following a meeting with Gilliam at which the director would offer his input, Stoppard would go off and some two months later would return a 120-page revised script. But Gilliam felt he was losing control. Stoppard's writing was also, to Gilliam, so exacting and intricately constructed that 'to remove a word is like pulling a stitch from a sweater'.

The two often disagreed, and Stoppard refused to meet regularly with Gilliam. At one session, Stoppard, in frustration, asked Gilliam 'just for today – on paper – let's do this. Then next year, do what you like with it.'[58] Nevertheless, Gilliam credited Stoppard with 'solving' the script, coming up with the key elements that held his otherwise amorphous narrative together. The original rambling story of a man swept up in a bureaucracy who finds freedom only through his dreams united the disparate elements. Two years after the film's release, Stoppard downplayed his role, saying he only put in a few jokes and adding that the film was 'too bleak and about 50 minutes too long'. He was nearly hissed off the stage when he made these remarks in front of students, he told one interviewer.[59] In fact, studio executives argued that the film was seventeen minutes longer than its contractual limit, precipitating a long and public battle over a studio cut versus a director's cut of the film – actually an American cut, since Gilliam had removed some eleven minutes from the two-hour, twenty-two-minute version first shown to Universal.

The film became an unexpected, if limited, hit for Universal and the script was nominated for an Academy Award, although it lost out to *Witness*. However, *Brazil* did win the LA Film Critics prize for best script, best director and best picture, beating Sydney Pollack's *Out of Africa*. The brouhaha with the studio pitted artistic independence against commercial control and, in the end, the movie, which satirized the abuses of authority, found its audience. The studio cut attempted to remove as much violence as possible in order to emphasize the humour and love story and make the protagonist more sympathetic.

For years, Stoppard had resisted the temptation to direct. He had enough to handle with writing, rehearsing, rewriting and overseeing changes to his various productions. In 1973, he had directed Garson Kanin's *Born Yesterday* at the Greenwich Theatre, but had politely refused other invitations. However, in 1985 a new company, in four separate units, formed at the National, with one group headed by the actors Ian McKellen and Edward Petherbridge, who wanted to restage *The Real Inspector Hound*. They invited Stoppard to direct; the opportunity to work with experienced actors in a theatre setting he knew well proved difficult to turn down.

Each acting group was independent and gave its actors equal billing.

Every member understudied roles and the company selected one production by vote. McKellen and Petherbridge sought to alter the rule of directors, rather than actors, that had marked the National since Olivier's retirement. They also sought to reverse the decline in the number of acting companies and invited four directors to join them, one of them Stoppard, whose play would be paired with Sheridan's *The Critic*, directed by the actress Sheila Hancock. Scheduled to appear after the immensely successful *Pravda* by David Hare and Howard Brenton, a product of the Eyre–Hare unit and the National's most popular drama (168 performances, averaging ninety-six per cent houses), the interest in a Stoppard work at the National would, of course, be high. The double bill of Stoppard and Sheridan in fact played to ninety-seven per cent audiences.[60] Stoppard directing added a *frisson* to the undertaking. His assistant director was Sheila Hancock, who directed Sheridan's play with Stoppard as her assistant director.

Petherbridge played Moon and Roy Kinnear starred as Birdboot. Ian McKellen was Inspector Hound. As a director, Stoppard took a guiding but always comic hand. Petherbridge recalled an early rehearsal when Stoppard stood up and addressed the cast: 'as you all know, this is a deeply existential comedy but what I shall chiefly be preoccupied about in rehearsals is getting as many laughs as possible.'[61] The pairing with Sheridan was inspired, since *The Critic* was a farcical presentation of dramatic theory and eighteenth-century theatre, with the hilarious Mr Puff. Both works were wicked caricatures, freely borrowing from other works (Sheridan from Shakespeare, Stoppard from Agatha Christie). 'English comedy has had to wait for Tom Stoppard to find a similar harnessing of earnest theory to lunatic fun,' wrote one critic in the programme.[62]

The Critic and *The Real Inspector Hound* also dealt with performance itself and found a means of dissolving the barrier between the two sides of the house, letting the onlookers into the stage action. Sheridan's play actually ending with a malfunctioning stage set that crashes down around the actors and audience. Yet the production exposes an important contradiction: in theatre, where everything is verbalized, the most profound moments often occur without words. There were parallels between Puff, the star-struck spectator, and Birdboot, the actress-struck critic literally drawn across the footlights.

In Sheridan's play, Puff attends a dress rehearsal; in Stoppard, the critics attend a first night. For both, the distance between reality and life evaporates. Sheridan was only twenty-eight when he wrote the play; Stoppard had been twenty-nine when *Rosencrantz and Guildenstern* premièred at the National.

Critics generally liked Stoppard's zestful, comic production, complaining only of the unsuitable vastness of the Olivier for *Hound*. Nevertheless, the production transferred successfully to the Odéon in Paris, opening for a short run on 18 February 1986 as *Le veritable Inspecteur Hound*. Stoppard wrote an accompanying article in *Le nouvel Observateur* and was himself the subject of an article about his preparations for the Paris performance, described in this manner: 'Picking his way between an industrial vacuum cleaner, a dead body and a wheelchair, Stoppard exits stage left pursued by stage-hand and bear.'[63]

While *The Real Inspector Hound* triumphed at the National, the revivial of *Jumpers* with Felicity Kendal was playing at the Aldwych, with a slightly altered text. The public thrilled to the production and the 'cadenzas of philosophic pastiche' exhibited by George in, for example, his demonstration of the theory of infinite series.[64] Despite the current acclaim, some interviews found Stoppard in reminiscent mood, commenting on the sixties. In one, he revealed: 'I'd really *love* to write a screenplay in the same spirit in which one writes a play for the theatre. Mick Jagger and David Bowie came to me about 18 months ago and said would you write us a film? And I thought, God, at last what a wonderful opportunity, something completely new.'[65] Nothing materialized, however, despite Stoppard thinking about it for a year.

Balancing the action in the theatre were cricket, tennis, fishing and life at Iver Grove with his children and Miriam. Their staff included a housekeeper, nanny and Stoppard's secretary, who also oversaw domestic administration. Miriam's own organizational skill was repeatedly tested; preparing for a holiday, she wrote a detailed two-and-a-half-page set of instructions concerning care of the children. She rose at 5 a.m. to plant a herb garden, in a typical display of her determination, although her energy and ambition embarrassed some in her family, notably her less energetic husband, whose own pace was more relaxed. His writing day now more typically began at noon.

A letter Stoppard wrote in the spring of 1985 sums up much of his secure, upper-middle-class life at this stage. Addressed to his mother and stepfather, it begins with a remark on the closing of *The Real Thing* after its sixteen months' run in New York and on tour. Some had expected the play to run for two years or more, but his plays generally did not meet with that success: 'They run out of genuine customers and after that the mass public sees right through them – nothing like as good as Neil Simon after all.' The 'dollar dream' is over and 'it's back to the real world', he says, which for him begins with the film script of J. G. Ballard's *Empire of the Sun*. *Jumpers*, however, has just marked its fiftieth performance, the actors giving a dinner for the producers and writer. Directing *The Real Inspector Hound* is about to begin, causing some regret, since he disliked rehearsing in July and August, 'not to mention the endless business of designing the sets and casting the play'. He also expresses apprehension as to whether or not 'the play is actually funny and if it is funny whether I am going to make it work. Writing is much easier.'

Most important is a planned two-week summer holiday at the Carnarvon Arms in Dulverton, which will allow the family to fish, play tennis and shoot clay pigeons: 'everybody in this family has a gun', except himself: 'I haven't bothered'. His main interest is fishing and he asks his stepfather if it might be possible to fish the Kennet, one of his favourite rivers, for two days in June. His son William shares his fishing passion. Oliver, studying physics at Bristol, joined his father for a brief weekend's fishing but had to return for exams. Edmund is captain of the Senior Colts cricket team, while William opened the batting for the First XI at his school, Caldicott. Stoppard then lists various planned trips, notably to talk to students in Bristol and an Amnesty International gathering in Bath. He also notes with pride that Anthony Smith has dedicated his novel about Sebastian Cabot's supposed discovery of America to him. He ends the summary with a survey of new developments at what he calls 'the Iver Grove leisure centre': floodlights are to be added to the tennis court, a stone garden around the swimming-pool has been finished, and a Caldicott School parents' party will offer ping-pong, snooker, cricket, tennis, croquet and swimming – but 'I suppose most of them will stick to drinking'.[66]

CHAPTER 15

ELOQUENT EQUATIONS

---

*As in other plays I've written, the first scene is supposed to be
virtually incomprehensible.*

Stoppard, 1989

Stoppard began one of his most complicated and poorly received plays
– *Hapgood* – in 1986, the same year he wrote the screenplay for *Empire
of the Sun* and completed a new version of Schnitzler's *Dalliance*, which
opened in May. He also finished his adaptation of *Largo Desolato* for the
Bristol Old Vic and became further involved in politics.[1]

On 17 February 1986, Stoppard organized a day-long roll-call at the
National Theatre for Soviet Jews prevented from leaving the Soviet
Union. Three years earlier, he had opened a Soviet Jewry exhibition at
the House of Commons, but now, for ten and a half hours, from a
freezing dawn to an icy dusk, Stoppard and a series of British actors,
writers, musicians, journalists, politicians and clergymen read out the
names of nearly 9,000 Soviet Jews – and for each name a drama
student dropped a red carnation on the gravel floor of a twisted stone
circle in front of the National Theatre. Pronouncing the names, in
temperatures that at one point reached -21° with the wind-chill factor,
was intended to symbolically release those prisoners less well known
than Anatoly Shcharansky, who had been freed the previous week.

Bundled in two coats, a sweater and a scarf, Stoppard was imper-
vious to the freezing temperature. Among over 200 well-known
personalities reading out names were Jeremy Irons, Anthony Hopkins,
Felicity Kendal, Andrew Lloyd Webber, Timothy West, Edward Fox,
Sir John Mills, Susannah York, Dr David Owen, Christopher Fry,
Kingsley Amis, John Braine, the Bishop of London and Twiggy. The
New York producer Emanuel Azenberg was asked to bring over

'names' from the United States, but Dustin Hoffman, Robert Redford and Mary Tyler Moore, among others, were unavailable. Senator Bill Bradley, however, agreed. On the flight over, Azenberg asked the senator why he was doing it. 'Three reasons,' was the reply: 'I believe in the cause, it's good politics and I'm going to have dinner with Tom Stoppard.' When Azenberg asked Stoppard the same question, his reply was: 'we get a million requests to do charitable things. But every once in a while you have to actually do something. So I chose to do this.'[2]

Another political issue that year was an incident with Beckett. Stoppard approached Beckett with a request to use a photograph of him for the *Index on Censorship* campaign against repression. Beckett agreed, but the advertising agency Saatchi and Saatchi doctored the picture to show Beckett with a gag in his mouth with the cut-line 'if Samuel Beckett had been born in Czechoslovakia, we'd still be waiting for Godot'. Stoppard, embarrassed by this unexpected use of the image, conveyed his apologies to Beckett, who replied in one sentence: 'Dear Tom, nothing against it, all best, Sam.'[3]

Stoppard soon confronted another aspect of his past: the time he spent in Singapore between 1939 and 1942. He had been working on and off as a freelance 'script doctor' and screenwriter since the mid-seventies, and the recent success of *Brazil*, Oscar-nominated for its screenplay, made Stoppard a high-profile, reliable writer who brought creativity and a glittering reputation to his projects. Hollywood had been making him offers for years. The movie producer Robert Shapiro held the rights to J. G. Ballard's Booker Prize-nominated, autobiographical novel *Empire of the Sun*, published in 1984. He and Stoppard were discussing other projects when Stoppard expressed interest in the work. In a May 1985 letter to his parents, Stoppard refers to the Ballard novel as 'very good' but 'rather depressing and close to home' because it is 'about a young boy whose family was caught by the war in Shanghai, and how he survived the war'.[4]

The link with Stoppard's past was evident in the story of the displaced family in Shanghai, overrun by the Japanese on 8 December 1941. Separated from his family (unlike Stoppard), the young hero survives four years in a Japanese prisoner-of-war camp, learning to be a wheeler-dealer, only to be reunited with his family at the end, when he finds he misses the security and camaraderie of the prison; later on, he wistfully returns to the liberated camp.

The novel contained a line that in many ways related to Stoppard's own pragmatic attitude to his life and understanding of the theatre. Jim, the young hero, realizes towards the end of the book, as the Americans attack Shanghai, that he must finally give up his battered wooden case of possessions which he had protected since his imprisonment at the Lunghua camp airfield. He must 'face up squarely to the present, however uncertain' which had been 'the one rule that had sustained him through the years of the war'.[5] This, too, had been Stoppard's attitude: to deal with the present in practical terms and not be trapped by the past – but at the same time, not forget it. Preparations for the film produced some uncanny connections for Stoppard, from his being attracted to everything American, as Jim is in the novel, to the set decoration of the boy's room at the family home in the International Settlement. The production team had put a chart of the flags of the nations on the wall: surprisingly, 'it was *exactly* the chart I'd had. Identical. Clipped from a magazine, I shouldn't wonder. Spooky.'[6] He also found books in Jim's room similar to ones he owned.

Stoppard began work on the script in the spring of 1985, offering his first version – 'I've called it a "film narrative" because "treatment" seems to mean different things to different people' – to Shapiro, now executive producer of the film for Warner Brothers. His submission was a description of the sequence of the unmade film, without the detail of a screenplay or any effort at dialogue. He saw the book's having only one hero, the young boy, as a problem; the emphasis, he argued, should be broadened. In tightening the storyline and discarding one or two incidents in the book, he had not, however, 'compromised at all on aeroplanes and milling hordes of extras'.[7] The first complete draft of the film, dated 7 January 1986, opens with a scene at an airfield, the young hero and his model aeroplane surrounded by groups of well-dressed Europeans gathered to see the remains of battle; their limousines with Chinese drivers line a grassy airfield. But war suddenly shatters the surreal opening, as Stoppard contrasts the reality of fighting with the idyllic life in Shanghai in 1937. Work on the script continued, but by February 1986, the original director, Harold Becker, was taken off the film, something of a shock to Stoppard.

Steven Spielberg took over, and when he and Stoppard first talked, 'we rather danced around each other'. They soon became good friends and worked intensely on subsequent drafts of the screenplay. There were, however, some differences of scale: 'Before Steven became involved, I was being very modest. I didn't write in a fly-over of P-51s – I'd no idea there were any available that still flew.'[8] Spielberg even found a small part for Ballard: he appears as a guest at a fancy-dress party. Stoppard began frequent communication with Spielberg, and by July 1986 he was sending detailed, page-by-page commentary on a third draft of the script dated 11 July 1986, containing additional dialogue by Menno Meyjes, a screenwriter Spielberg had brought on board. Stoppard's eye is sharp but sympathetic; regarding small changes to dialogue, he says: 'it's okay to be wrong about it but it's not okay to be casual about it . . . You're looking for my reaction to the big changes but it's the small things which depress me really.' What Stoppard particularly objected to was streamlining the story and characters: 'the general tendency is to simplify the tapestry in order to make way for a couple of bold patterns'.[9] When a revised third draft, dated 12 September 1986, reached him, Stoppard filed it away after glancing through to see if any of his changes had been incorporated. They had not.

Stoppard took an active role in the production, visiting Shanghai with Spielberg a year before principal photography began, as well as Spain, the location of the prison camp, and Ascot, Jim's home. Shooting began in late February 1987 with three weeks in Shanghai. The crew would be in England in late March. Script revisions continued, however, with Stoppard responding to a call from Shanghai in March, adding four new pages as late as 18 March 1987. One request was to find a new poem for use at the end, although Stoppard disliked the scene. His favourite was Dryden's translation of Horace, *Book III*, 'Ode 29', beginning 'Happy the man, and happy he alone', although he also included a passage from Swinburne's 'Garden of Proserpine', 'but it's not exactly optimistic'. Another choice was the First Epistle of Paul to the Corinthians (13:11), but 'I think it's too literary and pious', and Wordsworth's 'My Heart Leaps Up', which also 'ends up a bit pious also and, although the man/child bit is what I wanted, it's really a bit wimpy'. He ends by saying 'If you don't like the Dryden, I'll have to write the bloody thing myself and pretend it's old . . . If you don't like the Dryden do not despair – we have the technology.'[10]

A fourth draft of the script led to further suggestions, with Stoppard pointing to problems with chronology in the story, which resulted in confusion of the historical and emotional narratives. From page 148 of the script on, he suggests, it has lost its shape: 'it has been treated as though it were composed of interchangeable parts'. Again, Stoppard's eye was acute, telling Spielberg in April that, with Scene 144, 'it's a tiny thing but the sign should say "You are now entering the United States" (the word now was missing) because that's what border signs say. The designer won't notice this unless somebody tells him of the change.'[11] Problems with the camp scene led to more rewrites, bringing Menno to England, and the efforts of both writers to cut twenty pages or so from the camp section from the 2 February 1987, revised fourth draft. Stoppard invited Meyjes back to his home, where the two stayed up late working on the script; after Meyjes left, Stoppard stayed up to revise that section. Further work led to additional changes, with Meyjes assisting, although the fundamental shift, which made the rewrite possible, was Stoppard's: transposing the two main Basie–Jim scenes. In mid-May 1987, Stoppard, on the heels of Meyjes, flew to Spain to revise a final scene, the one where Basie dies. Shooting ended in Spain on 6 June.

Spielberg's decision to bring in Menno Meyjes led to a disagreement over whether or not the screen credit should be shared. Stoppard was clear: although Meyjes had contributed a number of moments which hardly appeared on the page but might have a disproportionate value in the film, it was not enough to justify sharing screen credit for no more than twenty-five pages of material. The dispute between Stoppard, Spielberg, Meyjes and Amblin Entertainment could not be settled and went forward to the Writers' Guild of America, who had to adjudicate the question of shared screen credit. Stoppard maintained that he was 'the first and last writer on this film and indeed am still working with the director on the day I write this statement' (4 August 1987), but while defending his position, he displayed characteristic generosity, ending his letter to the Writers' Guild: 'I don't want to be acrimonious about it'.[12] The Guild agreed with Stoppard, who received exclusive billing – and maintained his friendship with Spielberg.

In an interview given when the film was released in the winter of 1987, Stoppard reiterated his apolitical stance, although he admitted to being conservative in taste: 'All positions are overstated is my dictum, and I don't believe in demons.' Before the release of the film, he was with Spielberg in a Hollywood editing suite, an experience he found transformative:

> It's a wholly different art from writing I've discovered. On the page you feel you just have a certain line. But when you see the film you want to cut all over the place. . . . the grammar of filmmaking eludes me. Those leaves blowing into Jim's [the hero's] swimming-pool expresses the bleakness of the boy's soul better than any dialogue could. You can't just 'transliterate' from words to images. . . . another great thing about film is its fixedness where the great thing about plays is they can be changed. That fixedness of film is a relief and a luxury for a playwright, but most deceptive.

At times during the filming, he felt like 'a privileged tourist . . . [but] half the time I felt I was simply in the way. Occasionally, thank God, they'd need a word or a line I could supply, and I'd feel better.'[13]

An anecdote concerning the early stages of the film's development reveals Stoppard's priorities. As related by Stephen Frears, the British director, Stoppard's version of the script had been written before Spielberg took over the project. Spielberg brought in his own writers to beef up Stoppard's version and then showed it to David Lean, who politely told Spielberg that it was not very good and that he should get Stoppard back on the project. After the studio failed to lure him back, Spielberg himself reportedly called Stoppard to ask him to return. Stoppard at first said no, but then relented.[14]

When the film was released, Janet Maslin of the *New York Times* complimented Stoppard on his compression of the novel and his 'crisp and clever' dialogue which fashioned a movie of epic proportions and visually expressive power.[15] His ability to script the ideas and language of a young boy was also praised. His work melded with Spielberg's own talent for presenting childhood and spectacle.[16] Spielberg, impressed by Stoppard's skill as a screenwriter, retained him as a 'script doctor' for *Indiana Jones and the Last Crusade* and *Schindler's List*. His reported fee for his work on *Indiana Jones* was $120,000, but when it became a mega-hit, Spielberg sent him a thank-you bonus: reportedly one million dollars.[17]

> *Don't feel bad about it . . . In the end we all have our secrets.*
> *That's how we live.*
>
> Stoppard, *Dalliance*

Earlier that summer, Stoppard's second adaptation of a Schnitzler work had opened at the National: *Dalliance*, originally *Liebelei*, written in 1895. Schnitzler, the Austrian–Jewish writer–physician who would gain further renown in the 1990s for his novella *Dream Story* (*Traumnovelle*), used by Stanley Kubrick for his last film, *Eyes Wide Shut*, and for *La Ronde*, later adapted as *The Blue Room* by David Hare, was immensely popular during his lifetime (1862–1931) for his comic exposure of Viennese hypocrisy. *Dalliance* had been performed in London as *Light of Love* and was filmed by Max Ophuls in 1933. In Stoppard's new version, directed by Peter Wood, it ran in repertoire with Neil Simon's *Brighton Beach Memoirs*, directed by Michael Rudman, who was soon to marry Felicity Kendal. In its time, the play was considered controversial because it brought dalliances, frivolous romances with serious consequences, and duelling out into the open.

The plot of the play deals with a young rake whose affair with a married woman leads to a duel with her husband which he seems destined to lose. Determined to enjoy his last remaining hours, he takes up with an impressionable young Viennese girl, gets her pregnant and tries to avoid the consequences. The play is predictable and doesn't really take off until the final act, a tragic sequence in which the action shifts to the backstage area of a Viennese opera house. The young woman realizes her folly against the backdrop of a rehearsal of 'The False Hussar'. At one point, the entire orchestra troops across the stage for a tea break, while the heroine plays out the most tragic scene of her life. In the original, the set of Act Three was to be the same as Act Two, the top-floor flat of Christine and her father, a violinist, with the added venue of a graveyard. The move to the wings and stage of the Josefstadt theatre, with a tenor, soprano and off-stage orchestra in mid-rehearsal, was not Stoppard's idea but Peter Wood's. Stoppard thought it a wonderful concept, 'allowing for the counterpoint between Christine's tragic love and the romanticized love-play of the operetta', fulfilling a character's remark early in the play that 'Love is for operettas'.

An undercurrent of Wildean repartee and irony runs throughout *Dalliance* as characters exchange banter and barbs about love. When Fritz, the lover, receives the mail, his friend Theodore remarks, 'love letters? I say, you are in a state. Is this the post-coital one hears so much about?' Remarks about marriage and love are made with a tone that masks feeling with humour and mistakes sentiment for love. Theodore says: 'the trouble with real women is that we can't stand the ones who want us, and we're mad about the ones we can't have.' At other times, the comedy combines the *risqué* with wit. Mizi states: 'no man is a hero to a wardrobe mistress. They're all the same when they're waiting for their trousers.'[18] One of several changes Stoppard made to the play is the elimination of the suicide of Christine, the woman in love with the rake, Fritz. The death of the philandering Fritz, however, killed in a duel by his mistress's husband, is morally appropriate but bittersweet.

Reaction to *Dalliance* was negative, one viewer writing that the Stoppard–Schnitzler relationship was like 'two incurable romantics looking at each other over half a century both convinced that they are realists because they so much savour the tastes of the bitter sweet'.[19] Others saw the work as a class study, with a working-class girl falling for a young gentlemen inconsiderate enough to have himself killed in a duel over another woman. Stoppard was satisfied with the play until his third rewrite, which he did without any recourse to the German text 'or even necessarily the intentions of the speaker'. He also altered the ending. The original final line is a stage direction: '*He sinks to the ground sobbing.* I faithfully reproduced this, then impulsively added – thinking of Michael Bryant – "I wouldn't count on it".'[20]

Stoppard outlined his bolder steps with this adaptation in his 'Introduction'. Noting first the change of locale for Act Three, he then cites the shift in dialogue which at the end makes Christine a more forceful character, unlike the tragic figure of the original. Other changes meant sharper dialogue and efforts to 'tease more humour' out of the text. The play, thought lightweight, was best summarized by one character's description of a not-so-fine wine: 'You'll find this an affectionate little cup, with just a hint of promiscuity.'[21] A more scathing response appeared in the *Sunday Times*, referring to the 'stopparding of central European drama. We have had *On the Razzle* (or destroy Nestroy), and *Rough Crossing* (or mauling Molnár). Now we have Tom Stoppard's adaptation of Schnitzler's *Liebelei* . . .

Stopparding means that you take an obscure foreign play, open it up (i.e., add some action with or without dialogue which makes it say things its author never intended) and spice it up with some snazzy intellectual gags characteristic of plays by Tom Stoppard.'[22] Stoppard's own view was that no official version or authorial truth exists: you just did your work and sent the play out into the world to be criticized. He related that even his own son could not interpret his plays: studying *Professional Foul* for O Level in the early eighties, he received only a B and 'instantly turned to Physics!'[23]

Shortly before his fiftieth birthday on 3 July 1987, Stoppard was castigated again for his conservatism and his success. His dismissal of Brodie and his activism in *The Real Thing* had not been forgotten, nor had the contradictions of his writing plays criticizing the selfishness of political convictions. Journalists recalled his statement that his favourite line in modern drama was 'I'm a man of no convictions. At least, I think I am,' from Christopher Hampton's *The Philanthropist*, but one columnist pointed out Stoppard's pleasure in living 'the good life' and the way he chose to spend polling day in June 1987 – 'on a boat in Sweden with a millionaire friend'. The envious journalist noted that Stoppard lived in a marvellous house in Iver, Buckinghamshire and 'collects prints and first editions and plays cricket'.[24]

Success brought infamy as well as fame, and Stoppard found himself the model for two fictional characters: Tim Stripling in Clive James's satiric novel, *Brilliant Creatures* (1983), and the rich, witty and fêted playwright Miles Whittier, an object of envy for the hero in Peter Nichols's comic play, *A Piece of My Mind* (1987). In the former, Stripling is described as writing plays 'at such an intellectual altitude that only a symbolic logician could follow the plots'; his wife Naomi is a parody of Miriam and 'an interdisciplinary dynamo'. In the latter, Miles Whittier has written a comedy entitled *Starboard Home* in which 'Mahatma Gandhi, Rudyard Kipling, Anton Chekhov and Nellie Melba meet on a P&O liner'; yet the *bon mots* in Nichols's farce are clearly Stoppard's, for example, Miles' lines: 'When my first play went on at university, some undergraduate critic asked me what it was going on about. I said about 7.30 with a 3 o'clock matinée.'[25]

Stoppard's fiftieth birthday was an occasion for interviews and articles, the most informative by Janet Watts who, twenty-one years earlier, had played Ophelia in the original Oxford student production of *Rosencrantz and Guildenstern* at the Edinburgh Fringe. She had only one line and one scream: 'that was disgraceful', commented Stoppard. 'If I had known you better, she probably would have had three.'[26] The interview opened by describing the problems the young playwright encountered when he arrived in Edinburgh in August 1966 and his determination to get the play 'to sound the way he heard it in his head'.

At fifty, Stoppard was still youthful and as enthusiastic about his work as he had been in Edinburgh. And the striking grey tweed suit he wore to the 1966 production still had life, being worn by one of his sons. Two revivals of the play were currently running, one at the Piccadilly Theatre in London, the other off-Broadway. Watts lists Stoppard's output to date: fifteen stage plays, four adaptations, seven radio and television plays, one novel and five film scripts. He had just finished *Hapgood* and *Empire of the Sun*. His charm shines through the biographical summary, despite his misgivings at being interviewed. Michael Codron, Peter Wood and Miriam Stoppard all offer their views in the article, Miriam's being perhaps the most trenchant: Tom 'quite likes being left alone', suggesting that he often placed a certain distance between himself and even those closest to him. 'He appears not to need approbation, agreement, consolation. He has an internal certainty about himself which I am in awe of,' she adds. To celebrate *her* fiftieth birthday two months earlier, Stoppard, the unsympathetic but obedient opera-goer, had taken Miriam to Luxor for a performance of *Aïda*.

At one point in the interview, Stoppard defended his critical and commercial success, often attacked by the literati: 'I'm not saying I didn't want to be rich and famous: but that riches and fame happened to come with what I really wanted – which was some sort of confirmation that Yes, I actually could write.' Ending the piece is a reaffirmation of Stoppard's domesticity and emotionalism: 'Tom is a great toucher and squeezer and kisser and hugger,' says Miriam. 'He will fly home on the Concorde for a son's rugby match or birthday. And when I've mentioned the expense, he's said "what better way is there to spend the money?" '[27] Two years later, he expressed this view concisely: 'Support Václav Havel? Definitely. But not if it's a Saturday afternoon and one of my sons is playing in a football game.'[28]

Pinter, also quoted in the Watts article, reaffirmed Stoppard's independence and confidence: "Tom is his own man. He's gone his own way from the word go. He follows his nose. It's a pretty sharp one. Nobody pushes him around. He writes what he likes – not what others might like him to write. But in doing so he has succeeded in writing serious plays which are also immensely popular. You can count on the fingers of one hand those who have brought that off.'[29]

Three years later, Stoppard had a chance to comment on Pinter. For the *Sunday Times,* he contributed to a page of tributes for Pinter's sixtieth birthday, declaring that the triumph of *The Birthday Party* (which Stoppard saw in 1958) was that it changed the subject matter of contemporary drama. Characters who insisted on explaining themselves naturally on the stage marked a new phase in playwriting. Pinter broke the contract between the audience and the playwright and then he redefined it, says Stoppard, making the plays conform more closely to the way Pinter observed people behaving. Stoppard also teased Pinter. When he solicited Stoppard to support the renaming of the Comedy Theatre, the venue for many of his plays, as the Pinter Theatre, Stoppard enquired, 'Wouldn't it be easier to change your name to Harold Comedy?'[30]

In contrast to Pinter, who has almost made *not* giving interviews into an art, Stoppard is a consummate manipulator of the media. He both dislikes and values it, offering constant critiques of the level of journalism and debate within the media at the same time as he makes himself available to reporters, interviewers and television hosts. He knows that people watch, listen and read and that his own former experiences as a journalist often depended on the cooperation of his subjects. He understands the media's importance and is willing to submit to requests for a background piece on a new play, an interview before a revival is to open or simply a check-up prompted by a new honour or award. He also admits that, as an ex-reporter, he feels 'under an obligation to give different answers to each questioner. But I sometimes fear it means keeping things dangerously inexact.'[31] However, his accessibility to the press has no doubt added to his reputation, providing the public with a sense of his work, even if they have seen only a few of his plays.

Stoppard does not understate the problems of writing and the anxiety he experiences when he finishes – not over the work's success or production, but what he will do next. But while he is writing, he is 'like a man in a hair shirt. He sits up half the night,' followed by one, two or three despairing calls, says Peter Wood. This contradictory behaviour, on the one hand forging ahead with his ideas and on the other needing to test them against a trusted fellow worker such as Wood or Paul Johnson, seems to parallel his contradictory political character which both distrusts and supports political action.

His views on religion, politics, music and turning fifty completed the interview with Janet Watts, extended by a note from Felicity Kendal on Stoppard's sense of style: 'he hears a tune . . . There is always one way of saying it which is better than any other, and he knows it exactly.' Watts also notes his admiration for the poetry of Philip Larkin and Stoppard's own efforts at poetic expression – 'for domestic consumption only'. A poem he sent to Larkin received the Larkinesque approval of 'dismayingly good', which Stoppard vowed to use as a heading should it ever be published.[32] His admiration for a well-written poem actually makes him jealous and, for a moment or two, makes him feel he is not a proper writer at all. But the feeling doesn't last.

Another piece from the celebratory 'turning fifty' period complained that Stoppard, 'probably the richest, most successful and critically-admired playwright of his generation', was also the most 'frivolous and uncommitted'. 'Flak-jacket aphorisms' had become his way of deflecting attention from his true convictions and his consistent theme, the ability to hold any convictions at all. The greatest criticism is of Stoppard's personal detachment from his plays, his work 'spawned by his library'. But the author of this critical essay also acknowledges Stoppard's skill at dramatic craftsmanship and superb handling of language, reporting that yet another revival of *Rosencrantz and Guildenstern* was about to open in the West End on 16 June 1987. He then cites Peter Wood: Stoppard 'has an amazingly high-spirited reaction to language, an obvious exuberance in his use of it. It visibly thrills him.'[33]

But while he was receiving such 'reviews' on his fiftieth birthday, Stoppard continued to celebrate his enthusiasms, including cricket, his first essay on the sport ironically appearing in an American magazine, *House and Garden*. With suitable self-satire, he refers to himself as 'one of England's leading cricketing playwrights', and notes how the *Observer* published Ken Tynan's account of his cricketing for Pinter's XI in 1977 which 'put me on the map as a serious cricketer who had written a few plays during the football season'.[34] Suddenly, requests to review cricket books, publish his cricketing memoirs and even cover England's tour of Australia poured in. Encouraged, he began to play two or three times a year, resuming his position as wicket-keeper.

In his article, he explains the importance and practicality of cricket terminology, taking care with expressions like 'bowling a maiden over'. Stoppard defines cricket in one sentence, although it contains some 135 words. An account of his (limited) cricketing accomplishments follows, none of which would make it into *Wisden*; he calls himself a 'cricketing failure who drifted into show business'. Even captaining a team in Perth, Australia, grandiosely named the 'Rest of the World XI', competing against the 'Perth Festival XI', brought him limited glory. What distinguishes cricket and its heroes is that, unlike other sports, the batsman is allowed only one mistake. When he's out, he must wait for both teams' first innings to end before he can bat again and that can literally take days. He explains to his American readership that scoring no runs is known as making a duck, and that 'Gentlemen', always capitalized, were amateurs, 'Players' professionals.

As wicket-keeper, Stoppard saw the bats and behinds of many a star player, especially in various charity matches. In one, Ian Botham scored some 200 runs in about forty minutes; Stoppard scored nine. In a comic end to the essay, Stoppard confesses that his life has gone wrong: 'being in the theatre was never what I meant. What I meant was keeping wicket for England or at least for Somerset, which was where I lived when I left school.' At age ten, Stoppard recalls, he asked for and received a copy of Godfrey Evans's *Behind the Stumps*. At the time, Evans was wicket-keeper for England, and Stoppard watched him take a spectacular catch in 1948 at Trent Bridge, the Nottinghamshire cricket ground. The catch chastened Stoppard to such an extent that he had curbed his cricket playing ever since. Nevertheless, in 1987, Stoppard captained the fathers' cricket team at his son Edmund's prep school, while the boy himself led out the school XI. However, four years later, Stoppard was disgruntled with the modernization of the game and the proliferation of one-day matches, as well as unorthodox batsmanship:

> I love watching classical batsmen and I am upset by people who score
> a quick 30 with incredibly dangerous shots.

That's not the way I want the world to be. I want them to be out first ball, and I want the classical batsman to score centuries. It's a romantic attitude, but that's me. It's pretty much my attitude to life.[35]

Writing a play is to write some kind of equation; it's got to be an elegant equation.
Stoppard, 1978

Stoppard's metaphor is appropriate for more than his playwriting. It also summarizes his long-standing fascination with mathematics, which became his focus in preparing for his next full-length play, *Hapgood*. Stoppard turned to introductory works on physics after telling an audience in 1994 that he had only had one term of physics and that was when he was thirteen. He did no chemistry, but had a smattering of biology.[36] Nevertheless, because he wrote two plays dealing with science, the unproduced *Galileo* and *Hapgood* (plus an unproduced screenplay of Nicholas Mosley's complex novel on physics and morality, *Hopeful Monsters*, winner of the Whitbread Book of the Year in 1990, for Kathleen Kennedy of Spielberg's Amblin Entertainment), he is perceived as a playwright on science, as he admitted in a lecture at Caltech: 'One play may be thought an aberration, but two suggests purpose'.[37]

The initial idea for *Hapgood* had to do not with spies but with science, specifically mathematics. Stoppard was perplexed by the concept of mathematical certainty, which was undergoing revision: 'the mathematics of physics turned out to be grounded on *uncertainties*, on probability and chance. And if you're like me, you think — there's a play in that.'[38] He made this remark in 1988. Three years earlier, he had told Anthony Smith that 'I keep trying to find a play about mathematics. There is one somewhere but I can't find it.'[39] In frustration, he turned to physics and discovered quantum mechanics.

The very structure of *Hapgood* is the ironic representation of a scientific paper. 'In a normal spy thriller you contrive to delude the reader until all is revealed in the denouement,' Stoppard explained in a 1988 interview. The exact opposite happens in a scientific paper, 'in which the denouement — the discovery — is announced at the beginning. *Hapgood* to some extent ironically follows this latter procedure.'

Rather than a whodunnit, 'the story becomes *how* he did it'.[40] Kerner in *Hapgood* expresses this very point when he outlines the structure of a scientific paper to Hapgood, explaining that 'when I write an experiment I do not wish you to be *surprised,* it is not a *joke*'.[41] A puzzle followed by an answer is the scheme, and this is precisely what is done in *Hapgood*. Stoppard's fascination with quantum physics as expressed in the dual (wave-and-particle) nature of light was another impetus for the play.

On Bloomsday (16 June) 1986, Stoppard wrote to the physicist J. C. Polkinghorne, complimenting him on his book *The Quantum World,* a 100-page introduction to the subject, adding that 'I have had it in mind for a few years to try to write a play which would in some way take off from quantum mechanics, for reasons not unconnected with what you write on pages 7/8 (Your point is well taken.) I wonder if you would be willing to meet me?' In a self-deprecating way, Stoppard adds, 'Don't worry if you don't want to – I'm constantly being asked to do things for people writing about my plays, so I know what these letters are like.'[42] Nevertheless, the two began a friendship.

Pages 7 and 8 of *The Quantum World* explain the paradox that light is both a particle and a wave but that quantum theory had the explanation for this paradox within itself: light will be a wave or particle if examined for waves or particles. Light becomes what you look for, according to the argument Kerner presents in the play. Such a discovery, however, did not prevent writers from continuing to assert 'the unresolved mystery of wave particular identity'. The implication, which infuriates Polkinghorne, is that 'mathematics is intrinsically inferior as a mode of rational discourse to ordinary language (which cannot quite cope)'. 'No! Mathematics is the perfect language for this sort of exercise,' Polkinghorne exclaims: 'It shows its power by penetrating beyond the everyday dialect of wave and particle to the synthesis of a quantum field.'[43] This gave Stoppard a concept he could investigate.

Stoppard was also helped by another physicist, Richard Feynman, the imaginative Caltech professor whose reputation for clarity in the field of theoretical physics was unsurpassed. His introductory *Lectures on Physics* were renowned for their humour. Published in two volumes in 1963, the lectures provided further detail for Stoppard, who cites a passage from Feynman's lecture on 'Quantum Behaviour' as part of the epigram to *Hapgood*. But of more importance for Stoppard was Feynman's set of lectures given at Cornell in 1964 and published by the BBC the following year as *The Character of Physical Law*. Feynman outlined the general developments and discoveries in physics, but two chapters stood out: 'The Relation of Mathematics to Physics' and 'Probability and Uncertainty – the Quantum Mechanical view of Nature'. Stoppard cites a passage from the latter chapter, the sixth in the book, as his second epigraph to *Hapgood*. In the paragraph preceding the quotation, Feynman stresses that 'nobody understands quantum mechanics'. Relax, he tells his audience, as he begins to explain the behaviour of electrons and photons (light particles) in 'their typical quantum mechanical way' through 'a mixture of analogy and contrast'.[44] By stressing analogy and contrast, Feynman gives Stoppard a partial scheme for the organization of his play, by inventing 'the experiment with two holes', the firing of bullets into two different holes to show that they could never arrive at the same time or number: they arrive in lumps, what scientists identify as the 'probability of arrival'.[45] Feynman then shows what the situation would be if one used electrons, noting that they, too, would arrive in lumps like particles but that their 'probability of arrival' would be determined 'as the intensity of waves would be'. Electrons behave sometimes like a particle and sometimes like a wave: they behave 'in two different ways at the same time'.[46] He begins to explain the experiment with the two sentences Stoppard will use in his epigraph. What is also clear from the experiment is the impossibility of prediction. The 'future' Feynman concludes, 'is unpredictable', as the two-hole experiment proves and the Stoppard epigraph confirms:

> Any other situation in quantum mechanics, it turns out, can always be explained by saying 'You remember the case of the experiment with the two holes? It's the same thing.'[47]

Feynman supplies Stoppard with the structure of his play when he explains that 'the probability of any event in an ideal experiment . . . is the square of something', which he calls the 'probability amplitude'.[48] In the play, Kerner refers directly to the experiment of the two holes when he explains to Blair that what began as particles become waves because two beams of light mix together when you shine light through two little gaps side by side. But when you begin to look closely, the waves are actually particles again. Why? 'Because we looked. Every time we don't look, we get wave pattern. Every time we look to see how we get wave pattern we get particle pattern. The act of observing determines what's what,' Kerner explains. Nobody knows how it happens because light is continuous and discontinuous: 'The experimenter makes the choice. You get what you interrogate for.'[49] The very unpredictability of light and the future provided Stoppard with a metaphor to justify the contradictory and often unknown behaviour of his agents. 'Nine-tenths of the action' in the play, he would later write, 'was just a metaphor for the world of particle physics'.[50] So Hapgood can be the steely agent and middle-class, worrisome mother. Kerner can be a theoretical physicist committed to science and a double, or possibly triple, agent. Ridley can be both Hapgood's aide and main operative and a spy. These contradictions exist at the intersection between interference curves and probability curves outlined by Feynman in *The Character of Physical Law*. 'It is impossible to predict in any way', he explains, 'from any information ahead of time, through which hole the thing will go, or which hole it will be seen behind . . . physics is incomplete.'[51] This uncertainty is the principle that defines *Hapgood*, the impatience of audiences and the confusion of critical reaction.

Equally appealing to Stoppard was Feynman's belief that physics was an art. That it contained something metaphysical and beautiful, Fenyman stated in his *Lectures on Physics* from 1963 and this forms the first of the play's epigraphs:

> We choose to examine a phenomenon which is impossible, *absolutely* impossible, to explain in any classical way, and which has in it the heart of quantum mechanics. In reality it contains the *only* mystery.[52]

Stoppard knew, however, that this view of science would displease Polkinghorne, explaining that 'in the case of quantum mechanics the difficulty is in reconciling the mathematical languages with a common-sensical view of what is *possible*. Feynman who presumably understands the mathematics insists on being amazed and so do I . . .' Nevertheless, despite his difference of opinion with Polkinghorne, Stoppard included a portion of their correspondence in the Aldwych theatre programme for *Hapgood* in March 1988. Stoppard also sent his script to a variety of physicists so that no howlers would appear.[53]

Polkinghorne questioned Feynman's take-it-or-leave-it attitude towards the nature of physics and offered some pointers: for example, cyclotrons (cyclic particle accelerators) do not give boosts or even pulses of magnetic energy but 'move' incrementally. More importantly, he considered that Kerner's wish not to be surprised in his outline of the structure of scientific papers and discoveries would make him a pretty second-rate scientist. Stoppard replied that the physics still remained mysterious: 'after two weeks, the actors are still trying to work some of it out; not to mention the author'.[54]

Stoppard's attachment to Feynman was close, although they never met. He explained this when he lectured at Caltech in October 1994 on the topic 'Playing with Science'. During tryouts of *Hapgood* in Wimbledon before its London opening, before the first audience arrived, Stoppard borrowed a newspaper from the stage doorman and to his shock learned of Feynman's death. His grief was strong but also selfish: 'because I had an epigraph from Feynman in front of this play. In a sort of fan-club way, I had intended to send him my play – not really that he should read it: I just wanted this metaphysical connection between us.'[55] The earliest typescript of the play contained an epigraph cobbled from two of Feynman's texts, the first time he ever attached an epigraph to one of his works. Part of his attraction was to Feynman's personality, which Stoppard found captivating, through a BBC series on science and Feynman's reminiscences, published as *Surely You're Joking, Mr. Feynman!*

In 1989, when the play was being done in Los Angeles, Stoppard and his son Oliver, who was studying low-temperature physics at the time and to whom the play is dedicated, visited Caltech (the California Institute of Technology) to see where Feynman lived and worked. A call to the Vice-Provost and Professor of Physics, David Goodstein, led to a tour and, like every literary or cultural pilgrim, 'I looked around thinking, well, Feynman was here, and it's better than nothing being here myself for a while'.[56] The visit led to a request to lecture at Caltech, which Stoppard did in 1994. In his talk, he extended his ideas about science and art which *Arcadia* (1993) had just demonstrated: 'Science and art are nowadays beyond being *like* each other. Sometimes they seem to *be* each other.'[57] Stoppard also detailed his further encounters with science, meeting Professor Arthur I. Miller at an art and science conference and Benoit Mandelbrot, of Mandelbrot set fame, at an art exhibition, where he bought forty postcards of the set, '38 of which I never managed to think of anybody to send to'.[58] But what was crucial to Stoppard in his focus on literature rather than science was the way language, not numbers, works by association and metaphor.

By 1987, the script of *Hapgood* was ready and there were plans for a production that summer. However, Stoppard delayed the play for six months because Felicity Kendal was pregnant and he wanted her to play the title role. Preparing the actors for the play's challenge, while reinforcing the theme of espionage, Stoppard bought twenty-four micro-cameras in July 1987 to give to cast members as gifts. Michael Codron, who was producing the play, agreed to the delay – it would have a greater draw with Felicity Kendal in the lead – and the production was pushed back.

The complexities of the play meant simplifying the plot, Peter Wood always bringing up Rupert Bear, or possibly Winnie the Pooh. 'Peter is an advocate for the audience and tries to make the plays work for an imaginary spectator called Rupert who he believes was the bear of little brain. It's no good my telling him that was actually Pooh,' Stoppard explained to Michael Billington in March 1988.[59] He did, however, redouble efforts to clarify *Hapgood* without losing any elements of the plot or central metaphor. During the tryouts, Stoppard admitted that the play was the hardest he and Wood had tried to do: 'It was hard to find the tone of the play. The first scene started to turn out ironic and detached, a direction we didn't expect it to go.' The other problem was that it was the first play he had written 'where such a large part of the plot has to be kept in mind all the time'. The amount of information the audience had to take in and retain left little time for the 'more casual side, the jokes and so on. We put in more signposts for the humorous side to work.'[60] The twelve scene changes, from the public swimming-baths to the Regent's Park Zoo and a school rugby field, also made it a highly technical show.

Rumours of the complexities of the play were filtering out to the theatre community. At one point, Stoppard prepared notes, with this summary of the plot:

the play is about dualities and uncertainties and about two people pretending to be one person and one person pretending to be two people, and a cartload of such things and was perforce written in the hope that we would keep our eye on the cart rather than on the tottering five-legged horse behind it.[61]

While physics has shown – but not entirely explained – that electrons can be in two places at the same time, Stoppard's agents cannot. Or at least, only one can, because he has a twin, but then the puzzle ends when one of the twins is shot.

Despite the confusions, the text maintained a Stoppardian tradition: a reference to someone named Chamberlain, in this case a decoy agent driving a cab, but, of course, an allusion to his secretary. He also added a reference to his producer, Michael Codron, naming the rival school in a rugby match in which Hapgood's son plays St Codron's.[62] As for the name Hapgood, he just 'arrived at it. Happy and Good, perhaps. Or Happenstance. Perhaps good.'[63] He may, however, have intended a subtle pun, since Elizabeth Reynolds Hapgood was the English translator of Stanislavsky; the detective/agent in the play thus became a translator of dramatic action as well as language.

In an essay published in April 1988, Stoppard cited a moment from the beginning of *Hapgood* as one of his favourite, most captivating scenes: a swimming-pool's diving tower descending on to the semi-darkened stage, after crackling short-wave radio signals and red lights on a map had tracked the movements of various spies' cars. The silent, effortless descent of the diving tower was a visual marker that the action was about to begin. The point Stoppard makes is that no one could '*write* anything that good' and that the moments we remember 'from plays are moments which nobody wrote'. He further elaborates: 'A play in the theatre is an equation which is continuously changing and most of the variables are specific to the performance.' The play, as understood by Stoppard, 'is an attempt to convey an event, and the typewriter keyboard does not offer the notation which makes it possible to succeed'.[64] The playwright has an ideal performance of the work in his head and is no more than a guide for the actors and director, telling them how 'to proceed towards realising the event', although he is repeatedly surprised by the way 'the realisation of the event is constantly telling the writer how to proceed with the text'.[65] One reads the text to see the play which a performance makes possible.

Like *Night and Day*, *Hapgood* began with out-of-town tryouts, and one night, in Wimbledon, a woman came out baffled by the complexities of the play to find Stoppard leaning on the bonnet of his car, writing furiously. 'I didn't understand that at all,' she complained. 'I know, I know,' said an unhappy Stoppard, 'but I'm trying to improve it.'[66] A note from Stoppard to Nigel Hawthorne and Roger Lewis about Act One, Scene Two, at the zoo, noted that it's 'a frightful nuisance that a deliberately hard to follow scene is immediately followed by an inadvertently hard to follow scene'. The problem, he adds, is that the scene is 'too much about reactions' with an 'overspill' from the physics into the espionage plot. Furthermore, it seems a bit hurried, especially the passage 'Ridley delivered to my Russian control, I delivered to Ridley'. This had to be made utterly clear to the audience.[67]

The note elicited a four-page critical response from Nigel Hawthorne, beginning with a comment on the complexity of the opening scene at the zoo and how odd it seemed that Stoppard wanted Hawthorne and Lewis to 'reduce the degree of humanity and by doing so, your contention is that the scene will be easier to follow'. The opposite should be the case. Hawthorne then astutely analyses the relationship between Kerner and Blair and questions further why Felicity Kendal is told to make Hapgood colder and less approachable. 'Any thought of the four of us working as a "team" went out of the window weeks ago . . . You seem to be advocating the sacrifice of relationships to theories by telling us that the characters are getting in the way of the physics.'[68]

The result of this emphasis made the play harder to perform night after night; any energy had to be artificially injected, Hawthorne explains, because there are 'no emotional areas'. He also disliked the idea that he had to play his character, Blair, with more ruthlessness. He indicts Stoppard and Peter Wood for dominating the rehearsals by 'playing games with the cast to see how much of the play they understood'. Feeling patronized, Hawthorne resisted the direction of Wood and Stoppard and resented the way 'the invention [was] thrown on the responsibility of the actors at the last moment', while the director's heart 'never really seemed *in* the production'. The final paragraph summed up Stoppard's weaknesses and strengths with this trenchant sentence: 'I love you as a man and puzzle that the warmth you give out so constantly and effortlessly is excluded from your plays. You have written a brilliant but élitist play . . .'

Stoppard tried to explain the complicated hypothesis of the play: 'that the dual nature of light works for people as well as things, and the one you meet in public is simply the working majority of that person'. The condition was not so much a dual personality but that 'one chooses to be one part of oneself, and not another part of oneself. One has a public self and a submerged self.' Both are real, if contradictory, elements which reflect the uncertainly principle of physics. It's not multiple personalities, 'it's a complex personality only part of which runs the show'.[69] Kerner explains that reality is not an either-or, plus or minus situation: 'we're all doubles . . . . we're not so one-or-the-other'.[70]

Given this element in the play, Michael Billington examined Stoppard's own double identity in emotional as well as political terms, pointing out that Stoppard is as comfortable being the activist in the cause of human rights as he is being the 'I-don't-know man'. He is equally wary of being known as a committed playwright as he is of being thought indifferent towards science or social injustice. Such duality had surfaced early in Stoppard's writing when he invented the dual nonsense language of *Dogg's Hamlet* and the double language in *Cahoot's Macbeth*, used to subvert the official language of repression. 'Words', the Inspector acknowledges, 'can be your friend or your enemy, depending on who's throwing the book, so watch your language.'[71]

Despite the intense lead-up to *Hapgood*'s first night, Stoppard continued to entertain friends and manage family life. Emanuel Azenberg and Michael Brandman, his two American producers, visited him in January 1988; Stoppard arranged for them to see *A View from the Bridge* by Arthur Miller. Paul Newman and Joanne Woodward visited him during rehearsals in early February; the next evening, all three went to see the eighty-three-year-old John Gielgud in Hugh Whitemore's *The Best of Friends* at the Apollo and, the following day, *Andromache* at the Old Vic. He met with Sean Connery at the Grosvenor House Hotel in mid-February and two days later took Stephen Sondheim to Wimbledon to see the tryout of *Hapgood*. Miriam was in Singapore, returning at the end of the month for the first performance of *Hapgood* on 8 March at the Aldwych Theatre. A week later, Stoppard gave a lecture at King's College, Cambridge. Capping this intense two-month period of preparation and performance was the Royal Film Performance of *Empire of the Sun*, on 21 March 1988. Stoppard was in the 'line-up' at the Odeon Leicester Square to meet the Queen and Prince Philip. The following evening, the Pinters attended *Hapgood* and, four nights later, so did Steven Spielberg. On 22 April, his old friend from Bristol, Val Lorraine, attended; his mother came on the 29th, and Mike Nichols on 10 May. Stoppard was thriving at the social centre of a theatrical and film world and would continue to do so for more than a decade.

> *You can't tell one from the other when they're all in the same get up.*
> Stoppard, *Hapgood*

Hapgood depicts the unpredictability of individuals, doubled by the language itself as words themselves become puns, double agents in the play. The work explores the randomness behind our perceived realities as the spy story becomes a metaphor for theoretical physics.[72] Agents cross and recross London and meet or miss each other at the municipal baths, in a curious choreography whereby randomness attains a rhythm akin to a ballet. Peter Wood added a whistled tune and occasional drumbeats to accentuate the dance, as the actors' movements become blurred and we lose track of the simultaneous exchange of briefcases between two Russians and what we later learn are two Ridleys.

As the house lights went down in its original production, a street map was projected on to three hexagonal panels above the empty stage, allowing the audience to follow the route of a Russian agent driving across London (his route plotted by red lights on the map). The agent stops at the municipal baths as alarmed voices over a two-way radio announce that he is 'not Georgi'. But his actions are predictable: he enters one of four cubicles and exchanges a briefcase among various unseen actors. The actor playing the Russian also appears as his twin brother. Throughout the play, the behaviour of characters intentionally obscures their actual position at a given moment in the spy plot.[73] These Russians, however, are decoys: the true double agent Hapgood must track down is her assistant, Ridley, and *his* twin brother, although they are not shown together until an inter-scene between Act Two, Scene Two and Act Two, Scene Three. Early in the Aldwych run, Stoppard inserted the scene between Act One, Scene Three and Act One, Scene Four, to clarify identities. At constant play in the text is the principle from quantum physics that 'the act of observing determines the reality'.[74]

Women in *Hapgood* remain enigmatic: Elizabeth Hapgood combines the wit, cleverness and common sense of Stoppard's previous female characters. But, unlike her predecessors, she uses words to command rather than to attack men. She is an astute 'control' in the all-male British intelligence unit. She needs to be terse, pointed, authoritative. When she masquerades as her twin sister, the non-existent Celia (a third set of doubles in the work), she assumes an arty, sensual stereotype to trap a double agent. But another facet of her character is as a middle-class mother cheering on the sidelines of her son's rugby games, far from the manipulator who solves the riddle of Ridley and his twin.[75] Yet Stoppard admitted confusion over her character: 'I'm not sure quite what to make of the end of the play – the idea that Hapgood should rebound from Blair to Kerner is too simplistic, and yet Kerner remains the truest character and perhaps the one most likely to appeal to her, quite apart from the emotional tie of their parenthood.'[76] 'In the last scene', he continues, 'Hapgood has finished with Blair, finished with the secrets game, and is simply mother with a small m.'[77] Importantly, much of the non-espionage plot of the play turns on a child, another constant in Stoppard's work.

As 'Mother', with a capital M, Hapgood is always in command. Kerner, her former lover, Wates, the CIA agent, and Ridley, the double agent whom she shoots, all, in a curious way, seek her protection or seek to protect her. Hapgood has both a personal and a technical self, terms she uses to differentiate between her private and professional life. Vulnerable on the personal side, not the professional, she is dependent on her section chief, Blair, a surrogate father-figure. There is often a conflict between the personal and professional for Hapgood: on one occasion, she uses a government agent to deliver new rugby boots to her son.

Most critics hated the London production, Stoppard receiving the worst reviews of his career. For instance:

We are told more about Quantum Mechanics than any sane person ever needs to know.

It would need a seeing eye dog with A-level physics to guide most of us through what was going on.

There are almost no moments in the new play when feeling, synthesis, metaphor and wit coincide. Stoppard leaves his homework lying around on stage. . . . It is expertly played as an emotional striptease of boulevard comedy, a style which promises everything but conceals all.

Plays collapse under the weight of too much information or too much plot. An excess of both these things is what is wrong with Tom Stoppard's *Hapgood*. There is enough information here for a sixth-form lecture on quantum mechanics and enough plot for one novel by John le Carré or two by Len Deighton.

Hapgood . . . is a characteristic chess game without a board.

The *Mail on Sunday* satirized the work by supposedly sending a theoretical physicist from University College London to see the play. He came back praising the work, especially the profound line 'we understand the behaviour of a pebble and we understand the behaviour of a nucleus but we don't understand in between'.[78]

Such opinions were exceeded only by the *maître d'* of a nearby restaurant, Orso, who praised the show although he hadn't seen it. So many people were leaving at the interval and starting their suppers early that he and his staff could finish serving and leave work earlier than normal. The *Guardian* actually devoted an editorial to the play and its creation of 'delight and disbelief'. One of the more interesting remarks offered by a critic was that the play was 'a wistful Central European celebration of Englishness', suggesting Stoppard's Czech origins again. The same critic praised Stoppard as 'the particle playwright', the only one talented enough to accommodate two major playwrights, the playwright of learning and the playwright of wit. Milton Shulman, in the *Evening Standard,* summed up responses when he wrote that the play is 'less a whodunnit then a whothoughtit' – although others pointed out that the physics in the play was circa 1927, 'couched in metaphors and rhetoric some 30 years old'.[79] Stoppard's rumoured reaction to this reception was the backstage remark, 'I don't know how to write plays any more.' When questioned about the comment some years later, he replied evasively: 'who knows what one says? . . . I'm left with a sense that I never quite cracked it, but I was never depressed about it.' Others who knew him disagreed. *Hapgood* was his only major play not to win a London award.[80]

Stoppard understood the problems and tried to rectify them thirty-six hours after the opening by inserting four speeches into the text at the point where Hapgood moves from entrapment to warning and realizes the traitor is the person most anxious to help her son. After the play ended its London run, Stoppard continued to make changes, with a plan to battle the cool reception of the play. He told Codron in May 1988 that the reviews had promoted the idea that it was a difficult rather than an entertaining work. 'We are all a little bewildered and certainly frustrated by the combination of somewhat disappointed audiences and evidently satisfied customers. For my part I receive more and nicer mail for *Hapgood* than for anything I've written including *The Real Thing*,' he told the producer, suggesting a new display advertising campaign.[81]

In June 1988, Stoppard participated in a panel at the First International Festival of the Arts at the Graduate Center of the City University of New York. Fellow panellists were August Wilson, Athol Fugard, Tina Howard and Arthur Miller. The latter created a minor controversy by declaring that if he were to write *Death of a Salesman* today, it would not succeed on the stage. Its moral and social focus would not find a hearing. Fugard in particular objected to this assessment and Wilson, author of the Pulitzer Prize-winning *Fences*, also disagreed with Miller. Collectively, they agreed only on the dismal state of commercial theatre. Stoppard, however, was the optimistic voice among the playwrights, stressing the opportunities for play-wrights in non-profit and regional theatres, as well as the British subsidized theatre. The problem, he explained, was that 'there aren't enough good plays, not that there are too many for the economics to handle . . . I think all the pronouncements of the theatre's death are some kind of symbolism for some other earth somewhere.' He also reiterated his position that your work can lose its force if you become too aware of your editorial stance while you're trying to deal with 'the collision of human personalities on paper . . . the moment you say

"What is the challenge of the theatre today", you look down [and fall into a chasm]."[82]

On their return from a family fishing trip to eastern Canada in the summer of 1988, Stoppard attended Felicity Kendal and Michael Rudman's *Hapgood* party, alone. In September, he attended Jeremy Irons's fortieth birthday party and in October a reception for the American writer Joseph Heller in honour of his new book, *Picture This*. In early November, he appeared at a party given by Paul and Marigold Johnson while Miriam went to the English National Opera that evening, and in December, when he visited the Oliviers for Christmas drinks, Miriam again attended the opera. In mid-November, he went to LA for six days to work with Steven Spielberg on the filmscript of *A Far-off Place,* derived from Laurens van der Post's novel; it was never produced. When he returned, he tried to contact Sting about a possible project, pursuing more new avenues for his creativity and income.

You don't know fuck, all you know is to talk Greek.
Stoppard, *Hapgood*

For the Los Angeles production of *Hapgood* in April 1989, following its dismal West End run – it closed in September 1988, some six months after opening – Stoppard began to make changes which would become even more drastic when the Lincoln Center production opened in New York in 1994. The LA production, the US première of the work, débuted at the smaller Doolittle Theater because of renovations to the original venue, the Ahmanson Center. In preparation, Stoppard adjusted scenes, at first adding material to elaborate the switches and the science to enhance the text. An explanatory replay of the first scene, including slides of all the participants, was thought to clarify the action but was dropped by the time the play was performed in San Francisco in March 1990. But the question remained as to how far he should simplify the play for American audiences. Could he rely on the superb cast – Judy Davis as Hapgood, Simon Jenkins as Blair and Roger Rees repeating his role of Kerner – to convey the complexities of the work?

Stoppard found the need to explicate offended his aesthetic sense of the work. What has always remained 'the bottom line' for him, and which the play celebrates throughout and quantum mechanics confirms, is uncertainty. For Stoppard, irresolution has the ring of truth. Yet this is precisely what theatre-goers found difficult about the interweaving plot. In his other works, the lack of resolution was accepted as part of the nature of the world he outlined. It was enough to recognize the coexistence of competing ideas. To identify the problems or the issues through his wit and linguistic pirouettes was satisfaction enough: compare the debates in *Jumpers*, the dialogues in *Travesties* or even the encounters to come in *Arcadia*. But in *Hapgood*, the debate was not enough, perhaps because the science was too arcane, the proofs too complicated, and the idea of twins coupled with double and triple agents too confusing. Part of *Hapgood*'s appeal 'is the pressure you're under to work it out for yourself as it goes', he explained to a visitor, questioning whether or not the narrative should be smoothed out.[83]

The open-ended, unresolved condition that he found so compelling in paradox or the work of Beckett lost its efficacy and currency in a play filled with equations, positional geometry, the bridges of Konigsberg's paradigm and references to Leibnitz, Kant, Euler, Einstein and Bohr. But Stoppard also understood the practicalities of production and that he would have to alter the work for his Los Angeles audience. He also felt an urgency to move ahead, since he had a new project: the filming of *Rosencrantz and Guildenstern* in July. He had also just agreed to write the filmscript for John le Carré's *The Russia House*.

Although he had finished *Hapgood* two years earlier, he still expertly summarized its dominating concept: 'the idea was to use the dualities in quantum physics as a metaphor for the duality in people.'[84] He wanted to show how one can be here and there, or know and not know, at the same time. In his 'Crib' written for the Los Angeles production, he admits that 'the two pool scenes have occupied more time than the rest of the play put together and I don't think that they are any more sensible than they were when they were driving me mad last summer'. The entire mechanics of the plot remained inscrutable and 'don't remotely interest me, they're just a necessary nuisance to provide the opportunity to write about this woman who in Blair's words, is "a sort of double", and the way this bears upon her relationships with Kerner, Blair and Ridley'.[85] The world of 'both/and' that Hapgood accepts in the play, learned from Kerner's physics, is in contrast to the 'either/or' world followed by Blair, for whom it is inconceivable that one could operate equally for both sides. Blair cannot understand that 'we're all doubles . . . we're not so one-or-the other'.[86]

A year before *Hapgood* appeared, Ian McEwan's novel *The Child in Time* was published, with a female theoretical physicist as one of the key characters. Thelma Darke, married to a publisher, offers a declaration and indictment of the science-versus-art debate which Stoppard enlarges. Arguing that none of the great thinkers of the past has 're-invented the world and our place in it as radically and bizarrely as the physicists of this century', she declares that 'Shakespeare would have grasped wave functions, Donne would have understood complementarity and relative time . . . But you "arts" people, you're not only ignorant of these magnificent things, you're rather proud of knowing nothing.'[87] *Hapgood* strives to disprove this charge, using quantum mechanics as a metaphor for the state of individual relationships which Stoppard would elaborate in a 1994 article just prior to the play's opening at Lincoln Center.

Stoppard flew to Los Angeles for rehearsals, rewriting and run-throughs. After the baffling opening scene with the switching of briefcases in the bath house, he inserted a statement of explanation. An actor turned to the audience and announced 'Okay, I'm Wates and you want to know what the hell is going on here.' In rehearsal, the new monologue, ostensibly directed to off-stage CIA agents, lasted eighteen minutes. 'Interminable' and 'unendurable', Stoppard said afterwards. By opening night, it was reduced to seven minutes, although audiences still seemed confused. The production had Peter Wood directing, with the original sets by Carl Toms (transparent screens, floating architectural elements and giant projections), in the 1,005-seat Doolittle Theater at the LA Music Center.

The previews met with appreciative audiences, but when the regular run started, the audiences were sullenly silent: they had subscribed to the complete Ahmanson season, with the promise of tickets to *The Phantom of the Opera* in May, and were doing their duty by attending Stoppard's play. Critics were also uncomfortable with the work, offering wary admiration, the *Los Angeles Times* noting its elements of romance, sharp encounters and brisk exchanges: 'it's all tricky stuff . . . that lies somewhere between a John le Carré novel and a lecture on the law of physics. Obfuscation is the idea.' Its challenge was its insistence on 'those intelligent mile-a-minute dissertations that tackle politics to philosophy, dissolving in a kiss, a reprimand or a gunshot'. 'It's difficult to dismiss a play with this much substance, but stating ideas is not the same thing as successfully dramatizing them.'[88] Plans for a Broadway run were abandoned.

On the surface, Stoppard's personal life in autumn 1989 couldn't have been more secure. While he worked on revisions and adaptations, Miriam, at the peak of her popularity and prominence, rushed between television broadcasts, video productions and writing health-and-beauty books. She also became the 'agony aunt' for *TV Times* and began to reflect her success in a more visible, sophisticated image. She operated at a faster, indeed, frantic pace, more intense than Stoppard's; Diana Rigg commented at the time that 'if you ask a taxi driver, he will have heard of Dr Miriam Stoppard, but not necessarily of her husband'. This was something of a reversal, for the uncharitable believed that she had always been competitive with Stoppard, wanting to be as successful and rich as him. In the press, they were often cited as 'a Golden Couple. He looked brooding and handsome; she, always impeccably groomed and coiffed – notoriously wedded to her false eyelashes.'[89]

Always well dressed, Miriam did not hide her svelte physique. Her skill in managing a career, a romantic relationship with her husband and a family astonished most people, except herself. And Stoppard's construction of dramas around attractive, intelligent, powerful women such as Ruth in *Night and Day* who might, like Hapgood, be able to run the British secret service efficiently might have been disguised Valentines to his wife. Or so it seemed. As one friend said of the marriage: 'it was not all that perfect under the surface. He felt he had to look after the children too much and his work suffered.' Nor was Miriam amused when she endorsed a stop-smoking campaign and he refused to give it up: 'she thought it bad for her image'.[90]

As he needed to be in London during rehearsals for *Hapgood* in the winter of 1988, Stoppard had taken a flat in Chelsea. During that same period, Felicity Kendal was entering another difficult phase in her life, as her marriage to Michael Rudman was falling apart. According to one rumour, she had received anonymous letters reporting that he was having an affair, while their volatile relationship often exhibited itself in restaurants. There were also stories that Rudman was unhappy that she returned to acting so soon after the birth of their son, Jacob; she began rehearsals for *Hapgood* when he was less than a month old.[91]

Kendal, some ten years younger than Miriam, soon found a sympathetic ear in Stoppard. They found one another, gradually at first but then more intensely during and following the *Hapgood* period. By September 1990, Kendal had left Rudman. On Christmas Eve 1990, in a formally-worded statement to the Press Association from the Stoppards' lawyers, Stoppard and Miriam announced their legal separation. The statement also noted that they had 'amicably maintained separate residences for some time past'.[92] Stoppard and Kendal had been seen together frequently that autumn. The papers loved the story and tabloid reporters would camp out in front of Kendal's house with tape recorders and cameras at the ready. Contradictory headlines soon appeared, like 'Why I Won't be marrying Tom', or 'Playing for Real'.[93] People expected them to marry, but they did not; people expected them to live together, but they did not; even close friends could not puzzle out the true nature of their relationship.

> *Perhaps, after all those years in the theatre, real life took her*
> *by surprise.*
> Stoppard, *Undiscovered Country*

When Felicity Kendal's marriage to Michael Rudman broke up, she left their home in Maida Vale for a townhouse in Carlyle Square, not far from Stoppard's apartment in Chelsea. By November 1990, they were romantically attached. One journalist pointed out that they were beneficiaries of Margaret Thatcher's sudden resignation, since there was no space in the press for details of their liaison: everyone was writing about Thatcher. Another coined an unusual sobriquet for Stoppard: 'the theatre's romantic Tomcat'.[94] Despite publicity of their romance, Stoppard and Kendal would always maintain their privacy and separate residences. As their relationship flourished, he paid tribute to her presence by making Chelsea the home of Flora Crewe, the free-spirited English poet who visits India in *In the Native State*.

Miriam Stoppard was in a vulnerable position when the Kendal–Stoppard affair began, in mid-menopause, as she told a reporter, in the midst of re-thinking her career and adjusting to the idea of her youngest son leaving home.[95] In November 1990, she broke down during a speech at a luncheon to honour Jewish Women of Distinction when she criticized women putting down other women and the schisms that develop between them. With tears welling behind gold-rimmed glasses, she admitted, according to observers, that, 'Generally, life is dark and lonely, it's very easy to be isolated . . . we have to build bridges between ourselves'. Ironically, the previous year's guest of honour had been Felicity Kendal, who had converted to Judaism when she married Michael Rudman in 1983.

Shortly after *Hapgood*'s March 1988 opening, Stoppard arranged to buy a riverfront apartment; he had acquired a flat in Chelsea some months earlier. At about the same time, Miriam had a town flat near Piccadilly, because of her many London engagements. They continued to maintain their estate at Iver Grove, gathering there for weekend reunions with the children, although the tabloids began to offer coy theories and see cracks in their marriage, which coincided with problems in Kendal's marriage. She, too, soon took up residence in Chelsea.

SW3 was a coveted postcode, and Chelsea attracted celebrity residents. Stoppard, however, chose to live not in the neighbourhood of the King's Road, nor in the upscale sidestreets that blend into South Kensington, but in a new, ultra-modern complex built on former railway sidings across the river from the massive but unused Battersea power station.

Chelsea Harbour, a complex of apartments, businesses and restaurants, was entered by crossing Chelsea Creek at the end of Lots Road, past Bonham's auction house. Once past the sentry house, one encounters The Chambers: shops and offices, including, for a considerable time, the offices of Stoppard's agent, Peters Fraser & Dunlop. Behind the Hotel Conrad is a modest marina which forms the centre of the complex, giving the impression in autumn and winter of a rich seafront out of season. To the right of the marina, towards the Thames, is a massive tower-like structure called the Belvedere; next to it is a smaller, semicircular building, facing the Thames: Chelsea Crescent, where Stoppard has lived since May 1988.

Stoppard's top-floor apartment – several years ago, he upgraded from his original, L-shaped flat, to a larger one, later acquiring the flat above so that he had two floors, which he connected by a staircase – overlooks the Thames and Battersea Park through a broad expanse of glass and balconies. 'I bought the [original] flat within one hour of seeing it. I thought "Oh, sod this". I've never regretted it for an instant.'[96] The view from his new apartment, with its bedroom and study on the upper floor, and the river below, mitigates the noise from the descending jumbo jets preparing to land at Heathrow. Beneath him is a river bus stop for commuters. Looking across at Battersea Park, he may recall the legend that centuries ago the Britons battled the invading Roman army in mid-stream as they headed for London. They lost only when the wily Romans called up an elephant out of the Battersea woods: at the sight of this preposterous beast, the defenders of Chelsea fled.[97] Stoppard can also observe a large brass ball that moves up and down with the tides on top of the next apartment tower. He's been trying to figure out how it operates for some time.

Stoppard writes on the second floor, at a table angled towards the glass doors that open on to a patio and look out on the Thames. Functionally furnished with several large couches and low Indian tables, his workspace is a mix of scripts, books, video cassettes, a dictionary stand and papers. No computer is to be seen, although the overall image of the flat is of a functional workspace moderately stamped with his personality. The English watercolours, autograph letters and leather-bound first editions that surrounded him at Iver Grove are absent, replaced by functional chairs, bare walls, piles of books, numerous bookcases. It has the air of a work in progress rather than a finished production. Outside, on one balcony, squats a life-like statue of a wicket-keeper. Peter Stoppard gave the piece, by Patrick Barker, to his brother for his fiftieth birthday.

Unlike the mid-eighties, however, when Stoppard permitted limited interviews at Iver Grove, he grew uncomfortable with inviting journalists to his flat. Rather than see them at his Chelsea Harbour apartment, an escape and refuge from publicity, he preferred interviews to be conducted in restaurants, cafés, rehearsal rooms or offices at the National Theatre. One story was that he used to pass off a friend's house as his own. Miles Kington even wrote a play in 1995 in which Stoppard failed to turn up for an interview arranged to take place at his own home.[98] Entitled *Waiting for Stoppard*, and performed by the Bristol New Vic and then the Southwark Playhouse in London, the play shows how two reporters arrive at Stoppard's house to interview him but spend their time waiting for him to turn up while nasty, unexpected things happen to them. The play flattered the playwright, but his agent was less amused and asked to review the script. Kington immediately wrote to Stoppard to declare there was nothing harmful in the work; Stoppard rang him back and left a recorded message telling Kington to ignore his agent and be as rude about him as he liked.[99]

Stoppard continued to work on movies in addition to writing and revising *Hapgood* in 1987–8, doing an uncredited 'polish' on Steven Spielberg's *Always*, which was released in December 1989, and writing the script for *The Russia House*, released in England in February 1991. 'I got into writing films precisely because I couldn't think of a play to write . . . If John le Carré has given me the plot and the characters, I would say that my problems are over.'[100] *The Russia House* also extended his interest in espionage for what became the first US non-co-production to be filmed in the Soviet Union. Until October 1989, when filming began, most movies needing a Russian setting had been shot in Finland. But in this work, because of the opportunity to actually film in Russia, Moscow and Leningrad almost overshadowed the stars, Sean Connery and Michelle Pfeiffer. *Variety* praised the film, writing that 'Shepsi's [the director] physicalization of Tom Stoppard's tight, sometimes structurally playful script is confident and convincing'.[101] Echoing *Hapgood*, the name of Connery's character is Barley Blair, while the text deals with smuggling a controversial manuscript by a leading physicist, describing Soviet nuclear capabilities, out to the west.

Spies, writing, film and theatre formed an irresistible nexus for Stoppard, as he made clear during a November 1988 appearance on *The Late Show with Clive James*. In discussion with Lord Annan, Professor Norman Stone and James, Stoppard explained that he had always thought being a reporter was equivalent to being a spy: you were in fact 'a spy with credentials', always 'in on the stuff' before the public. There was also a thrill to this sort of work, and from his earliest success, *Rosencrantz and Guildenstern*, through *The Dog it Was* and *Professional Foul* to *The Russia House* and *Hapgood* (plus, most recently, his film script of Robert Harris's *Enigma*), he has had a fascination with espionage and spying. He was intellectually attracted to spies and their systems, observing that men and women seem to be temperamentally, rather than politically, attracted to such activity. But what absorbed him most was the hypothesis that all evidence, even contradictory, will substantiate any conclusion you want to reach.

Confirming this view of espionage, Stoppard excitedly cited Peter Wright's 1987 autobiography, *Spycatcher*, which had initially been banned in Britain. Wright, the first scientific officer of MI5, later held a senior post in the counterespionage section until his retirement in 1976. Stoppard found *Spycatcher* one of the most fascinating books he had read (much of it deals with Wright's effort to uncover a mole at the highest level of MI5) and disclosed that he had bought three copies in New York and read one of them straight through on the flight home, 'the fastest ride ever back from the US'. What struck him most forcibly was the way the mathematical logic of Wright and MI5 often contradicted experience. Life, as Stoppard reminded everyone on the show, is often unclear and does not accept the law of the excluded middle: it is untidy and 'unconvincing as a plot'. Wright, however, could not allow for this in his account of the agency's activities, and he and MI5 often dismissed or neglected the messy parts. Stoppard, in *Hapgood*, made sure they were there. Stoppard also revealed a secret of his own on the show: that he desperately wanted to learn Russian in his youth, because he was 'mad for a girl who was studying it'.[102]

CHAPTER 16

AN ENGLISH EDEN

―――――

It was quite fun walking around above the Bazaar
Darjeeling and reading the names of these houses which are
called Killarney Lodge and Gleneagles.
Stoppard, 1991

Was India an English – or possibly Scottish – Eden? In his recollection of the country, Stoppard seemed to think so. Between 1988 and 1995, India would take over from spies as his central focus, with his radio play *In the Native State*, a visit to Darjeeling in 1990 and his stage play *Indian Ink*. 'I felt I should be able to use my own experience of India to write something about the ethos of the British Empire,' he explained; he wanted to write 'the ethics of empire'.[1] His artistic and personal re-encounter with the country marked an engagement with the past during an uncertain present. Stoppard found in India a world that balanced stability with change, while providing him with a new direction in his writing. Personally and artistically, India saved him a second time.

This period of re-engagement not surprisingly coincided with his involvement with Felicity Kendal. The week *In the Native State* was to air, the *Radio Times* had as its cover story 'Felicity Kendal on her Great Love Affair'. Those expecting a scoop on her relationship with Stoppard were surprised to learn that her 'love affair' was with India. Stoppard's decision to write about it was a way of confronting and evaluating his past, and had been partly triggered by Kendal's own experiences there. *In the Native State*, and its subsequent expansion into *Indian Ink*, provided a means of integrating his memory of the past with the progress of his writing. The dedicatee of the published radio play was, appropriately, Kendal, who also took the lead role.

In December 1990, Stoppard returned to India alone, placing his images of India within 'their physical reality' to see 'how the scale of things has changed'. When he returned to his boarding-school and visited the room he had lived in, he was startled by its ordinariness and small size, 'not really worthy of the intensity of the emotions I felt and associated with it'. His trip, which lasted almost two weeks and took him from Madras to Darjeeling, had an important impact, re-introducing him to a changed country which altered his sense of his past. Setting *In the Native State* in the dual time frame of 1930 and 1990, he chose an early period preceding his residence there (1942–6). But his nostalgia, intensified by his research for the play, increased his desire to re-experience India, and coincided with an invitation from a film festival in Madras to show his film of *Rosencrantz and Guildenstern*. Yet, as he recalled his youth in India, Stoppard also remembered his marginalized position: because the family was Czech, not English, they belonged neither to the world of the British Raj nor to India. Precisely because of this social limbo, he was able to under-stand and recover India aesthetically, and his visit enabled him to clarify recollections of the past which might otherwise have produced a patina of sentiment.

In the winter of 1989, Stoppard's personal life had not yet formally altered. With two large dogs, his wife and fourteen-year-old son Edmund still at home in Iver, Stoppard preoccupied himself with a New York production of *Artist Descending a Staircase* and the rewrites for *Hapgood*'s April première in Los Angeles. An interview for *Vanity Fair* conducted in late February 1989, but not published until May, revealed a domestic Stoppard troubled by the *fatwa* against Salman Rushdie, the nine-month sentence just given to Václav Havel and the contrast between Havel and himself as he sat in his palatial home surrounded by leather-bound copies of his work and the first editions of others'. Smoking Silk Cuts in an odd Central European manner – tilting the lighted tip upwards and then sipping, so to speak, the cigarette from below – Stoppard at fifty-one seemed at once relaxed and on edge, admitting his insecurity in areas of supposed knowledge: 'All my time is spent concealing what I don't know,' he lisped, referring to the supposed intellectualism of his plays.[2]

He also admitted frustration over the lack of a big idea for his next play, although he reports that he had just read James Gleick's *Chaos* and was gathering ideas for another work – which would become *Arcadia*. By late December 1989, the Stoppards again went *en famille* to Scotland to fish, possibly their last full family outing. Domestic stability temporarily defined his private life, although the changes were occurring which a year later would result in their lawyers formally announcing that the Stoppards had separated. But in the winter of 1989, while he puzzled over the unsuccessful production of *Artist* in New York – it closed after only thirty-six performances – and Miriam whistled about from office to studio to television station, Iver Grove remained a gathering place and refuge.

For more than a decade, Stoppard had resisted efforts to stage *Artist*, preferring its life as a radio drama, first broadcast on BBC Radio 3 on 14 November 1972. In 1988, Stoppard reluctantly agreed to let Dan Crawford, 'impresario', and Tim Luscombe, director, stage the play at the King's Head, an Islington pub theatre. It was a hit when it opened in August and in December transferred to the Duke of York's Theatre in the West End. Emanuel Azenberg saw the production and thought it would work in New York. He organized a production with a cast that included Paxton Whitehead, Harold Gould, John McMartin and Michael Cumpsty. Tim Luscombe was to direct. It opened at the Helen Hayes Theater, but closed after a short run. Its radical structure made it difficult for the New York public to follow, even though *Playbill* printed a chart to simplify the complicated time shifts defining each of the eleven scenes, and showed, the philosophical Azenberg explained, that sometimes Stoppard's hold on an audience was tenuous.

'Artist Ascending an Airplane' was the subtitle of a comic interview with Stoppard conducted in late November 1989 in British Airways' first-class lounge at Kennedy Airport, as the uncomfortable playwright – he was suffering from a serious toothache – waited for a flight to London. The play was due to open in New York in four days. Stoppard had recently been to Duke University in Durham, North Carolina, where the pre-Broadway run of *Artist* took place (Azenberg lectured there on occasion). Commenting on the structure, Stoppard hopes that the audience will read the *Playbill* chart before the play begins. He explains that the play was his first effort at writing a romantic drama, and comments on his resistance to putting it on the stage. But Tim Luscombe persisted and 'I felt it was priggish to keep on saying no'.[3]

Unusually, he did not attend rehearsals, only the final run-through. It was fine and he agreed that the visual would now enhance the oral dimension of the work. Writing radio plays was still enjoyable but he was already a year late with a new work (which would become *In the Native State*) because of the projected film of *Rosencrantz and Guildenstern* which was due to begin shooting in January/February 1990.

He was supposed to be travelling to Zagreb to scout locations for his film, but his dental problem required a detour to London. He explained to the interviewer that the film will *not* be 'a filming of the play's text'. He was directing because he was the only person willing 'to commit the necessary violence to this well-known stage play . . . At least the director wouldn't have to keep wondering what the author meant. It just seemed that I'd be the only person who could treat the play with necessary disrespect.'[4]

The film was supposed to have begun shooting on 30 January the previous year, with Sean Connery, Roger Rees and Robert Lindsay, but Connery had pulled out. The new cast was Richard Dreyfuss, Gary Oldman and Tim Roth. 'The money was for a Sean Connery film, not a Tom Stoppard film,' he adds ruefully. Stoppard's screenplay of *The Russia House* was also being filmed with Connery as the star. Stoppard reports that he was also completing the script of E. L. Doctorow's *Billy Bathgate*. Such work, he explains, is extremely enjoyable because the other writers have done all the labour:

> I find it difficult to invent a story situation and people. I only seem to come up with a full-length stage play every three, four or five years. And they don't take four years to write. They're a year of one's life. I like to keep occupied – and also, it's one's livelihood.[5]

Before leaving, Stoppard mentions the failure of *Hapgood* to be staged in New York, although he suggests that Lincoln Center and Greg Mosher, the director, might mount it.

While Stoppard was revising *Hapgood* and preparing to film *Rosencrantz and Guildenstern*, reports also hinted at a possible new play dealing with his childhood, when his family fled Nazi-occupied Czechoslovakia for Singapore and India. This would eventually focus on India, however, and become the story of the poet Flora Crewe in *In the Native State*. At this time, he also started work on the earliest drafts of *Arcadia*.

*

Stoppard's public profile in the UK at this time continued to grow, with his appointment on 3 August 1989 to the Board of Directors of the National Theatre. (He would be reappointed for his third term in 1998.) For years, he had been involved with the National not only as a practising playwright and public supporter, but more immediately as part of the 1988 search committee to find a new director to succeed Peter Hall, who ran the National from 1973 until 1988. The committee's choice was Richard Eyre, who would continue in the post until September 1997, when he was succeeded by Trevor Nunn.

Location shooting for *Rosencrantz and Guildenstern are Dead* did not actually begin until April 1990; until then, Stoppard occupied himself with script matters and a series of visitors. In late March, it was Havel, now President of the Czech Republic, arriving in London to open an East European Forum at the ICA at which George Steiner and Timothy Garton Ash also spoke. The Stoppards joined Havel for dinner at 10 Downing Street with the Prime Minister, John Major. A few weeks later, Stoppard's friend, the opera director Robert Carsen, arrived from Paris and they went to see a production of *Lady Windermere's Fan* at the Bristol Old Vic and Peter Wood's production of Sheridan's *School for Scandal* at the National Theatre. The spring was divided between theatre visits (*The Crucible, The Duchess of Malfi, Three Sisters*), opera at Glyndebourne, cricket at Lord's, and a Rolling Stones concert. During this time, his friendship with Jagger solidified. They had first met in 1984 and, through a variety of shared interests, including cricket, books and mutual friends like Paul Johnson and Harold Pinter, Stoppard and Jagger developed a friendship, Stoppard discovering that Jagger's theatricality and showmanship were balanced by a seriousness, conservatism and, as the photographer Cecil Beaton noted, 'an analytical slant'.[6] Several years later, Stoppard came up with the name for Jagger's 1997 tour, 'Bridges to Babylon', and he would soon undertake the screenplay of *Enigma*, the World War II novel by Robert Harris on which Jagger had purchased an option.

During the spring and summer of 1990, a season of Stoppard's radio plays was broadcast on BBC Radio 3. But soon another activity competed for his attention in the spring of 1990: the organization and dispersal of his manuscript archive, possibly anticipating his forthcoming separation from Miriam and the need for additional funds.

Stoppard contacted Sotheby's for an appraisal of his papers and possible management of the sale. Not one for constant filing or ordering his material, he needed Sotheby's organizational skill. Working with Stoppard's secretary, Sotheby's diligently listed the materials, which included correspondence, manuscripts, production notes, television scripts and screenplays, among other items, housed in the renovated stables at Iver Grove, a process that took nearly six months.

By June of the following year, Sotheby's reported that there were no serious offers for the material from any of the institutions they had approached and suggested that Stoppard consider offering the papers to the British Library. He had some qualms about that move, however, even when Sotheby's suggested an arrangement whereby he could sell the material to the British Library at a fee £50,000 below that offered to other institutions. Stoppard balked, but eventually the material would be purchased in 1991 and, in a second stage, 1993 by the Harry Ransom Humanities Research Center at the University of Texas, Austin. The sale naturally generated a strong reaction in the press, who blamed the Texans for glibly throwing money at English writers. Editorials and columns similarly castigated English institutions, including the government, for not preventing the removal of such cultural material from the country. *The Times* dismissively asked: 'What do we care if the laundry-lists of the literati are sold to Texas?' The answer, not surprisingly, was a great deal.[7] Underscoring the issue was Pinter's September 1993 deposit of his own archive at the British Library, an event that received national praise. The archive that Stoppard sent to Austin included manuscripts, correspondence, reviews, theatre programmes, photographs and legal documents. Various additions to the archive by Stoppard since 1993, plus the acquisition of ancillary collections, now make the Ransom Center the essential repository of his papers.

*Smith: What's the big difference between the stage and film
versions of* Rosencrantz and Guildenstern are Dead?
Stoppard: That I left out half the lines.
Sid Smith, 'Script Jockey', 1991

Michael Brandman, a Hollywood producer who had successfully
made a series of television movies of stage plays, had originally contacted Stoppard in 1986 about filming *Rosencrantz and Guildenstern*. A
much earlier attempt to film the play, initiated by John Boorman and
MGM in 1968, for which Stoppard wrote various scripts, had been
aborted. But now, with the possibility of Sean Connery signing on as
the Player, money was forthcoming and work got under way. Stoppard
had previously succeeded in retrieving the film rights to the work,
although it reportedly cost him $500,000 dollars.[8]

Unsure of how to actually make a movie but eager to learn, some ten
years earlier Stoppard had taken David Puttnam to lunch to quiz him
on technique, as he was beginning to feel 'the pangs of an intermittent
desire to make a film myself'.[9] From Puttnam, he discovered that all a
director needed to know was what he wanted the picture to look like:
its colour tones and atmosphere. 'Go up to your lighting cameraman
and tell him the name of a movie you want your film to look like' was
the advice. To Peter Biziou, his cinematographer, Stoppard repeatedly
murmured the name of Sergio Leone, whose spaghetti westerns
inform elements of the action, pace and look of *Rosencrantz and
Guildenstern*, from the opening sequence onwards.[10] Once the look
was established, all he needed was a team of creative technicians on
whose expertise he could rely; bluffing was out, Stoppard insisted.

Stoppard soon reworked the script, editing, extending and com-
pressing scenes. He repeated that no other director would take such
liberties with the text: 'it needed to be done by someone who was
prepared to do the necessary violence to this supposed modern classic.
That really narrowed it down to me.'[11] After twenty-five years, he also
felt that some parts of the play were repetitive, and that certain lines,
mainly the Player's, did not belong in the film. Because he could
change the frame of the work – in the theatre, you have a consistent
medium shot, fairly wide angle – Stoppard could emphasize different
features in the film: close-ups, contrasting angles, overhead shots and

filtered light were all possible. When an important six-line speech brought the film to a halt, he ruthlessly cut it. He also added more Shakespeare to provide greater continuity for the story (in the play, there were only approximately 250 lines from *Hamlet*) and eliminated about half the original play.

He added a number of visual delights: the verbal tennis match between Rosencrantz and Guildenstern near the end of Act One occurs on an empty, Felliniesque court; a paper airplane effortlessly flies through various scenes; a hamburger makes its silent début in Elizabethan drama. These gags function to reveal virtually all the laws of physics to the medieval travellers, who ignore them. Newton's apple falls, Archimedes' bath overflows, and balls, feathers and flower-baskets display the principles of energy and gravity. One joke that didn't 'fly' was the plan to make Rosencrantz play the opening bars of Beethoven's Fifth by accidentally rattling broken banisters. The musical director said no.

The location for the movie was to be Toronto and its environs, especially the Scarborough bluffs above Lake Ontario. This was mainly on account of cost (being cheaper than either Ireland or Yugoslavia) and the tax situation of the then Player, Sean Connery. The movie was designed to be shot inside a studio, although changes meant that more than half of it would be shot outside, 'but in various ancient-type, Danish-type buildings in downtown Toronto. Preparing a film is like one of those kayak races: you just keep going even when it's upside down.'

Connery's participation was instrumental in securing finance for the movie. But a month or so before shooting was to begin in January 1989, Connery informed Stoppard that a throat illness might prevent him appearing in the film. Stoppard cut short a Christmas vacation and flew to Los Angeles to tell Connery that he would wait for him to improve; Connery, forbidden to talk, communicated through his wife, who read notes written by her husband over the phone to Stoppard. Connery withdrew from the film. Stoppard suggested there was a commitment, adding that the producers were uninsured. If they didn't make the film, they would lose the £500,000 already spent. Connery took umbrage when the producers threatened to sue, stating: 'but for this throat, I would have sued Stoppard out of the country', to which Stoppard answered in a letter to *The Times*: 'He is confusing different parts of his anatomy. Connery paid up because he didn't have a leg to stand on.'[12] Azenberg negotiated with Michael Ovitz, who represented Connery, and the matter was settled out of court. Connery, in the meantime, signed a lucrative contract to star in *The Hunt for Red October.*

Finance for the film became problematic after Connery pulled out, although two days after the non-meeting with Connery, Stoppard signed Richard Dreyfuss after dining with him and visiting him at home with his producer. Dreyfuss, however, could not do the film for a year and another delay was necessary. Dreyfuss's participation, for much less than his usual fee (which, Stoppard quipped, was larger than their entire budget), would guarantee critical kudos but not distribution success. The producers stood to lose a million dollars. Azenberg said 'let's kill it'. Brandman said no, and Stoppard said he wanted it done and would stand for one third of the potential loss. Azenberg then agreed to do it and they shook hands. The film lost a million dollars, despite its critical success, and Stoppard wrote a cheque to cover his share. And although it was a financial disaster, it became a minor classic which the three were proud to include on their résumés.

With Richard Dreyfuss signed as the Player, the movie needed a younger cast: Gary Oldman took the role of Rosencrantz and Tim Roth that of Guildenstern. Brandman's wife, Joanna Miles, played Gertrude. Lowering the ages by a generation was actually a positive move, Stoppard realized. It also brought a modern element to the film. His decision to develop a western motif meant borrowing features which intentionally confused the locale – a nondescript but dramatic landscape of sheer cliffs and verdant woods interrupted by a rough castle defined the setting, all actually shot in Yugoslavia after all. To set the mood, the movie opens with country-and-western music as two figures languidly ride along a sensational cliff, Rosencrantz stopping to pick up a gold coin on the ground and then becoming engrossed in tossing the coin to test the probability of heads versus tails. Stoppard originally wanted the opening to be set on a seashore, but they found nothing suitable along the Adriatic coast. Instead, they shot the scene in a cement quarry in Zagreb. They retained the spaghetti-western motif, which runs throughout the movie with evocative costumes and haunting but stylized music. The theme even found its way into the promotion of the film, the British posters showing only 'two boots and a noose' and copy that boasted the 'original buddy movie'.[13]

Stoppard's inexperience as a director showed up early in the production process. 'After a few days of shooting,' he recalled, 'the producer came up to me and said "The camera isn't moving very much". It was at that point that I realised that it wasn't moving at all. I was doing seaside photography.' Thanks to his cameraman and cinematographer, however, motion and point of view shifted throughout the film – 'but only because I had the sense not to pretend that I knew how to do something that I couldn't do'.[14]

Richard Dreyfuss remembers a different experience. From the beginning, Stoppard possessed an 'absolutely secure certainty of what he was doing'; he knew what he wanted, why he did certain things with the camera and why he wanted the pacing in a certain manner. Stoppard himself remarked that once he had written the work as a screenplay, 'I had defined the kind of film it ought to be in my mind'.[15] This was evident even during the two weeks of rehearsals in London prior to the cast and crew going to Zagreb to film in the old castle. The vibrancy of Dreyfuss's own performance as the Player – he always had in mind how Donald Wolfit would have done it – partly derives from Stoppard's sense of assuredness and his decision to let the actors handle the roles the way they wanted. For Dreyfuss, it was a creative and challenging time since the role was so different from others he had done. The character of the Player was immensely 'inhabitable'.

Two brilliant ideas stood out, Dreyfuss remembers: the use of the Czech mime group who produced 'theatrical magic', and Gary Oldman's work as Rosencrantz, inventing various nuances and details. To enhance the movement of the acting troupe, Stoppard located a choreographer who had done the same thing for the Croatian National Theatre's production of the play twenty years earlier. Stoppard also hired a Yugoslavian puppet master, Zlatko Bourek, who had been performing his '15 Minute Hamlet' for years.

A tight budget meant limited takes, with only four or five retakes permitted. The shooting schedule was also curbed to only thirty-eight days. Stoppard had to be strict with the schedule, admitting that since he had no experience as a director, he did not know how long things took. He erred on the side of caution. However, post-production was a different story. Enamoured of the technology, he reduced pauses, sped up the action, altered colour and enhanced sound, things that could not be done in the theatre. 'I came in on-time and below budget in Yugoslavia, but I overspent at Pinewood because in the dubbing the schedule meant nothing to me. After about seven days I had a message from California to say could I please stop behaving as if this was an expensive film.'[16]

After it was completed, he also explained that he hardly ever examined 'the how-to part. I just try to get on with it.' The practical Stoppard ruled: he didn't theorize about how it ought to be. 'We just looked around, and liked this and didn't like that.' Recalling an evening with Stephen Frears and Christopher Hampton at BAFTA (the British Academy of Film and Television Arts) in late September 1990, he recounted a question from an American writer on writing scripts. She was having problems making her scripts adhere to the technique she had been taught. A film script, she knew, should be between 115 and 120 pages long, with a secondary plot on page 71. 'I was completely out of my depth,' Stoppard recalled, 'I didn't have a clue what she was on about.'[17]

Prior to general release, the film won the prestigious Golden Lion award at the Venice Film Festival, beating Martin Scorsese's *Goodfellas* and Jane Campion's *An Angel at My Table*. Gore Vidal's announcement of the winner, however, brought whistles, shouts and general distress at the closing press conference. Italian journalists were dismayed that Marco Risi's *Boys on the Outside* was passed over; English-speaking journalists were upset that Jane Campion's movie was dismissed to second place. Insiders reported that Vidal, as chairman of the judges, had pushed a divided jury to accept his favourite. The audience poll actually favoured Scorsese's tale of American gangsters, yet Vidal reigned and, when he presented the award, he began by saying: 'in every country, democratic or totalitarian, language has been so debased in this century that it is very difficult to communicate anything complex at all in life, or in art. The prize I am about to give is a tribute to the force of the mind, of wit and of logic in human affairs.'[18] Stoppard's film was the first British entry since Olivier's *Hamlet* of 1948 to win the Golden Lion, a work which ironically had cut out the parts of Rosencrantz and Guildenstern.

In November 1990, Stoppard wrote an article about the film, recalling Sean Connery's withdrawal three weeks before filming in

Toronto was to have begun. Retelling the search for locations, he mentions other disappointments and false trails: a trip to Budapest; a visit to Athens, to convince Vangelis to do the music (he didn't); and a journey to Dubrovnik 'to audition the ocean' (it almost failed). Budapest supposedly had a standing set from a *Hamlet* production and wild horses on the Hungarian plains, but in fact they found neither. Dubrovnik did have the Adriatic and the proper backdrop, but in the end they chose neither location because of tight money and a tighter shooting schedule. Even the ocean was dropped in the middle of shooting. Elsinore became a combination of two castles near Zagreb, while the ocean became the cement quarry.

The experience taught Stoppard 'a valuable lesson in pragmatism on every scale'. For example, a theatre set is built to last a year; a film set, days or possibly hours. Vaughan Edwards, his production designer, quickly changed doors in walls or complete interiors, and shooting the film created less stress than putting on a play. 'To spend ten hours concentrating on perhaps three minutes of the script was a new experience and on the whole a more enjoyable one.' And when he got something right, it stayed that way, although this was curiously both the pleasure and displeasure of film for him and its main difference from the theatre, which in the end he missed. Several years earlier, in answer to a set of questions from students at St Andrews, Stoppard had explained why he preferred to write for the stage rather than film: in the theatre, 'one can control the disposition of the forces. The frame doesn't change. All the lines have to find their proper weight. In film and television a line might be said in close-up or long-shot or off-screen . . . [and] most of the time other considerations determine the choice.'[19]

The film was not a popular success in America, where it was released in the winter of 1991, one critic complaining that 'the words have the effect of absorbing all thought. The realism of the settings . . . also doesn't help. Rather, it calls attention to the abstract nature of the play without supporting it.'[20] English critics were equally unreceptive, commenting on fatigue from the language and suggesting that, without the support of a stage, the Shakespearean tradition loses its point while the humour turns to slapstick. *Sight and Sound* felt the adaptation lacked the briskness of the original. That the dumb show or play-within-a-play should be the most striking cinematic moment in the film is a paradox of Stoppardian proportions, the writer added.[21] However, attendances benefited from the release the previous month (April 1991) of Zeffirelli's *Hamlet*. Directing the film version of *Rosencrantz and Guildenstern,* gave Stoppard temporary cachet as a film-maker.

Before the movie was released in England in late May, Stoppard had another important work before the public: *In the Native State,* which aired on BBC Radio on 21 April 1991, starring Felicity Kendal. The play embodied the classic Stoppard conflict of sense and sensuality: 'heat had its way with me,' the heroine says at one point.[22] Initially, Stoppard had intended to write a conversation between a poet and a painter. At the same time, he was thinking about a play about the Raj, India during the time of the British Empire. The two ideas coalesced, aided by Kendal's own recollections of India. The first thing he wrote was Flora's poem which opens *In the Native State.*[23]

Wangle the Daimler!
Stoppard, *In the Native State*

In the Native State focuses on a 1930 visit to India by an English poet, Flora Crewe. The work took more than three years to complete (it was a year late in delivery) and differed from his original intention to write a play on the 'ethics of empire'. He considered writing about a woman having her portrait painted while writing a poem about the painter: 'you had this loop between artist and artist,' he explained to an interviewer.[24] But the pattern of composition was the same: enthusiastic commitment, followed by growing obligation, topped by a sense of burden, and relief when it was done. 'I think the cart has always been pulling the horse. I wrote my first novel by owing it to someone.'[25] He had accepted a commission to do an hour-long play for the BBC Globe Theatre in 1987, although he regretted the decision because of the one-hour restriction. In the end, the season, broadcast in 1988, did not contain a contribution from him. Feeling guilty, he still promised to deliver and over the course of three years and an exchange of jokey postcards between himself and Tydeman he reported his progress. The principal delay was the filming of *Rosencrantz and Guildenstern.*

However, when the film was finished in July 1990, he set to work in September and delivered the text in October 1990. He also managed to include two name jokes in the work: one a reference to the ubiquitous Chamberlain, the other, Eldon Pike, whose last name matched that of his editor at Faber and Faber, Frank Pike.

For the work, Stoppard again read widely, from Forster's *A Passage to India* to numerous autobiographies, histories and biographies, including *Autobiography of an Unknown Indian* by Chaudhuri and Mark Tully's *No Full Stops in India,* plus the work of V. S. Naipaul. Charles Allen's *Scrapbooks of the Raj* were wonderful sources, with old photographs and advertisements from the era. He also read the two-volume *Up the Country* (1866), letters written by Emily Eden from India between 1837 and 1840 to her sister Eleanor (a name shared by Flora's sister in the play). Emily Eden, forty years old and unmarried, accompanied her brother, Lord Auckland, the new Governor General of India, on an official 'progress' up country. The thirty-month tour, which included Auckland's French chef in the entourage of several thousand, began in Calcutta and headed for Cawnpore, Delhi, Simla and Futtehpore-Sickrey, where the rajah led them into a brilliantly illuminated hall fitted 'up in the oddest way with French chandeliers of green and purple and yellow glass'.[26] Old-fashioned mirrors and English prints hung on the walls.

Emily Eden's letters comment as much on life in England as India. Thanking her sister for a packet received on 30 October 1837, Eden writes: 'I think the young Queen a charming invention, and I can fancy the degree of enthusiasm she must excite. Even here we feel it.' A month later, she tells her sister that a rajah sent her and a friend 'two very picturesque camels and camel drivers to sketch in the morning' and later that afternoon begged their acceptance as gifts.[27] Details on opium godowns (warehouses), formal balls, the jewels of rajahs, tent camps, city travel and life in the country occupy her. Everywhere is luxury amid poverty: 'the throne [of the Prince of Lucknow] is gold, with its canopy and umbrella and pillars covered with cloth of gold, embroidered in pearls and small rubies. Our fat friend the prince was dressed to match his throne . . . and there were jugglers and nautch-girls and musicians, all working at their vocations during breakfast.'[28]

More than a travelogue, however, *Up the Country* provides moments of insight and concern about time, journeying and the future. Writing on 10 December 1838, Eden provides this remarkable self-assessment:

> I never know exactly where we are in our story, for I keep so many anniversaries it puts me out. So many people have married, and died, and gone home, that it is really incredible that we should have been here so long, and yet are kept here still. Something must be done about it, because it is a very good joke; but life is passing away and we are in the wrong place.[29]

The vividness of the feeling as well as language, plus the convention of letters written to a sister, may have given Stoppard a clue for the structure he would follow in both the radio and stage versions of the play. The passage which concludes both versions, referring to the Queen's ball in Simla on 25 May 1839, is taken from Volume II of Eden's diary and summarizes her surprise that the Indians 'do not cut all our heads off and say nothing more about it'.[30] The following passage, for 26 May 1839, begins: 'the aides de camp are about as much trouble to me as so many grown-up sons. That sedate Captain P. followed me to my room after breakfast, and thought it right to mention that he had proposed to Miss S. on Thursday, and had been accepted', but he no sooner leaves than another officer visits her with *his* love tale.[31] The persistent admiration of soldiers and others also became a theme in the life of Flora Crewe, Stoppard's poet.

Despite the rich history in the Eden diary, Stoppard discarded most of it for the character of Flora, becoming 'more wrapped up in my characters than in previous plays, particularly Mrs. Swan and her feelings for her elder sister [Flora]'.[32] He also spent a fair amount of time writing Flora's poetry. The play, he explained, 'began as odd pages, dialogue and stuff. I kept trying to find what play they belonged to ... then I found the idea of her poetry so perversely enjoyable I went on writing her poetry far longer than you'd believe.'[33] Dedicated to Felicity Kendal, it is itself a kind of poem to her and their respective Indian pasts, dealing with feelings, love and art. *Indian Ink* would be dedicated to the memory of Laura Kendal, Felicity's mother.

Stoppard spent the five days it took to record the play in January 1991 in the studio with John Tydeman, the director. He spent half the time listening to the actors and the other half reading Peter Ackroyd's massive new biography of Dickens. He liked to hear what the actors did with his script at first and then made polite suggestions to the director and actors such as 'Do you mind if I change that word?' He interrupted to correct emphases, as when he asked Kendal to put more emotional weight on the word 'mangrove' in the erotic poem spoken by the heroine which opens scene sixteen of the play: it's 'not there entirely accidentally. It has a gender connotation too,' he intimated.[34]

There was one awkward incident with Dame Peggy Ashcroft. Ashcroft arrived believing that she would also be playing her character in an important flashback scene. But the voice of a twenty-three-year-old was clearly outside the range of the eighty-plus actress. But 'that's the chief reason I accepted the role,' she snapped. 'Besides, this is radio. The audience won't see me.' She tried and, while emotionally right, her voice was not. Stoppard took her aside and gallantly explained that he originally conceived the character of the younger Mrs Swan as someone totally different from the eighty-year-old she had become. Ashcroft cried – but then brightened, laughed and philosophically said: 'Ah well! It was worth trying.'[35] Between the recording and the broadcast in April, Peggy Ashcroft died; this was her last acting performance.

Ashcroft featured in a mini-controversy regarding Stoppard and Kendal. One of the publicity shots for the production, reproduced in the tabloid *Today,* showed Ashcroft standing between Stoppard and Kendal. The journal hailed the photo as the first picture of the couple together since they had denied rumours of a relationship. The production team at the BBC thought the treatment of the photo in bad taste, one adding that it made Peggy Ashcroft look like a female Pandarus. Kendal was at the time starring in a West End play, *Hidden Lives* (for which she won the *Evening Standard*'s best actress award), about a career woman with a crumbling marriage. A month after the taping of *In the Native State*, in February 1991, Kendal's divorce from Rudman became official; Stoppard's divorce from Miriam would not come through until February 1992.

Rasa, an ancient Sanskrit term, is perhaps the key concept of *In the Native State* and expresses the love possibly, or possibly not, consummated between Das, the Indian painter, and Flora Crewe. Das explains that *Rasa* is 'juice. It's taste. It's essence . . . *Rasa* is what you must feel when you see a painting, or hear music; it is the emotion which the artist must arouse in you', a state of heightened awareness or delight.[36] Originating with the early writer Bharata, *Rasa* has nine specific sentiments, from *shingara*, the erotic, to *adbhuta*, the wondrous. Stoppard discovered *Rasa* accidentally. Early for an appointment one afternoon in London, he was browsing through a Charing Cross bookshop when he came upon a book on Indian art that described the various kinds of *Rasa* with their corresponding colours and deities:

> It's quite alarming how casually one trawls the ocean for things that end up important in one's work. I wasn't engaged in a systematic search, [*Rasa*] wasn't something I would have inevitably come across ... This is my new system. I just blindly stumble forward, relying on destiny to bring me what I need. I'm completely shameless that way. I just grab what I need while I'm working on it.[37]

In the play, the exchange of *Rasa* between Das and Flora creates tension and danger, since an Anglo-Indian relationship was forbidden; the existence of the nude miniature of Flora suggests an affair, though it is inconclusive. The painting definitely possesses *Rasa*, the means for the emotions to harmonize and a condition Flora constantly desires. Her personal quest, set against the multiple perspectives of a Hindu painter, an Indian rajah, a British captain, an eager American scholar and the reminiscences of her sister in England sixty years later and of the painter's son, Anish, create an absorbing work that questions the Empire, love and the nature of both painting and poetry.

But Stoppard does not sacrifice the comic; it's present not only through the repartee and misunderstandings between Das and Flora, but through the curious blend of Anglo-Indian phrases known as 'Hobson-Jobson'. Soon the two hold a contest to demonstrate how many pseudo-dialect words they can cram into one sentence. Flora manages: 'I went doolally at the durbar and was sent back to Blighty in a dooley feeling rather dikki with a cup of char and a chit for a chotapeg.'[38] And for comic contrast, there is the intrusive drawl of Eldon Pike, Stoppard's parody of an academic. Mrs Swan, Flora's sister, complains about the footnotes in Pike's edition of *The Selected Letters of Flora Crewe*, 'far too much of a good thing ... to be constantly interrupted in a Southern drawl by someone telling you things you already know or don't need to know at that moment. I hear Mr Pike's voice every time I go to the bits at the bottom of the page.'[39]

Pike's voice-overs form a contrasting commentary on Flora's actions, providing chapter and verse for her allusions and references, eliminating the romance of her actions. When Stoppard revised the radio play for the stage and retitled it *Indian Ink*, Pike became a biographer as well as an editor, present on stage. In the radio play, his role permits various internal time shifts to occur, so that when he footnotes one of her letters, Stoppard's stage directions re-create that scene: '*Flora's letter becomes an immediate presence – we can hear her pen scratching now and then, and insects, distant life, etc. – but when her letter takes us into an event, the sound-plot turns into the appropriate accompaniment.*'[40]

This India is cemented to a colonial past: 'they read the *New Statesman* and *Time and Tide* and the *TLS* as if they were the Bible in parts,' Flora exclaims to her sister with surprise.[41] The import of these scenes is to show cause *after* effect; so, for example, we witness her lecture and original meeting with Das long after we have seen them together.

The politics of empire is kept remarkably low-key throughout the work and characteristically Stoppardian: distant, amusing, and not terrifically shattering. While Das tries to rally Flora's sensibility to matters of Indian culture and identity, she is dismissive, even with the ideas of Joshua Chamberlain, whose lectures on political theory in Jummapur 'caused the Theosophical Society to be suspended for one year'. All Flora can offer is an open mind: 'Political theories are often, and perhaps entirely, a function of temperament.'[42] Nevertheless, she repeatedly attempts to stop Das being a stereotypical Indian, parroting Anglo-Indian views. But perhaps it is all England's fault for having robbed India of its culture: 'The bloody Empire finished off Indian painting! . . . The women here wear saris made in Lancashire.'[43] An angry Flora responds by pointing out that India accepted and even emulated the Empire and that that was its downfall: 'you *are* an Indian artist, aren't you? Stick up for yourself,' she tells him.[44]

Combining the views of Emily Eden with various histories and his own sense of India, plus the likely recollections of Felicity Kendal, *In the Native State* successfully renders the British attitude and experience of the country through the personality of a poet that is equally affective and moving. Flora Crewe, with her unfulfilled desire, is one of Stoppard's most successful and impassioned women.

Stoppard did not go back to India to research the play. In a characteristic move, he returned to India and Darjeeling only *after* the play was done (cause following effect again). Needing snapshots for his visa, he mused with an interviewer – they were lunching at the Ritz because of another engagement Stoppard had there later that day – whether or not a camera might be at hand: 'Perhaps the Ritz has got a photographer, and I'll have this unique picture of a man with a champagne glass leering into the camera with waiters in the background.' The pair discovered Margaret Thatcher was lunching just a few feet away. After her departure, the interviewer remarked on the apparent lack of security and the possibility of an assassination attempt, to which Stoppard replied, 'In her case I would seriously consider throwing myself in the path of the bullet.' Why the heroism? 'I am susceptible to very beautiful women,' he replied, rapidly undercutting his remark by saying, 'this is a ridiculous interview, and I am going to regret every word I say.' He then suggested a system of alternative typefaces to indicate in print whether people were being indiscreet or jokey.[45]

Stoppard's support of Mrs Thatcher occasionally got him into trouble, especially with the left. He tried repeatedly to clarify it by indicating that he valued what she brought to politics when she first arrived, but after she sent a congratulatory twenty-first birthday message to the tabloid *Sun* and the social consequences of her economic policy became more evident, he altered his view. But in 1993, he explained why he originally liked her and liked her still:

> She restored a kind of credibility to politics . . . I was absolutely tremendously pleased by Mrs Thatcher not because of what she espoused but because she seemed to have either a strange innocence about what was sayable or a strange courage about what ought to be said.[46]

Three important articles about his youth resulted from Stoppard's visit to India.[47] Details and memories of his life in Darjeeling from his earliest days at school to his mother's occupation as manager of the Bat'a shoe store in the hill town fill the texts. Writing *In the Native State* initiated an unusual period of retrospection for Stoppard. Rewriting the radio play as a stage drama, *Indian Ink*, extended his fascination with the country, expanded by a short return visit to India in the winter of 1998–9. Stoppard's unexpected 1994 encounter with a young relative in a Prague hotel and trips to Zlín in 1998 and 1999 continued his almost inescapable recovery of the past.

For Stoppard, art has directed his life: only after writing *In the Native State* did he feel ready to return to India. From that period on, from roughly 1988 to the present, he has been moving in a slow, gliding arc back to his origins, probing, observing and addressing the issues that such a return might raise. It was hardly an accident that *Arcadia* would consider questions of the past through its transparent structure of a divided time-frame, further concentrated in *The Invention of Love* through the convention of the older and younger Housman.

> *I don't trust writers who wax confidently about what they do*
> *and why they do it.*
>
> Stoppard, 1992

Early in May 1991, Stoppard went to see Molière's *The Miser* at the National Theatre, directed by Steven Pimlott. He loved it and began to think about theatre again rather than the movies, although he had a contract with Universal to direct his next original work for the screen. 'I started wishing I had a play which Richard Eyre would like. I began to get itchy. I thought that this was the place I wanted to be. But that's the trouble, I want to be everywhere.'[48] This itchiness would result in his next two plays for the National: the smash hit *Arcadia,* directed by Trevor Nunn, and the erudite but magnificently acted *The Invention of Love,* to be directed by Richard Eyre.

During the spring of 1991, Stoppard was working on the film script of E. L. Doctorow's *Billy Bathgate.* His screenplay of *The Russia House* opened in February to good reviews and he recalled that his meetings with Connery were not tense but 'cordial', despite their disagreement over filming *Rosencrantz and Guildenstern.* Even le Carré was pleased with the result, and its success meant that Stoppard received a sizeable percentage of the profits as well as his fee.

Billy Bathgate was more characteristically a Hollywood story. Stoppard wrote the screenplay for Touchstone Pictures before the director, Robert Benton, who had filmed *Kramer vs. Kramer,* was selected. Hollywood insiders predicted that the film would be a disaster since the shooting schedule had to be extended, personality clashes were reported and a new ending was shot. Stoppard met Benton once and the director said he was happy with the screenplay, which accurately reflected the novel, although it dropped the comic presence of Billy Bathgate's first-person commentary. Stoppard did not hear from Benton after this meeting and did not visit the set since he was not invited. He understood changes had been made to the script, but he was not consulted. Benton never contacted him and left out several speeches, which Stoppard, piqued, vowed to use in another film, although he never did.

Another film project at this time was *Schindler's List*. Spielberg asked Stoppard to do some script edits to the screenplay by Thomas Keneally, author of the novel, and Steven Zaillian. They consisted of modest, individual dialogue changes and suggestions for one or two transitions, such as the arrival at the Kraków train station of various prisoners from rural areas and a shot of a grey stripe stamped across a registration card with the stripe then bleeding into a bright yellow ink with the title 'Sept 1939'. Stoppard appears to have revised an important episode covering pages 120 to 180 in draft, titled 'SSL 154', when Schindler discusses with his assistant, Stern, the preferential treatment of Jews destined for his factory. 'I collect Jews,' he states at one point, articulating his new resolve and control of his factory. This moment and others in the script show Stoppard re-ordering scenes, as well as dialogue. He added a new scene, Schindler walking in a cemetery with a priest and remarking that these are not suicides but 'victims of a great murder'. Among the script pages in the Stoppard archive is Schindler's speech before the guards and workers as the surrender is announced: 'You have survived. Some of you have come up to me and thanked me. Thank yourselves (and turning to the guards), thank *you*.' The scene with a young girl presenting Schindler a ring inscribed with a saying from the Talmud – 'Whoever saves one life saves the world' – follows.[49] The direct impact of these scenes, written or revised by Stoppard, was to show a more poignant and a more detached Schindler, creating greater ambiguity in his characterization.

A month after the broadcast of *In the Native State*, Stoppard went to Prague, where *Travesties* was being performed at the Realisticke

Theatre in a translation by President Havel's press secretary. Havel himself attended, his secretary acting as Stoppard's translator. 'After a party I was given a lift home by the lord mayor of Prague, who is the translator of *Hapgood* and *Rosencrantz*,' Stoppard reported. He met a further establishment figure who had translated *Lord Malquist and Mr. Moon*. The effect was stimulating because, remarkably, the outsiders – the translators, literary types, intellectuals – were now in command of the ship of state: 'The people in steerage [former political dissidents] are not actually chained to the bilges. It was quite exhilarating.'

The day after the performance, Stoppard was taken to the presidential palace to observe Havel inspecting the palace guard, resplendent in newly designed uniforms chosen by a friend of Havel's who had won an Oscar for the costumes in *Amadeus*. 'In a curious way, *Travesties* itself was the most earthbound experience, because there were other things that were so much more dramatic and exaggerated.'[50] The 1991 palace visit made him feel as though he were in a play 'and all you had to do was write it. Except that I would be writing his [Havel's] play, instead of mine.' 'Actually,' he continued, 'in Prague I felt I was in a play by Dürrenmatt, because the people holding the reins of power had no sense that they were connected to the rooms they were inhabiting. The minister of defence was actually a literary critic, I think. But he looked every inch a minister of defence. Perfect casting I thought.'[51]

Stoppard refused to see any symmetry in his return to the Czech Republic: 'I am not that way inclined. I don't stand gasping at the wonderful emotional symmetry of my life ... I am aware of the implied ironies, but in a detached sort of way ... when I went to Prague in 1977, there was no sense of going back, just of going to another interesting country and situation.' The important change was seeing Havel: when he first met him in 1977, he was between prison sentences, with fear and suspicion hovering everywhere; this time, he was installed in the presidential palace. Ironically, Stoppard's distanced view of the importance of the Czech Republic would change when he returned in 1994 and again in 1998 and 1999, in search of his Jewish past.

Throughout this period, Stoppard always kept a note of the Jewish holidays. His appointment books indicate the specific days for Rosh Hashana or Yom Kippur, not necessarily out of observance but out of his secretary's concern that he and Miriam and the boys knew.

Although he was indifferent to his Judaism, he was not unaware of its cycles and rituals, if only in broad terms. Such codes, recorded in his diaries, form a type of identity-mapping which over the next several years would lead back to his Czech past and a desire to know his background more thoroughly. Stoppard gradually realized the need to go beyond invention to history.

At the end of 1991, Stoppard was maintaining his involvement with politics and human rights. In mid-November, he participated in the twenty-four-hour vigil in support of Salman Rushdie which marked his thousandth day under a death threat. As one of the three vice-presidents of PEN, Stoppard delivered a letter to 10 Downing Street on the Rushdie affair, accompanied by William Cooper and A. S. Byatt.

By his own standards, Stoppard admitted that the Thatcherite decade was 'leanish'. After his hit *The Real Thing* in 1982, his Molnár adaptation, *Rough Crossing,* encountered rocky seas, while *Hapgood,* despite its respectable run at the Aldwych, was hardly a critical success. Its revised Los Angeles version never made it to New York. But the nineties began with a success, *In the Native State,* and he would quickly move on to a triumph, *Arcadia.* He was evolving, moving in new directions and overcoming what Michael Billington referred to as the defects of his virtues, exposing the emotional foundations of his intellectual superstructures. *Rasa,* 'the emotion which the artist must arouse in you', would permeate his work for the next ten years.[52]

CHAPTER 17

THE CLASSIC ROMANTIC: SHAKESPEARE IN LOVE

―――――

*Playwrights teach nothing about love, they make it pretty,
they make it comical or they make it lust. They cannot make
it true.*

Stoppard, *Shakespeare in Love*

Love, truthful or otherwise, artistic or personal, shaped Stoppard's life in the late eighties and early nineties. A conflict had long been at the heart of Stoppard's work, between subjectivity and objectivity, personality and knowledge. Stoppard characteristically supported both views, as his early works *Artist Descending a Staircase* and *Travesties* demonstrated. But now, at the beginning of the nineties, he again questioned their values, starting with *In the Native State,* and then more fully in *Arcadia* and *Indian Ink.* Coinciding with this debate and its dramatization were personal matters that challenged his own sense of convention and the past.

In late February 1991, after Kendal's divorce papers came through, journalists again pursued her and Stoppard, suggesting that they would soon marry. When Stoppard's own divorce from Miriam was finalized exactly a year later, many were convinced a celebrity ceremony must be imminent. It didn't happen, possibly because they feared it might disrupt their professional lives, although they chose to lead a life together marked by frequent appearances at openings, galas and festivals. Publicity followed them, although they often tried to avoid it. Even friends were not sure they were still together at times, one telling Nigel Dempster that 'basically they can't live with each other, but they don't want to live without each other'. An entry in Stoppard's daybook for early December 1991, referring to Iver Grove, marks his detachment from the past in a neutral tone; it reads 'Sort out & Split up house'.[1]

Miriam took refuge, as she always had, in work. Her public image demanded it, as well as her role as 'the doyenne of do-it-yourself well-being', as one writer phrased it. She had written a long list of self-help and health books, and spent almost two decades presenting programmes with titles like *Don't Ask Me, Don't Just Sit There* and *So You Want to Stop Smoking*. In 1991 she achieved a new coup, being selected by the BBC to host a live morning news and chat programme originating in Manchester called *People Today*. Gracious, personable, commanding, there was nevertheless 'a flinty undertone to the charm designed to keep people on their toes'.[2] Yet she was also emotional and prone to crying in public, although one observer noted that 'there is a controlled, positively Thatcheresque quality about even her crying'. She cried when presenting her first television series, the health show, *Where There's Life*, especially when the handicapped or terminally ill were discussed; at the Jewish Care's Women of Distinction luncheon in November 1990; and at the plight of her younger sister, a comprehensive schoolteacher. 'I'm both soft and tough,' she explained: 'that's not extraordinary – that's how most women are. It's just that I own up to both sides.' Yet she told a newspaper reporter that she had decided not to take her make-up off at night because she thought it unseemly that her husband should see her without benefit of cosmetics. She later defended herself by saying make-up was not bad for your skin. 'You don't *need* to wash it off at night. My point was a medical one.'[3]

The public, however, was not always sympathetic. The super-achieving Stoppards possessed a knack 'for getting up people's noses', one writer unflatteringly wrote.[4] When Stoppard decamped, empathy was tempered for those who thought the superwoman had received her comeuppance. Constant stories of their lifestyle, success and triumphs created just a touch of public cynicism when the scandal went public. Miriam herself was aware of this and by early October 1991 she was seeking to change her profile from the energetic over-achiever, trying too hard and offering smug how-to-do-it advice. A streamlined figure with newly lightened auburn hair in an upswept style (reminiscent of Felicity Kendal, one wag pointed out) greeted a visitor in a Mayfair hotel where she conducted interviews. A week before she was to start her BBC news programme, she exuded confidence and good looks as she prepared to challenge the reigning

ITV morning programme, *This Morning*. A year into her separation from Stoppard, she defended him, telling the guest 'I will hear nothing bad about Tom. I would hate him to be upset.' Noting that the family still gathered at Iver Grove at weekends, she nevertheless admitted that her life 'is full of pauses'. Off-handedly, she says she doesn't work for the money, but 'because the process of working makes you feel secure'.[5] Her new, slimmer figure is not the result of her break-up, but due to her schedule, which often limits her eating. She admires the reaction of her children to the separation, praising their astuteness and balance. She admits that a *rapprochement* with Stoppard would be unlikely, but optimistically believes that things will work out for the better.

Two years later, she was proven right, reporting that her new relationship with Sir Christopher Hogg, former chairman of Courtaulds, non-executive chairman of Reuters and then a director of the Bank of England, was perfect. Their interests in business and fitness established common bonds, but more importantly, he provided a calmness for her, accentuating a need to be more reflective and tranquil. There was no pressure or drive to succeed, she explained in 1993. The 'chatelaine of a Palladian mansion, tireless campaigner on health issues, TV presenter, . . . author and glamorous wife' had changed. She expressed her style in this *bon mot*: 'The only difference between me and other people is I don't like vacuums. If there is an empty hour I fill it with work.'[6] Acknowledging that she was back at her desk five days after her first son was born and seven days after her second, she now saw how unnatural such a drive was and what its cost must have been. All it represented, she mused, was an 'awful dissatisfaction . . . that constant kind of striving'.[7]

Along with this new, relaxed and certainly satisfied self, came more praise for her former husband. 'Without his [Stoppard's] encouragement I wouldn't have done television, I wouldn't have written books, I probably wouldn't have persisted in industry':

> When I first met Tom, I had a feeling of inferiority. I felt like a fish out of water, I suppose. I didn't feel I had any place among the literati and glitterati, I was insecure. I remember asking him which women he admired most. He named a few, writers and businesswomen; the sort of woman that I later became . . . the more I did, the more he approved

and the happier he was . . .Tom likes women who are independent, who can take care of themselves and have lives of their own. He *likes* working women. He likes to be left alone.

His approval of her various ventures was fundamental to Miriam's success, which had been defined by work because, she explained, 'work has been the source of more controllable happiness than anything else'. Admitting that she was not the perfect mother because she put work above family, she credits Stoppard for the children's well-being: 'the children didn't suffer because Tom is a wonderful father . . . my regrets now are all to do with not being there with the children'. Yet she married a man 'who just loved blue stockings and encouraged me in spades. It was a repetition of the pattern with my parents', that is, working hard to gain her husband's love and approval as she had done with her parents.[8]

She maintained her allegiance to Stoppard. In early May 1993, she went with friends to see his latest hit, *Arcadia,* starring Kendal, and she took aim at carping reviews of his work: 'there's only one line they take on Tom – and that's *snide.*' She claimed she didn't feel any rejection, rationalizing Stoppard's actions by saying 'of all the things one can't help, one certainly cannot help falling in love. I don't disapprove of that.' No longer bitter, she stressed her own regrets and mistakes and the importance of Stoppard in her life. On the clarity of his plays, she reported that 'Tom used to say occasionally: "Now you're a typical member of the audience; what does *this* mean to you?" And I'd get it right only 50 per cent of the time.'[9] She declared a new happiness in the spring of 1993 and a change in emphasis in her life. For the first time in years, she had no television series. Her more patient attitude meant she had given up the urge to drive herself and be in control, and she had become a more sympathetic individual. Stoppard, by contrast, seemed as driven as ever, working on three new plays in the period from 1991 to 1995.

The papers would not let up. In November 1992, one headline read: 'Stoppard seals love for Felicity with a starring role', hyping the part she would play in *Arcadia*. The column, however, focused not on the play but a sighting of Kendal with her former husband. The two had attended a charity première. But the next day she and Stoppard attended a champagne supper party in London to celebrate the thirty-year partnership of Merchant–Ivory and 'they seemed extremely happy – and affectionate towards each other'.[10]

Stoppard was diverted by other projects, notably a 'pre-production polish' on Richard Attenborough's film *Chaplin*. The script's history was murky, beginning with an original version by Bryan Forbes that was tossed aside when Attenborough and his co-producer, Diana Hawkins, hired William Boyd. He worked on a new script over the next seven months, only to learn that five weeks before principal photography was to begin, the studio and Attenborough thought Stoppard should take a look. In March 1991, Attenborough called on Stoppard, who revised certain parts; the studio, however, pulled out, to be replaced by an independent film company who wanted further revisions, notably the addition of Chaplin's years in exile in Switzerland. They hired William Goldman to write the extra scenes. The arbitrated screen credits list Boyd, Forbes and Goldman. Stoppard was uncredited.[11]

Another film project hit a roadblock: in early November 1992, the original production of *Shakespeare in Love* stalled. Stoppard became involved with the script in 1991, approached by Universal Studios to review the version by Marc Norman. The film was originally to be an American production with American actors; Ed Zwick, whose credits included *Legends of the Fall*, *Glory* and *The Siege*, was to direct. Norman was a veteran Hollywood scriptwriter of more than twenty years' standing: his productions included *Cutthroat Island* and *Waterworld*. The screenplay originated in 1988, when Zackeray Norman, the screenwriter's son, called his father from Boston, where he was taking a theatre course, and suggested a film about the young Will Shakespeare, inspired by a torrid love affair to pen his first romantic tragedy, *Romeo and Juliet*. After a while, Norman consulted Zwick and they pitched the idea to Universal, who gave them the go-ahead; they would also be the film's producers.

The original idea was that Shakespeare was starved of attention, love and work. Norman imagined Shakespeare speaking American street lingo, but that didn't work, and Norman lacked the background or knowledge to set the film in the Elizabethan period. He turned to an expert, Professor Stephen Greenblatt, then at Berkeley, to confirm that his approach to Shakespeare's life had merit. Greenblatt graciously agreed, even with the notion that if Shakespeare were alive today he would be a screenwriter.[12]

The completed script went to Universal in 1991 and they called in Stoppard to make it more Shakespearean. At first he hesitated, fearing that he would be going over old ground again and would be typecast as 'that writer of Shakespeare'. What interested him, however, was the opening scene of Shakespeare practising his signature to break his writer's block. Norman's page struck Stoppard with the kind of tone and humour he extended to the script as a whole, with details like a Shakespeare mug from Stratford-upon-Avon that appears in the opening scene. The aim, Stoppard later explained, was to show Will Shakespeare not as an icon but as 'a feisty young man who's a genius but isn't treated like a genius'.[13] Without the need for historical accuracy, Stoppard could be free to invent the past as he had done so often, beginning with *Rosencrantz and Guildenstern* and then in *Travesties* and *The Invention of Love*. His approach to the past was that 'all supposed historical truths are temporary, meaning they're always there to be modified in the light of subsequent discoveries'.[14]

The original version was quite different from the finished shooting script. The heroine was named Belinda, not Viola, and the movie began with dogs quarrelling over rubbish in front of the Rose Theatre's stage. A victorious dog leaps on to the stage, knocking over an easel with a torn placard that reads 'The Admiral's Men . . . the Lamentable Tragedy of . . . the Robert Reveng'd'. The opening words of the film are Fennyman's to Henslowe, whose feet are in the fire: 'You dog! Why do you howl when it is I who am bitten?' (in the finished script, this begins 'You mongrel!'). In this draft, Shakespeare's play is called 'Romeo and Ethel, The Bandit's Daughter' and contains an equal number of detailed comic moments – such as Shakespeare rushing through the streets of London, overhearing the preacher Makepeace speaking in a jumble of Shakespearean lines; he pulls out his quill, dips it in a vial of ink he carrys in a bag attached to his belt and makes a note on the cuff of his shirt (in the film, he is shown merely pausing to make a mental note).

Another comic moment occurs when Henslowe walks into a tavern and passes Thomas Nashe and John Lyly, two arguing scholars – 'If Augustine was a neoplatonist I'm a water spaniel.' He then passes a producer and a writer:

Producer   . . . just needs a polish – more heart – a few jokes – different ending – you can do it.

Writer   Ask Ellison.

Producer   He wrote it.[15]

Other elements that mark the literary character of this draft, toned down in the final version, include Lord Wessex purchasing a pamphlet – sold like an evening paper – from the young John Webster, with the headline, 'Famous writer done to death! Horrible murder!' and a woodcut of Marlowe's murder in the Deptford Tavern, and Will stopping before a poster announcing the play which reads:

Romeo and Juliet
with Mr. Fennyman as the Apothecary

Will takes out his 'loaded quill' and starts to write underneath this, 'by W. Sha . . .'[16] One comic exchange remained: when Ned Alleyn tells Will that Marlowe died not because he was thought to be Will but in a fight over a tavern bill, Henslowe bursts in with 'The bill! Oh vanity, vanity!' Alleyn responds, 'Not the billing, the bill!'[17]

    This draft ends with Queen Elizabeth splashing through the puddle, while her courtiers try to undo their capes and she mutters, 'too late, too late'; we then cut to an interior of the theatre with Wessex claiming Belinda as his wife. She departs, stops to look back at Will, who steps towards her but is detained by Burbage. Suddenly, four men approach Henslowe from the audience, one with a manuscript. Henslowe recognizes them: 'Ah, Mr. Lyly, Mr. Nash, Mr. Chapman, Mr. Dekker. I hear you have a play,' he says, as the Renaissance dramatists materialise.[18]

    The next scene takes place outside the theatre. Will and Burbage are besieged by a dozen would-be Juliets, who have overheard the pair say they need a new actress. Taking command, Burbage announces auditions in an hour and then turns to tell Will that 'the Master of the Revels requests a comedy after Christmas, for Twelfth Night'. (Queen Elizabeth makes this request in the finished film.) Will answers 'Yes. A comedy,' and the stage directions read 'He clasps Burbage on the shoulder and the two of them go back to the Curtain like Bogart and Rains at the end of "Casablanca".'[19] Will's voice-over offers a synopsis of what will be *Twelfth Night*. In the epilogue to this, the second draft of the film, there is a storm and Belinda washes ashore. She wakes up and meets a sailor who has with him a native, 'painted and almost naked'. She asks where she is and the answer the sailor offers is 'America'. The final words are Belinda's: 'America! Well, good.'[20]

Julia Roberts signed up after looking at the revised script and Universal forwarded $4.5 million for pre-production as the cast and crew moved to England: once Stoppard had transformed the words, it had to become an English production to sustain its authenticity. Filming was to begin at Pinewood Studios. Roberts, however, insisted on working with Daniel Day Lewis, star of *My Beautiful Laundrette* and *A Room with a View* and winner of the 1989 Best Actor Oscar for *My Left Foot*; according to the papers, another source of her interest was a possible romance between the two. But he declined, even after Roberts flew to his home in Ireland to persuade him. Roberts, also unhappy working with Ed Zwick, considered Ralph Fiennes, Colin Firth and Paul McGann as possible co-stars but found all of them inferior. She pulled out, shutting down the set on 20 October 1992, causing consternation in the British film industry since it was a big-budget project involving a crew of more than two hundred. 'Julia jilts the Bard', read one headline.[21] Other studios soon expressed interest, but Universal insisted that they be reimbursed the $4.5 million advanced out of a total production budget of $25 million. Most backed out because the up-front costs were too high for a movie many thought would be only a modest hit, appealing to an older crowd.

Norman and Zwick continued to search for a new Belinda and Shakespeare. They approached Winona Ryder, Jodie Foster and Meg Ryan. Ryder was the keenest but terms could not be worked out. Gwyneth Paltrow came on board, supposedly after she saw the script while house-sitting at Ryder's apartment and immediately called her agent. No Shakespeare had yet materialized, although at one point Mel Gibson was interested, but wanted his own production company to rewrite the part to reflect a mid-life crisis. Norman objected and the script sat around until Harvey Weinstein of Miramax appeared.

Weinstein loved the script so much that he paid off the $4.5 million to Universal but demanded the picture be made his way. That meant replacing Zwick with his choice, the British director John Madden who had scored a hit with *Mrs Brown*. Weinstein also wanted Paltrow, who had been in *Sliding Doors* and *A Perfect Murder*, plus other Miramax films, for the female lead. She insisted on a role for her then boyfriend, Ben Affleck. Weinstein agreed and Affleck took the part of Ned Alleyn. But the movie, still to be made in England, needed more theatrical in-jokes, caricatures and *doubles entendres* and so Stoppard was called in again, supplying these features and more, even admitting to stealing a 400-year-old gag attributed to the first actor to play the gravedigger in *Hamlet*. He also modernized the dialogue, mixing verse with modern speech, low comedy with high passion. He introduced several secondary characters, as well as Christopher Marlowe, Shakespeare's rival. Apparently Stoppard also had a hand in persuading Rupert Everett to play the part, but when he first agreed, Everett asked that his name should not be included in the credits because he thought the movie had little chance of being a hit.

Stoppard did his usual research for the film, reading a number of studies on Shakespeare's life and the situation of theatre owners and buildings in London. At the time, the foundations of the Rose Theatre in London, where Shakespeare's early plays were performed, had just been discovered and he visited the site. The scale of the theatre surprised him. One of the early issues in revising the script was how Shakespeare would speak. Would he sound like Shakespeare the great writer or like a youthful, ink-stained hack? Stoppard resolved the problem by giving him a line from Act Two, Scene Two of *Hamlet* as his first line of dialogue and then slipping into modern syntax: 'Doubt thou the stars are fire, doubt that the earth doth move . . .', to which Henslowe, the producer, curtly replies: 'No, no, we haven't the time. Talk prose. Where is my play?'[22]

Stoppard also added some mischief, maintaining his playful references to Boot and Chamberlain, this time within the same paragraph. Early in the film, Henslowe, accompanying Will, anxiously tells him, 'Well, I am a dead man and buggered to boot. My theatre is closed by the plague these twelve weeks, my company is playing the inn-yards of England, while Burbage and the Chamberlain's Men are invited to court.'[23] Other antics include Will telling Marlowe that he loves his early work, then spitting out the title of his new, yet to be written play, *Romeo and Ethel, the Pirate's Daughter*.[24] Marlowe offers Will suggestions for the plot:

Marlowe	Romeo is . . . Italian. Always in and out of love.
Will	Yes, that's good. Until he meets –
Marlowe	Ethel.
Will	Do you think?
Marlowe	The daughter of his enemy.
Will (*thoughtfully*)	The daughter of his enemy.[25]

In this work, even the boatman rowing Will down the Thames to Viola de Lesseps's mansion is an aspiring writer who offers up his memoirs in manuscript: 'It wouldn't take you long to read it. I expect you know all the booksellers,' he pleads. In the tavern scene, Stoppard parodies an out-of-work Los Angeles actor when he offers the daily special of 'pig's foot marinated in juniper-berry vinegar served with a buckwheat pancake'.[26]

The final scenes are also Stoppard's, who, like Will, was frantically rewriting the ending virtually until shooting began. A romantic comedy in which the boy did not get the girl troubled many, yet 'the whole point was that the experience led him to write the greatest love tragedy of all time, not the greatest love comedy'. Instead of the final shots of the shipwreck and Gwyneth Paltrow on the beach, Stoppard had in mind 'a sort of ghostly Manhattan . . . as she walked off – but that was a ghostly skyscraper too far'.[27] Stoppard realized that the concluding shipwreck would set the tone for the next play Shakespeare would write, on command from Queen Elizabeth: 'tell Shakespeare something more cheerful next time, for Twelfth Night'.[28]

One Stoppardian change to the script was not accepted. It dealt with the playbill announcing the performance of *Romeo and Juliet*. It lists the producers, theatre managers, actors and title, but not the author. Stoppard wanted Shakespeare to go over and write his name in, as in the second draft of the film script, but Madden convinced him that the apparently doomed love affair would devastate Will and he would be in no mood to add his name. In the film, Will does not even glance at the poster when, distraught, he walks out of the theatre on his way to the boat dock and the home of Viola de Lesseps. Lovesickness over billing? 'I thought it a very poor reason,' Stoppard said.[29] The scene, however, comically confirms what Henslowe tells Fennyman early in the film when he barges in during a rehearsal at the Rose Theatre and asks the owner, pointing to Will, 'who is that?' 'Nobody. The author,' is the reply.[30] What Stoppard sought to show was that many things in the theatre were much the same then as they are today.[31]

Following one month's rehearsal for the principals, shooting took place in February and March 1998 in Surrey's Shepperton Studios, with a full-size replica of the Curtain, used by the Lord Chamberlain's Men. The set was later dismantled and presented to Judi Dench, to become part of a theatre school. With typical production logic, the last scene was shot first. One of the technical challenges was how to present realistic images of the Elizabethan period yet avoid a dark or sombre look, since interiors in that period were so underlit. The compromise was to make sure that the faces would always be well lit, the director of photography, Richard Greatrex explained. Similarly, the sets were always seen and did not disappear in the gloom, and, because the story was complex, it was necessary to maintain a simplicity in the way the film looks, while characters were separated from the background by the lighting. Shot in widescreen in order to capture the appropriate depth and yet maintain low light levels – period lighting was mostly candles or lanterns – it also met John Madden's requirement of a movable, flexible 'pick it up and run camera' which could not be achieved with an anamorphic set-up (differing magnification of the same image).[32]

One additional problem was the title. *Shakespeare in Love* was thought by studio executives to dissuade rather than invite viewers. Shakespeare, they argued, meant study, examinations and the classroom. They proposed *Thou Art My Girl*, and *How Should I Love Thee*, among others. In the end, the studio reluctantly went with the original, crossing their fingers. From its original screenings through to the Academy Awards, the movie was an international success.

Stoppard's interest in political causes did not abate. On 14 February 1992, he participated in a large gathering at Stationer's Hall, joining Nadine Gordimer, Martin Amis, Seamus Heaney and Derek Walcott in condemning the *fatwa* against Salman Rushdie. In a prepared speech, Stoppard expressed his outrage against the suppression of human rights. We are not writers closing ranks for literature, he said, nor is the issue free expression in writing. It was, rather, a matter of liberty and justice, and he quoted Isaiah Berlin. The issue was to question the premise and the rights assumed by the Iranian government. 'I have never been comfortable with the idea that words have a preferential status over and above the discomfort they may give others,' he declared.[33] Yet literature was not the only way to cause offence. Of course what had been done to Rushdie 'has been intrinsically unjust' and must be opposed, but writers should not be expected to do the job that statesmen should perform: seeing that such injustice be overturned. Such public gatherings had little immediate impact on the situation, but Stoppard felt it necessary to show his support.

Despite the backdrop of domestic turmoil, the period from 1993 to 1995 was a remarkable one for Stoppard. The preceding decade had seen his stock fall and he needed a hit. Not only did he have one with *Arcadia*, praised by the critics, public and prize-givers, but there was a successful revival of his work, beginning with *Travesties* produced by the RSC. It starred Antony Sher, played to sell-out houses in September 1993 (making Stoppard the only living playwright to have two major productions running simultaneously on the main stages of the National and the RSC) and transferred from the Barbican to the Savoy in the West End. The production ran until June 1994. *Arcadia* also transferred, to the Haymarket. Stoppard then had a smash in New York with the previously unsuccessful *Hapgood,* revised and improved, while *Indian Ink,* the rewritten *In the Native State,* would become a ten-month hit in the West End, opening at the Aldwych in February 1995, and running simultaneously with *Arcadia* at the Haymarket. On 14 December 1995, an immensely engaging revival of *Rosencrantz and Guildenstern* would open with Alan Howard and Simon Russell Beale at the National, topping off his successes.

But there was still concern over Stoppard's appeal, expressed by the West End producer Duncan Weldon (who oversaw the transfer of *Travesties* to the Savoy and co-produced *Arcadia* with Michael Codron when it moved to the Haymarket). The audiences for Stoppard's plays, even in the West End, he remarked, remained modest in comparison to those for the playwrights of forty years ago. At the Barbican, *Travesties* was seen by approximately 40,000 people and roughly the same number saw *Arcadia* at the National. Both figures would, of course, increase with their West End transfers. But 'in the old days, if Binkie Beaumont put on a new Rattigan or Coward, he could expect to do as much as two years at the Globe, and have an audience of half a million'.[34]

During this period, Stoppard also wrote the new narration for the Glyndebourne concert version of *The Merry Widow*, contributed several uncredited rewrites to *Schindler's List*, worked on a screenplay of Nicholas Mosley's novel, *Hopeful Monsters*, adapted Jerome K. Jerome's Victorian tale *Three Men in a Boat* for radio (he had previously adapted it for television in 1975 – and elements of it would appear in *The Invention of Love*) and drafted a full-length animated film version (unproduced) of *Cats*. Understandably, by February 1995 he could tell Mel Gussow that his 'version of retirement' would be 'to be a poet, by which I mean I don't want to stop work, because I love work, but my ideal form of retirement would be to spend six months on a poem, which I then wouldn't have to show anybody'.[35] Among all these shows, however, only one was an original work: *Arcadia*. In December 1995, he told a reporter that he was in the midst of a new work, though currently 'blocked'. This would become his 1997 hit, *The Invention of Love*.

At the beginning of this renewal, a debate over Stoppard persisted: was he a gifted dramatist who fulfilled Olivier's definition of the theatre as 'the first glamouriser of thought', or was he just a showman taking up Alfred Hitchcock's notion that theatre is just life with all the dull bits removed?[36] In the eleven years since *The Real Thing*, his output had been thin and he had missed his goal of a major new work by the age of fifty: all he had were a number of adaptations, a successful radio play and one original play, *Hapgood*, which left audiences and critics confused.

CHAPTER 18

BYRON IN A LAPTOP

*It's the best possible time to be alive, when almost everything
you thought you knew is wrong.*
Stoppard, *Arcadia*

When he turned to chaos theory as a metaphor in his first major play
since his experiment with quantum mechanics of 1988, *Hapgood,*
Stoppard gambled that those who disliked physics might nevertheless
be seduced by chaos. His reputation had suffered and several papers
were pointing out that he needed a hit. His own background in physics
was limited to half a term at Pocklington, aged thirteen, when he pored
over the textbook, attempting to catch up, and scored forty per cent,
enough to impress the teacher, although 'he did not realise that I had
managed this without any understanding of what was behind the
numbers or why'.[1]

This initiated a general interest in science, however, which took
form in his fascination with the moon landings (in *Another Moon
called Earth*) and then shifted to mathematics, Galileo, geometry (in
Every Good Boy) and, finally, Heisenbergean physics with *Hapgood.*
The failure of that work didn't deter him. Hugh Whitemore's 1986
play, *Breaking the Code,* made him want to find out more about Alan
Turing. *Shadow Makers,* a 1989 film about the Los Alamos atom bomb,
furthered his interest. His disappointment with the lack of actual
scientific explanation in the film was exceeded by his unhappiness with
the oversimplification that characterized the work. In addition to the
concerns of *Hapgood* and *Arcadia,* he continued to improve an unproduced film script for Paramount about physics, based on Nicholas
Moseley's novel, *Hopeful Monsters.*

When asked to explain his interest in science, Stoppard had no clear-cut answer. He had always been intrigued by science and maths and enjoyed reading about them, although he admitted that 'the relationship between a mathematical or scientific idea and drama may not really exist legitimately'. Beckett was in some ways a model: he, too, was fascinated by mathematics and the paradoxes it generated, using them to structure his plays. Stoppard forced the union of science and drama 'to gratify on one hand my own interest and tastes and on the other hand my profession'. Such concerns coalesced in his 'discovery' of chaos theory.

In an interview in the *Irish Times*, Stoppard remarked that the first germ of the new play came in the 1980s, when he read Peter Quennell's book on Byron, but that he always begins with an idea, an 'intellectual idea. The characters come at what is really a second or third stage. They happen when I find the story to contain the things which I want to write about.'[2] In another comment, he noted that various ideas joined together and the issue was to establish a balance between the improbable concepts: chaos theory seemed a bit too abstract and unmanageable, 'so where I really kicked off was the classification between the classical and Romantic temperaments, or classical and Romantic anything else – which was mirrored by developing tastes in landscape gardening, with the Lord Byron theme emerging as a knock-on from that.'[3]

Another nineteenth-century source was Thomas Love Peacock. In the play, set in the Romantic and modern periods, a pretentious academic named Bernard, tracing the mysterious actions of Byron, uses the name Peacock (also, coincidentally, Ken Tynan's middle name) to disguise himself from a popular novelist he has slammed in the press who is also visiting the same country house. The trick fails, but Thomas Love Peacock remains in *Arcadia,* as author of a fictional letter detailing life at Sidley Park in the 1830s. He also supposedly describes the hermit of Sidley Park in an article in the *Cornhill Magazine.*[4]

The references to Peacock are not gratuitous; Stoppard used a copy of a letter by him from the Huntington Library in California as part of his research. But more important is the allusion to Peacock's 1815 novel, *Headlong Hall*, providing a reference to what may be the closest fictional parallel to *Arcadia*. Peacock's book has its own set of disputatious writers, scientists and landscape architects who anticipate the ensemble of *Arcadia* and gather at the country estate of Harry Headlong for a weekend. Among the objects sent to Headlong Hall to stimulate the philosophical debates are books, mathematical instruments, telescopes, quadrants, air-pumps, drawing books, scenery for a private theatre and myriad other objects, many of which seem to find their way into *Arcadia*. Chaos without theory might describe Peacock's listing of the objects in his fiction: 'all was bustle, uproar, and confusion; yet nothing seemed to advance', while science suddenly becomes a matter of velocity, projectiles and speed.[5]

Landscape gardening is especially important as a topic in the novel. The task of Marmaduke Milestone, 'picturesque landscape gardener', is to redesign Headlong Hall, which has 'great capabilities in the scenery' but wants 'shaving and polishing . . . clumping and levelling'. References to Capability Brown and Humphrey Repton anticipate discussions of landscape in *Arcadia*, as do Milestone's efforts to add a Chinese bridge and pagoda. Headlong Hall is appropriately and comically referred to as a 'terrestrial theatre of universal deterioration', evoking images of decay if not entropy.[6]

Two poets vie with two critics in the novel, while one indefatigable 'compounder of novels', Miss Philomela Poppyseed, offers to share her new work with all of them. Paralleling Septimus from *Arcadia* is Mr Panscope, a chemical, botanical and geological wizard, partly a take-off of Coleridge. Anticipating Bernard is Mr Escot, who believes in the perfectibility of man through the increase of knowledge, although not necessarily through science: 'Profound researches, scientific inventions: to what end?' he ponders in an effort to analyse the value of progress, complaining to Mr Foster, as Bernard does to Valentine, that 'you present to me a complicated picture of artificial life, and require me to admire it'. Foster responds like Valentine: 'in the process of time, moral science will be susceptible of mathematical demonstration'.[7] Debates on literary reputation, the role of critics and the pernicious influence of periodical criticism round out parallels with *Arcadia*. There is even a dance to complete the story. Only Byron and the hermit are absent.[8]

A further source was found in the library of Stoppard's friend, the British historian, political writer, former editor of the *New Statesman* and one-time neighbour of Stoppard's in Iver, Paul Johnson. Stoppard went to visit Johnson in 1990 when he was looking for a new idea: 'He has a lot of books. And looking at them I said: "I'm sure there's a play about the difference between Romantic and classical attitudes and eras." He had some books on Byron on that shelf. I even think I borrowed one or two. I acquire knowledge little by little . . . [and] it often turns out I own the books at home years before I need them."[9] As it turned out, he had books on landscape gardening, mathematics and even hermits. Ten years earlier he had been given a book on garden follies and grottoes.

The Byron interest led to another level of enquiry, since Byron's daughter, Ada, was considered by many to be a mathematical genius. Robert May, the Oxford professor who advised Stoppard on science in *Arcadia* and reviewed a draft of the play as early as December 1992, drew his attention to a recent study of Ada which detailed her meeting with Charles Babbage and her knowledge of his Analytical Engine, an early computing machine. Ada's tutor, William Frend, was also scientifically talented and knew many mathematicians. Although Stoppard denied basing the character of Thomasina on Ada, parallels exist which establish a further link to Byron. Stoppard's son, Oliver, a physics student at Bristol, would often forward papers, journals or books that might assist his father, including a paper entitled 'Mathematical Chaos and Strange Attractors' from *Structures and Strangeness*.

Direct antecedents for Stoppard's play were few, although Louise Page's *Adam was a Gardener* was produced in 1991. That play shuttled back and forth between the present and the early nineteenth century and used fashions in landscape gardening as a metaphor for broader emotional and cultural divisions. The title came from Kipling. Stoppard's work is more complex, given his use of science and chaos theory as well as academic sleuthing and Byron. The shuttling back and forth in Stoppard's work is art's attempt to delay the bleak ending established by time moving only in one direction and entropy controlling all. When the past and present merge in the final sequence of *Arcadia*, it is the temporal counterpart to the play's artful blurring of a set of distinctions and antitheses.

Lindsay Clarke's 1989 Whitbread Prize-winning novel, *The Chymical Wedding*, the story of a modern researcher working in a country house on the papers and books of the landed gentry, also has clear connections with *Arcadia*. The hero, Alex Darken, is trying to establish the facts about a girl of unacknowledged genius whose work had been burned and who may have been involved in certain sexual scandals. Alternate chapters describe what actually happened and Darken's attempts to reconstruct the past and to some extent relive it. Although the overall pattern is similar to *Arcadia*, the historical period shifts from 1809 to 1848 and it is set in the Norfolk village of Munding, not Derbyshire. The Agnew family, with their large home and library, are at the centre of this landscape adventure, and the presence of a Victorian scholarly clergyman, Edwin Frere, and a clerically minded modern scholar, the hero, balance the action in the two time-frames of the novel.

One additional and crucial source was the literary sensation of 1990, A. S. Byatt's novel *Possession*. The plot and structure of *Arcadia* owe much to this work, beginning with its use of purloined letters stolen from the Victorian poet Randolph Henry Ash's copy of Vico, which a budding researcher, Roland Michell, has read at the London Library. *Arcadia* deals with the discovery of letters by the scholar–critic Bernard Nightingale which supposedly prove Byron's murder of the minor poet Ezra Chater in a duel held in 1810 at Sidley Park, Derbyshire. *Possession* and *Arcadia* both rely on a dual time structure. Part of *Possession* is contemporary, focusing on the literary sleuthing of Roland and Maud Bailey, and part is historical, dealing with Ash and his love affair with Christabel La Motte. Stoppard follows a similar structure in *Arcadia*, dividing the time between 1809 and 1989. Each work is also a detective story, with Roland and Maud attempting to piece together the Randolph–Christabel connection, while Bernard and Hannah try to unravel the story of Byron and Chater as well as the identity of the hermit of Sidley Park. Time in both works is also cyclical.

Possession and *Arcadia* both enjoy satirizing academics and their scholarly certainty, showing how often they are incorrect. The end of the novel vividly confirms this. After the 'capture' of Mortimer Cropper, entrepreneurial scholar *par excellence*, holding letters stolen from the grave of Ash, the scholars gather to open the strongbox only to discover a letter by Christabel La Motte which documents her illegitimate daughter by Ash. They find out that the daughter lived and married without knowing her true parents. They also learn that Ash never even knew he had a daughter and died in ignorance, since La Motte's letter detailing the child's life was never sent.[10] This tragic news satisfies the scholars' need for an ending, providing a conclusion to the novel. But in a postscript dated 1868, Byatt reveals that they are wrong and exposes the incompleteness of their evidence. Ash *did* know of his daughter and met her, asking the child to tell her 'aunt' (Christabel La Motte) that 'you met a poet, who was looking for the Belle Dame Sans Merci'.[11] But the child forgot and the message was never delivered, and the scholars, despite their research, were no wiser. A similar exposé of scholarly assumptions takes place in *Arcadia* with the correction – to his horror, after the papers have printed such headlines as 'Bonking Byron shot Poet' – of Bernard's theory that Byron murdered Chater in a duel.[12]

A sentence in *Possession* summarizes a good deal of what Stoppard dramatizes in *Arcadia*: 'Roland's find had turned out to be a sort of loss.' Bernard Nightingale makes the same discovery, although in a much more theatrical and horrified manner, when he exclaims 'Fucked by a dahlia!' as documents shatter his nifty theory proving that Byron killed Chater. Hannah Jarvis actually explains the link between the novel, the play and their parallel quests when she describes their originating motives: 'Comparing what we're looking for misses the point. It's wanting to know that makes us matter.'[13] A possible pun exists in the word 'matter', meaning both material substance and something important; a further meaning derives from printing: type that is set up or composed ready for typesetting. Maud's supposition after she reads the two stolen letters by Ash anticipates both Hannah's statement and Stoppard's plot: 'The dates fit. You could make up a whole story. On no real evidence. It would change all sorts of things. La Motte scholarship. Even ideas about [her poem] *Melusina*. That fairy topic. It's *intriguing*.'[14] It is no surprise to learn that Stoppard told Byatt he had pinched the plot of *Arcadia* from her novel.[15]

> *The unpredictable and the predetermined unfold together to*
> *make everything the way it is.*
> Stoppard, *Arcadia*

The title of *Arcadia* was for Stoppard a potent metaphor, although he originally wanted to call the work by its full Latin tag: *Et in Arcadia ego.* Lady Croom, in Scene One, translates the phrase as 'Here I am in

Arcadia', rather than 'Even in Arcadia here I [Death] am', the Latin tag in Poussin's painting of shepherds uncovering a tomb with the inscription.[16] Stoppard wanted the presence of death in the title, but brevity and box-office sense prevailed: 'death is now in the title only by imaginative extension,' he confessed.[17]

The principal source of Stoppard's understanding of chaos theory was James Gleick's *Chaos*, extracts from which appeared in *The New Yorker*. Gleick provides a clear exposition of chaos not only in terms of scientific advances but in terms of the individuals who understood, often tangentially or accidentally, how a science of chaos might exist. One of them was Mitchell Feigenbaum, who in 1975 developed the idea of scaling and the use of mathematical clues for the emergence of chaos. From chaos theory, Stoppard borrowed the notion of geometric convergence and periodic doubling for the structure and content of his play.

Entropy, the dissipation of energy, also interested Stoppard. The physicist Richard Feynman described it as the decreasing availability of energy in the universe, a troubling characteristic of the world. Thomasina observes it when she tells her tutor that when you stir jam in rice pudding, it will not come together again if you reverse the motion, the first of various allusions to entropy in the play.[18] Stoppard elaborates the idea that the energy in any system will slide towards disorder and dissipate throughout the play, often through the simplest of images; Valentine, for example, explains to Hannah that 'your tea gets cold by itself, it doesn't get hot by itself . . . it will take a while but we're all going to end up at room temperature'.[19]

Another element of chaos theory was the idea of 'strange attractors', points in space that define the behaviour of dependent systems which pull one object to another. They become engines of information as they conflate order and disorder, 'efficient mixers'; according to physicists, they also create unpredictability. When coupled with the butterfly effect, tiny differences in input that result in overwhelming differences in output, they formulate the theoretical basis of Stoppard's play.[20] In *Arcadia*, the strange attractors not only plot graphs but are the unplanned-for elements that disrupt Newtonian systems. As Chloë tells Valentine late in the play, the universe is deterministic, or tries to be: 'the only thing going wrong is people fancying people who aren't supposed to be in that part of the plan'.

'Ah. The attraction that Newton left out,' Valentine replies.[21] The lines reverberate with biographical significance, given Stoppard's relationship with Kendal.

Stoppard also elaborated, as the persistent metaphor for art in the play, an image cited by Gleick but also one the playwright had already used: dance, specifically the waltz which Thomasina hopes Septimus will teach her, a sure sign of romance.[22] This is set off against the country dance to be held at Sidley Park, which Chloë mentions to Bernard in Scene Two of the play. The 3/4 time of the waltz sets a mathematical order for the play which echoes as an aesthetic counterpoint to the mathematics of the iterated algorithms developed by Valentine. Introduced to England in 1812, the year of the play's final scene, the waltz was called by Byron the 'Muse of motion', as well as 'seductive' and 'voluptuous' in his poem 'The Waltz'. In *Arcadia,* the waltz is a harmonious movement in the shape of a triangle, both across the floor and in the style of its musical conducting. The Sierpinski triangle, the name for the equilateral triangle that is the simplest structure to generate an algorithm and an example of a fractal (the visual objects that result from iterated algorithms), is one of the key designs of the play and in chaos theory, because it duplicates the structure of the relationships and movements of the characters. Blocking of the play frequently emphasized the triangular positionings of the characters.[23]

In the final scene of the play, Septimus teaches Thomasina to waltz; Hannah and Gus also dance. The two time periods converge for the audience, but not the characters, who, while simultaneously on stage, have no sense of each other. They only hear the music, embodying an image Mahler tried to express in the third movement of his Second Symphony. This, Mahler explains, was

> like the motions of dancing figures in a brilliantly lit ballroom into which you look from the dark night outside and from such a distance that the music is inaudible . . . Life may appear senseless to you.[24]

But life and the dance are anything but senseless at this moment in Stoppard's play; it is the instant when the audience, watching the moving characters, discovers that life – at least on stage and regardless of time – *has* meaning, symbolically uniting the classical and the Romantic, stasis and flux. Strange attractors collapse order and disorder as the characters formally and sensually move about the stage. The dance is the triumphant, visual celebration of Thomasina's early observation that things cannot be stirred apart, set against the inescapable backdrop of the dissipation of energy.

Stoppard thought that the dance which concludes the orderly chaos of the seventh scene of the play would manipulate, educate and entertain all at once. His source may have been Congreve, who ends *The Way of the World* with a dance, or even Sheridan, who functions as a dramatic reference point for the play. The waltz, once thought to be scandalous because it involved holding your partner, was the natural and anticipated climax for the play, since it had been mentioned as early as Scene Two, preceded by the motif of music which operates throughout the work. However, it was again rock rather than classical music that Stoppard listened to when writing *Arcadia*, specifically the Rolling Stones' 'You Can't Always Get What You Want'. He originally wanted that song to end the play, to give the dance a more modern element, actually writing the recording, which opens with the massive sound of a boys' choir, into the script. The musical director of the National Theatre surprised him when he explained that the song wasn't a waltz; 'but I always wanted to have the Rolling Stones at the end. I wanted them all to come to the play,' Stoppard lamented.[25]

> *Nature has played a joke on the mathematicians. The*
> *nineteenth century mathematicians may have been lacking*
> *in imagination, but Nature was not.*
>
> F. J. Dyson, 'Characterizing Irregularity'

Critics repeatedly praise Stoppard's skill in making his audiences believe they understand more than they do. He has an uncanny ability to bring his audience along with him as he explores complex scientific and moral ideas, doing so through dramatic structure, language and character. As his figures expound concepts as diverse as Fermat's theorem, Newcomen's engine, the second law of thermodynamics or, indeed, chaos theory, Stoppard always presents a dramatic situation or context to vivify the ideas. Valentine's exposition of chaos theory to Hannah in Scene Four of Act One, for example, occurs while Bernard 'is going through the library like a bloodhound'. As if to underscore the art-versus-science theme in the play, Valentine uses the exchange to expound the history of mathematics.[26] To maintain the ideas of overlap, recursiveness and non-linearity, Stoppard keeps the scene numbers throughout the play sequential but divides the work into two acts. But he also condenses: Scene Seven is actually made up of numerous small scenes, a kind of iterated algorithm (a formula whereby you feed the solution back into the equation and then solve it again, as Valentine states;[27] the resulting parabola produces a picture of the data) of repeated moments altered by small, incremental changes which have gradually assumed a plotted shape. Scene Seven is actually the opening of Act Two, the process being another way of maintaining unity in the text during the time shifts of the play. Yet the conflicts between the characters in *Arcadia* display Stoppard's technique of collision between premeditated structures and spontaneity.

What Stoppard believed was the strongest aspect of the play was not the physics, landscape history or Byron, but the story, which he called 'a thriller and a romantic tragedy with jokes', adding that 'the architecture of the play is what has made it work'.[28] The appeal of the play, as he understands it, is on the narrative level, which is funda-mental; in an undated postcard note written while revising the play, he underlined the phrase 'Simple narrative must be prime'.[29] As if to reinforce this, Septimus, amid the overlapping time-frame of the play, responds to Thomasina's confirmation that they are doomed because of heat loss by saying, 'this is not science. This is story-telling.' Stoppard might interject 'Precisely', but Thomasina doesn't even listen to Septimus: 'Is it a waltz, now?' she asks. He answers, 'No.'[30]

Looping describes the recursive function of non-linear mathe-matics, a form of periodic doubling which in mathematical terms becomes iterated algorithms, the mathematical feedback that enlarges exponentially. Feedback becomes a way of making pictures, as Valentine understands, answering Thomasina's question, 'if there is an equation for a curve like a bell, there must be an equation for one like a bluebell, and if a bluebell, why not a rose?' The answer to both is, as Valentine explains, how 'the unpredictable and the predetermined unfold together to make everything the way it is. It's how nature creates itself on every scale, snowflake and the snowstorm.'[31] The complex behaviour of simple systems is another formulation of the condition that one scientist described as the strange behaviour of 'deterministic dynamical systems' which give rise to motions that are 'essentially random'.[32]

Valentine neatly expands the method when he explains the Coverly set, Thomasina's formulas. And he does so with a single finger: Hannah's, as she presses a key on his computer: 'See? In an ocean of ashes, islands of order. Patterns making themselves out of nothing.' He continues, 'I can't show you how deep it goes. Each picture is a detail of the previous one, blown up. And so on. For ever. Pretty nice, eh?'[33] Valentine achieves this by putting Thomasina's equations through the computer a few million times more than she managed by herself with a pencil, a situation analogous to that in which Mitchell Feigenbaum used his HP65 calculator in 1975 to discover that there was a fixed number marking the period-doublings, the splitting of two cycles into four cycles into eight and so on, that led to his understanding that 'the numbers were converging geometrically'.[34] The system which led to chaos possessed an inherent order as scaling became an important element of the geometric convergence. Some quality was being preserved while everything else changed, a structural comment appropriate to Stoppard's play.

The transition to chaos followed a mathematical pattern which a diagram confirmed for Feigenbaum: two small wavy forms and one big one. Bifurcation, which Feigenbaum could predict, would create oscillation in populations, the very problem Valentine is studying with the game books on grouse at Sidley Park. The numbers, which Valentine understood and Thomasina intuited but could not prove, predicted when a change or period doubling would occur. 'She didn't have the maths, not remotely. She saw what things meant, way ahead, like seeing a picture,' Valentine explains to Hannah.[35]

Thomasina's efforts to describe the fractal geometry of a leaf presage the mathematics of Benoit Mandelbrot, who discovered fractals when he worked for IBM in the 1970s (fractals being the uneven surfaces generated by successive subdivisions). The leaf itself is a recursive element in the play, first brought on stage by Gus at the end of Scene Two, when he gives Hannah an apple. Septimus mentions it in Scene Three. Stoppard's sense of doubling is so strong that Thomasina virtually quotes Mandelbrot. Criticizing Hobbes's celebration of

Euclidian geometry, Thomasina exclaims: 'Mountains are not pyramids and trees are not cones.' Mandelbrot, at the opening of his groundbreaking study *The Fractal Geometry of Nature*, writes: 'clouds are not spheres, mountains are not cones . . .'[36]

The development of multiple scaling patterns involving recursive numbers established universality between different systems. Self-similarity – symmetry across scale – meant parallels and doubling, a constant degree of irregularity over different scales.[37] Irregular systems would behave similarly, although not identically, as Stoppard, dividing his play into 1809 and 1989, demonstrates by moving towards coalescence rather than chaos in Scene Seven, when the two periods overlap without interference on the stage.

Stoppard's cigarettes may have helped him understand the complexities of chaos. An inveterate chain-smoker, he was notorious for stubbing out a cigarette after one or two puffs and then lighting another. This, he calculated, was equivalent to smoking with a very long filter. Interviewed about his smoking and informed of the effectiveness of nicotine patches, he responded by saying he treats 'this as information of mainly historical interest'. The reporter then pressed him:

> 'How many [cigarettes] do you smoke a day?'
> 'Oh, no. Steady on. I'm not Rousseau, you know.'
> 'Is smoking associated with writing for you?'
> 'Yes. And with drinking coffee, and having had a meal, and talking on the telephone. And, indeed, with being between cigarettes. I have no self-exculpation on this, except to say that I enjoy every single one . . .'[38]

But Stoppard probably felt satisfied that smoke rings, clouds and other forms that scientists could not understand before chaos theory, now had a structure based on fractal geometry and the scaling phenomenon. This development, elaborated in *Arcadia*, results from the recursive symmetries between different levels of a system. Understanding correspondences across scales of different lengths (the events of Thomasina and Septimus in 1809 and those of Hannah and Bernard in 1989, for example) establish the regularities of a chaotic system. The complex interactions performed by the actors and understood by the audience of *Arcadia* enact the very process of chaos.

In our seats, we follow the behaviour of the system as the play becomes the visual expression of iterative formulae which change incrementally.[39]

You can't stick Byron's head in your laptop! Genius isn't like your average grouse.

Stoppard, *Arcadia*

Chaos theory was not the only science in the play. There were also binary contrasts between classical and Romantic, formal and picturesque landscape gardening, Newtonian science and the chaotic shape of nature, objective inquiry and egoistically driven research. These divisions are often, and comically, expressed through the opposition between Bernard's forceful views and those of the more objective Valentine: 'Fifty-five crystal spheres geared to God's crankshaft is my idea of a satisfying universe,' Bernard says dismissively; 'I can't think of anything more trivial than the speed of light. Quarks, quasars – big bands, black holes – who gives a shit?'[40]

Stoppard did, for one. Through his characters, he explains why fractal geometry, thermodynamics and Newcomen's steam pump matter. When the sound of a steam engine is heard in the second act, Stoppard introduces the science of heat, thermodynamics. Illustrating Newton's flaws and the importance of chaos, Stoppard indicates that change will occur until the capacity for change is spent; disorder increases at the expense of information, a variation of the Second Law of Thermodynamics. So the quest by Bernard to find documents to back up his theory of Byron's duel with Chater halts when crucial letters are destroyed. Stoppard also elaborates the idea of Time's Arrow and the concept of the dissipation of energy and heat (the Second Law of Thermodynamics), simply but effectively illustrated by Thomasina's interest in stirring jam into rice pudding.

Landscape gardening, expressing the contrast between classical and Romantic worlds, is another focus of the play. Indeed, Stoppard's interest in distinguishing between the classical and the Romantic was an early impetus for writing the play, which explores Hannah's concern with the decline of reason into emotion. The Enlightenment is 'a century of intellectual rigour turned in on itself', and 'the history

437

of the garden says it all, beautifully', she asserts.[41] Through Hannah's 'reading' of landscape-gardening changes and her mistakes (namely in the origin of the hermit of Sidley Park), Stoppard astutely and accurately represents the shifting geometry of the English garden between the eighteenth and early nineteenth centuries, using the picturesque as his bridge.

Stoppard draws his character Richard 'Culpability' Noakes from two of the best-known English landscape gardeners, Lancelot 'Capability' Brown, nicknamed for his habit of pronouncing that client's acres had 'capabilities', and Humphrey Repton, who used 'red books' (large drawing books bound in red morocco) to depict scenes as they were and how they might be improved. Until about 1740, according to Hannah the garden researcher and popular novelist, Sidley Park enjoyed a 'formal Italian garden which included topiary, pools, terraces, fountains and box hedges'.[42] By 1760, this had changed, when a follower of Capability Brown eliminated this 'sublime geometry', replacing it with a green sward up to the walls of the house and a ha-ha. The illusion was that the garden extended indefinitely from the house into the countryside. Stoppard added a gazebo, classical boat-house, Chinese bridge and shrubbery to Brown's design.

Noakes – Stoppard may have borrowed the name from Christopher Hampton's *The Philanthropist*, where he appears as a college don[43] – brings the picturesque into Sidley Park's transformation. Based on the paintings of Salvator Rosa, this is a scenery of 'gloomy forest and towering crag, of ruins where there was never a house'. It involves a fallen obelisk rather than a delicate Chinese bridge, a hermitage rather than a classical boat-house. A fourth landscape stage in the play is that of the *parterre*, a regular arrangement of patterned flower-beds established by Noakes next to the house, 'a consolation for the picturesque catastrophe of the second and third distances'.[44] Picturesque gardens looked new by looking old, as if they had been neglected for centuries, and allowed one to experience the dangers of solitude in safety. Such artificial landscapes, however, excluded any vision of rural hardship or social oppression and were called 'arcadias' by creators and historians of English landscape gardens. The garden of Sidley Park is a metaphor for chaos theory, since it melds the predetermined, the designed, with unpredictable, natural growth. The symmetry of the classical garden confronts the irregularity of the

Romantic in the play, which the National Theatre programme, with its numerous citations and mini-histories of gardens, made clear. Stoppard understood that his audiences might need some background for the developments discussed on stage.

Hannah's focus on the supposed hermit of Sidley, his hermitage constructed by Noakes when he remodelled the garden, becomes the centrepiece of her study of 'the nervous breakdown of the Romantic Imagination'.[45] 'The genius of the place,' Bernard exclaims when Hannah describes the hermit. 'That's my title!' she responds. Stoppard quietly borrowed the phrase from John Dixon Hunt's *The Genius of the Place, The English Landscape Garden 1620–1820*.

Stoppard's own early encounters with gardens helped formulate his interest in the subject. When he arrived in England in 1946, he lived near and visited Chatsworth, celebrated for its elegant gardens that encompassed four periods of design. Soon afterwards, Stoppard's Nottinghamshire boarding-school, the Dolphin School, temporarily moved to a Derbyshire country house, Okeover. Stoppard admired the type of landscape Hannah rails against – 'the best box hedge in Derbyshire was dug up for the ha-ha so that the fools could pretend they were living in God's countryside' – and claimed 'I love the grass going from the door straight through to the horizon'. He partly achieved this at Iver Grove with the construction of a ha-ha.[46]

> *The theatre is not about listening to tracts, it is about*
> *listening to stories.*
> Stoppard, 1993

Before a director was chosen for *Arcadia*, Stoppard had already committed the play to the National. He had been a Board member since 1989 and informally agreed to write a play for the theatre, which meant it had a home before a word had been written. He had known Trevor Nunn for years, having worked with him on Mrozek's *Tango* for the RSC in 1965 and *Every Good Boy* in 1977, and in 1974 he was to have directed *Travesties*. However, other obligations prevented him from following through, 'so we had a joint venture on hold'.[47]

The selection of Nunn raised eyebrows at the RSC. He had directed only one play there in the previous eight years, remaining artistic director emeritus, and had never directed at the National. He was now associated with megahits in the West End, but had also been noted for uncovering the core of feeling inside complex intellectual structures which many thought was necessary for Stoppard's new play. Nunn astutely observed that despite Stoppard's fascination with exile and displacement, he actually wrote 'much more emotionally than he thinks he does'. The subtext of the characters' lives in *Arcadia*, Nunn believed, was as fascinating as the 'carapace they had constructed for themselves'. For Nunn, the play became one about 'the collision of two different worlds', showing how two sets of people from different centuries might change each other in the course of the action. As Michael Billington also noted, 'at this tricky stage of his career [Stoppard] needs someone who can excavate the emotion underneath the intellectual wordplay'.[48]

Further gossip created additional controversy over Nunn's selection: the actress Imogen Stubbs, Nunn's wife, had apparently fallen out with Richard Eyre's wife, the television producer Sue Birtwhistle, over Stubbs's new television series which Birtwhistle was producing. Complicating matters was Stoppard's wish to do a play for Richard Eyre, director of the National. Eyre would have to wait until 1997, when, in his final year at the National and as his final play, he would direct *The Invention of Love*. For Stoppard and Nunn, meanwhile, production became a question of getting together to discuss actors and auditions; it was a difficult play to cast because they needed young actors who could do things very well.

While at the Royal Shakespeare Company – he was Director from 1968 to 1986 – Nunn had developed a talent for grand and impressive productions, most visibly in the eight-hour *Nicholas Nickleby* which he co-directed with John Caird and which won five Tony Awards when it transferred to New York. Nunn's reputation for gala productions grew after he left the RSC with hits like *Les Misérables*, *Cats*, *Starlight Express* and *Aspects of Love*. *Porgy and Bess*, *Così fan tutte* and *Peter Grimes* at Glyndebourne confirmed his skill with opera. His move to the National was considered a coup and was greatly anticipated. The combination of Nunn and Stoppard had box-office appeal.

Nunn felt qualified to do *Arcadia* 'because at Cambridge I studied at the feet of Dr Leavis', who had a 'notorious squabble' with C. P. Snow in the early sixties on science versus art. 'I happen to think Leavis was on the wrong side of the argument. But I recognized in *Arcadia* a clear set of references to it.' Nunn gave the example of Bernard learning that there is a Chater in the British Library's database but that he is a botanist and certainly not a poet 'like our Ezra'. When he finds out they are the same man, Bernard shouts, in an effort to save his theory, that Chater wasn't a botanist, but a poet! This, says Nunn, illustrates how limiting our current views are: 'in modern thinking scientist and artist are two branches of study'. He also admits that the science in the play, 'everything concerned with mathematics and chaos theory and the second theory of thermodynamics and quantum physics and relativity . . . panicked me no end'. He was more confident with Hannah, however: 'I can say that I had an invigorating dinner sitting next to Germaine Greer once that obviously contributed to defining the character of Hannah.'[49]

The science in the play was a challenge to the cast as well as the audience. Samuel West, who played Valentine in the original production, and Emma Fielding, Thomasina, visited the Oxford laboratory of Professor Robert May in their attempt to understand chaos theory and mathematical modelling. Stoppard met May, a mathematical biologist, at the *Daily Telegraph* science party in 1992. One of May's graduate students, Alun Lloyd, actually developed the 'Coverly Set' for Fielding's character, a simple mathematical formula that can create the complex leaf shape her character sought by number-crunching. The original programme for *Arcadia* reproduces the formula and diagram. May also gave a three-and-a-half-hour seminar for Stoppard, Nunn and the cast on chaos theory and attended the first preview – which ran ten minutes over three hours and forced Stoppard to cut. The programme for the National's production contains a brief essay by May entitled 'From Newton to Chaos'.

Stoppard felt that, more than with any of his other plays, he had this one right. It had to do with falling upon a story that suited the narrative structure and ideas he wanted to develop: 'I feel for once that I stumbled on to a really good narrative idea. *Arcadia* has got a classical kind of story and, whether we are writing about science or French maids, this whole thing is about story-telling first and foremost.'[50] He emphasized this point when he explained that the two time periods of the play occurring simultaneously was the result more of dramaturgy than anything else. After doing A and then B and then A and then B, 'just at the point the audience thinks it can guess what's coming next, you have to fool them'. This he calls 'the pragmatism of the theatre' and it dominates his conception of drama.[51] One curious pragmatic matter concerned the tortoise. The National received several letters from distracted playgoers saying that they couldn't appreciate the work because they feared that Septimus's tortoise, 'Plautus' in the 1809 sections, 'Lightning' in the 1989 scenes, was going to tumble off the table. A cruelty-to-animals league threatened some form of action, until it was revealed that 'Plautus' was a radio-controlled imitation tortoise expertly built by the props department.

The detective story, which had for so long intrigued Stoppard, became important again, the mystery taking on a twofold character: did Byron kill Chater in a duel, and who was the hermit of Sidley Park? Detection and scholarly research are linked. Bernard's theory that Byron decamped for the continent because of his encounter with Chater, which thrills him because he envisions a future on *The Breakfast Show* and unbridled fame, parallels Hannah's search for the hermit of Sidley Park. Valentine's search through the game books of Sidley also involves a mystery as he analyses the grouse populations to see if his calculations conform to the mathematical understanding of nature, which doubles Thomasina's search for a mathematical formula for a leaf. The mystery of the ordinary and everyday is his and Thomasina's quest, which Stoppard suggests chaos theory, through its predictions of the irregular, can unravel. This is another, higher-level detective story, which Thomasina had predicted: if you could stop every atom and 'your mind could comprehend all the actions thus suspended, then if you were really, *really* good at algebra you could write the formula for all the future; and although nobody can be so clever as to do it, the formula must exist just as if one could'.[52]

The grand mystery Stoppard is able to present in mundane terms is the fate of the universe, made marvellously clear at one point through the overlapping conversations of Septimus, Thomasina, Hannah and Valentine. Unbounded by time, their astonishing cross-talk reaches over history. As Thomasina tells Septimus she has no more room to extend her 'rabbit equation' in her lesson book, Augustus begins to draw the models and Valentine explains to Hannah what algorithms can reveal about the future, and they are in turn interrupted by

Thomasina correcting Septimus's understanding of what algebra might reveal.[53] The blended conversation, with neither set of characters aware of the other despite similar actions, is the dramatic expression of the rice pudding image at the outset of the play. But overlapping does not mean duplication. Elements correspond but do not copy each other, which is a key element of chaos theory. A lot of the time, the correspondences are not quite right and their not quite matching is the source of humour in the play. The only object that could possibly, and does, live from 1809 to 1989 is the tortoise. But even he is not entirely the same, since his name changes from Plautus to Lightning.

In rehearsal, Stoppard seemed to be the victim of chaos. He couldn't reduce the running time to the required three hours, telling Michael Billington that 'I can't get the bloody thing down to 3 hrs. – it's 3'5", so I cut 5 mins. And that night it comes out at 3'5" again – is this Quantum or Chaos? The interesting question never to be answered is: if I put all the cuts back, will it still come out at 3'5'?' The programme for the original production reads 'Length: about 3 hours, including 20 minute interval'.[54]

But worry over either the running time or the science in the play was unnecessary. The integrated structure and engaging detective story, and the balance between the characters of 1809 and 1989, worked perfectly. Again, children were at the centre of the work: the thirteen-year-old Thomasina in the early scenes and the younger Gus in the modern portion of the play. (Children have increasingly become the emotional and moral centre of many of Stoppard's plays, from *Every Good Boy* to *Hapgood* and *Arcadia*; he finds in them an instinctive natural justice uncorrupted by experience.)

The production stressed the contrast between Bernard Nightingale, the impulsive, ambitious, caustic Sussex don, over-eager to prove the murder of the poet Chater at the hands of Byron, and the sceptical but inquisitive novelist, Hannah Jarvis. Bill Nighy's impassioned performance and Felicity Kendal's comic but poised characterization in the original production powerfully played off each other, the former supposed to represent reason besotted by imagination, the latter the creator of fiction drawn to research and fact. Kendal, in particular, grew into the role, which Stoppard thought she played better after a month: 'she was absolutely individual and different from the person who had been Hannah when the play opened.'[55] The doubling of love in the work – Thomasina's for her tutor Septimus, the mute Augustus for the writer Hannah – reinforced the unity between the time periods. The work displayed not only the intellectual games Stoppard had been known for, but the new emotional energy that first surfaced in *The Real Thing*.

However, critics writing in advance of the play's opening warned potential audiences that the emotional Stoppard would probably not appear. They emphasized the difference between the man and his plays, commenting that in person he *was* emotional and caring, though on stage he seemed to be the metaphysician who responded more to abstract ideas than human contradictions, placing concept ahead of character. New theories were advanced that his principal theme was not language, the nuances of history or science, but fear, the fear 'of living in a teeming chaotic universe where truth is relative, moral absolutes are shaky and God is provisional'.[56] Stoppard had first voiced this view in *Lord Malquist and Mr. Moon*: the world 'got huge, disproportionate to the human scale, it's all gone rotten because life – I feel it about to burst at the seams . . . it's all got too *big*'.[57] It was Rosencrantz and Guildenstern living in an inexplicable world.

Stoppard had been defensive about his own feelings for too long, but in *Arcadia,* as he confronts chaos and entropy, he also confronts the power of emotions. 'I was', as he would explain four years later, 'a repressed exhibitionist. I found emotional self-exposure embarrassing' – a product of his Central European past and English upbringing. He also declared that the older he got, the less he cared about 'self-concealment'.[58] Many productions of *Arcadia* stressed the high comedy rather than the existential despair, although there *is* compassion and sentiment buried under the high-octane repartee. 'Play up the pain and let the comedy, usually there in abundance, look after itself,' is the advice Billington offered.[59] One director who listened was Peter Wood, whose production of *Arcadia* opened in August 2000 at the Chichester Festival. His was a more intellectual than emotional reading, although it exposed some of the narrative flaws in the work.

Despite being the first new play in five years by a playwright whose romantic partner was the leading lady, there was no glitzy first-night audience, no special performance for the champagne-and-caviar crowd and no giant after-show party, since the National was publicly funded and knew that taxpayers would be upset. The audience was mostly made up of subscribers, who enjoyed the Wildean repartee as much as the ingenious display of time. Their response to lines like Lady Croom's 'Do not dabble in paradox, Edward, it puts you in danger of fortuitous wit'; or Septimus declaring 'there is no more to be said about sexual congress', with Thomasina then asking 'Is it the same as love?' which brings the riposte 'Oh no, it is much nicer than that'; or Thomasina asking 'Septimus, do you think God is a Newtonian?' 'An Etonian? Almost certainly, I'm afraid,' frequently interrupted the first-night performance.[60]

Advance publicity, and there was a great deal of it, neatly divided itself between the upmarket magazines which speculated on the play and whether or not Stoppard would return to form, and the downmarket journals which focused on his relationship with Felicity Kendal. The play, however, also seemed to divide the journals along class lines. Broadsheets like *The Times* were ecstatic. The morning before the play opened, the paper devoted half a page to a careful explanation by its science correspondent of the complex time-and-motion mechanics of the play, and led the field with a rave review, referring to the work as leaving 'the impression of a novel by le Carré rewritten by Stephen Hawking in collaboration with Groucho Marx'. The *Guardian* and *Telegraph* concurred.

But Jack Tinker of the *Daily Mail* complained that the play was 'too clever by about two-and-three-quarters' and Nicholas de Jongh in the *Evening Standard* suggested that 'barriers to understanding loom large . . . Such simple concepts, so pretentiously arranged . . . the play staggers beneath the weight of its intellectual garb . . . the snob hit of the season,' he concluded. However, Benedict Nightingale of *The Times* expressed the majority view:

> Any man on the Clapham omnibus reading this review should instantly hijack the vehicle and drive it to the National's box-office . . . . the piece comes as close as any to fulfilling [Stoppard's] creative aim . . . the perfect marriage of ideas and high comedy.[61]

Michael Billington noted that the set, an elegantly curved room designed by Mark Thompson, and background of Sondheimish piano chords, upped the emotional ante in the play, which, in Stoppardian style, 'theatricalises his themes'. The essential theme was that of ideas renewing themselves as 'mathematical discoveries glimpsed and almost to view will have their time again'.[62]

Science writers were naturally eager to comment on the play following its triumphant opening. Roger Highfield in the *Daily Telegraph* praised the science precisely because it was entertaining as well as accurate. The sub-atomic world of *Hapgood* baffled scientists as much as playgoers, he remarked. The new science of chaos, which focuses on the chaotic but visible world, seems more understandable. The insensitivity of Newton's laws of motions to time and unpredictability was the starting-point of the play. Non-linear maths shattered this world, Highfield notes, but fractal geometry supplements chaos theory as the irregular is shown to be beautiful. Clouds and cauliflowers are shown to be similarly constructed. It all works: the play is 'a virtuoso display of science portrayed in dramatic form, not simply decoration'. The *Guardian* published 'Tom Stoppard's Science: A Playgoer's Guide' along with its interview of the playwright by Nigel Hawkes. Other papers did the same, seeking to ease any public anxiety that a failure at A Level physics or neglect of maths would reduce their enjoyment of the play. Other critics were eager to celebrate the return of Stoppard to the front ranks of British dramatists.[63]

Several writers could not resist resurrecting the Pinter–Stoppard rivalry, largely because, having not had a hit for ten years, each suddenly had a new success, *Arcadia* and Pinter's *Moonlight*, which was followed by Pinter taking a role in remounting his 1975 *No Man's Land* and the revival of Stoppard's *Travesties* by the RSC. Their return to form was cause for celebration but also competition, and the inevitable contrasts appeared: Pinter spare and modernist; Stoppard postmodern and rococo; Pinter the minimalist, hard and obscure; Stoppard the classicist, cerebral and subtle; obscenities in one, wit in the other; Pinter produced on the fringe, Stoppard in the subsidized theatre. But if Pinter was the tramp and Stoppard the dandy, they had both returned and done so by recovering their styles of the seventies 'as if released from the political obligations imposed upon them by the 1980s'.[64]

Pinter's *Moonlight* succeeds as a play without words, desolation and loss poignantly poised on the stage; Stoppard's *Arcadia* triumphs by its time shifts as chaos theory supplements art theory and politics, as in the earlier *Travesties*. Humour, gaiety, quips and puns challenge the audience. But some were still dismissive: 'sophisticated cabaret artistry' was one summation, compounded by criticism that Stoppard still could not cope with love or inner feelings. Yet the work is dazzlingly eclectic. Pinter, however, takes over where Stoppard leaves off; when the party is over, the characters must confront the mess – in silence. Seven years later, the rivalry persists, the occasion of Pinter's seventieth birthday being the cause of further comparisons pitting Stoppard's 'baroque, intellectual playfulness' against the 'spare seriousness of Pinter'. Stoppard seems determined to 'fill his plays with the entire history of western ideas', while Pinter focuses only on the thing itself, the working out of a specific situation.[65]

Sales of *Arcadia* at the National Theatre Bookshop during its run exceeded all other plays in print, including Shakespeare. One account reported an astonishing 6,000 copies sold in the first three weeks of the run, a figure not often reached by a play during its existence in print.[66] Transferring to the Theatre Royal, Haymarket in the spring of 1994, by the final curtain in June 1995, *Arcadia* had played for 431 performances.

> *There is another geometry which I am engaged in*
> *discovering by trial and error, am I not?*
> Stoppard, *Arcadia*

The day after the opening of *Arcadia* (14 April 1993), Stoppard gave a 'Platform' at the National. He began with a series of introductory remarks, again citing the magical disappearance of Ariel in the Oxford production of *The Tempest* and the importance of understanding that a play is an event, not a text. He then asked the audience to present their questions in alphabetical order: 'Is there anyone here whose name begins with A and has a question? I'll answer any questions, including "Who are you?"' he offered.[67]

Rather than reassuring the audience that he absolutely understood what *Arcadia* was about, he left doubts, suggesting that 'the text provides the occasion for something more mysterious to transcend it'. He recalled his remark to an American midwest university audience in the early 1970s that he had never written anything to be studied, a remark that startled them. He stressed that, as an event, not a text, a play's success depended on collaboration and the contribution of others. And although he writes about intellectual matters, he did not pretend to be an intellectual.

Stoppard defined himself as a playwright whose job is to get ideas on to the stage through character and situation. Peter Wood, in the audience, pointedly asked him why a man who writes as well as he does was fascinated by people who don't write well, the exception being Flora Crewe in *In the Native State*. Stoppard responded by admitting he had never thought about the fact that people in his plays write things, and that *In the Native State* earned strong reviews, adding that Flora writes poetry and that 'nearly all the time it took to write the play was taken up writing the poem she's trying to write'. The reviews, he added, were generous about 'this "pastiche" I'd written'.[68] When asked to talk about his indebtedness to Beckett, Stoppard interrupted the questioner with, 'I paid it back.' Other queries focused on his reasons for writing and his admiration for Oscar Wilde. As the time for ending approached, he asked for a final question: 'Anyone's name begin with Z?' A man stood up: 'I don't believe you,' Stoppard snapped. Unfazed, the gentleman asked how he would reply to the question, 'Who are you?' 'Talking of Samuel Beckett as we were,' Stoppard answered, 'I would reply, "Very well", pretending to have misheard.'

Two months after *Arcadia* opened, Fermat's theorem was solved after some 358 years. Professor Andrew Wiles, a British mathematician based at Princeton, outlined his formula for solving the problem in Cambridge on 23 June 1993. Using elliptical curves, Wiles essentially solved Fermat's statement that x to the nth power plus y to the nth power *never* equal z to the nth power if n is greater than 2, which Stoppard restates in this manner: 'when x, y and z are whole numbers each raised to power of n, the sum of the first two can never equal the third when n is greater than 2'.[69] Fermat challengingly wrote: 'I have found an admirable proof of this theorem but the margin is too narrow to contain it.' Septimus gives the problem of finding the proof to Thomasina in the first scene of the play and Thomasina does, in a fashion, provide a solution: 'the answer is perfectly obvious . . . there is no proof, Septimus. The thing that is perfectly obvious is that the note in the margin was a joke to make you all mad.'[70] Some mathematicians agreed.

When news of Wiles's solution was made public, the National felt it had to take steps to enlighten its audience. Meetings were called, with a printed insert for the programme being the likeliest solution, reported the *Daily Telegraph*. Stoppard, however, preferred more drastic measures: reprinting the programme with the original article outlining the discovery, by Adrian Berry, the *Telegraph*'s science writer, in the front and centre.[71] None of this dampened the popularity of the play.

> Septimus: *When we have found all the mysteries and lost all the meaning, we will be alone, on an empty shore.*
> Thomasina: *Then we will dance. Is this a waltz?*
> Stoppard, *Arcadia*

Lowering the stage lighting tempers the optimism of the dance at the end of the play, reinforcing the shadow of extinction, a combination of Time's Arrow and entropy. It is the gradual shift to room temperature. Despite our pleasure in the final scene of the play, we and the universe are running down. The final moments embody an orderly chaos, as the visualization of period doubling occurs, with co-existence of two different periods, preceded by internal references to fractal patterns through the interplay of character and props. The same geometric spheres, folios and drawings from 1809 remain on the study table next to a computer and Hannah's research books as visual reference points for the crossing of time in the 1989 sections of the play.

The success of *Arcadia* was assured, not only by terrific box-office sales, but by critical acceptance. Many of Stoppard's fellow dramatists also praised the work, Arnold Wesker writing to tell him how he admired the play and that 'the image of dancing before life (and the universe) go cold on us was quite moving'.[72] Harold Pinter, Princess Margaret, Peter Shaffer, Patrick Stewart and Mick Jagger all celebrated the work. Old friends and new came to the early performances: from Bristol, Val Lorraine and Anthony Smith, and from Texas, Tom Staley, Director of the Harry Ransom Humanities Research Center.

Arcadia was soon being produced throughout the world, including a Zurich production directed by Peter Wood in October 1993, followed by productions in New York and then San Francisco. American universities soon devoted symposia to the play, coordinated with its production. The University of Pennsylvania invited Stoppard to lecture on the play in February 1996; Berkeley's Mathematical Sciences Research Institute invited him to speak on 'Mathematics in *Arcadia*' in February 1999; and in January 2000, Stanford University asked him to address undergraduates in the Introduction to Humanities course for which *Arcadia* was the set text. Websites proliferated, with study guides, glossaries, and landscape histories linked to discussions of physics, Byron and hermits.

In February 1998, *Arcadia* premièred at the Comedy Theatre in Prague, with a Czech translation published by the Theatre Institute to mark the occasion, as well as a visit by Stoppard. On 30 November 1998, *Arcadia* was the play selected by the prestigious Comédie-Française as the first work by a living foreign playwright ever to be performed there. Champagne and speeches heralded the event, with speeches by Chris Smith and Catherine Trautmann, culture ministers of Great Britain and France, preceding the performance. Translated by Jean-Marie Besset, the work had difficulty finding a proper audience, however, and actually lost money at the box office, although Stoppard was recognized widely as a writer of '*théâtre des idées*', a philosophically minded playwright who naturally appealed to the French, according to Trautmann.[73]

Because each production differed, Stoppard frequently participated in the new rehearsals. For Peter Wood's Zurich production, for example, the set differed not only in angles and planes but in the kind of room and atmosphere. It was shabby, with a mural of an idealized sort of Poussin/Claude landscape on the back wall facing the audience. But the mural was a scrim (a gauzy material allowing light to penetrate), so it would occasionally disappear and reveal the terrace of the garden outside. When characters walked back into the room, the wall would become solid, showing the picture of the landscape. Stoppard thought this was brilliant.[74]

Following this period of new stagings in the spring and summer of 1993, with a revised and successful *Travesties* at the Barbican and *Arcadia* at the National and then the West End, Stoppard became increasingly candid about his writing style and process. In an October 1993 interview, he explained, for example, how unreliable is his writing practice as a form of documentation. Working with a fountain pen and writing in longhand with innumerable versions of each page, he finds it necessary to maintain order by dating the individual pages and adding page numbers. In order to look back at a previous page, after he's written, say, the fourteenth version of the dialogue, he can tell the order of the previous pages by date. But it was easy to get the dates wrong when working on something continuously; even his numbering was often wrong. An attempt to reconstruct his process of composition in detail would not be accurate, he explained with a touch of impish satisfaction.[75]

Travel and theatre-going marked Stoppard's frantic pace after the success of *Arcadia*. In mid-October 1993, for example, he jetted off to Austin, Texas, for a speech at the Ransom Humanities Center, plus an academic conference and lecture to drama students. Four days later, he was in San Diego to confer with Jack O'Brien on the new production of *Hapgood* for Lincoln Center. On his return to London, he went to see Pinter's *Moonlight*; two days later, on 28 October, he and Felicity Kendal attended an event at Buckingham Palace and the next day he was off to Auckland, New Zealand and then Australia for the opening of several of his plays and to lecture. On his return, he lunched with the Prince of Wales and dined with John Cleese on the same day. The year ended with a party at the Jaggers'.

Arcadia marked a watershed. It reaffirmed Stoppard's importance in the theatre, not just in Britain but beyond. But if his reputation was firmer, his personal life was less so. By late 1993, his relationship with Kendal seemed unsteady. Partially reconciled with Rudman because of their young son, she told the press that 'he's wonderful, Michael. We always spend Christmas together, always. We spend every weekend together, more or less. We have a very, very close relationship', a statement that hardly satisfied Stoppard, although she claimed that they were also close.[76] A photo showing Kendal, Rudman and their young son Jacob returning from a holiday in Nice appeared in the *Daily Mail* of 11 August 1993. The short accompanying story noted that *The Good Life* was being repeated again on television and that Kendal was taking a break from her performance in *Arcadia*. One observer remarked: 'I think she sees herself as a moralist in an immoral world', a view akin to that, dramatically at least, of Stoppard. They also shared a deep commitment to children, although she admitted that she did not suit marriage: 'I'm just difficult to be with, I'm always absolutely sure I'm right.'[77] Stoppard at one point apparently called her 'a bossy blonde', an ungenerous way of saying she was pragmatic, efficient, practical, brisk, shrewd and realistic.[78] Professionally, Kendal was also encountering a few problems: the critics disliked her 1994 television series *Honey for Tea* and the BBC cancelled the show after six episodes. Yet she and Stoppard would remain together for another four years, despite the complexities of Kendal's role as mother, actress and celebrity.

CHAPTER 19

NEW YORK, PRAGUE

I'll cable New York. 'Disembarked. Don't worry.'
Stoppard, *Rough Crossing*

Stoppard's return to New York in 1994 was a triumph, with not one but two hits. The success of *Arcadia* made him a hot property, although his major achievement was not his current London success but his former flop, *Hapgood*. Beginning with a successful production of *Rough Crossing* in October at Princeton University's McCarther Theater, something of a Stoppard festival occurred, with the revised *Hapgood* opening in December 1994 at Lincoln Center and then *Arcadia* débuting there in March 1995. Stoppard had a triple triumph and was the first playwright ever to have two hits running at Lincoln Center at the same time: the extended run of *Hapgood* (closing on 26 March 1995) overlapped with the beginning of *Arcadia* on 2 March. One critic calculated that for three Wednesdays and Saturdays, both plays could be seen on the same day, as a matinée and an evening performance.

The New York production of *Hapgood* opened the 1994–5 season of the Lincoln Center Theater Company. The not-for-profit and partly public-funded theatre, New York's equivalent to London's National Theatre, did not rely on the box office alone for survival, but had a stable list of subscribers who were eager, it turned out, to see a new Stoppard play. Only in this environment could the risk of *Hapgood* be undertaken.

Stoppard protested at the expensive nature of staging a Broadway show, whereby 'unless you're a smash hit, you've somehow failed. *Angels in America*, for example ended up *technically* a failure as far as economics. Which is insane. I mean, what do you have to do?'[1] But

Stoppard and others underestimated public interest in his work, no doubt increased by the phenomenal success of *Arcadia* in England and his renewed reputation. André Bishop, artistic director of the Lincoln Center Theater, actually apologized by letter to subscribers unable to purchase tickets for the run of *Hapgood* and announced a two-week extended run to accommodate demand. A second extension would follow. In fact, the show sold out within six days of the box office opening on 17 October 1994, with the first extension selling out in ninety minutes. By 4 December, when the play opened, all tickets for the entire twelve-and-a-half-week production had gone.

Hapgood was 'a kind of struggle from the word go and I was still dealing with it at Lincoln Center, trying to explain, simplify. We started off by referring to it as a melodrama, and once it was so labelled, I felt much more comfortable with it, because it is melo-dramatic. It's not satiric about the spy business. It operates on a heightened, slightly implausible level of life'– and is probably the only play of Stoppard's in which somebody shoots somebody else on stage.[2] Stoppard rewrote large chunks of what he called 'his loose tooth', removing eight pages from the original script and reworking certain key monologues once he knew that Stockard Channing would star and the production would proceed.

Stoppard had, in fact, first approached Channing in 1988 for the Los Angeles production but she was committed to a film, *Meet the Applegates,* and had to refuse. After seeing her in the 1992 London production of John Guare's *Six Degrees of Separation,* he sent her a note: 'Is it too late for *Hapgood*?'[3] Further letters passed between them until they met and she suggested Jack O'Brien, a friend and Artistic Director of the Old Globe Theater in San Diego, should direct. He had done a successful revival of *Damn Yankees* in New York and was a good friend of Emanuel Azenberg, Stoppard's Broadway producer. O'Brien had actually met Stoppard four years earlier in New York, at Azenberg's request, because O'Brien wanted to do a production of *Rough Crossing*. The rights were not available, however; when Stoppard found out, he was genuinely sorry and told O'Brien at a breakfast meeting in New York where they also discussed the possibility of doing *Hapgood* on the west coast (although the LA production at the Ahmanson would pre-empt them). O'Brien and Stoppard unexpectedly discovered a mutual interest in trout fishing and the next night surprised each other at a performance of *M. Butterfly* by David Henry Hwang, which they both disliked, although Stoppard was circumspect in his criticism until O'Brien burst out with 'it's bullshit!' Stoppard's laughter trumpeted through the lobby. When Stockard Channing called from London to see if he'd be interested in directing *Hapgood*, O'Brien jumped at the chance.

O'Brien recalled his initial reaction to Stoppard as 'one of the two or three most seductive people I've known in my entire life'. He meant that he could manage to bring out what he wanted from directors and actors. But O'Brien also felt intimidated 'because he [Stoppard] has this most facile and available intellect. But you begin to realize what an amazingly generous person he is. And before long, I had one hand on my hip, saying, "Come on, Tom, what the hell does *that* mean?" '[4] O'Brien had a clear vision of *Hapgood*, which turned it into a success: he realized that the relationships of the spies 'are not dissimilar to what happens in theatre bonding' between a director and his actors and between the actors themselves: 'you know you can trust them and so you go *deeply* into an instant rapport and you stay there!' Often, this is 'very sexy; that's why theatre people are falling in and out of love with each other'.[5] O'Brien saw that the relationships in *Hapgood* were all about passion and survival skills plus 'quickly made, quickly judged relationships that pack intensity into a very short period of time'.[6] But while he knew he could make the work sexy, he didn't understand what it meant.

O'Brien also sensed the fundamental if hidden emotion in Stoppard's work, and that his diffidence, gentlemanly behaviour and emotional reserve were ways of protecting it. Stoppard, one of the most generous and appealing companions, doesn't give this off; rather, his public persona is more likely that of 'a brilliant, complex intellectual machine' who ironically is unaware of these two contradictory projections. O'Brien was convinced that he could make *Hapgood* 'delicious'.

André Bishop and Bernard Gersten, executive producer of the Lincoln Center Theater, quickly agreed to the Stoppard–Channing–O'Brien project, although it had to be put on hold for a year because Channing had another movie commitment. The delay displeased Lincoln Center, but it allowed O'Brien and Stoppard more time to meet and think about the work. Not only were cuts and modifications made to the text, but Stoppard outlined the complex chronology of the action at least five times to O'Brien. Clifton Davis as Wates, David Lansbury as Ridley and David Strathairn as Kerner joined Channing in the all-American cast which Stoppard requested.

Hapgood, of course, deals with twins, actual, imagined and atomic. New York had a restaurant called Twins across from the more famous Elaine's on Second Avenue between 88th and 89th Streets. The owners and staff comprised twenty-eight sets of identical twins. Stoppard went for pizza and found the place fascinating, although Trevor Nunn expressed fear that the restaurant might turn up in a future Stoppard play, recalling the line from *Hapgood* where Kerner says 'an electron is like twins, each one unique, a unique twin'. To which Hapgood replies, 'its own alibi'.[7]

As part of the pre-opening publicity, Stoppard wrote an article for the *New York Times* under the inelegant headline, 'Spy Stuff as a Metaphor for the World of Physics'. Billing the play as a comedy thriller – a hook that no doubt clarified the nature of the revised play for New York audiences – Stoppard summarized the importance of Richard Feynman in his thinking about physics. He surveyed the science-versus-art debate and how it differed from his use of historical characters in previous works like *Travesties*. 'The fact remained that "Hapgood" had its origins in my sudden fascination with quantum physics as expressed in the dual (wave and particle) nature of light . . . the spy stuff, merely nine-tenths of the action, was just a metaphor for the world of particle physics.'[8] But now, the subject appeared every-where, in novels, newspapers and possibly even comic strips. He still had the urge to send his manuscript to Feynman, implicitly consenting to the divide in culture between artists and scientists, or, as he typified it, 'Pink Floyd' on one side and science on the other. He never did post the work to Feynman, and that, writes Stoppard, revealed, or rather confirmed, something about the continued separation – more than six degrees – between dramatists and physicists.

Although this impulse passed, Stoppard records in the article his unexpected discovery of chaos theory 'not long after "Hapgood" opened'. In 1989, this new field of science caught his imagination, but back then, 'chaos-playwriting was lonely work'. *Arcadia* 'turned out to be mainly about Byron and landscape gardening (on the surface of course) and I can report that I felt no urge to mail it to a famous mathematician' – because he was no longer impressed with himself for 'mixing a little real science into my art'.[9] The two were actually more like each other than he first realized.

In October that year, Stoppard had been invited to speak at Caltech and gave a lecture entitled 'Playing with Science' in which he made a similar argument that his knowledge of science was general but he knew enough to apply it as a metaphor. Although he emerged from school with little formal science training, he was considered to be some sort of expert because he has written two plays with science in them: 'One play may be thought an aberration, but two suggests purpose. Don't be misled, however. My next play is about India,' he warned his audience.[10]

To generate interest in *Hapgood*, not that they needed to, Lincoln Center sponsored a round-table on art and science, held on 14 December 1994. Participating were a Nobel Laureate in chemistry, Dr Ronald Hoffman, Diane Ackerman, naturalist and writer, and Dr Melissa Franklin, a particle physicist. Oliver Sacks and the poet John Hollander asked questions from the audience. Predictably, it was a sell-out. In further preparation for the opening, Stoppard published a short article, 'The Matter of Metaphor', in the *New Theater Review* published by Lincoln Center, in which he countered the view that the 'two Cultures' divide still existed, explaining that an interest in science among general readers was growing. Indeed, he credits his *lack* of scientific knowledge as the source of his excitement for the central image in *Hapgood*, the dual nature of light, a concept wearily familiar to anyone who had studied physics at an advanced level.

The metaphoric potential of dualities excited him. He comically explains that:

> *Hapgood* is not 'about' physics, it's about dualities. No – let the playwright correct the critic in me – *Hapgood* is not about dualities, of course, it's about a woman called Hapgood and what happened to her and to the people around her between Wednesday morning and Saturday afternoon one week in 1989 just before the Berlin Wall was breached.[11]

The physics, he added, 'is not invented, though it is intended to be artful'. The play actually has more to do with espionage than physics and in looking around for a real world to express the metaphor, he 'hit upon the le Carré world of agents and double agents'. He mentions that le Carré, whom he came to know, went to see the play but managed to avoid mentioning the work 'which I immediately recognized as the height of courtesy. Espionage buffs – or even real spies – will conclude that Mrs Hapgood must be working for MI Five-and-a-Half.'[12]

The New York production of *Hapgood* differed from both the London and Los Angeles versions: 'it's an American *Hapgood* with American actors', without baggage from previous productions, he explained to Mel Gussow.[13] Once he began to think of it as a melodrama, he felt more comfortable with it. Although not a satire, it nevertheless operates on a slightly 'implausible level of life'.[14]

Jack O'Brien's vision for the play, to be performed in the small, 299-seat Mitzi E. Newhouse Theater at Lincoln Center, a theatre three-quarters in the round, meant a more intimate and involving production. He also understood that 'sex was the subtext that powered the production. It was Chekhovianly sexy'.[15] O'Brien also met head-on Stoppard's fondness for obscurity by seeking clarity in the production: 'he loves words that don't explain themselves. He loves the sound of them. His thrill is to hide from you as an audience' – a comment partly based on Stoppard's habit of lurking in the back of a theatre during previews, making notes, observing nuances, changing his point of view and then passing on comments to the director, lighting engineer, designer and actors.[16] O'Brien added that 'Tom writes this play as if it were a film. He says about a character that the next time he moves, he's somewhere else. And I was determined to do that, to make it possible to switch the scenes at a lightning pace, and keep the narrative going.'[17]

Stockard Channing explained in *Theater Week* that '*Hapgood* is a *film noir*. That's how Tom always envisioned it', and this became a further key to its success. The critics loved it and Channing's performance as Hapgood, although there were, of course, dissenters. Leading the way was Robert Brustein, never sympathetic to Stoppard's work. After acknowledging Stoppard's handling of science, he writes that 'his grasp of human behaviour is less sure'; while the motives are clear, 'the plot is cloudy'. The evening possesses everything 'except a coherent dramatic purpose. None of the characters has much emotional life.' David Richards of the *New York Times* was dismissive largely because he didn't understand it.[18]

The then Chair of Lincoln Center, Beverly Sills, was seen leaving a performance of *Hapgood* at the intermission, a source of considerable gossip. In response, she quickly fired off a letter to Bernard Gersten, insisting that she loved the play but that the air in the theatre was a bit stuffy and her husband was feeling ill.[19] Others, however, had less difficulty staying and praised the work, as well as Channing, 'whose mix of brains, humour, vulnerability and classy style make her a perfect Stoppard heroine', according to one critic. John Simon in *New York Magazine* summed up the Stoppard challenge: 'A trying chap this Stoppard. He is either more intelligent than anybody else writing plays these days, or at least smart enough to have convinced the rest of us that he is, which comes to the same thing.' The source of this is mixed identity: 'he probably sees himself as Tom, the heir to all those clever drawing room comedies but also as Tomáš, who might have been the homonymous hero of Kundera's *The Unbearable Lightness of Being*. Central European existentialist as all hell. So Stoppard wonders about the other side of things.'[20] Stoppard himself was so pleased with the production and Channing's performance that he granted her the film rights for the work, although it has yet to be produced.

What accounted for the success of the play, with *USA Today* trumpeting it as the 'best British import', more 'dazzlingly intricate and emotionally moving than in its original London production'?[21] Part of the reason was its powerful mix of intellectualism and intrigue, women and espionage, precisely the blend that would appeal to a large segment of New Yorkers. Stoppard had also updated the text slightly, with comments that forecasted the downfall of the Soviet Union. It had been ten years since a major Stoppard play had been produced in New York, the last being his Broadway hit, *The Real Thing*. Limited access to the play – it was part of a subscription series in a small theatre in a major complex – also increased its appeal to the public. The harder tickets were to obtain, the more people wanted them.

The staging was more imaginative and successful than the London production. The atmospheric mood of battleship greys and dirty linen whites which suffused the set generated a mysterious quality. Even the air looked thick and slightly soiled, one critic remarked, exactly right for the subject matter, confusions and mix-ups in the play. The revised text seemed up-to-date and emphasized more clearly that everyone is two or more people, with the anarchist shielding a member of the bourgeoisie, while inside every Communist there is a capitalist wanting to get out. The giant projections devised by Wendall K. Harrington, which slithered across the rear wall and floor and out towards the audience, and the spare sets by the distinguished designer Bob Crowley, matched the interest and fast-paced direction generated by O'Brien.

Three factors contributed to the outstanding success of the play, according to O'Brien: the chemistry among the actors, the extraordinary design by Bob Crowley and the brilliant jazz score composed by Bob James. Coupled with this was O'Brien's direction which emphasized a witty, deft, tongue-in-cheek style, rejecting anything grim or pompous. He succeeded in liberating the play from its seriousness and turned it into a hit.

> *Thank God, what a relief. Go to Prague. We don't want*
> *you here.*
> Message on Stoppard's answerphone

Stoppard missed the first night preview of *Hapgood* in New York, but for a good reason. Václav Havel had invited him to participate in a round-table discussion with Arthur Miller and Ronald Harwood (then President of PEN) as part of the 61st Congress of the International PEN association. Stoppard would have to miss the first preview and he cabled Jack O'Brien to tell him he felt he should go to Prague. The message on his answering machine was clear: 'Thank God, what a relief. Go to Prague. We don't want you here.' The cast could do their first preview without the author watching, which was a vast relief. He did make it to the second, however.[22] Stoppard's participation on the PEN panel became more than an opportunity to share ideas on the fate of the theatre. The trip to Prague also unveiled a startling revelation about his past.

The round-table, actually held outside Prague, at Plzeň, allowed Stoppard, then vice-president of PEN England, and the others to outline their writing practices, theatrical origins and view of politics in the theatre. The contrasting range of experience actually found a common ground, Havel's dissident and political background equalling Miller's critique of American moral life and Stoppard's unrepentant revision and criticism of theatre as a craft. Stoppard began by noting his favourite American dramas, *Death of a Salesman* and *The Front Page*, and the role of American writing at the outset of his career. Between the ages of eighteen and twenty-five, 'American literature in general was much more potent for me than contemporary English literature at that time.'[23] He then addressed the question of politics in the theatre and admitted that, for him, 'all political questions resolve themselves into moral questions.'[24] He also explained that the arts in general laid down a 'matrix of our moral sensibilities, whereby we make the moral judgments on society'. Miller agreed, adding that 'when politics is used in a play purely on its political level, it at best can have a short interest. It's when it does engage that moral element in the political conflict that it has a chance to become real drama and last beyond its moment.'[25]

In the ensuing dialogue, Havel profiled life in the Czech Republic and the reception of theatrical works in a climate of repression and obstruction. Exploring a certain resentment between politicians who have power and intellectuals who have no practical responsibilities, Harwood, as chair, prompted Havel to articulate the way the state might mitigate these differences. Before he could do this, however, Harwood recounted that when he visited Havel some months ago at his office and asked him if he was writing plays, he responded by saying no, only research. 'Picasso said that every picture was only research,' Stoppard interjected.[26] Miller then surveyed the minimal presence of intellectuals in American political life and the complete absence of artists.

Stoppard outlined his experiences in England, where the artist had 'roughly speaking . . . elevated a recreation into a career and was getting away with it'. With his middle-class background, he did not at first experience the alienation or separation from such a world experienced by other artists, although in the early years of his career as a playwright he did feel uncomfortable 'in the company of my elder brother, who worked for a living and I got money for doing what I did, which seemed to be a very different situation'.[27] Even his appointment in 1989 to the Board of the National Theatre caused anxiety:

> I thought – what do you mean, join the board? I'm a writer. The board
> talks about how to spend the money, and whether they should have a

new elevator or a new car park, the politics of the National Theatre . . . including the infrastructure, without which there is no theatre. After a few weeks, I thought this is right, and I became a sort of converted harbour light, but not wholly so. Even now, I don't feel at home doing what is, in the most general sense of the word, politics.[28]

Stoppard went on to elaborate his position that it is not the artist's duty to change the world. The theatre, he argued, does not have to have political or social ambitions. It has the ability to perform that function but is not defined by it: 'one tends to talk about plays and playwrights as if they have some kind of sacred duty at all times and in all societies. I plead guilty to having written a lot of things which had no such ambition and certainly no such effect.'[29] For Stoppard, playwriting is a craft not a platform. Havel concluded the discussion by reminding everyone of the distinctive role played by the theatre in responding to the Communist regime and its downfall in the so-called 'Velvet Revolution' which itself was a theatrical pastiche: 'it had the structure of an ancient drama at the same time of a fairy-tale and then again of a musical.'[30]

Harwood recalled that the playwrights travelled to Plzeň in the presidential motorcade, speeding through villages and making the usually two-hour trip in something like forty minutes. Stoppard was impressed with the authority of the motorcade and its ability to command the roads, turning to Harwood at one point and saying, 'I could get seriously used to this.'[31] Near the town, the entourage stopped for an early dinner, rather like 'Louie the XIV, with the people gawking', Harwood remembered. When they arrived at Plzeň, the nineteenth-century theatre was full, with nearly 800 people in the audience. Havel's impish manner was such that he went on stage first and, with some fanfare, announced the other participants, who stood behind a curtain which rose as they stepped forward. Havel structured the entire evening, from the curtain-raiser to the topics brought forward for discussion. Afterwards, the ten-car motorcade with its police outriders sped back to Prague, although Havel branched off to his residence to prepare his weekly radio broadcast.

Stoppard and Harwood continued on to their hotel, where a young man had been waiting in the lobby for several hours. This was Alexandr, the grandson of his mother's sister Berta, as he would later find out. The visitor had travelled from another town to see him, having read in the papers that Stoppard was visiting. The young man's English was poor and at 2 a.m. Stoppard was not entirely sure what was wanted, although an old photo album spoke for itself. Placing it on the hotel counter, Alexandr opened it to reveal a picture of Stoppard and his brother ('Tomáš and Petr') with the family spaniel in the garden of their first English home.

Images from the past suddenly materialized on the counter of the reception desk: the Beck children in 1914; his mother in 1927, aged sixteen and wearing a flapper outfit, and again in the 1930s, glamorous in a fur-collared coat. 'The fact that my mother was beautiful had escaped me, and the realization was shocking.'[32] He soon realized that his mother had four older sisters and an older brother. Their names were Wilma, Berta, Anny, Irma and Ota. He learned their fate from Šarka, the daughter of Jaroslav, one of his aunt Wilma's two sons (the other was named Milan). The next morning, when he saw Stoppard, Harwood recalled that he 'was instantly pleased to make that connection' with his past.

Stoppard's Jewish quest had begun in 1993, when Šarka, the great-granddaughter of his aunt Wilma, wrote to his mother from Germany, proposing to visit her in Devon. His mother, however, panicked because her husband, Kenneth Stoppard, would not have been receptive to this re-attachment to a Central European, Jewish past. As a result, a meeting took place at the National Theatre, where Stoppard was working on *Arcadia*, involving his mother, his half-sister Fiona, her daughter, Šarka and himself. Šarka wrote down a family tree for Stoppard of his mother's generation: this was 'the first time, at least in my memory, that my Czech family had been given names and relationships'. And it was at that moment that Stoppard learned of his complete Jewish identity, not just on his father's but his mother's as well. He also uncovered for the first time the fate of his aunts: Wilma and Berta, both of whom had married gentiles, died at Auschwitz; Anny, unmarried, died at Riga. Ota, the older brother, survived. Irma, childless and a widow, was nearly ninety and dying in Argentina, where she had gone to live after her marriage.

Stoppard soon learned that all his grandparents died at the hands of the Germans. Julius and Hildegard Sträussler, his father's parents, were part of a 'transport' of Moravian Jews taken to Terezin and then

463

transported to Riga in Latvia, where they died. Regina and Rudolf Beck, his mother's parents, died in Terezin in April and July 1944, while Stoppard and his brother were at school and his mother was managing the Bat'a shoe store in Darjeeling. His own identity was becoming clearer:

> 'Šarka, were we Jewish?'
> 'What do you mean?'
> I adjusted.
> 'I mean, how Jewish were we?'
> 'You were Jewish.'
> 'Yes, I know we were Jewish, my father's family . . .'
> 'You were completely Jewish.'[33]

Border Crossings

Throughout his life, Stoppard had been crossing borders, whether from Czechoslovakia to Singapore, Singapore to India, or India to England. He had travelled abroad a great deal, west to the States and beyond to the Pacific Rim, and east to Russia or back to the Czech Republic. But he had also travelled across boundaries, and the 1993 discovery that his mother was Jewish, confirmed by later discoveries after her death, was perhaps the most important. Such knowledge made little difference to him, he has said, although he was compelled to return to Zlín more than once, in search of his past.

Stoppard should not be blamed for his indifferent reaction to the discovery of his Jewish past. Judaism seemed accidental and contingent in Kenneth Stoppard's world, which he mythologized as uncompromisingly British. In England, Stoppard had accepted a double life, wherein his mother visibly differed from her English husband, spoke the language with a pronounced accent and behaved in a more emotional manner, yet sought to make her Czech-born sons English. However, Stoppard's own unique speech and recall of his 'exotic' past constantly singled him out as 'other', though not necessarily Jewish. Silence about his past and that of the Jews of Europe was the rule as he and his brother sought to live a better life under the guidance of a thoroughly English stepfather in post-war Britain. They learned to contain themselves, partly because that was the new norm and partly because 'Jewishness was a form of unfreedom and determination'.[34] Effacing one's Jewishness was the key to becoming English.

The fear of rejection was a silent worry instilled by Stoppard's mother as much as by the culture. To prevent it, the idea was to become as English as possible in an effort to eliminate the stigma of being a Czech Jew, which would have been a grave embarrassment to Kenneth Stoppard. Questions about the past, about the death of his father or their departure from Zlín were inappropriate: sadness, anger and disappointment over the past were to be held in check. 'Parents looked to us to redeem their histories. We were to provide the validation for their survival. At the same time we owed it to them to be happy,' Victor Seidler explains in his memoir, *Shadows of the Shoah*. To fit in with English culture and not call attention to oneself as a Jew was the goal. 'Becoming English' was a way of securing one's safety and may partly explain, psychologically, Stoppard's love for and promotion of England and its culture in his plays. It was part of an unconscious desire to fit in. One result was the myth that his background was not very different from others'. As Seidler writes of himself, with overtones for Stoppard, 'Because I did not want to be different, at some level I did not really want to know about the very different histories my family had or to experience the loss.'[35] Only as an adult did Stoppard accept the uniqueness of his identity and past.

Ironically, Shakespeare's era, like Stoppard's, was preoccupied with Jewish questions. As the English of the sixteenth and seventeenth centuries worked to reinvent what it meant to be English, the increasingly anxious English defined themselves by whom they were *not*, and very often that was Jewish. Focusing on Jews became a way of exploring troubling questions about themselves. The Jews influenced English ideas about nationhood, identity and difference. 'Englishness would not be same as it is without the existence of Jewishness,' one scholar concludes.[36]

The post-war period was similar in that the concept of an English identity was being rewritten. In the theatre, the opposition was between Noël Coward and John Osborne. But with Stoppard, one found a writer who, while not outwardly Jewish (indeed, not even autobiographical in his work), taught the English something about England, beginning with his use of Shakespeare and then moving on to his re-inventions of Wilde, Sheridan and even Shaw, appropriately Irish writers assimilated into English society. An Englishman in Zurich (Carr in *Travesties*), a moral philosopher battling continental philosophers in *Jumpers*, another English philosopher taking on Central Europe (Anderson in *Professional Foul*), the English Thomasina, Septimus, Bernard and Hannah constructing English myths for foreign behaviour and departures (Byron to the continent, Chater to the West Indies), and finally Housman, who discovers his errors or at least disappointments in Dieppe, all reveal how border crossings define one's home identity. By battling the foreign, one reclaims one's Englishness. Fashioning this approach was a Czech-born Jewish writer, who although dispossessed of a home until he was eight, had nevertheless established an almost unassailable position in his articulation of an English cultural identity – which in Stoppard's hands is not above parodying itself, as when Das in *Indian Ink* begins to lyricize about Bloomsbury, to the chagrin of Flora Crewe.

But of course, the desire to remain silent about the past and downplay its force could not last. Buildings as well as narratives hold memories and connect us to the past, as Stoppard discovered when he made his journeys to Darjeeling in late 1990 and Zlín in 1998. Returning to these sites reconnected him to the past and helped him understand that he had a history that reached back too far to remember but not to imagine. Once Stoppard and his brother learned of their mother's connection with Zlín, they had to visit. History, via Stoppard's relatives and his mother's past, caught up with him and both forced and allowed him to speak. 'Another country', his 1999 article, summarized what he had discovered.

In this file is perhaps the only preserved photograph of
your father.
Dr Emil Máčel, Zlín

In May 1998, Stoppard extended his quest to restore a hidden identity when he and his brother travelled to Zlín via Vienna to meet Dr Emil Máčel and revisit their family home. A retired chemical engineer, Dr Máčel had for several years studied the fate of the Jewish employees of Bat'a and had been in correspondence with Stoppard's mother since

1994, unbeknownst to Stoppard. She had written back to Dr Máčel, explaining that there were so many mixed marriages that the matter of being Jewish had lost importance. In her own family, the ratio was fifty–fifty. Being Jewish did not matter in her own life until it disrupted it and set her on a course of displacement and loss. Sanctuary in England, where her sons would be safe, and forgetting the past was her resolution. But her experiences in Czechoslovakia, where she sought religious anonymity, sadly taught her this was impossible. 'Hitler made her Jewish in 1939,' Stoppard sharply wrote in 1999.[37]

In a November 1997 letter to Stoppard, Dr Máčel told him of what is perhaps 'the only preserved photograph' of Stoppard's father, found in his personnel file at the Bat'a archive; Dr Máčel also summarized his brief correspondence with Stoppard's mother. Stoppard and his brother Peter decided that they must recover the photo and their family history after a fifty-nine-year absence.

Dr Máčel, hobbled by a stroke, still proudly and graciously escorts visitors around Zlín, and lives in a modest apartment building built by the Communists on the outskirts of the city. Without an elevator, he slowly walks up to the third-floor apartment where, in a small room next to a tiny kitchen, he has a computer and an incomplete set of files, all that is left of the records of former Jewish employees of the Bat'a corporation. Complementing the Bat'a materials is a painting, by Dr Máčel's brother, of Dr Eugen Straüssler, based on the photo discovered in the company's records. It shows an attentive figure with a high forehead, dark, round glasses, and a mouth with full, sensuous lips, looking to the left. A combination of intellect and emotion emerges, suggested by the eyes and lips. Few photographs of Dr Straüssler survive, although by chance some footage unexpectedly surfaced in May 2000, showing what appears to be the opening of a clinic at the Bat'a Hospital in the mid-thirties and capturing a well-dressed and engaging Dr Straüssler directing dignitaries into the building.

With Dr Máčel, Stoppard and his brother found the family home in May 1998, a small brick cube of a building in the tract of homes constructed by Bat'a for its employees not far from the main hospital. They photographed the house with the two brothers outside, unable to enter. They visited the hospital and revisited the town, now dominated by a somewhat dismal commercial centre called the Centrum with small businesses, restaurants with genuine 1950s decor and the ubiquitous McDonald's. On the far hillside to the north, Bat'a apartment buildings for workers – advanced for Europe in the 1930s – are arranged in modernist formation. The Hotel Muscova, constructed in 1933 along contemporary lines, looms over the former twelve-storey corporate offices built in 1938 and the now empty Bat'a factory.

But Stoppard wasn't satisfied; there still remained unanswered questions, especially about his father. In April 1999, he went back to Prague, this time visiting the widow of Dr Albert, the chief physician at the Bat'a Hospital, who had hired Dr Sträussler. She recounted the events of 14 March 1939, when Dr Albert called a meeting of the Jewish doctors at his home, having received a call from a Bat'a director earlier that day, warning him that the Germans had crossed the frontier. The Sträusslers had been prepared by the company for such an event, his mother receiving her first passport in September 1938 and, in February 1939, an advance of £30 from the firm for the anticipated transfer to Singapore. On the 14th, the day of Dr Albert's meeting, the family received its health permit to travel and an instruction from Dr Albert: 'you have to get out, right now'.[38] Dr Albert's two daughters also shared their memories of his father with Stoppard. On the spur of the moment, Stoppard decided to return to Zlín following a visit to the Pinkas Synagogue in Prague in the company of Šarka and her father, Jaroslav. The fifteenth-century synagogue has the names of nearly 80,000 Bohemian and Moravian Jews killed by the Nazis inscribed on its walls. Among them are the names Sträussler and Beck.

Back in England, another piece of the puzzle unfolded: Stoppard was unexpectedly contacted by a survivor from the Singapore period who turned out to be one of the last individuals to see his father and who was able to throw light on his father's death. Leslie Smith contacted Stoppard after reading an account of his past, and Stoppard went to visit him in Wales. It was Smith who had driven Dr Sträussler to the docks for his fateful departure. He knew several captains and managed to get Sträussler and his friend, Mr Heim, on board one ship, which was attacked by Japanese aircraft and sunk in the strait between Sumatra and the island of Bangka as it steamed towards Australia only hours before Singapore was overrun on 15 February 1942. Fifty-seven years later, Stoppard had solved the mystery of his father's fate and added another fragment to his own identity.

*I feel an aversion toward the trail my people followed and
yet I am myself the desert through which Israel wanders.*
Otokar Fischer, Czech poet, 1923

Stoppard's mother very rarely talked about their past and failed to tell her two sons that she had siblings or that they had died in concentration camps. Even her own parents' destiny was unclear. In a private note to Ken Tynan, written while Tynan was researching his 1977 profile of the dramatist, Stoppard explained that his mother believed that British chauvinism might put the newly named Stoppard boys at a disadvantage if much was made of their foreignness. Furthermore, 'my mother always made out that we were sent to Singapore because of the Jewish grandparent' that they had heard about on their father's side, 'but we were Jewish by race. My mother didn't consider herself Jewish, she wasn't a religious woman,' Stoppard explained in a 1999 interview. He added that 'one of the reasons she buried the traces was that my stepfather wasn't sympathetic. She was a conforming woman and she deferred to his preference.'[39]

When she remarried and moved to England, she ceased to acknowledge any Jewish background: 'She had a completely practical sense, which I think was misplaced, that bringing her two little boys to England, she felt we would have had a hard time at school if we were Jewish. I think she was completely wrong.' Peter Stoppard added in 1998 that 'there was always the suspicion that we were Jewish, but mother always said, oh well, not really, only in part. People didn't care about that. There was a Jewish grandfather, that sort of thing. Yes, father had Jewish grandparents or something,' was all she would say.[40]

Some thirty years after arriving in England, however, Stoppard's mother felt guilty for apparently cutting off her sons from their past, while at the same time claiming she never really did so. Perplexed about his origins, Stoppard asked his mother to write a memoir of their beginnings, which she began in a sketchy fashion in 1981. Stoppard, however, did not confirm his mother's Jewish identity and the fate of her sisters and brother until he met Alexandr Rossa in the hotel lobby in Prague in 1994 and saw the photographs that established the Jewish identity of Martha Becková and confirmed the existence of her siblings and their tragic fate in the concentration camps.

Understandably, Stoppard recalls nothing of his time in Czechoslovakia, having left at age two. He has also said that he spoke no Czech at home, although his brother confirms that their parents used a kind of infant Czech to communicate with their sons. It is hard to imagine that he did not pick up some vocabulary, at least by the time he left Singapore in 1942 and arrived in India. Stoppard's Czech consciousness began to grow in the 1970s and he declared in a 1978 interview that 'I'm as Czech as Czech can be'. More recently, in 1998, he said that in the last ten years his 'Czech-ness' had become stronger than it had ever been in childhood, a desire to understand his past being stimulated in part by his mother's death, on 11 October 1996.[41]

Various return visits to the country – notably the 1994 trip to participate in the PEN seminar with Arthur Miller and Václav Havel and visits in February 1998 for the première of *Arcadia*, in May 1998 with his brother to Zlín and in spring 1999 to Prague and Zlín again – confirm his statement. However, he also admitted in a 1998 Prague interview that when he wrote *Professional Foul* in 1978, 'Czech-ness was brought into my life when I didn't know what to do with it'. But increasingly throughout his work, whether through his adaptations of the plays of Havel, support of Charter 77, protests against the imprisonment of dissidents, writing *Cahoot's Macbeth* or *Professional Foul*, Stoppard has never forgotten his Czech origins, which emphasize the constant doubleness of his life.

CHAPTER 20

MULTIPLE FASCINATION

It's a sad story, isn't it, my hopeless quest for simplicity.
Stoppard, 4 April 1995

On 26 March 1995, Stoppard held a cast party at O'Neal's restaurant on West 64th Street near Lincoln Center in New York: it was unique but consistent with his attraction to doubles because *two* casts were invited, one from *Hapgood*, which had had its run extended, and the other from *Arcadia*, which began previews on 2 March and would open on the 30th. It was a typical gesture of Stoppard's generosity and delight with the two productions. It also confirmed the ironic loss of his hope to write simple plays as two of his most complex works successfully made their way across the stages of Lincoln Center. More accurate than any wish to write 'simple' plays was his remark in New York's *Village Voice*: 'Entertaining and dealing with metaphysics are the same thing. They're simultaneous activities. Theatre is a recreation. It can be much more, but unless it's recreation, I don't see the point of it.'[1]

New York's premier not-for-profit theatre seemed to Stoppard the proper home for *Arcadia*, although Emanuel Azenberg disagreed. Azenberg saw *Arcadia* in London on its second night and thought it the best new play he had ever seen, apart from *Death of a Salesman*, which he had seen as a child. He immediately told Stoppard he wanted to take the show to Broadway, but Stoppard was hesitant: institutional theatre might be a better place for it, because he knew they would do *all* his plays, while commercial theatre only 'cherry-picked' the best. Azenberg gave him four reasons why *Arcadia* should go to Broadway: first, Lincoln Center could only do the play with an American cast: their rule is not to use imported actors; second, casting of American actors by a British director was chancey at best and often too quickly done; third, the performance had to be better than it was in England, since the worst notice you could get was that the American production was inferior to the English; and fourth, it was the wrong theatre from the point of size and publicity.

Stoppard disagreed and gave Lincoln Center the go-ahead. The very week *Arcadia* was to open at the Vivian Beaumont Theater in Lincoln Center, Neil Simon declared that he, too, was avoiding Broadway, heading downtown with his latest work and no longer putting his plays in to mid-town theatres where soaring production costs and inflated ticket prices ruled. David Mamet and Edward Albee soon joined the protest. Proof of the inflation and dangers of Broadway productions would occur that May with the collapse of *On the Waterfront*, a three-million-dollar production, after eight performances. The British shows that did dominate Broadway that winter were all spectacular: *Hamlet, Les Misérables, Cats, Phantom of the Opera, Sunset Boulevard*; as was the Lincoln Center's production of *Arcadia*.

'A seasoning of chaos and a pinch of thermodynamics following a dash of quantum mechanics' was Stoppard's summary of the play in 'The Matter of Metaphor', his essay in Lincoln Center's *New Theater Review*.[2] This time, without the assistance of Professor Robert May, who had instructed the London cast in chaos theory, Stoppard took on the task of lecturing his actors on fractals and algorithms; it was a challenge, since he had to put himself through a refresher course on what he knew about regular irregularity. In an interview preceding the opening, he reiterated a by-now-characteristic position in an effort to defuse charges of intellectualism: 'Art has a purpose which doesn't get as much attention as it ought to. The primary reason for its existence is as recreation.'[3] The message was that Stoppard wrote prismatic comedies in which language celebrated the certainty that there are no certainties.

The New York production of *Arcadia*, directed by Trevor Nunn, began previews in early March 1995, with its all-American cast which included Blair Brown, Billy Crudup and Robert Sean Leonard. There was some criticism that the American actors were uneven in their use of English accents. Rufus Sewell, the marvellous Septimus in the original London production two years earlier, was actually in New York at that time, acting in Brian Friel's *Translations*, although that play closed after only a few performances. Stoppard, who attended a number of the rehearsals, reacted to the Americans' unease in their English roles by preparing, as he so often did, notes for the actors which he didn't realize actually intimidated them. Robert Sean Leonard, Valentine in the production, noted that Stoppard 'forgets that actors are often terrified of writers. He finds that so strange.'[4] But Stoppard's concern with detail, whether it was props or music, was constant, according to the designer, Mark Thompson.

Arcadia featured a semicircular stage surrounded by a scrim on which a pastoral scene based on Poussin's *Spring* appeared, reminiscent of a Renaissance tapestry. At the centre of the screen, Eve held an apple in her palm, offering it to Adam. As the lights went down, a circle of light embracing Adam and Eve remained. That, too, faded as the curtain rose on the scene of Thomasina Coverly and her tutor, Septimus Hodge, studying at opposite ends of a long table. 'Septimus, what is carnal embrace?' is the wonderfully comic first line.[5] The production visually and dramatically showed how logical science and irrational love share an unpredictability. The play's confrontation and integration of matters erotic, pastoral and algebraic found affirmation in art, although in a universe that was slowly winding down. Stoppard, however, did make some concessions to his audience. The mock headline 'Bonking Byron Shoots Poet' became pure New Yorkese: 'Byron Bangs Wife, Shoots Poet'.

New York's reaction to the play was not as direct. Some left at the interval. Others who had already seen the London production missed its sensuality, but stayed. Lady Croom in the New York production was awful; the young males quite good. Audiences seemed to take away the science but not the emotion. 'In London you knew you were seeing a masterpiece,' said Azenberg; in New York, you weren't sure about anything. Vincent Canby reproachfully declared that the work was no more than 'a reasonable American facsimile' of the London production. One member of the audience pointed out the error of Septimus's mispronunciation of Fermat, sounding the final *t*: he knew French and so he should use the correct, French pronunciation, 'FER-MAH', wrote the observer.[6] The play, although nominated for a Tony as Best Play, lost to Terence McNally's *Love! Valour! Compassion!*. However, it did earn the New York Drama Critics' Circle award for Best Play of the 1994–5 season. The show ran until the end of August in repertory, although *Variety* noted in July that *Grease* was packing in audiences while *Arcadia* was not.

Lincoln Center at first hoped that the success of *Arcadia* might mean a transfer to Broadway and a possible American tour, as had happened with the British production, which, following its West End transfer, toured Britain for six months. However, the modest success of the play in New York and failure to win the Tony for Best Play made a transfer or tour unlikely. By May 1995, the executive producer of Lincoln Center, Bernard Gersten, decided the play was too logistically and intellectually complex to tour, which gave new force to the lobbying efforts of Carey Perloff of ACT to produce the play in San Francisco. Negotiations for the rights to *Arcadia* took on fresh urgency since the pre-production schedules for casting and design required an early decision if the American Conservatory Theater was to mount the play. Perloff finally got the green light from Kenneth Ewing in Tuscany when the Tonys were announced and *Arcadia* lost.

With characteristic generosity, Stoppard – generally uncomfortable in explaining his work – answered a series of queries from Perloff about the play, including her question concerning what Septimus laments when he says at the end 'when we have found all the mysteries and lost all the meaning, we will be alone, on an empty shore'.[7] Did he mean 'when we have answered all the mysteries (and then lost those answers in the endless search for meaning), we will be lost'? Stoppard replied:

> Yes, sort of 'Found' = found out, seen through, solved, answered. But in solving the mysteriousness of mystery (by for example maths), we lose its deeper meaning, psychic meaning. It's like . . . NASA can't solve the *meaning* of the moon, they can only demonstrate it's not made of cheese (I found out to my cost and slight embarrassment that the whole sentence says the same thing to me even if you transpose 'mystery' and 'meaning').[8]

Arcadia opened in San Francisco in October 1995, its first US production outside New York. It had already been seen in Germany, Belgium, Denmark, South Africa, Macedonia, Slovenia, Sweden and Poland.

Stoppard on Broadway had not been an outright success (the successful *Hapgood*, of course, played at Lincoln Center). *Rosencrantz and Guildenstern* and *Travesties* were hits, although the latter was something of a struggle to maintain at the box office until it won its Tony. *The Real Thing* in 1984 was something of a sensation because of its stars – Jeremy Irons and Glenn Close – and subject matter. The direction of Mike Nichols also added lustre. Stoppard understood that only subsidized theatre, with built-in assurance of subscription audiences guaranteeing box-office support, could afford his large-cast productions: *Jumpers* required nineteen, including the acrobats; *Travesties* eight; *Hapgood* nine; *Arcadia* thirteen; *Indian Ink* fifteen, plus two groups of servants and questioners; *The Invention of Love* needed twenty-three. Even *Rosencrantz and Guildenstern* required eighteen actors plus nine members of the court. Compared to Harold Pinter, David Hare or even Peter Nichols, a Stoppard play was an extravaganza.

Stoppard's greatest successes in America seemed to be in regional centres: Los Angeles, Philadelphia or San Diego, in subscription theatres such as the Ahmanson, the Wilma or the Old Globe. He enjoyed continued success at the American Conservatory Theater in San Francisco, beginning in 1968 with a production of *Rosencrantz and Guildenstern are Dead* and extending to *Arcadia* in 1995 and the American premières of both *Indian Ink* in February 1999 and *The Invention of Love* in January 2000. The appeal of Stoppard for a director and the public, Carey Perloff suggests, is that 'underneath that dazzling surface, Stoppard's work keeps coming back to a few very simple and powerful questions', through his confrontation of romantic misunderstandings and 'how hard it is to be with someone, to forge a relationship with someone that feels true'.[9]

While Stoppard maintained his involvement with the New York production of *Arcadia*, he worked on another project that required a US focus – this time, in Hollywood. In February 1994, Stoppard became the principal screenwriter for Steven Spielberg's project to produce a full-length, animated film of *Cats*. From the first, the studio was aware of the challenges involved in transferring a London stage hit, and what would soon become the longest-running Broadway musical of all time, to the screen. Numerous memos stressed that while the structure would be the same – a series of poems introducing a series of individual cats – translation into a film would be difficult.

Emotion and storyline would have to compensate for the loss of theatricality.

Working first with Trevor Nunn, who had directed the original stage version, and then Andrew Lloyd Webber and Spielberg, Stoppard fashioned a provisional first draft in late April 1994. This version was the result of reworking a fifty-page treatment by Nunn which Stoppard had received in February 1994. Nunn introduced a new storyline based on the old one, with the addition of a kidnap plot. Stoppard told the studio that he would consult Lloyd Webber (who would be executive producer) about this version, but that he anticipated few objections, in which case, his own role would be minimal and Nunn could claim main authorship of the film-story. Stoppard saw himself providing only some additional dialogue.

The restructuring, however, proved to be more challenging. By 1 May, a rewritten script, now mostly by Stoppard, appeared, with Lloyd Webber, Stoppard and Spielberg in agreement on the thematic focus: the emotion of the movie should emanate from the mirror relationship between Demeter and Grizabella, which the stage version treated as background. It was necessary to intensify the moment when Demeter sees a vision of what life would be like if she allowed herself to be seduced by Macavity's jewels and promises. Stoppard offered a practical suggestion: they should increase the screen time Demeter spends with Grizabella and intensify Demeter's responsibility for Macavity taking Old Deuteronomy, and hence her responsibility for his rescue.

Providing an intriguing view of the corners and crannies of a London cat's world would improve the beginning. To an unnamed executive, it 'screams movie' in its early look at Macavity's lair and the museum of ancient cats. Stoppard then proposed a new title sequence, opening with a large, old cat sleeping on Tower Bridge, which prevents the bridge from opening. The time is the 1930s. Jellyorum joins Old Deuteronomy, the cat on the bridge, who gradually awakens as they are both transformed into semi-human embodiments of their personalities. They slide down as the bridge splits open and the main title appears over the frame of the two cats righting themselves, two-legged. The next shot, number 23, moves to a panorama map of London which remains as the backcloth to the title sequence. Stoppard's skill is clearly in seeing things in parts, yet visualizing their sequence and continuity to establish theme.

Setting up the physical world in the film was not a problem; the bigger challenge was to figure out the mythology of the thematic world in such a way that it would not detract from the film's entertainment value. Another troubling issue was length. The first draft of the screenplay (1 May 1994) was ninety-nine pages and assumed to be ninety minutes long. But 'even if the script works in terms of running time, as a story, it feels longer than it should' and had to be cut.[10] As soon as Old Deuteronomy has been kidnapped, the story slows down and some songs are too short. Stoppard, in a pencilled comment on the script, writes 'no' at the suggestion of condensing some of the action, such as Macavity's thefts. However, timed out at 100 minutes and 24 seconds, it was too long; musical numbers had to be condensed and some secondary characters possibly eliminated. Together, Stoppard and Lloyd Webber worked carefully to cut script and time in an effort to get it down to approximately eighty-five minutes.

Stoppard paused in his work on the script from mid-June to mid-July when he went to New Zealand and then Australia to help with a production of *Arcadia*. He reported to Spielberg, however, that he spent '4 days in Tahiti with "Cats"' but admitted that the new agenda for Macavity made for some difficulties with the plot. Reducing the screen time by fifteen minutes was also problematic. Back in London, he told Spielberg that a studio head wanted to fly him back to Hollywood for a day, which he could certainly do, 'but perhaps an hour on the phone is almost as good'.[11] However, prolonged script development and further complications relating to cost, plus the suggestion that other writers should be brought in (notably from Pixar, the makers of *Toy Story*) to 'punch up' Stoppard's script, plus the politics of the studios that pitted Universal against Spielberg's Amblinmation (part of Amblin Entertainment), which at the time was being folded into the new Dreamworks, led to the cancellation of the project in late 1994. It remains unproduced.

There is only one thing more charmless than a dramatist
quoting himself, and that is a dramatist misquoting himself.
Stoppard, 1984

While *Arcadia* prepared for its New York début, Stoppard involved himself with the West End opening of *Indian Ink,* his reworking of *In the Native State.* His return to India in late 1990, after the radio play was completed, prolonged his interest in the topic; his promise of another West End production to Michael Codron made delivery an obligation. The success of the radio play meant that audiences had had a taste of Stoppard's treatment of the subject. The decision to cast Felicity Kendal in the role of Flora Crewe again, along with Art Malik as Das, meant an immediate box-office draw and advance sales for the show were phenomenal, helped, of course, by the success of *Arcadia,* which continued its run at the Haymarket. Stoppard, with Michael Codron, assembled the old gang: Peter Wood directed, Carl Toms did the design and Mark Henderson did the lighting.

Differences from the radio play were noticeable, since Stoppard took more chances with that work. Structurally, the radio play presented nineteen scenes without a break. The stage play consists of two acts with a series of scenes that effortlessly flow into each other but are not divided up. Moments overlap as characters stand next to each other from two different time periods but do not see each other; time slides easily from 1930 to the present. In the radio play, there is a scene in England and then a scene in India, one succeeding the other. In the stage play, scenes and characters vividly and physically overlap, similar to the final scene of *Arcadia,* where the two time periods co-existed with characters from both centuries using the same props on the same table.

One way Stoppard constructed the overlapping time shifts in *Indian Ink* was to have Eleanor Swan in London in the 1980s silently reading her sister's letters from 1930 describing a dak bungalow, while we hear Flora's voice behind her and off to the side, wandering about the bungalow in Jammapur in 1930. Eleanor then wanders off and Flora sits at the same table. In this way, the fluidity of time finds physical expression. The staging also allowed the audience to be part of the creative understanding of the work, matching what they had seen with what was said while also trying to figure out whether it held up.

Stoppard also made some structural and textual changes to the poetry for the stage play. *In the Native State* opens with Flora reading her sensuous poem about heat. *Indian Ink* postpones the poem until after Flora has established her presence in India, her relationship with Das and her sister's association with the biographer Eldon Pike. The text of the poem also differs slightly, Stoppard removing the reference to 'a woman in a blue dress' and substituting 'a woman in a house of net/that strains the oxygen out of the air'.[12] However, in their suggestiveness, both versions prefigure how Flora becomes a woman 'without secrets', which her sister and Das's son, Anish, confirm as they uncover her identity and desires.

At one point in the play, Eleanor Swan also explains to Anish that her sister's weakness was romance and that it was quite possible that Flora had a romance with Das or Durance or the Rajah of Jummapur, 'or someone else entirely. It hardly matters, looking back. Men were not really important to Flora. If they had been, they would have been fewer. She used them like batteries. When things went flat, she'd put in a new one.'[13]

For the stage play, Stoppard also expanded the role of the American professor, Eldon Pike, who not only offers verbal footnotes to Flora's life, but goes to India to search for additional information. Stoppard enjoys satirizing his enthusiastic pursuit of Flora Crewe and easy misunderstanding of so-called 'facts'. There are also many more references to real people in the play, including Madame Blavatsky and Louis MacNeice. Flora's poem about heat also contains a new, direct reference to Indian ink. Surprisingly, Stoppard did not read Paul Scott's *The Jewel in the Crown*, or watch the television adaptation of the work before writing the play. Most of his reading was factual: histories, autobiographies and biographies, although he did reread *A Passage to India* by E. M. Forster, which he felt was necessary since the play is set in 1930 and the novel appeared in 1924. Flora actually asks Das if he has read Forster's novel.[14] Other sources were Charles Allen's *Scrapbooks of the Raj* and Nirad C. Chaudhuri's *Autobiography of an Unknown Indian*.

In the radio play, history is announced or declared, but in the stage play it is presented. Emily Eden is a case in point. Scene Thirteen of *In the Native State* contains several explanatory passages by Pike about Emily Eden and her background, beginning with Flora's discovery in the dak bungalow 'among a box of dilapidated railway novels a book of letters written from India a hundred years ago by an English spinster – hand on my heart – to her sister Eleanor in London, and this is now my only reading'.[15] The scene reappears in Act Two of *Indian Ink*, and later Eleanor Swan refers to Eden in discussion with Anish in London. In the stage play, she actually gives Anish Flora's copy of the book because 'it belonged to your father. It has his name in it,' altering the provenance of the book.[16]

Stoppard ends both the radio and stage plays with an excerpt from Eden's diary, one of the few outright political statements in the play. Expressing her contempt for colonial rule in a passage dated 25 May 1839, Eden describes a ball to honour Queen Victoria at which one hundred and five Europeans were surrounded by some three thousand Indians, who bowed if a European came near them. Upset at the power exerted by the colonials, she wonders why the Indians don't destroy them and be done with it.

During the previews for the London production, to make the point perhaps too clearly that she and Das had probably slept together, Flora wakes up in bed wearing Das's shawl. But this seemed too obvious and was cut. *Rasa* was even more crucial than in the radio play because it had to be visually represented through gestures and actions. A nude bedroom scene called for the forty-eight-year-old Felicity Kendal to appear naked on stage for the first time in her career, a mini-scandal – at least in the tabloids. The move was justified, Kendal explained, because of the play; her part called for it during the scene when she becomes ill; though the scene in the radio play of her being painted in the nude by Das was absent in the stage version. Kendal's nudity 'lasts less than a minute. She walks from a bathroom door to a bed, and is obscured by a mosquito net', one theatre critic disappointedly wrote. And one paper felt compelled to report that 'Ms. Kendal has an enviably slim figure, but she is no Sharon Stone or Cindy Crawford' and that her action 'to appear nude in middle age . . . reveals a woman of courage and great inner confidence'.[17] What the relationship between Nirad Das and Flora Crewe reinforces is the Stoppardian theme that falling in love can occur through, or even because of, the commingling of ideas. In *Arcadia*, Septimus and Thomasina fell in love through the beauty of mathematics. Here, it is through the characters 'appreciating the eroticism of a really good idea'.[18]

Stoppard made changes to the *Indian Ink* script right up until the opening night on 27 February 1995. He re-ordered scenes in the second act and for several nights during the previews, he and Peter Wood tried an alternative ending which didn't work. Another change from the radio play was the addition of the apricot which Flora seductively and boldly eats without washing or peeling when visiting the Rajah of Jummapur immediately after their discussion of erotic art, which we overhear in *In the Native State* but do not see or hear in *Indian Ink*.[19]

Like *Arcadia*, *Indian Ink* is partly a detective story and partly a romance. The detective motif continued the farcical misinterpretation of the past by academics. When Eldon Pike, the ambitious editor/biographer of Flora Crewe, wonders about Flora's dream concerning 'the Queen's Elm. Which Queen? What elm? Why was she dreaming about a *tree*?', Eleanor Swan instantly deflates him with the remark that it was only a pub on the Fulham Road. 'Thank you,' he replies, adding 'this is why God made writers, so the rest of us can publish'.[20] In comic revenge for his blunders and tenacious research, Anish Das and Eleanor Swan agree *not* to tell Pike about the watercolour nude Anish's father had painted of Flora. His father would not want it known, 'not even in a footnote', Anish says. 'Good for you. I don't tell Mr Pike everything either,' Eleanor Swan impishly remarks.[21]

Pike and his footnotes originated with Stoppard's idea of writing a novel where everything happened in the footnotes – as Nabokov did in *Pale Fire*. It actually connects with the theme of a commentator making points about the material which he is part of – not that different, Stoppard pointed out, from the critics in *The Real Inspector Hound* or Rosencrantz and Guildenstern, who are themselves living footnotes commenting on the action of their play. It is the device of 'having a voice outside the play, though belonging to a character in the play', he explained.[22] This also describes Stoppard's remarkable double act – part of, and apart from, England, simultaneously English and Czech, British and Central European, non-Jewish and Jewish, in the centre and marginalized.

Indian Ink opened quietly, without the customary author interviews, and got away with being something of a slender work, certainly lacking the density of *Arcadia*. Nevertheless, it was by Stoppard, with his leading lady, Felicity Kendal, in the starring role. Critics were generous, noting the warm russet glow of Peter Wood's production and admiring the 'atmosphere of mellow lucidity' in opposition to the 'witty dazzle' of *Arcadia*.[23]

Comparisons to previous treatments of Anglo-Indian relations in E. M. Forster and Paul Scott's *The Raj Quartet*, however, complained of Stoppard's sparse treatment of political complexities and personal predicaments. Praise was given, instead, to his focus on the aesthetic drawbacks of imperial influence, underscored by Das painting Flora in westernized style – which she rejects. Not even art is in its native state as Flora discovers – which one viewer made clear in a letter to Stoppard telling him that during the time of the play, no one referred to the *Times Literary Supplement* as the *TLS*. The play was a success, however, and played for ten months.[24]

The *Observer* ran a feature gauging Stoppard's prominence, divided into the 'case for' and the 'case against'. The 'case for' praised 'the ageless bright boy of the British theatre', describing him as the 'witty defender of the language as befits the Czech son of a shoe salesman and a staunch advocate of human rights. Good bloke, national treasure.' The case against read 'guilty of allowing generations of middle-class, semi-educated London theatre-goers a smug sense of intellectual adequacy with smart dramas' and complained that *Indian Ink* was wildly overpraised. The account ended with Stoppard's 'Falling words': 'I don't mind as long as you're not doing Harold Pinter instead.'[25]

I am a fatal victim of multiple fascination.

Stoppard, 1986

In the mid-nineties, Stoppard extended his interest in multiple genres and forms with new work, beginning with the filmscript for the animated *Cats*, an attempt at adapting *Arcadia* for the screen, a restaging of *Rosencrantz and Guildenstern* at the National and an adaptation of Chekhov's *The Seagull* for Peter Hall. He also laboured on a revised screenplay of *Shakespeare in Love*, now in the hands of Miramax, a film adaptation of Robert Harris's *Enigma* for Mick Jagger and a new play, *The Invention of Love*, which would première in October 1997 at the Cottesloe Theatre of the National. A revival of *The*

Real Thing at the Donmar Warehouse in May 1999 and the American première of *The Invention of Love* in San Francisco in January 2000 kept him active, while rumours of a new work dealing with nineteenth-century Russian writers circulated, possibly fallout from his work on Chekhov and youthful neglect of reading the Russian novelists. A New York production of *The Invention of Love* opened in the early spring of 2001, sponsored by the Lincoln Center. Any spare time was taken up by rehearsals, lectures or interviews.

Behind all this activity, however, lay his dissolving relationship with Felicity Kendal and short-lived rumours of a renewed 'friendship' with Mia Farrow. The split with Kendal began in mid-1997. At the time, the fifty-one-year-old actress was looking after not only her nine-year-old son, Jake, from her marriage to Rudman, and Charlie, her twenty-four-year-old son from her first marriage, but also her father, who had been in a London nursing home for three years, paralysed by a stroke. Her mother had died in 1992; and her father, then aged eighty-four, had an affair with her mother's nurse. But when questioned about her relationship with Stoppard in a February 1997 interview, Kendal restated the ground rules: she doesn't talk about Tom. 'We have a pact never to talk about each other. We can't. It's an agreement . . . I'm very old fashioned in that I have a tremendous need to protect a certain area.'[26]

The papers did not share that sentiment, but tracking Kendal netted only such cryptic remarks as 'I love many people and Tom is one of them' and 'I don't suit marriage'. She soon returned to her former husband, Michael Rudman. Asked in July if she and Stoppard had broken up, Kendal replied: 'Have a nice day'.[27] Her pledge with Stoppard – that neither would talk about the other – remained, and was maintained when her autobiography *White Cargo* was published in the summer of 1998. Her relationship with Stoppard is not mentioned even once in the narrative, although his name appears on the back jacket flap, along with four other playwrights.

Before the Stoppard–Kendal relationship broke up, there was a slightly tongue-in-cheek piece focusing on the failure of British libraries to retain the manuscripts of important contemporary writers. Libby Purves begins her critique with mock-horror that Stoppard's letters from Kendal had probably been lost to the nation. The 'dastardly Americans have bought this literary archive' which is securely resting on an air-conditioned shelf in Austin, Texas, the columnist complained. Not only were such essential documents as the Kendal–Stoppard letters inaccessible, but other revealing materials such as Stoppard's 'invitation to the wedding of Lady Sarah Armstrong-Jones' had also been whisked away from prying English eyes. Stoppard couldn't resist a reply. Four days later, his disingenuous statement appeared in *The Times*, with a hint of triumph matched by a tone of impregnable seriousness and scholarship: 'As students of journalism may already suspect, my valuable collection of letters from Felicity Kendal is not yet lost to the nation, and serious researchers must apply to me.'[28]

Stoppard spent his sixtieth birthday in July 1997 with Mia Farrow in Annamoe, County Wicklow, where she was working on a film and staying in a cottage with three of her children on the estate of John Boorman, Stoppard's old friend. Relaxed and informal, the two enjoyed the Irish countryside. The papers made much of the attachment but little other than friendship was revealed. Little was also made in the press of his turning sixty, other than his admitting to a reporter that 'I'm evidently dying of something – until about 12 o'clock every day'. He continued with his writing practice of beginning at about midday and going through to about midnight: 'I never work in the morning unless I'm in real trouble,' he quipped.[29]

Despite her separation from Stoppard, Kendal played the role of Madame Arkadina in his adaptation of *The Seagull* for Peter Hall at the Old Vic in the summer of 1997. Kendal had joined Hall's troupe, which attempted to restore the idea of a London repertory company devoted to the classics in contrast to the National and RSC, for a season at the Old Vic. She had just played the lead in Pinero's *Waste* for Hall before undertaking the role of Arkadina. This was the seventh time Hall had directed Kendal; just six months earlier, she had been in his production of Feydeau's *Mind Millie for Me*.

A play that often falls into the mists of Russian melancholy, *The Seagull* in Hall's production was comic and alert, aided, of course, by Stoppard's bracing adaptation. He again worked from a literal translation, this time by Joanna Wright, and contributed a series of running jokes based on quotations from *King Lear*, as well as *Hamlet*. For example, Konstantin tells Dr Dorn in Act Four, echoing Hamlet to Horatio, that 'life out there is harder than is dreamt of, Doctor, in your philosophy'. He also made his own comic contribution in lines like 'having no backbone, he was able to bend both ways', mocking Trigorin's tendency for sexual sharing.[30]

Stoppard balanced faithfulness to the original with his own brisk wit, enhancing the tragicomic mood of the work and infusing a contemporary sensibility; this new version of the play, Sheridan Morley remarked, 'might have been written 100 days instead of 100 years ago'.[31] With Dr Dorn, for example, declaring that 'I've lived a pick-and-choose sort of life', the use of such contemporary language seemed equal to the modern thrust of the production – as does the withering question Arkadina asks her son, Konstantin: 'Since when has the exhibition of a morbid personality been a new art form?' And in a line echoing the frustration of Rosencrantz ('Incidents! All we get is incidents! Dear God, is it too much to expect a little sustained action?!'), Nina tells Konstantin that 'there isn't much *action* in your play, it's all – you know – *lines*'.[32] Stoppard's conception of the work is, indeed, comic, following Chekhov's own view that the play is 'a comedy with much talk about literature and five tons of love'.[33]

In a programme note, Stoppard clarified the nature of what he had done: 'a translation as scrupulous as a ledger – that is, where everything on the Russian side of the line is accounted for on the English side, sentence by sentence . . . would have its purpose. But the spoken art has imperatives which are unforgiving. In the theatre the question, "what is translation" is replaced by "what is translation for?" and the answer is that it is for the event.' The translation is for the actor, the speaker. At a rehearsal, the translator has more to think about than an author, Stoppard adds, noting as well that the great quartet of plays by Chekhov are 'still the exempla of modern drama which is modern in the sense of insisting on being explored before it can be acted'.[34]

In his introduction to the published version of the play, Stoppard goes into greater detail about his text, proud to engage with Chekhov's language and world, while joining such other contemporary 'adapters' as Michael Frayn and David Mamet. He explains that while he worked from the literal translation made by Joanna Wright, he also had his eye on four other versions, and then cites a fifth, Pam Gems' text used for the 1994 National production, which he finds the most unconventional but closest to his own attempt. What he admires in Gems' work is the effort to convey the sense of the action rather than the literal word. But, again, he stresses that the translator works for the actor and that theatre is, above all else, a spoken art. In this case, the translator/adapter may, indeed, have been working for Kendal, who received generally favourable notices for her performance. And in his rationale of adapting, Stoppard again displays his practical understanding of theatre and the pragmatics of production.

Unrequited and illusionary love dominate discussions on the artificial nature of writing in *The Seagull*. Konstantin, overreacting to his mother's rejection of his art, cries, 'I've lost everything. She doesn't love me – I can't write any more – I've lost all hope.'[35] They make up, but the next moment the heartbroken Trigorin enters and Madame Arkadina must again comfort a shattered heart. The production of *The Seagull* revealed that the characters who show any capacity for change are tragic, while those who remain locked inside their own egos are comic. Yet Kendal's performance was highlighted as showing self-absorption without forfeiting sympathy, while Michael Pennington's Trigorin was suitably smug at the same time as he exposed his moral weaknesses. The entire production succeeded in showing what people were feeling but failing to say.

Stoppard's work on Chekhov made him mindful again of the challenges of translation and dovetailed with his study of Housman. He repeatedly experienced the difficulties of the genre, working, as he had in the past, from literal translations in order to fashion his own adaptations. Housman's view of translation, that a work should be accurate rather than poetic, was actually an antidote to Stoppard's practice. Yet he would have most likely applauded Housman's belief that 'to determine what an ancient author actually wrote is, in a small but significant way, to repossess a lost certainty, to be enabled once again to see things as they really are'. A single sentence by Housman encapsulates his view of textual criticism, which *The Invention of Love* elaborates: 'textual criticism is a science, and, since it comprises recension and emendation, it is also an art'.[36] But although his translations admitted virtually no lacunae, Stoppard found that Housman's life did, and those gaps became the source of his next play.

Don't let me put you off, my objections are a mere detail.
Stoppard, January 1999

'Can a play show us the very truth and nature of love?' This question, posed by Queen Elizabeth to Viola in *Shakespeare in Love*,[37] in many ways summarizes the issues Stoppard had been facing throughout his career. Through the voice of Will Shakespeare and his play *Romeo and Juliet* (how ironic that film, rather than drama, has finally given Stoppard the opportunity to become Shakespeare, a role he'd sought since his first major work), he showed how 'nature and truth' are *not* 'the very enemies of playacting', but the opposite.[38] The ability to do so partly derived from his new self-awareness and conviction that love was the deepest form of knowing and drama the most direct way of expressing it.

At the same time as Stoppard was writing about love and finding himself in the limelight, he was paradoxically letting down his guard, feeling that it was 'okay' to reveal more of himself. Self-protection was less necessary and he was ready to live 'without secrets', as Flora Crewe writes in *Indian Ink*.[39] In a 1998 lecture, he confirmed this: 'as I get older, I am less concerned about concealing myself in my plays – consequently, they are more emotional'. The reasons for this shift were varied, beginning with a clearer understanding of his past, a sense, perhaps, of his age and a realization that hiding himself frankly didn't matter any more. This began in earnest with his comments in 1997 to Benedict Nightingale and then gradually, but with increasing frequency, in other interviews and articles, culminating in his essay of September 1999, 'Another country'. Critics also began to detect a change in his plays, citing a 'defiant optimism' in his work and a 'new note of warmth and acceptance of disorder and unpredictability'. And as he began to 'open up', Stoppard even began to acknowledge that his life was uncommon:

> I've had quite an interesting life by some standards. I was born on one continent, brought up in the Far East, became English when I was 8 and so forth. I mean, it's not uninteresting.[40]

The cause for this shift was a confluence of personal events, beginning in 1993–4 with the recovery and confirmation of his Jewish past, followed by the death of his mother in October 1996, his break-up with Felicity Kendal in 1997 and the writing of *The Invention of Love*. The death of Stoppard's stepfather in July 1997, and his feeling, after his return to Zlín in 1998 and again in 1999, that the past must and *could* be dealt with, also contributed to his decreased self-protection.

The situation of Anish Das, outlined by Stoppard in *Indian Ink*, curiously parallels what he experienced regarding this altered identity. Anish doesn't feel Indian in the play: he went to school in England, married an Englishwoman, continues to live there and thinks of himself as an English painter. But a good part of his journey is the discovery of his own Indianness through meeting Eleanor Swan and learning about his father's life. Such an understanding provides him with another, richer identity. Stoppard went through a similar process as he uncovered his own Jewish identity. The parallels are striking, as *Indian Ink* was composed in 1994–5 and Stoppard's earliest suggestions of his mother's Jewish past occurred in 1993; the following year he met his distant relative in a Prague hotel and after his mother's death in 1996, he discovered her correspondence with Dr Máčel in Zlín.

The collective impact of these events, at the same time as he was earning such honours as a knighthood (June 1997) and being celebrated as the first living foreign playwright ever to have a work performed at the Comédie-Française, plus winning an Oscar for co-writing *Shakespeare in Love*, and, in May 2000, being elevated to the prestigious Order of Merit bestowed by the Queen, affected Stoppard in such a way as to make him feel more secure about revealing himself. Another paradox: the more established he felt in England, the more he could reveal his 'otherness'. Doubleness now entailed not the hiding of one self from another, but their co-existence. Turning sixty in 1997 may have made him more anxious to discover his past for his own sake, as well as for his brother and their children.

Two interviews from this time particularly capture the new Stoppard. When previously asked about his past, he carefully avoided answering the question. There had been a persistent sense of protecting something, about veering farther away, rather than towards, the shaping events and formative moments of his life. But in a 1997 interview with Benedict Nightingale, Stoppard fully outlined his new-found candour. Confronted by the observation that his plays had become less emotionally guarded, he reluctantly and comically admitted that

> Yes, you can't all be wrong. And it's not difficult to work out. I'm a very shy, private person and I camouflaged myself by display rather than by reticence. I became a repressed exhibitionist. I found emotional self-exposure embarrassing – and now I don't, or less so. The older I get, the less I care about self-concealment.[41]

In the same article, he admitted that his reticence had been replaced by a willingness to illuminate the past through his own efforts to understand it and a concern for posterity. With age comes a certain insouciance about what others' expect, and Stoppard cited what he considers to be one of the great movie lines: Tommy Lee Jones's rejoinder to Harrison Ford in *The Fugitive*. Pursued by Jones to the edge of a waterfall, Ford shouts in desperation, 'I didn't kill my wife!' An indifferent Jones answers, 'I don't care.' Time is limited, Stoppard said, and you 'have to choose what matters. And part of me is beginning to say "I don't care".'[42] Stoppard soon dropped his signature interview style, which began with questioning the premise of a question and ended by questioning the question itself, while in between he used words with nonchalant vividness. The old view was that 'Stoppard doesn't write plays, he builds glittering theatrical erector sets – wit-strewn, mirrored theatrical mazes that alternately baffle and delight audiences with high-wire linguistic pirouettes and bizarre twists'.[43] The new perspective was that he was grappling with emotional issues that needed to be faced.

Critics suddenly noticed that Stoppard had not been well-served by productions of his work. They had too often stressed the high comedy at the cost of his existential despair and fundamental humanism, which emerged from his awareness of the discontinuity between our imagination and human condition. Thomasina in *Arcadia* illustrated this clearly through her imaginative perceptions concerning maths and heat; Bernard illustrated it comically through his wrongheaded but enthusiastic pursuit of Byron's supposed duel with Chater. One critic in 1997 suggested that Stoppard actually hides 'a very serious case of cosmic depression'. Stoppard is expert in concealing his disorder, as his interviews, lectures, talks and plays constantly show. He tries hard to say little, his plays active efforts to disguise his own insights and attitudes. 'I wouldn't dare to write about most of the things I write about were I not a playwright,' Stoppard has said.[44] But his glittering surface conceals despair if not death, a reading of Stoppard that coincides with his newly open self.

By November 1998, Stoppard felt comfortable about announcing his new self-awareness. As he has aged, he has shed 'layers of protection' and cared less about what he has revealed of himself: 'I was extremely protective when I started writing, very shy and self-conscious. But I'm quite surprised with this degree of losing shyness,' he admitted.[45]

Stoppard's interview with Lyn Gardner took place just before Christmas 1998 and was published, with the headline 'The Heart in the Closet', in the new year. It opened by repeating the by now conventional view that his plays are about thinking, not feeling, and that audiences leave the theatre with a good deal more information about chaos theory but not the heart. Ideas, rather than people, had always fired up Stoppard's writing; let the actors provide the emotion, he has implied. But despite his denial that the events of his life are in his work – 'My opinions may filter through, but never my life' – he was beginning to admit that some connections did exist.[46]

Links between a writer's life and work do not interest him, he says in the interview, although he quickly undercuts his own remark: 'Do I really mean that?' He acknowledges that such connections certainly interest others and that the very essence of *Shakespeare in Love* is the relationship between the playwright's life and work. But he again rejects any connection between his facile manner with English and the linguistic skills demonstrated by the émigrés Conrad and Nabokov, claiming that, unlike these two cases, English was *always* his first language. He does admit, however, that the family was sent to Singapore because of their Jewishness: 'My mother always made out that we were sent to Singapore because of the Jewish grandparent, but we were Jewish by race.' This was also where he defensively explained that 'My mother didn't consider herself Jewish, she wasn't a religious woman'.[47] He then mentions his 1994 encounter at a Prague hotel and the discovery that his mother had two further siblings he had never heard of. Yet, he still maintains he had no curiosity about his past, at least in his early years in England and during the early part of his career.

The apex of Stoppard's self-discovery was his September 1999 article in *Talk*, 'On turning out to be Jewish' reprinted in the *Sunday Telegraph* on 10 October 1999. Its title in the UK underscored his distinct sense of foreignness: it read 'Another country'. In both versions, the article is an important confrontation with his past and its impact on his life. Interestingly this occurs visually, through the photographs of the Beck family which begin the article, corroborating a remark on mathematical theory he had made earlier that year: 'I understand it pictorially', rather than intellectually.[48] So, too, does he understand his family's past, especially as he looks at early family pictures which suddenly contain a fifth girl, his mother, aged three, in 1914. Confronted by these visual records, he discovers his own past; documents and mere names are less immediate than images.

Stoppard's removal of his protective self was not, however, complete. There was still an unwillingness to embrace his Jewish origins and Czech past which made his visits to the Czech Republic and encounters with history all the more complicated. On the one hand, Stoppard *wants* to know that background but on the other he is reluctant to seize it. This ambiguity was acutely evident in his *Talk/Sunday Telegraph* essay, when he wrote that when he and his brother came home from school, 'my mother would see us off by pushing bags of toffee at us. But for every home-made cake and knick-knack she gave out, my mother held back much more, whole histories.'[49] He still referred to himself and his brother Peter as 'half-Jewish' when describing his youth and relationship with his stepfather, despite the revelations in his *Talk/Sunday Telegraph* article that his mother was not 'Catholic', as she wrote on her employment application at Bat'a, but Jewish.

Stoppard makes it clear that the signs of the past he had uncovered in Prague, Zlín and elsewhere had 'the power to move, but not to reclaim' him; he could not give up his English name for his Czech origin.[50] This occurs with no small amount of embarrassment, acknowledging that his early denial of his sense of his Jewish past was an 'almost wilful purblindness, a rarely disturbed absence of curiosity combined with an endless willingness not to disturb [his] mother by questioning her'.[51] He honestly admits his 'self-reproach' at not wanting to know more from his mother, a condition 'not helped by my current state of mind now that I'm Jewish. I feel no more Jewish than I felt Czech when, 22 years ago, I went to Prague for a week to do my English bit for Charter 77.'[52]

*I was busy being English and seldom thought about these
mysterious distant relatives.*

Stoppard, 1999

Edward Said claims that 'all families invent their parents and children,
give each of them a story, character, fate and even a language'.[53]
Stoppard's invention, generated out of his mother's fear that the
family's true identity might undo their security in their new home, and
his step-father's determination to sever any links with the Central
European, Jewish past of his two stepchildren, enveloped Stoppard
throughout his youth and adulthood. It meant a distancing from, if
not denial of, his Jewish roots, and the formation of a set of remarkable
paradoxes: an unusually strong British identity, although he didn't
sound English; plays that succeeded in establishing an Englishness
while possessing qualities critics and the public found to be foreign
(excessive wit, absurdity); an eagerness to include history but a
tendency to fictionalize historical figures; a determination to re-create
the past while distrusting it. His work also contained a subversive
aspect, a character or situation that consciously worked to undermine
a convention or cliché. His parody of genres, love of pastiche and
hidden bleakness – 'we're all going to end up at room temperature' –
further distinguished his work from his contemporaries. Beckett
'decked out' might be an informal way of understanding his work,
much of it an elegant and sophisticated elaboration of Nell's remark in
Endgame that 'nothing is funnier than unhappiness'.[54] But Stoppard is
unsure of how to react to his reconstructed past. He can write about it,
but can he accept it? Not, perhaps, until he can dramatize it in a play.

A series of losses began to accrue, starting with his mother, who died
on 11 October 1996. She and Stoppard's stepfather were living at the
time in Devon. At eighty-five, she was suffering from cancer and her
final words to him, spoken from the front passenger seat of his car as
he drove her to hospital for the last time, expressed frustration and
worry: impatiently, she said, 'And Tom hasn't got any sweets!' Sweets
were to her 'a surety against the likelihood of my falling asleep at the
wheel on my journeys back to London,' he explained.[55] A curious
response to her death was the reconstitution of his Czech identity. 'I

feel the torch has been passed on to me to be Czech,' he told an interviewer in December 1996:

> A few days after I returned from her funeral service I was invited to a reception, an annual event held by the Czech ambassador in London. I never go to these things. I don't like receptions; I'm always too busy and too behind with my work. But I came back from the funeral and suddenly wanted to go. I suddenly felt Czech. So, I went and I was Czech for a couple of hours.[56]

In 1968, when the armies of the Warsaw Pact invaded Czechoslovakia, Stoppard was indifferent. Jose, his then wife, was incredulous that he didn't get upset by it as a Czech. He, however, 'had no special feeling other than the general English one of impotent condemnation ... I knew I was – used to be – Czech but I didn't feel Czech.' That year, he had some money for the first time and spent it on first editions of Austen, Dickens and Waugh and started to collect nineteenth-century English landscape watercolours while living at River Thatch in Bourne End: 'I felt I was about as English as you can get.'[57] His 1977 trip to Prague to write about human rights and Charter 77 also had little impact on rekindling his Czech identity.

In his *Talk/Sunday Telegraph* article, Stoppard seems distant and objective about the discovery of his Jewishness, reminding one of Jonathan Miller's waffling line in *Beyond the Fringe* when asked his religion: 'I'm not a Jew, exactly,' he replies, 'I'm Jewish.' Similarly, the critic John Lahr remembered his mother telling him about his father, the actor Bert Lahr: 'John, your father was not Jewish. He was a star.'[58] When asked if he was Jewish during his Bristol years, Stoppard would respond in a similarly jokey manner. The *Talk/Sunday Telegraph* article, however, contains a tone of self-reproach, not about his religion but concerning his father, originating in his failure to feel a greater sense of loss over his father's death. Not caring about how his father died, or that he died, seems to be the centre of the essay. Judaism still seems something he keeps apart from himself, alternately an irritant and an identity, and he is slightly dismissive of its importance, hesitant to confront its importance because it might undo his own self-perception or established image. He has discovered who he is, but equivocates over its acceptance. He is Jewish and he isn't.

This curiously parallels the situation of the Austrian dramatist Arthur Schnitzler, two of whose plays Stoppard had adapted for the National in 1979 and 1986. All his life, Schnitzler neither denied his Jewishness nor asserted it. Denial was to him demeaning; assertion led to self-deluding vanity. There may be something similar in Stoppard, who never denied that there was Jewishness in his past, on his father's side. He furthermore strongly and publicly defended the rights of the refuseniks and Soviet dissidents, leading the roll-call of dissidents at the National Theatre in 1986, which convinced many that Stoppard was Jewish – otherwise, why would he take such an interest in the lives of Soviet Jews?

Stoppard has said that he became 'habituated to the unexamined idea that although . . . there was some Jewish blood in me (my father's father?), enough to make me more interesting to myself, and to have risked attention from the Nazis, it was not really enough to connect me with the Jews who died in the camps and those who didn't.'[59] This admission of being Jewish at a distance is crucial. He believed he could be, or not be, a Jew, just as he could choose to be or not be Czech. But Stoppard didn't make such a choice about being English. That was something he always wanted to be. His comic skills gave him a strategy to achieve a nervous freedom both to be and not to be like other men. His talk about his neutrality, taking no sides, allowed him to explore both sides of an issue without fear and is part of his ambivalency or desire to hide his identity, behaviour partially inherited from his mother. Conceivably, Stoppard's belief that one can never truly or completely know the past and his corresponding satire of biographers or historians in his work originates in his suspicion of what they may uncover. Better to argue that they will always misrepresent.

But it may be even more complicated, and Schnitzler may again be helpful. All his writing life, the Austrian dramatist observed the Jewish condition with a kind of involved indifference. There is a telling passage in his autobiography: 'even if you managed somehow to conduct yourself so that nothing showed, it was impossible to remain completely untouched; as for instance a person may not remain unconcerned whose skin has been anaesthetized but who has to watch, with his eyes open, how it is scratched by an unclean knife, even cut until the blood flows.'[60] In the past, Stoppard had said flat out that he

494

was not Jewish, something one can do rationally but perhaps not emotionally or psychologically.

Contributing to Stoppard's absorption with his past may be his discomfort with his xenophobic stepfather, who was determined to keep it out of their home, disliking blacks, Irish, Yanks and Jews, according to Stoppard. Kenneth Stoppard's reaction to the perceived 'tribalization' of his stepson in associating with Jews, especially in the seventies and eighties, led to the shocking request for Stoppard to give back the Stoppard name and revert to Sträussler. Stoppard's cool reply – 'it's not practical' – displayed his resistance to renouncing his English identity.[61] He expressed this view at the ceremony of his knighthood in December 1997: 'I was instantly proud. I have felt English almost from the day I arrived, but the knighthood puts some kind of seal on that emotion,' he declared. His only regret was that his mother had died the year before.[62]

Stoppard has long operated as a double act, becoming his own 'unique' or unidentical 'twin', as the physicist Kerner explained in *Hapgood*. Through the denial and acceptance of his past, Stoppard has led a kind of double life that complements rather than cancels each element, whether that is his Czech origin and English identity, or his Jewish parentage and indifferent attitude towards religion. Such doubleness, however, is natural, as Kerner again elaborates in the play which may be an important expression of Stoppard's own state of mind. And now it seems that Stoppard's second self, his Jewish self, is beginning to emerge.

One might claim that Stoppard wants the identity but not the knowledge of being Jewish, a doubleness that is hardly new for Jews: 'to be a man is a drama; to be a Jew is another. Hence the Jew has the privilege of living our condition *twice over*,' the French–Romanian philosopher E. M. Cioran wrote.[63] Stoppard encounters this doubleness which challenges him to both escape and embrace his Judaism, creating not a double act but a double consciousness. Interestingly, he has not been, and does not plan to go, to Israel, unlike David Hare who has not only been but has written a monologue, *Via Dolorosa*, about it. Borrowing the language of battle, Stoppard summarized the situation by deflecting the issue to nationalism, not religion: 'Englishness had won and Czechoslovakia had lost,' reads the final sentence of his 1999 article.[64] But as Emanuel Azenberg remarked, 'we who are on the inside of the outside, never forget our position on the margin. You can't forget and always want to get in.' Stoppard 'discovered who he is – but he isn't, but he is, but he isn't. That's his dilemma.' The question he faces, said Azenberg, is 'What is it you *don't* want to be, Tom?' Jewishness, an identity he did not invent, may be an identity Stoppard doesn't want. Ironically, some thirty-three years earlier he wrote of his character Moon that he 'sometimes wanted to be a Jew but had only the most superficial understanding of how to go about it'.[65]

I knew I was – used to be – Czech, but I didn't feel Czech.

Stoppard, 1999

Stoppard addressed the issue of his renewed Czech identity when he lectured at the Prague Theatre Institute in February 1998 and attended the opening of *Arcadia* (*Arkádia* in Czech) at the Divadlo Komedie (Comedy Theatre). In his talk, Stoppard expressed how complicated his feelings had become about his Czech origins, more so in the last ten years than in his childhood. Noting that his mother had wanted him and his brother to assimilate and become English schoolboys, he also acknowledged the irony that she spoke English with a Czech accent until she died. He also admitted that 'Czech was brought into my life when I didn't know what to do with it', referring to the period when he wrote *Professional Foul*. In the late sixties, he had read *The Garden Party* and *The Memorandum* and felt that they were plays *he* wanted to write.[66]

One way in which Stoppard sustained a link with his Czech past was through his theatre practice. Many of his dramatic habits, from his use of absurdism as a form of subterfuge for conveying serious ideas to the importance of disguise and employment of cross-talk as a means of dramatic presentation, are key concepts in Czech Authorial Theatre, where the theatre-makers themselves took on the authors' responsibility in shaping and presenting the work, often using material from history refashioned for the stage. The non-linear presentation of action, called 'text appeal', also emerged, often with spoken dialogue mixed with songs, much as Stoppard used them in *Jumpers* or *Travesties*.

Stoppard's stress on the practical dimension of the theatre extended his link with modern Czech drama, which also emphasized the importance of direct address to the audience, often through theatrical display. The anti-reductionist aspect of Czech theatre equalled Stoppard's theatrical purpose: it was to be a vehicle of thought and ideas, marrying forms to the sophisticated expression of thought. In addition to technique, both Stoppard and Czech theatre also explored social, philosophical, political and comedic issues. However, because it was necessary to protect the individual from repressive action in Czechoslovakia during the Communist period, self-concealment was required. This appealed to Stoppard too, although for personal rather than political reasons. 'Don't show them who you are' became a mantra for both Czech dramatists and the English playwright.

In the Czech theatre, language always had two meanings: the stated and the implied, the former dealing with the immediate situation, the latter with metaphoric and interpretative 'readings' of the words. The cynicism of Czech society resulted from the constant suspicion generated by a repressive regime; and two of Stoppard's favourite devices, parody and irony, became the dramatists' natural responses. Display through language, gesture, costume or mask became a protective way of encoding the self, simultaneously exposing and hiding; this became something of a feature in Czech theatre and certainly describes much of Stoppard's writing.[67]

These dramatic habits outline a lineage, unconscious as well as conscious, between the work of Stoppard and contemporary Czech drama. He read Havel as early as 1967, provided an introduction for *The Memorandum* in 1981 and adapted *Largo Desolato* for the Bristol Old Vic in 1986. The cooperation between author and director/cast in rehearsal and performance that characterized Czech theatre and made theatre a collaborative undertaking was precisely what Stoppard himself undertook, without the theorizing and politics. And during the so-called 'period of normalization', the wonderfully ironic term for the Soviet control of the Czech Republic (c.1969-89), when Authorial Theatre became linked with dissidents and political opposition, the theatres literally became forums for the exchange of liberal ideas and views opposed to the regime. During the 1989 uprisings that led to the fall of Communism, theatre people orchestrated the main demonstrations of the revolution. In the intervening years, with various productions of Stoppard's plays produced in the Czech

Republic, he has begun to influence a number of younger playwrights. Ladislav Smoljak's absurdist satire *Little October*, for example, possesses a *Travesties*-like structure and plays with history. Set in a Czech prison in the 1920s, Lenin, his wife and other historical figures define the political life of freedom and repression.[68]

Parallels between Czech theatre and Stoppard's writing existed from the beginning of Stoppard's dramatic career, coincidentally marked by the appearance of Tynan's influential article on Prague theatre in April 1967, the very month *Rosencrantz and Guildenstern* premièred at the National Theatre. As his past became more focused, Stoppard's need for disguise lessened. But this was not clear-cut. Obstacles appeared everywhere to delay the public reclamation of his 'Czechness'. His resistance to his Czech past held fast through his 1999 narrative of family history, underscored by the unexpected 1996 request, only days after his mother died, from his stepfather to 'return' the Stoppard name. Of course, he refused, although he reported that as soon as he 'went to the bad', the first sign of which was turning out to be 'arty', he and his stepfather became estranged. Indeed, while his mother would excitedly attend his plays whenever possible, his stepfather never did. Kenneth Stoppard died in July 1997, nine months after Stoppard's mother. And despite returning to recover a Czech past that had been erased, it was too late; Stoppard could not, indeed, would not change.

A sign of England's hold on Stoppard were the honours that surfaced in 1997 and 1998. The most significant was his knighthood, announced in June 1997. At first he did not believe it, and when it was corroborated, he expressed anxiety: 'Oh no, not yet' was his immediate reaction, 'but then I ended up with maybe 100 letters and that completely transformed my attitude. I felt very proud and rather bashful.'[69] Stoppard was the first dramatist to be knighted since Terence Rattigan in 1971, although Pinter had been approached by John Major but declined.

Awards continued to come: on 12 April 1997, just before the announcement of his knighthood, the French government honoured Stoppard, along with Christopher Hampton and David Hare. Each received the insignia of *Officier des Arts et Lettres* for his contribution to Anglo-French culture. The following year, the Comédie-Française selected *Arcadia* as the first play by a living foreign playwright to be added to its repertoire. (A time limit previously prevented works by foreign playwrights from being performed there, but the statute was altered in 1994.) The French playwright Jean-Marie Besset translated and adapted *Arcadia*. It was not the first play of Stoppard's to be performed in French, however; fifteen of his other works were produced, *Arcadia* having itself been performed in Paris earlier in 1998, at the Théâtre du Vieux-Colombier on the Left Bank. In the introduction to the French translation of the play, Besset observes with Gallic wit that 'written by a British author of Czech origin, this is, so to speak, an almost French play'.[70]

Matching these honours would be the success of Stoppard's new play, his first since *Arcadia*: *The Invention of Love* would première at the Cottesloe Theatre at the National on 1 October 1997, transferring to the larger Lyttelton stage in December, where it remained in rep until April 1998. Remounted at the Haymarket in the West End in November 1998, it continued for a further six months, its appeal lying in the interplay between textual scholarship, Latin poetry and love.

CHAPTER 21

CAMOUFLAGED BY DISPLAY

———

People like myself appear to have promoted a recreation into
a career.
Stoppard, 1994

A garden provides camouflage while allowing for display. The Chelsea Physic Garden is no exception. The oldest existing botanical garden in England, it began when the Worshipful Society of Apothecaries could no longer rely on the belladonna found in Islington or wild bugloss spotted on the banks of ditches near Piccadilly for their medicines. Three and a half acres in Chelsea, far from London's smoke, aided by sun and good soil, answered their needs after they lost their building in the Great Fire of 1666.

The garden soon prospered and a high wall was built to keep out thieves and the wind. Fruit trees and four Cedars of Lebanon, the first seen in England, were planted. By 1722, however, the apothecaries were facing financial difficulties and the fate of the garden was in question. Sir Hans Sloane, who had founded the British Museum, stepped in, conveying the property to the Society of Apothecaries in perpetuity. His only requirement was that for forty years, fifty specimens, all grown in the garden and no two alike, were to be dried, mounted, labelled and sent to the Royal Society. Sloane also introduced Philip Miller, the author of *The Gardener's Dictionary*, as gardener in 1722. Soon, the garden became celebrated throughout Europe and visited by such botanists as Linnaeus and Joseph Banks.

Today, the Physic Garden is a rambling area entered from either Swan Walk or the Chelsea Embankment, with gravel paths passing exotic plants and flowers. Rising above the patrons in the centre is a large marble statue of Sloane, commissioned by the Society of

Apothecaries in 1757. In this urban oasis, Stoppard has held three large garden fêtes in the past several years, the first occurring in September 1997, to celebrate his knighthood and sixtieth birthday. The afternoon was cloudless as Stoppard, dressed in a black velvet suit with a silk scarf, greeted nearly four hundred guests, who ranged from Princess Margaret to Andrew Lloyd Webber, Jeremy Irons, Simon Callow, Diana Rigg and Judi Dench. Others included Piers Paul Read, Bob Geldof, Nicholas Mosely and the film producer Katherine Kennedy, as well as Peter, Richard and Fiona Stoppard, Kenneth Ewing, Anthony Smith and Isabel Dunjohn. There was also Val Lorraine, his former Bristol landlady, as well as Harold Pinter and Timothy West.

The invitation for the gathering two years later was characteristically low-key:

Tom Stoppard will be
– At Home –
at The Chelsea Physic Garden
66, Royal Hospital Road, SW3,
on Saturday September 4th 1999
– between Noon and Sunset –

The purpose was to celebrate such recent successes as his Oscar, but, more importantly, it was a chance for Stoppard to let a lot of people know that he hadn't forgotten them. It also allowed him to announce the birth of his first grandchild, a daughter named Eden, born to his son Barnaby and his wife. The crowd was as mixed as at his earlier fête: among the guests were Miriam with Barnaby, Harold Pinter, Lady Antonia Fraser, Christopher Hampton, Michael Frayn, Mike Nichols, Simon Gray, John Wood, Peter Hall, John Boorman and Tom Staley. Also present were Lady Berlin, the widow of Sir Isaiah Berlin, and Alastair Macaulay, theatre critic of the *Financial Times*. A third party in the late summer of 2001 was, again, a celebratory social event.

Given Stoppard's enjoyment of the outdoors, his pleasure over-seeing the seventeen acres at Iver Grove and the importance of gardens in *Arcadia*, the Chelsea Physic Garden, not far from his Chelsea Harbour apartment, was an appropriate location for the three galas. The outdoor stations offering food, drink and roving musicians added to the near-carnival, if not theatrical, environment. The parties displayed the social Stoppard in full Chelsea bloom.

*Oxford in the Golden Age! . . . what emotional storms, and
oh what a tiny teacup.*
Stoppard, *The Invention of Love*

A month after the first of those parties, Stoppard's new play appeared, reflecting his long interest in the classics. He had read Greek until he was seventeen, but found Latin more exciting, the writing richer; had he gone to university, he thought he might have read classics.[1] In his Housman play, Stoppard duplicated the time shifts of *In the Native State*, *Arcadia* and *Indian Ink*. But what attracted him to Housman was the by now familiar Romantic–classical contest: 'It's *Arcadia* again. I just realised there was something basically dramatic in the man who was two men': classicist and poet. 'What I was interested in was the idea of two people in one – the Latin scholar and the poet, the classical and the romantic.' But this work differs from others in that it is character-based: 'I've always started with an idea before, often quite separate from whoever was in the play. This time I've started with whoever is in the play.'[2]

The structure, however, posed problems. His research, which began in late 1991 when he read a complete edition of Housman's translations and poetry, followed by three volumes of his criticism, seemed unstoppable. When asked about his new work in December 1995, he admitted that he was stumped: he was in a position 'to do an excellent radio documentary. But I can't find the play I have.'[3] Stymied, he reported that he had worked on the play for two or three months in 1991 and then for three months in 1995. In between, he told Richard Eyre that a play on Housman was under way – but it had still not crystallized.

For diversion, he turned to working on a screenplay of *Hapgood* for Stockard Channing, but that, too, proved tricky and was put aside. Unlike his experience with the film of *Rosencrantz and Guildenstern*, where he happily chucked things out and added new elements, he was indecisive about how to film *Hapgood*. In December 1995, he participated in rehearsals for the National's revival of *Rosencrantz and Guildenstern* starring Alan Howard and Simon Russell Beale, and had other projects on the go, including a new film in collaboration with Mick Jagger.

'I worked closely with Stoppard on the second draft of *Enigma*. I don't want to be a carping busybody, but sometimes you've got to be a sounding board,' Mick Jagger proudly declared, referring to a new venture he and Stoppard planned: a screenplay of Robert Harris's 1995 novel, *Enigma*.[4] Jagger had purchased the rights to *Enigma* and approached his friend Stoppard knowing of his interest in spies and espionage. Early that November, before Jagger bought the option, Stoppard was about to visit Jagger at La Fourchette, his early eighteenth-century château in the Loire, when Jagger's office asked Stoppard to bring out a copy of Harris's novel. By chance, Stoppard said, he had an advance copy and would bring it. Jagger read it and quickly took an option, although it would be six years until the film would be released. The papers reported that Stoppard was to do the screeenplay, although the process was protracted and prolonged, taking longer to produce, some suggested, than the Second World War itself. By the summer of 1998, however, Stoppard and Jagger were at the Cannes film festival, trying to sell the film, directed by Michael Apted. Stoppard, long a lover of codes, actually figured out how to break the Enigma code: he read numerous books on it, 'so to try to calm him down was difficult', Apted reported.[5]

Produced with difficulty and, ironically, principally German financing – the movie focuses on Bletchley Park's efforts to crack the Nazis' Enigma code before their U-boats could destroy supply convoys from the United States destined for England – the film created a minor controversy with its suggestion that a Pole at Bletchley Park might have been a traitor rather than celebrating the contribution of Polish intelligence to cracking the code. Stoppard, offended, criticized the allegations as unfounded. The Pole in the novel and film was invented and should not have affronted the heroism of Polish exiles during the war.[6] Stoppard's main concern was the double enigma: the signals the mathematics whiz Tom Jericho (played by Dougray Scott) must decipher and the mysterious fate of Claire, who abandons him and may have joined the enemy.

Opening night, a Royal Première at Leicester Square on 24 September 2001, in aid of the Prince's Trust, was a success. Jagger attended with his daughter Elizabeth; they had both appeared fleetingly in the film itself (Jagger in RAF uniform at a dance hall). Apted, Stoppard, Bill Wyman and Ronnie Wood joined the Prince of Wales for the highly publicized charity evening.

The future perfect I have always regarded as an oxymoron.
Stoppard, *The Invention of Love*

The Invention of Love is about a real person, both an advantage and disadvantage for Stoppard. He decided to write about Housman long before he knew anything about the poet's personal life. Indeed, he had hoped to discover that Housman had been in love with a cruel mistress, perhaps as Housman's hero Propertius had been. But what he read in a reproduced page from Housman's diary, written when Moses Jackson, the great unrequited love of Housman's life, was going to India, surprised him. Housman noted the times of the arrival and departures of the boat in each port, as in '*His boat arrives Bombay 8.45*'. Suddenly, 'a sense of suppression, of unhappiness, just came off the page – even in reproduction,' he explained.[7] This became the key to Housman's character for Stoppard. In the play, Housman sublimates his passionate love for the heterosexual Moses Jackson into a love of classical scholarship.

The borrowing from his earlier work was again evident, since his engagement with the classics returned Stoppard to several of his earlier interests: university life, academic gamesmanship, translation, literature and, of course, language. A passage in *Indian Ink* anticipated the subject of the new play:

> The only poet I *know* is Alfred Housman . . . He hauled me through 'Ars Amatoria' when I was up at Trinity . . . When it comes to love, he said, you're either an Ovid man or a Virgil man – *omnia vincit amor* – that's Virgil – 'Love sweeps all before it, and we give way to love' – *et nos cedamus amori*. Housman was an Ovid man – *et mihi cedet amor* – 'Love gives way to me'.

The speaker is not the poet Flora Crewe but the Resident, the chief colonial officer of Jammapur. Flora responds that, unlike Housman, she's 'a Virgil man', causing the Resident to reply, 'Are you? Well, it widens one's circle of acquaintance.'[8] Another recursive element in *The Invention* is the reference to Jerome K. Jerome's novel *Three Men in a Boat*, which Stoppard had adapted for television in the mid-1970s and for radio in the 1990s. The first appearance of the young Housman is in a boat on the River Isis in Oxford with Moses Jackson, their friend

Pollard and a dog; the stage direction reads 'three men in a boat row into view'.[9] The play cuts across time and opens with the elder (dead) Housman about to enter a boat rowed by Charon as he prepares to cross the River Styx, followed by his encounter with his younger self at Oxford on the River Isis in a punt with Jackson and Pollard.

Stoppard takes the repetitive structure of the play further when, towards the end of the first act, he reworks snatches of dialogue, as well as images, ideas and events taken from pages one to forty-five in the Faber edition into a two-and-a-half-page passage. The concentrated dialogue from the end of page forty-six to the top of page forty nine manages to condense virtually the first act, reversing the scaling of self-similarity seen in chaos theory and presented in *Arcadia*. There, events, through their replication, get larger; in *The Invention of Love*, they become more concentrated. For the audience, it seems as if the play shrinks and starts twice. Stoppard even repeats this process in the last nine pages of the text, when he intersperses, within new material, key phrases and dialogue from Act One. These are like small eddies within the larger eddies of the play which, at its end, finishes a circuit with the older Housman standing by the side of the river, repeating the water/river imagery throughout the work, and from *Arcadia*: at the end of that play, Septimus declares that 'when we have found all the mysteries and lost all the meaning, we will be alone, on an empty shore'. Housman's final line in *The Invention of Love* is: 'How lucky to find myself standing on this empty shore, with the indifferent waters at my feet.'[10]

Having studied Latin up to A Level standard at Pocklington, Stoppard could read it easily, with the occasional crib, although when he arrived at Bristol to begin his newspaper career he wasted no time in heading to George's bookshop to sell his Homer, Caesar and Catullus. But translations and their variety fascinated him. As a playwright, he had a practical interest in translation but found adaptation more appealing to his sense of language. His own practice of producing adaptations shows how he has been able to transform literal translations into his distinctive style. After working on *Indian Ink*, Stoppard returned to investigate Housman's ideas of translation, as well as his life. For five years, he reread the classics, studying Propertius and Catullus, as well as researching life at Victorian Oxford and its personalities.

Among his sources was Norman Page's life of Housman. Page warned at the outset of his account that one of the dangers of biography was its tendency to make too much sense out of a life. Stoppard agreed, but found such curious details as Housman leaving his black boots to his college servant more telling than other, more generalized actions.[11] Stoppard also studied nineteenth-century aesthetics and its relation to homosexuality and classical culture.

Stoppard's review of classical literature led to some important discoveries, notably a collection of lost fragments by Greek tragedians, plays that survived only because somebody quoted or paraphrased them. There was also a fragment from Sophocles which compared love to a piece of ice held by children: 'Love is like a piece of ice.' 'I thought, "That's good. The more you grip it, the quicker it melts."' After the première of *The Invention*, however, he realized he was completely wrong, which was what was so interesting:

> The right meaning, as I discovered after the first night, was even more wonderful. It's to do with the fact that ice, as it freezes, sticks to the skin, and it hurts when you pull it away. So when I got to the bottom of this quotation, it turned out to mean 'it's like love because it hurts to hold it as it freezes and it hurts when you try to get rid of it . . .' which accords even more sharply with one's experience, I would say.[12]

The context of the line in the play supports his new explanation: the younger Housman claims he does not know what love is. The older replies, 'Oh but you do' and recounts the way copied-over fragments preserved important passages from the past, including Sophocles' single sentence on love: it reads love 'is like the ice held in the hand by children'. 'A piece of ice held fast in the fist. I wish I could help you, but it's not in my gift.' Enthusiastically, the young Housman replies, 'Love it is, then, and I will make the best of it.'[13] The classics provided Stoppard not only with material but metaphors.

Again, he followed his rubric of writing fiction about real people, carefully summarized near the end of the play when Wilde and Housman meet, although factually they never did. Explaining that he based the details of a poem on the report of a suicide in the *Evening Standard*, Housman defends his source. Wilde recoils:

Wilde   Oh, thank goodness! That explains why I never believed a word of it.

AEH   But it's all true.

Wilde   On the contrary, it's only fact. Truth is quite another thing and is the work of the imagination.

More background evidence from Housman incites Wilde to declare that 'art deals with exceptions, not with types. Facts deal only with types.'[14] This is the characteristic Stoppard dilemma: facts alone are deadly and need to be enlivened by the imagination, yet they resonate with interpretative possibilities: the première of the play in September 1997, for example, coincided with the centenary of Wilde's release from Reading Gaol.[15]

> *Many of my plays are about unidentical twins, about*
> *double acts.*
> Stoppard, November 1998

Stoppard finessed the structural problems of the play's two time periods by creating two Housmans, the older (seventy-seven in the play), movingly and vigorously played in the original production by John Wood, and the younger played by the emotional and energetic Paul Rhys. Wood, in his seventh Stoppard play, was at first not excited by the role: when he heard about the topic, he thought 'there's an unpromising subject, a minor poet who lived like a hermit and was staggeringly rude.'[16] Reading the text changed his mind and for the production Wood was at the top of his form in the clarity and speed of his delivery and in the modulation of his voice, which varied from the venomous, when discussing rival scholars, to the confessional, when speaking of his curtailed love, subsiding at times to a whisper when his heart breaks. Rhys vividly portrayed the nervous cleverness of Housman in his twenties. This memory play gave Stoppard an extraordinary range of emotions to present, plus the advantage, as he explained, that 'all kinds of confusions, inaccuracies and cheating can be attributed to the character rather than to the author' – as he did in *Travesties*.[17] Where else but in a Stoppard play would it seem perfectly normal for Virgil and Jerome K. Jerome to meet?

The interaction between the older and younger Housman is in itself a drama of deep emotion underscored by their extended dialogue at the conclusion of Act One, the older Housman longingly addressing Moses Jackson, whom he sees in the distance, with, 'I would have died for you but I never had the luck!' With innocence touched by desire, the younger Housman believes that one can be both a poet and a scholar; the older, however, tells him it's not possible: 'No. Not of the first rank. Poetical feelings are a peril to scholarship.' His tone hides his own despair at having curbed his heart both poetically and personally.[18]

The question Stoppard addresses was fundamental, and linked his three latest works, *Arcadia*, *The Invention of Love* and *Shakespeare in Love*. 'Is love ever the real thing?' – and if so, if you believe it to be so, do you or should you act on it? Love, he believes 'is an abstraction, it's never real in the way a coffee cup is. I'm not a romantic.'[19] Perhaps, but his characters are romantic, or at least struggle to be, as Stoppard makes clear when Housman encounters Wilde in Dieppe.

The meeting of the two should have actually happened. When Stoppard discovered that Housman's first trip abroad occurred the same year Wilde went abroad after leaving jail, he was ecstatic, especially when he also found that Housman went to Naples, thinking that they were both in Naples at the same time: in fact, they missed each other by a week, but 'I was not to be thwarted by a mere detail like that', although in the end he settled for their meeting in Dieppe.[20] The scene, one of the most important in the play, displays Stoppard's habit of fictionalizing real people and the limitations of biography, a quality Wilde aphoristically praises near the close of the play when he declares that 'biography is the mesh through which our real life escapes'.[21]

Wilde's view reflects Stoppard's on biography, in which he celebrates the inventive if it is truthful: 'the fictional biographer as I conceive him is a biographer who tells the truth without being enthralled to the facts . . . in biography, though not in classical scholarship, there is no special virtue in accuracy if it is not the right kind of accuracy.'[22] Stoppard playfully illustrated this in the work by naming a young clerk, a contemporary of Housman's at the patent office, Chamberlain, which raised a query in the *Housman Society Journal*'s review of the play: 'why choose the name Chamberlain for the one character who is invented?'[23] The answer, of course, was that it was the name of Stoppard's secretary.

Wilde is held up as the figure who, despite his suffering and fall, has lived, whereas Housman is only the hollow figure who had 'colleagues', not friends. Of course, Stoppard had already drawn on Wilde as early as 1974, in *Travesties*. Stoppard adapted Wilde's comment that the way to atone for being 'occasionally a little over-dressed' is by being 'immensely over-educated', to read that Wilde may be 'a little overdressed but he made up for it by being immensely uncommitted'.[24] 'My route to Wilde left out the politics; what I valued was style raised to genius,' Stoppard explained to one interviewer.[25]

In *The Invention of Love*, Stoppard presents Wilde as a tragic rather than narcissistic figure. 'He sacrifices himself to self-fulfilment, if that's an intelligent statement,' said Stoppard. When he died, Housman was acknowledged by a memorial service at Trinity College, Cambridge and a lead editorial in *The Times* but 'he failed in life – emotionally, if not intellectually. Though Wilde crashed in flames, and ended as a disgraced, pathetic maladjusted poverty-stricken wreck, he had the successful life,' Stoppard claimed, and this is the view the play supports.[26] One dazzling line in the play expresses the situation acutely: 'Better a fallen rocket than never a burst of light.' Wilde had earlier declared that 'the betrayal of one's friends is a bagatelle in the stakes of love, but the betrayal of oneself is lifelong regret. Bosie is what became of me.' The selfishness, vindictiveness and egotism of Bosie 'are merely the facts. The truth is he was Hyacinth when Apollo loved him . . . he is the only one who understands me.'[27]

Textual criticism in the play is shown to be an art as well as a science, with Housman making grand claims for its virtues. In a bravura piece of writing, Stoppard gives power and importance to the solitary study of individual words, lines and manuscripts. In the midst of the older Housman's powerful dialogue with the younger, he offers an apologia for textual criticism, which he calls 'a science whose subject is literature'. It requires 'reason and common sense, a congenial intimacy with the author, a comprehensive familiarity with the language, a knowledge of ancient script . . . almost anybody can be a botanist or a zoologist. Textual criticism is the crown and summit of scholarship.' But at the end, all Housman can say to Wilde in celebration of his career is that his life was 'marked by long silences.

The first conjecture I ever published was on Horace. Six years later I withdrew it.' Although caustic criticism, a sharp tongue and a vilification of inadequate scholars defined his scholarly self, repression, hesitation and love withheld defined Housman's private self. Wilde may declare that 'to do it is nothing, to be said to have done it is everything' but he in fact did it: he lived; Housman, to his endless regret, did not.[28]

The central conceit of the play is that love is a necessary invention. Wilde explains: 'before Plato could describe love, the loved one had to be invented. We would never love anybody if we could see past our inventions. Bosie is my creation, my poem. In the mirror of invention, love discovered itself. Then we saw what we had made – the piece of ice in the fist you cannot hold or let go.' The stage direction at this point is simple but powerful: '*He weeps.*' Painfully, Housman recognizes his own inadequacies, although Wilde tries to support him: 'You are right to be a scholar. A scholar is all scruple, an artist is none . . . I made my life into my art and it was an unqualified success . . . I made art a philosophy that can look the twentieth century in the eye.'[29] The scene pits *allegro* against *penseroso*.

A genuine love of learning is one of the two delinquencies
which cause blindness and lead a young man to ruin.
Stoppard, *The Invention of Love*

The Latin and Greek in the play challenged the actors and audience, as well as the author, and the cast benefited from a lecture on pronunciation and scansion.[30] Assisting Stoppard with his study were two classicists from the University of Newcastle: Dr Peter Jones, author of the popular book *Learn Latin* (originally a series in the *Daily Telegraph*, beginning in 1997) and Professor David West, a Latin specialist known for his prose translation of Virgil's *Aeneid*. Both were also instrumental in establishing and running Friends of the Classics, a national group established in 1990 to promote and popularize the study of Latin and Greek as well as classical studies; the organization also hoped to strip the subject of its élitist image. As early as 1967, Stoppard had met the poet and translator Tony Harrison, and the meeting had made him briefly regret his peremptory disposal of his classical texts some thirteen years before. Harrison later helped Stoppard clarify classical references in *The Invention*.

Again, the play was late, but not inordinately so. Stoppard, who had discussed the work with Richard Eyre in early 1994, explained that one reason for this habit of delay was that 'I can't shake off this idea each time that I can't possibly write anything until I've worked out exactly what's going to happen and why. I tend to start writing a play at the point where I just give up in despair and just *start* and hope that something works itself out.'[31] Like his other works, *The Invention of Love* required originality in its staging. Eyre, who sensed the usual Stoppardian collision between plot and idea (his difficulty with plot often leading Stoppard to rely on other texts like *Hamlet* or *The Importance of Being Earnest*), not only imaginatively developed the entrances and exits of the boats in the play, but also worked closely with Anthony Ward, the designer, to construct clever projections on the curved back wall to evoke everything from a library and a sports field to a billiard room and the hills of Shropshire. This was remarkably effective in the small Cottesloe Theatre at the National, but when the play transferred to the West End, the projections were gone and seven minutes were cut from Act One to streamline the action.

Critics were divided over the play. Hoping for the seamless structure of *Arcadia* and its effortless knowledge, they found instead a dense work that focused on the minutiae of classical translation, academic squabbles and repressed love in an all-too-obvious form of divided time. The general consensus was that earlier works like *Jumpers* or *Travesties* linked intellectual conceits with dramatic ideas while displaying dazzling aplomb. *The Invention of Love* lacked their theatrical rigour and zest. It was too didactic and not dramatic enough, argued David Benedict in the *Independent*.

Charles Spencer in the *Evening Standard*, however, found the work to be vintage Stoppard with the added value of flattering the viewer's intelligence. The play made the audience feel as well as think, balancing intellectual rigour with emotion. He praised Richard Eyre's direction, noting that in the intimate Cottesloe Theatre (this was the first of Stoppard's plays to be performed there), Eyre was both sympathetic and imaginative in his directing. Indeed, 'only the combination of Stoppard's writing, Richard Eyre's direction and John Wood's acting could bring a modern audience close to tears over these matters, or could enthral it with the thousand-word lecture on Horace, *Odes* IV. i.'

Such action, of course, is ironic and theatrical, since in reality Housman was a quiet, austere teacher who would have emptied theatres. The sources of Housman's wistfully elegiac lyric poems, however, take on new significance as the play exposes the dilemma of his sexuality, which resulted in 'emotional refrigeration'. The scene in Act Two in which Housman falteringly offers up his love for Jackson was one of the most powerful and poignant Stoppard has ever written, according to Spencer. Michael Coveney in the *Daily Mail* favoured the 'distilled cabaret of High Victorian aesthetics on Oxford lawns' as Jowett, Pater, Ruskin and Pattison play croquet. This equalized the presentation of Housman as the 'stifled romantic and demonic classicist'.[32]

The acting of John Wood, magisterial as the elder Housman, and the romantic portrayal of his younger self by Paul Rhys saved the play for many from becoming a tedious exercise in textual scholarship filled with arcane fragments and obscure references. The enthusiasm of one reviewer over the scene at the end of Act One, where the older and younger Housman meet on a park bench and discuss classical poetry, was such that he described it as done with 'such passion, wit and verve, you feel like signing up for a classics course on the spot'.[33]

Some, however, found fault with its history, noting, for example, that Stoppard incorrectly emphasizes Moses Jackson as Housman's only 'lover', when evidence suggests he had some vital experiences in Italy, especially with one Venetian gondolier. Others felt the theme too simple: that Housman's error was to be a poet who lived a long life without having lived. Still others felt the play was crammed with too much detail: 'The Latin learning is laid on with a trowel. At the same time, the jokes are very good.' This assessment, by Michael Billington, expresses the weakness and strength of the work: the lottery of literary survival and the power of passion were now constant Stoppard themes and 'for all his cerebral qualities [he] is at his best when he endorses private passion'.[34]

Unfavourable notices were equally strong, the most controversial by David Sexton, Literary Editor of the *Evening Standard*, who wrote a highly critical review, although the theatre critic of his own paper, Nicholas de Jongh, hailed the work as 'the most emotionally powerful and enthralling play of the year'. Sexton, by contrast, found it 'com-pletely insufferable. I would rather have spent the evening in a darkened cell. Standing in a corner, facing the wall.'[35] It was tedious, false and boring, but since many found it riveting, its faults must be taken 'to be representative of theatre altogether'. Sexton proceeded to dismantle the play and production, from eidetic images of the athletic Moses Jackson to the imaginary games of croquet and billiards. He found the shouting of the actors equally off-putting, especially because they enunciated for audience effect: 'every line is an attempted gag – both in the writing and the delivery'. The result was the absence of motivation and presence of *only* theatrical gesture. The shy and retiring Housman appeared dramatic and flamboyant. Exposition rather than drama meant little or no animation of the characters. Lectures replaced speeches and impersonation replaced character Sexton concluded. The theatre itself was 'an anachronism preserved by piety, subsidy tourism – and those collusive reviewers', he claimed at the end.

Audiences, however, were enthusiastic and it did well at the box office, transferring to the West End. One evening during its opening run, Peter Hall, Edward Albee and Princess Margaret attended. The latter summoned John Wood to dine with her and told him that she 'was confident that the play was bursting to get into a larger space. I didn't know whether that was royal speak or she was saying, "You are overacting".'[36] The play won the Best New Play Award from the *Evening Standard* that year.

In a 'Platform' presentation at the National on 10 October 1997 and a 29 October 1997 lecture at the London Library entitled 'The Invention of Love and Not only Love: Reflections on "Biographical Fiction" ', Stoppard stressed the duality of Housman's life as the romantically minded poet and analytical scholar. At the 'Platform', he admitted that when he first began to read about him, he had no idea of Housman's homosexuality. He also emphasized his fascination with what he calls 'the combination of two competing not conflicting temperaments . . . which perhaps I detected in myself', the classical and romantic.[37]

He repeated his distrust of biography and its essentialist attitude but went ahead and wrote about Housman as he had previously written biographically about Joyce, Wilde, Carr, Lenin, Rosencrantz,

Guildenstern and a host of others, the logic being that if biography is usually in error, why not capitalize on its faults and make truthful fiction out of supposed fact? Yet the mysterious, dramatic elements of Housman's life, his failure at his Oxford finals and later disappearance for a week from his Bayswater flat do not even enter Stoppard's play. His focus is unrequited love.

Stoppard expanded his ideas on the freedom of biography in his London Library lecture held at the Royal Geographical Society lecture rooms, for which all 750 tickets were sold out. He began by admitting, however, that his title had been 'whimsically provided' to meet a printer's deadline before he had even the faintest idea of what he would say. Nevertheless, it provided a useful guiding light as he explained that 'I have a practice but I have no theory, let alone a thesis – my only expertise is in theatre which is a much more pragmatic business than is often thought.'

Stoppard illustrates his 'impudent claim' that there is no special virtue in biographical accuracy via his sly approval of the most inaccurate Housman biography, Maude M. Hawkins' *A. E. Housman, Man Behind a Mask*. It has none of the virtues of the more detailed, factual work by P. G. Naiditch, nor the congeniality of the life by Norman Page, but it conveys several truths about Housman. That, for Stoppard, is of supreme value and he only partially jests when he says that Hawkins 'would be *my* first choice as my biographer, maximum inaccuracy being the only possibility of a silver lining to an appalling cloud'. This follows from his belief that a fictional treatment of Housman filled with inaccuracies might 'deliver the man as truthfully as a much fatter book of carefully deployed fact'.

He points out his own inventions in the Housman story. Chamberlain, for example, Housman's homosexual office mate at the Patent Office, is based on a real colleague named Maycock who was not homosexual but wrote Housman an admiring letter. Housman did not say he moved because someone spoke to him on the train to work one day, but it was representative of him. The croquet game in the play between Jowett, Pater, Ruskin and Pattison could not have taken place since Ruskin had fallen out with Pater, who was not speaking to Jowett because of a scandal involving sonnets which passed between two men, a scandal which had, in fact, occurred five years *before* the scene. All of the above supports Stoppard's statement that in literature 'the fictional biographer . . . is a biographer who tells the truth without being enthralled by the facts'.

US productions of *The Invention of Love* began with its première at ACT in San Francisco in January 2000, with Stoppard participating in rehearsals and providing minor script changes. A production followed at the Wilma Theater in Philadelphia which prompted a lengthy and critical essay/review in the *New York Review of Books*. The author, a classicist, objected to Stoppard's failure to show adequately the division within the younger and older Housman, between the poet and the scholar; the play seemed only to show Housman ageing. The actual division in the work was that between Housman and Wilde. The essay also indicted Stoppard's misuse of intellectual matter in the play: such 'trimmings . . . are ultimately anti-intellectual; he loves to show and audiences love to watch – brilliant analytical minds humbled by messy, everyday emotions'. Stoppard, we are told, is 'the dithyrambic sort – a romantic at heart' who believes that Housman's devotion to the 'life of the mind was a repressive reaction to, and a sublimation of, his failed love for Jackson' and without value for itself. Stoppard's interest in intellectuals and their lives is no more than 'garnish for his essentially romantic, pop vision', while his audience is 'hungry' only for 'sentimental fantasies'. The work, he concludes, is a disappointing 'one-sided play about this fascinatingly two-sided figure'.[38]

Uncharacteristically, Stoppard chose to respond. In a letter published on 21 September 2000 in the *New York Review of Books*, he countered the critic's understanding of the play, objecting to the characterization that the work presents only a dry-as-dust view of Housman. Stoppard declares that he in fact reveres Housman for his devotion to the recovery of ancient texts and objects to the linking of the repression of one's self-will, required of a textual critic, with repression of Housman's emotional life. He does agree, however, that the celebratory Housman, the light versifier and gourmand, are underpresented in the work, and that Wilde is a foil to the classical scholar. But Wilde is *not* the real hero of the play; indeed, who is a hero remains an unanswered question. Stoppard finally objects to the fatuous thesis that intellectuals lead less interesting or complex emotional lives than others.

The critic, Daniel Mendelsohn, hadn't finished, offering a lengthy rejoinder, beginning with the flawed nature of Stoppard's response. The play did not, he repeats, find a solution to the 'two Housman' problem; the contest in the play is not between Housman the romantic poet versus the classical scholar, but Housman the scholar and Wilde the poet. This is unfair and works against Housman, since Wilde's persona was much more flamboyant and public. Stoppard further-more continues to punish intellectuals, his so-called reverence for them tempered by his 'romantic' elevation of the heart over the head. The playwright's ambivalence about people who pursue knowledge for its own sake perfectly mirrors that of most people; 'hence his popularity', Mendelsohn adds. One who had genuine convictions that intellectual passions could, in and of themselves, provide a satisfying life would not, he continues, have found necessary 'the erotic humiliation' of Henry in *The Real Thing*, the *auto-da-fé* of Thomasina in *Arcadia*, and the presentation of Housman as a man who, despite his stunning academic accomplishments, constantly cries out that he wishes he had died for his beloved, which, of course, Wilde did.[39]

Stoppard's long reply of 19 October 2000 begins with four lines in Latin from Catullus, establishing his credentials as at least a part-time classicist. In his lengthy answer to Mendelsohn, he exhibits his scholarly side and familiarity with the slightly arcane elements of classical texts, providing two dense footnotes to display his erudition. Demonstrating that Housman did not sunder poetical feeling (or 'self-repression') from scholarship through a contextual reading of Housman's Cambridge Inaugural Lecture, Stoppard then ironically but clearly explains that he did, indeed, know that Housman was a classicist. He then reiterates his opposition to the argument that Wilde supposedly represents the successful personality which Housman failed to live up to for himself. Rather, Housman 'was simultaneously a gratified man and a disappointed one'.[40] Stoppard also makes it distinctly clear that he does not disdain Housman's intellectualism for overriding his emotions. To the contrary, it is the tension in Housman 'between different sorts of success and failure' that expressly interests him. Housman's 'failure' is actually understood as a complement to his intellectual and poetical self-fulfilment 'which is Housman's triumph'.

Mendelsohn's sarcastic reply – 'Tom Stoppard in his defensive mode reminds me of the mythic monster: for every head you chop off, ten grow back. In this case, however, each batch of ten makes more noise, and yet has less bite, than the single head it replaces' – repeats the charge that Stoppard finds the vibrant Wilde a hero and the pedant Housman a failure. Stoppard's defence is no more than 'hair-splitting', 'straw-man arguments' and misconstrued jokes. Mendelsohn ends with a dig at Stoppard's lack of awareness of when he is losing an audience, his protestations reminding Mendelsohn of the A-grade student who received a B: 'The fuss! The protestations! The quasi-Talmudic interpretations of interpretations, and critiques of critiques!' Mendelsohn proposes to let readers/audiences decide by attending (or not) a production of the play scheduled for Lincoln Center Theater in New York in 2001.

Why did Stoppard bother to respond to Mendelsohn? He seems to have taken offence at the suggestion, also levelled at Housman, that he divorces feelings from intellect. In his defence of Housman, he is defending himself and, again, displaying the new, unguarded Stoppard, unafraid to take on an opponent of his work. With the protective wall down, Stoppard can respond to one of his critics, contradicting his usual, comfortable position of either (a) disregarding all criticism because his responsibility is to create, not interpret, or (b) saying that he simply doesn't know. In this instance, he *does* know and is absolutely clear about it, offering documentation and sources to contradict his opponent, despite his own complaint concerning the way others, especially biographers, have used such sources. Stoppard the Pocklington debater is much in evidence. More basic is his understanding that feelings and ideas have a common source and form of expression; they are dispossessed of a contestatory or cancelling element as one might have earlier and more easily argued. Taking the unexpected step of responding to his critic, Stoppard defends the idea that the emotional and the analytical co-exist in a single writer and that life and art can be united, not separated.

The play concludes with Housman elder telling Housman younger that the first love poet was not Propertius but Cornelius Gallus, little known because only one line of his has survived. But that one line is a monument because it concentrates the contradictions of love; it invents love. The play ends with Housman repeating the first Latin words of the play, *ripae ulterioris amore,* 'And they stretched out their hands in desire of the further shore'.[41] The play has explained, illustrated and demonstrated the invention, though not the completion, of love. And Stoppard, while allowing Wilde the glitter and the intensity of life, still maintains respect for Housman's iron reserve and sense of privacy. The title might have another resonance, however, linked more personally to Stoppard. The play's focus on someone falling in love with another who could not fully reciprocate that love may be connected with Felicity Kendal. He may have then felt compelled to invent what he no longer possessed.

Why should I write a play? I don't have to write a play, do I?
But somehow, I think that's what I'm here for, so I'd better
do it.

Stoppard, March 1999

Stoppard's anxiety over writing another play was suspended by turning to film, which dominated his work following the success of *The Invention of Love*. While shooting was being completed for John Madden's production of *Shakespeare in Love*, Stoppard continued with other projects, notably *Vatel,* a French costume epic directed by Roland Joffé. Starring Gérard Depardieu, Tim Roth and Uma Thurman, it is a seventeenth-century story of a celebrity chef and master of the revels, François Vatel, and an account of a weekend in 1671 during which the perfectionist must prepare an extraordinary three-day banquet-cum-spectacle to ingratiate the disliked Prince de Condé with France's King Louis XIV. Politically and financially, this is an important step for the prince, who desperately needs the support of the king; in turn, the king needs the prince's military knowledge to fight the Dutch. Court intrigues interfere with Vatel's plans, but his overreaction to the delayed delivery of seafood, disrupting the final dinner, is extreme: he kills himself.

Stoppard's interest in writing the screenplay, adapting the original French version by Jeanne Labrune, relates to his concern over whether the artist as a perfectionist can survive in society. Yet he includes his rapier humour. When the prince is impolitic enough to beat the king at cards, one onlooker whispers, 'the Prince could lose everything.' 'Not', the reply comes, 'if he plays his cards wrong.' Decadence and privilege define the film, which opened at the Cannes Film Festival in

May 2000 to unfavourable reviews and was released throughout Europe between May and November, with a US release in December. Stoppard was also busy making uncredited script changes to Tim Burton's *Sleepy Hollow,* adjusting the original script by Kevin Walker. Released in Great Britain in January 2000, the film met with a modest reception.

In preparation for the Oscars – *Shakespeare in Love* was nominated for thirteen – Stoppard wrote a new work, a sketch to be presented at the Miramax dinner held the night before the awards ceremony on 20 March 1999. Released in December 1998, the film had more nominations than any other picture that year and went on to win seven – not only the Academy Award for Best Picture of 1998, but also Oscars for Best Screenplay, Best Actress, Best Supporting Actress, Best Art Direction, Best Original Music or Comedy Score and Best Costume Design. But Stoppard's skit may have been the highlight of the gala.

Miramax traditionally throws a party the night before the Oscars, dragooning its stars into improvising scenes from one another's movies. Judi Dench put on a red wig to play Brenda Blethyn's brassy blabbermouth in *Little Voice.* Roberto Benigni put on Joseph Fiennes's costume from *Shakespeare in Love* and shouted 'I want to kiss your Golden Globes!' (The movie had already won three Golden Globe awards, including best screenplay.)[42] Gwyneth Paltrow imitated Benigni's character in *Life is Beautiful,* donning a plastic nose and glasses. The highlight, however, was Stoppard's burlesque, 'Two Gentlemen of Queens', a satire of the two heads of Miramax, Harvey Weinstein and his brother Bob. Geoffrey Rush played Harvey Weinstein, Matt Damon his brother.

The set-up in Stoppard's lampoon was the brothers' first meeting with former *New Yorker* editor (and Stoppard's friend) Tina Brown, to discuss her new magazine, *Talk.* Questioning the seventy-five million dollars needed to start the project, Harvey corrects his brother: that's not start up, that's her salary'. At that point, Gwyneth Paltrow entered, playing Brown, bubbling with a fresh idea: if Monica Lewinsky will have Bob Weinstein's baby and deliver by November, it will make the Christmas cover. Brown, in the audience, and the Weinsteins loved it.

At the Oscar ceremony the following night, a surprised Stoppard was droll in his acceptance speech for the Oscar for best screenplay (shared with Marc Norman): 'I feel like Benigni,' he began. Benigni had spontaneously jumped up on his seat and flailed his arms when he won. 'I feel like Benigni . . . on the inside.' Gracious in thanking the Academy, he also acknowledged the presence of Kenneth Ewing, his agent of more than thirty years, who had accompanied him to Los Angeles. He also thanked his four sons. A photo taken later that night at the Miramax party at the Polo Lounge of the Beverly Hills Hotel captured a glowing, tuxedoed Stoppard clutching his Oscar with his left hand, while his right held a mobile phone close to his ear.

The popularity of the film leading up to the Oscars overshadowed some sniping in the press, which included objections to Stoppard's altering the chronology of Shakespeare's plays (*Twelfth Night* did not follow *Romeo and Juliet*, as the film suggests at its end), the false idea that a love affair of Shakespeare's inspired *Romeo and Juliet* rather than his reading of Arthur Brooke's 3,000-line poem of 1562, *The Tragicalle Historye of Romeus and Juliet*, and the fact that in 1593, when the film is set, Shakespeare had been married for more than ten years.

An additional contretemps involved the possible borrowing of the story from a 1941 comic novel entitled *No Bed for Bacon* by Caryl Brahams and S. J. Simon, reissued in the late 1980s. A Shakespearean spoof, the novel tells of Lady Viola Compton who disguises herself as a boy to satisfy her ambition to act and falls in love with young William Shakespeare, who is struggling to get a play written, entitled *Love's Labour's Won*. A chance meeting with Francis Bacon gives him new direction and help with the plot, while his love affair eliminates his writer's block. In response to remarks about this possible plagiarism, Stoppard wrote that Marc Norman, who penned the original draft of the screenplay, had never heard of the comic novel and that although he, Stoppard, owned a copy of the book, he did not use it for the film: 'both book and screenplay draw from the same well of Shakespeareana', he explained. The overwhelming consensus was that the film was a 'generous comedy which interweaves its multiple strands and styles with dazzling Stoppardian assurance'.[43] A new lawsuit began in October 2001, brought by two screenwriters arguing copyright infringement over an unproduced script entitled 'The Dark Lady'.[44]

Theatre people especially praised the film, with Peter Brook's response indicative: 'in the film, Stoppard out-Stoppards himself . . . it's more than astonishing. The magic of the film is that it shows us what Shakespeare might have done if he could have made a film.' What was most stunning, Brook added, was the way Stoppard enfolded the making of a new play within Shakespeare's own life and within Stoppard's own film in a totally convincing manner. Richard Dreyfuss described *Shakespeare in Love* as '*the perfect*' Stoppardian experience: 'it is far better an audience pleasing experience than any of his plays . . . all of his talents were put to best use in this piece. No one else could have written this – that particular moment, that attitude, that joke.' He reached millions with the work, which is graceful, generous, loving, funny: 'When was Tom Stoppard ever able to lay out his own intelligence and wit to an audience that didn't feel like there were only ten people in the audience who get the joke?' Frequently interviewed about the movie – Stoppard has long recognized the importance of publicity and the press for his projects – he prepared a stock answer to the most frequently asked question, 'If Shakespeare were alive today, would he be writing movies?' 'No,' he replied, 'he'd be rewriting them.'[45]

> *The 'Marseillaise'. That's unusual, isn't it? – for the Queen's Jubilee.*
>
> Stoppard, *The Invention of Love*

In October 1998, Stoppard purchased a house in France, in the town of Lacoste, perched on a mountain spine overlooking farmlands leading to Bonnieux. He had been retreating to France since the early sixties and on several previous occasions came close to locating a home. He finally chose Lacoste, the location of the Marquis de Sade's ancestral castle, recently purchased by Pierre Cardin. John Malkovich, one of Stoppard's neighbours, has lived in the area for several years.

A hilltop settlement in the sloping hills of the Lubéron, forty minutes by car east of Avignon, twenty minutes from Cavaillon, Lacoste is one of the most romantic and historical sites in France. The narrow streets paved in *calade* stone lend a consistency of colour and style to the site. The ruins of the château, dating mostly from the sixteenth to eighteenth centuries, dominate the landscape. The Marquis de Sade sought refuge there, in his grandfather's château, from 1774 until his arrest in 1778. Avignon, where Petrarch studied and glimpsed Laura, the source of his unrequited love and greatest love poetry, is a short distance away. The valleys of the Vaucluse stand in the distance, with the Rhone, where van Gogh spent his most creative years, to the west. Surrounding the village are the wooded hills of the Lubéron mountains and numerous Roman ruins. At the top of Lacoste's hill is a quarry that is now a performance and meditation space. This area of Provence had appealed to Stoppard ever since his visits to the region with Anthony Smith and other Bristol journalists in 1961. A photo from that trip shows a cavalier Stoppard perched on the edge of an ancient well, writing on a pad, while several of his friends sit about, relaxing in a courtyard in a rented villa in the Vaucluse. Stoppard's home on a village street in Lacoste needed some renovation and he was eager to get rid of the black bathroom the former owner had put in. He graciously offered it to the previous owner, who gladly accepted it for her new home.

A month after his purchase, France formally honoured Stoppard with the Comédie-Française performance of *Arcadia*. Although the play, directed by Philippe Adrian, received mixed reviews, its choice symbolized his importance as a dramatist in France.[46]

Work on new screenplays and overseeing the remounting of *The Real Thing* for its first revival in a major London theatre since 1982 preoccupied Stoppard for most of the following year. The screenplays for *Enigma*, *Sleepy Hollow* and *Vatel*, plus further investigations in his family's past, prevented him from working on a new play.

The reception of a new production of *The Real Thing* at the Donmar Warehouse dispelled any sense of public discomfort with Stoppard's persona or the play. Those put off by the erudition of *The Invention of Love* were delighted by the naturalism and emotion of the revival. Praised by the critics for its fluent direction by David Leveaux and wonderful acting by Stephen Dillane, whose ironic attitudes exposed his unearned and self-serving romanticism (and who won the *Evening Standard* Best Actor Award), and Jennifer Ehle, equally passionate and intelligent, the play was a hit. A West End transfer in January 2000 was followed by an April opening on Broadway for fifteen weeks at the Ethel Barrymore Theater with same cast (made possible by an exchange programme between American and British Equity).

Stoppard not only attended rehearsals and faxed changes to the script from France, where he had gone for a short vacation, but sat through previews and constantly consulted with the director and actors on nuances, shifts and alterations to improve the production. The papers celebrated its success, especially in capturing the exhilaration and agony of love. Critics were suddenly praising the introspective and self-revealing character of the play, seeing it as a window on Stoppard's feelings, finally withdrawing the criticism that he is unable to write about the emotions. Billington concisely summed up the new view: 'Stoppard is really a romantic who uses cerebration as a shield against emotional excess.'[47] The play in this new production was about the breakdown of Henry's defences, somewhat akin to the change that Stoppard himself was undergoing in the mid-nineties.

Two days before *The Real Thing* was to open in London, Stoppard participated in a remarkable event: a 'Platform' on *Rosencrantz and Guildenstern* at the National Theatre which reunited the original cast. The evening was held in conjunction with the NT 2000 poll, a survey of actors, playwrights, directors, journalists and other theatre professionals asked to nominate the 100 top plays of the twentieth century, in which *Rosencrantz and Guildenstern* tied with Noël Coward's *Private Lives* at number seven.[48] A year-long series of Platforms charted the progress of drama through the century, one devoted to each play on the list. In one of his many silent acts of financial support – he had over the years supported scholarships, theatre students and programmes – Stoppard contributed to the funding of the series.

On 25 May 1999, John Stride (the original Rosencrantz), Edward Petherbridge (the original Guildenstern) and Stoppard appeared on the stage of the National Theatre – actually the set of *Private Lives*, then in repertoire – to revisit the first production of the play. After retelling stories about the chaotic original production in Edinburgh in 1966, Stoppard and the actors relived the National Theatre production, reading several sections and, at one key point, co-opting Stoppard to join them as the Player for a reading of the concluding section of the play. It was a triumph, personally and dramatically, especially after Genista McIntosh, Executive Director of the National, encouraged Stoppard, the hesitant actor, to perform.

Continuously in demand as a speaker, and with his work con-tinuously in revival, in new as well as traditional performances – *Jumpers* was produced in Nottingham in the summer of 1999 and

Albert's Bridge performed as 'A Musical Play' in Shaftesbury, adapted by Anthony Smith with music by David Lyon in November 1999 – Stoppard's work and profile had no chance to recede.

*I'm deeply resistant to change; I can't bear what happened
to English sentence structure after the eighteenth or
nineteenth centuries.*
Stoppard, 1998

Stoppard continued to work and oversee the production of his plays as the new century started, spending nearly a month in San Francisco on two separate trips, guiding the preparations for the January 2000 American première of *The Invention of Love*. Attending early cast readings and then rehearsals, Stoppard was frequently deferred to, even when the actors thought that a gesture here, or an additional word there, might enhance the clarity of the text. Willing to listen, Stoppard just as readily said 'no' to various suggestions, although he worked with the director, Carey Perloff, to make the text accessible to American audiences. The imaginative staging satisfied Stoppard's sense of the play, which received national attention.

In the midst of the preparations, he spoke on *Arcadia* at Stanford University and flew to San Diego for a day to meet with the cast of *The Seagull* in Jack O'Brien's production for the Old Globe. Stoppard agreed with O'Brien's delightful vision of *The Seagull* as 'a Russian version of *Hay Fever*, the characters drunk on theatre'. With *The Seagull* cast, Stoppard worked to remove any lingering 'Englishisms' from the script and, once again admiring Chekhov's compression, expressed wonder over how Chekhov moved from this moment to that in four lines. 'It would have taken me four pages,' he said, adding that despite Chekhov's talent, he didn't find him intimidating. Stoppard further explained that 'every text is capable of producing a dull evening. I mean, that's why theatre is so terrifying: the text guarantees nothing.'[49] By March, he was back in London, speaking on 'Writing Plays for Fun or Money' at the Athenaeum.

In late February 2000, rumours of a new relationship circulated in the papers. Stoppard had apparently been going out with a stunning, forty-eight-year-old ex-model born in Japan of American-Japanese parents who had spent her childhood in Hawaii, where she moved at the age of four. The exotic Marie Helvin moved to England and at one time was married to the photographer David Bailey, whom she met at nineteen when she went to his Regent's Park studio house for a shoot; since her divorce from him in 1985, she had been romantically linked to the Pakistani cricketer Imran Khan, the novelist Salman Rushdie and the British actor Neil Pearson. She and Stoppard met through mutual friends; for many years, Helvin had been a close friend of Jerry Hall and Mick Jagger. Stoppard and Helvin began to be linked in the papers.[50] However, other rumours emerged: that Stoppard was actually seeing another woman, an actress whom the papers had confused with Marie Helvin. This second, mystery figure might also be named Marie. Whatever the case, the papers had clearly not lost interest in Stoppard's romantic life.

Stoppard, in fact, was never allowed out of the spotlight. *Arcadia* appeared on the A Level syllabus in autumn 2000. He was interviewed by Richard Eyre for *Changing Stages*, the BBC television series on modern British theatre. At one point, Eyre remarked that Stoppard had written more than even Proust; Stoppard replied, 'More jokes, too.'[51] A new-found personal happiness accompanied his increased success.

New York was soon to celebrate Stoppard again, with the Broadway transfer of *The Real Thing*. The opening-night audience in New York was packed with A-list celebrities, including Jerry Seinfeld and his wife, Tina Brown and Harold Evans, the actors Philip Seymour Hoffman, Geoffrey Rush and Patrick Stewart and the singer Moby. Regis Philbin, host of *Who Wants to be A Millionaire?*, the actress Marisa Tomei and President Clinton's former spokesperson George Stephanopoulos joined the crowd and the after-show party at the Tavern on the Green in Central Park. The production won three Tonys: one each for Stephen Dillane and Jennifer Ehle as Best Actor and Best Actress and one for the play as Best Revival. The renewed success of the play, which had run for 566 performances in 1984, confirmed its continued appeal. Sixteen years later, the purpose and attraction of the play was unmistakable: 'Love. Passion. Marriage. Adultery. Get them all in the right order and you've got THE REAL THING.'[52]

Such success brought further attention, including an incident on a bus: unable to find a cab one night in New York, Stoppard hopped on an Eighth Avenue bus but lacked a Metro card or the right change. Realizing this, he told the driver he had to get off because he couldn't pay. A lady in the middle of the bus, overhearing the exchange, suddenly interrupted and in a loud voice said, 'I think I owe you more than $1.50, Mr Stoppard.' Five women immediately opened their purses for the needed fare and treated him like a child, introducing him to the rest of the bus as the writer of *Shakespeare in Love*. The driver, Stoppard added in his comic retelling of the tale, was not impressed – he had probably not seen the movie. The episode underlines the point that, in America, Stoppard is better known as a screenwriter than playwright. In England, his prominence as a playwright balances his success as a screenwriter. In November 2000, he was chosen to present the first Charles Wintour Award – now worth £30,000 – to the Most Promising Playwright as part of the *Evening Standard* Theatre Awards. In 1967, Stoppard had shared the Most Promising Playwright award with David Storey. Wintour was the *Evening Standard* editor who turned down Stoppard as a reporter when he could not name the then Home Secretary. Although Stoppard did not get the job, Wintour long took credit for creating Tom Stoppard the playwright, according to his daughter.[53]

Returning to England after his New York success, Stoppard went to France to work on his new play, rumoured to be a nine-hour production focusing on nineteenth- century Russian socialists – 'not all of them but some of them', he noted – tracing the lives of three characters over a twenty-five-year span. He explained to a *New York Times* reporter that 'in defence, I'm thinking of it as three plays. I'm telling everyone it's a trilogy.'[54] The title of the work is *The Coast of Utopia*, a phrase which echoes Stoppard's love of Shakespeare, since it alludes to *Twelfth Night* and the arrival of Viola and Sebastian after their shipwreck on the coast of Illyria. Appropriately, Stoppard has Will Shakespeare begin this play at the end of *Shakespeare in Love*. The *Coast of Utopia* consists of three sequential, self-contained plays, *Voyage*, *Shipwreck* and *Salvage*, and traces several key players in the drama of Russian radical opposition before and after the European revolutions of 1848: Alexander Herzen, founder of Russian populism, Michael Bakunin, an early anarchist, the writer Ivan Turgenev and Vissarion Belinsky, an erratic young critic who died young. Although the play has more than fifty characters, with action moving from Bakunin's country estate to Moscow, St Petersburg, Paris and London, it concentrates on the private lives of romantic exile and the social duty of the artist.

Originally intended to be an exploration of the remarkable relationship between Isaiah Berlin and the Russian poet Anna Akhmatova, derived from their extraordinary meeting in Leningrad in 1945, Stoppard shifted his new work back to the Decembrists of 1825 and the revolutionary writer and aristocrat Herzen, one of Isaiah Berlin's favourite Russian authors. It is possible that reading Michael Ignatieff's 1998 biography of Berlin stimulated Stoppard to consider such a subject, moving not only back in time from Berlin's experiences in 1945 but to the romantic exile Herzen, who, despite his popularity as a novelist and essayist in Russia, left that country in 1847 for exile in Europe, where he remained until his death in 1870, living thirteen of those years in England.

Stoppard would find three elements of Herzen's thought appealing: first, his belief that literature could be a tool for improving society, that philosophy must be practical, expressed by his axiom 'action not knowledge is the aim of man', and that so-called 'logical fact cannot fully acknowledge real fact' or life as it is lived. Hence the need to push aside simple fact for complex experience: 'reality is not a lecture, not a sermon, but life,' Herzen wrote.[55] And Herzen's exile in England and Europe might be said to loosely parallel Stoppard's, at least in theory, while his interest in nineteenth-century Russian life shows him turning eastwards, this time to satisfy his persistent interest in Russian rather than central European culture. Thirdly, Herzen also believed that 'in a suppressed society, the artist is more important than in a free society, more attention is paid to the artist'.[56] Coinciding with this interest was the news, in September 2001, that although Stoppard's work had been banned in Russia since 1977, when *Every Good Boy Deserves Favour* appeared, his works had been kept and read in a secret archive of the Russian State Library.[57]

Work on the Herzen project had been slow with research, structure and continuity a continual challenge as Stoppard investigated the intricacies of Russian political life, recalling his remark to Michael Billington when working on an earlier drama. Encountering the critic on the steps of the London Library while balancing an armload of books, Stoppard quipped, 'Just returning my new play.'[58] Drafts of the three Russian plays were sent to Trevor Nunn who will direct the production, scheduled for the National's twenty-fifth anniversary season, in the summer of 2002. However, the complicated play brought on thoughts of writing simpler works. Next time, Stoppard told an interviewer, he hoped to come up with a story that required no research. Having seen the recent revival of *The Real Thing*, he remarked 'how easy it was in those days when all I had to do was sit down and start writing instead of first reading for a year and a half.'[59]

Truth does not yield to a single antithesis but is as graduated as a Russian court. This is the promise held out by art to biography,' Stoppard said in 1997. 'When in doubt, speculate. Enter the picture. It's not only allowed, it's inescapable,' he added.[60] The reference to Russia and biography are apt given Stoppard's interest in Herzen and hesitancy over biography. Herzen was himself an aristocrat and familiar with the Tsar's court where the hierarchy was notorious: courtiers, ministers and aristocrats had well-defined roles and status that could not be violated. Discriminations of rank were observed, tested and reasserted, as Tolstoy so clearly represented in *War and Peace*. Stoppard's analogy between the complex levels of truth in a biography and the ranks of a Russian court reminds one, of course, of the challenges biography faces in its attempt to reveal its subject. But the potential of art to grasp such intricacies shapes the biographer's quest.

> *The further back we look, the stranger are the ups and*
> *downs of reputation. Is anybody safe?*
> Stoppard, 'Reflections on Hemingway', 1984

Stoppard has achieved fame, but is his reputation secure? The question occasionally bothers him. Honours, both foreign and national, have accrued, and attention to his work has been constant since his first, overnight success. But critics still worry about his intellectualism and attraction to the erudite at the expense of entertainment. 'Is my seriousness compromised by my frivolity . . . or my frivolity redeemed by my seriousness?'[61] This query, which he posed to himself years ago, cannot yet be definitively answered.

Despite new honours, including the prestigious Order of Merit announced in May 2000 and an honorary degree from Cambridge University in July 2000, Stoppard does not overlook the milestones of his friends. He honoured the retirement of Frank Pike, his editor for nearly forty years at Faber, by inviting Pike and Anthony Smith, who had originally introduced the two in 1962, to lunch at the Ivy in November. Less than a month later, he was back at the restaurant for the seventieth birthday party of Peter Hall, joining Harold Pinter, Alan Ayckbourn, Richard Eyre, Trevor Nunn, David Hare, Judi Dench and Maggie Smith.

His critical reception, however, continued to puzzle the public. Response to *The Invention of Love*, first understood as an exercise in Latin and Greek rather than an examination of love, stressed its esoteric, rather than experimental, elements. Reaction to the restaged *The Real Thing* praised its emotional core. The immensely successful New York production of *The Invention of Love*, directed by Jack O'Brien, emphasized more vividly the homosexual element and erotic loss in the play. O'Brien sought to give the play a less muted performance and to 'unlock its mystery from the inside – not to impose something on it'. The play 'had to be translated into things that had appetite'.[62] Opening on 29 March 2001 and produced by Lincoln Center Theater at the Lyceum on West 45th Street, *Invention* earned a Tony Award for Richard Easton as Best Actor and another for Robert Sean Leonard – who had been in the 1995 Lincoln Center production of *Arcadia* – as Best Featured Actor. The play was also nominated for Best Play and Stoppard flew to New York to introduce the play to the Tony and television audience. It lost to *Proof* by David Auburn, but *Invention* did win the New York Drama Critics' Circle Award for Best Play.

Two days before the opening, Stoppard spoke at the Young Men's Hebrew Association on 92nd Street in Manhattan, a well-known literary centre. But the 900 plus audience found Stoppard doing something unusual: for the first time, he was not going to lecture or be interviewed. He took 'the soft option' of reading from his works. 'I don't do voices,' he announced, but then proceeded to read excerpts from *The Invention of Love*, and *Arcadia*, while offering comments on *Cahoot's Macbeth* and its problematic structure which at one point was 'like two men carrying a rolled carpet: the play sagged and the audience was bottoming out in the middle.' He then decided to add policemen after the first ten minutes of the work providing the missing tension. He ended the successful evening by describing his new play and its focus on the birth of the Russian intelligentsia.[63]

Another New York success for Stoppard was the Central Park production of his adaptation of The Seagull. Directed by Mike Nichols and starring Meryl Streep (who had not been on the stage for twenty years) as Madame Arkadina, Kevin Kline as Trigorin, Marcia Gay Harden as Masha, Natalie Portman as Nina and Philip Seymour Hoffman as Konstantin, the play was an immediate hit. Bob Crowley, who also designed the Lincoln Center Theater's Invention of Love, successfully evoked Sorin's estate and Trigorin's stage, partly by using nearly two dozen Chekhovian white birch trees. The 12 August 2001 première of the play at the open-air Delacorte Theater was an event and audiences lined up overnight to acquire the free tickets. Even the previews were sold out.

The first-choice text had not been Stoppard's but the version by the American playwright Richard Nelson; Streep's preference for Stoppard's adaptation won out, however. In rehearsal, a Russian scholar from Yale assisted by translating from Chekhov's original so that the actors could supplement the Stoppard edition. Anna Deavere Smith acted as the production's dramaturg. The idea to do the play at Joseph Papp's Public Theater was Meryl Streep's, and she had called Mike Nichols to see if he would direct. Early in February 2000, they did a first readthrough; they then called the Public Theater to confirm that they would produce. The movie commitments of Natalie Portman delayed the production until the summer of 2001. Fans had to line up no later than 6 a.m. for the 1 p.m. distribution of tickets; some arrived the night before. Rumours of a revival on Broadway in autumn 2001 circulated among the cognoscenti.

During the Broadway production of The Real Thing, critics celebrated the 'opening' of Stoppard's heart, although others persisted in their indictment of his work and its impact: 'there's no one like Tom Stoppard for making you feel both spoiled and inadequate as an audience'.[64] Others felt he never overcame the title of flashy dilettante, or complained that he turned away from social problems. In defence of the latter charge, he explained that it was a matter of temperament and that while art does a great deal, affecting 'the moral sensibilities of a society . . . it does so in a subterranean way'.[65] Only the attention Stoppard received for *Shakespeare in Love,* which cut across age and education barriers, balanced the view that he was an intellectual's writer, requiring an advanced degree in order to be fully appreciated. Yet his prismatic comedy constantly challenges, in language that celebrates the certainty that there are no certainties – and always with panache: 'I've never written a play which isn't supposed to make the audience laugh . . . I don't think of theatre as night school.' What he has always sought to avoid is the situation described to him by a New York publicist of a show he once visited: 'They're laughing but they're not enjoying themselves.'[66]

An incident at the end of May 2001, however, epitomized the fragility of reputation. Stoppard had been asked to make the opening remarks at the Royal Academy of Arts Annual Dinner, a gala event at Burlington House held the day after the nominations for the Turner Prize were announced. The art world was alight; the invitation read 'white or black tie with decorations' and, although Lord Attenborough won for the most decorated chest, Stoppard appeared wearing his Order of Merit. Joining Sir Nicholas Serota, Director of the Tate and chairman of the Turner Prize jury, were Lord Puttnam, Sir Paul Smith, Peter Blake, Bjork, Vivienne Westwood and numerous gallery directors, dealers, collectors and politicians. Stoppard, speaking informally from headline notes, proceeded to lambast conceptual art and the YBA (Young British Artists) of the day. Directly or indirectly, he criticised Tracey Emin, Damien Hirst and Marcus Harvey, complaining about artists who do not complete their own projects – several, like Hirst, assign the completion of works to assistants. He argued that 'the term artist isn't intelligible to me if it doesn't entail making'. In referring to Emin, who displayed her soiled underwear at last year's Turner Prize competition as part of her unmade bed project, Stoppard added 'from there it is but a hop skip and a jump to Tracey's knickers'.[67] Tracing conceptual art back to Duchamp, whom he approved for making a valid attack on prevailing cultural values, Stoppard contrasted Duchamp's work with that of the conceptualists and installation artists who were the new orthodoxy only because they were hailed by the art establishment. Their protests against society had less value because their art was only self-validatory. The audience was stunned; Sir Nicholas looked steely. 'I looked across at Nicholas Serota and I occasionally wondered if he'd throw his bread roll at me,' Stoppard said afterwards.[68]

A pandemic of criticism rained down as Stoppard's opponents at last had proof of his conservative, reactionary and bourgeois taste. Editorials, articles, columns and letters appeared, castigating Stoppard's support of figurative or representational art and absence of a postmodern vision. For several weeks, the controversy between contemporary and traditional art raged. To suggest that the intellectual basis of conceptualism was suspect and that it lacked craftsmanship ignited many. The artists Gilbert and George were cornered and asked if they had ever met Stoppard. They replied that they once went to one of his plays, 'but we didn't last long – there were too many words. So we left.'[69] Stoppard was suddenly seen as a playwright who was 'a generation divider, to the middle class, middle aged and reasonably educated, he provides a comforting experience, reinforcing their values with his so-clever dialogue and brittle repartee'. Variously labelling his talk 'a tirade', 'feeble outburst' and 'jealous tantrum', columnists isolated Stoppard from the new.[70] A defence was required and Stoppard himself provided it.

An article by Stoppard headlined 'Thinking is not enough: art involves making, too' began by recalling the informal description provided to him of what he was to present: essentially a toast for the guests. The morning after, he was the scourge of modern art, compared to Sir Alfred Munnings and his 1949 speech denouncing Picasso and Henry Moore. This entire reaction has been 'dispiriting', Stoppard writes, because he wanted his speech to be only a suggestion that a fault line had been crossed 'when it had become unnecessary for an artist to make anything, when the thought, the inspiration itself, had come to constitute the achievement'.[71] 'I decided to keep value judgments out of it,' he adds, noting that he spoke 'off the cuff' but that the press coverage and letters he received made it clear that 'merely to describe the phenomenon is to be taken to be attacking it'.

Turning to classical Greece, Stoppard then defended his position by pointing out that the idea of the artist carried the sense of skill, manufacture and technique, whether poet or painter: 'from Praxiteles to Pollock (not to stop there), the artist was somebody who made something'. The shift towards subjectivity gave 'escalating offence to the older idea of art as the pursuit of objective truth', although the personal action of a maker of something remained part of the meaning of 'artist'. This what has been 'jettisoned . . . in triumph' and this was what upset him: 'a work of art may be no more than a mental act, complete at the moment of inspiration'. We have now the 'repudiation' of value as well as making. But there is a problem, which a reference to Thomas Love Peacock's novel *Headlong Hall* clarifies: the issue of whether or not unexpectedness can exist when you walk around a garden a second, third or fourth time. He had been walking around the garden of modern art since 1917, he writes. Hirst and Emin are, indeed, more complicated than he may have implied in his remarks, which he insists were not designed as 'Hirst-and-Emin bashing'. But he maintains that conceptual art is no more than 'thought exhibited . . . But so is a Turner, he of the Prize. So is art itself. The thought varies in profundity. The rest, the making, is, or was, the hard part.'[72]

To no one's surprise, Stoppard's article did not end the matter. Mark Lawson in the *Guardian*, eager to defend Stoppard as a modernist *manqué* who *could* understand the new art, nevertheless found the playwright's defence less than convincing. To say that modern art has abandoned the idea of the artist as a maker is not entirely correct, yet Lawson praises Stoppard for raising the issue of whether it is necessary for the artist to make anything at this time when thought alone constitutes the achievement. But Stoppard's article does not exhibit the instinctive conservatism reported in his speech by the papers. For Lawson, 'the narrowness of the division between thinking and making becomes apparent' when one considers architecture. No one expects an architect to be a glazier. Who did the riveting is not an issue. Other talents, in fact, put the ideas of screenwriters or even novelists into final form, whether directors or editors. Even the dramatist is someone who is both a creator and collaborator. And Stoppard should worry not about art which is 'hands-free' but that which is 'ideas-free'.[73] Blasts and counterblasts continued, even if Stoppard first thought his remarks were meant to be harmless observations. Ironically, at the beginning of the very month in which the controversy occurred, a performing arts facility named the 'Tom Stoppard Centre' opened at Pocklington, his former grammar school.

Part of the pleasure and the excitement is the translation of
the text into an event.
Stoppard, May 2001

Tom Stoppard has moved from a 'double act' to a double consciousness, aware of both his English and Czech origins, his identity and
non-identity as a Jew. 'Happiness' may remain 'equilibrium', as Henry
remarks in *The Real Thing*, but Stoppard is less sure of how to shift
one's weight. His balance in the last six years or so has been tested by
the discovery of his family's past and the unsettling challenges of new
work. The balance he seeks may exist only in the pronunciation of his
name, which stresses both syllables equally: STOP-PARD, he insists,
with the accent shared equally.

Stoppard is successful, but is he popular? One theatre historian
explained why he was not, or at least why there remains suspicion over
his success. While the British like irony in the theatre, they are
uncomfortable with the absurd. Stoppard can be flip as well as ironic,
a unique Central European combination originating in a sense of
darkness, if not despair. Furthermore, he is full of ideas, not
characters. Attending a Stoppard play means one must remain alert.
Among the intelligentsia, he is both successful and popular, but
among the general public he is not. A retired British naval intelligence
officer formerly stationed in Russia explained the problem: Stoppard
is too smart and his public is put off, if not offended, by his show of
knowledge. His audience attends the National Theatre or the Royal
Shakespeare Company, not the West End. The public suspects his
work because it is full of 'chattering heads' and the plays themselves are
very unEnglish, reflective of more Central European than English
attitudes. His closest predecessors are Irish: Congreve, Sheridan,
Wilde, Shaw and Beckett – all of them 'outsiders'. But what makes it
difficult for the public to dismiss him is that along with the wit and
intelligence comes laughter. This makes his surreal and absurdist
pieces, as well as his 'realistic' ones, unique. He presents serious fun, an
apparent but appealing contrast that, owing to his success in film, may
mean increasingly larger audiences in the theatre.

News that *The Coast of Utopia* will involve nineteenth-century
Russia excites the intelligentsia but only arouses the curiosity of his

general audience. But Stoppard seems compelled to write wittily about serious matters and with as much determination as Trigorin who, in Stoppard's adaptation of *The Seagull,* proclaims that 'day and night I'm driven by one constant thought. I must be writing – I must be writing – I've scarcely finished one story before – God knows why – I have to write another . . . I can't do anything else.'[74] Although Stoppard may not entirely share Trigorin's urgency (deadlines and obligations push him on), the intensity is the same. Answering the question 'why do I write?', Stoppard replied: 'it's my identity, is all I can say.'[75]

In inventing dramatic truth, Stoppard teases history. But he never allows his audiences complacently to replace scepticism with certainty in a world where believable disbelief is so mischievously expressed. As Archibald Jumper tells Crouch, 'the truth to us philosophers . . . is always an interim judgment',[76] a precept Stoppard constantly reframes in the world of theatrical action.

NOTES

INTRODUCTION

1. *Indian Ink*, 5; *The Invention of Love*, 96.
2. Stoppard on inaccuracy in Charles Spencer, 'What Tom thinks of Oscar', *Daily Telegraph*, 27 February 1999; Stoppard to the author, 27 May 1999.
3. *Indian Ink*, 61.
4. Stoppard, 'Tom Stoppard on a dazzling new writer…', *Scene* 18, 9 February 1963.
5. Virginia Woolf, 'Notebooks', quoted in Hermione Lee, *Virginia Woolf* (London: Chatto, 1996), 10.
6. Stoppard in Mel Gussow, *Conversations with Stoppard* (New York: Grove Press, 1995), 3. Hereafter referred to as Gussow.
7. Stoppard in Michael Blowen, 'Talking chaos with Tom Stoppard', *Boston Globe*, 11 September 1996.
8. Stoppard, 'No symbolism', in Benedict Nightingale, 'Rosencrantz and Guildenstern are Back', *New York Times*, 17 May 1987; Stoppard, 'Pragmatic Theater', *New York Review of Books*, 23 September 1999.
9. Stoppard in Paul Delaney, ed. *Tom Stoppard in Conversation* (Ann Arbor: Univ. of Michigan Press, 1994), 96. Hereafter referred to as Delaney.
10. *The Invention of Love*, 93.
11. Stoppard in Louise East, 'Enter a free man', *Irish Times*, 16 January 1999. Stoppard was in Dublin for a production of *Arcadia* at the Gate Theatre.
12. *Arcadia*, 75.
13. Stoppard in Charles Spencer, 'What Tom thinks of Oscar'; Stoppard in Delaney, 57.
14. Christopher Hampton, *The Philanthropist* (London: Faber and Faber, 1970), 55. The play, combining a satire of academic life with romantic misunderstanding, premièred at the Royal Court Theatre in July 1970.
15. Stoppard in Roger Hudson et al., 'Ambushes for the Audience: Towards a High Comedy of Ideas', *Theatre Quarterly* 4 (May 1974); rpt. in Delaney, 57.
16. *Plays for Radio*, 171-2.
17. Stoppard in 'Sunday Morning', CBS TV, 28 February 1999; Stoppard in Michael Elkin, 'Tom Terrific', *Jewish Exponent* (Philadelphia), 3 February 2000.
18. Stoppard to Lyn Gardner, 'The Heart in the Closet', *Guardian*, 16 January 1999.
19. *Hapgood*, 10.
20. Richard Ellmann in Thomas Wright, 'In the mouth of fame', *Times Literary Supplement*, 9 February 2001.
21. Arthur Koestler quoted in Ian Buruma, *Anglomania: A European Love Affair* (NY: Random House, 1998), 274. In this useful review of European fascination with England, Buruma explains that so many rootless cosmopolitans became Anglophiles, individuals like the art historian Nikolaus Pevsner, the economist F. A. Hayek, and the philosopher Isaiah Berlin, because Britain 'combined a strong national culture with a relatively open, liberal society' (279). He neatly summarizes the paradox when he writes that 'No one was more English and yet less English at the same time' than Berlin (274).
22. Stoppard in Benedict Nightingale, 'Long haul for a laidback lad', *The Times*, 26 September 1997.
23. Virginia Woolf, 'Stopford Brooke', *Times Literary Supplement*, 29 November 1917, in *The Essays of Virginia Woolf*, ed. Andrew McNeillie (London: Hogarth Press, 1987), II: 184; *The Invention of Love*, 51. My italics.
24. *Cahoot's Macbeth*, 193.

CHAPTER ONE DESERTS OF BOHEMIA

1. Derek Sayer, *The Coasts of Bohemia: A Czech History* (Princeton: Princeton University Press, 1998), 16.
2. *Ibid.*, 6.
3. *Ibid.*, 158.
4. For Stoppard's self-description as a 'bounced Czech', see Tynan's profile, 'Withdrawing with Style from the Chaos', *Show People* (New York: Simon and Schuster, 1979), 64, which originally appeared in the *New Yorker* of 19 December 1977. In his 1977 television play *Professional Foul*, Stoppard has Grayson, a sports reporter, declare the following over the phone to London, detailing a football match: 'There'll be Czechs bouncing in the streets of Prague tonight as bankruptcy stares English football in the face . . .' (*PF* 164).

   Other transformations that surrounded Stoppard included the renaming of his city. In 1948, Zlín became Gottwaldov, after Klement Gottwald, the first Communist President of Czechoslovakia. The Bat'a industries which anchored the town were nationalized and renamed Svit at that time. At the end of Communist rule, the city reverted to Zlín.
5. Letter of appointment to Dr E. Straüssler from Dr B. Albert, 1 February 1932.
6. Stoppard recounts the scene in his article 'On turning out to be Jewish', *Talk*, September 1999, published in the UK as 'Another country', *Sunday Telegraph*, 10 October 1999. Hereafter referred to as 'Another country'.
7. For an account of Jewish indifference towards Judaism and assimilationist attitudes, see Saul Friedlander, 'In the Shadow of National Socialism', *The Jews of Bohemia and Moravia*, ed. Wilma Abeles Iggers (Detroit: Wayne State University Press, 1992), 349-53.

   On intermarriage in the Beck family, see Stoppard, 'Another Country'.
8. Richard Lamb, *The Drift To War 1922-1939* (New York: St Martin's Press, 1991), 248; Kurt Weisskopf, *The Agony of Czechoslovakia '38/'68* (London: Elek Books, 1968), 113.
9. George F. Kennan, *From Prague After Munich: Diplomatic Papers 1938-40* (Princeton: Princeton University Press, 1968), v.
10. For the percentages of Czech economic loss as a result of the Munich agreement, see Joseph Rothschild, *East Central Europe between the Two World Wars* (Seattle: University of Washington Press, 1974), 132; for arms production by the Czechs which went to the Germans, see Lamb, *The Drift to War*, 265.
11. Sayer, 115.
12. *Ibid.*, 116.
13. Tomás Masaryk, 'On the Czech Jews', Iggers, 334; Franz Kafka, 'Tagebuch, 24 December 1911', *ibid.*, 290.
14. Joseph C. Pick, 'The Economy', *The Jews of Czechoslovakia: Historical Studies and Surveys* (Philadelphia: Jewish Publication Society of America, 1968), I: 420. Two other volumes complete this essential study for grasping the history and conditions of Jews in Czechoslovakia. Jan Bat'a, however, was not as sympathetic as his official actions may have indicated: after the Munich agreement, he actually went to Germany to meet with Hermann Göring, although possibly to discuss some agreement should Germany invade Czechoslovakia. See Thomas J. Bat'a, with Sonja Sinclair, *Bat'a: Shoemaker to the World* (Toronto: Stoddart, 1990), 143.
15. See Bat'a, *ibid.*, 37, 57. This autobiography of the son of the founder of the international shoe company provides some useful historical information of the survival of the company during and after the Nazi occupation of Czechoslovakia. Bat'a also relates an encounter with a Jewish student at a school in Switzerland in 1929, who warned him of the threat to Czechs and Jews from Hitler; he drew a swastika on a bathroom mirror, saying 'You're going to see a great deal of this emblem.' (21).
16. Letter to the author from Dr Emil Máčel, Zlín, Czech Republic, 14 July 1998. Dr Máčel is a chemical engineer formerly employed by the Bat'a Shoe Company.
17. Stoppard, 'Another country', reprints both photographs.
18. The prescient act of removal by Bat'a of the Straüsslers and other Jews avoided encountering such unhappy incidents in Zlín as when, in the late spring of 1939, sixty-three high-school students from Prague visited the Bat'a works. German authorities arrested several students when they voiced criticism of a movie. When one tried to escape, he was shot; the others were

sent back to Prague, but when they went through the Reich-controlled territory of north Moravia, the entire class was arrested for shouting 'Heil Moskau' instead of 'Heil Hitler' and held in prison at Sumperk. As of 6 June 1939, their fate remained unknown according to the American Consul General (Kennan, 182).

19. On the issue of Jewish emigration between the Munich Agreement of September 1938 and the German occupation of Bohemia and Moravia, see Kurt R. Grosmann, 'Refugees to and From Czechoslovakia', *The Jews of Czechoslovakia*, II: 575-7. On the question of the fate of Jews in Czechoslovakia, see Jiri Fiedler, 'From the History of the Jewish Communities in Bohemia and Moravia', *Jewish Sights of Bohemia and Moravia* (Prague: Sefer, 1991), 5-40; Iggers; and Ezra Mendelsohn, *The Jews of East Central Europe Between the World Wars* (Bloomington: Indiana University Press, 1983).

For a more personal account, see *Letters from Prague, 1939-1941*, compiled by Raya Schapiro and Helga Weinberg (Chicago: Academy Publishers, 1991), an account from Prague of the fate of a Jewish family during the German occupation. Martha Gellhorn's novel *A Stricken Field* (1940; London: Virago, 1986) vividly narrates the conditions of refugees in Prague in 1938.

20. Tom Stoppard to the author, 27 May 1999, London. The conversation is also the source of the phrase 'they were "not Jews to themselves"'. Stoppard makes the same point in 'Another country'.

21. Tom Stoppard, Prague Theatre Institute Lecture, 7 February 1998. Video archive, Prague Theatre Institute.

CHAPTER TWO LAVENDER STREET

1. H. D. Harben, 'Singapore', *Travellers' Singapore: An Anthology,* compiled by John Bastin (Kuala Lumpur: Oxford University Press, 1994), 232. Hereafter, *Travellers' Singapore.*

2. Kipling, *From Sea to Sea*, I: 250. 'Singapore is another Calcutta, but much more so', he added in the next sentence.

3. Mona Gardner, 'The Singapore Military Base' (1939), *Travellers' Singapore*, 250.

4. Norman Edwards, *The Singapore House and Residential Life, 1819-1939* (Singapore: Oxford University Press, 1990), 101.

5. Peter Stoppard to the author, 23 June 2000.

6. H. D. Harben, 'Singapore', *Travellers' Singapore*, 232-3.

7. Noel Barber, *Sinister Twilight: the Fall of Singapore, 1942* (London: Collins, 1968), 31.

8. Stoppard, Prague Theatre Institute Lecture; Stoppard in Janet Watts, 'Stoppard's half-century', *Observer*, 28 June 1987.

9. Peter Elphick, *Singapore: The Pregnable Fortress* (London: Hodder & Stoughton, 1995), 273.

10. Richard Gough, *The Escape from Singapore* (London: William Kimber, 1987), 59-60.

11. Elphick, 275.

12. Joseph Kennedy, *When Singapore Fell: Evacuations and Escapes, 1941-42* (New York: St Martin's Press, 1989), 23, 26.

13. *Ibid.*, 27.

14. Barber, 213.

15. Dr Emil Máčel quoting Mr Josef Varmuža in a letter to the author dated 16 February 1999. Mr Varmuža originally described the incident in a letter to Dr Máčel of 8 April 1995; Stoppard, 'Another country'.

C. M. Turnbull in his *History of Singapore 1819-1988*, 2nd ed. (Singapore: Oxford University Press, 1989), 182. Of the forty-four ships trying to leave during this period, all but four were sunk within two days of their departure. It is possible that Dr Straüssler was on one of the four small vessels that left that night: the *Malacca, Sin Kheng Seng, Wo Kwang* and the *Trang*. The *Malacca* was attacked on the 14th by enemy aircraft, causing sufficient damage for her captain to scuttle the vessel (Gough, 83-4, 218).

16. Watts, 'Stoppard's half-century'.

17. 'Another country', 193.

18. Gussow, 130-1.

19. *Ibid.*, 132, 131.

20. 'Another country', 242-3.
21. Jan Morris, 'Darjeeling', *Among the Cities* (New York: Viking, 1985), 108.
22. Stoppard, 'Going back', *Independent*, 23 March 1991.
23. Geoffrey Kendal in Felicity Kendal, *White Cargo* (London: Michael Joseph/Penguin, 1998), 20. Geoffrey Kendal at the time was heading a touring company of British actors sent out to entertain the troops.
24. On the social geography and culture of the hill stations, see Dane Kennedy, *The Magic Mountains: Hill Stations and the British Raj* (Berkeley: University of California Press, 1996), 3-9.
25. Hazel Innes Craig, *Under the Old School Topee* (London: British Association for Cemeteries in South-east Asia, 1990), vi. Stoppard himself consulted this useful 186-page account.
26. Quoted in Watts, 'Stoppard's half-century'; Stoppard, 'Going back'.
27. Stoppard, *ibid*. The occasion for Stoppard's return was an invitation from the Indian Film Festival to present *Rosencrantz and Guildenstern* in Madras. He went, having for some time wanted to revisit the country, but only after he completed *In the Native State*.
28. *Ibid*.
29. *Plays for Radio*, 106.
30. Stoppard, 'Going back', 28.
31. *Ibid.*, 25.
32. *Ibid*.
33. *Ibid.*, 26.
34. *Ibid.*, 27.
35. Delaney, 242.
36. 'Another country', 221.
37. Stoppard in Stephen Schiff, 'Full Stoppard', rpt. Delaney, 218-19. The interview originally appeared in *Vanity Fair*, No. 52, May 1989.

CHAPTER THREE ET IN ARCADIA EGO

1. Delaney, 233.
2. Stoppard, 'Something to Declare', *Sunday Times*, 25 February 1968.
3. On Kenneth and Martha Stoppard, Peter Stoppard to the author, 14 December 1998, 23 June 2000; on fashioning Tom Stoppard as British, see 'Another country'. In this article, the first extensive autobiographical essay Stoppard has written, he curiously refers to himself and his brother as 'half-Jewish' despite proving that his mother was not 'Catholic', as she wrote on her employment record, but Jewish; at one point in the article, he refers to her as a 'Jewess' (193).
4. Peter Stoppard to the author, 26 May 1998.
5. Cyril Connolly in Robert Hewison, *In Anger: British Culture in the Cold War 1945-60* (New York: Oxford University Press, 1981), 14.
6. Stoppard, 'Late to read, early to rise', *The Times*, 12 September 1992.
7. Duchess of Devonshire, *The House: A Portrait of Chatsworth* (London: Macmillan, 1982), 226.
8. Stoppard in Matt Wolf, 'Playing on the Pastoral', *Mirabella*, May 1995.
9. Stoppard in Mark Amory, 'The Joke's the Thing', *Sunday Times*, 9 June 1974. Hereafter cited as Amory; Stoppard with Roy Plomley on 'Desert Island Discs', recorded 8 January 1985 and broadcast on 12 January. National Sound Archive, British Library.
10. Stoppard in Michael Pye, 'A Very English Kind of Celebrity', *Daily Telegraph*, 31 March 1995; Stoppard on 'Desert Island Discs'.
11. P.C. Sands, C.M. Haworth and J.H. Eggleshaw, *A History of Pocklington School, East Yorkshire, 1514-1980* (Beverley: Highgate Publications, 1988), 7. Hereafter cited as *History*. I am grateful to Mr David Gray, former Headmaster of Pocklington School, and Mr A. D. Nuttall, Second Master, for their generous hospitality and assistance during my June 1998 visit to the school. They, and other members of the staff and students, enthusiastically shared with me the history, legends and geography of the school which proudly continues its centuries-long traditions.
12. Stoppard in 'What's All this About', *Newsweek*, 7 August 1967; Stoppard in Amory.
13. Pocklington School brochure, *Virtute et Veritate* [nd], 2.
14. *History*, 109-10.

15. *Ibid.*, 162.
16. J.G.L., 'Sixth Form Society', *Pocklingtonian* LIV: 2 (1953), 24-5.
17. Gussow, 13-14, 35.
18. Gussow, 3.
19. Stoppard in anon., 'Juggler to the British Stage', *Observer*, 14 November 1982.
20. Stoppard in Ken Tynan, 'The Man in the Moon', *Sunday Times*, 15 January 1978. This is a condensed version of Tynan's *New Yorker* profile with some additional details.
21. *The Pocklingtonian*, Lent 1954, 20.
22. Stoppard, 'Platform', National Theatre, 14 April 1993: [4]. Transcript provided by the National Theatre.
23. *History*, 119, 207-8.
24. *History*, 120.
25. Peter, who graduated in the summer of 1953, had a distinguished career at Pocklington, becoming a School Prefect in his senior year, graduating in the Middle VIth form with Moderns, being a member of the Antiquarian Society and progressing from the Second to the First XI. He also shared the French Declamation Prize and won prizes in Modern Studies. His General Certificate was in English and History.
26. R.G., 'Characters of the XI', *The Pocklingtonian*, Summer Term, 1953 (LIV), 14. Stoppard recalled an American student named Crump at the school *c.*1950 who dressed in full baseball catcher's outfit to play cricket: 'We sneered at him all summer and hurled cricket balls at him for his namby-pamby American ostentation', although Stoppard later acknowledged the usefulness of his protective outfit. Stoppard, 'Going to Bat for Britain', *House and Garden*, November 1987, 159.
27. *Ibid.*, p. 16.
28. R.G., 'Characters of the XI', *The Pocklingtonian* LV (1954), 13.
29. Stoppard in Michael Owen, 'Razzle dazzle Stoppard', *Evening Standard*, 28 August 1981.
30. Stoppard and Clive Exton, *The Boundary* (London: Samuel French Ltd, 1991), 10. The play was originally broadcast on the BBC's 'The Eleventh Hour' on 19 July 1975.
31. Stoppard interviewed by Melvyn Bragg on the TV programme, 'The South Bank Show', rpt. in Delaney, 120. The programme was originally broadcast on 26 November 1978.
32. *History*, 162.
33. Stoppard on 'Desert Island Discs'.
34. Peter Stoppard to the author, 14 December 1998.
35. Stoppard in Delaney, 53. The interview first appeared in 1974.
    His attitude towards Pocklington has altered: in March 1996, Stoppard returned to the school as a distinguished guest to meet with students, tour the grounds and announce his support of their Performing Arts Centre Appeal, a campaign to construct a new and badly needed music and theatrical complex.
36. *History*, 177.
37. Stoppard in Watts, 'Stoppard's half-century'. The title puns on the cricket term for scoring fifty runs, as well as Stoppard's age.
38. Peter Stoppard added that 'the main feature of our house was that you never actually felt you wanted to bring friends there'. Peter Stoppard to the author, 23 June 2000.
39. The literary past of Bristol was as varied as it was distinguished: Pepys and Pope visited and wrote about the city. Daniel Defoe supposedly interviewed the original shipwrecked sailor for *Robinson Crusoe* at the Landger Trow pub on the Bristol docks. Thomas Chatterton and Robert Southey were born there; Coleridge lectured and lived there in 1795-6 and was married at St Mary Redcliffe, the imposing parish church with its 300-foot spire favoured by Elizabeth I. Coleridge first met Wordsworth there in the late summer of 1795. In the 1790s, Bristol was thought to be the second city of the country and the first port of the kingdom, boasting several newspapers, publishers, theatres, Assembly Rooms, lecture halls and a large municipal lending library – on account of its population of prosperous merchants, shipowners, lawyers, manufacturers and shopkeepers and the city's status as the leading exporter/importer of sherry and packager of tobacco – as well as one of the centres of the slave trade for the New World. Other notables of the city included the novelist Charles Kingsley who attended school in Bristol,

the scientist Humphrey Davey, the historian Macaulay and, perhaps most importantly for Stoppard, Dr W. G. Grace, the great Victorian cricketer, who practised medicine there for a time.

40. The principal story was 'The Idyll of Miss Sarah Brown'; the dice game was from 'Blood Pressure'. Both stories appeared in Runyon's 1932 collection, *Guys and Dolls*. For an account of the musical and an upbeat narrative of Runyon's life, see Jimmy Breslin, *Damon Runyan* (New York: Ticknor and Fields, 1991), especially 399-400. The 1955 movie *Guys and Dolls* starred Marlon Brando and Frank Sinatra. The '6 to 5' quotation is from Runyon's story, 'A Nice Price'.
   Three of Stoppard's early short stories appeared in *Introduction 2: Stories by New Writers* (London: Faber and Faber, 1964) published in 1964 and discussed below (chapter 5).

41. Stoppard outlines his reading in 'Late to read, early to rise'.

42. Stoppard to Richard Hoggart, 'Writers on Writing: Tom Stoppard', TVS [Television South], 1983. Macdonell was born in India, wrote drama criticism in 1919 for the *London Mercury* after being invalided out of the army and found overnight fame after the publication of *England, Their England* in 1933. For the cricket match, see chapter VII.

43. Delaney, 53.

44. *Ibid.*, 91.

45. Evelyn Waugh, *Scoop* (1938; Harmondsworth: Penguin, 1985), 13, 155.

46. Stoppard, 'Late to read, early to rise'.

47. Geoffrey Reeves in Tynan, *Show People*, 59.

48. Stoppard in Peter Lewis, 'How Tom went to work on an absent mind and picked up £20,000', *Daily Mail*, 24 May 1967.

49. Dr John Wilders in Kate Kellaway, 'Tom's foolery', *Observer*, 6 July, 1997.

50. Denis Frost in Watts, 'Stoppard's half-century'.

51. David Foot, interview, 23 October 1997.

52. A. C. H. Smith in Amory; Smith to the author, 26 May 1998.

53. Stoppard, 'Saint Nick – the facts', *Western Daily Press*, 24 December 1957; 'A Child's First Concert', *Bristol Evening World*, 22 November 1958.

54. Stoppard in Hunter Davies, 'Stoppard Goes', *Sunday Times*, 23 April 1967.

55. Isabel Dunjohn, letter to the author, 21 May 1998.

56. Keith Harper in Watts, 'Stoppard's half-century'.

57. W. J. Bomford in letter of 20 May 1998.

58. David Foot, interview, 23 October 1997.

59. Bomford, 20 May 1998.

60. See Delaney, 54. John Fleming in *Stoppard's Theatre: Finding Order Amid Chaos* (Austin: University of Texas Press, 2001) records that Stoppard worked for the *Western Daily Press* until late 1958 and began work with the *Bristol Evening News* in January 1959. See Fleming, note 10 to chapter 1.

61. Stoppard, 'To speak of two Hamlets', *Western Daily Press*, 5 June 1958.

62. Stoppard, 'The Definite Maybe', *The Author* LXXVIII, Spring 1967, 18.

63. Stoppard, 'And now a preposterous New Year', *Western Daily Press*, 1 January 1962.

64. Bomford, 20 May 1998.

65. Hilton Tims, letter of 14 May 1998.

66. Keith Harper in Watts, 'Stoppard's half-century'; Tomik Straussler [Tom Stoppard], 'A Slave to a Mural', *Western Daily Press*, 1 March 1961.

67. Amory, 66.

68. Mike Nichols in Peter Applebome, 'Always Asking, What is This Really About', *New York Times*, 25 April 1999.

69. Mel Gussow, 'The Real Tom Stoppard', *New York Times*, 1 January 1984.

70. Delaney, 17.

71. 'Another country', 15.

72. Stoppard in Jerry Tallmer, 'Rosencrantz's Friend', *New York Post*, 8 December 1967.

73. Stoppard to Mark Lawson, 'Front Row', BBC Radio 4, 31 May 1999.

74. Stoppard, 'Harold Pinter: the poet of no-man's-land', *Sunday Times*, 7 October 1990.

75. Gussow, 136.

76. Anon., 'Homely Interest', *Evening Standard*, n.d. Gordon Dickerson Collection, Harry Ransom Humanities Research Center (hereafter HRC, University of Texas, 18.2.

77. Kenneth Tynan, 'Ondine', *Observer*, 23 October 1955.

78. Anon., 'Now an Angry Young Hamlet in Bristol Production', *The Times*, 24 April 1958.

79. Gussow, 'The Real Tom Stoppard'.

80. On O'Toole at the Bristol Old Vic, see Nicholas Wapshott, *Peter O'Toole: A Biography* (London: New English Library, 1983), 38-43.

81. Stoppard, 'Act II . . . in which Tom Stoppard tries another profession', *Western Daily Press and Bristol Mirror*, 13 September 1958. This is Stoppard's newspaper account of his dramatic début. He refers to it also in a letter to A. C. H. Smith of October 1965.

82. Stoppard, 'In front of the Curtain', *Not in the Script: Bristol Old Vic, Anecdotes on stage and off* (Bristol: Redcliffe Press, 1992), 7. In October 1965, at a televison taping of one of his plays, Stoppard recalled his walk-on when he re-encountered Emrys James, who had a small part in Stoppard's play.

83. Stoppard in Delaney, 54; Anthony Smith, 'Silence, Exile, Cunning', Lecture, University of Texas, Austin, 14 October 1994. This talk has been published in a slightly revised form under the same title in the *London Magazine* n.s. 40 (June-July 2000), 57-74.

CHAPTER FOUR   AT THE PARAGON

1. Stoppard to Joost Kuurman, 'An Interview with Tom Stoppard', *Dutch Quarterly Review of Anglo-American Letters* 10 (1980-1), 44.

2. Stoppard, 'Platform', National Theatre, 14 April 1993: [5]. See also Stoppard, 'Something to Declare'.

3. Stoppard, 'The event and the text', in Delaney, 200. In the same lecture, he explains that the theatre doesn't work as parable but metaphor (207).

4. Stoppard to Jon Bradshaw, 29 November 1976, correcting material for an interview that appeared in *New York Magazine* in 1976, HRC. See also the interview in Delaney, 94.
   On the state of the theatre in 1956 and its new programme of social change, see Dan Rebellato, *1956 and All That: The Making of Modern British Drama* (London: Routledge, 1999), especially chapters 1-3.

5. Kuurman, 44.

6. Stoppard, 'Platform', National Theatre, 14 April 1993: [4].

7. A. C. H. Smith, 'Arts page', *The 60s in Bristol*, ed. James Belsey (Bristol: Redcliffe, 1989), 39.

8. Smith in Amory.

9. *Ibid.*

10. *Ibid.*

11. Stoppard to Isabel Dunjohn, January 1961.

12. Stoppard to Dunjohn, July 1960.

13. Stoppard to Dunjohn, July 1960.

14. Delaney, 91.

15. Stoppard, 'A Slave to a Mural', *Western Daily Press*.

16. Stoppard, 'Grandmother Courage', *Western Daily Press*, 13 November 1961. A background article on Brecht and his life in the theatre by B. S. Johnson appears on the same page.

17. Stoppard, 'The Tense Present – Harold Pinter', *Western Daily Press*, 8 January 1962.

18. Stoppard, 'After Wesker – is the horse so thirsty?' *Western Daily Press*, 30 October 1961.

19. Stoppard, 'Who's talking of Jerusalem?' *Western Daily Press*, 15 January 1962.

20. Stoppard, 'Double focus – the plight of the sane lunatic', *Western Daily Press*, 13 November 1961.

21. Stoppard, 'Late to read, early to rise'.

22. Stoppard, in Michael Pye, 'The Arts: A very English kind of celebrity', *Daily Telegraph*, 31 March 1995; Stoppard, 'Reflections on Ernest Hemingway', *Ernest Hemingway: The Writer in Context*, ed. James Nagel (Madison: University of Wisconsin Press, 1984), 21-2, 26.

23. Stoppard, 'Reflections on Ernest Hemingway', 19-27. On the Hemingway play never written, see Delaney 133.

24. Stoppard to Dunjohn, July 1960.

25. Stoppard, 'The Articulate Peasant, A Profile of John Steinbeck', *Men Only and Lilliput* 75, November 1960, 72-5.
26. Stoppard to Smith, 1963, HRC; Marlowe quoted in Tynan, *Show People*, 90; Stoppard to Ronald Hayman, 'First Interview with Tom Stoppard', 12 June 1974 in Ronald Hayman, *Tom Stoppard* (London: Heinemann, 1977), 1.
27. Delaney, 91.
28. Smith, 'Silence, Exile, Cunning'.
29. Stoppard to Dunjohn, 1960.
30. Stoppard to Dunjohn, 1962.
31. Stoppard to John Hale, 15 October 1960; John Hale to Stoppard, 16 October 1960. Bristol Old Vic, Theatre Collection, Bristol University.
32. In a 1967 interview, Stoppard reversed the order of submission. See Stoppard, 'The Definite Maybe', 19: 'with misgivings and deprecating noises, I sent him [Ewing] *A Walk on the Water*, explaining that it was, of course, rather passé compared with the one acter'. The order of events shifts again in 'Ambushes for the Audience', where Stoppard indicates that he sent *A Walk on the Water* to Ewing and not *The Gamblers*. See Delaney, 55.
33. Charles Landstone to John Hale included in letter sent to Stoppard, 14 February 1961, HRC.
34. Stoppard in Delaney, 55; Stoppard, 'The Definite Maybe', 19.
35. Delaney, 55.
36. For Ramsay on the early work of young playwrights, see Delaney, 55; on Ramsay and *Rosencrantz and Guildenstern*, see Colin Chambers, *Peggy: the Life of Margaret Ramsay, Play Agent* (1997; London: Methuen, 1998), 210.
37. Jeremy Brooks to Peggy Ramsay, 16 November 1964, HRC. Brooks apparently learned of the work from Derek Marlowe, who was in Berlin with Stoppard; John Tydeman to the author, 27 May 1998. Stoppard's commitment to Ewing extended to the Academy Awards in 1999, when Ewing was singled out in the audience by Stoppard for praise when he received his Oscar for best screenplay for *Shakespeare in Love*.
38. Ewing to Stoppard, 29 January 1962. HRC.
39. Stoppard in Michael Billington, *Stoppard the Playwright* (London: Methuen, 1987), 17. See also Delaney, 55.
40. Stoppard, 'The Definite Maybe', 18.
41. Delaney, 55.
42. Stoppard, *The Gamblers*, HRC; several passages in Hayman, *Tom Stoppard*, 28-31.

A further passage directly anticipating the dialogue of *Rosencrantz and Guildenstern* is the following, from p. 27 of the MS:

P. Everything I have has been taken from me. Except my life. They're taking that tomorrow. It's usual.
J. It's compulsory.
P. Conclusive
J. And after tomorrow?
P. Nothing
J. They can take no more.
P. It is enough.
J. And for what?

Even more like a section of *Rosencrantz and Guildenstern* is this exchange from p. 31:

J. That's right, keep your chin up.
P. My spirits.
J. One is dependent on the other?
P. There is a connection.
J. Exactly
P. A definite link?
J. Precisely

P.   Elastic tendons . . . from my chin. Down the throat, round to the back, down the spine. The left leg . . . the ankle.

J.   The left leg?

P.   My spirits are in my left shoe.

J.   As low as that?

P.   They fell out of a hole in my sock.

J.   What wd happen if there was a hole in your sole?

P.   A nervous grey pool of spirits around my feet

43. Gussow, 13-14.

44. *The Gamblers*, MS, 4-5.

45. Delaney 55, 59.

46. *The Gamblers*, MS, 24.

47. Harry Corbett to Stoppard, n.d., *c.* 1961/62, HRC.

48. Michael Hardwick to Script Editor Drama, 8 January 1962, BBC Written Archives; Kenneth Ewing to Stoppard, 29 January 1962, HRC; Michael Bakewell to Ewing, 22 June 1962, BBC Written Archives.

49. Stoppard to Dunjohn 1961; June 1961. (Stoppard rarely dates his letters, preferring such headings as 'Tuesday I think' or nothing at all.)

50. Stoppard, 'Vox Britannicus, In Another Country', *Village Voice*, 3 May 1962. Curiously, Stoppard uses virtually the same title for his 1999 autobiographical essay 'Another country'. Anthony Smith provides a similar account of their New York adventures in 'Silence, Exile, Cunning'.

51. Stoppard in Tallmer, 'Rosencrantz's Friend'.

52. Smith, 'Silence, Exile, Cunning'.

53. Stoppard, 'Vox Britannicus, In Another Country'.

54. Stoppard, 'Lenny Goes Limey', *Village Voice*. The date of the article is 1 May 1962 but it was not published until the 10th; Stoppard, 'Death by Satire', *Western Daily Press*, 30 April 1962. Peter Cook, in Harry Thompson's biography, tells a comic story of Bruce turning up at his apartment after being kicked out of his hotel during his tour and needing some heroin. Cook travelled about London searching for questionable doctors to fill a questionable prescription. No luck. He returned to tell Bruce, who was calm and said 'Oh, that's cool . . . I'd like some chocolate cake.' 'And I got quite cross and said "I'm willing to traipse all over London at three in the morning to look for heroin, but chocolate cake is out of the question."' This was in 1962, 'when chocolate cake was not so freely available', he added. Harry Thompson, *Peter Cook* (London: Hodder & Stoughton, 1997), 131.

55. Stoppard to Smith, May 1962, HRC.

56. Stoppard to Dunjohn, undated letter June 1962.

57. Stoppard to Dunjohn, undated letter June 1962.

58. Stoppard to Dunjohn, spring 1962.

59. Stoppard to Dunjohn, undated letter July/August 1962.

60. Stoppard to Smith, 30 August 1962, HRC.

61. Stoppard in Amory. In the same article, Stoppard reverses himself criticising his early work as inadequate, calling it 'indefatigably facetious. There is a sort of second-rate journalism that presents the journalist more than the subject. I did that.'

CHAPTER FIVE SWINGING LONDON

1. Stoppard in Duncan Fallowell, 'Theatrical incest and acquisitive lust', *The Times*, 23 August 1985. The following are illuminating on the sixties: Robert Hewison, *Too Much: Art and Society in the Sixties 1960-1975* (London: Methuen, 1986); Arthur Marwick, *The Sixties: Cultural Revolution in Britain, France, Italy and the United States, c.1958-1974* (New York: Oxford University Press, 1998); David Alan Mellor and Laurent Gervereau, eds, *The Sixties: Britain and France, 1962-1973* (London: Philip Wilson, 1997), this last with remarkable illustrations.

2. Stoppard to Smith, 30 August 1962. HRC; Stoppard in Amory.
3. For Stoppard as the 'Mod Pre-Raphaelite', see Lewis, 'How Tom went to work on an absent mind and picked up £20,000'. Fallowell, 'Theatrical incest and acquisitive lust'.
4. Tynan in the *Observer*, 14 May 1961, quoted in Thompson, *Peter Cook*, 109.
5. Peter Cook in Thompson, *Peter Cook*, 115.
6. For an account of some of these developments, see Charles Marowitz, 'Notes on the Theatre of Cruelty', *Theatre at Work: Playwrights and Productions in the Modern British Theatre*, ed. Charles Marowitz and Simon Trussler (London: Methuen, 1967), 164-85; Peter Brook, *The Empty Space* (1968; London: Penguin, 1990); Tim Brassell, 'Post-War Theatre: Some Contemporary Currents', *Tom Stoppard: An Assessment* (London: Macmillan, 1985), 24-34; Martin Esslin, *Brief Chronicles: Essays on Modern Theatre* (London: Temple Smith, 1970), especially 'Brecht and the English Theatre', 84-96. Of course, Esslin's *Theatre of the Absurd* (1961; 3rd ed., London: Penguin, 1980) is equally important.
7. Stoppard to Smith, 30 August 1962, HRC.
8. Stoppard to Dunjohn, August/September 1962.
9. Derek Marlowe in Tynan, *Show People*, 66.
10. Stoppard to Dunjohn, September 1962.
11. Peter O'Toole to Stoppard in Wapshott, *Peter O'Toole*, 93, 101.
12. *Ibid.*
13. Stoppard to Dunjohn, September 1962.
14. Stoppard in Amory.
15. Stoppard, 'Spades in Hades', *Scene* 1, 14 September 1962. Neither of these first two reviews are signed. His third, however, 'Twelve years without trousers' (*Scene*, 21 September 1962) is. Critics have made little of Stoppard's work at *Scene*, the exception being Neil Sammells, *Tom Stoppard: The Artist as Critic* (London: Macmillan, 1988), 16-39.
16. Stoppard, 'Theatre Reviews', *Scene* 3, 28 September 1962.
17. Stoppard, 'Waiting for Scofield', *Scene* 10, 15 November 1962. A later column addresses the matter of directors fiddling with Shakespeare and opens with the line that Shakespeare has 'become less and less of an actor's bandstand and more and more of a director's playground'. 'Tom Stoppard on why directors monkey about with Shakespeare', *Scene* 23, 20 April 1963.
18. Stoppard, 'O'Toole of Arabia', *Scene* 6, 19 October 1962.
19. Stoppard, 'Tom Stoppard on a dazzling new writer…'.
20. James Saunders, *Next Time I'll Sing to You* (New York: Dramatists' Play Service, 1963), 29. The play premièred at the Questors Theatre, Ealing in June 1962 and opened at the New Arts Theatre in London on 23 January 1963 presented by Michael Codron. It transferred to the Criterion in Piccadilly Circus on 25 February 1963. In November 1963 it opened at the Phoenix Theater in New York; *Rosencrantz and Guildenstern*, 66.
21. *Rosencrantz and Guildenstern*, 80.
22. *Next Time I'll Sing to You*, 34.
23. *Rosencrantz and Guildenstern*, 66.
24. *Next Time I'll Sing to You*, 39.
25. *Rosencrantz and Guildenstern*, 28.
26. *Next Time I'll Sing to You*, 40.
27. *Ibid.*, 39.
28. *Ibid.*, 12.
29. Stoppard, 'Tom Stoppard on a dazzling new writer . . .', 47.
30. Delaney, 96.
31. *The Real Inspector Hound*, 24.
32. Stoppard would of course soon understand the power of reviews when Ronald Bryden's rave of *Rosencrantz and Guildenstern* at the 1966 Edinburgh Festival was read by Tynan, leading to the play's National Theatre début in April 1967.
33. William Gaskell in Stoppard, 'Theatre Now', *Scene* 21, 23 March 1963.
34. *Ibid.*
35. Gussow, 3-4.
36. Gussow, 4.

37. *Ibid.*, 4; Stoppard in Delaney, 71. Of course, the idea of a critical double began in Bristol when Stoppard would appear twice on the same Arts Page, first as 'Tomik Straussler' and then as 'Tom Stoppard'.

38. Delaney, 71; *The Real Inspector Hound*, 59. Another fan of the name was Christopher Hampton whose character James Boot appears on pages 29-30 of *The Philanthropist* (1970).
    Stoppard's preference for the name may also be a sleight-of-hand reference to Beckett who in his prize-winning poem 'Whorscope' refers to 'the brothers Boot' in line three, which in turn may refer to the English apothecaries who today are known as 'Boots'. Of course, the opening scene of *Waiting for Godot* also involves boots. In *The Invention of Love*, reference is made to A. E. Housman's boots which, despite their old-fashioned style and small size, he left to his college servant (*The Invention of Love*, 104).

39. Stoppard, 'Who Killed Peter Saunders?', *Scene* 15, 24 December 1962.

40. Stoppard, 'How Much Rubbish does your Money Buy at the Theatre?', *Scene*, 23 March 1963.

41. Stoppard in Letters, 1963 file, HRC.

42. Stoppard to Smith, April/May 1963, HRC. Useful in covering this period of Stoppard's life is John Fleming, 'Tom Stoppard: His Life and Career before *Rosencrantz and Guildenstern*', *Library Chronicle of the University of Texas at Austin*, 26 (1996), 111-61.

43. Stoppard in Fleming, 118.

44. Of *Happy Days*, Stoppard complained that 'nobody comes and nobody goes', the play 'the testing point of Samuel Beckett's independence of stage conventions'. *Happy Days* is the 'ultimate distillation' of Beckett's earlier work but as a statement has 'left the theatre behind' in his failure to write a drama. Stoppard, 'The ultimate distillation', *Scene* 10, 15 November 1962. For Stoppard's reference to Henry James see Stoppard to Isabel Dunjohn, ? Easter 1963.
    Stoppard wrote a lengthy piece praising Jack McGowran's one-man Beckett show *End of Day* in *Scene* for 25 October 1962. The title is 'Crying till you Laugh'.

45. Stoppard to Dunjohn, 6/7 June 1962.

46. Stoppard to Dunjohn, 30 October 1962; Stoppard to Dunjohn, Spring 1962.

47. Stoppard to Dunjohn, undated letter ? 1963.

48. Stoppard in Lewis, 'How Tom went to work …'; Stoppard to Dunjohn, ? April 1963. References to Easter (14 April 1963) in the letter suggest it was written near that date. The last issue of *Scene* appeared that month.
    There is a certain irony in Stoppard's remark since he writes his plays in longhand with a pen. At one point he dictated these ms. versions into a tape recorder and his secretary would then type them out for further revision.

49. *Introduction* 2, 12.

50. *Ibid.*, 123.

51. *Ibid.*

52. *Ibid.*, 126-7.

53. *Ibid.*, 127.

54. *Ibid.*, 128.

55. *Ibid.*, 129.

56. Derek Marlowe in Tynan, *Show People*, 65; Stoppard in Tallmer, 'Rosencrantz's Friend'.

57. Smith to the author, December 1998.

58. Stoppard to Dunjohn, ? September 1963, from Zagreb.

59. Stoppard to Smith, late Oct./early November 1963, HRC; Stoppard, *Funny Man*, HRC, Sc.III: 2; also in Fleming, 120.

60. Stoppard to Smith, October 1963, HRC; Stoppard, 'Introduction', *Television Plays*, vii.

61. Stoppard to Smith, October 1963, HRC, Stoppard to Smith, November 1963, HRC; Stoppard in Delaney, 56.

62. Stoppard to Smith, Summer 1963. HRC.

63. Stoppard to Dunjohn, June 1963.

64. *Ibid.*

65. Ewing quoted in Tynan, *Show People*, 66.

66. Delaney, 219

67. Stoppard to Smith, autumn 1963, HRC.

68. Stoppard to Smith, ? November 1963, HRC.
69. Stoppard, 'Introduction', *Plays for Radio*, vii.
70. Stoppard to Smith, autumn 1963, HRC. When Stoppard heard of the new BBC series in November 1963, he encouraged Smith to follow his lead and submit material. The format appealed to him because 'one can approach something as short as that in the spirit of attacking an article – there is no sense of a great *project* hanging over one's head, a thing which I find is responsible for many things being left unwritten'.

    The producer furthermore reported that if one is weak on plot and good on dialogue, then so much the better: 'I have a tremendous difficulty in seizing a "plot" but am happy to tackle a "situation". Stoppard to Smith, ? November 1963, HRC.
71. Stoppard, 'Introduction', *Plays for Radio*, vii.
72. Stoppard acknowledged Imison's significance when he spoke movingly at his funeral in February 1993. For Stoppard as punk journalist, see quote in Billington, *Stoppard The Playwright*, 16.

CHAPTER SIX BERLIN COWBOY

1. Stoppard to Smith, May 1964, HRC.
2. Stoppard, 'Life, Times: Fragments', *Introduction 2*, 129.
3. Stoppard, 'On the Little Theatres', *Scene* 8, 1 November 1962. Stoppard reviewed a production of *The Trigon* by James Broom Lynne.
4. Stoppard to Smith, ? July 1964. HRC. Stoppard contracted to do the book during the spring of 1964.
5. Stoppard to Smith, October 1965, HRC.
6. Stoppard to Smith, 12 October 1965, HRC.
7. Stoppard to Smith, January 1964, HRC.
8. Stoppard to Smith, January 1964, HRC; Stoppard in Delaney, 228.
9. Stoppard to Smith, October/November 1963, HRC.
10. Tynan, *Show People*, 69.
11. Delaney, 22-3.
12. For a brief account, see *Shouting in the Evening: British Theatre 1956-1996*, ed. Cathy Henderson and David Oliphant (Austin, Texas: Harry Ransom Humanities Research Center, 1996), 182. Saunders did not actually arrange for the reading; rather, the actors who came from the Questors to Berlin for the performance of the new work returned to Ealing enthusiastic over Stoppard's play and chose to put it on. Saunders, interview, London, 10 May 1999.
13. Saunders, interview.
14. Stoppard to Smith, May 1964, HRC; Stoppard to Smith, 22 June 1964, HRC.
15. Stoppard to Smith, 22 June 1964, HRC.
16. *Lord Malquist*, 158.
17. Stoppard elaborated his film career in a letter of 22 June 1964 to Smith: 'I, and Derek Marlowe and Piers Read have all been acting in the film-makers film, doing crazy things. I'm sure it's all crap. After working with Boorman I am sceptical (not to say contemptuous of these way-out boys (Nice as they are) who do "crazy" and "free" cinema, i.e, one-take-regardless, no script , no plot, all images, outlandish cuts and pretentious action'. HRC.
18. Stoppard to Smith, Spring 1964, HRC.
19. Klaus Mann in Michael Farr, *Berlin! Berlin!* (London: Kyle Cathie, 1992), 145.
20. Brecht in Peter Brooker, 'Key Words in Brecht's Theory and Practice of Theatre', *The Cambridge Companion to Brecht*, ed. Peter Thomson and Glendyr Sacks (Cambridge: Cambridge University Press, 1994), 187; Stoppard, 'Author's Note', *Jumpers*, 11.

    A month after Brecht's death in August, 1956, the Berliner Ensemble made its first visit to London, performing *Mother Courage*, *The Caucasian Chalk Circle* and *Trumpets and Drums* at the Palace Theatre. English playwrights like John Arden, Edward Bond and, to a lesser extent, John Osborne were affected by the original productions. The visit also encouraged the formation of the English Stage Company at the Royal Court because it stimulated the desire to have an English company extend some of its production values. Theatrical designers in Britain were similarly influenced as they abandoned a fussy realism in favour of austere, evocative sets and actors shifted from Stanislavskian introspection to a greater awareness of characters as social representatives. Peter Hall, among others, shifted his directorial perspective to incorporate a view Brecht fondly quoted from Marx: 'the philosophers have only *interpreted* the world in various ways; the point, however, is to change it'. The year of the Berliner Ensemble visit, Stoppard was beginning to write theatre reviews for the *Western Daily Press*.

21. Stoppard to Smith, June 1964, HRC.
22. Stoppard to Smith, June 1964, HRC.
23. Peter Brook, 'Introduction', Peter Weiss, *Marat/Sade* (London: Calder & Boyars, 1965), [6]. Brook's own startling production of the play would open in London in 1964.

    Other German plays produced in London that Stoppard saw were Max Frisch's *The Fire Raisers*, which played at the Royal Court in 1961, and a 1963 production of Friedrich Dürrenmatt's *The Physicists* by the Royal Shakespeare Company. Other German sources for *Rosencrantz and Guildenstern* include scenes Brecht wrote into *Romeo and Juliet* and other additions to the classics, rather than W. S. Gilbert's 1891 burlesque, *Rosencrantz and Guildenstern*, excerpted in the programme for the National Theatre's 1967 production of Stoppard's play.
24. Peter Weiss in *Materialien zu Peter Weiss' Marat/Sade*. (Frankfurt: Suhrkamp, 1967), 99, quoted in Michael Patteson, *German Theatre Today* (London: Pitman Publishing, 1976), 69. Stoppard says that his plays emerge out of 'an ongoing debate with myself' and that he writes drama because 'dialogue is the most respectable way of contradicting myself' (Delaney, 7).
25. For both references, see Stoppard to Smith, May 1964, HRC.
26. Ewing cited in Felicia Hardison Londré, *Tom Stoppard* (New York: Frederick Ungar, 1981), 6. The name of the rejected television play Londré cites is incorrect, however.
27. Delaney, 94-5.
28. Stoppard to Smith, 22 June 1964, HRC.
29. Ewing to Stoppard, 2 May 1964, 7 July 1964, HRC.
30. Stoppard to Smith, late summer, 1964, HRC. In the same letter he refers to his novel as 'a tour/investigation/examination of contem young-lib-intellectual pretension, dichotomy, syndrome, prejudices, humor, mores and manners'. He would like to call it 'A Short Walk Around the Block', but is 'worried about "Block" being American'. (*Ibid.*)
31. Charles Marowitz, 'Rosencrantz and Guildenstern', *Confessions of A Counterfeit Critic: A London Theatre Notebook 1958-1971* (London: Eyre Methuen, 1973), 123. For Esslin on *Rosencrantz and Guildenstern*, see Hayman, 32, and Ruby Cohn, *Modern Shakespeare Offshoots* (Princeton: Princeton University Press, 1976), 211; Saunders on Esslin, interview.
32. Alfred Emmet, 'Followthrough: Rosencrantz in Embryo', *Theatre Quarterly* 15 (March-May 1975). Emmet, a member of the Questors Theatre, added that this version of Stoppard's play takes place during Act IV, Scene IV of *Hamlet* and cites a programme note which reports that Stoppard is working on a full-length play of which the one-act piece forms a part.
33. Stoppard, 'The Definite Maybe'.
34. Stoppard, *ibid.* Also see Marowitz, *Confessions of a Counterfeit Critic*, 123. The rewritten work would be performed in August 1966 at the Edinburgh Fringe Festival by students in the Oxford Theatre Group. For details, see the next chapter; Stoppard in Delaney, 57.
35. Stoppard, *Rosencrantz and Guildenstern meet King Lear*, HRC.
36. *Ibid.*, 44.
37. For a chronicle of the play, see Stoppard, 'The Definite Maybe'. For a textual summary of the play, see Fleming, 'Tom Stoppard: His Life and Career before *Rosencrantz and Guildenstern*', 1996, 139-46; Stoppard to Smith, early 1965, HRC. Jose Stoppard added to the question of identity and the characters of Rosencrantz and Guildenstern when she responded to Stoppard's remark that he didn't identify with either character: 'Oh, but they're very much him', she retorted. Jose Stoppard in Lewis, 'How Tom went to work…'.
38. Stoppard to Smith, 22 June 1964, HRC.
39. Stoppard to Smith, July 1964, HRC.
40. Stoppard to Smith, July 1964, HRC. Quoted in *Shouting in the Evening*, 182.
41. Richard Ellmann, *Oscar Wilde* (Markham, Ontario: Penguin/Viking, 1987), 346. According to

Jean-Joseph Renaud, Wilde, wearing a green carnation, began his curtain speech by saying, after a pull on his cigarette held in a mauve-gloved hand, 'Ladies and gentlemen, it's perhaps not very proper to smoke in front of you . . . but it's not very proper to disturb me when I am smoking'. Henry James, in the audience, found such behaviour and remarks arch. Wilde attended rehearsals, as Stoppard would do, offering suggestions and rewrites on the spot.

42. Stoppard to Smith, July 1964, HRC.
43. *Ibid.*
44. Stoppard in Patti Hartigan, '"Rosencrantz" the movie has the Stoppard stamp', *Boston Globe*, 17 February 1991. Both Dylan songs appeared in 1965, the first on *Highway 61 Revisited*, the second on *Bringing It All Back Home*. Piers Paul Read recalled Beatles songs playing repeatedly in Stoppard's room. Read to the author, 10 December 1998.
45. Stoppard to Smith, ? September 1964, HRC.
46. Stoppard to Smith, ? October/ November 1964, HRC.
47. Stoppard to Smith, August 1964, HRC.
48. Stoppard to Smith, ? October/November 1964, HRC.
49. Piers Paul Read interview, London, 10 December 1998.
50. For the 'primitive cool' of Jagger, see Christopher Sandford, *Mick Jagger* (London: Victor Gollancz, 1991), *passim*. Sandford notes that Joyce's *Ulysses* provided the hook line of 'Paint It Black', 'I turn my head until my darkness goes' (89).
51. Jose Stoppard in John Knight, 'Saturday Night Sunday Morning', *Sunday Mirror*, 18 December 1966; *New Yorker*, 4 May 1968.
52. Jose Stoppard in Lewis, 'How Tom went to work...'; Stoppard, *ibid.*

CHAPTER SEVEN ROSENCRANTZ ON THE ROYAL MILE

1. Stoppard in Billington, 'Indelible Ink', *Guardian*, 8 February 1995; Stoppard in Delaney, 57; Stoppard in Peter Orr, 'Interview', British Council, 21 September 1972, National Sound Archive, British Library.
   In the programme for the original 1966 production, Stoppard further explained how in writing the play 'it became necessary to establish them [Rosencrantz and Guildenstern] first within the context of Hamlet and this establishing process drove them further and further back into the action of "Hamlet" until – somewhat to the author's surprise – they emerged out of the other end, i.e., before their entry into "Hamlet". He then offers this interpretation of the two characters: 'Rosencrantz and Guildenstern are a curious and rather appealing couple, customarily thought of as "unsympathetic", as spies and accessories to the evil plot against Hamlet. However nothing in the play indicates a shared guilt with the King; they are told little, they obey orders, and are somewhat bewildered, having been thrust into a situation which is nothing to do with them, and what they hardly understand. Because of this they have the air of occupying a level above the action, a different level of reality. It must have been this which makes Wilde (in *De Profundis*) refer to them as immortal characters whose reported death is merely part of the play's mechanics. They march on'. 'The Play', *Rosencrantz and Guildenstern are Dead*, World Première, Cranston Street Hall, programme note, 24 August 1966, HRC.
2. Saunders to Stoppard, 14 April 1965, HRC.
3. For Stoppard on Jeremy Brooks's objection to plays dealing with minor characters in Shakespeare, see Orr, 'Interview'.
4. Brooks to Stoppard, 4 May 1965, HRC.
5. Brooks to Stoppard, 22 July 1965, HRC.
6. Stoppard in Jon Bradshaw, 'Tom Stoppard Nonstop', in Delaney, 93. Another account appears in Keith Harper, 'The Devious Route to Waterloo Road', *Guardian*, 12 April 1967.
7. Jose Stoppard in Knight, 'Saturday Night Sunday Morning'.
8. Ewing to Stoppard 15 September 1965, HRC.
9. Brooks to Stoppard, 22 July 1965, HRC.
10. Richard Findlater to Stoppard, 19 June 1964, HRC.
11. Tom Stoppard, 'David Warner', RSC Profiles, 1965. Warner's *Hamlet* opened at Stratford in late August 1965. For an account of the production and its impact see David Addenbrooke, *The*

Royal Shakespeare Company: The Peter Hall Years (London: Kimber, 1974), 129-32 and Sally Beauman, *The Royal Shakespeare Company* (Oxford: Oxford University Press, 1982), 281-83. Both accounts stress Warner as a disaffected sixties teenager, apathetic but pitted against the establishment of Elsinore. Crowds of young people gather at the stage door to glimpse their new hero who projected a Hamlet bewildered and affronted by the way his elders let down his generation. To the young audience's delight, he often mumbled his lines. Peter Hall directed.

12. Richard Imison, 'Playwrights for the Arabic Service', BBC Written Archives. The date of the poem is 7 July 1965.

13. Ewing in Delaney, 219.

14. Stoppard to Smith, 12 October 1965, HRC.

15. Stoppard. *A Student's Diary*, 4: 5. BBC Written Archives. Hereafter identified by script number.

16. *A Student's Diary*, # 14: 6.

17. *A Student's Diary*, # 23: 5.

18. *A Student's Diary*, # 23: 8.

19. *A Student's Diary*, # 33: 4.

20. *A Student's Diary*, # 25.

21. On hospitals and illness see Stoppard, 'A Separate Peace', broadcast on TV in August 1966; Jose's training as a nurse may have provided him with some additional source details.

22. *A Student's Diary*, # 138: 1.

23. Interestingly, after the first third of the series had been written, Stoppard actually worked with suggestions from H. F. Duckworth, Arab Programme Organiser and Mr Rizq on the development of the plot and the hero Amin, pulling him 'down to a more credible level'. Furthermore, he felt that the dialogue became more natural as the situations became more natural. But this was not at the loss of their English comedy and orientation, experiencing English situations rather than merely reporting them. And once *Rosencrantz and Guildenstern* opened in April, the need for continuing this arrangement ceased.

24. Stoppard to Smith, September/October 1966, HRC.

25. Stoppard to Smith, 12 October 1965, HRC.

26. *Ibid.*

27. Stoppard in Giles Gordon, 'Tom Stoppard Interview', Delaney, 20. The interview originally appeared in *The Transatlantic Review* 29 (1968).

28. Stoppard to Smith, 5 June 1966, HRC; Stoppard to Smith, July 1964, HRC.

29. BBC Memo, 20 December 1965; Stoppard to a Ms Alexander, ? August 1966. BBC Written Archives.

30. Keith Williams to Stoppard, 25 February 1964, BBC Written Archives.

31. Stoppard, 'A Separate Peace', *Television Plays*, 9; 'Introduction', *ibid.*, vii.

32. Trevor Nunn in Sheridan Morley, 'New challenge for non-stop Trevor Nunn', *The Times*, 28 June 1977.

33. Stoppard in David Gollob and David Roper, 'Trad Tom Pops In', Delaney, 159. The interview originally appeared in *Gambit* 10 (1981). See also the references in *Inside the Royal Court Theatre, 1956-1981*, ed. Gresdna A. Doty and Billy J. Harbin (Baton Rouge: Louisiana State University Press, 1990), 47-8, 156.

34. Rebellato, 78. For Gaskill's views on staging, see pp. 87-8. Rebellato's study refreshingly challenges the received view of an unexpected 'revolution' in British drama in 1956. For accounts of the Royal Court, see Philip Roberts, *The Royal Court Theatre, 1965-1972* (London: Routledge & Kegan Paul, 1986); *Inside the Royal Court Theatre* and Philip Roberts, *The Royal Court Theatre and The Modern Stage* (Cambridge: Cambridge University Press, 1999).

35. The 1964 season also included Peter Wood's production of *The Master Builder* and George Devine's production of *Play* by Beckett. In 1965, Wood, who would become Stoppard's favoured director, would direct a very successful production of Congreve's *Love for Love*, with Olivier as Tattle. In that production, John Stride played Valentine. Edward Petherbridge had appeared in Shaffer's *The Royal Hunt of the Sun*. The former would be the National Theatre's original Rosencrantz, the latter, the original Guildenstern.

36. Stoppard in Richard Corballis, *Stoppard: The Mystery and the Clockwork* (New York: Methuen, 1984), 169. Stoppard's not knowing Polish and Nunn's remark were quoted to me by Ronald

Bryden, 5 June 1999.

37. Slawomir Mrozek, *Tango*, trans. Nicholas Bethell, adapted by Stoppard (London: Jonathan Cape, 1968), 10. A few lines later, she exclaims 'follow suit or I put in the boot', using a favourite Stoppardian reference.

38. Brook, *The Empty Space*, 55.

39. For a synopsis of the play, see Arthur Robinson, 'Rosencrantz and Guildenstern', *Precious Nonsense* 39 (1993). This is the newsletter of the Midwestern Gilbert & Sullivan Society, located in North Aurora, Illinois.

40. Oscar Wilde, *De Profundis*, quoted in programme for *Rosencrantz and Guildenstern are Dead*, National Theatre, London, 1967.

41. Stoppard recalled the event in a 1993 interview for the Oxford magazine *Isis*, remembering that the text had 'some odd lines which were simply repeated and some were missing. In 1966 everybody was on the look out for the Theatre of the Absurd and these very curious lines struck the reader as being par for the course for plays which were being written at the time. So when I arrived during rehearsal, this dedicated band of actors were speaking all the typos – they were trusting but bewildered. We sorted that out and did the show pretty well'. Stoppard, '*Arcadia* Regained', *Isis*, Trinity, 1993.

42. Watts, 'Stoppard's half-century'.

43. Stoppard in Janet Watts, 'Tom Stoppard', Delaney, 45. Originally, this interview appeared in the *Guardian*, 21 March 1973; David Mamet in Rick Groen, 'The Interview', *Globe and Mail*, 11 June 1999.

44. Watts, 'Stoppard's half-century'; Stoppard in Delaney, 17.

45. Stoppard, 'Programme Note', *On the Razzle*, Edinburgh Festival, 13 August 1981. Royal National Theatre Archive.

46. Stoppard, 'The Play', Playbill, *Rosencrantz and Guildenstern are Dead*, Oxford Theatre Group, 24 August 1966, HRC.

47. Stoppard, 'Programme Note', *On the Razzle*.

48. Stoppard, *Lord Malquist*. Stoppard in Tallmer, 'Rosencrantz's Friend'.

49. Press release, Fraser and Dunlop, August 1966, HRC.

50. Anthony Blond to Stoppard, 27 June 1967, HRC.

51. *Lord Malquist*, 56.

52. *Ibid.*, 52.

53. Stoppard in Mel Gussow, 'Stoppard Refutes himself Endlessly', Delaney, 31. The interview/article originally appeared in the *New York Times*, 26 April 1972. Another, longer version of the article appears in Gussow, 1-9; Christopher Hampton, *The Philanthropist* (London: Faber and Faber, 1970), 28.

54. *Lord Malquist*, 52-3.

55. *Ibid.*, 54.

56. Stoppard in Benedict Nightingale, 'Long haul for a laidback lad'.

57. See Aristotle, *Rhetoric* in *The Complete Works of Aristotle*, ed. J. Barnes, 2 vols (Princeton: Princeton University Press, 1984), Sect. 1355a; ii.2154; Cicero, *Academica* in *De natura deorum* and *Academica*, trans. H. Rackham. (London: Heinemann, 1933), ii.3, 7-9.

58. *Lord Malquist*, 32, 54.

59. *The Real Thing*, 60; Stoppard, 'Playwright-Novelist', *New Yorker*, 4 May 1968.

60. *Lord Malquist*, 53.

61. *Ibid.*, 36.

62. *Ibid.*, 187, 8, 11.

63. *Ibid.*, 98.

64. Stoppard in Delaney, 70-1. The headnote to the 42-page typescript of 'Murder at Mousetrap Manor', another working title for the play, reads: 'The mousetraps came over with the Conqueror and retain the old pronunciation , i.e., Moos'e-tra. This is respected by everyone except Inspector Hound who insensitively refers to the family as mousetraps', HRC.

65. Stoppard in Tynan, *Show People*, 67.

66. Stoppard, *Lord Malquist*, screenplay pp 26, 47, HRC.

67. Allan Wright, 'Scathing Review of Tom Stoppard's New Play', *Scotland on Sunday*, 25 August

1966; Douglas F. Blake, 'Rosencrantz and Guildenstern', *Stage and Television Today*, 1 September 1966.

68. Harold Hobson, 'The Lost Revolution Edinburgh Festival Theatre', *Sunday Times*, 11 September 1967; Codron in Watts, 'Stoppard's half-century'.

69. Tom Stoppard, 'Festival Comment', programme, *On The Razzle*, Edinburgh Festival, 13 August 1981. Royal National Theatre Archive, London. Some thirty-two years later, Stoppard recalled the events at a National Theatre 'Platform' with John Stride and Edward Petherbridge; he reminisced as much about the 1966 Edinburgh production as the 1967 National production.

Fleming questions whether or not Stoppard's novel was actually published by the time of the first production, citing a letter that postdates the Edinburgh première in which Stoppard wonders if the novel was yet out. Nevertheless, Stoppard may have still believed that the novel and not the play would make his reputation. See Fleming, 159.

70. Ronald Bryden to the author, 5 June 1999.

71. Bryden, 'Wyndy Excitements', *Observer*, 29 August 1966.

72. Stoppard in Delaney, 17.

73. David Marks in Thomson Prentice, 'Stoppard returns to where it began', *Sunday Standard* (Edinburgh), 9 August 1981.

CHAPTER EIGHT THE OLD VIC AND A NEW PLAYWRIGHT

1. Stoppard in Michael Owen, 'Razzle dazzle Stoppard', *Evening Standard*, 28 August 1981.

2. Peter Lewis, *The National: A Dream Made Concrete* (London: Methuen, 1990), 27.

3. Stoppard on meeting Tynan in Shusha Guppy, 'Tom Stoppard the Art of Theatre VII', Delaney, 184. Originally published in the *Paris Review*, Winter 1988. On Tynan's speech and Stoppard's reaction, see also Stoppard in Vicky Payne, 'Tom Stoppard', *BBC Worldwide* (September 1993). *Rosencrantz and Guildenstern* would stay in the repertoire of the National Theatre for the next four years. For a description of the 'huts' of the National, see Lewis, 7-8.

4. Tynan's quotation appears in John Lahr, 'The Whirlwind', *New Yorker*, 7 August 2000; John Mortimer, 'Introduction', *Olivier at Work* (London: Royal National Theatre and Nick Hern Books, 1989), 10.

Tynan, who visited Prague in February 1965, probably introduced Stoppard to the work of Havel. 'Czech Discoveries' by Tynan appeared in the *Observer* of 7 March 1965. In a letter to thank the British Ambassador to Czechoslovakia at the time, Tynan writes 'what hits one of course all the time is the virtual impossibility of uttering a word, either on stage or screen, that can't be interpreted politically'. Tynan, *Letters*, ed. Kathleen Tynan (London: Weidenfeld and Nicolson, 1994), 318.

5. Tynan in John Elsom and Nicholas Tomalin, *The History of the National Theatre* (London: Jonathan Cape, 1978), 149. Tynan made the remarks in a speech to the Royal Society of the Arts, 18 March 1964. For Olivier on Tynan, see *Olivier at Work*, 48.

6. Tynan, *Letters*, 362, 363, 327.

7. For Stoppard on the bed, see Kathleen Tynan, *The Life of Kenneth Tynan* (London: Weidenfeld and Nicolson, 1987), 262; for Stoppard's eulogy, see *ibid.*, 405.

8. Peter Nichols, *Diaries 1969-77* (London: Nick Hern Books, 2000), 46. Olivier in *The Life of Kenneth Tynan*, 217.

9. Olivier to Tynan, *ibid.*, 221; *ibid.*, 406.

10. Nichols, *Diaries*, 29.

11. Stoppard in Delaney, 20-1, 16-17.

12. Derek Goldby in Sue Francis, 'Tonight's the night for Derek', *Yorkshire Post*, 11 April 1967, 12.

13. Stoppard in Delaney, 180.

14. Stride in Cheryl Faraone, 'An Analysis of Tom Stoppard's Plays and Their Productions (1964–1975)', Dissertation, Florida State University, August 1980, 32; Goldby, in Faraone, 33.

15. Stoppard in Delaney, 180; retold by Stoppard at the National Theatre 'Platform' on *Rosencrantz and Guildenstern*, 25 May 1999. For a description of the rehearsal space at 10a Aquinas street and the anxiety of auditioning for Olivier and Tynan, see Kendal, 242-5. Photographs of the space appear throughout *Olivier at Work*.

16. Petherbridge to the author, London, 27 May 1999.
17. Petherbridge to Angus McKechnie, 1 November 1983.
    McKechnie went on to run the immensely successful National Theatre 'Platform' series which, on 25 May 1999, saw Stride, Petherbridge and Stoppard revisit the original production of *Rosencrantz and Guildenstern*.
18. Stride, Petherbridge and Goldby interviews in Faraone, 34-5.
19. Petherbridge to McKechnie, 1 November 1983.
20. Tynan, 9 March 1967, HRC.
21. The text, used in rehearsal for the National Theatre production but cut before the first performance, reads, after Horatio's speech through to the end of the *Hamlet* text, as follows:

FORTINBRAS	Go, bid the soldiers shoot.
	(*The Bodies are picked up: a peal of ordnance is shot off. A death march begins and continues until the stage is empty except for the two Ambassadors.*)
	(*Pause. They move downstage. They stop.*)
AMBASSADOR	Hm. . . .
2nd AMB	Yes?
1ST AMB	What?
2ND AMB	I thought you –
1st AMB	No.
2nd AMB	Ah.
	(*Pause*)
1st AMB	Tsk tsk . . . .
2nd AMB	Quite.
1st AMB:	Shocking business.
2nd AMB	Tragic . . . (*he looks in the direction of the departing corpses*) . . . four . . . . just like that.
1st AMB	Six in all.
2nd AMB	Seven.
1st AMB	No – six.
2nd AMB	The King, the Queen, Hamlet, Laertes, Rosencrantz, Guildenstern, and Polonius. Seven.
1st AMB	Ophelia. Eight.
2nd AMB	King, Queen, Hamlet, Laertes, Rosencrantz, Guildenstern, Polonius, Ophelia. Eight.
	(*They nod and shake their heads.*)
	(*Looks about.*). Well . . . One hardly knows what to . . . .
	(*From outside there is shouting and banging, a Man, say, banging his fist on a wooden door and shouting, obscurely, two names.*)
	(*The Ambassadors look at each other.*)
1st AMB	Better go and see what it's all about . . .
	(*The other nods.*)
	(*They walk off together. The Tragedians' tune becomes audible – far away.*)
	(*The house lights come up until they are as bright as the lights on the empty stage.*)

22. Stoppard, *Rosencrantz and Guildenstern are Dead* (London: Faber and Faber, 1967), 95-6; (New York: Grove Press, 1967), 126.
    Certain errors remained in the text. For example, the two protagonists still talk about being paid in guilders, although they are in Denmark, where the currency is crowns. Stoppard explained that when he was writing the first draft, he got confused between Holland and Denmark and never did bother to check which country used which currency.
23. Petherbridge to the author, London, 27 May 1999.

24. Stoppard in Cyril Dunn, 'Footnote to the Bard, Briefing', *Observer*, 9 April 1967.
25. Stoppard in Tim de Lisle, 'Re-enter Stoppard', *Sunday Telegraph*, 3 December 1995.
26. Frank Wedekind's *Spring Awakening*, written in 1891, was the catalyst for Lord Chandos's remark. See *The Life of Kenneth Tynan*, 228. Chandos opposed a production of the play by the National.
27. Peter Lewis quoting himself in Lewis, 27.
28. Harold Hobson, 'A fearful summons', *Sunday Times*, 16 April 1967. Jasper Rees, 'Arts Interview: Tom Stoppard', *Independent*, 2 December 1995.
29. Ronald Bryden, 'Theatre: Out of their world', *Observer*, 16 April 1967.
30. Petherbridge to the author, 27 May 1999; Tom Stoppard in John Dodd, 'Success is the Only Unusual Thing about Mr. Stoppard', Delaney, 12. The article originally appeared in the *Sun*, 13 April 1967. Stoppard repeats the story with a slight variation in Lewis, 27. Interestingly, a similar thing happened to O'Toole and the screening of *Lawrence*, which he left, because of anxiety, at its première. He did not see the entire film until some twenty years later, on a hotel television in Jordan. See Wapshott, *Peter O'Toole*, 93; Smith to the author, 22 August 1997.
31. Joe Orton, 'April 1967', *The Orton Diaries*, ed. John Lahr (1986; London: Methuen, 1998), 135.
32. Kenneth Williams, *The Kenneth Williams Diaries*, ed. Russell Davies (London: HarperCollins, 1993), 314, 315. Another critical view of the play is that of Michael Billington, drama critic of the *Guardian*. In 1987 he recalled his initial reaction, 'hooked by the surface brilliance' but wary that the characters could extend their energy for three acts on the theme of the senseless universe. He hadn't changed his idea much by 1987: 'the wordplay is overstretched' and 'a one-act idea is being teased out'. Furthermore, 'the essential innocence of truly great drama is missing'. Billington, *Stoppard The Playwright*, 37-8.
33. Tom Stoppard in Owen, 'Razzle dazzle Stoppard'.
34. Stoppard in Benedict Nightingale, 'Interview: Tom Stoppard', Thames Television, 1976.
35. Stoppard, 'Author's Note', *Rosencrantz and Guildenstern are Dead* (London: Samuel French, 1995), 3; Stoppard, 'Tom Stoppard to Saml. French', HRC.
36. The plays of 1967, in order, were Strindberg's *The Dance of Death*, *Rosencrantz and Guildenstern are Dead*, Chekhov's *Three Sisters*, Shakespeare's *As You Like It* and Molière's *Tartuffe*. Olivier directed the Chekhov, Tyrone Guthrie the Molière. For a listing of the National Theatre's plays from 1963-1988, see Tim Goodwin, *Britain's Royal National Theatre: The First 25 Years* (London: National Theatre and Nick Hern Books, 1988). Also useful is Simon Callow, *The National Theatre and Its Work 1963-1977* (London: Royal National Theatre and Nick Hern Books, 1997).
37. Stoppard in Knight, 'Saturday Night Sunday Morning'.
38. Stoppard in Lewis, 'How Tom went to work…'.
39. Petherbridge and Stride in Anthony Holden, 'Rosencrantz and Guildenstern on Tour', *National Theatre On Stage Magazine* [1967], n.p.
40. This apocryphal story was repeated by Stoppard at the National Theatre 'Platform' on *Rosencrantz and Guildenstern*, 25 May 1999.
41. Stoppard in Davies, 'Stoppard Goes'.
42. *Ibid.*
43. Stoppard in Lewis, 'How Tom went to work…'.
44. On the Italian version, see the unsigned article, 'Female Rosencrantz in Stoppard Play', *The Times*, 22 February 1968; Frederic Raphael, 'Introduction', Arthur Schnitzler, *Dream Story*, trans. J. M. Q. Davies (London: Penguin, 1999), xv-xvi. Schnitzler achieved early fame for his prose sketches of a man about town entitled *Anatol*. He was thirty; Stoppard was twenty-nine when he succeeded with *Rosencrantz and Guildenstern*. Another parallel is that of changed names. Zimmerman was the family name before Schnitzler, just as Straüssler was the family name before Stoppard.
45. Stoppard in Judith Boyd, 'Theatre: Tom Stoppard Back on Home Ground', *Bath and Wiltshire Evening Chronicle* (Bristol), 25 September 1976. Cf. his remarks on his use of Wilde in *Travesties* and *Hamlet* in *Rosencrantz and Guildenstern* in Anthony Smith, 'Tom Stoppard in Conversation', British Council recording taped on 17 December 1976: 'I'm still feeling slightly shifty about my apparent dependence on other people's work'.

46. *Enter a Free Man*, 10.
47. Stoppard in William Hedgepeth, 'Playwright Tom Stoppard: Go Home, British Boy Genius!', *Look Magazine*, 26 December 1967.
48. Garry O'Connor, 'Stoppard and Savary', *Financial Times*, 18 October 1967.
49. Goldby in Faraone, 43.
50. Clive Barnes, 'Theatre: 'Rosenkrantz [sic] and Guildenstern are Dead', *New York Times*, 17 October 1967. On the Michael Stewart play, see John Chapman, 'Rosencrantz and Guildenstern are Dead Is a Most Delightful Prank', *New York Daily News*, 17 October 1967.
51. Peter Kihss, 'Pulitzer to Styron Novel; No Prize Given for Drama', *New York Times*, 7 May 1968.
52. On sailing first class, see Stoppard in 'What's this All About?' *Newsweek*, 7 August 1967; Stoppard in Tallmer, 'Rosencrantz's Friend'.
    Another version of the story has Stoppard at an after-opening party at Sardi's in New York reading the advance and very positive reviews of the play, then turning to Jose and mockingly interviewing himself. 'Question: What's the play about, Mr Stoppard? Answer: It's about to make me rich'. Delaney, 'Exit Tomás Sträussler, enter Sir Tom Stoppard', *The Cambridge Companion to Tom Stoppard*, ed. Katherine E. Kelly (Cambridge: Cambridge University Press, 2001).
53. For these opinions on Stoppard's appeal, see Delaney, 210-20.
54. Stoppard, 'Playwright-Novelist'.
55. Stoppard, 'Another Moon called Earth', 51. The play was first broadcast on BBC in June 1967 with John Wood as Bone.
56. *Lord Malquist*, 32.
57. Stoppard, 'M is for Moon', *Plays for Radio*, 17; Stoppard to Blond, 12 October 1965, HRC; Stoppard in Lewis, 'How Tom went to work…'.
58. William Foster, 'Commitment is only to deadlines', *Scotsman*, 6 July 1974.
59. Stoppard to Smith, ? March 1968, HRC.
60. Trevor Nunn to Stoppard, 14 July 1969, HRC.
61. Stoppard, 'Treasure Island', *Architectural Design* (June 1969), 33. His contribution was part of a series where various people were asked to name one place in England that had a special quality for them.
62. Quoted in Tynan, *Show People*, 65.
63. Nichols, *Diaries*, 29, 32.
64. Quoted in Delaney, 220.
65. Delaney, 21.
66. Stoppard, 'Something to declare'.
67. Stoppard in Delaney, 56.
68. Michael Codron to Stoppard, 22 May 1968, HRC.
69. Rees, 'Arts Interview: Tom Stoppard'.
70. Stoppard in Delaney, 181; Stoppard in Delaney, 59-60.
71. The phrase about witnesses is Mel Gussow's in 'Stoppard Refutes Himself Endlessly', Delaney, 32; on *The Real Inspector Hound*, see Stoppard in Delaney, 60.
72. Stoppard in Delaney, 60; Stoppard, 'Who Killed Peter Saunders? Tom Stoppard on thriller boom', *Scene*, 24 December 1962. A comic exchange on drink in Stoppard's article (30) parallels one in *The Real Inspector Hound* (27).
73. Stoppard in Delaney, 59.
74. Susan Rusinko, *Tom Stoppard* (Boston: Twayne, 1986), 69.
75. Ronald Bryden, 'A critic's nightmare', *Observer*, 23 June 1968.
76. *The Real Inspector Hound*, 24.
77. *Ibid.*, 40.
78. *Ibid.*, 41.
79. Father Robert Foley to Stoppard, October 1975, HRC.
80. *The Real Inspector Hound*, 24.
81. *Ibid.*
82. Stoppard in Delaney, 63, 59.
83. *The Real Inspector Hound*, 44.

84. Bryden, 'A critic's nightmare'; Harold Hobson, 'Critics through the Looking Glass', *Sunday Times*, 23 June 1968; Irving Wardle, 'Theatre: A grin without a cat', *The Times*, 22 June 1968; on the *Rosencrantz and Guildenstern* parody, see Bryden, *ibid.*
85. Jose Stoppard in Lewis, 'How Tom went to work...'.

CHAPTER NINE SWINGING FROM AN EPIGRAM

1. On 1 July 1969, for example, Stoppard received an invitation from Anthony Smith to a cricket match in Surrey on 27 July. In the memo, addressed to Clive Barker, Tim Corrie, Reggie Smith and Stoppard, are also the names 'Miriam Moore-Robinson (barber-surgeon), Peter Moore-Robinson (vet)'. Smith to Stoppard, 1 July 1969, HRC.
2. Stoppard to Smith, December 1969, HRC.
3. *Plays for Radio*, 54.
4. *Ibid.*, 64.
5. *Ibid.*, 69.
6. *Ibid.*, 75.
7. Kate's response to Albert's speech on wanting her to be happy may express the pathos of what Jose felt: 'I've begun talking to myself, over the sink and stove ... I talk to myself because nobody else listens, and you won't talk to me, so I talk to the sink and the stove and the baby, and maybe one day one of them will answer me'. *Plays for Radio*, 75.
8. *Plays for Radio*, 98, 82.
9. For an elaboration of this reading, see Clive James, 'Count Zero Splits the Infinite', *Encounter* (November 1975). In *The Real Thing* Henry tells Annie 'I don't believe in behaving well. I don't believe in debonair relationships .... I believe in mess, tears, pain, self-abasement, loss of self-respect, nakedness' (*The Real Thing*, 71).
10. Corinna Honan, 'I felt inferior in Tom's world, now I love a man who makes me feel so happy', *Daily Mail*, 30 April 1993; Delaney, 217.
11. Miriam Stoppard in 'Playwright's wife admits turning off patient's life', *Daily Telegraph*, 19 November 1975.
12. David Lister, 'Arts Diary', *Independent*, 13 June 1998.
13. Delaney, 48.
14. Stoppard in Jerry Tallmer, 'Tom Stoppard Pops In On the Cast', *New York Post*, 26 August 1972.
15. *Rosencrantz and Guildenstern*, 21; *Jumpers*, 38. A later reference occurs in *Artist Descending a Staircase*, when the artist Martello explains that 'to the Incas, who had never seen a horse, unicorns had the same reality as horses, which is a very high degree of reality' (*Artist Descending a Staircase*, 41).
16. In the late twelfth century, a grant of the manor was made to the House of Clavering which lasted until the late fourteenth century, when the Black Death wiped out the Claverings and the manor transferred to the Dean and Chapter of Windsor. By the end of the seventeenth century, Iver was acknowledged as an advantageous country residence, the *Index Villaris* of 1690 listing the seats of a baronet, a knight and more than three gentlemen. In the eighteenth century, the grand home known as Richings owned by Lord Bathurst had more than its share of literary greats and statesmen, being favoured by Pope, Prior, Addison, Congreve and Gay, who left their verses inscribed on a bench in the park. The grounds were often called Arcadian and boasted a canal 555 yards long, a cave with a spring and miniature arbours spotted throughout the park. See W. H. Ward and K. S. Block, *A History of the Manor and Parish of Iver* (London: Martin Secker, 1933), 200-1.
17. Miriam Stoppard in Pauline Peters, 'The Unstoppable Stoppard', *Sunday Times*, 15 June 1980; Clive James, *Brilliant Creatures* (London: Jonathan Cape, 1983), 188.
18. Janet Watts, *Guardian*, 21 March 1973.
19. Harold Pinter to Stoppard, 25 August 1969, HRC.
20. Stoppard in Delaney, 187. On 'PINTA', see Stoppard in Amory. Pinter actually used that name to sign his earliest published poetry, according to Michael Billington in *The Life and Work of Harold Pinter* (London: Faber and Faber, 1996), 29.
21. Pinter's introduction can be heard on 'Direct Experience', 1985, National Sound Archive, British

Library, T7730R. BDI. This was the Dawson Scott Memorial Lecture given for PEN at the Purcell Rooms, London.

22. See notes from Pinter to Stoppard dated 4 January 1970 and 11 May 1970 at HRC for further details on their cricket connection. Also see Tynan's account of the Pinter cricket match, with Stoppard as wicket-keeper, in *Show People*. Stoppard himself discusses cricket in his 'Going to Bat for Britain'.

23. Pinter on Stoppard's independence in Watts, 'Stoppard's half-century'. Stoppard celebrates Pinter in Stoppard, 'Harold Pinter: the poet of no-man's-land', *Sunday Times*, 7 October 1990.

24. Stoppard in Amory.

25. Stoppard as quoted by Paul Johnson to the author, 15 December 1998.

26. Boorman to Stoppard, 19 April 1971, HRC; Stoppard to Peter Bart, 28 May 1971. Stoppard goes on to address three main problems: no sense of growing jeopardy for Galileo, the overly complicated politics of the church and the disappearance of Galileo's wife and daughter in the story, Furthermore, Brecht condemned Galileo for his recantation; Stoppard celebrates the scientist for his intellect, commitment to truth and humanity. For a detailed discussion of the screenplay and playscript, see Fleming, *Stoppard's Theatre: Finding Order amid Chaos*.

27. Stoppard to Michael Eisner, 13 June 1993, HRC.

28. Stoppard in Barry Norman, 'Tom Stoppard and the contentment of insecurity', *The Times*, 11 November 1972.

29. Ed Berman, 'How long is an Ephemeron?', *Ten of the Best British Short Plays*, ed. Ed Berman (London: Inter-Action Imprint, 1979), xi, x. This introduction to a collection of ten plays performed by Inter-Action, including works by James Saunders, Wolf Mankowitz, Harold Pinter and Tom Stoppard, is the most detailed history of the Inter-Action theatrical movement to 1978. Additional information from an interview with Berman, London, 20 May 1999.

30. Stoppard in Watts, 'Stoppard's half-century'.

31. Stoppard, 'Yes, we have no bananas', *Guardian*, 10 December 1971.

32. *Ibid.*

33. *Ibid.*

34. Stoppard, 'Preface', *Dogg's Hamlet, Cahoot's Macbeth*, 8. Stoppard reorganized *Dogg's Our Pet* as part of *Dogg's Hamlet*, a work which conflates two separate pieces: *Dogg's Our Pet* and *The Dogg's Troupe 15-Minute Hamlet*. *Dogg's Our Pet* appears separately in *Ten of the Best British Short Plays*, 79-94.

35. Stoppard, *Dogg's Our Pet* 15, 17. At the conclusion of the performance, Stoppard sent notes to all those on the set. Ros Asquith, who painted scenery, received one which read 'Ros. Cube. Tom', Cube, of course, means 'thanks' in the language of the play. Ros Asquith, 'Tom Stoppard', *City Limits*, 19-25 October 1984.

    Stoppard's fascination with language would find prose expression in his review of a supplement to the *Oxford English Dictionary*, vol.1, A-G, which appeared in *Punch*, 13 December 1972, 893-4. The review is comic, cites Wittgenstein and believes the book should not 'be reviewed so much as unveiled, not so much noticed as ogled'.

36. *Rosencrantz and Guildenstern*, 41. Cf. 'we'll stoop to anything if that's your bent . . .' (*Rosencrantz and Guildenstern*, 24).

37. Stoppard to Smith, 5 July 1968, HRC.

38. Beckett makes his remark in the final lines of *The Unnamable*. For Wood on Stoppard's wealth, see Amory.

39. Stoppard in Norman, 'Tom Stoppard and the contentment of insecurity'. While it is correct that Stoppard knew few academics, he probably heard about many, including Donald MacKinnon, who, according to George Steiner, was the model for George Moore in *Jumpers*. MacKinnon was an eccentric philosophy don who often conducted tutorials from his bath or rolled up in an oriental carpet. See Peter J. Conradi, *Iris Murdoch: A Life* (New York: Norton, 2001), 124-5. Conradi cites Steiner as his source for the Stoppard/MacKinnon connection in the notes.

40. Stoppard in Gussow, 14.

41. Stoppard in Norman, *ibid.*

42. Lewis, 59.

43. *Ibid.*, 60, 58.

　　For Stoppard, only the National could meet the play's demand for a large cast, complicated sets and actors who could not only swing from trapezes but perform long philosophical monologues with humour and panache. He was right and found what he needed in the production team of Peter Wood, the director, and Patrick Robertson, the designer. Use of the revolve stage with a wall-sized television screen added lustre to the production; acrobats from Kirby's Flying Ballet, Black Boys Inn, Sussex added action.

44. Stoppard in Amory.

45. Stoppard quoted in Tynan, *Show People*, 47.

　　Stoppard's candidate for the funniest line in English appears in a Ben Travers farce: 'arrest several of these vicars', claiming that the word 'several' is 'the funniest word in the English language, but it has to be the right context'. Stoppard in Amory.

46. Tynan, *Show People*, 92.

47. *Ibid.*, 93. Stoppard summarizes the fiasco in Norman, 'Tom Stoppard and the contentment of insecurity'. He adds that 'when it was all over, they never said a word'.

48. Stoppard in Norman, *ibid.* The quote cites a John Baxter, which appears to be a misprint for John Dexter, or Stoppard's memory may be faulty.

　　One of Tynan's memos dated January 1972 addressed the issue of the play's length, the awareness of the audience to the plot and the implausibility of some of the characters' reactions: 'Why doesn't George or Bones react to the news of a body?' 'Instead of following the plot-line, they go off into routines about "softly softly" and "Bones the Osteopath". At this point we stop taking the murder plot seriously, with very bad effects on [what] follows . . . I know Tom's objections to this, but I still maintain that to set up a whodunit and not reveal whodidit is very confusing. The audience will feel cheated'. Tynan, *Letters*, 506-7.

　　A certain mythology about the role of Tynan in reshaping the play has grown up, however, which Stoppard addressed in a 1993 letter to the *Financial Times*, 22 April 1993:

> Sir, in his review of *Arcadia*, Malcolm Rutherford unwittingly perpetuates a myth about *Jumpers* (Order and Chaos in *Arcadia*, April 15). I owed a lot to Kenneth Tynan and profited from his scrutiny, but it is quite untrue that he cut the play by an hour during rehearsal, unilaterally or otherwise or needed to.
>
> At a working dinner after the first preview, Tynan, the director Peter Wood and I discussed cuts and I shortened the play's coda by about 10 minutes. The main casualty incidentally was Tarzan played by Alan Mitchell who is Jellaby in *Arcadia*.
>
> Tom Stoppard
Iver Grove, Iver, Buckinghamshire

A few weeks after the opening, however, a grateful Stoppard delivered a decanter to Tynan with a note that read 'it comes with love, thanks and a sincere appreciation of your influence on *Jumpers* in those last days. It is s.r.o. and . . . it would not have got there I think without your intervention'. Stoppard in *The Life of Kenneth Tynan*, 396.

49. Brook in Anthony Smith, *Orghast at Persepolis* (New York: Viking Press, 1972), 27. Smith provides the fullest account of Brook and the *Orghast* production. For an additional view, see Geoffrey Reeves, 'The Persepolis Follies of 1971', *Performance* 1: 1 (New York Shakespeare Public Theatre, 1971). Reeves was Brook's assistant director.

50. Ted Hughes, Peter Brook in Stoppard, 'Orghast', *Times Literary Supplement*, 1 October 1971. The source of Brook's remark is *The Empty Space*, 15.

51. Peter Wood in Peter Lewis, 'Doubles match that's lasted 20 years', *Sunday Telegraph*, 12 February 1995; Wood, *Jumpers* programme, National Theatre, September 1976.

52. Wood in Lewis, *ibid.*; also see Delaney, 175 for an expanded account of the incident.

53. Michael Hordern with Patricia England, *A World Elsewhere: The Autobiography of Sir Michael Hordern* (London: Michael O'Mara Books, 1993), 155, 157, 158. Hordern had first worked with Stoppard in 1963 on the television production of *A Walk on the Water* and later in the play's revised format for the West End as *Enter a Free Man*, directed by Frith Banbury, which premièred on 28 March 1968.

54. Stoppard, 'Something to declare'. An example Stoppard cites of movement are the white butterflies released at the end of Peter Brook's production of *US*, the last one set aflame as it escaped: the impact was electric.

55. *Jumpers*, 18.

56. *Ibid.*, 21.

57. Martin Esslin in 'Kaleidoscope', BBC Radio 4, 22 September 1976. Esslin also notes Stoppard's use of literary or painterly models in his work. For *Jumpers*, of course, it is analytical philosophy.

58. *Jumpers*, 50-1.

59. *Ibid.*, 46; 71.

60. Stoppard in Delaney, 23.

61. Delaney 39-40; *Jumpers*, 24.

62. *Jumpers*, 63, 51-2.

63. Gussow, 13-14.

64. *Jumpers*, 24.

65. Diana Rigg in Margaret Tierney, 'Marriage Lines', *Plays and Players* (March 1972).

66. *Jumpers*, 42; Gussow, 13.

67. Tynan, *Show People*, 97; Stoppard disputes this story. See his letter to the *Financial Times*, 22 April 1993, above in note 48.

68. Irving Wardle, 'Jumpers', *The Times*, 3 February 1972; Milton Shulman, 'At the Old Vic', *Evening Standard*, 3 February 1972.

69. Nichols, *Diaries*, 225.

70. Stoppard in *Evening Standard*, 5 March 1979.

71. A. J. Ayer, 'Love among the logical positivists', *Sunday Times*, 9 April 1972. Cf. *Jumpers*, 44. Stoppard on Hordern and Jonathan Miller in Amory. For Hordern's view of the play and delight in playing the role, see Hordern, *A World Elsewhere*, 155-60.

   Ayer displayed the authority of his academic credentials at a later period as reported in the biography of him by Ben Rogers. In 1987, while Ayer was visiting the Manhattan home of lingerie magnate Fernando Sanchez, he heard a woman hollering that the boxer Mike Tyson was in the process of assaulting a woman in an adjoining bedroom. At age seventy-seven, the buoyant Ayer sprang into action and discovered the fighter attacking the model Naomi Campbell. Ayer ordered him to stop. 'Do you know who the fuck I am?' Tyson yelled. 'I'm the heavyweight champion of the world'. 'And I am the former Wykeham Professor of Logic', Ayer replied. 'We are both pre-eminent in our field; I suggest we talk about this like rational men'. As their conversation ensued, Campbell escaped. Reported in Ben Rogers, *A. J. Ayer: A Life* (London: Chatto & Windus, 1999), 344.

72. *Jumpers*, 81, 78.

73. *Ibid.*, 11.

74. For a summary of changes to the text of *Jumpers*, see Anthony Jenkins, 'Introduction: From Page to Stage', *Critical Essays on Tom Stoppard*, ed. Jenkins (Boston: G. K. Hall, 1990), 3-7. Every performance posed challenges, of course, and the evening of 5 July 1973 was no different. That night the plastic-bag routine did not work because the bag was not marked to indicate how to open it. The actors guessed wrongly and had to improvise a sort of mime to cover the difficulty, winding up by laying the plastic bag *over* the corpse to carry it off rather than placing him inside.

CHAPTER TEN ARTIST ASCENDING A STAIRCASE

1. Sean Day-Lewis, 'Extreme example of "Don't Know" man', *Daily Telegraph*, 8 July 1972. The show aired on 7 July 1972 and was rebroadcast in 1978. Also see Celia Brayfield, 'Stoppard: I think I'm a don't know', *Evening Standard*, 5 August 1978.

2. *Artist Descending a Staircase*, 16.

3. Diana Maychick, 'Stoppard Ascending', Delaney, 232. Originally published in the *New York Post*, 26 November 1989. Also see Katherine E. Kelly, 'Tom Stoppard's *Artist Descending a Staircase*: Outdoing the "Dada" Duchamp', *Comparative Drama* 20 (1986), 191-200.

4. *Artist Descending a Staircase*, 26.
5. Delaney, 233.
6. For a discussion of this controversy and Stoppard's written defence, see chapter 21.
7. *Artist Descending a Staircase*, 21.
8. *Ibid.*, 22.
9. Chesshyre, 'Tom Stoppard, Putting on the Ritz', *Daily Telegraph*, 18 February 1991.
10. *Artist Descending a Staircase*, 21; *Travesties*, 22.
11. *Artist Descending a Staircase*, 22; *Travesties*, 24-5.
12. *Artist Descending a Staircase*, 43.
13. Peter Hall, *Peter Hall's Diaries*, ed. John Goodwin (London: Hamish Hamilton, 1983), 100-1.
14. Stoppard in 'Stoppard's new electric notion', *Evening Standard*, 24 May 1974.
15. Tom Stoppard in Foster, 'Commitment is only to deadlines'. Stoppard in 'Stoppard's new electric notion', *Evening Standard*, 24 May 1974. Earlier, Stoppard had noted that his play was due in three months, and confidently said: 'Once I've cracked it then three months is all right but if not it can take three years'. Stoppard in 'Bricklayer named Stoppard', *Evening Standard*, 13 April 1973.
16. Carl Toms, who died on 4 August 1999, also designed *Night and Day*, *The Real Thing*, the 1984 West End revival of *Jumpers* and *Hapgood*. A student of Oliver Messel, Toms also worked for the English Stage Company at the Royal Court. His style blended the opulent and the naturalistic. His talent was understood as designing from the word up: 'the playwright's style seems to be his guideline', wrote Clive Barnes in the *New York Times*, praising a 1974 production of Terence Rattigan's *French Without Tears*. Toms also designed for the opera, notably at Glyndebourne.
17. Anthony Smith, *Zero Summer* (London: Eyre & Spottiswoode, 1971), 40.
18. *Artist Descending a Staircase*, 23.
19. *Ibid.*
20. *Ibid.*, 24; 25; 25, 26.
21. Stoppard is slightly misleading on the origin of the play, in one interview saying that as early as 1960 Smith pointed out to him the coincidence of Tzara and Lenin both being in Zurich at the same time during the First World War and that he only discovered many years later that Joyce was also there. In October 1969, Stoppard was reading Wittgenstein, quoting from him in a postcard to Smith. Stoppard was then working strenuously on the play, attempting to finish it before 1 January 1970, when he had to begin a film script of *Rosencrantz and Guildenstern*. In a December 1969 note to Smith, he admits that he is alternately pleased and disappointed with his progress: 'I haven't done much despite working much, sometimes two days for one speech (which I will end up re-writing)', HRC.
22. Stoppard, 'Programme Note', *Travesties*, Royal Shakespeare Company, June 1974.
23. Peter Wood in Ronald Hayman, 'Peter Wood', *The Times*, 8 June 1974.
24. Delaney, 63, 59.
25. Stoppard in Delaney, 59; Oscar Wilde, 'The Decay of Lying', *The Artist as Critic: The Critical Writings of Oscar Wilde*, ed. Richard Ellmann (New York: Vintage Books, 1970), 299; *Travesties*, 46.
26. *Artist Descending a Staircase*, 43; *Travesties*, 46.
27. *Travesties*, 47.
28. *Ibid.*, 62, and cf. 50.
29. *Ibid.*, 79.
30. *Ibid.*, 52; 74.
31. Stoppard in Dan Sullivan, 'Young British playwright here', *New York Times*, 29 August 1967.
32. *Travesties*, 64, 65.
33. *Ibid.*, 66.
34. 'In London', he added, 'we got S by doing $n(t-m)$, where m is most of the 15 minutes, but it wasn't as much fun'. Stoppard, 'Playing with Science', *Engineering & Science*, LVIII (1994), 12.
35. Stoppard in Ronald Hayman, *Tom Stoppard* (London: Heinemann, 1977), 9-10, 12.
36. Stoppard in Smith, 'Tom Stoppard', *Flourish*, RSC Club News-sheet, 1974 [2]. In the same interview, Stoppard suggests that 'art is changed a great deal more by society than it changes

society', a view expressed in *Travesties* by Carr (*Travesties*, 74).

37. Stoppard in Ross Wetzsteon, 'Tom Stoppard Eats Steak Tartare with Chocolate Sauce', *Village Voice*, 10 November 1975; Stoppard in 'Stoppard's new electric notion'.

38. Hugh Herbert, 'Domes of Zurich', *Guardian*, 7 June 1974. *Travesties* opened on 10 June 1974.

39. *Travesties*, 18.

40. But a problem still existed: how to get the characters off the stage and Carr on. Wood solved it by having the stage empty of characters one by one, except for Joyce, who picks up a fallen slip written by Lenin, reads it out loud and then hands it to the anxious Lenin while speaking to him in three languages – French, German and Italian. Joyce, as Lenin is about to leave, utters the first real sentence in the play: 'It's perfectly all right!' (*Travesties*, 20). In response, Lenin departs and Joyce, alone, attempts a limerick. Cecily the librarian enters to quiet him; he puts on his hat, picks up his walking stick and leaves. Old Henry Carr appears and the scene shifts from the library to his room.

   While Wood found means to enliven the text through physical movement, Stoppard would solve the dramatic moments. They were stymied, for example, by how to convey Carr's discovery of Lenin's possible use of a wig to disguise himself in his escape from Switzerland back to Russia. First, they tried Carr looking directly at Lenin and his wife, but it didn't work; Wood then suggested that Carr might creep up on the Lenins, pretending to read a book, and eavesdrop. That didn't work, even after John Wood as Carr tried it. Confusion followed until Wood suggested bringing down a large screen on which images of Zurich and Lenin and Russia were later to be projected, to show a silhouette of Carr listening to the Lenins. Stoppard objected because the idiom of the frolicking between Carr and Cecily which precedes this moment is in 'the idiom of Feydeau'. The silhouette device was in another idiom altogether. They pondered, fretted and admitted defeat, Stoppard punningly stating: 'Your interpretation is right, the theatrical convention is right. My carp seems to have led us into deep waters'. But then a solution, or hook, appeared: Wood mimed Carr creeping behind the bookcases, climbing the library ladder and peering over the top of a screen as the Lenins plot. When Tzara spots him and cries out, the Lenins catch him and an embarrassed Carr creeps down the ladder and moves out of their range. Lenin knows his plot has been uncovered.

41. Herbert, 'Domes of Zurich'.

42. Stoppard in 'Leftover from "Travesties"', *Adam International Review* 42 (1980), 11-12. On textual changes between the rehearsal script, published text and tape recordings of performances of the play, see Philip Gaskell, *From Writer to Reader: Studies in Editorial Method* (Oxford: Oxford University Press, 1978), 245-62.

43. *Travesties*, 48.

44. Michael Billington, 'Travesties', *Guardian*, 11 June 1974; Benedict Nightingale, 'Carried away by his own mental helter-skelter', *New Statesman*, 17 June 1974; Michael Coveney, 'Travesties', *Financial Times*, 11 June 1974; James, 'Count Zero Splits the Infinite'.

45. Stoppard in Smith, 'Tom Stoppard'.

46. Mrs Henry Carr to Stoppard, 17 August 1974; 8 September 1974, HRC.

47. A list of differences between the London and New York performance versions, plus the published edition of the play, exists in HRC.

48. Doris Cole Abrahams (of the Merrick Group) to Stoppard, 2 December 1975, HRC.

49. Robert Lantz to Kenneth Ewing, 12 December 1975, HRC. Further citations to this letter.

50. Stoppard, 'A Memo on Travesties for the attention of anybody directing it', 12 August 1976, HRC.

51. Stoppard to Parone, 11 August 1976, HRC.

52. *Travesties*, 69.

53. *Travesties*, 36; *Arcadia*, 21. Arcadia premièred at the National on 13 April 1993, *Travesties* was revived at the Barbican on 16 October 1993.

54. Antony Sher, *Beside Myself: An Autobiography* (London: Hutchinson, 2001), 248.

55. *Ibid.*

56. *Ibid.*, 249.

57. *Ibid.*, 249-50. For an example of Stoppard's concern with the delivery, rhythm and beat of a passage, see 250 and the line 'like the man who bet 6d on the Titanic sinking'. At a celebratory

dinner at Joe Allen's after the successful press night, Stoppard ordered 'a duck salad and a Caesar salad as the main course. The waiter was momentarily confused. "So that's two salads." Tom replied, "Yes, sorry, I save my creativity for my work."' (*Ibid.*, 252.)

58. *Ibid.*, 252.
59. Stoppard in Alfred Hickling, 'A clever play on words', *Yorkshire Post*, 26 November 1993; Stoppard in Charles Spencer, 'Stoppard, master of the play on words', *Daily Telegraph*, 8 September 1993. In his revision, Stoppard also improved the scene documenting Lenin's attitude to art.
60. *Travesties* typescript, Royal Shakespeare Company, Archive, Stratford.
61. *Travesties* (London: Faber and Faber, 1975), 60, 56-7, 58. This edition, despite the copyright date [no new year of publication is indicated], incorporates the revisions made to the 1993 RSC production which opened on 16 October according to a statement on p. vii.
62. But the train did not always work. At the performance of 28 January 1994, the carriage became disconnected from the engine just before it reached the door. As the show report records, 'pushed off by Mr. Martin and assisted by stage staff'. The next day is the note, 'could the train have a 30,000 mile service, please?' An earlier comic note is that a balloon from the production of *The Winter's Tale* floated down at the end of the interval: 'managed to catch it before taking up the lights for Part Two' of *Travesties*. This rescue was exceeded only by another entry: 'only managed to get one overboot onto Mr. Sher's quick change during the final dance' but 'very good show this evening & set looking in very good shape'. 12 November 1993. RSC Archive.
63. Stoppard in Hickling, 'A clever play on words'; Stoppard in Peter Lewis, 'Tom's gallimaufry', *Sunday Times*, 12 September 1993.
64. Peter Hall, *Diaries*, 116.
65. Stoppard in 'Tom Stoppard: The House of Bernarda Alba', *Plays and Players*, April 1973.
66. Robert Brustein, 'Plaudits and brickbats', *Observer*, 25 March 1973; Irving Wardle, 'The House of Bernarda Alba', *The Times*, 23 March 1973.
67. Stoppard in Jon Bradshaw, 'Tom Stoppard Non-Stop', *Sunday Telegraph*, 10 July 1977.
68. Michael Billington, 'Born Yesterday', *Guardian*, 21 April 1973.
69. Delaney, 178.

CHAPTER ELEVEN MARZIPAN CLOCKS

1. Peter Hall in Watts, 'Stoppard's half-century'; my italics.
2. *Dogg's Hamlet*, 152.
3. Stoppard in William Foster, 'Commitment is only to deadlines', *Scotsman*, 6 July 1974; Stoppard, 'When Auden said his poetry didn't save one Jew from the gas chamber . . .', in Watts, *Guardian*, 21 March 1973. Stoppard was upset that his remark became the headline for the interview; a year later, in *Theatre Quarterly*, Stoppard qualified his statement to mean the short-term not long-term efficacy of art. See 'Ambushes for the Audience', Delaney, 66-7.
4. *Dirty Linen*, 75.
5. *Ibid.*, 83.
6. *Ibid.*, 83
7. *Ibid.*, 84.
8. *Ibid.*, 86.
9. *Ibid.*, 86.
10. *Ibid.*, 93.
11. *Ibid.*, 105.
12. *New-Found-Land*, 123.
13. *Dirty Linen*, 137.
14. *Ibid.*, 94.
15. Atticus, 'Exit Tom, Enter Edgar', *Sunday Times*, 22 May 1977.
16. *Night and Day*, 89; *The Real Thing*, 227. *Night and Day* also contains an internal reference to Stoppard's earlier play: re 'the public washing of dirty linen which represents freedom to an English editor' [*Night and Day*, 84].
17. Originally a medical secretary working for Miriam Stoppard at Syntex, Jacky Chamberlain –

later Matthews – had previously studied drama part-time and was an unpaid worker for a while at the Questors Theatre. She began working full-time for Stoppard in 1975.

18. Stoppard, 'National Pride', *Evening Standard*, 30 September 1976.

19. *Index*, vol. 4, no. 2, 62; *Cahoot's Macbeth*, 205.

20. Quoted in Clayton Yeo, 'The abuse of psychiatry in the USSR', *Index on Censorship*, vol. 4 (1975), 66. Fainberg was a Fine Arts specialist. For an overview of the situation concerning human rights and psychiatric abuse in Russia, see Joshua Rubenstein, *Soviet Dissidents, Their Struggle for Human Rights*, 2nd ed. revised and expanded (Boston: Beacon Press, 1985) and Sidney Bloch and Peter Reddaway, *Psychiatric Terror: How Psychiatry Is Used to Suppress Dissent* (New York: Basic Books, 1977).

21. *Every Good Boy*, 30.

22. Stoppard, 'Preface', 'Every Good Boy Deserves Favor', *Every Good Boy Deserves Favor and Professional Foul* (New York: Grove Press, 1978), 7. 'Favor' is the American spelling used by Grove Press. All citations refer to this edition.

23. *Every Good Boy*, 7.

24. *Ibid.*, 23.

25. Delaney, 153.

26. *The Gamblers*, typescript, 3, HRC.

27. *Every Good Boy*, 5.

28. *Ibid.*, 6.

29. *Ibid.*, 17.

30. *Ibid.*, 22.

31. Václav Havel, *The Garden Party*, trans. Vera Blackwell (London: Jonathan Cape, 1969) 50.

32. *Every Good Boy*, 23.

33. *The Invention of Love*, 38.

34. *Every Good Boy*, 27–8.

35. *Ibid.*, [13].

36. Stoppard, 'Dirty Linen in Prague', *New York Times*, 11 February 1977. All further references are to this appearance of the article.

37. Stoppard, 'Prague: the story of the Chartists', *New York Review of Books*, 4 August 1977. The excerpts are from p. 15. For a dramatic account of the writing, attempted distribution and suspenseful seizure of Charter 77, see Eda Kriseova, *Václav Havel, The Authorized Biography*, trans. Caleb Crain (New York: St Martin's Press, 1993), 108-34.

38. Stoppard, 'The face at the window', *Sunday Times*, 27 February 1977.

39. Will Cohu, 'High Spirits and Gloomy Spectres', *Sunday Telegraph*, 16 May 1999.

40. Kenneth Tynan, 'Theatre Abroad: Prague', *New Yorker*, 1 April 1967, 99; Martin Esslin, 'Czechoslovakia: The Explosive Decade', *Plays and Players* 8 (August 1971), 22.

41. *Dogg's Hamlet* is actually a conflation of *Dogg's Our Pet*, which was first performed in December 1971, and *The Dogg's Troupe 15-Minute Hamlet*, which was written for performance on the double-decker bus owned by Ed Berman's Inter-Action travelling theatre group.

42. Stoppard, 'Introduction', *Tom Stoppard: Plays 3* (London: Faber and Faber, 1998), viii. Stoppard wrote this introduction in 1993. He also refers to the idea of dancers visiting Prague in 'Trad Tom Pops In', Delaney, 156.

43. Stoppard, 'Play of the Week', *BBC2: Autumn Season* (1977), 10.

44. *Ibid.*; Stoppard in 'Trad Tom Pops In', Delaney, 157. The interview originally appeared in *Gambit* in 1981.

45. Stoppard in Milton Shulman, 'The Politicizing of Tom Stoppard', Delaney, 111. The article originally appeared in the *New York Times*, 23 April 1978.

46. Delaney, 112.

47. *Professional Foul*, 60.

48. *Ibid.*, 78.

49. *Ibid.*

50. *Ibid.*, 87.

51. Delaney, 155.

52. *Professional Foul*, 90.

53. Havel in Tynan, *Letters*, 502.
54. *Ibid.*, 93.
55. *Ibid.*, 90, 56.

CHAPTER TWELVE CZECH MATES

1. Delaney, 155.
2. Jasper Rees, *Independent*, 2 December 1995; Stoppard declared he was 'as Czech as Czech can be' in Shulman, 'The Politicizing of Tom Stoppard', Delaney, 110; Stoppard in Michael Hollinger, 'The Good Words of Tom Stoppard', *Seven Arts Magazine*, January 1997, n.p. On similarities and differences between Havel and Stoppard, see Marketa Goetz-Stankiewicz, *The Silenced Theatre: Czech Playwrights Without a Stage* (Toronto: University of Toronto Press, 1979), 43-5, 1-15.
3. Stoppard, 'Prague: the story of the Chartists'.
4. Delaney, 212.
5. Václav Havel, 'Introduction', *Summer Meditations on Politics. Morality and Civility in a Time of Transition*, trans. Paul Wilson (London: Faber and Faber, 1992), xv.
6. Tynan, *Show People*, 75. Tynan describes it as 'the principle of the thermos flask: it contains heat without radiating it' (78).
7. Václav Havel, 'Politics and the theatre', *Times Literary Supplement*, 28 September 1967.
8. Authorial in this context means that theatres circumvented censorship by authoring their own, often semi-improvisational works in response to the audience. Skits, monologues, lectures and banter, reminiscent of the cabaret style, replaced traditional theatrical structures. See Dennis Beck, 'The Czech Authorial Studio Theatres 1968-89', dissertation, University of Texas, 1998.
8. Stoppard to Havel, 29 May 1984, HRC.
10. Michael Simmons, *The Reluctant President: A Political Life of Václav Havel* (London: Methuen, 1991), 195, 31; Stoppard in Chesshyre, 'Tom Stoppard, Putting on the Ritz'; Havel, 'The Power of the Powerless', *Open Letters: Selected Writings 1965-1990*, ed. Paul Wilson (New York: Knopf, 1991), 209. The essay, originally written in October 1978, had a profound impact on Eastern Europe.
11. Havel wrote that:

> I felt that Stoppard's play was close to our theatre not only in its intellectual sophistication and its clever multilayered meaning but also because it pointed (more than Beckett the metaphysician did, of course) to the moral and social dimension of human existence (the theme of betrayal). After all, my plays, too, gave our theatre that general direction – and it's no accident that in the Czech intellectual context, this comes up again and again. Later I saw *Rosencrantz and Guildenstern* in a large theatre on Broadway; it was marvellously acted and the audience was lively and responsive, yet I still think the play belongs more properly in a small, 'high profile' theatre and that a touch of nightclub or cabaret atmosphere in the performance setting would not hurt it a bit. Everything in that play is properly turned on its head, everything is paradoxical, and so I think that its 'high' meanings would resonate well in a somewhat obscure, 'low' setting, the kind of atmosphere that the Balustrade worked with (mainly before the renovations) and the kind that probably best serves the plays of Ionesco and Beckett as well.

> Václav Havel, *Letters to Olga*, trans. Paul Wilson (New York: Knopf, 1988), 135-6.

12. *The Garden Party*, 50; *Jumpers*, 81; *Hapgood*, 62; *The Memorandum*, 57, 58.
13. Jiri Nemec in Paul Wilson, 'Introduction', Václav Havel, *Letters to Olga*, trans. Paul Wilson (New York: Knopf, 1988), 13.
14. Michael Konupek in Stoppard, 'My friends fighting for freedom', *Daily Mail*, 20 October 1977.
15. Henry Popkin, 'Germany 1: Signoret goes on trial', *Sunday Times*, 17 February 1980. For an account of Havel's imprisonment, see John Keane, *Václav Havel: A Political Tragedy in Six Acts* (London: Bloomsbury, 1999), 288-99.
16. Stoppard, 'Prague's Wall of Silence', *The Times*, 18 November 1981, reprinted as 'Open letter to President Husák', *An Embarrassment of Tyrannies: twenty-five years of Index on Censorship*, ed. W. W. Webb and Rose Bell (New York: Braziller, 1998), 104-6. The accompanying photo of

Stoppard in *The Times* shows him standing, appropriately, next to a poster of *Night and Day*, his play about journalism and dictatorship.

17. Stoppard, 'Introduction', Václav Havel, *The Memorandum*, trans. Vera Blackwell (New York: Grove Press, 1967), vii.

18. Fred Hauptfuhrer, 'Playwright Tom Stoppard may have his "Dirty Linen"; Wife Miri has her own Company', *People*, 4 July 1977.

19. Miriam Stoppard in Vickie Mackenzie, 'Best prescription for coping with a very busy life', *Observer*, 18 September 1977.

20. Tynan, 'The Third Act', *New Yorker*, 14 August 2000. The comment appears in an excerpt from Tynan's recently published journals.

21. Stoppard in 'Stoppard, The '77 Tour', *Time Out*, 29 April 1977.

22. *Night and Day*, 81, 82.

23. Stoppard writes, in *The Times*, 11 August 1977:

> An unclosed shop is a state of affairs where if, for example, I want to publish my own paper, all I need is wealth, which may indeed have to be enormous if I want my own *Daily Express* but not so enormous if I want my own *Iver Heath Bugle*, or for that matter, my own *Socialist Worker*. If I don't have the money I can try to raise it and neither Mr. Victor Matthews nor Mr. Kenneth Morcan can stop me. This is called freedom of expression.
>
> A closed shop, by contrast, is where if he wanted to work for a paper, all he has to do 'is to avoid offending some person or group in a position to withdraw my right to do so, on that paper or any other. This is called absence of freedom of expression'.

24. Robert Birley, 'Freedom of the Press: an historical perspective', *Index on Censorship* 5 (Spring 1976), 32-40.

25. Michael Codron interview, London, 15 December 1998.

26. Milne's death was paralleled by that of the war correspondent Nick Tomalin, whom Stoppard knew from his days on *Scene*.

27. Waugh, *Scoop*, 155.

28. *Night and Day*, 60.

29. *Ibid.*, 60, 40.

30. *Ibid.*, 40.

31. *Ibid.*, 54.

32. *Ibid.*, 68.

33. *Ibid.*, 94.

34. Peter Wood in Philip Gaskell, 'Night and Day', *Textual Criticism and Literary Interpretation*, ed. J. McGann (Chicago: University of Chicago Press, 1985), 173. Hereafter cited as Gaskell. For New York performances, Stoppard actually rewrote Ruth's lines to read: 'I was meant to be one of those women who blow smoke into the faces of strong men in smart nightclubs – hip first to the microphone'. The full passage is on p.172 of Gaskell's essay.

35. Stoppard, *Night and Day* (New York: Grove, 1979), 51-2.

36. Gaskell, 172.

37. Changes to the text occurred throughout rehearsal and tryouts; in the end, there would be five editions of the play, essentially incorporating 177 changes, including four major alterations and nineteen added speeches. The 1999 reissue of the play in *Tom Stoppard: Plays 5* (London: Faber and Faber) reprints the first, unrevised 1978 edition of the play. For an account of the textual changes, see Gaskell.

38. Peter Wood quoted in Gaskell, 167. Collaboration between Stoppard and Wood fostered many of the changes, some of them designed to tighten the action (a form of rehearsal editing), explain a reference or improve a joke. Late in the play's development, eight short speeches were added to the fourth and fifth edition to illuminate Wagner's deception of Carson. Minor changes included the word 'breakfast' in Mageeba's comment that 'I think it would be to his [Colonel Shimbu] advantage now to come to the breakfast table with a reasonable and peace-loving man', which appears on p. 79 of the 1978 first edition but was dropped in the second edition, reinserted in the third and finally deleted in the fourth and fifth.

39. *Night and Day*, 1979 edition, 51-2.

40. Gaskell, 168-9.
41. *Scoop*, 68-9, 96-7.
42. Stoppard in Gaskell, 175.
43. Gaskell, 177; Peter Wood to the author, 8 June 1998; Gaskell, 176.
44. Gaskell, 178.
45. Steve Grant, 'Night and Day', *Plays and Players* 26 (1979).
46. Peter Hall, *Peter Hall's Diaries*, ed. John Goodwin (London: Hamish Hamilton, 1983), 475.
    In New York, where *Night and Day* opened in late November 1979, following a première in Washington, one particular line in the play began to receive spontaneous applause. At the time, American hostages were being held in Iran and the public was frustrated at America's impotent foreign policy. The line was President Mageeba's reply to Wagner's question as to whether he would seek military aid from the US and Britain. 'I'd be a fool to do that. Your record of cowardice in Africa stretches from Angola to Eritrea'. (*Night and Day*, 80.) The audience regularly interrupted with applause.
47. Gussow, 51.
48. For a summary of critical responses, see Susan Hollis Merritt, *Pinter in Play* (Durham, NC: Duke University Press, 1990), 232-7.
49. Delaney, 133; *Night and Day*, 91.
50. Stoppard, 'Is it true what they say about Shakespeare?' *International Shakespeare Association Occasional Paper No.2* (Oxford 1982), 9. This is a thirteen-page pamphlet.
51. Stoppard, 'Pragmatic Theater', *New York Review of Books*, XLVI (23 September 1999), 10.
    Apart from the prize money, there was a stipend that allowed Stoppard to select a student to study for a year at a German university.
52. *Cahoot's Macbeth*, 192.
53. Stoppard, 'But it's a pity it had to sag', *Bristol Evening World*, 20 October 1959.
54. Stoppard, 'The Wrong Door', *Western Daily Press*, 18 January 1961.
55. Stoppard, 'Confessions of a screenwriter', *Today's Cinema*, 3 February 1969, 5. For details on his effort with the screenplay and his overall career in film, see Ira B. Nadel, 'Stoppard and Film', *The Cambridge Companion to Tom Stoppard*.
56. Stoppard in Nancy Shields Hardin, 'Interview', *Contemporary Literature* XXII (1981), 163. On the debate concerning Stoppard's script, see Edith de Rham, *Joseph Losey* (London: André Deutsch, 1991), 242-3. Pauline Kael in de Rham, 244.
57. Stoppard in John Preston, 'Stoppard's dramatic turn', *Sunday Telegraph*, 7 October 1990.
58. Stoppard to Dirk Bogarde, 10 December 1977, HRC.
59. Stoppard in Ray Connolly, 'Atticus: Stoppard in Greenland', *Sunday Times*, 20 January 1980.
60. Stoppard in Tom Buckley, 'Stoppard Adapting Graham Greene's *The Human Factor*', *New York Times*, 14 July 1978.
61. Michael Billington, 'In search of the real Tom Stoppard', *Guardian*, 11 May 1991.
62. Stoppard in Mel Gussow, 'Stoppard's Intellectual Cartwheels now with Music', Delaney, 132-3. Originally appeared in *New York Times*, 29 July 1979; Stoppard in Peter Hall, *Diaries*, ed. John Goodwin (London: Hamish Hamilton, 1983), 446.
63. *Undiscovered Country*, 144.
64. *Ibid.*, 94; Delaney, 190.
65. For a summary of such changes and a detailed if unsympathetic reading of the play, see Corballis, *Stoppard: The Mystery and the Clockwork*, 174-80. On Peter Wood's inventive treatment of a scene change from a garden to a mountain hotel, see Delaney, 203.
66. Delaney, 129.
67. *Cahoot's Macbeth*, 188, 191.
68. Delaney, 131, 143.
69. Delaney, 138.
70. Ward and Block, *A History of the Manor and Parish of Iver*, 203.
71. See the British edition of *House and Garden* for August 1962 and, more particularly, John Cornforth, 'Iver Grove, Buckinghamshire', *Country Life* CXXXIV (15 August 1963), with its impressive photographs. Ward and Block's *History* features the house, which the architectural historian Ackerman, writing in 1824, described as having 'a boldness and a masculine feeling . . .

which is the result of a breadth of parts', providing the entrance front with its dignity and grandeur, unusual in such a small or modest-sized house. (Cf. Cornforth, *ibid.*) The cramped feeling of the front was the price paid for the boldness, with the pilastered centrepiece requiring a seven rather than five-bay front. The effect is described as 'restless', linked to the cramping; historians have therefore favoured James as the architect rather than Hawksmoor or Vanbrugh.

72. Delaney, 220.
73. Stoppard in David Lewin, 'Laugh? I could have spied', *Mail on Sunday*, 13 November 1988.
74. Margaret Thatcher quoted in 'Profile: Tom Stoppard', *Independent*, 13 June 1987.

CHAPTER THIRTEEN INCURABLE SEMANTIC

1. Stoppard, 'Tom Stoppard on the KGB's Olympic Trials', *Sunday Times*, 6 April 1980. Stoppard in Delaney, 64.
2. Stoppard in Joost Kuurman, 'An Interview with Tom Stoppard'.
3. Stoppard in Fallowell, 'Theatrical incest and acquisitive lust'. Stoppard provides a further description in Delaney, 220.
4. Gussow, 'The Real Tom Stoppard'.
5. Stoppard in Delaney, 263; Gussow, 23.
6. Stoppard, 'Across Nestroy with Map and Compass', Programme Note, *On the Razzle*, National Theatre, 22 September 1981.
7. *On the Razzle*, 101, 105.
8. *Ibid.*, 112.
9. *Ibid.*, 74, 118.
10. *Ibid.*, 114, 115.
11. *Ibid.*, 129, 131.
12. Stoppard in Phyllis Ruskin and John H. Lutterbie, 'Balancing the Equation', *Modern Drama* 26 (1983), 549. This is an interview and summary of Stoppard's role as playwright-in-residence at San Diego State University in 1981.
13. Even more troubling is that 'something which starts off complete . . . is then thrown into a kind of spin dryer which is the process of staging the play', Stoppard, 'Pragmatic Theater', 8. For his equation, see page 10. For another perspective on the practical Stoppard, see Carree Ryan, 'Translating *The Invention of Love*: The Journey from Page to Stage for Stoppard's Latest Play', *Journal of Modern Literature* XXIV (2000-1), 197-204. The essay focuses on Stoppard's adjustment of the text for American audiences.
14. Benedict Nightingale, 'Theatre', *New Statesman*, 2 October 1981; Michael Billington, 'On the Razzle', *Guardian*, 23 September 1981.
15. Jack Kroll, 'On the Razzle', *Newsweek*, 15 November 1982.
16. Owen, 'Razzle dazzle Stoppard'; anon., 'Juggler to the British Stage', *Observer*, 14 November 1982.
17. Stoppard in Owen, *ibid.*
18. Gussow, 68.
19. Stoppard, 'The Event and the Text', The Whidden Lectures 1988, McMaster University, transcribed by Doreen DelVecchio, *Ta Panta* 6 (Hamilton, Ontario: McMaster University Faculty Association, 1988), 18. This lecture was given 24 October 1988.
20. Stoppard in Ruskin and Lutterbie, 'Balancing the Equation', 544. Stoppard repeated this example of misunderstanding Frisch in 'The Event and The Text', *Ta Panta* (1988), 19 and in his 1999 article, originally a lecture at the New York Public Library, 'Pragmatic Theater',10.
21. Ruskin and Lutterbie, *ibid.*, 546-7.
22. *Ibid.*, 547. The importance of pragmatism in his work is reaffirmed in 'Pragmatic Theater', 8, 10.
23. 'Pragmatic Theater', 8.
24. Ruskin and Lutterbie, *ibid.*, 551, 553.
25. Kendal, *White Cargo*, 26.
26. *Ibid.*, 40-1.
27. *Ibid.*, 283, 306.
28. *Ibid.*, 177.

29. *Ibid.*, 209.
30. *Ibid.*, 270; Kendal in Fionnuala McHugh, 'I lived a sheltered but exotic life', *The Times*, 18 August 1990.
31. *White Cargo*, 292, 293.
32. Sheridan Morley, 'On the Razzle', *London Theatre Record* 1 (1981) (originally published in *Punch*); Sammells, ix.
33. See Geoffrey Wansell, 'Tom Stoppard, Man of the Week', *Sunday Telegraph*, 3 February 1985.
34. Anthony Powell, *Journals 1982-1986* (London: Heinemann, 1995), 40.
35. *The Real Thing*, 81.
36. Paul Delaney, *Tom Stoppard: The Moral Vision of the Major Plays* (London: Macmillan, 1990), 114; Stoppard in Michael Owen, 'Is this for real, Tom?', *Evening Standard*, 15 October 1982.
37. Stoppard in Owen, *ibid.*
38. Benedict Nightingale, 'On the couch', *New Statesman*, 26 November 1982.
39. *The Real Thing*, Broadway Edition (Boston: Faber and Faber, 1984), 32-3. This edition incorporates Stoppard's latest changes to the text. Minor updates were made to the work for the London and Broadway production of 1999/2000.
40. Ortega y Gasset in W. H. Auden, *A Certain World: A Commonplace Book* (New York: Viking Press, 1970), 86.
41. Gussow, 65.
42. Stoppard, 'The Event and the Text', lecture, Boca Raton, Florida, 13 March 1982, cited in Delaney, *Tom Stoppard: The Moral Vision of the Major Plays*, 105.
43. Stoppard in Delaney, 109.
44. Delaney, 175.
45. Gussow, 28.
46. *The Real Thing*, 64, 71. *The Invention of Love*, 51.
47. *The Real Thing*, 81.
48. *The Real Thing*, 24.
49. Stoppard in Delaney, 213-4. Stoppard elaborates his enthusiasm for oldies from the sixties in a 1989 interview reprinted in Delaney, 225-6.
50. *The Real Thing*, 44, 61.
51. Stoppard on 'Desert Island Discs'.
52. Stoppard, *Love for Three Oranges*, typescript, Bancroft Library, University of California at Berkeley, MSS 84/52.: 2. Also see Frank Corsaro and Maurice Sendak, *The Love for Three Oranges: The Glyndebourne Version* (London: Bodley Head, 1984), which curiously does not contain Stoppard's libretto. Rather, it reproduces the illustrations for the production and a series of conversations between Corsaro and Sendak on the staging.
53. *Love for Three Oranges*, II.1, 16.
54. Stoppard, 'Trad Tom Pops In', in Delaney, 164. In the next sentence, Stoppard explained that 'a fairly simple question about morality, if debated by highly sophisticated people, can lead to almost any conclusion'. On wanting to write a 'quiet play', see John Barber, 'Stoppard finally achieves ambition', *Daily Telegraph*, 1 December 1982.
55. Delaney, 195.
56. *Arcadia*, 7.
57. Delaney, 16.
58. *Ibid.*, 195.
59. Gussow, 73.
60. *The Real Thing*, 51.
61. Frank Rich, 'Stoppard's Real Thing in London', *New York Times*, 23 June 1983.
62. Comments from the *Observer* and *The Times* in Mary Blume, 'Tom Stoppard: Words, Words, Words and Music', *International Herald Tribune*, 17 December 1982; Michael Coveney, 'The Real Thing', *Financial Times*, 17 November 1982.
63. Hare cited in 'Making a shameless play for riches', *Independent*, 13 June 1987; Blume, 'Tom Stoppard: Words, Words, Words and Music'.
64. *The Real Thing*, 45-6, 50.

CHAPTER FOURTEEN BROADWAY TO BRAZIL

1. Emanuel Azenberg, interview, New York City, 9 June 1999.
2. Stoppard in Blume, 'Tom Stoppard: Words, Words, Words and Music'.
3. Gussow, 68.
4. Gussow, 'The Real Tom Stoppard'.
5. Azenberg, interview.
6. Gussow, 74.
7. Gussow, 'The Real Tom Stoppard'; *Where are they Now?*, 106. The passage appears in a section where Stoppard transposes an event he recalls from the Mount Hermon School in Darjeeling.
8. Stoppard, 'Author's Note', *The Real Thing* (London: Samuel French 1986), [4].
9. Samuel G. Freedman, 'Stoppard Debates the Role of the Writer', *New York Times*, 20 February 1984.
10. *Ibid.*
11. Gussow, 110.
12. The letter, addressed to Gordon Davidson of the Mark Taper Forum in Los Angeles, interprets the last two scenes in the play and reads in part

> Annie's attachment to Henry gets loosened because he starts to take their relationship for granted, doesn't feel he has to prove anything at which point she meets Billy. Henry's discovery of Billy is the 'virginity' which Charlotte said he still had to lose and his immediate danger is that it will affect him in a way as to make him even less of a rival to Billy; but he recognizes this and attempts, successfully to 'behave' in the way which would get her back. . . . finding herself loved by both men, and the second one turning out to be merely the sort of accident which happens away from home, especially in rehearsal, (hoist by her own petard), . . . she feels responsible for drawing Billy that far in .
>
> (Stoppard, HRC)

The Los Angeles production of *Hapgood* opened in 1989.

13. *The Real Thing*, 64.
14. Viveca Lindfors to Stoppard, HRC. George Tabori was a Hungarian-born novelist and dramatist and Ms Lindfors's fourth husband.
15. John Simone to Stoppard, HRC 15.7. Simone was a designer/tailor in New York and friend of Stoppard's.
16. Delaney, 228; cf. *Ibid.*, 189.
17. *Ibid.*, 194.
18. Robert Lantz to Stoppard, 6 December 1983, HRC.
19. *Jumpers*, 38.
20. Blume, 'Tom Stoppard: Words, Words, Words and Music'.
21. *The Dog it Was*, 171-2.
22. *Ibid.*, 164.
23. *Ibid.*, 181, 190.
24. Stoppard in Lewin, 'Laugh? I could have spied', *Mail on Sunday*, 13 November 1988.
25. Stoppard confirmed this in Lewin, *ibid.*
26. *The Dog it Was*, 192.
27. *Lord Malquist*, 21.
28. *Squaring the Circle*, 191-2, 257.
29. *Ibid.*, 239.
30. *Ibid.*, 214.
31. *Ibid.*, 193. Aristophanes anticipated Stoppard in using the quadrature in drama. In *The Birds*, he introduces Meton, an astronomer, who brings with him a ruler and compasses to fashion a construction 'in order that your circle may become square'.
32. *Squaring the Circle*, 193.
33. Stoppard in 'Introduction', *Squaring the Circle* with *Every Good Boy Deserves Favour* and *Professional Foul* (London: Faber and Faber, 1984), 9.
34. *Ibid.*, 10.
35. *Ibid.*, 9.

36. *Ibid.*, 9, 10.
37. *Ibid.*, 12.
38. *Ibid.*, 14.
39. *Ibid.*, 15.
40. Stoppard to Václav Havel, 29 May 1984, HRC. Another letter to Havel, also at HRC, from 25 February 1985, outlines the difficulties of adapting *Largo Desolato.*
41. Stoppard, 'Havel', *Bristol Old Vic Magazine*, typescript, 29 September 1986, HRC.
42. Stoppard on 'Front Row'.
43. Delaney, 194.
44. Stoppard in Michael Owen, 'Tom Storms back to the National', *Evening Standard*, 12 October 1984.
45. Stoppard in Asquith, 'Tom Stoppard'.
46. Delaney, 17.
47. Stoppard in Owen, 'Tom Storms back to the National'.
48. Peter Sherwood, 'Tricks of the trade', *Times Literary Supplement*, 9 November 1984.
49. Stoppard in Karine Schaefer, 'About the Play, *Rough Crossing*', *Playbill* (Princeton: McCarther Theater), 25 October-13 November 1994. Michael Maggio directed.
50. Sheridan Morley, 'Rough Crossing', *Punch*, 7 November 1984.
51. *Rough Crossing*, 12.
52. *Ibid.*, 47.
53. *Ibid.*, 63, 51, 63.
54. Benedict Nightingale, 'Fine Frenzy', *New Statesman*, 9 November 1984. Nightingale is no doubt responding to the delivery of the line, which in the 1985 edition of the play and the 1991 Faber reprint, *Rough Crossing and On the Razzle*, correctly reads '*Festina lente*' (40, 33).
55. Michael Billington, 'Villains of the Piece', *Guardian*, 9 November 1984; Michael Ratcliffe, 'Curse of the Dodo', *Observer*, 4 November 1984.
56. 'Report of Burglary', *Evening Standard*, 30 August 1984.
57. The mistaken arrest at the outset of the film already existed in the script, but Stoppard introduced the name and the single-letter mistake – 'Buttle' for 'Tuttle' – that connects them. See Terry Gilliam, *Gilliam on Gilliam*, ed. Ian Christie (London: Faber and Faber, 1999), 111. Also useful is the original first draft of the screenplay: Terry Gilliam and Charles Alverson, *Brazil*, ed. Bob McCabe (London: Orion Books, 2001). On Stoppard's contribution, see Jack Mathews, *The Battle of Brazil* (New York: Crown Publishers, 1987), 28-9.
58. Stoppard in Jack Mathews, *The Battle of Brazil*, 28. This account of the confrontation between Gilliam and Universal Pictures over the US version of the film which was seventeen minutes too long contains useful background material as well as an annotated version of the director's cut of the script. Also useful is *Gilliam on Gilliam*, ed. Christie.
59. Stoppard in Peter Buckley, 'Tom Stoppard: Boy Genius Grows Up', *New York Daily News*, 17 May 1987.
60. Lewis, 186.
61. Petherbridge, interview, London 27 May 1999.
62. James Morwood, *The Life and Works of Richard Brinsley Sheridan* (Edinburgh: Scottish Academic Press, 1985) in programme, Tom Stoppard's *The Real Inspector Hound* with R. B. Sheridan's *The Critic* (1985), [10].
63. Simon Banner, 'The trick of being calmly nervous', *The Times*, 24 February 1986. The allusion, of course, is to the stage direction in Shakespeare's *The Winter's Tale*, III.iii, which reads '*Exit pursued by a Bear*'.
64. Ian Stewart, 'Infinite Leapfrog, The Plays of Tom Stoppard', *Country Life* (August 1985).
65. Stoppard in Fallowell, 'Theatrical incest and acquisitive lust'.
66. Stoppard to his parents, 16 May 1985, HRC.

CHAPTER FIFTEEN ELOQUENT EQUATIONS

1. For a discussion of *Largo Desolato*, see chapter 14.
2. Azenberg, interview.
3. Material on the controversy and the *Index on Censorship* is campaign located in Stoppard materials at the Royal National Theatre Archive dated 20.6.86.
4. Stoppard, 16 May 1985, HRC.
5. J. G. Ballard, *Empire of the Sun* (London: Gollancz, 1984), 199.
6. Stoppard in Champlin, 'New Day Dawns for "Sun" Writer Tom Stoppard', *Los Angeles Times*, 10 December 1987.
7. Stoppard to Robert Shapiro, 27 June 1985, HRC.
8. Stoppard in Champlin, *ibid.*
9. Stoppard in memo to Spielberg, 21 July 1986, HRC.
10. Stoppard to Spielberg, 18 March 1987, HRC.
11. Stoppard to Spielberg, 23 March 1987, 1 April 1987, HRC.
12. Stoppard to the Writers' Guild of America, 4 August 1987, HRC.
13. Stoppard in Richard Freedman, 'Author Stoppard's wartime experiences nearly mirrored those of "Empire's" hero', *Newark Star Ledger*, 24 January 1988.
14. Stephen Frears in Rob Baker, 'A Few Words from Tom Stoppard', *Women's Wear Daily*, 18 May 1987. The story appears with slightly different wording in Chesshyre, 'Tom Stoppard, Putting on the Ritz'.
15. Janet Maslin, 'Wartime Exploits, Empire of the Sun', *New York Times*, 9 December 1987.
16. For Stoppard on the representation of children and *Empire of the Sun*, see Michael Billington, 'Stoppard's Secret Agent', Delaney, 196-7. The interview was originally published in the *Guardian*, 18 March 1988.
17. Stephen J. Dubner, 'Inside the dream factory', *Observer*, 21 March 1999. This is a report of a visit to the offices of Steven Spielberg just before the Oscars. Stoppard unexpectedly drops in while the journalist is present.
18. *Dalliance*, 6, 16, 37.
19. David Nathan, 'Too much dalliance for the National', *Jewish Chronicle*, 6 June 1986.
20. Stoppard in Nicholas Shakespeare, 'A New Wineskin from Old Vienna', *The Times*, 17 May 1986.
21. *Dalliance*, x, 19.
22. John Peter, 'For disservices rendered', *Sunday Times*, 1 June 1986.
23. Stoppard in Shakespeare, 'A New Wineskin'; Interestingly, the following year an educational programme on BBC2 entitled *A-Level Studies: English* focused on Stoppard. Michael Billington and Michael Coveney discussed his works, with extracts from *Rosencrantz and Guildenstern, The Real Inspector Hound* and *The Real Thing*. The date of broadcast was 27 April 1987.
24. 'Profile: Tom Stoppard', *Independent*, 13 June 1987.
25. Clive James, *Brilliant Creatures*, 188; Peter Nichols, *A Piece of My Mind* (London: Methuen 1987), 42, 24.
26. Stoppard in Watts, 'Stoppard's half-century'.
27. *Ibid.*
28. Stoppard in Mervyn Rothstein, 'A One-Act Dialogue Starring Tom Stoppard', *New York Times*, 26 November 1989.
29. Watts, 'Stoppard's half-century'.
30. Stoppard, 'Harold Pinter: the poet of no-man's-land'; Stoppard in 'Tin Man with the golden touch', *Sunday Times*, 31 January 1999.
31. Stoppard in Champlin, 'New Day Dawns for "Sun" Writer Tom Stoppard'.
32. Watts, 'Stoppard's half-century'.
33. 'Profile: Tom Stoppard', *Independent*.
34. Stoppard, 'Going to Bat For Britain'.
35. Stoppard in Chesshyre, 'Tom Stoppard, Putting on the Ritz'.
36. Stoppard, 'Playing with Science', 5.
37. *Ibid.*
38. Stoppard in Delaney, 179.

39. Stoppard to Smith, 5 January 1985, HRC. Stoppard also said that 'the trigger for the play was the notion that duality in particle physics had some sort of correspondence to duality in human personality'. Stoppard in Billington, 'Stoppard's Secret Agent'.
40. Delaney, 181.
41. *Hapgood*, rpt. with corrections (London: Faber and Faber, 1988, 1994; 'Broadway edition') 40. Unless otherwise noted, this edition will be used. It differs from the 1988 first edition, which more fully explains the physics in the play. The 'Broadway Edition' reflects Stoppard's rewrites for the 1989 American première in Los Angeles and the 1994 New York production at Lincoln Center. References to the first edition are indicated as 1988.
42. Stoppard to J. C. Polkinghorne, 16 June 1986, HRC.
43. J. C. Polkinghorne, *The Quantum World* (London: Longman, 1984), 7-8.
44. Richard Feynman, *The Character of Physical Law* (Cambridge, MA: M. I. T. Press, 1967), 129. The BBC publication appeared in 1965.
45. *Ibid.*, 131-2, 138.
46. *Ibid.*, 138.
47. *Ibid.*, 130.
48. *Ibid.*, 144.
49. *Hapgood*, 10.
50. Stoppard, 'Spy Stuff as a Metaphor for the World of Physics', *New York Times*, 27 November 1994.
51. Feynman, *The Character of Physical Law*, 146.
52. Richard Feynman, *The Feynman Lectures on Physics* (1963; Reading, MA: Addison-Wesley Publishing, 1977), I, 37.2.
53. Stoppard to J. C. Polkinghorne, 5 January 1988, HRC.
54. Stoppard to J. C. Polkinghorne, 26 January 1988, HRC.
55. Stoppard, 'Playing with Science', 4. This was a lecture given at Caltech on 20 October 1994. Stoppard gives another account of discovering the obituary in 'Spy Stuff as a Metaphor for the World of Physics'.
56. Stoppard, 'Playing with Science', 5.
57. *Ibid.*, 9.
58. *Ibid.*
59. Delaney. 195.
60. Stoppard in Michael Owen, 'Spy society', *Evening Standard*, 4 March 1988.
61. Stoppard, 'Hapgood says "All right. We can do this"', 2, HRC.
62. *Hapgood*, 5, 16.
63. Gussow, 94.
64. Stoppard, 'The text's the thing', *Daily Telegraph*, 23 April 1988.
65. *Ibid.*
66. Stoppard in John Preston, 'Stoppard's Dramatic Turn', *Sunday Telegraph*, 7 October 1991; another anecdote from the same try-out run had a patron accosting Stoppard in the car park, asking him if he was connected with the production. 'Loosely' was his answer. Michael Billington, 'Joker over the abyss', *Guardian*, 2 April 1993.
67. Stoppard to Nigel Hawthorne and Roger Lewis, 1 August 1988, HRC. He also complained that he thought the scene was 'now too much about reactions. The physics used to have more air and pace to itself, more focus'.
68. Nigel Hawthorne to Stoppard, 1 August 1988, HRC.
69. Gussow, 78-9, 80.
70. *Hapgood*, 62.
71. *Cahoot's Macbeth*, 191.
72. See P. G. W. Davies and J. R. Brown, eds., *The Ghost in the Atom* (Cambridge: Cambridge University Press, 1986).
73. For details on the staging of *Hapgood*, see Anthony Jenkins, 'Moles and Molecules: Tom Stoppard's *Hapgood*', *Critical Essays on Tom Stoppard*, ed. Jenkins, 164-74.
74. *Hapgood* 1988, 12.
75. See Doreen Thompson, 'Stoppard's Idea of Woman: Good, Bad or Indifferent?', *Critical Essays on Tom Stoppard*, ed. Jenkins, 194-203.

76. Tom Stoppard, 'Hapgood Crib', HRC. This nine-page commentary on the play was likely prepared after the London premiere in 1988 but before the Los Angeles production of 1989 at the Doolittle Theater. For the 1994 New York production, Stoppard produced no such guide, although he and Jack O'Brien, the director, met at various times to discuss the work, Stoppard stressing to O'Brien the simple chronology of the events in the work.

77. *Ibid.*, 8.

78. Jack Tinker, *Daily Mail*, 9 March 1988; quoted in Delaney, 193; Michael Ratcliffe, *Observer*, 13 March 1988; Francis King, *Sunday Telegraph*, 13 March 1988; Sheridan Morley, *Punch*, 25 March 1988. Adam Edwards/Leonardo Castillejo, *Mail on Sunday*, 20 March 1988.

79. Adam Edwards, *Mail on Sunday*, 20 March 1988; E. Pearce, review in *Encounter*, 1988. Milton Shulman, *Evening Standard*, 9 March 1988; Tom Wilkie (Science Correspondent), *Independent*, 23 March 1988.

80. Stoppard in '*Arcadia* Regained', *Isis*, Trinity, 1993.

81. Stoppard to Michael Codron, 16 May 1988, HRC.

82. Stoppard in Leslie Bennetts, 'Five Top Playwrights in a Dialogue', *New York Times*, 18 June 1988.

83. Delaney, 222.

84. Delaney, 216.

85. 'Hapgood Crib', HRC.

86. *Hapgood*, 62.

87. Ian McEwan, *The Child in Time* (London: Jonathan Cape, 1987), 44-5. 'As far as I can make out', she continues, 'you think that some local, passing fashion like modernism – modernism! – is the intellectual achievement of our time. Pathetic!'

88. Sylvie Drake, 'A Conspiracy of Spies in "Hapgood",' *Los Angeles Times*, 14 April 1989.

89. Delaney, 217; Deirdre Fernand, 'Playing for Real', *Sunday Times*, 5 May 1991.

90. Fernand, *ibid.*

91. *Ibid.*; Lynn Barber, 'Felicity Kendal – All Things Nice', *Observer*, 23 February 1997.

92. Michael Harvey, 'Stoppards to separate', *Press Association Newsfile*, 24 December 1990. The columnist Baz Bamigboye, in the *Daily Mail* of 14 November 1992, summarized the start of their relationship in this way: 'it was towards the end of *Hapgood's* run that the couple's friendship became deeper'. See chapter 17, note 10.

93. Michael Owen, 'Why I won't be marrying Tom', *Evening Standard*, 1991; Fernand, 'Playing for Real'.

94. Lynn Barber, 'Base thoughts', *Independent*, 25 November 1990; Mark Lawson, 'Tomcat's new tale', *Independent*, 10 April 1993.

95. Honan, 'I felt inferior in Tom's world'.

96. Stoppard in Chesshyre, 'Tom Stoppard, Putting on the Ritz'.

97. Thea Holme, *Chelsea* (New York: Taplinger, 1971), xvii.

98. Jasper Rees, 'Arts Interview', *Independent*, 2 December 1995.

99. Miles Kington, 'Tom Foolery, Waiting for Stoppard', *Time Out*, 1-8 November 1995.

100. Stoppard in Chesshyre, 'Tom Stoppard, Putting on the Ritz'.

101. J. S. Cart, 'The Russia House', *Variety*, 17 December 1990.

102. Stoppard on 'The Late Show with Clive James', BBC 2, 11 November 1988.

CHAPTER SIXTEEN AN ENGLISH EDEN

1. Delaney, 89, 229, 240.

2. Delaney, 214.

3. Stoppard in Mervyn Rothstein, 'A One-Act Dialogue Starring Tom Stoppard', *New York Times*, 26 November 1989.

4. Stoppard in Peter Brunette, 'Stoppard finds the right man to direct his film', *Los Angeles Times*, 20 February 1991.

5. Rothstein, 'A One-Act Dialogue Starring Tom Stoppard'.

6. Cecil Beaton in A. E. Hotchner, *Blown Away: The Rolling Stones and the Death of the Sixties* (New York: Simon & Schuster, 1990), 275. Beaton met the Stones in Morocco.

7. Libby Purves, 'Books before archives', *The Times*, 10 December 1996.

8. Chesshyre, 'Tom Stoppard, Putting on the Ritz'.
9. Stoppard in Sally Giles, 'Tom Foolery', *City Limits*, 16-23 May 1991. Stoppard also recounts his meeting with Puttnam in Chesshyre, *ibid.*
10. Kevin Jackson, 'Tiffin and sympathy', *Independent*, 2 February 1991.
11. Stoppard in Preston, 'Stoppard's dramatic turn'.
12. Tom Stoppard, 'Connery dispute', *The Times*, 13 October 1990.
13. Geoff Brown, 'Tell the truth, face the consequences', *The Times*, 23 May 1991. The cover of the Faber and Faber screenplay (London, 1991) shows a colour still of Roth and Oldman standing like two condemned outlaws in the old west, with thick ropes around their necks.
14. Stoppard in Lyn Gardner, 'The Heart in the Closet', *Guardian*, 16 January 1999.
15. Richard Dreyfuss, to the author, London, 26 May 1999; Stoppard, in Alan Franks, 'Stoppard stoppered', *The Times*, 29 June 1999.
16. Stoppard in Franks, 5.
17. Stoppard in Brunette, 'Stoppard finds the right man to direct his film'; Stoppard in Preston, 'Stoppard's dramatic turn'. The formula still holds. A Canadian writer whose book was optioned was told to write a 120-page script: a page equates to one minute of screen time, a scene is half a page. Jan Wong, 'Fifth Column', *Globe and Mail* (Toronto), 24 September 1999.
18. Gore Vidal in 'Gored', *The Economist*, 22 September 1990.
19. Stoppard, 'To Film or Not to Film', *Première* (November 1990); Stoppard, questionnaire, HRC.
20. Vincent Canby, 'Rosencrantz and Guildenstern are Dead', *New York Times*, 8 February 1991.
21. Peter Aspden, 'Rosencrantz and Guildenstern are Dead', *Sight and Sound* n.s. 1 (1991), 58.
22. *In the Native State*, 20.
23. Gussow, 120, 135.
24. Jackson, 'Tiffin and sympathy'.
25. Stoppard in Russell Twisk, 'Stoppard basks in late Indian summer', *Observer*, 31 April 1991.
26. Emily Eden, *Up the Country: Letters written to her Sister from The Upper Provinces of India* (London: Richard Bentley, 1866), II, 203.
27. *Ibid.*, I, 11, 19–20.
28. *Ibid.*, I, 87.
29. *Ibid.*, II, 1.
30. *In the Native State*, 83.
31. *Up the Country*, II, 117-8.
32. Delancy, 239.
33. Stoppard in Elizabeth Brodersen, '*Indian* Inspiration', *Words on Plays: Indian Ink* (San Francisco: American Conservatory Theater, 1999), 12. The quotation can also be found in Delaney, 249.
34. Delaney, 253.
35. Peggy Ashcroft in John Tydeman, 'Stoppard conjures a play from the air', *Daily Telegraph*, 27 February 1995.
36. *In the Native State*, 23.
37. Stoppard in Brodersen, '*Indian* Inspiration', 14.
38. *In the Native State*, 11.
39. *Ibid.*, 18-19.
40. *Ibid.*, 29.
41. *Ibid.*, 31.
42. *Ibid.*, 35.
43. *Ibid.*, 45.
44. *Ibid.*, 44.
45. Stoppard in Chesshyre, 'Tom Stoppard, Putting on the Ritz'.
46. Stoppard in *Venue* (Bath), 4.
47. Stoppard, 'Going Back'; 'In search of childhood', *Daily Mail*, 4 May 1991; 'Late to read, early to rise'.
48. Stoppard in Michael Owen, 'Stoppard and the nearly man', *Evening Standard*, 17 May 1991.
49. Stoppard, *Schindler's List* 154, [1991], 174, HRC.
50. Stoppard in Franks, 'Stoppard stoppered'.

51. *Ibid.*

52. Michael Billington, 'In search of the real Tom Stoppard'; *In the Native State*, 23.

CHAPTER SEVENTEEN THE CLASSIC ROMANTIC: SHAKESPEARE IN LOVE

1. Nigel Dempster, 'Mail Diary', *Daily Mail*, 1 March 1995; Stoppard, diary, HRC uncatalogued.

2. Zoë Heller, 'Sex and drugs and on a roll', *Independent*, 14 July 1991.

3. *Ibid.*

4. Honan, 'I felt inferior in Tom's world'.

5. Miriam Stoppard in Diana Hutchinson, 'Smug, pompous, over-the-top . . . Miriam's views about herself', *Daily Mail*, 2 October 1991.

6. Honan, 'I felt inferior in Tom's world'. Also see Nigel Dempster, 'Mail Diary', *Daily Mail*, 5 January 1993.

7. Honan, 'I felt inferior in Tom's world', 23.

8. *Ibid.*

9. *Ibid.*

10. Baz Bamigboye, 'Stoppard seals love for Felicity', *Daily Mail*, 14 November 1992. The gossip columnist adds that 'it was towards the end of *Hapgood*'s run that the couple's friendship became deeper. When Miss K. separated from Mr Rudman, she surprised the showbiz world by turning to Stoppard as a shoulder to cry on. When she eventually divorced, her love grew for Stoppard who by that time had split from TV personality Dr Miriam Stoppard after 18 years'.

11. William Boyd provides a detailed account of the process in 'Give credits where they're due', *The Times*, 12 December 1992.

12. Marc Norman in Patrick Pachecho, 'Putting Genius in its Place: Tom Stoppard and Writer Marc Norman took the bard off his pedestal so they could put him back on top of it', *Los Angeles Times*, 12 December 1998.

13. Stoppard in Patrick Pacheho, 'Putting Genius in its place'.

14. Stoppard in Sarah Lyall, 'The muse of Shakespeare imagined as a blonde', *New York Times*, 13 December 1998.

    Stoppard's fanciful dialogue in a letter to Isabel Dunjohn actually anticipates Stoppard's comic treatment of Shakespeare. Set in a coffee cellar in Montmartre, Byron enters, supposedly reading T. S. Eliot:

Lord B	Now is the winter of our discontent (poor booby has not realised that someone has put the wrong dust jacket on his book.)
Dalmation	That's Shakespeare, you nit.
Lord B	Where?
(As the light strengthens we see that Shakespeare is indeed sitting in the corner.)	
Dalmation	There.
Shakespeare (drunk)	Where is Miss Hathaway?
Lord B	Gone for a bucket.
Dalmation	You furrow browed romantic looking gett. You mean, done, done for a ducket.
Shakespeare	I can use that. (Gets out quill).
Dalmation	You already did you twit.

The exchange continues for another half page as Anne Hathaway returns with a bucket, Byron drops more bon mots and Shakespeare reaches again for his quill.

15. Stoppard, 'Shakespeare in Love, a Screenplay from the original screenplay (June 1992) by Marc Norman', second draft. Typescript (September 1992), 7, 24-5.

16. *Ibid.*, 97, 112.

17. *Ibid.*, 120.

18. *Ibid.*, 129.

19. *Ibid.*, 130.
20. *Ibid.*, 130-1.
21. 'Julia jilts the Bard', *Evening Standard*, 20 October 1992; 'Stoppard returns to the stage', *The Times*, 2 November 1992; Mr Pepys, 'Hathaway went thataway', *Evening Standard*, 27 October 1992.
22. Marc Norman, Tom Stoppard, *Shakespeare in Love* (London: Faber and Faber, 1999), 6. All further citations refer to this edition of the film script. The humour in the line is that it is written by Hamlet to Ophelia but read in the play by Polonius.
23. *Ibid.*, 7.
24. *Ibid.*, 30.
25. *Ibid.*, 30.
26. *Ihid*, 67, 27.
27. Stoppard in Elizabeth Gleick, 'The Scene Stealers', *Time*, 25 January 1999.
28. *Shakespeare in Love*, 150.
29. Stoppard in Paula Span, 'Trusted to put his words in the Bard's mouth', *The Record* (Bergan County, NJ), 4 January 1999; originally a *Washington Post* wire-service story.
30. *Shakespeare in Love*, 49-50.
31. For Stoppard on the anachronisms in theatre life then and now, see Gary Dretzka, 'Stoppard and Norman on the same page with Shakespeare', *Chicago Tribune*, 23 December 1998.
32. Technically, they used Super 35, 'doing an anamorphic squeeze at the interneg stage in postproduction'. This way, there would not be any underexposure in any part of the frame, gaining sharpness by not using any diffusion. Yet he worked extensively with soft lighting and Vision 500T film because it 'saw into the shadows better . . . and controlled the highlights better'. The result was vivid, rich and dramatic. Richard Greatrex in 'Shakespeare's Writer's block', *In Camera*, October 1998.
33. Stoppard, 'What is to be done?' Stationer's Hall, London, 14 February 1992. Videotape, National Sound Archive.
34. Duncan Weldon in Franks, 'Stoppard stoppered'.
35. Gussow, 135.
36. Michael Billington, 'Joker above the Abyss', *Guardian*, 2 April 1993.

CHAPTER EIGHTEEN BYRON IN A LAPTOP

1. Stoppard in Roger Highfield, 'Chaos, Stoppard's dramatic turn-on', *Daily Telegraph*, 23 May 1994.
2. On Stoppard's discovery of chaos theory, see John Fleming, 'A Talk with Tom Stoppard', *Theatre Insight* 10 (December 1993); Stoppard in Blowen, 'Talking Chaos with Tom Stoppard'; Stoppard in *Irish Times*, 16 January 1999. In a 1997 interview, Stoppard said that *Arcadia* worked because he had 'ended up with a story which had a quite independent appeal as a structure irrespective of how I was writing the dialogue . . . the sequence of incidence seemed to develop a momentum, and that's really what I meant about getting it right'. Stoppard in Hollinger, 'The Good Words of Tom Stoppard'.
3. Stoppard in Hickling, 'A clever play on words'.
4. *Arcadia*, 26.
5. Thomas Love Peacock, *Headlong Hall* in *The Novels of Thomas Love Peacock*, ed. David Garnett (London: Rupert Hart-Davis, 1963), I: 13-14.
6. *Ibid.*, 18, 21; 20.
7. *Ibid.*, 48, 50.
8. Another striking similarity between *Headlong Hall* and Stoppard's work is the passage from *Artist Descending a Staircase* which celebrates the uniqueness of the artist. Escot in Peacock's novel anticipates Beauchamp's remark that in any community of a thousand, nine hundred will do the work, ninety will be doing well, nine will be doing good and 'one lucky dog painting or writing about the other nine hundred and ninety-nine' (*Artist*, 43). Escot explains that 'ninety-nine in a hundred are occupied in a perpetual struggle for the preservation of a perilous and precarious existence while the remaining one wallows in all the redundancies of luxury that can be wrung from their labours and privations'. (*Headlong Hall*, 51).

For another precursor, see Lionel Monkton's 1909 Edwardian musical comedy, *The Arcadians*, the story of an Edwardian falling from a plane and landing in the classical world of Arcadia. His adventures return him to London with a number of the Arcadians. A racecourse and restaurant figure importantly in the amusing story.

9. Stoppard in Jerry Tallmer, 'The High-Tech Human Heart', *Hapgood Playbill* (December 1994), 84.

10. A. S. Byatt, *Possession* (1990; London: Vintage, 1991), 499-504. Further citations refer to this edition. An additional source, not in structure but in its concern with chaos theory, is Robert Littell's novel, *The Visiting Professor* (London: Faber and Faber, 1993), in which a Russian chaologist stuns a Prague conference with his experiments in dynamic systems and chaos.

11. *Possession*, 510.

12. *Arcadia*, 74.

13. *Possession*, 470; *Arcadia*, 88; 75.

14. *Possession*, 49.

15. A. S. Byatt to the author, 13 June 2000. Byatt made her remark to me after a panel on biography held at the University of London which also included Richard Holmes and Lawrence Norfolk. Byatt's later novel, *The Biographer's Tale* (2000), extends her exploration of the confusions and uncertainties that plague biographers.

16. On the problematics of this phrase, see Erwin Panofsky, '*Et in Arcadia Ego*: Poussin and the Elegiac Tradition', *Meaning in the Visual Arts* (Garden City, New York: Doubleday, 1957), 295-320. The phrase itself is not classical but first appeared in the early seventeenth century in Italy. For a briefer discussion of Poussin and his relation to *Arcadia*, see Kevin Jackson, 'A Little Place in the Country', *Independent*, 22 April 1993.

17. Stoppard in Matt Wolf, 'Playing on the Pastoral', *Mirabella*, May 1995, 61.

18. Richard Feynman, *The Character of Physical Law* (Cambridge, MA: M. I. T. Press, 1967), 121.

19. *Arcadia*, 78.

20. See Brian Davies, *Exploring Chaos: Theory and Experiment* (Reading, MA: Perseus Books, 1999), 8, 11; James Gleick, *Chaos* (New York: Penguin, 1987), 134, 139-42, 8, 20-3.

21. *Arcadia*, 73-4.

22. Dance, cited in Henry's cricket-bat speech in *The Real Thing*, is a crucial metaphor throughout Stoppard's work, representing movement in time and space plus the stylized interchange of ideas and emotions. *Arcadia* represents this most clearly in the preparations for the country dance in the grounds of Sidley Park in the contemporary portion of the play (although the characters dress in Regency outfits), matched at the end with Thomasina's learning how to waltz for her seventeenth birthday. Septimus, long in love with her, teaches her, leading to a kiss. And then the two periods cross, although one is invisible to the other, joined only by the movement of the bodies, themselves a metaphor of the behaviour of chaos theory and heat exchange.

   There is a similar dance at the end of *Travesties*, where Joyce has been talking about art which will exist in a separate realm where it will 'dance for some time yet and *leave the world precisely as it finds it*'. (*Travesties*, 63). *Jumpers*, one could argue, is all dance, from the opening acrobats to the swinging Dotty. The original idea of *Professional Foul* was that a ballroom-dancing team would be going to Prague, not a football team (Delaney, 156). Dance, for Stoppard, gives physical grace to the complexity of idea and character expressed through the liveliness of his writing.

23. Throughout his work, Stoppard has relied on triangular relationships, beginning with Rosencrantz, Guildenstern and Hamlet and continuing with Dotty, George and Archibald Jumper (*Jumpers*), Hapgood, Kerner and Blair (*Hapgood*), Annie, Henry and Billy (*The Real Thing*) and, finally, A. E. Housman the younger, Housman the elder and Moses Jackson (*The Invention of Love*). The triangle was Stoppard's instrument of choice in *Every Good Boy*, as well as in his own musical career: Stoppard played the triangle in his school band in Darjeeling.

24. Mahler in a 26 March 1896 letter to Max Marschalk in Gleick, *Chaos*, 163. The translation of the letter on p. 180 of the *Selected Letters of Gustav Mahler*, ed. Alma Mahler, enlarged by Knud Martner, trans. Eithne Wilkins et al. (London: Faber and Faber 1979) differs slightly.

25. Stoppard in 'Stoppard: A Play in Three Acts', *Pennsylvania Gazette* (April 1996), 28. See also

Fleming, 24. Of the Stones, only Jagger attended, on 3 July 1993.

26. *Arcadia*, 44, 45.

27. *Ibid.*, 44.

28. Stoppard, 'A Play in Three Acts', *Pennsylvania Gazette*, 1 April 1996.

29. Stoppard, undated postcard, HRC.

30. *Arcadia*, 93.

31. *Ibid.*, 47, 37, 47.

32. Philip Holmes in Davies, *Exploring Chaos: Theory and Experiment*, 11.

33. *Arcadia*, 76.

34. Gleick, *Chaos*, 172.

35. *Arcadia*, 93.

36. *Ibid.*, 84; B. Mandelbrot, 'Introduction', *The Fractal Geometry of Nature*, Updated and Augmented (New York: W.H. Freeman and Company, 1983), 1. The book originally appeared in 1977 as *Fractals: Form, Chance and Dimension* and included Mandelbrot's original essay, 'How Long is the Coast of Britain?', using fractals to establish an answer. For a dramatic, visual portrait of fractals, see John Briggs, *Fractals: The Pattern of Chaos* (New York: Touchstone Books, 1992). For images of fractals as art, see www.deepleaf.com/fractal.

37. Gleick, *Chaos*, 98.

38. Stoppard in Lawson, 'Tomcat's new tale'.

39. See N. Katherine Hayles, *Chaos Bound: Orderly Disorder in Contemporary Literature and Science* (Ithaca: Cornell University Press, 1990), 170-1.

40. *Arcadia*, 61.

41. *Ibid.*, 27.

42. *Ibid.*, 23-4.

43. Hampton, *The Philanthropist*, 33.

44. *Arcadia*, 12; 89.

45. *Ibid.*, 25.

46. *Ibid.*, 27; Wolf, 61.

47. Fleming, 19.

48. Billington, 'Joker above the abyss'.

49. Trevor Nunn in Don Shewey, 'Certain Personal Elements, Notes on Biography and Theatre', *New Theater Review* 12 (1995), 6-7. Published by Lincoln Center Theater, New York.

50. Stoppard in Highfield, 'Chaos: Stoppard's dramatic turn-on'.

51. Stoppard in Fleming, 'A Talk with Tom Stoppard'.

52. *Arcadia*, 5.

53. *Ibid.*, 77-8.

54. Stoppard to Billington, 9 April 1993, HRC. Programme, *Arcadia* (London: National Theatre, 1993) [12].

55. Stoppard in Gussow, *Conversations with Stoppard*, 138. Several critics, however, felt the recast production of the play for the Haymarket Theatre in the West End in May 1994 was more effective because Joanne Pearce's Hannah and Roger Allam's Bernard were 'more convincing literary duellist[s]'. 'Nunn sheds new light on world of literary duellists', *Evening Standard*, 24 May 1994. Charles Spencer in the *Daily Telegraph* was equally praiseworthy: 'I have never left a new play more convinced that I'd just witnessed a masterpiece', 'Stoppard's thrilling workout', *Daily Telegraph*, 26 May 1994.

56. Billington, 'Joker above the abyss'.

57. *Lord Malquist*, 18.

58. Stoppard in Benedict Nightingale, 'Long haul for a laidback lad'.

59. Billington, 'Joker above the abyss'.

60. *Arcadia*, 11, 4, 5.

61. Benedict Nightingale, 'Ideas meet their comic match', *The Times*, 14 April 1993; Jack Tinker, 'Another lesson in whims and conceit at the knee of too-clever Mr. Stoppard', *Daily Mail*, 14 April 1993; Nicholas de Jongh, 'Complicating the meaning of life in Stoppard's Arcadia', *Evening Standard*, 14 April 1993.

62. Michael Billington, 'Hand on heart and tongue in cheek', *Guardian*, 14 April 1993.

63. Roger Highfield, 'Stoppard solves the problem', *Daily Telegraph*, 15 April 1993; Simon Jenkins, '(Pause). Enter Two Writers', *The Times*, 30 October 1993. After summarizing the fallow decade of the eighties for both Stoppard and Pinter, Jenkins celebrates their magisterial return with *Arcadia* and *Moonlight*.

64. Jenkins, '(Pause). Enter two writers'.

65. Bryan Appleyard, 'Plenty left to shout about', *Sunday Times*, 5 November 2000.

66. Kate Kellaway, 'Seeking the script for success', *Observer*, 23 May 1993.

67. Sandra Barwick, 'If anyone asked you who you are . . '., *Independent*, 17 April 1993.

68. Peter Wood, 'Stoppard in *Arcadia*', 'Platform', National Theatre, 14 April 1993. Transcript, Royal National Theatre archive, [6].

69. *Arcadia*, 3.

70. *Ibid.*, 6.

71. 'The National Theatre', *Daily Telegraph*, 25 June 1993; Adrian Berry, 'Number's Up for Fermat's Last Theorem', *Daily Telegraph*, 24 June 1993. For an account of the history and solution to Fermat's theorem, see Simon Singh, *Fermat's Last Theorem* (1997; London: Fourth Estate, 1998). Andrew Wiles's proof of the theorem, considered the world's most famous mathematical problem, ran to over 1,000 pages. Ironically, and perhaps dramatically, Wiles's original Cambridge paper had a serious gap, the construction of a Euler system. He was able to complete his proof by removing the Euler system and developing the hypothesis that certain Hecke algebras are local, complete intersections. See Singh, 299.

72. Wesker to Stoppard, 5 May 1993, HRC, uncatalogued material.

73. Catherine Trautmann in Nicholas Powell, 'The French fail to stage a good argument', *Financial Times*, 6 December 1998. On the failure of *Arcadia* at the Comédie-Française, see Susannah Herbert, 'Comédie-Française is gripped by mutiny', *Daily Telegraph*, 21 January 1999.

74. Fleming, 22.

75. *Ibid.*, 21.

76. Barber, 'Felicity Kendal – All Things Nice'.

77. *Ibid.*

78. *Ibid.*

CHAPTER NINETEEN NEW YORK, PRAGUE

1. Stoppard in Bob Ickes, 'Surely you're joking, Mr. Stoppard!', *New York Magazine*, 9 January 1995.

2. Gussow, 106.

3. Stoppard in John Heilpern, 'Stockard does Stoppard', *Vogue*, December 1994.

4. Jack O'Brien to the author, Globe Theatre, San Diego, CA, 8 May 2000; O'Brien in Ickes, 'Surely you're joking, Mr. Stoppard', 39.

5. O'Brien to the author, 8 May 2000.

6. *Ibid.*

7. *Hapgood*, 41.

8. Stoppard, 'Spy Stuff as a Metaphor for the World of Physics'.

9. *Ibid.*

10. Stoppard, 'Playing with Science', 5.

11. Stoppard, 'The Matter of Metaphor', *New Theater Review* 11 (1994), 4. Published by Lincoln Center Theater, New York.

12. *Ibid.*

13. Gussow, 78.

14. *Ibid.*, 196.

15. O'Brien to the author, 8 May 2000.

16. Jack O'Brien in Joseph Hurley, 'The director's art', *Irish Echo* (7-13 December 1994), 24. Stoppard's behaviour at the rehearsals for *Indian Ink* and *The Invention of Love* for the American Conservatory Theater in San Francisco in February 1999 and January 2000 were no different, as the author observed. Stoppard also favours a pen with a light on it to jot down his notes.

17. O'Brien to Hurley, 'The director's art', 24.
18. Stockard Channing, *Theater Week*, 2 January 1995; Robert Brustein, 'Intellect into Passion', *New Republic*, 30 January 1994; David Richards, 'All Roads lead to Mother in a game of Spy versus Spy', *New York Times*, 5 December 1994.
19. Ickes, 'Surely You're Joking, Mr. Stoppard!'. A response by the theatre manager pointed out that the temperature was actually kept lower than usual to ensure no overheating.
20. Christopher Rawson, 'McNally! Stoppard! Molière! On Broadway', *Pittsburgh Post-Gazette*, 28 February 1995. John Simon, 'Half Good', *New York Magazine*, 2 January 1995. Simon adds that '*Hapgood* is a play I simply couldn't follow in performance. So I bought the text, and had the privilege of not being able to follow it that way either'.
21. *USA Today*, 30 December 1994.
22. Gussow, 95.
23. Stoppard in 'Not Only About Theatre', *Theatre Czech* 9 (1995), 41. The entire article, pp. 38-48, summarizes the dialogue among the three playwrights and chair.
24. *Ibid.*, 43.
25. *Ibid.*, 44.
26. *Ibid.*, 45.
27. *Ibid.*, 45.
28. *Ibid.*, 45-6.
29. *Ibid.*, 46.
30. *Ibid.*
31. Ronald Harwood to the author, 21 June 2000.
32. 'Another country'.
33. *Ibid.*
34. Victor Jileniewski Seidler, *Shadows of the Shoah: Jewish Identity and Belonging* (Oxford: Berg, 2000), 8. This is an intriguing account of growing up as the son of refugees in post-war Britain and the effort to reclaim a Polish–Jewish identity.
35. *Ibid.*, 25, 27.
36. James Shapiro, *Shakespeare and the Jews* (New York: Columbia University Press, 1996), 4 and *passim*. Shapiro also adds that 'Englishness has in part defined itself by the wholesale rejection of that which is Jewish', referring both to the expulsion of the Jews in 1290 and their return in the seventeenth century.
37. 'Another country'.
38. *Ibid.*
39. Gardner, 'The Heart in the Closet'.
40. Tom Stoppard in 'Sunday Morning', CBS News, 28 February 1999; Peter Stoppard to the author, 14 December 1998.
41. Tom Stoppard in Delaney, 110; Stoppard, Prague Theatre Institute Lecture. The occasion was a discussion to mark the première of *Arcadia* by the Divadlo Komedie (Comedy Theatre), the first Stoppard play to be performed in the Czech Republic since *Travesties* in 1991.
   Interestingly, up to June 1998, Stoppard's plays were not available in Czech, with the exception of *Arcadia*. During the seventies, of course, his work was not allowed to be performed, since he was intensely critical of the repressive regime that jailed Havel and others. The list of Stoppard plays performed in the Czech Republic is brief: *Rosencrantz and Guildenstern* in 1971, *Entera Free Man* in 1978, *Rosencrantz and Guildenstern* again in 1989, *Enter a Free Man* again in 1990, *Travesties* in 1991 and, finally, *Arcadia* in 1998.

CHAPTER TWENTY MULTIPLE FASCINATION

1. Stoppard in Randy Gener, 'Unstoppered Stoppard', *Village Voice*, 4 April 1995. With seeming reluctance, Stoppard admits in the same interview that 'I find complexity attractive'. Stoppard expressed interest in the simple play as early as 1974, telling Ronald Hayman that following *Travesties*, 'what I'd like to write now is something that takes place in a whitewashed room with no music and no jumping about . . '. In a *Paris Review* interview of 1988, he said: 'I would like to write a very simple play, perhaps with two or three people in one setting . . '. *Arcadia* is his

complicated response to that wish.

2. Stoppard, 'The Matter of Metaphor'.

3. Stoppard in Jack Kroll, 'Mind over Matter', *Newsweek*, 3 April 1995.

4. Gener, 80.

5. *Arcadia*, 1.

6. Vincent Canby, 'Stoppard's Comedy of 1809 and Now', *New York Times*, 31 March 1995, Carole S. Appel to Stoppard, 28 March 1995, HRC, uncatalogued. Stoppard answered by hand.

7. *Arcadia*, 94.

8. *Ibid.*, 94; Carey Perloff to Stoppard, 29 September 1995; Stoppard to Carey Perloff, n.d. *Arcadia* files, American Conservatory Theater, San Francisco.

9. Carey Perloff in 'An Interview with Carey Perloff on *Indian Ink*', *Words on Plays: Indian Ink* (San Francisco: American Conservatory Theater, 1999), 57, 58.

10. Studio memo, *c.* May 1994, HRC.

11. Stoppard to Steven Spielberg, 12 July 1994, HRC.

12. *In the Native State*, 1; *Indian Ink*, 11. In the stage play, Flora wore a blue print dress.

13. *Indian Ink*, 79.

14. *Ibid.*, 30.

15. *In the Native State*, 52-3.

16. *Indian Ink*, 59, 78.

17. Bill Hagerty in Catherine O'Brien, 'Stripping away the years', *Today*, 1 March 1995; Catherine O'Brien, *ibid.*

18. Carey Perloff in 'An Interview with Carey Perloff on *Indian Ink*', 58. In the same interview, Perloff, Artistic Director of ACT, pointed out that one of her goals for the play was 'to make language hot. Appreciating Stoppard's writing isn't really an intellectual experience' but the appreciation of the 'eroticism of ideas and of art'.

19. *In the Native State*, 68-9; *Indian Ink*, 65.

20. *Indian Ink*, 4.

21. *Ibid*, 79.

22. Gussow, 121.

23. Peter Kemp, 'Flinging Mangoes at the Resident's Daimler', *Times Literary Supplement*, 17 March 1995; Vincent Canby of the *New York Times* referred to the play's 'soothing wit' and 'leisurely charm which are not the kind of virtues reviewers look for in Mr. Stoppard. They want fireworks'. Vincent Canby, 'Visiting "Arcadia's" Kindly Cousin in London', *New York Times*, 20 April 1995.

24. This did not mean, however, a quick transfer to the US. In fact, it did not première until February 1999 at the American Conservatory Theater in San Francisco, with Art Malik in the cast. Stoppard attended rehearsals, made minor changes to the script and lurked about the theatre making notes, clearly enjoying the process.

25. Stoppard in *Observer*, 'Thrown from the Balloon: those that almost made it . . .' 17 December 1995.

26. Kendal in Barber, 'Felicity Kendal – All Things Nice'.

27. Kendal in 'Felicity finds love the second time around', *Mail on Sunday*, 21 March 1999; Kendal in Anne Shooter and Paul Bracchi, 'Irish eyes are smiling as Stoppard and Mia go strolling', *Daily Mail*, 2 July 1997. By October 2000, Kendal was starring with Frances de la Tour in Noel Coward's *Fallen Angels*, directed by Michael Rudman, with whom she was reunited. Public fascination with her continues; see Celia Brayfield, 'The Test – Felicity Kendal', *The Times*, 26 October 2000, an assessment of her life and career. She scored 61 per cent.

28. Purves, 'Books before archives'; Stoppard, letter to *The Times*, 14 December 1996.

29. Stoppard in Bryan Appleyard, 'So what's it all about, Mr. Stoppard?' *Sunday Times*, 21 September 1997; Stoppard in Richard Mowe, 'The Word made flesh', *Scotsman*, 29 October 1995.

30. *The Seagull*, 59, 58.

31. Sheridan Morley, 'A breathtaking version of The Seagull', *International Herald Tribune*, 14 May 1997.

32. *The Seagull*, 20, 12; *Rosencrantz and Guildenstern*, 118; *The Seagull*, 9.

33. Anton Chekhov in Benedict Nightingale, 'The Seagull', *The Times*, 12 May 1997.

34. Stoppard, 'An English Seagull', *The Seagull*, programme (London: Peter Hall Company of The Old Vic, 1997), 6,7. Opening night for the production was 9 May 1997; first preview was 28 April 1997. The director of Stoppard's 1988 *Hapgood* in New York, Jack O'Brien, presented Stoppard's adaptation of *The Seagull* at the Old Globe Theater in San Diego in February 2000, envisioning the work as a Russian version of Noël Coward's *Hay Fever* with the characters drunk on theatre.

35. *The Seagull*, 45.

36. A. E. Housman, 'On certain corruptions in the *Persae* of Aeschylus', *The Classical Papers of A. E. Housman*, ed. J. Diggle and F. R. D. Goodyear (Cambridge: Cambridge University Press, 1972), I: 165; Housman, 'The Application of Thought to Textual Criticism', *Selected Prose*, ed. John Carter (Cambridge: Cambridge University Press, 1961), 131.

37. *Shakespeare in Love*, 95.

38. *Ibid.*

39. *Indian Ink*, 11.

40. Stoppard, Prague Theatre Institute Lecture; Michael Billington, 'Indelible Ink', *Guardian*, 8 February 1995. Stoppard in Hollinger, 'The good words of Tom Stoppard'.

41. Stoppard in Benedict Nightingale, 'Long haul for a laidback lad.

42. *Ibid.*

43. Thomas O'Connor, 'Welcome to the World of Tom Stoppard', Delaney, 227. The interview originally appeared in the *Orange County Register*, 2 April 1989.

44. Stoppard in Appleyard, 'So what's it all about, Mr. Stoppard?'.

45. Stoppard in Alastair Macaulay, 'The man who was two men', *Financial Times*, 31 October 1998.

46. Gardner, 'The Heart in the Closet'. Both Michael Billington and Mel Gussow, in their biographies of Pinter and Edward Albee, found that there were closer connections between the plays and the lives of their subjects, despite the repeated disavowals of links by their respective subjects.

47. *Ibid.*

48. Stoppard in conversation with Robert Osserman at University of California, Berkeley, 19 February 1999. The topic was 'Math in *Arcadia*'. See 'Another country'.
    Stoppard, asked by Tina Brown for a piece on the current British theatre for her new magazine, *Talk*, replied that he had nothing to say on the subject. He did, however, have some thoughts on his personal life. 'On turning out to be Jewish'/'Another country' was the result. See Michael Elkin, 'Tom Terrific', *Jewish Exponent*, 3 February 2000.

49. 'Another country'.

50. *Ibid.*

51. *Ibid.*

52. *Ibid.*

53. Edward Said, *Out of Place: A Memoir* (New York: Knopf, 1999), 3. Compare passages in V. S. Naipaul's novel, *The Enigma of Arrival* (Harmondsworth: Penguin, 1987): 'to be what I wanted to be, I had to cease to be or to grow out of what I was' says the narrator (221). When that is not possible, however, it leads to hiding 'the cause of his incompleteness from himself', referring to the writer Alan in the novel (260).

54. *Arcadia*, 78; Beckett, 'Endgame', *Endgame and Act without Words: Collected Works of Samuel Beckett* (New York: Grove Press, 1970), 18.

55. 'Another country'.

56. Stoppard in Hollinger, 'The good words of Tom Stoppard'.

57. 'Another country'.

58. Jonathan Miller in Ronald Bergan, *Beyond the Fringe . . . and Beyond* (London: Virgin Books, 1989), 40; John Lahr, *Show and Tell: New Yorker Profiles* (New York: Overlook, 2000) in *New York Times Book Review*, 26 November 2000.

59. 'Another country'.

60. Arthur Schnitzler, *My Youth in Vienna*, trans. Catherine Hutter (New York: Holt, Rinehart and Winston, 1970), 7.

61. 'Another country'.

62. Stoppard in Robin Young, 'Wood and Stoppard Honoured at Palace', *The Times*, 13 December 1997.

63. E. M. Cioran, *The Temptation to Exist*, trans. Richard Howard (London: Quartet Books, 1987), 80. In the same passage, Cioran adds that the Jew 'is the man who will never be *from here*, the man from somewhere else, the stranger *as such* who cannot unambiguously speak in the name of the natives…'.

64. 'Another Country'.

65. Azenberg, interview; *Lord Malquist*, 28.

66. Stoppard, Prague Theatre Institute Lecture.

67. See the following for an account of modern Czech theatre: Paul I. Trensky, *Czech Drama since WWII* (White Plains, New York: M. E. Sharpe, Inc., 1978); Marketa Goetz-Stankiewicz, *The Silenced Theatre: Czech Playwrights without a Stage* (Toronto: University of Toronto Press, 1979); Jarka M. Burian, *Modern Czech Theatre* (Iowa City, Iowa: University of Iowa Press, 2000). Also helpful is Beck, 'The Czech Authorial Studio Theatres, 1968-1989'.

68. On current Czech theatre, see Carol Rocamora, 'A Glimmer of Satire Amid Freedom's Obscurities', *New York Times*, 17 December 2000.

69. Stoppard in Nightingale, 'Long haul for a laidback lad'.

70. Jean-Marie Besset quoted in Ben Macintyre, 'Stoppard Makes Paris Stage History', *The Times*, 27 November 1998; see also Besset's French adaptation of *Arcadia*, 'Une échappée de lumière dans la grisaille des temps' (Paris: Actes Sud-Papiers, 1998), [1].

CHAPTER TWENTY-ONE CAMOUFLAGED BY DISPLAY

1. Gussow, 86.

2. Stoppard in Macaulay, 'The man who was two men'; Gardner, 'The Heart in the Closet'; Stoppard in Hill, 'The poet punts down the Styx'.

3. Stoppard in de Lisle, 'Re-Enter Stoppard'.

4. Mick Jagger in *USA Today*, 29 December 1997.

5. Robert Harris describes the process in 'Enigma in the making', *Sunday Times*, 30 September 2001, noting that Stoppard expressed interest in the script in 1995, making pages of notes on the novel which he then pummelled Harris with in his Chelsea Harbour apartment. Three months later, Stoppard asked Harris to give him a tour of Bletchley Park, near Milton Keynes. Jagger tagged along. Stoppard then wrote the first draft in twelve weeks, arriving for a weekend visit to Harris in May with this version and a mechanical parrot for the children. This draft was more complicated than the novel, however. A second version, with an action ending (a submarine exploding in Scotland), appeared and then interest in the film stopped.

Over the next four or five years, a series of directors turned down the film, despite Jagger's efforts; his resistance to changing the story to include an American hero did not advance his cause. In October 1997, Stoppard and Michael Apted met. Apted had directed *Coal Miner's Daughter* and *Gorky Park*, plus Granada Television's *Seven Up* series. They agreed on more script changes. Within five months, Stoppard completed draft three. By the summer of 1998, a final conference between Stoppard, Apted and Harris occurred; by November, however, no financing had been found, and no star. Apted then took on the new James Bond film *The World is Not Enough* and the principals – Stoppard, Jagger, his partner Victoria Pearman and Harris – waited another year.

Twelve months later, with Apted now a bankable director because of the success of the Bond film, Stoppard told Harris – at the *Literary Review* Bad Sex Award evening – that Senator Films from Germany would put up the money; shooting would begin in May. Kate Winslet, Saffron Burrows, Jeremy Northam and Dougray Scott signed on, Winslet replacing Natasha Little. Shooting actually began in April 2000, but not at Bletchley Park: it was felt to look insufficiently like itself. The locale was a nearby mansion, Chichely Hall. But in the end, Harris was satisfied: 'it is not merely an old-fashioned British film: it is an unfashionable British film'. Others did not entirely agree, one critic commenting that Stoppard's dialogue seemed more 2001 than 1941 and that 'Dame Barbara Cartland would have come up with acceptable exchanges between Mr Scott and Miss Burrows' (Peter McKay, 'Don't let the home front go to ruin', *Daily Mail*, 8 October 2001). Others, however, have found it a quintessential British story, well-crafted and patriotic, although Apted lamented that 'here's a film about England beating Germany in the war – and

Germany paid for it'. Apted in Geoffrey Macnab, 'First Night: two riddles wrapped in a mystery', *Independent*, 25 September 2001.

    For Apted on Stoppard's enthusiasm for codes, see Alison James, 'Finding the Key to Tale of Intrigue', *Birmingham Post*, 27 September 2001. Jagger, however, actually purchased a four-rotor Enigma encoding machine at Sotheby's in 1995; Stoppard explained to him how it worked.

6. Stoppard, 'No reason for Polish concern over film', *Daily Telegraph*, 4 October 2001.
7. Stoppard in Macaulay, 'The man who was two men'.
8. *Indian Ink*, 46.
9. *The Invention of Love*, 4.
10. *Arcadia*, 94; *The Invention of Love*, 102.
11. Norman Page, *A. E. Housman: A Critical Biography* (London: Macmillan, 1983), 7; Stoppard, 'The Invention of Love and Not Only Love: Reflections on Biographical Fiction', Lecture, London Library, 29 October 1997.
12. Stoppard in Macaulay, 'The man who was two men'.
13. *The Invention of Love*, 43; stylistic differences exist with the passage in the first edition.
14. *The Invention of Love*, 92-3.
15. Wilde was released on 19 May 1897; *The Invention of Love* opened on 25 September 1997. The long Wilde–Stoppard connection began with Wilde's praise of Rosencrantz and Guildenstern in *De Profundis*, cited by Stoppard in the programme of the April 1967 production at the National. Stoppard's use of *The Importance of Being Earnest* for *Travesties* is well known, and elements of Wilde's dialogue appear throughout Stoppard's work until Wilde himself crops up in *The Invention*. Stoppard may have furthermore known of the Rosencrantz and Guildenstern situation Wilde sought to construct once he arrived in Dieppe in 1897. Travelling under the pseudonym of Sebastian Melmoth, Wilde reported to Ada Levenson that it might be better 'that Robbie [Ross] should stay here under the name of Reginald Turner, and Reggie under the name of R. B. Ross. It should be better that they should not have their own names'. Wilde in Ellmann, *Oscar Wilde*, 496.
16. John Wood in Mel Gussow, 'John Wood at the National: Tom Stoppard's Acting Alter Ego', *New York Times*, 14 January 1998.
17. Stoppard in Rasselas, *Sunday Times*, 5 October 1997.
18. *The Invention of Love*, 46, 36.
19. Stoppard in Peter Conrad, 'Thomas the think engine', *Observer*, 1 November 1998.
20. Stoppard in Alastair Macaulay, 'The man who was two men'.
21. *The Invention of Love*, 93.
22. Stoppard, 'The Invention of Love and Not Only Love: Reflections on Biographical Fiction', London Library Lecture, 29 October 1997.
23. Kate Shaw, 'The Invention of Love', *Housman Society Journal* 23 (1997), 10.
24. Oscar Wilde, 'Phrases and Philosophies for the Use of the Young', *The Artist as Critic*, 434; *Travesties*, 74.
25. Stoppard in Peter Conrad, 'Thomas the think engine'.
26. Stoppard, *ibid.*
27. *The Invention of Love*, 96, 94-5, 95.
28. *Ibid.*, 38, 95, 93.
29. *Ibid.*, 95, 96.
30. To assist in studying the work, a website devoted to translations of the Latin phrases in the play exists. It contains a detailed glossary of the terms in the play, with reference to a Latin Dictionary on the web. On page one of the site is a photograph of a Latin Translation Party. See www/netaxis.com/~fountfam/Invention%20of%20Love/Latin.htm.
31. Stoppard in Elizabeth Brodersen, '*Indian* Inspiration'.
32. Jeremy Treglown, 'Those who can, teach also', *Times Literary Supplement*, 10 October 1997; David Benedict, 'Don't shoot the messenger', *Independent*, 7 March 1998; Charles Spencer, 'Stoppard triumphs magna cum laude', *Evening Standard*, 2 October 1997; Michael Coveney, 'Sheer poetry from Tom', *Daily Mail*, 2 October 1997.
33. Robert Gore-Langton, 'The Invention of Love', *Daily Express*, 2 October 1997.
34. Michael Billington, 'Passion amid scholarship in juicy Stoppard', *Guardian*, 2 October 1997. The

TLS wrote that Stoppard's more recent plays 'sometimes feel less postmodern than postgraduate: theatre for the tertiarily-educated'. (Treglown, 'Those who can, teach also'.)

35. Nicholas de Jongh, 'Stoppard brings to life the sadness of being a lonely poet', *Evening Standard*, 2 October 1997; David Sexton, 'Theatre? I'd rather spend the night in a dark cell', *Evening Standard*, 16 February 1998.

36. John Wood in Mel Gussow, 'John Wood at the National'.

37. Stoppard, 'The Invention of Love', 'Platform', National Theatre, 10 October 1997. Audio tape.

38. Daniel Mendelsohn, 'The Tale of Two Housmans', *New York Review of Books*, 10 August 2000.

39. Stoppard, '"The Invention of Love": An Exchange', *New York Review of Books*, 21 September 2000; Daniel Mendelsohn, 'Reply', *ibid.*

40. Stoppard, 'On "The Invention of Love": Another Exchange', *New York Review of Books*, 19 October 2000. Mendelsohn's reply immediately follows.

41. *The Invention of Love*, 100, 5.

42. Roberto Benigni in George Rush and Joanna Molloy, 'Spielberg, Benigni: A "beautiful friendship"', *New York Daily News*, 22 March 1999.

43. Stoppard, 'Tom Stoppard's response', *Evening Standard*, 4 February 1999; Katherine Duncan-Jones, 'Why, then, O brawling love!', *Times Literary Supplement*, 5 February 1999. Another writer, Faye Kellerman, claimed in a writ that Stoppard and Norman took the film from her 1989 novel, *Quality of Mercy*, about Shakespeare falling in love with a Rebecca Lopez, a Portuguese Jewess.

44. 'Federal Judge Orders Trial to Proceed in Copyright Case against Oscar Winner "Shakespeare in Love", Entertainment Wire, 4 October 2001. The plaintiffs submitted their script to Universal Pictures in March 1991; Stoppard's co-writer Marc Norman began writing *Shakespeare in Love* in April 1991. The film earned $298 million world-wide.

45. Peter Brook to the author, London, 28 May 1999; Richard Dreyfuss to the author, London, 26 May 1999. Stoppard in Andrew Billen, 'A play about myself? It's not a subject I have any appetite for', *Evening Standard*, 27 January 1999.

46. For an account of the event and a special performance of the work for the French and British Ministers of Culture, see Chapter 20.

47. Michael Billington, 'The Real Tom Stoppard'.

48. Each contributor was asked to nominate ten English-language twentieth-century plays they considered 'significant'. One hundred and eighty-eight authors were nominated, with 377 different plays. Arthur Miller was the most nominated author, closely followed by Pinter and Beckett. *Rosencrantz and Guildenstern* tied with Noël Coward's *Private Lives* at number seven. The first ten plays in the survey were 1. *Waiting for Godot*; 2. *Death of a Salesman*; 3. *A Streetcar Named Desire*; 4. *Look Back in Anger*; 5. *Long Day's Journey into Night*; 6. *The Crucible*; 7/8. *Private Lives* and *Rosencrantz and Guildenstern are Dead*; 9/10. *Angels in America* and *The Caretaker*. Number 22 in the listing was *Arcadia*; number 61 was *Jumpers*. NT 2000 poll published as a brochure. National Theatre Archive.

49. O'Brien to the author, Old Globe Theatre, San Diego, CA. 8 May 2000; Tom Stoppard in Anne Marie Welsh, 'Stoppard in Love', *San Diego Union-Tribune*, 6 February 2000.

50. She and Stoppard continued to be an item for some nine months after their meeting. See Adam Helliker, 'Marie proves to be the real thing for Tom', *Sunday Telegraph*, 12 November 2000. Also see Nigel Dempster, 'Sir Tom finds a new leading lady', *Daily Mail*, 8 March 2000 and 'People of the Week', *Sunday Times*, 12 March 2000. Ed Stoppard, the playwright's son, refers to his father's relationship with Helvin in Cassandra Jardine's interview, 'We're like a Disney movie', *Daily Telegraph*, 2 July 2001.

51. Richard Eyre, 'Shall I compare thee to a summer holiday resort?', *Guardian*, 4 November 2000. The series was shown on BBC television in November–December 2000. In the book on which the television series is based, Eyre devotes eight pages to Stoppard. See Richard Eyre and Nicholas Wright, *Changing Stages* (London: Bloomsbury, 2000), 303-11. At the end of his discussion, Eyre congratulates Stoppard for entering 'mellow greatness', adding that 'no modern playwright since Ibsen has made such sense of late middle-age. This is Stoppard's gift to the next generation. Which isn't, in fact, much younger than him: not that it ever was' (311).

52. Advertisement, 'The Real Thing', *New York Times*, 13 February 2000.

53. Stoppard in Mamie Healey, 'Stoppard making sense', *Time Out* (New York), 13-20 April 2000; Anna Wintour in 'Standard Awards Wintour', *Evening Standard*, 7 November 2000.

54. Tom Stoppard in Bernard Weinraub, 'When Stoppard sends his "Love", San Francisco Reciprocates', *New York Times*, 2 February 2000; Stoppard in Robin Pogrebin, 'For Stoppard, a Play must be just that: Play', *New York Times*, 18 March 2001. With typical panache, Stoppard added 'I don't read Russian. I don't know how to write about Russians. I don't know what I think I'm doing, but I'm doing it anyway'.

55. Alexander Herzen in Monica Partridge, *Alexander Herzen* (Paris: UNESCO, 1984), 35, 42, 41.

56. Stoppard in Louis East, 'Enter a Free Man', *Irish Times*, 16 January 1999. Stoppard was in Ireland for the première of *Arcadia* at the Gate Theatre.

57. William Peakin and Mark Franchetti, 'Moscow's secret library comes in from the cold', *Sunday Times*, 9 September 2001. The Nobel Prize-winning poet Joseph Brodsky translated *Rosencrantz and Guildenstern* into Russian *circa* December 1970 and sent it to the Foreign Literature Magazine (*Inostrannaja Literatura*). It was not published; rediscovered in the late 1980s, its survival surprised even Brodsky, who gave permission for the translated play to appear in the journal in the same year Jevgeny Arye directed the work at the Mayakousky Theatre in Moscow. The play has since been published as a separate book: *Rozenkranc i Gil'denstern mertvy*. (Moskva: Azbuka, 2000). For details see Yurij Fridshtejn, *Rozenkranc, Gil'denstern i druzie Izdatel'sstvo*. (Sankt-Peterburg: Azbuka, 2000); also helpful is David MacFadyen, *Joseph Brodsky and the Baroque* (Montreal: McGill Queen's Press, 1998) 136. Arye emigrated to Israel in the early nineties and began the Gesher Theatre there. One of its first productions was the Brodsky translation of *Rosencrantz and Guildenstern*.

58. Michael Billington, 'The Play of the Week: Two to A T', *Guardian*, 16 December 1995.

59. Stoppard in Toby Zinman, 'Knowledge is Power', *Citypaper* (Philadelpha), 13–20 January 2000.

60. Stoppard in 'The Invention of Love and Not only Love: Reflections on Biographical Fiction', London Library Lecture, 29 October 1997.

61. Stoppard repeats it again in Appleyard, 'So what's it all about, Mr. Stoppard?'.

62. Jack O'Brien in Robin Pogrebin, 'Going from Steel Mill to Campus', *New York Times*, 20 May 2001.

63. Kathleen Sharp, 'Tasting Tom Stoppard', *Big City Lit*, April/May 2001.

64. Michael Coveney, 'Head scratching in Stoppard's Arcadia', *Observer*, 18 April 1993. Coveney also makes the point that Stoppard's 'humanist insistence as a writer' elevates 'footnotes in cultural history'. hence the importance of Rosencrantz and Guildenstern, Henry Carr or even Flora Crewe, who just failed to sit for Modigliani.

65. Stoppard in Kroll, 'Mind over Matter'.

66. Stoppard in Pogrebin, 'For Stoppard, a Play Must Be Just That: Play'; Stoppard in Michael Hollinger, 'The Good Words of Tom Stoppard', *Seven Arts* (January 1997), [4].

67. Stoppard in Nigel Reynolds, 'Stoppard tears strips off "self-indulgent artists"', *Daily Telegraph*, 1 June 2001. Stoppard failed to note Marcus Harvey's new painting, a picture of several dildos with the title *Ann's Summer Party*.

68. Stoppard in Reynolds. Ironically, Stuart Pearson Wright, the twenty-five-year-old winner of Britain's leading portrait painting prize, the BP Portrait Award for 2001 with *The Six Presidents of the British Academy*, said at the announcement of the award that Sir Nicholas Serota should be sacked for championing conceptual art. 'The figurative painters are on the outside, shut out', said Pearson Wright. See Nigel Reynolds, 'Sack Tate chief, says prize artist', *Daily Telegraph*, 20 June 2001. The following day, an article called 'Art at the Crossroads' opened with 'For many years, British art has been Sir Nicholas Serota's oyster', but that was all changing, thanks in part to Stoppard's speech and its aftermath. 'Art at the Crossroads', *Daily Telegraph*, 21 June 2001.

Stoppard's views should not startle those familiar with his early attitudes towards abstract art. In interviews given in the early seventies relating to his play, *Artist Descending a Staircase*, he expressed a similar opinion. See Delaney, 37.

69. Janet Street-Porter, 'Over the last five years people of all ages have flocked to see the kind of art Tom Stoppard despises', *Independent*, 5 June 2001.

70. These terms and the passage referring to 'a generation divider' are all from Janet Street-Porter's

article. Another anti-Stoppard article is Rosie Millard's 'Silly old Tom Stoppard', *The Times*, 8 June 2001.

For a counter view see Howard Jacobson, 'I know what art is for – but what are Gilbert and George exactly?' *Independent*, 9 June 2001, or the letter by the artist Ken Howard in the *Daily Telegraph*, 21 June 2001. Howard admitted his prejudice, however: he had been commissioned to do a portrait of Stoppard. The novelist Robert Harris defended Stoppard in the largely sympathetic piece entitled 'Profile: Sir Tom Stoppard, Enemy of the Puerile', *Sunday Telegraph*, 3 June 2001. The article notes that a playwright with 'conservative sympathies' is a rarity in the theatre – and that Stoppard sometimes finds it difficult to support left-wing causes.

71. Stoppard, 'Thinking is not enough: art involves making, too', *Daily Telegraph*, 15 June 2001. The essay also appears as 'Making it', in the *Times Literary Supplement*, 15 June 2001.

72. *Ibid.*

73. Lawson, Mark, 'Art needs ideas (and artisans)', *Guardian*, 16 June 2001. For a considered response to Stoppard's article and critique that conceptual art is the child of Dada, not Duchamp, see the letter by John S. Warren in the *Times Literary Supplement*, 22 June 2001, 17. The heading reads 'Tom Stoppard and Conceptual Art'.

74. *The Seagull*, 32.

75. Stoppard, 'Arcadia', 'Platform', National Theatre, London, 14 April 1993. Transcript.

76. *Jumpers*, 81.

BIBLIOGRAPHY

WORKS BY TOM STOPPARD

Arcadia Reprint with corrections (London: Faber and Faber, 1993)

Artist Descending a Staircase and *Where are They Now: Two Plays for Radio* (London: Faber and Faber, 1973)

The Boundary With Clive Exton (London: Samuel French Ltd., 1991)

Cahoot's Macbeth in *The Real Inspector Hound and Other Entertainments* (London: Faber and Faber, 1993)

The Coast of Utopia: 'Voyage', 'Shipwreck', 'Salvage' (London: Faber and Faber, 2002)

Dalliance and *Undiscovered Country* (London: Faber and Faber, 1986)

Dirty Linen in *The Real Inspector Hound and Other Entertainments* (London: Faber and Faber, 1993)

The Dog it Was that Died in *Plays for Radio 1964–1991* (London: Faber and Faber, 1990)

Dogg's Hamlet in *The Real Inspector Hound and Other Entertainments* (London: Faber and Faber, 1993)

Enter a Free Man (1968; London: Faber and Faber, 1993)

Every Good Boy Deserves Favor and *Professional Foul* (New York: Grove Press, 1978)

Hapgood Broadway Edition (Reprint with corrections. London: Faber and Faber, 1994)

In the Native State (London: Faber and Faber, 1991)

Indian Ink (London: Faber and Faber, 1995)

The Invention of Love 2nd edition (London: Faber and Faber, 1997)

Jumpers (New York: Grove Press, 1972)

'Life, Times: Fragments', 'Reunion', 'The Story', in *Introduction 2: Stories by New Writers.* (London: Faber and Faber, 1964)

Lord Malquist and Mr. Moon (London: Anthony Blond, 1996; Faber and Faber, 1980).

Night and Day (London: Faber and Faber, 1978)

Plays for Radio 1964–1991 (London: Faber and Faber, 1990)

Rosencrantz and Guildenstern are Dead (London: Faber and Faber, 1997; New York: Grove Press, 1967)

Rough Crossing and *On the Razzle* (London: Faber and Faber, 1990)

The Real Inspector Hound and Other Entertainments (London: Faber and Faber, 1993)

The Real Inspector Hound and *After Magritte* (New York: Grove Press, 1975)
The Real Thing (London: Faber and Faber, 1982; Broadway Edition, reprint with corrections, London: Faber and Faber, 1991)
The Seagull by Anton Chekhov, a New Version by Tom Stoppard (London: Faber and Faber, 1997)
Shakespeare in Love With Marc Norman (London: Faber and Faber, 1999)
Squaring the Circle in *Television Plays 1965–1984* (London: Faber and Faber, 1993)
'A Student's Diary', BBC Written Archives
Television Plays 1965–1984 (London: Faber and Faber, 1993)
Travesties (London: Faber and Faber, 1974)
Undiscovered Country in *Plays 4* (London: Faber and Faber, 1999)

ARTICLES BY TOM STOPPARD

'Confessions of a Screenwriter', *Today's Cinema* 3, February 1969: 5
'The Definite Maybe', *The Author* 78 (1967): 18–20
'"Dirty Linen" in Prague', *New York Times*, 11 February 1997: 27
'The event and the text', 1988 in *Tom Stoppard in Conversation* ed. Paul Delaney (Ann Arbor: University of Michigan Press, 1991) 199–211
'The face at the window', *Sunday Times*, 27 February 1977: 33
'Going back', *Independent Magazine*, 23 March 1991: 25–30
'In search of childhood', *Daily Mail,* 4 May 1991: 17, 19
'Is it true what they say about Shakespeare?', International Shakespeare Association Occasional Paper No. 2. (Oxford: Oxford University Press, 1982)
'Late to read, early to rise', *The Times*, 12 September 1992: 17
'On turning out to be Jewish,' *Talk*, September 1999: 190–4, 241–3. Reprinted as 'Another country', *Sunday Telegraph Magazine*, 10 October 1999: 14–19, 20–1
'Playing with science', *Engineering and Science* LVIII (1994): 3–13
'Playwrights and professors', *Times Literary Supplement*, 13 October 1972: 12–19
'Pragmatic theater', *New York Review of Books*, 23 September 1999: 8, 10
'Prague: the story of the Chartists', *New York Review of Books* 24, 4 August 1977: 11–15
'Reflections on Ernest Hemingway' in *Ernest Hemingway: The Writer in Context* ed. James Nagel (Madison: University of Wisconsin Press, 1984) 19–27
'Something to Declare', *Sunday Times*, 25 February 1986: 47
'The text's the thing', *Daily Telegraph*, 23 April 1988
'Yes, we have no bananas', *Guardian*, 10 December 1971: 10

OTHER SOURCES

CALLOW, SIMON, *The National Theatre and Its Work 1963–1977* (London: Royal National Theatre and Nick Hern Books, 1997)

CHAMBERS, COLIN, *Peggy, the Life of Margaret Ramsay, Play Agent* (1997; London: Methuen, 1998)

CORBALLIS, RICHARD, *Stoppard: The Mystery and the Clockwork* (New York: Methuen, 1984)

DAVIES, BRIAN, *Exploring Chaos, Theory and Experiment* (Reading, MA: Perseus Books, 1999)

DAVIES, P. G. W. AND BROWN, J. R., eds, *The Ghost in the Atom* (Cambridge: Cambridge University Press, 1986)

DELANEY, PAUL, ed. *Tom Stoppard in Conversation* (Ann Arbor: University of Michigan Press, 1994) 57

——, *Tom Stoppard, The Moral Vision of the Major Plays* (London: Macmillan, 1990)

ELSOM, JOHN AND TOMALIN, NICHOLAS, *The History of the National Theatre* (London: Jonathan Cape, 1978)

EYRE, RICHARD AND WRIGHT, NICHOLAS, *Changing Stages* (London: Bloomsbury, 2000

FARAONE, CHERYL, 'An Analysis of Tom Stoppard's Plays and Their Productions (1964–1975)', Dissertation, Florida State University, August 1980

FEYNMAN, RICHARD, *The Character of Physical Law* (Cambridge, MA: M. I. T. Press, 1967)

——, *The Feynman Lectures on Physics* (1963; Reading, MA: Addison-Wesley Publishing, 1977)

FLEMING, JOHN, 'Tom Stoppard: His Life and Career before Rosencrantz and Guildenstern', Library Chronicle of the University of Texas at Austin, 26 (1996)

FLEMING, JOHN, *Stoppard's Theatre: Finding Order amid Chaos* (Austin, Texas: Ransom Humanities Center and the University of Texas Press, 2001)

GLEICK, JAMES, *Chaos: Making a New Science* (New York: Penguin, 1987)

GOODWIN, TIM, *Britain's Royal National Theatre, The First 25 Years* (London: National Theatre and Nick Hern Books, 1988)

GUSSOW, MEL, *Conversations with Stoppard* (New York: Grove Press, 1995)

HALL, PETER, *Peter Hall's Diaries*, ed. John Goodwin (London: Hamish Hamilton, 1983)

HAYMAN, RONALD, *Tom Stoppard* (London: Heinemann, 1977)

JENKINS, ANTHONY, 'Introduction, From Page to Stage', *Critical Essays on Tom Stoppard*, ed. Anthony Jenkins (Boston: G. K. Hall, 1990)

LEWIS, PETER, *The National, A Dream Made Concrete* (London: Methuen, 1990)

LONDRÉ, FELICIA HARDISON, *Tom Stoppard* (New York: Frederick Ungar, 1981)

MROZEK, SLAWOMIR, *Tango*, trans. Nicholas Bethell, adapted by Tom Stoppard

(London: Jonathan Cape, 1968)

NICHOLS, PETER, *Diaries 1969–77* (London: Nick Hern Books, 2000)

RUSINKO, SUSAN, *Tom Stoppard* (Boston: Twayne, 1986)

SAMMELLS, NEIL, *Tom Stoppard: The Artist as Critic* (London: Macmillan, 1988)

SHER, ANTONY, *Beside Myself, An Autobiography* (London: Hutchinson, 2001)

TYNAN, KATHLEEN, *The Life of Kenneth Tynan* (London: Weidenfeld and Nicolson: 1987)

TYNAN, KENNETH, *Show People* (New York: Simon and Schuster, 1979)

——, *Letters*, ed. Kathleen Tynan (London: Weidenfeld and Nicolson, 1994)

ACKNOWLEDGEMENTS

Many have played important roles in this study, from backstage managers to set designers and directors. The most crucial has been Michael Earley, publisher and editor *extraordinaire*, who not only 'produced' this project from the start but worked continuously on its behalf, calling, enquiring and even tracking down past and present actors in the drama. His support and enthusiasm have been constantly valued, as well as his generosity in making sure I was up to date on the latest theatrical news. Philippa and Christopher Earley also helped in numerous ways. Brenda Maddox, friend and fellow biographer, always shared with me the expected and unexpected dilemmas of biographical research. Michael Billington is to be thanked for encouraging me to speak to Tom Stoppard about writing this biography late one afternoon in Austin, Texas, while his timely bulletins on the state of the London theatre repeatedly keep me in touch with new directions and developments.

Others who helped include Peter Wood, who graciously hosted me at his remarkable priory in the Somerset hills, Richard Eyre, who explained to me the complicated history of recent British theatre, and John Tydeman, who kindly recounted the challenges of Stoppard's work in the radio studio. James Saunders, who chose the unusual Tramshed pub in Islington for our lengthy meeting, detailed Stoppard's days in Berlin, while Frank Pike, formerly of Faber and Faber and Stoppard's editor for nearly forty years, explained to me the many challenges of preparing dramatic texts for publication. Miriam Stoppard also offered useful information. The Royal National Theatre has, from my first request, been welcoming and I especially want to thank Nicola Scadding, former archivist of the theatre's Archives, Fiona Welsh, former Press Officer, Angus MacKechnie, producer of the NT 2000 series, Patsy Rodenberg, distinguished voice coach at the National, and Toby Radford, Manager of the National Theatre Bookshop, and his staff.

Edward Petherbridge and John Stride were each kind enough to recount for me moments in the performance history of *Rosencrantz and Guildenstern are Dead*, as was Simon Russell Beale. John Wood, who threw me off guard by greeting me in his dressing-room at the Haymarket during the West End production of *The Invention of Love* with the challenge 'What is a *literary* biography?' and then compounded the situation by mistaking me for the Housman expert P. G. Naiditch, is also to be thanked for his generosity in summarizing a career performing Stoppard. Richard Dreyfuss, who puzzled me with his question posed in a late-night, upscale South Kensington supermarket, 'Do strawberries have carbohydrates?', was unselfish with his time and remarkable knowledge of movie production. Ed Berman, at his tilted desk on the HMS *President* floating on the Thames, shared with me many stories of Inter-Action and its theatrical history.

Fiona Stoppard kindly met me in Hampstead to recall the warmth of her mother and the repeated generosity of her half-brother. Colin Chambers shared with me his comprehensive understanding of recent theatre history, while Sheridan Morley, Peter Brook and Timothy West, at the time President of the Society for Theatre Research, gladly answered questions. Ronald Harwood generously shared with me stories of Stoppard in and out of the theatre, while Ron and Marilyn Bush fearlessly wandered with me about Chelsea Harbour, all three of us neophyte sleuths. Alan Bell, former Librarian of the London Library, provided a place to work, resources, and friendship. At the National Portrait Gallery, Jill Summerhill, archivist, and Terence Pepper, Curator of Photography, assisted at crucial moments. John Wyse Jackson of Sandoe (Books) Ltd. also helped, as did the photographer Mark Gerson. Staff at the London Theatre Museum were welcoming, and writer Jonathan Croall also assisted.

Others to thank begin with Andrew Gasson, friend and bibliophile, who gallantly drove through the English countryside while sharing with me his knowledge of cricket. Our afternoon at the Oval was for me an education that defined both a pokey and a pudding. Mr and Mrs Geoffrey Bridges graciously allowed me to tour the house and grounds of Iver Grove. David Gray, former Headmaster and A. D. Nuttall, Associate Headmaster, Pocklington School, Yorkshire were marvellous hosts as well as guides to Stoppard's former school.

Michael Codron was especially generous, sparing me time during a busy theatrical season to recount some of the many adventures in staging Stoppard in the West End. Paul and Marigold Johnson kindly invited me to their London home to recount life in Iver and their long friendship with Stoppard. Jackie Kavanagh and Neil Summerhill of the BBC Written Archives at Caversham helped to locate some early Stoppard material, while John Oliver at the British Film Institute patiently answered questions. The ebullient Gordon Dickerson kindly shared his expansive knowledge of theatre life with me, while Kenneth Ewing, Stoppard's agent for many years, provided me with insights into the career of the dramatist. Jacky Matthews, Stoppard's assistant, has been unstintingly helpful and enthusiastic, always willing to listen to yet another request. Tom Stoppard has been from the first a sceptical but supportive witness to the entire project, who surprised me at one of our encounters with the question, 'So, when is it to be done?'

In Bristol, the following have been instrumental and without them this account could hardly have been written: Anthony Smith, novelist and dramatist, repeatedly went beyond the call of dramatic or any other duty, and has been, from our first meeting at Temple Mead, friend, mentor, host, Bristol guide and resource *sans pareil*. His belief in the project has been an important contribution to its completion. Peter and Lesley Stoppard, of Long Ashton, have also been wonderful guides to the Bristol past and present of the Stoppards, although I may not have listened as carefully as I should have to Peter's constant warning to keep it short. Isabel Dunjohn kindly provided me with details about Stoppard's early life and journalistic endeavours; David Foot recounted for me Stoppard's valiant efforts as a cub reporter in police court and attempts at sports writing.

The late Val Lorraine, former Old Vic actress and close friend of Stoppard's, spent hours with me narrating life at Grosvenor Lodge and reliving the many theatrical parties she hosted; she also graciously allowed me to explore the house and learn its history. Sarah Morris, Keeper of the Theatre Collection at the Department of Drama, University of Bristol and George Brandt, former Professor of Drama at Bristol, also filled me in on important details, while staff at the Bristol Old Vic valiantly tried to retrieve records for me. They were stymied by Mother Goose. A visit to the storage area, located directly beneath the stage, would have disrupted that afternoon's Christmas matinée of *Mother Goose*; entertainment triumphed over research.

In the Czech Republic, I again benefited from the assistance of many, beginning with Mirka Potuckova, head of the Foreign Department of the Theatre Institute, Prague; Professor Milan Lukas of the Theatre Department, Charles University, also shared his understanding of Stoppard's reception in the Czech Republic with me. Dr and Mrs Emil Máčel of Zlín were outstanding instructors in matters Czech, providing me with an extraordinary introduction to the city of Zlín, the history of Bat'a shoes and the fate of its many Jewish employees. Dr Máčel's research into the lives of Bat'a employees during and after the war was one of the key archives for this study. The hospitality of Dr Máčel and his wife was also much appreciated, allowing a Canadian traveller a glimpse of Czech life past and present. Marek Jacina, former translator for President Havel and his wife, and present at a meeting between Stoppard and the president, has been especially helpful and generous in aiding my grasp of modern Czech issues. His residence in Vancouver was an unexpected but delightful discovery. Marketa Goetz-Stankievich, formerly of the Department of Slavonic Studies at the University of British Columbia and an expert on Havel's drama, has also been a remarkable resource from the beginning of this project and is to be thanked for her expert translation of an important document.

In the US and Canada, I want to thank especially Thomas F. Staley, Director of the Harry Ransom Humanities Research Center at the University of Texas – who, after soundly beating me on a Texas tennis court, finally revealed to me the title of Stoppard's then newest play. Katherine Mosley, able archivist of the Stoppard collection at HRC, was always ready to help; Mellisa Miller, who educated a neophyte in theatre studies, also took the time to explain some of the performative challenges of mounting a Stoppard play. Also assisting at HRC were Cathy Henderson, Associate Librarian, and Richard Oram, Librarian. Will Goodwin was a further resource; Rachel Howarth assisted ably in the HRC Reading Room, as did Pat Fox.

Also in Texas, John Fleming, of Southwest Texas State University, San Marcos, eagerly shared with me his expertise of Stoppard and knowledge of the archive. Thanks as well to Dennis Beck, formerly of Austin, Texas and Prague, but now at Bradley University, whose research on Czech Authorial Theatre was invaluable and who managed to educate me in the history of contemporary Czech theatre one afternoon in a dismal Prague apartment. Alan Friedman and his wife, Elizabeth Cullingford, had the patience to listen to my tales, while their hospitality during my frequent visits to Austin made every visit a delight. Charles Rossman happily sat through frequent recitations of research progress. Zulfikar Ghose, formerly of Bristol, now of Austin, was also helpful in recalling the challenges of producing the Arts Page of the *Western Daily Press* (Bristol) edited by Anthony Smith and Stoppard.

Others who were generous in sharing their marvellous sense of theatre history, acting and performance were Hersh Zeifman, Toby Zinman and Katherine E. Kelly. Paul Delaney was especially kind: a generous and exceptionally knowledgeable Stoppard scholar, he willingly provided references, guidance and aid in locating sources and constantly displayed an expertise little matched in Stoppard studies. Wendy Steiner, of the University of Pennsylvania, also helped, as did Professor Robert Osserman of the Mathematics Research Institute, Berkeley. Richard Corballis offered ideas, material and information drawn from his own work on Stoppard and kindly took the time to forward much useful material to me, as did John Harty, III. Ronald Bryden, now of Toronto, was also an invaluable source.

Emanuel Azenberg of New York took time to share with me tales of producing Stoppard for Broadway; Mel Gussow of the *New York Times* assisted by answering questions and clarifying details; Tom Cott of Lincoln Center Theater, New York, and David Lefkowitz of *Playbill*, New York offered crucial details on Stoppard's Gotham career. Carey Perloff, Artistic Director of the American Conservatory Theater, San Francisco, kindly let me review production records and let me attend rehearsals of two Stoppard productions. She also shared with me the satisfactions of directing a playwright of intellectual power and immense dramatic skill. Jack O'Brien of the Globe Theater, San Diego recounted for me the challenges of the New York production of *Hapgood* and how he worked with Stoppard in reshaping the play. He also revealed useful details on the casting, lighting and music of the production, while sharing a portion of his encyclopaedic knowledge of contemporary American theatre. Soheyl Dahi, Glenn Horowitz, Tracey Jackson, Laura Barnes and Pati Cockram all helped in valuable ways.

597

In Vancouver, Pamela Dalziel listened, talked, challenged and travelled, at one point literally following Stoppard by his shirttails; she is to be thanked for her constant support and belief in this project from its inception (and for her wisdom in deflecting me from another project). Ian McAndrew and Annie Murray were both outstanding research assistants who managed to locate numerous materials that significantly aided the book and its completion. Carmen DesOrmeaux has continually displayed a remarkable flair and enthusiasm for research, discovering difficult details and helping to complete the manuscript in various ways. Jocelyn Godolphin assisted with library research when it was most needed. Sherrill Grace, friend and colleague, encouraged and supported; Dominique Yupangoo played a crucial role in the last-minute preparation of photos. Dr Jeffrey Claman, David Evans, Tony Dawson, Lisa Quinn and Ramona Montagnes all provided assistance at critical moments in writing this book, from explaining various psychiatric concepts to writing better sentences, occasionally in the passive voice. Francis R. Andrews, Director of the University of British Columbia's Writing Centre, is to be thanked for his computer expertise and for the Centre's assistance in preparing the manuscript. At Methuen, Max Eilenberg has edited with care, while Sarah Hulbert provided expert copy-editing and Nicky Pearce saw the book through to completion.

My children, Ryan and Dara, who easily shifted from an interest in music to the theatre, and my mother, Frances Sofman Nadel (who at ninety-one decided it was finally time to read *Sons and Lovers*, as well as *The Importance of Being Earnest*), were consistent listeners and a largely willing audience. The dedication of my late father, Isaac David Nadel, to his own projects and industriousness have remained an inspiration.

Without the generous support of the Social Sciences and Humanities Research Council of Canada and the University of British Columbia's committee on research, this project would not have been possible. My thanks to both. And mindful of the Inspector's remarks in *Cahoot's Macbeth* that 'words can be your friend or your enemy, depending on who's throwing the book', any errors or confusions remain, of course, my own.

Ira Nadel
Vancouver

INDEX